Hillier's Fundamentals of Automotive Electronics 2nd Edition

V.A.W Hillier I.Eng. MIRTE, FIMI

™ Nelson Thornes
a Wolters Kluwer business

First published in 1987 as Fundamentals of Automotive Electronics by:
Hutchinson Education
Reprinted in 1989 by:
Stanley Thornes (Publishers) Ltd
Second edition published in 1996 as Hillier's Fundamental of Automotive
Electronics by:
Stanley Thornes (Publishers) Ltd

Reprinted in 2001 by:
Nelson Thornes Ltd
Delta Place
27 Bath Road
CHELTENHAM
GL53 7TH
United Kingdom

07 / 13 12

A catalogue record for this book is available from the British Library

ISBN 978 0 7487 2695 0

Page make-up by Florence Production Ltd

Printed and bound in Slovenia by DELO tiskarna by
arrangement with Korotan - Ljubljana

Contents

Preface

When the first edition of this book was written in 1986, I suggested that in the next few years electronic devices would replace systems that had been used on motor vehicles for many years. Although growth was predicted, the evolution far exceeded the forecast for the decade. This rapid change was forced on vehicle manufacturers by international pressure for a cleaner environment, so as more stringent regulations were legislated, vehicles had to be designed to satisfy the requirement.

It was fortunate that during this period rapid developments also took place in the electronics industry; these enabled suppliers to produce cheap sophisticated silicon chips and manufacture compact reliable computers. As electronic components became readily available they were incorporated into vehicle control systems, first into engine management and then into other vehicle systems. Today all the main circuits incorporate some form of electronic device. This use has spread to many other parts; some of these may be considered as desirable essentials, but many others have been introduced as gadgets or gimmicks to attract potential buyers.

Viewed against this background, it was necessary to update, amend and enlarge the original material to reflect the changes that had taken place in industry and in the training field. In this second edition the original objectives have been retained; these include the need to present the subject to potential electromechanical technicians in a style that is easy to understand. When this book is used in conjunction with my other books, it will help the reader to gain a basic knowledge of the motor vehicle; this foundation will enable the pursuance of more detailed studies of modern systems and testing techniques.

To minimize repetition each book focuses on a target objective; this book concentrates mainly on electrical and electronic features, *Fundamentals of Motor Vehicle Technology* on the construction and operation of mechanical systems and *Motor Vehicle Related Studies* for NVQ on the science and related studies aspects.

The subjects covered relate to the electrical features outlined in the syllabus for an NVQ in Vehicle Mechanical and Electronic Systems. It will be suitable for students preparing for various examinations set by the City and Guilds of London Institute, BTEC and other examining bodies. In addition the book will provide valuable support material for automotive electronic courses and personal study activities.

Treatment of the subject is varied to suit the requirement of the reader and with this in mind it is anticipated that the appropriate sections will be used to match the course of study. The book is divided into two parts, Principles and Applications. It is intended that the first part should be read and studied as and when required. Where applicable cross-references are made to minimize repetition of fundamental principles.

The electronic world has created many mysteries for the newcomer to the subject and these are often created by the use of technical jargon. In this book I have intentionally used some of this modern-day language to show its meaning and give its relation to descriptions of working principles of typical applications.

Acknowledgements

During the time that this book was being researched, considerable assistance was given by many friends in various companies. In particular I wish to thank and acknowledge the technical assistance and material supplied by:

British Standards Institution
Champion Sparking Plug Co Ltd
Fluke (UK) Ltd
Ford Motor Co Ltd
Toyota (GB) Ltd
Ital Audio Ltd
Lucas Rists
Lucas Yuasa Batteries Ltd
Robert Bosch Ltd
Rover Group
Saab (Great Britain) Ltd
Sun Electric U.K. Ltd
Trafficmaster plc

Though many of the drawings are based on commercial components, they are mainly intended to illustrate operational principles. For this reason, and because component design changes so rapidly, no drawing is claimed to be up to date. Readers should refer to manufacturer's publications for the latest information.

Manufacturers use many different electrical layouts and it is impossible in a book of this size to include all of them. The layouts and circuits chosen for treatment are intended to establish the working principle of a typical system. With this introduction other systems can be studied and understood.

Although an outline of test procedures is given, no claim is made that the material in the book represents the approved tests applicable to a certain model or type of vehicle. Rapid changes in electronics means that vehicle manufacturers must be responsible for this service.

Many diagrams have been simplified to help the reader and, in most cases, the graphical symbols conform to the recommendations made by the British Standards Institution in BS 3939 and the International Electrotechnical Commission (IEC).

V.A.W.H.
May 1996

Part A

Principles

1 Electrical principles

Just like any other subject, electrical and electronic systems obey certain basic rules and laws. To avoid constant repetition throughout the book, the common features have been brought together in this section. This is intended to enable the main principles to be established before they are applied to the individual circuits and components.

A reader who has studied basic electrical theory at school should find that this section revises the important facts associated with the world of electricity.

1.1 Circuit fundamentals

Electric charge

The word 'electric' is derived from a Greek word *ēlektron* which means amber. As long ago as 600 BC it was known that when this yellow translucent fossil resin was rubbed with a silk cloth, the amber was then able to attract to it particles of dust. Today, a similar effect can be produced after passing a plastic comb through your hair – the comb will attract small pieces of paper.

Experiments performed around the year 1600 indicated that other materials could be 'charged with electricity'. Also, observations showed that when small particles, such as two pith balls, were charged from an electrified material, they would react in different ways when placed close together. When they were each charged from a similar source they would repel each other, but when one was charged from a resinous material and the other ball was charged from a vitreous substance (e.g. glass) the two charged particles would then be attracted together.

In 1747 Benjamin Franklin introduced the names *positive* and *negative* to distinguish between the two *electrical charges*. Vitreous materials were said to acquire a positive charge and resinous substances a negative charge.

He thought the electrical flow passed from a high potential positive to a lower potential negative source. The choice was unfortunate because a later discovery proved that small electrical charges called electrons moved from negative to positive. By this time many electrical rules and laws had been established, so today the *conventional flow* from positive to negative is applied whenever basic laws have to be used. Actual flow from negative to positive is called *electron flow*. The form of energy produced by rubbing a material is called *electrostatics*. In a motor vehicle this type of charge is generated at places where friction occurs, e.g. clutch and brake. These charges can build up in a vehicle, especially on a hot dry day, so the occupants can sometimes detect these static charges as they conduct or *discharge* the static electricity to the ground.

Today electric energy is obtained normally from a battery or generator and this form of energy is called

1

electric current to distinguish it from electrostatics. Although the energy is obtained from a different source, the behaviour of both forms is similar.

Electrons and protons

Objects around us consist of various formations of atoms bonded together to form molecules. A molecule of water consists of two atoms of hydrogen and one atom of oxygen; this combination is indicated by the chemical symbol H_2O.

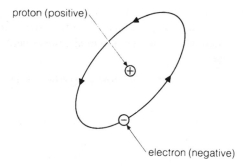

Fig. 1.1 Hydrogen atom

Examination of an atom under a powerful microscope shows that it is built up of very minute particles. A hydrogen atom (Figure 1.1) consists of a *proton*, at the *nucleus* (centre) and one *electron*, which orbits around the proton at high speed. The electron is the lightest particle known at this time; its mass is only about 0.0005 of the mass of the hydrogen atom or stated another way, 9×10^{-28} g.

Each electron carries a small negative charge and this balances the positive charge held by the proton. The two opposite charges make the atom electrically neutral.

Other materials have different combinations of electrons and protons. A copper atom has 29 electrons; these move in four different orbits around the atom's nucleus. This central region consists of protons and other particles called *neutrons* which have no electrical charge.

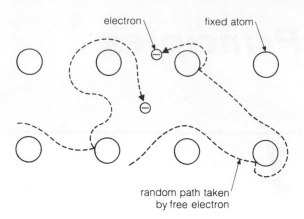

Fig. 1.2 Copper atom

Conductors

Some of the electrons in metallic materials are not bonded tightly to their nucleus; instead they drift at random from one atom to another, Figure 1.2. Materials that have a number of these free electrons make good conductors of electricity because little effort is needed to persuade the electrons to move through the tightly-packed atomic structure.

Copper is a very good conductor of electric current so this metal is often used as a material for an electric cable.

Insulators

Insulation materials have no loosely-bound electrons, so movement of electrons from one atom to the next is very difficult. Insulators therefore do not, in general, conduct electricity. However, no material is a perfect insulator because all materials will allow some electron movement if the force is large enough.

Attraction and repulsion

Electrical charges of the same polarity mutually repel one another, whereas charges of opposite polarity attract one another. This behaviour may be likened to that produced by two magnets. When two groups of electrons are brought together, a force exists which attempts to separate the two groups.

The size of the force produced between two electrically charged bodies was studied by the French scientist Coulomb in 1775. To honour his work, the SI unit of electrical charge is called the *coulomb* (C).

This unit is the quantity of charge which passes a section of a conductor in one second when the current flowing is one ampere (A). (The ampere is defined at a later stage on page 6.)

Potential

The potential indicates the amount that a body is electrically charged.

When two bodies are equally charged with electrical energy of the same polarity, e.g. positive and positive, a force is needed to move the two bodies together. The work done in applying this force over a given distance is the *electrical potential*.

Electrical potential is similar to air pressure. Consider as an example a car tyre. To inflate the tyre, work has to be done and this work is stored in the tyre by virtue of its pressure. When you push against the tyre it will deflect and the amount of work needed to do this is calculated by multiplying the force by the distance moved. The amount of work done is an indication of the potential, i.e. a measure of the quantity of energy stored in the tyre.

Electrical potential is based on the 'work per unit of charge'. The *joule* is the unit of work and the coulomb the quantity of charge, so potential is expressed in *joules per coulomb*. To honour the early work of the Italian scientist Volta, the unit of potential is named the *volt*.

$$1 \text{ volt} = 1 \text{ joule per coulomb}$$

Potential difference (p.d.)

The concept of potential difference can be visualized by extending the example of the tyre. Consider two tyres; one at low pressure and one at high pressure. If a hose joins the two tyres together, then air will flow from the high pressure tyre to the low pressure tyre until both pressures become equal. The rate of flow of energy will depend on the pressure difference or as applied to electricity, the potential difference.

P.D. is measured from some reference point and, when this is established, the potentials of the two points can be compared to determine the difference.

Using conventional flow, positive (+) to negative (−), electrical energy is considered to move from a point of high potential to a point of lower potential. If a point A has a higher potential than a point B then work is required to move a positive charge from B to A.

The potential difference between the two points A and B is one volt if the work done in taking one coulomb of positive charge from B to A is one joule.

From this definition it follows that the charge (in coulombs) on an object is proportional to its potential difference (in volts).

Electromotive force (e.m.f.)

A battery and generator are both capable of producing a difference in potential between two points. The electrical force that gives this increase in p.d. at the source is called the electromotive force. The unit of e.m.f. is the volt.

The terminals of a battery and generator are called positive (+) and negative (−) and these relate to the higher potential and lower potential respectively.

1.2 Electrical symbols, units and terms

Diagrams of electrical systems are shown in pictorial or theoretical form; in the latter, graphical symbols are used to indicate the various items that make up the circuit.

Many separate parts are used in an electrical system of a motor vehicle, so a convention is needed to enable people to understand the graphical symbols. In the past there has been considerable confusion because each country used its own standard. Nowadays many countries have adopted the recommendations made by the International Electrotechnical Commission (IEC).

In the UK the British Standards Institution (BSI) recommend that the symbols shown in BS 3939:1985 should be used. A selection of the main graphical symbols is shown in Table 1.1.

Many manufacturers in this country have an overseas parent company so this means that they adopt the standard set for that country. Circuit diagrams of these vehicles contain some strange symbols so care must be exercised when using the diagrams.

Electrical units

Table 1.2 shows the main electrical units used in this book.

Description	Symbol
Direct current Alternating current	
Positive polarity Negative polarity	+ –
Current approaching Current receding	⊙ ⊕
Battery 12V (Long line is positive)	
Earth, chassis frame Earth, general	

Description	Symbol
Conductor (permanent) Thickness denotes importance Conductor (temporary)	
Conductors crossing without connecting	
Conductors joining	
Junction, separable Junction, inseparable Plug and socket	o ●

Description	Symbol
Variability; applied to other symbols	
Resistor (fixed value)	
Resistor (variable)	
General winding (inductor, coil)	
Winding with core	
Transformer	

Description	Symbol
Diode, rectifying junction	
Light emitting diode	
Diode, breakdown; Zener and avalanche	
Reverse blocking triode thyristor	
Transistor pnp npn	

Description	Symbol
Lamp	⊗
Fuse	
Switch ('make' contact, normally open)	
Switch ('break' contact, normally closed)	
Switch (manually operated)	
Switch (two-way)	
Relay (single winding)	
Relay (thermal)	
Spark gap	
Generator ac and dc	
Motor dc	
Meters; ammeter, voltmeter, galvanometer	

Description	Symbol
Capacitor, general symbol	
Capacitor, polarized	
Amplifier	

Description		Symbol
Junction f.e.t.	N-type channel	
	P-type channel	
Photodiode		
Thyristor		

Table 1.1 Electrical symbols (BS 3939: 1985)

Unit	Symbol	Electrical property
Ampere	A	Current
Ampere-hour	Ah	Battery capacity
Coulomb	C	Electrical charge
Farad	F	Capacitance
Hertz	Hz	Frequency (1 Hz = 1 cycle per second)
Volt	V	Potential difference or electro-motive force
Watt	W	Power (watt = volt × ampere)

Table 1.2 Electrical units

The electric circuit

The conduction of electricity in metal is due to the drift of free electrons from a lower potential to a higher potential (Figure 1.3). Since many electrons are involved and the space for the drift is large, then the actual speed of movement of any one electron is very slow; it is only about 6 mm per second.

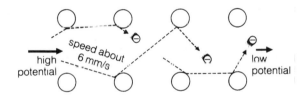

Fig. 1.3 Electron flow from high to low potential

As the electrons move, they collide with atoms in their path and the resultant impact causes the temperature of the metal conductor to increase.

A battery is used in Figure 1.4 to start electron movement and provided that a *closed circuit* (completed path) exists then electrons will flow around the full system.

The electron drift around a circuit is similar to the ball movement in a pipe circuit partially filled with ball bearings (Figure 1.5). When the first ball is struck with a hammer, the force of impact is transmitted to the other balls in turn until all balls are moving around the complete pipework system. To sustain this motion a provision must be made to recharge the balls with energy. The effect of the hammer is performed by a battery in an electrical circuit.

When the movement of the balls has to be stopped, the pipework system is interrupted by a valve. This action is similar to the electrical switch. Switching on and off closes and opens the circuit to the flow of electrons.

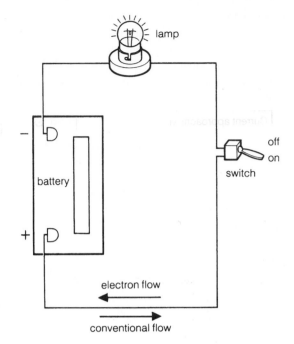

Fig. 1.4 Closed circuit

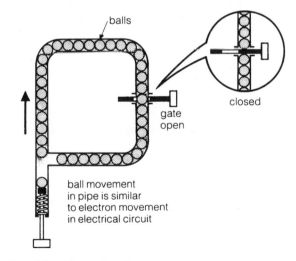

Fig. 1.5 Pipe circuit

Electron movement gives an energy flow called *electric current*. Although the existence of electric current flow was known many years ago, the direction was assumed to be from a higher potential (+) to a lower potential (−); an assumption which has since been proved to be incorrect.

Ampere (A)

The ampere is the unit of electric current flow and is the rate of electron movement along a conductor. A coulomb is the quantity of electrons so when one coulomb passes a given point in one second then the current is one ampere.

$$1 \text{ ampere} = 1 \text{ coulomb per second}$$

Various standards have been used in the past to define the ampere; nowadays it is defined in terms of the force between conductors. If two parallel conductors are placed a given distance apart, then when current is passed through the conductors, a force is set up which is proportional to the current.

Watt (W)

The watt is a unit of power and applies to all branches of science. It is equivalent to work done at the rate of one joule per second. (One joule is the product of the force, in newtons, and the distance, in metres. $1 \text{ J} = 1 \text{ Nm}$.)

A power of 1 W is developed when a current of 1 A flows under the 'pressure' or p.d. of 1 V.

$$\text{power} = \frac{\text{energy supplied (joules)}}{\text{time (seconds)}}$$

$$= \frac{\text{voltage} \times \text{current} \times \text{time}}{\text{time}}$$

Hence   watts $= \text{volts} \times \text{amperes}$

Ohm's Law

In 1826 Ohm discovered that the length of wire in a circuit affected the flow of current. He found that as the length was increased, the current flow decreased and from these findings he concluded that:

Under constant temperature conditions, the current in a conductor is directly proportional to the p.d. between its ends.

Today this statement is known as *Ohm's Law*.

Resistance

From Ohm's Law the relationship between p.d. (V) and current (I) is:

$$\frac{V}{I} = R$$

In this case, R is a constant which changes only when the length or the material of the conductor is altered.

Evidence shows that the value of the constant is related to the conductor's opposition to current flow, so R is called the resistance and is given the unit name of *ohm* (symbol Ω).

The ohm is the resistance of a conductor through which a current of one ampere flows when a potential difference of one volt is across it.

In practical work the expression $V/I = R$ is often called Ohm's Law. Rearranged it gives:

$$V = IR \quad \text{or} \quad \text{volts} = \text{amperes} \times \text{ohms}$$

If two of these values are known, the third can be calculated, so this expression has a number of practical uses.

When the resistance of a conductor is the main property, it is called a *resistor*.

The resistance of a conductor is determined by its material, temperature and dimensions, namely cross-sectional area and length.

The SI unit of *resistivity* of a material is the ohm-metre. This is the resistance in ohms of a 1 metre length of material having a cross-section of 1 square metre. Table 1.3 shows typical values for some pure metals arranged in the order of resistivity; best conductor is placed first.

Substance	Approximate resistivity (ohm m at 20°C)
Silver	1.62×10^{-8} (or 0.000 000 0162)
Copper	1.72×10^{-8}
Aluminium	2.82×10^{-8}
Tungsten	5.5×10^{-8}
Brass	8×10^{-8}
Iron	9.8×10^{-8}
Manganin	44×10^{-8}
Constantin	49×10^{-8}

Table 1.3 Resistivity of some materials used for electrical conductors

Although silver is the leader in respect of electrical conductivity, the lower cost of copper makes this a suitable material for a cable carrying electrical currents.

Since the resistivity is based on the dimension of 1 metre, the effect on cable length and cross-sectional area can be deduced. This shows that a proportional increase in resistivity occurs when either the length is increased or the cross-sectional area is decreased.

Most metals also increase their resistivity when the temperature is raised, so these metals are said to have a *positive temperature coefficient*. Conversely if the resistivity decreases with an increase in temperature then the material has a *negative temperature coefficient*; carbon behaves in this manner.

REMEMBER

Electrical units

term	symbol	unit of:
ampere	A	current flow
volt	V	e.m.f. or potential difference
watt	W	power
ohm	Ω	resistance

Circuit resistors

Motor vehicle circuits often consist of a number of components which behave like resistors controlled by switches and connected to an electrical supply. Resistors can take many forms; they can be a lamp or be a part of some other energy-consuming device.

Basic understanding of circuit behaviour may be helped if the effect of resistors on voltage and current flow is considered.

Resistors may be connected in series, in parallel, or a combination of both.

Resistors in series

Placing two resistors in series (Figure 1.6) means that the full current must pass through each resistor in turn. When they are connected in this end-to-end manner, the total resistance of the two resistors is the sum of their values, so:

$$R = R_1 + R_2$$
$$R = 2 + 4 = 6\ \Omega$$

Assuming the resistance of the cables is negligible, by applying Ohm's Law the current flow can be calculated.

$$V = IR$$

$$I = \frac{V}{R} = \frac{12}{6} = 2\ \text{ampere}$$

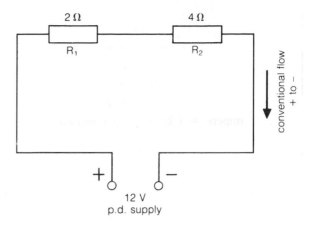

Fig. 1.6 Resistors in series

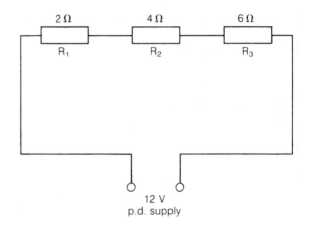

Fig. 1.7 Three resistors in series

In this case, a current of 2 A will pass through each resistor and around the whole circuit.

Inserting an additional resistor of 6 Ω in series with the other two (Figure 1.7) will now give a total resistance of:

$$R = R_1 + R_2 + R_3$$

Figure 1.8 shows two resistors in series with an ammeter and a voltmeter positioned to measure the current and p.d. respectively. It will be seen that the ammeter is fitted in series with the resistors and this means that all current flowing in the circuit must pass through the ammeter, no matter where the meter is inserted in the circuit.

Energy is expended driving the current through a resistor so this causes the potential to drop. The voltage drop (decrease in p.d.) when the current passes through R_1 can be found by applying Ohm's Law:

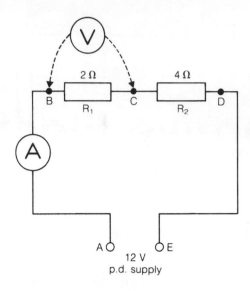

Fig. 1.8 Voltage distribution

$$V = IR$$

$$= 2 \times 2 = 4 \text{ volts}$$

A voltmeter, connected as shown, will register the voltage drop. In this case it will register 4 V, so the p.d. applied to R_2 will be:

$$12 - 4 = 8 \text{ V}$$

By moving the voltmeter around the circuit, the voltage distribution can be determined:

Voltmeter position	Potential difference (V)
AE = BD	12
BC	4
CD	8

The voltmeter is a useful meter for locating an unintentional resistance that has developed in a circuit.

Figure 1.9 shows a simple lighting circuit consisting of a lamp, of resistance 4 Ω, connected to a switch and battery. This lamp requires a current of 3 A to give its full brilliance, but if the cable between A and B develops a 'high resistance' of 2 Ω then the current flow will be reduced to 2 A and the brightness of the lamp will be reduced.

Using a voltmeter to measure the voltage drop of the cable AB will show a reading of 4 V instead of 0 V which is the value expected if the circuit is in good condition. In this case it is obvious that the lamp will

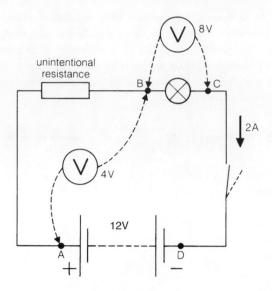

Fig. 1.9 Unintentional resistance in the circuit

not be so bright, because the p.d. across it is only 8 V instead of 12 V.

Resistors in parallel Connecting resistors in parallel (Figure 1.10) ensures that the p.d. applied to each resistor is the same. Current flowing through the ammeter is shared between the two resistors and the amount of current flowing through each resistor will depend on the resistance of that part of the circuit.

Applying Ohm's Law to find the current flow in each resistor:

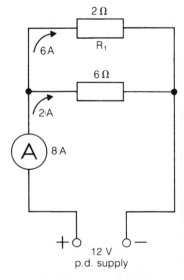

Fig. 1.10 Resistors in parallel

$$I = \frac{V}{R}$$

Current flow through $R_1 = \frac{12}{2} = 6 \text{ A}$

Current flow through $R_2 = \frac{12}{6} = 2 \text{ A}$

Total current flow $= 6 + 2 = 8 \text{ A}$

When calculated in this way, the current through each branch circuit can be found easily. Also it is possible to find the value of a single equivalent resistor (R) which would give the same total current flow as that which passes through both resistors. Applying Ohm's Law:

$$R = \frac{V}{I}$$

$$R = \frac{12}{8} = 1.5 \text{ }\Omega$$

The *equivalent resistance* of a number of resistors R_1, R_2, R_3 can also be found by applying the expression:

$$\frac{1}{R} = \frac{1}{R_1} + \frac{1}{R_2} + \frac{1}{R_3}$$

Figure 1.11 shows a circuit consisting of two lamps in parallel, both controlled by a switch. Arranged in this manner both lamps operate at full brilliance because the battery p.d. of 12V is applied directly to each lamp. Failure of the filament of one lamp has no effect on the other lamp, whereas a break in any part of a series circuit would cause complete failure of all parts of the circuit.

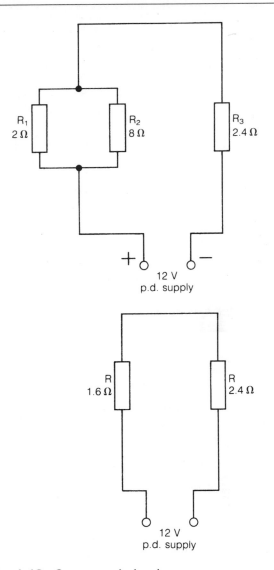

Fig. 1.12 Compound circuit

Compound circuit (series–parallel circuit) This circuit uses resistors, or other components connected so that some parts are in series and other parts are in parallel (Figure 1.12).

When calculating the current flow in these circuits, it is imagined that the parallel resistors are replaced by a single resistor of equivalent value so as to produce a series circuit.

Equivalent resistance of R_1 and R_2 is found by:

$$\frac{1}{R} = \frac{1}{R_1} + \frac{1}{R_2} \quad \left[\text{or } R = \frac{R_1 R_2}{R_1 + R_2}\right]$$

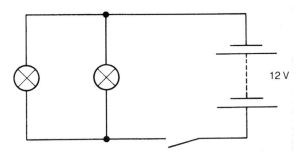

Fig. 1.11 Lamps in parallel

$$\frac{1}{R} = \frac{1}{2} + \frac{1}{8}$$

$$\frac{1}{R} = \frac{4 + 1}{8} = \frac{5}{8}$$

$$5R = 8$$

$$\therefore R = \frac{8}{5} = 1.6 \ \Omega$$

The two resistors R_1 and R_2 working together in parallel give the same current flow as one resistor of 1.6 Ω.

$$\text{Total resistance of circuit} = 1.6 + R_3$$

$$= 1.6 + 2.4$$

$$= 4 \ \Omega$$

Current flow is given by applying Ohm's Law:

$$I = \frac{V}{R} = \frac{12}{4} = 3 \ A$$

Consideration of the current flow through R_1 and R_2 shows that 3 A is shared by both resistors. This current divides according to the resistor values – the higher the value, the smaller the current.

$$\text{Current flow through } R_1 = \frac{R_2}{R_1 + R_2} \times I$$

$$= \frac{8}{10} \times 3 = 2.4 \ A$$

Current flow through $R_2 = 0.6$ A

This result may be verified by using the p.d. values applied across R_1 and R_2.

Voltage drop across R_3:

$$V = IR$$

$$V = 3 \times 2.4 = 7.2 \ V$$

So p.d. across R_1 and $R_2 = 12 - 7.2$

$$= 4.8 \ V$$

Therefore the current flow through R_1:

$$I = \frac{V}{R}$$

$$I = \frac{4.8}{2} = 2.4 \ A$$

and current flow through R_2:

$$I = \frac{4.8}{8} = 0.6 \ A$$

Having mastered the way of finding the voltage and current distribution in simple circuits, more complex circuits can now be investigated. Normally these are a collection of simple circuits, so each sub-circuit can be viewed in turn to determine the current and voltage readings. Figure 1.13 shows a typical example.

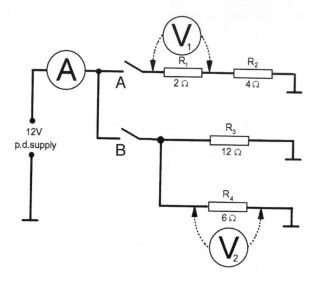

Fig. 1.13 Compound circuit

Example

Calculate the readings on the ammeter and volt-meters V_1 and V_2 when:

switch A is closed and switch B is open;
switch B is closed and switch A is open;
both switches are closed.

Calculate the resistance of the full circuit.

Solution
When only switch A is closed:

total resistance of R_1 and $R_2 = 2 + 4 = 6 \ \Omega$

$$\text{current through ammeter} = \frac{V}{R} = \frac{12}{6} = 2 \ A$$

$$\text{reading on voltmeter } V_1 = IR = 2 \times 2 = 4 \ V$$

When switch B is closed:

$$\text{current through } R_3 = \frac{V}{R} = \frac{12}{12} = 1 \ A$$

current through R_4 $= \dfrac{V}{R} = \dfrac{12}{6} = 2$ A

current through ammeter $= 3$ A

full supply p.d. acts on R_4 so reading $V_2 = 12$ V

When both switches are closed:

total current $= 2 + 3 = 5$ A

reading on V_1 $= 4$ V

reading on V_2 $= 12$ V

Resistance of full circuit $= \dfrac{V}{I} = \dfrac{12}{\text{full current}} = \dfrac{12}{5}$

$= 2.4\ \Omega$

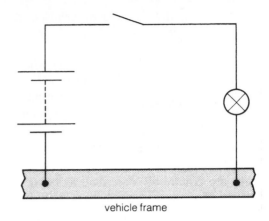

Fig. 1.15 Earth return circuit

Circuit terms

Insulated return The simple circuit shown as Figure 1.14 connects the lamp to the battery and uses a switch to control the 'supply' from the battery via the *feed wire*. To complete the circuit, the cable joining the lamp to the battery acts as a return for the *supply current*. These terms relate to conventional flow.

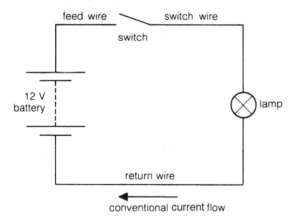

Fig. 1.14 Insulated return circuit for supply current

The term *insulated return* is used whenever an insulated cable provides the return path for the current.

Earth return In this case the vehicle frame or 'earth' provides the return path for the current (Figure 1.15). Advantages of this system are: reduced cost, lighter weight and simpler circuit layout.

Extra precautions must be taken with this system to prevent chafing of the feed wire cable insulation by a sharp part of the vehicle's frame or body. If this occurs, the supply current will be conducted to earth so, unless

the circuit is protected by some form of fuse, a fire can be started. (See 'short circuit' below.)

Most vehicles have an earth return system; the exceptions are the special-purpose vehicles such as petrol tankers that have a high fire risk; these use an insulated return layout.

A simpler diagram is obtained when the earth symbol is used (Figure 1.16).

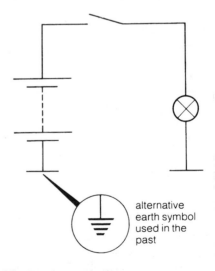

Fig. 1.16 Earth symbols

In North America the term *ground* is used instead of 'earth'.

Earth polarity The negative terminal of the battery shown in Figure 1.16 is connected to the frame. This arrangement is called *negative earth* and is commonly used on the majority of modern vehicles. Reasons for this choice will be covered at a later stage (see page 185).

In the past, vehicles used *positive earth* whereby the vehicle frame was of positive potential.

Damage to electrical components containing semi-conductor devices will occur if the battery is incorrectly earthed.

Circuit faults

Failure of an electrical system is often caused by a circuit fault. Two common faults are considered at this stage.

Open circuit   A complete circuit is needed if current is to flow around the system. An *open circuit* exists when the circuit is interrupted either intentionally or unintentionally. A switch 'opens' the circuit by breaking the supply wire and a similar effect is produced when either a poor terminal connection or a broken cable stops the current flow (Figure 1.17).

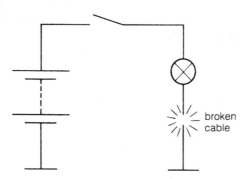

Fig. 1.17 Open circuit

Short circuit   When the feed- or switch-wire insulation is damaged and the conductor touches the metal frame, some or all of the current will take this 'easy' path to earth. This alternative path offers the current a short path back to the battery, so the term *short circuit* is used to describe this condition (Figure 1.18).

The extent of the short-to-earth, i.e. the resistance of the alternative path, governs the p.d. that is left to act on the lamp in Figure 1.18. As the resistance in the short circuit path is reduced, the p.d. across the lamp is also reduced so the effect of the voltage reduction will be a proportional decrease in the lamp brilliance.

A *dead short* describes a very low resistance path to earth. When this occurs the very high current flow that results will soon make the cable glow red-hot. This melts the plastic covering of the cable and often starts

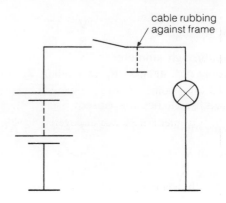

Fig. 1.18 Short circuit

a fire. Some circuit-protection device such as a fuse is needed if this danger is to be avoided.

REMEMBER

Total resistance of **resistors in series**:

$$R = R_1 + R_2$$

Equivalent resistance of **resistors in parallel**:

$$\frac{1}{R} = \frac{1}{R_1} + \frac{1}{R_2}$$

OR

$$R = \frac{R_1 \times R_2}{R_1 + R_2}$$

$$R = \frac{\text{p.d. across resistors}}{\text{total current through parallel resistors}}$$

$$R = \frac{\text{p.d.}}{\dfrac{V}{I_1} + \dfrac{V}{I_2}}$$

Voltage drop (or IR drop) = current × resistance

$$V = IR$$

Earth return – vehicle frame is part of circuit
Insulated return – separate cables for feed and return currents
Open circuit – circuit is interrupted, no current flows
Short circuit – some current takes a shorter path than intended

1.3 Magnetism and electro-magnetism

Magnetism

As long ago as 600 BC it was known that lodestone would always point in one direction when it was suspended. The name *magnet* was derived from the place where this magnetic iron was discovered – Magnesia in Asia.

Because of its directional capabilities, the two ends of a magnet were called North and South. Perhaps the name 'North seeking' would have been more appropriate in view of the fact that the Earth acts as a large magnet itself (Figure 1.19).

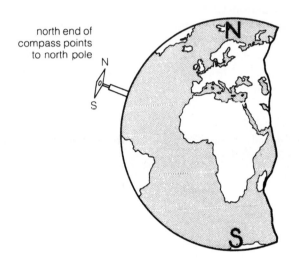

Fig. 1.19 Earth as large magnet

Later discoveries showed that the magnetic effect of lodestone was due to the iron deposits in the stone. Iron can be strongly magnetized, so this metal, along with nickel and cobalt, is called *ferro-magnetic*. Steel is also ferro-magnetic but it is more difficult to magnetize although it retains its magnetism far better than iron.

A magnet made from a metal that retains its magnetism is called a *permanent magnet*. Today, special steel alloys containing cobalt, nickel or aluminium are used to make strong permanent magnets.

Metals having no iron content, i.e. non-ferrous metals, are commonly described as being non-magnetic. However, some of these materials do show slight magnetic properties when exposed to a very powerful magnet.

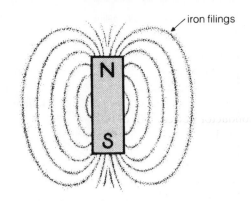

Fig. 1.20 Magnetic field

Magnetic field   Iron filings scattered on a sheet of paper placed over a magnet (Figure 1.20) form a pattern due to the presence of a magnetic field. This is an invisible region around a magnet which produces an external force on ferro-magnetic objects. The iron filings are more concentrated towards the end of the magnet, so this shows that the field is strongest at these points. The two ends of the magnet are called *poles*: north pole (N) and south pole (S).

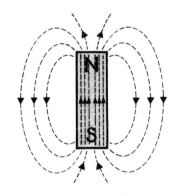

Fig. 1.21 Magnetic field pattern

Figure 1.21 shows that the iron filings arrange themselves to form a series of lines which extend from one pole to the other. These lines are called magnetic *lines of force*.

Attract and repel action   When a magnet is moved towards a suspended second magnet (Figure 1.22) the effect is that:

Like poles repel each other
Unlike poles attract each other

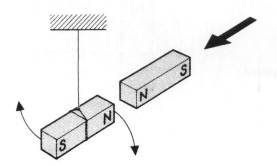

Fig. 1.22 Action when two opposing poles are brought together

When this experiment is performed under a sheet of paper containing iron filings, it is seen that the 'unlike poles' of the magnets combine together to make a larger magnet and as a result the lines of force pass directly from one magnet to the other. This action produces an external force that makes it difficult to hold the magnets apart.

An opposite effect results when either N and N, or S and S, are brought together. In this case the field of one magnet opposes the field of the other magnet and observation of the filings shows that the lines of force are bent as the magnets come together. The external force pushing the two magnets apart is related to the 'bending' of the lines of force; the greater the field distortion, the larger the magnetic force produced.

The direction of a line of force can be found by using a small compass, which is a magnet pivoted at the centre for rotation purposes. By positioning the compass in various places in the field, the lines of force can be mapped out (Figure 1.23).

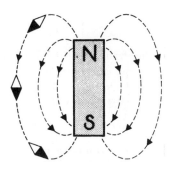

Fig. 1.23 Mapping a magnetic field

Magnetic flux Lines of force passing from N to S indicate a region of magnetic activity around a magnet. This activity is produced by a magnetic flux. The presence of this magnetic region is detected by the effects it produces.

Sometimes it is said that magnetic flux flows around the magnet from the N pole to the S pole where it then passes internally through the magnet to return to the N pole. This statement suggests movement but, unlike electricity, no flow actually takes place.

Magnetic flux density The density is the strength of a magnetic field at a given point. It is measured by the force that the field exerts on a conductor through which a given current is passed.

A ferromagnetic material, placed in a magnetic field (Figure 1.24), provides an easier path for the magnetic flux than through air. An iron frame concentrates the flux where it is required and gives an increased flux density. Iron accepts a magnetic flux easier than air, so iron is said to have a higher *permeability* than air.

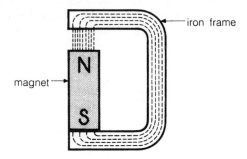

Fig. 1.24 Iron frame concentrates flux

Magnetic screening There are cases where a magnetic flux must be either contained, or excluded, from a given region. An iron ring, placed in a strong magnetic field, has a region within the ring that is *screened* or *shielded* from the magnetic flux (Figure 1.25).

Magnetic theory Various theories relating to the internal changes that take place in a metal when it becomes magnetized have been advanced over the years. The modern view is called the *domain theory*.

Earlier in this book (page 2) the movement of electrons in an atom was described. This showed that electrically charged electrons orbited around a nucleus at a high speed.

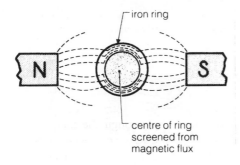

Fig. 1.25 Magnetic screening

The domain theory suggests that when all electrons of one particular atom are moving in the same direction, then magnetism is produced which makes the atom into a tiny atomic magnet. When an atom has an equal number of electrons moving in opposite directions, then it receives no charge from the electrons and no magnetic effect is produced.

A ferromagnetic metal, such as iron and steel, has a composition that consists of a number of domains of 'atomic magnets' arranged so that each group has a common magnetic axis. In Figure 1.26 each arrow represents an atomic magnet; the arrow head indicates the N pole.

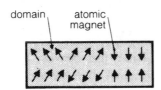

Fig. 1.26 Unmagnetized

When the metal bar is gradually magnetized from some external source, the atomic magnets slowly rearrange themselves. When the external field is very strong, the magnetic axes of all atomic magnets will coincide with the direction of the external field (Figure 1.27). When this is achieved, the maximum magnetic strength is obtained and no further increase is possible: this condition is called *magnetic saturation*.

Fig. 1.27 Magnetized

In the case of soft iron, the removal of the external field causes some of the atomic magnets in certain domains to return to their original position. As a result, only a few domains remain aligned with the axis of the bar, so the magnetism that remains is very small. This partial magnetism is called *residual magnetism*; the polarity of the magnetism is set by the external field previously applied.

Demagnetization A permanent magnet will 'lose' its strength if it is exposed to heat or vibration, because these effects allow the atomic magnets to settle back in their preferred positions. To avoid this, a magnet should have a *keeper* when it has been removed from a component. The keeper becomes an *induced magnet* (Fig. 1.28).

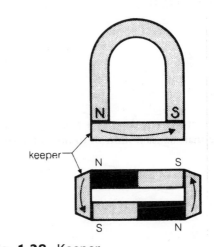

Fig. 1.28 Keeper

Reluctance This term is similar to the term 'resistance' as applied to an electrical circuit, except that reluctance refers to a magnetic circuit.

Figure 1.29 shows how the reluctance of an air gap is reduced when two poles of a magnet are bridged by a piece of iron.

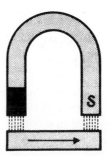

Fig. 1.29 Reluctance

REMEMBER

Magnetism
- Around a magnet there is an invisible magnetic field
- Like poles repel, unlike poles attract
- Iron has a high magnetic permeability
- Permanent magnets will lose their strength if they are exposed to heat or vibration
- Reluctance is the opposition to a magnetic field

Electromagnetism

In 1819 Prof. Oersted discovered that a wire carrying an electric current deflected a nearby compass needle. Further investigation showed that the direction of the needle deflection depended on whether the compass was placed under or over the wire and also on the direction of the current (Figure 1.30).

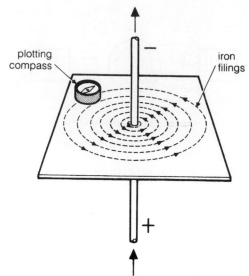

Fig. 1.31 Iron filings show presence of magnetic field

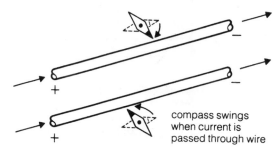

compass swings when current is passed through wire

Fig. 1.30 Compass shows presence of magnetic field

The movement of the compass needle showed the existence of a magnetic flux around the wire. This can be seen from an experiment shown as Figure 1.31. Iron filings, scattered on a sheet of paper, rearrange themselves into a series of concentric rings when current flows in the circuit and the paper is gently tapped. The direction of the flux can be determined by using a plotting compass.

If the current is reversed, a similar pattern is formed but the compass needle points in the opposite direction.

The direction of the flux can be found by imagining a corkscrew placed around the wire. As current flows along the wire, the direction of the screw indicates the direction of the magnetic flux (Figure 1.32). Known as *Maxwell's Screw Rule*, the method has many practical applications.

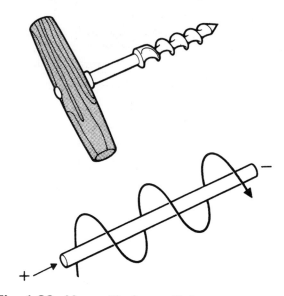

Fig. 1.32 Maxwell's Screw Rule

The electromagnet When current is passed through a wire that is wound to form a coil, a magnetic flux is produced (Figure 1.33). This flux can be concentrated by placing a soft iron core in the coil. In Figure 1.34 the direction of the current (conventional flow) is shown by the symbols • and +; these represent the point and tail of an arrow that points in the direction of the current (Figure 1.35).

On closing the switch a magnetic flux is set up around each winding. Since the windings are placed

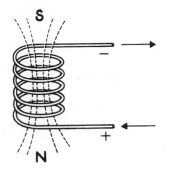

Fig. 1.33 Magnetic flux in coil

close to each other, the flux blends together to form a common pattern centred around the iron core. This action makes the iron into a magnet; the polarity of the magnet is governed by the direction of the current in the winding.

The relationship between current direction and magnetic polarity can be determined quickly by the *right-hand grip rule*. (This should not be confused with Fleming's rule described on page 21.)

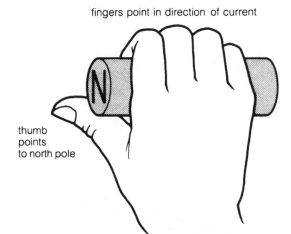

Fig. 1.36 Right hand grip rule

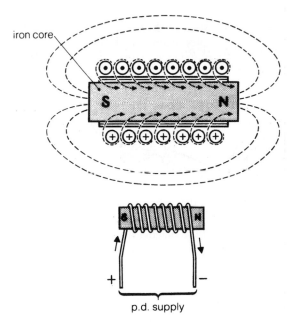

Fig. 1.34 Electromagnet

Fig. 1.36 shows that when the fingers point in the direction of current flow, the thumb points to the north.

An alternative method is shown as Fig. 1.37. The symbols representing N and S indicate the direction of the current in relation to the magnetic polarity.

The strength of an electromagnet depends on two things; the amount of current that flows through the winding and the number of turns which make the coil. Multiplying these two together gives the unit 'ampere-turns', so if 5 A flows through a coil winding having 1000 turns, then the magnetic strength will be equivalent to 5000 ampere-turns.

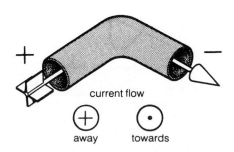

Fig. 1.35 Symbols to represent direction of current

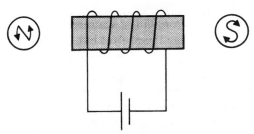

Fig. 1.37 Symbol method of showing polarity

Electromagnetic components

One advantage of an electromagnet is that it can be turned on and off at will. To provide this feature, the core must lose its magnetism quickly, so for this reason iron is preferred to steel for the core material.

The solenoid This device is used commonly on vehicles to produce movement from an electrical signal, e.g. to control a remote switch or operate a door-locking system.

A solenoid consists of a coil of wire wound around a cylinder into which is fitted a sliding soft iron plunger. A spring holds the plunger away from the coil when the unit is not in use (Figure 1.38).

When current is supplied, the magnetic effect attracts the plunger into the centre of the winding and movement of the plunger operates the appropriate switch or mechanical linkage.

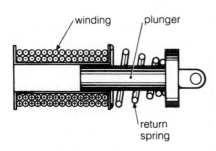

Fig. 1.38 Solenoid

Electromagnetic relay Some electrical systems require a small current to control the flow of a large current: this duty can be performed by a relay.

One type of relay (Figure 1.39) consists of an L-shaped frame on to which is hinged an *armature*. A coil, consisting of many turns of very fine enamelled wire, is wound around the soft iron core and a pair of heavy-

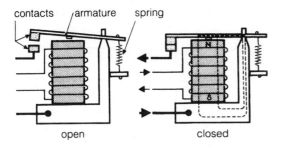

Fig. 1.39 Electromagnetic relay

duty contacts are connected, in series, to a separate circuit which carries a large current.

When a small current is supplied to the coil winding, the core becomes a magnet. At this point the armature is attracted to the magnet and this causes the main contacts to close.

The voltage at which the contacts close can be altered by varying the strength of the spring.

1.4 Electromagnetic induction

After 1819, when Oersted discovered that magnetism could be produced by an electric current, many scientists searched for a method to establish the reverse effect. It was not until 1831 that Michael Faraday achieved this goal: he showed that electricity could be produced from magnetism. By a series of experiments he demonstrated the principles from which the generator and many other automobile components have been developed.

Faraday's experiments

One of the most important experiments is shown as Figure 1.40. The apparatus he used consisted of a coil wound around a paper tube and to the winding he connected a galvanometer (an instrument for detecting the presence and direction of an electric current).

Faraday noticed that when he plunged a magnet into the coil the galvanometer needle moved, Also he saw that as he removed the magnet from the coil the galvanometer needle flicked in the opposite direction. The needle behaviour showed that current was generated

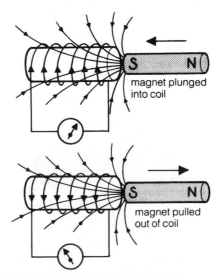

Fig. 1.40 Electromagnetic induction

only when the magnet was being moved. Furthermore this experiment demonstrated that the direction of the current depended on the direction of movement of the magnet.

Whenever current is generated in this way it is called *electromagnetic induction.*

The conclusion made by Faraday was that current is induced into a circuit when a coil winding cuts a magnetic line of force formed around a magnet. Today this conclusion can be expressed as:

An electromotive force is induced whenever there is a change in the magnetic flux linked with the coil.

Faraday discovered that the electromotive force (e.m.f.) induced in the coil winding depended on:

1) number of turns in the coil;
2) strength of the magnet;
3) speed with which the magnet cuts the coil windings.

Another of Faraday's experiments is shown as Figure 1.41. The apparatus was a coil, wound around a soft iron core, which was positioned between two permanent bar magnets. When he moved the magnets in the direction of the arrows, the galvanometer needle deflected one way, and when he brought the magnets together, the needle moved in the opposite direction.

In this case the induced currents were produced by the changes in the density of the magnetic flux through the coil. The strength of the e.m.f. induced in this manner is proportional to the rate of change of the flux linked with the circuit.

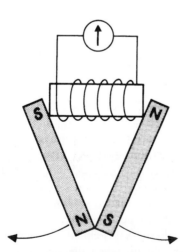

Fig. 1.41 Electromagnetic induction

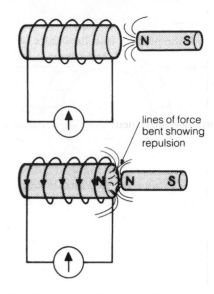

Fig. 1.42 Apparatus for showing Lenz's law

It is found that when the iron core is removed, the magnetic flux in the region of the coil is decreased, so this results in a reduction in the e.m.f.

Lenz's Law In 1834 Lenz stated a law which is related to electromagnetic induction. This law is:

The direction of the induced current is always such as to oppose the change producing it.

This law can be explained by the apparatus shown as Figure 1.42. When a magnet is plunged into a coil, an induced current is generated.

According to Lenz's Law this current will always have a magnetic polarity which will repel the magnet, so in this case the current in the coil will form a N pole at the end nearest the magnet.

Mutual induction Faraday's iron ring experiment (Figure 1.43) showed that a coil could be used instead of a magnet to induce a current into an independent coil.

He used an iron ring and on opposite sides of this ring he wound two coils: a primary and a secondary. He connected the primary coil to a battery and switch and the secondary coil he joined to a galvanometer.

On closing the switch, the build-up of magnetic flux in the iron ring induced a 'momentary' current into the secondary and this caused the galvanometer needle to kick over. Opening the switch gave a similar effect except the needle kicked in the opposite direction to show a current flow in the reverse direction. He concluded that the breaking of the primary circuit causes

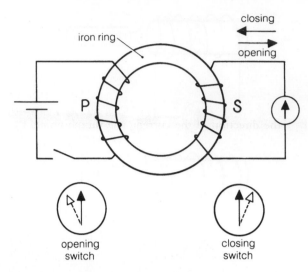

Fig. 1.43 Mutual induction

the magnetic flux to decay and the change of flux which results *induces a current* into the secondary coil.

Faraday varied this experiment by using two coils, wound on a piece of wood, placed side by side. The result was similar except that a lower current was induced. The decrease in current was due to the reduced

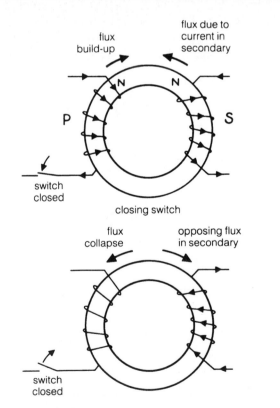

Fig. 1.44 Direction of current in secondary

flux concentration brought about by the loss of the iron core.

The term *mutual induction* is used when one coil or conductor induces an e.m.f. into a separate coil or conductor.

Lenz's law also applies to mutual induction so in Figure 1.44 the direction of current in the secondary depends on whether the switch is opened or closed. Closing the switch causes the magnetic flux to build up in a clockwise direction so, by applying Lenz's Law, the induced current in the secondary gives an anti-clockwise magnetic flux. Once this is established, the right-hand grip rule indicates the current direction in the secondary.

Opening the switch causes the magnetic flux to decay so the induced secondary current will set up a flux in a clockwise direction. This produces a current in the secondary circuit which flows in the opposite way to that obtained when the switch is closed.

Self-induction On opening the switch to break the primary circuit (Figure 1.44) it is seen that a spark jumps across the switch contacts just as the contacts separate. The spark shows that a current of high voltage in excess of about 350 V is induced back into the primary by the decay of the magnetic flux. This effect is called *self-induction* and the e.m.f. causing the effect is termed *back-e.m.f.*

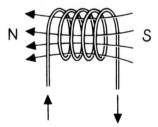

Fig. 1.45 Magnetic field set up by current in coil

Whenever a current flows through a coil (Figure 1.45) a magnetic field is set up. (If the current is either increased or decreased then the back-e.m.f., caused by self-induction, will oppose the change. This is another case of Lenz's Law and is the reason why, in the experiment shown as Fig. 1.44, it takes a relatively long time for the current to build up to its maximum in the primary after the switch is closed. Conversely, an interruption of the circuit when the switch is opened will quickly produce a large secondary current.

In vehicle ignition systems a sparking plug is used in the place of the galvanometer shown in Fig. 1.44, and a contact breaker replaces the switch. By connecting a capacitor in parallel with the contacts, arcing is minimized so a rapid break in the circuit can be obtained.

Induction in a straight conductor A further example of electromagnetic induction is shown in another of Faraday's experiments. This involves the movement of a straight conductor through a magnetic flux (Fig. 1.46). An e.m.f. was generated when the conductor was moved in a direction which cuts the magnetic flux.

A few years after this experiment was demonstrated, Fleming introduced a simple rule to show the relationship between the directions of the field, current and conductor.

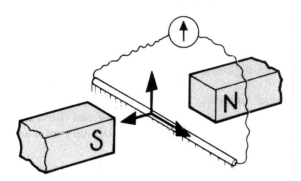

Fig. 1.46 Induction in a straight conductor

Fleming's right-hand rule (dynamo rule) This is applied to electromagnetic induction and is shown by Figure 1.47. This rule may be expressed as:

> ***When the thumb and first two fingers of the right-hand are all set at right angles to one another, then the forefinger points in the direction of the field, the thumb to the direction of the motion and the second finger points to the direction of the current.***

This can be summarized as:

thu**M**b	**M**otion
fore**F**inger	**F**ield
se**C**ond finger	**C**urrent (conventional flow)

Another rule is credited to Fleming which is used with motors. This will be applied at a later stage in this chapter (page 26).

(page 26).

REMEMBER

Electromagnetism

- Maxwell's screw rule can be used to find the direction of a magnetic flux
- Right-hand grip rule uses the fingers to point in the direction of the current; the thumb points to the north
- Strength of an electromagnet depends on ampere-turns

Induction

- Faraday discovered that an induced e.m.f. depended on:

  a) number of turns
  b) strength of magnet
  c) cutting speed

- Lenz's law states that the magnetic polarity of an induced current always opposes the main field
- mutual induction – when a varying magnetic flux around a conductor induces an e.m.f. into *another* conductor
- self-induction – when a varying magnetic flux around a conductor induces an e.m.f. into *that* conductor – this causes a *back-e.m.f.*

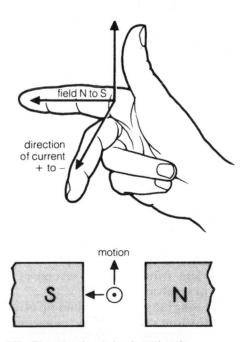

Fig. 1.47 Fleming's right-hand rule

The alternating current generator

A simple dynamo is shown as Fig. 1.48. This consists of two magnetic poles of a field magnet and a conductor bent to make a loop. Each end of the loop is joined to a slip ring which makes contact with a carbon brush.

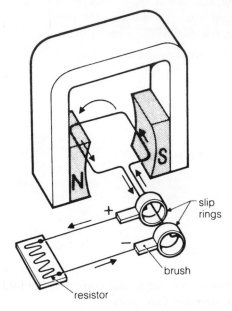

Fig. 1.48 Simple dynamo

When the conductor loop is rotated, an e.m.f. is generated and this drives a current around the circuit (Figure 1.49).

The direction of the current, as found by Fleming's right-hand rule, is shown by the arrows and symbols · and +. Although the current induced in side A flows in the opposite direction to side B, the loop of the conductor ensures that the flow in the circuit at this instant is unidirectional.

As the conductor coil moves away from the dense magnetic flux region, shown as position 1, the output gradually falls. At position 2 both conductors are moving in the direction of the flux so neither conductor is cutting any of the imaginary lines of force. Since the flux is uncut, no current will be generated at this point.

In position 3 the coil is situated in a dense flux region so maximum output will be obtained, but at this point the direction of the current in each conductor will be opposite to the flow indicated in position 1.

The e.m.f. output of a generator is shown by the graph (Figure 1.50). It is seen that the e.m.f. will cause the current to flow in one direction and then reverse to flow in the opposite direction. This type of current is called *alternating current* (a.c.).

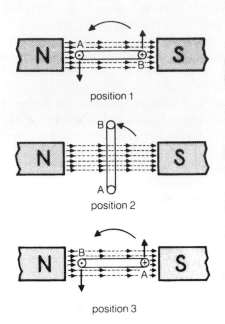

Fig. 1.49 Coil position and current flow

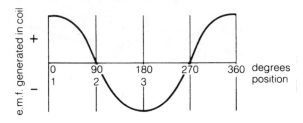

Fig. 1.50 E.M.F. generated in coil

Alternating current

Waveform terms When the conductor starts its motion from a vertical point (position 2, Figure 1.49), the e.m.f. will vary as shown in Figure 1.51. This shape of curve is called a *sine wave* and when something moves or varies its output in this way the term *sinusoidal* is used.

One complete turn (360°) of the conductor loop gives one complete wave and this is called a *cycle*. The time required to complete one cycle is termed its *period* (or *periodic time*).

A study of the e.m.f. output at a given instant (the *instantaneous voltage*) shows that it builds up to a *peak voltage*, then decreases to zero and reverses to build up to give a peak voltage of opposite polarity. The vertical distance between the two peaks is known as the *peak-to-peak voltage*. This should not be confused with the *amplitude*, which is the vertical distance from the horizontal axis of the graph to the peak.

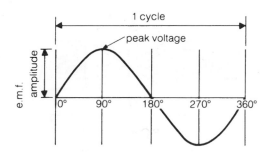

Fig. 1.51 Sine wave

When the conductor is rotated beyond 360° the e.m.f. cycle is repeated. The number of complete cycles that occur in one second is called the *frequency*; the SI unit for frequency is the *hertz* (1 cycle/second = 1 Hz). A generator frequency depends on its speed of rotation: the faster the speed, the higher the frequency.

For many applications such as battery-charging, the alternating current must be *rectified* so that the current is made to flow in one direction only. This undirectional flow, or *direct current*, is achieved when the negative half-wave of the sinusoidal wave is transferred to the positive side of the graph axis (Figure 1.52). This change is called *full-wave rectification*.

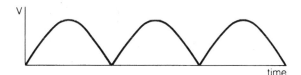

Fig. 1.52 Full-wave rectification

The e.m.f. from an a.c. generator is not sinusoidal when the poles are shaped to provide a uniformly distributed flux (Figure 1.53). In this case the conductor moves in a dense flux for a large angle of movement so this gives a non-sinusoidal waveform (Figure 1.54)

By rounding-off the pole shoes as shown by the broken line, the sharpness of the corners at A and B in Figure 1.54 can be reduced.

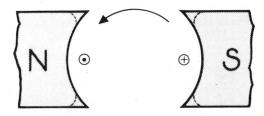

Fig. 1.53 Uniformly distributed flux

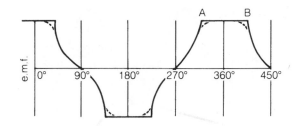

Fig. 1.54 Non-sinusoidal waveform

Current flow The instantaneous e.m.f. gives a proportional current flow through an external circuit of resistance R. The power (volts × amperes) or heating effect produced by this output is given by:

$$\text{power (W)} = VI$$

where V = volt and I = current (ampere)

From Ohm's Law, V = IR so:

$$\text{power} = (IR) \times I = I^2R$$

This shows that the power is proportional to the square of the current, i.e. when the current is doubled, the power is increased four times.

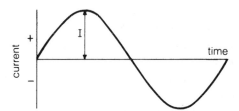

Fig. 1.55 A.C. waveform

Consider the current shown by the waveform in Figure 1.55. To obtain the heating effect of this current a graph of I^2R is plotted (Figure 1.56). This curve shows that the heating effect is unaffected by the direction of the current. By rearranging the various parts of the curve it is possible to make a rectangular pattern. The height of this rectangle represents the *effective value* of the a.c. current, i.e. the value of the direct current which would give the same heating effect in the same resistance.

Another name for the effective value of an alternating current is the *root-mean-square* (r.m.s.) value of the current. Alternating current test meters measure the r.m.s. value of either the current or the voltage.

Sometimes the term *average current* is used. As the name suggests this is the mean current that flows during

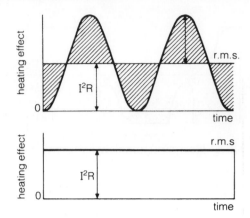

Fig. 1.56 R.M.S. value of sinusoidal current

the cycle and should not be confused with the r.m.s. value.

For sinusoidal waves:

average value = 0.637 maximum value

r.m.s. value = 0.707 maximum value

Waveforms can be examined by using a *cathode ray oscilloscope* (CRO).

Impedance A back-e.m.f. caused by self-induction, develops when the direction of current is reversed. This effect prevents an a.c. current building up to that which would be obtained from a constant d.c. supply.

Impedance of a circuit is the 'opposition' it gives to the flow of alternating current. It is expressed in ohms and calculated by:

$$impedance = voltage/current$$

The frequency of an a.c. current affects the impedance of the circuit.

Multi-phase a.c. The current delivered by the conductor coil of a simple generator is a single-phase a.c. This means that the output e.m.f. and current corresponds to a single wave as shown in Figure 1.55.

If three conductor coils, A, B and C in Figure 1.57 were equally spaced and connected as shown to four terminals, then the coils will reach their peak e.m.f. at different times.

Output of each coil, measured between the common neutral (N) and the appropriate terminal A, B or C, will give a sinusoidal wave but the waves will be 120° out-of-phase. Figure 1.58 shows a three-phase output obtained from this layout and in this graph the cycle of each phase is emphasized.

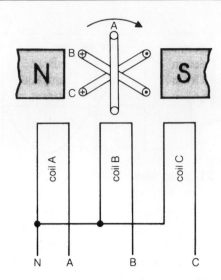

Fig. 1.57 Three coils to give three-phase output

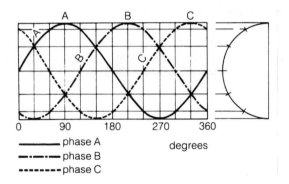

Fig. 1.58 Three-phase output

When a three-phase output is rectified, a smoother current is achieved than that obtained from a single phase.

1.5 Electromagnetic equipment

Eddy currents

In a dynamo, the conductor coils are normally wound on a soft-iron former called an *armature*. The iron concentrates the magnetic flux where it is needed and forms a part of the magnetic 'circuit'.

If the cylindrical armature were made in one piece, rotation of the armature would cause an eddy current to be generated within its iron core. The direction of flow of the current can be obtained from Fleming's right-hand rule and in Figure 1.59 it shows how the current makes a path around the armature.

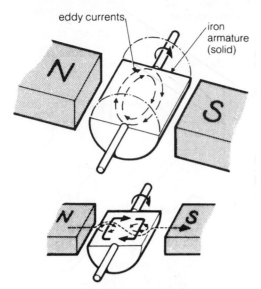

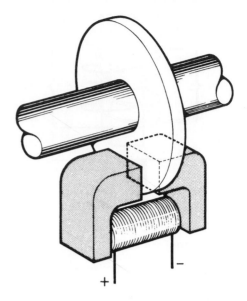

diagram shows bending of main
flux by the eddy currents — this
causes resistance to motion

Fig. 1.59 Eddy current

In addition to the problem of heat created by the dissipation of electrical energy, the magnetic effect of the eddy current makes it more difficult to revolve the armature. This is because the eddy current sets up its own magnetic flux as described in Lenz's law. Since the N pole of the flux from the eddy current is moving towards the N pole of the main field, a repulsion action results.

Electric machines should have a high efficiency, so steps are taken to avoid the internal energy loss due to eddy currents. This is achieved by making the armature, or similar core devices, from thin iron stampings (Fig. 1.60). Each is coated with varnish for insulation purposes.

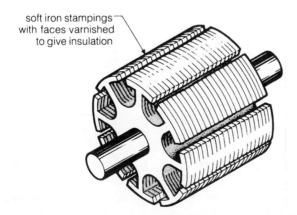

soft iron stampings
with faces varnished
to give insulation

Fig. 1.60 Armature construction

Fig. 1.61 Eddy current brake

Eddy currents can be usefully employed in a number of ways. They can be used to damp the needle movement of a test meter and as a brake retarder to resist the rotation of a disc connected to the road wheels (Figure 1.61).

Drag on the disc of a retarder is produced when the main field is energized; the stronger the field, the greater the drag on the disc.

The transformer

A transformer is a device for stepping-up or stepping-down the voltage.

It consists of two windings, a primary and a secondary, which are wound around a laminated iron core as shown diagrammatically in Fig. 1.62. If a higher voltage is required from the secondary, the secondary winding must have more turns than the primary. The relationship between turns and voltage is:

$$\frac{\text{secondary voltage}}{\text{primary voltage}} = \frac{\text{secondary turns}}{\text{primary turns}}$$

It has been stated that induction must be accompanied by a change in magnetic flux, so providing the primary receives an alternating current the output from the secondary will be a.c. at a voltage governed by the *turns ratio*, due to mutual induction (page 19).

A transformer does not give 'something for nothing': an increase in voltage is balanced by a proportional decrease in current.

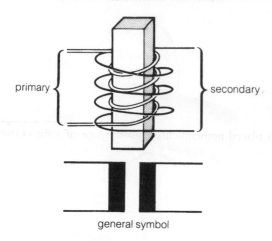

Fig. 1.62 Transformer

The electric motor
When current is supplied by a battery to a conductor placed in a magnetic flux, a force is produced which will move the conductor (Figure 1.63)

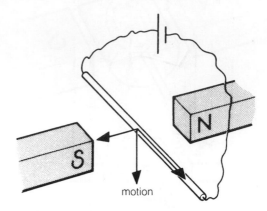

Fig. 1.63 Force on conductor

Fleming's left-hand rule (motor rule) This gives the relationship between the field, current and motion. Similar fingers to those used for the right-hand rule (page 21) are employed to give the various directions as follows:

fore**F**inger **F**ield
thu**M**b **M**otion
se**C**ond finger **C**urrent

The cause of the turning motion can be seen when the lines of magnetic force are mapped (Figure 1.64). This shows a current being passed through a conductor and the formation of a magnetic field around the conductor. This field causes the main field to be bent and the repulsion of the two opposing fields produces a force that gives the motion.

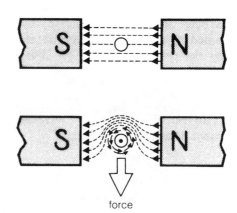

Fig. 1.64 Bending of main field

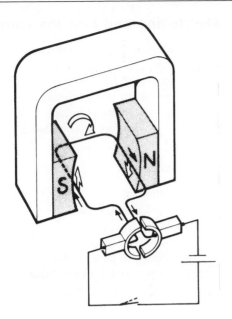

Fig. 1.65 D.C. motor

Figure 1.65 shows the construction of a simple direct current motor. The conductor is looped to form a coil and the ends of this coil are connected to a *commutator* (a device to reverse the current in the coil each cycle as it rotates). Carbon brushes rub on the commutator to supply the coil with current.

Since the two sides of the coil in this construction act as two conductors, a greater turning moment

(torque) is achieved. In Figure 1.64 the field distortion is shown, and if the lines of force in this diagram are considered to be rubber bands, then the principle of the motor movement can be seen.

Hall effect devices

In 1879 Edward Hall discovered that when a magnet was placed perpendicularly to the face of a flat current-carrying conductor, a difference in potential appeared across the other edges of the conductor. This event is called *Hall effect* and the p.d. produced across the edges is termed the *Hall voltage*.

Figure 1.66 shows the principle of the Hall effect. In Figure 1.66.(a) the vertical edges of the plate have equal potential so the voltmeter registers zero. But when the plate is placed in a magnetic field (Figure 1.66(b)), a p.d. across the edges is shown as a steady reading on the meter.

Hall voltage depends on the current flowing through the plate and on the strength of the magnetic field. When the current is constant, the Hall voltage is proportional to the field strength. Similarly, if the field strength

REMEMBER

Electric motor

- a physical force acts on a current-carrying conductor when it is placed in a magnetic field
- *Fleming's left-hand rule* – applied to motors to show the relationship between

  a) motion – thumb
  b) field – forefinger
  c) current – second finger

- Motion of an electric motor is caused by the bending of the main magnetic field by the flux around the conductor
- Commutator in a motor reverses the current in a conductor as it moves from a North to a South pole to maintain cyclic motion

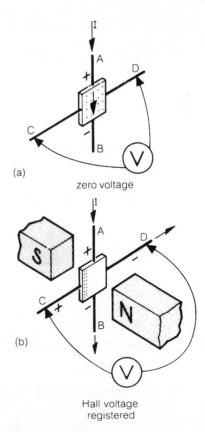

Fig. 1.66 Hall effect

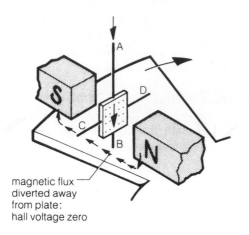

magnetic flux
diverted away
from plate:
hall voltage zero

Fig. 1.67 Hall effect sensor

is constant, the Hall voltage is proportional to the current flowing through the plate.

With common metals such as copper, the Hall voltage is very low, but when a semiconductor is used a much higher voltage is achieved. The polarity of the plate edges depends on the type of semiconductor; a p-type has the opposite Hall voltage p.d. to an n-type (see page 44).

The magnetic field which gives the Hall effect does not act as a generator of energy; instead it acts in the form of a control or switch.

In motor vehicle work this switching feature is utilized as a circuit breaker and trigger in one type of electronic ignition system. Switching is achieved by using a slotted metal 'chopper' plate to interrupt the magnetic field (Figure 1.67) to produce an ON/OFF voltage at the connections CD.

Another application of the Hall effect is for measuring the strength of a magnetic field.

REMEMBER

Hall effect

- When a flat current-carrying conductor is placed in a magnetic field, there is a difference in potential across the other edges
- Hall effect can be used as a switch to trigger the spark in an ignition system
- Switching is controlled by a chopper plate – no Hall voltage is produced when the chopper plate diverts the magnetic field away from the unit

1.6 Measuring and test instruments

There is a large range of electrical test equipment available to the electrician. This equipment may be divided into two main categories: basic instruments used by all electricians and special test sets to measure or check the performance of specific items of vehicle equipment. At this stage the former category is considered.

Basic test instruments

Moving-coil milliammeter This is a galvanometer with a scale graduated to show a current in milliamperes (1 mA = 0.001 A).

Figure 1.68 shows the construction of this type of meter which resembles, in basic principle, the layout of a motor. There is a permanent magnet with two shaped pole pieces and between these is placed a fixed iron cylinder. This concentrates the magnetic field and makes the lines of force radiate from the cylinder centre.

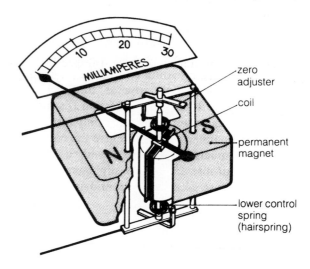

zero
adjuster

coil

permanent
magnet

lower control
spring
(hairspring)

Fig. 1.68 Moving-coil milliammeter

The coil is wound on an aluminium former: this is pivoted on jewelled bearings and attached to a pointer which registers on an evenly-spaced scale. The actual number of turns on the coil, and the gauge of the wire, are governed by the purpose for which the instrument is to be used.

By using an aluminium former, the damping effect of the eddy current allows the pointer to register a reading without oscillating to and fro. This 'dead beat' action is obtained by the opposition of the magnetic flux set up by the current induced into the former when it moves in the main field.

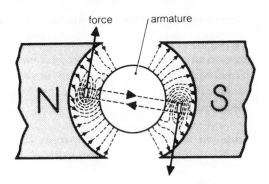

Fig. 1.69 Bending of magnetic flux by current

When current is passed through the coil (Figure 1.69), the flux distortion causes the coil to move. The angle of movement is controlled by two hairsprings which are wound in opposite directions to compensate for thermal expansion. These control springs conduct the current to the coil and their strength governs the current required to give a full-scale deflection (FSD).

A moving-coil meter can be used only with d.c. and must be connected so as to give the correct polarity; terminals are marked + and −.

This type of instrument is easily damaged by overload because excessive current damages the hairsprings.

Moving-coil ammeter Having described the milliammeter it would appear that the meter could be scaled-up to read amperes: this would result in a clumsy inefficient meter. Instead the milliammeter is modified to suit the range required by fitting a resistor of low value in parallel with the meter to *shunt* (by-pass) the major part of the current away from the meter (Figure 1.70).

By selecting a shunt resistor of suitable value, it is possible to vary the range of the meter to suit the application. The normal ammeter has an internally connected shunt to suit the range but when this meter is to be used to measure a high current, e.g. a starter motor current of about 200 A, an external shunt may be fitted (Figure 1.71).

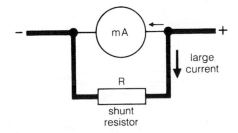

Fig. 1.70 Moving-coil ammeter

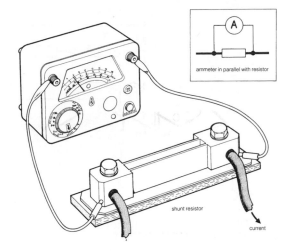

Fig. 1.71 Using shunt resistor to measure large current

Since an ammeter is always placed *in series* with the circuit components, the meter must have a low resistance: it must not restrict the current flowing in the circuit.

Moving-coil voltmeter The current flowing through a milliammeter is proportional to the p.d., so by changing the scale it is possible to use the meter as a millivoltmeter.

When a larger voltage is to be measured, a resistor is fitted in series with the meter to prevent damage from an excessive current. This high-value resistor, called a *multiplier* is fitted internally and the meter is scaled accordingly (Figure 1.72)

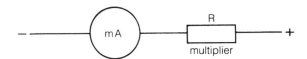

Fig. 1.72 Multiplier resistor for measuring voltage

A voltmeter is used *in parallel* with a circuit component. It should have a high resistance across which the p.d. is to be measured, so as to give an accurate reading without influencing the circuit it is measuring.

Multirange meters Since the milliammeter forms the basic meter it is possible to construct a multirange test meter to cover various ranges.

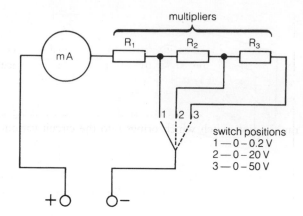

Fig. 1.73 Multirange voltmeter

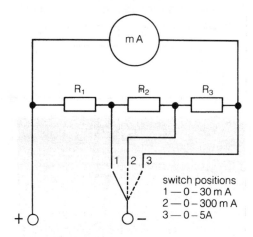

Fig. 1.74 Multirange ammeter

one piece is attached to the spindle and the other piece cut in the form of a taper and fixed to the meter body. A pointer, secured to the spindle, registers on a scale having unequal spacings. A hairspring provides the control force required for the range of the meter.

When current is passed through the coil the two pieces of iron become magnetized and similar poles are set adjacent to each other. The repulsion of the 'like'

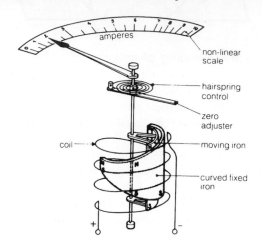

Fig. 1.75 Repulsion-type ammeter

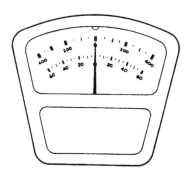

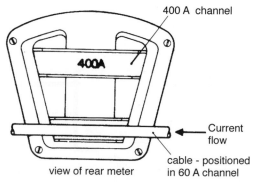

Fig. 1.76 Induction-type meter

Figure 1.73 shows a circuit of a multirange voltmeter which incorporates a switch to select the appropriate voltage multipliers. A typical meter of this type has ranges 0–0.2 V, 0–20 V, and 0–50 V.

A multirange ammeter circuit is shown as Figure 1.74. This uses a universal shunt which has tappings to obtain the various current ranges.

Before using this type of meter, it is wise to initially select a higher range than the maximum expected current so as to avoid overloading the meter.

Moving-iron meters This is a cheaper type of meter which can be used with either d.c. or a.c. currents.

There are two types of moving-iron meter: one operates on magnetic repulsion and the other on magnetic attraction.

Figure 1.75 shows a repulsion-type meter. It consists of a coil which is placed around two pieces of soft iron:

poles moves the inner piece of iron towards the narrow end of the taper.

On this type, needle damping is achieved by some form of air vane or dashpot.

Moving–iron meters can be used either as a voltmeter or ammeter by adding suitable shunts or multipliers.

The induction ammeter This relatively cheap meter is clipped on to the outside of a cable and it registers the current flowing in the circuit (Figure 1.76). It has the advantage that it does not require cable disconnection so it can be quickly fitted, but its accuracy is poor compared with a normal meter.

The instrument measures the magnetic flux around a cable which is set up when current is passing through it.

The ohmmeter Many multimeters incorporate a circuit for measuring the resistance of a component.

To provide this feature the milliammeter is switched into a circuit which incorporates a small battery and variable resistor (Figure 1.77)

The zero on the ohms scale on the meter is set to coincide with the full deflection of the pointer.

Before the instrument is used the test leads are connected together and the variable resistor is adjusted to balance the battery voltage: this gives a zero reading on the ohms scale. After carrying out the initial setting, the test leads are connected to the resistance to be measured.

The principle of the ohmmeter is based on Ohm's law: $R = V/I$. For a given voltage it is seen that the resistance is inversely proportional to the current, i.e. as the current increases, the resistance decreases. Scaling the meter in the opposite direction to normal practice, and calibrating the scale by using known resistance values, it is possible to provide a meter which measures resistance in ohms.

The range of an ohmmeter is increased by using a multi point switch which brings into the circuit various multiplier resistors.

Analogue multimeters These meters register the reading by a pointer and calibrated display, i.e. an *analogue display*

Figure 1.78 shows a battery-operated, hand-held multimeter suitable for voltage, current and resistance measurements of a.c. and d.c. systems.

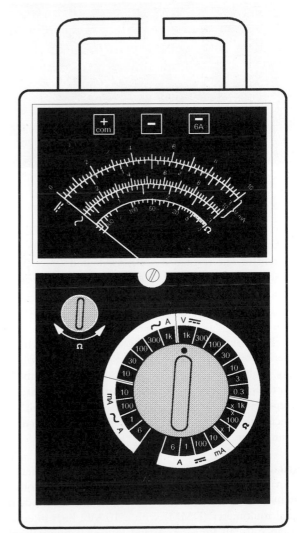

Fig. 1.78 Multimeter

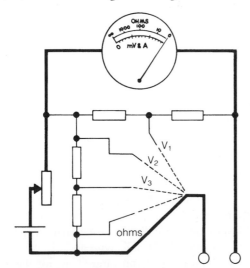

Fig. 1.77 Circuit of multimeter

A rotary switch selects the measurement unit and scale range. Typical ranges are:

DC voltage: 0.3 V, 3 V, 10 V, 30 V
AC voltage: 10 V, 30 V, 100 V, 300 V, 1000 V
DC current: 50 μA, 10 mA, 100 mA, 1 A, 6 A
AC current: 10 mA, 100 mA, 1 A, 6 A
resistance: 10 kΩ, 1 MΩ, 10 Ω

The instrument shown is based on a 40 μA moving coil meter. Test leads connect to two of three sockets provided in the case: these are arranged to give one common negative and two positive for either current or voltage/resistance measurement. Each test lead has either an insulated test prod or crocodile clip; these can be quickly changed to suit the application.

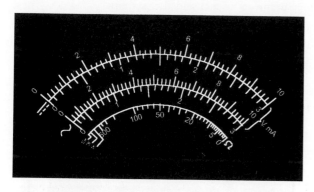

Fig. 1.79 Multimeter scales

In common with other instruments, each scale is used to register more than one range (Figure 1.79) e.g. the right-to-left resistance scale, calibrated 0 – 10, is used for three ranges; 1 Ω, 100 Ω, 1 kΩ. In these cases the indicated reading is multiplied by 1, 100 and 1000 respectively, hence the multiplier sign on the rotary switch.

When using a multimeter care must be taken to prevent damage to the meter and circuit component. Many multimeters use fuses to protect the instrument against excess current, but these will not safeguard a current-sensitive circuit especially if the circuit is subjected to the large currents associated with resistance measurement.

Digital multimeters   The ease of use of digital meters has made this type very popular for testing automotive systems. Compared with the analogue type, the modern digital multimeter (DMM) with a 10 MΩ high internal resistance (input impedance) and low operating voltage (3.5 V) 'draw' less current from the device being tested;

> ## GOOD PRACTICE
>
> **Multimeters**
> Special care is needed when
>
> - measuring voltages above 50 V
> - testing electronic systems to avoid damage to circuit components: the range switch must not be changed when the instrument is connected in the circuit
> - measuring voltage to ensure that the meter is not switched to either resistance or current ranges
> - making resistance, continuity or current measurements, to ensure that the circuit is de-energized by switching the meter to a voltage range before taking the reading
> - selecting the range: if the value is unknown, it is advisable to initially select a higher range and then work downwards
> - instrument is not being used: it should be set to 1 kV range
> - measuring current because it is possible to overload the instrument

in consequence the meter is less likely to damage delicate computer circuits.

Figure 1.80 shows one of the range of Fluke® digital meters made specially for the automotive service industry.

In addition to the basic test functions that allow measurement of voltage, current, resistance and continuity, the meter shown also incorporates the following features:

- *analogue bar graph*: indicates variable input voltage signals such as those given by sensors used for signalling exhaust oxygen content and throttle position;
- *frequency measurement*: resistors handling pulsed d.c. signals from engine manifold sensors and a.c. cycles associated with speed sensors;
- *dwell meter*: measures dwell angle as required during ignition tests;
- *duty cycle*: verifies operation of vehicle components such as electronic feedback carburettor and exhaust gas recirculation (EGR) valves;
- *speed measurement*: indicates rotational speed in rev/min for most electronic systems;
- *temperature*: measures temperature up to 980°C/ 980°F by means of a thermocouple bead probe;

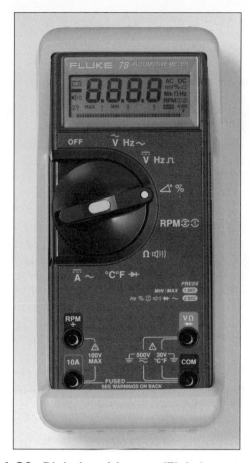

Fig. 1.80 Digital multimeter (Fluke)

- *min/max*: allows the highest and lowest readings to be captured for all meter functions;
- *continuity beeper*: audible 'beep' tone allows circuits and components, including diodes, to be easily checked for continuity and short circuits.

These features alone make the instrument extremely versatile, and with the purchase of extra probes and accessories it is possible to conduct an even wider range of tests.

Using a low-drain meter circuit, and 'sleep' mode that switches off the 9 V battery when not in use, it is claimed that a long battery life of about 2000 hours is achieved. The instrument is housed in a tough plastic case and is fused to protect it from high current.

Typical ranges used for testing MV systems are:

DC voltage range: 40 mV – 1000 V
AC voltage range: 400 mV – 750 V
DC current ranges: 4 mA – 10 A (5–400 A with probe)
resistance: 40 – 400 Ω; 400 Ω – 40 MΩ

SAFE PRACTICE

The meter protection devices do not safeguard the vehicle circuit, so you must make certain that the range you intend to select will not damage the circuit. Also you must NOT select the resistance range when you intend to test sensitive semiconductor circuits. If you do the current from the battery in the meter may damage the component.

Use of test meters
Intelligent use of the three basic meters: voltmeter, ammeter and ohmmeter generally allows the cause of a fault to be quickly diagnosed. The method of performing these tests is considered at this stage.

Voltage checks The p.d. at various parts of a circuit can be determined by connecting a voltmeter between 'earth' and the main points of the circuit as shown in Figure 1.81. A 'good' circuit gives meter readings (1 to 4) similar to battery p.d. and reading (5) will be zero.

Normally tests should start at the source of power and follow the circuit through to earth. In motor vehicle work this is not always possible because some points are inaccessible. For convenience the initial reading is taken at the source and then this is compared with the p.d. across the circuit component: in the case of the circuit shown in Figure 1.81, this will be the lamp. If the voltage differs by more than the recommended amount, further readings should be taken at exposed connection points nearer the source to locate the fault.

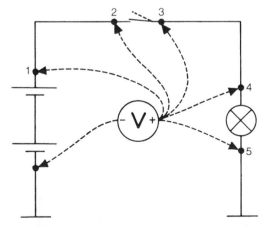

Fig. 1.81 Circuit testing with voltmeter to check lighting circuit

Two fault types identified by this check are: open circuit and high resistance. In Fig. 1.81, an open circuit at the switch will give a zero reading at point (3) whereas a high resistance at this point will show a p.d. at (3) less than that indicated at (2). For example, if the reading at (2) is 12 V and at (3) the p.d. is 8 V, then this shows the presence of a resistance causing a voltage drop of 4 V across it. This drop or loss of voltage will cause the light to dim.

Volt-drop test   This is carried out by mounting a volt-meter in parallel with a part of the circuit: any reading shown on the meter indicates the p.d. across that part. In the previous example a volt-drop across points (2) and (3) will show 4 V (Figure 1.81). Note that when volt-drop testing all sections of a complete circuit, the sum of all volt-drop readings will equal the battery p.d.

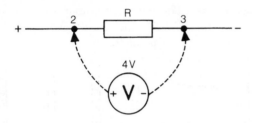

Fig. 1.82 Volt drop test

Measurement of resistance   The ammeter/voltmeter method of measuring resistance can be used if an ohmmeter is not available.

If the value of the resistance in Figure 1.83 is to be found, then the meters should be connected as shown

in the diagram. Assuming the volt-drop across the resistance is 4 V and the current is 2 A, then by applying Ohm's law ($R = V/I$) the resistance is 2 Ω.

Resistance measurement by using a Wheatstone Bridge
The bridge arrangement was devised by Charles Wheatstone in 1843 for finding the value of an unknown resistor.

Today the bridge circuit is used for this task and for detecting a resistance change in a part of an electronic circuit.

Figure 1.84 shows a Wheatstone Bridge; it consists of four resistors connected to form four arms of the bridge. Current is supplied by a battery cell and a centre-zero galvanometer, connected across the bridge, shows the difference in potential between points (a) and (b).

Closing the switch causes current to pass across the bridge by taking the two paths as indicated by I_1 and I_2. The current passing along each path is governed by the total resistance of that section of the circuit compared to the total resistance of the alternative path.

If all resistors are of equal value, then the voltage drop across R_1 is similar to R_3. In this case the p.d. at (ab) is zero and a *null deflection* of the galvanometer shows that the bridge is *in balance*.

Other combinations of resistors can be used. When the resistor values produce a balanced bridge, then it indicates that:

$$\frac{R_1}{R_2} = \frac{R_3}{R_4}$$

The bridge method may be used to find the value of an unknown resistor. The bridge is formed by placing resistors of known values at R_2, R_3 and R_4 and the

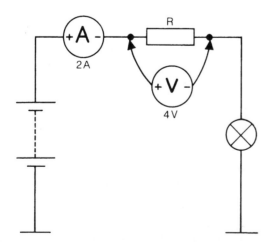

Fig. 1.83 Measurement of resistance

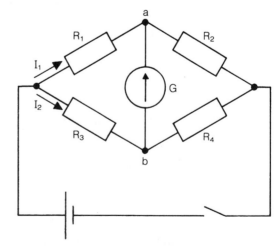

Fig. 1.84 Wheatstone Bridge

unknown resistor at R_1. The value of R_2 is then varied until the galvanometer shows a zero reading. The unknown resistor's value is given by:

$$R_1 = R_2 \times \frac{R_3}{R_4}$$

A Wheatstone Bridge circuit can also be used to demonstrate the effect of temperature on a resistor. If heat is applied to one of the resistors of the bridge, then the galvanometer will show that the bridge becomes out of balance.

This feature can be used to compensate for changes of temperature in a bridge network of resistors. If R_2 in a bridge circuit was an active resistor in a circuit, e.g. a resistor in the air-flow meter of a fuel injection system, then a change in temperature of this resistor would produce a measurement error. This is avoided by fitting, at R_4, a resistor similar to that used at R_2 and arranging its situation in the component so that both resistors operate at the same temperature. In operation this layout will ensure that the change of resistance of R_2 and R_4 will keep the bridge in balance.

Potentiometer The resistance of a conductor of uniform cross-section is directly proportional to its length.

This can be demonstrated by the layout shown in Figure 1.85. In this case the resistance, as indicated by the potential difference, is measured by a voltmeter. As the voltmeter contact is slid along the wire from 1 to 5, the p.d. registered on the meter decreases proportionally to the distance l.

The p.d. across length x is:

$$\frac{x}{l} \times \text{(p.d. across length } l\text{)}$$

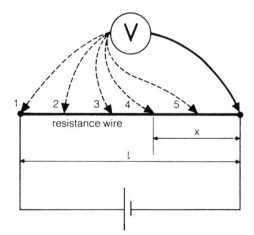

Fig. 1.85 Potentiometer

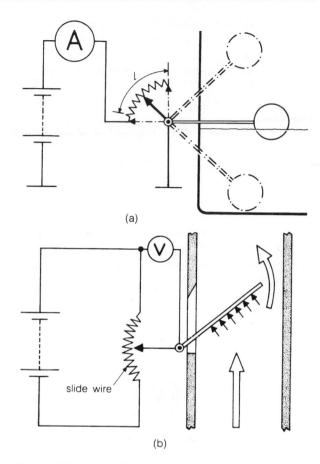

(a)

(b)

Fig. 1.86 Use of potentiometers

This is the principle used in a *slide-wire potentiometer*.

In scientific activities, a potentiometer is often used as an instrument to measure e.m.f., whereas in the automotive world a potentiometer is commonly used as a sensor to indicate the position of a moving part of a system.

Figure 1.86 (a) shows a simple application of a potentiometer used to indicate a fuel level. In this case, the resistance wire is wound around an insulated former, to increase the length of the wire, and a sliding contact, attached to a float, is used to pass the current to earth. The meter in the circuit is an ammeter which is calibrated to indicate the fuel level.

As the fuel level rises, the contact slides over the wire to decrease proportionally the resistance and increase the current flow.

An alternative circuit, shown in simplified form in Fig. 1.86 (b)) can be used to indicate the position of a part such as a flap or throttle valve in an air intake system. This circuit uses a constant current and utilizes the change in p.d. to indicate the position of the contact on the slide wire. The change in p.d. can be registered on a voltmeter or can be used as a signal voltage to indicate, to an electronic control unit, the flap or valve position.

1.7 Capacitors and resistors

Capacitors

A capacitor, or condenser as it was called in the past, is a device for storing electricity for a limited period.

The common type of capacitor consists of two electric plates separated by an insulator called a *dielectric* and represented by the symbol shown in Figure 1.87.

The ability of a capacitor to hold a charge can be demonstrated by using a large capacitor. After charging the capacitor for a few seconds by connecting it to a high voltage d.c. supply, it is possible to obtain a spark when the terminals are connected together. In the past, this storage ability made capacitors attractive for building up high-voltage electrical energy.

Fig. 1.87 Capacitor symbol

Action of a capacitor The action of a capacitor is similar to the water 'capacitor' shown in Fig. 1.88(a).

When the pump operates, water is taken from chamber B and is delivered under pressure to chamber A. This causes the piston to move against the spring until a point is reached where the maximum pump pressure equals the spring pressure. At this stage the capacitor is fully charged so if both taps are turned off, energy is stored for future use.

To discharge the 'capacitor', the pump is disconnected and the two sides of the 'capacitor' are interconnected by a pipe (Figure 1.88(b)). On opening the tap, the energy is released and the 'capacitor' is returned to its natural state.

The operation of an electrical capacitor is shown in Figure 1.89. When the switch is closed, electrons flow from the negative battery terminal to the capacitor plate A. As this flow takes place, a similar number of electrons move from plate B to the battery. Gradually the plates become charged and the p.d. across the plates is increased. This charge process continues until the

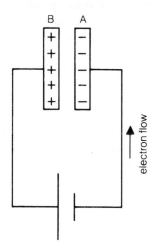

Fig. 1.89 Capacitor action

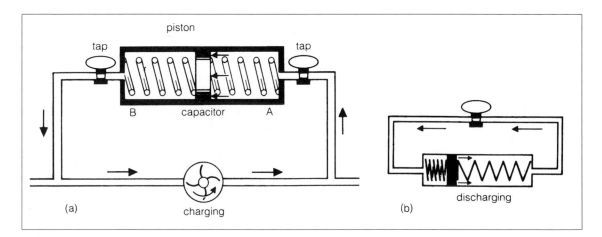

Fig. 1.88 Action of capacitor

capacitor p.d. is equal to the battery p.d. At this point the negative charge at plate A opposes any further flow of electrons.

When the battery is disconnected and the two plates are bridged with a wire, the electrons flow out of plate A and back into plate B. This flow continues until the two charges on the plates becomes equal.

Capacitance Earlier in this book (page 3) it was stated that the quantity of electricity is proportional to its potential difference. Experiments with capacitors show that the ratio between the quantity of charge accepted by the plates, and the p.d. produced across the plates, is the capacitance of the part. This is stated as:

$$C = \frac{Q}{V}$$

where C = capacitance, farads (F); Q = quantity of charge, coulombs (C); V = potential difference, volts (V).

The unit of one farad is very large, so small capacitors used on motor vehicles are rated in:

microfarad μF or 1×10^{-6} (a millionth part)
nanofarad nF or 1×10^{-9}
picofarad pF or 1×10^{-12}

Capacitance depends on a number of factors which include the dielectric material and the plate area.

Dielectric Capacitance can be greatly increased when certain insulation materials (dielectrics) are placed between the plates. The electronic structure in these materials is activated by the charge on the plate and in consequence the dielectric encourages the plates to accept a greater charge.

Materials commonly used for a dielectric are mica, waxed paper and, in the case of an electrolytic capacitor, a paste of ammonium borate. Solid materials are ruined if a spark passes through the dielectric whereas liquid materials recover after the p.d. is reduced. This means that the type of capacitor selected for a given task is governed by the maximum voltage of the system in which it is to be used.

Capacitors normally used in motor vehicle work have a dielectric which completely fills the space between the plates to give a large capacitance and is made very thin. Since the dielectric is an insulator, the safe working voltage may be increased as the thickness is increased.

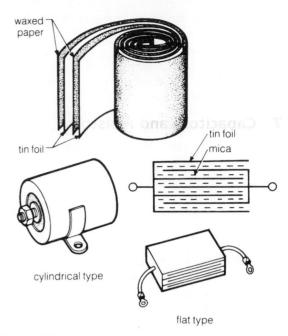

Fig. 1.90 Capacitor construction

Area of plates The larger the plate area, the greater the capacitance. So as to save space, the two plates are either rolled to form a cylindrical shape or stacked to give a number of rectangular plates with each alternate plate connected in parallel with the others (Figure 1.90)

Electrolytic capacitor This type consists of two aluminium cylinders with a paste of ammonium borate between them (Figure 1.91).

It is called electrolytic because when a current is passed from the anode (A) to the cathode (C), a reaction takes place which liberates oxygen. This combines

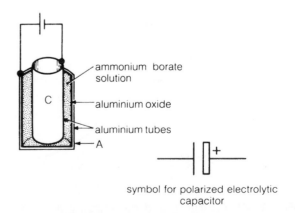

Fig. 1.91 Electrolytic capacitor

with the aluminium to form an aluminium oxide dielectric over the inner surface of (A).

After the dielectric has formed, it becomes a capacitor – the cylinder (A) as one plate and the paste as the other 'plate'. Since the dielectric is very thin, a very large capacitance is obtained.

Two precautions must be taken with this type: the oxide layer will break down if the voltage exceeds the value stated on the case. Also the polarity of the p.d. must not be reversed.

An alternative design of electrolytic capacitor uses two aluminium foils interleaved with paper soaked in ammonium borate and fitted into an aluminium container.

RC time constant It takes a given time to charge or discharge a capacitor, so by altering either the supply voltage or capacitance it is possible to obtain any given time interval. The supply voltage and hence the current flow to a capacitor can be controlled by fitting a resistor in series with the capacitor. In this case the time interval for the charge or discharge cycle to take place is called the RC time constant:

$$\text{time} = \text{resistance} \times \text{capacitance}$$

or

$$T = RC$$

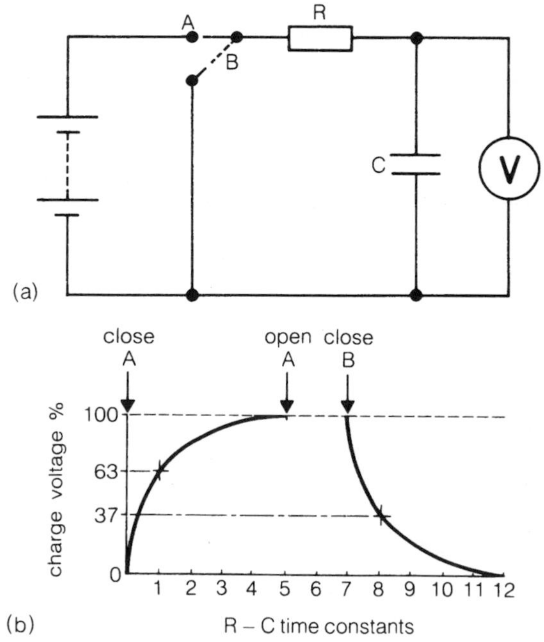

(a)

(b)

Fig. 1.92 Charging and discharging a capacitor

The product of R and C represents one RC time constant. In one time constant a capacitor will charge to about 63% of its total charge or discharge to about 37% of its total charge. To fully charge or discharge a capacitor takes about five RC time constants.

The charging and discharging action is shown in Figure 1.92(a). When the switch is moved to A the capacitor begins to charge and this continues until the p.d. across the capacitor is equal to the battery voltage (Figure 1.92(b)).

Moving the switch to B discharges the capacitor at a rate which initially is quite rapid, but after about one RC time unit, the rate slows down and the discharge is more gradual.

Increasing the value of either the resistance or the capacitance in the circuit increases the time taken to charge, or discharge, the capacitor; i.e. the RC time constant is increased.

Use of capacitors Capacitors are often used in alternating current and radio circuits because they can handle alternating currents. A direct current cannot be passed through a capacitor. The proof of this is shown in Figure 1.93.

When the switch is set at position A, the current gives a positive charge to the plate C. Moving the switch to position B causes the plate C to lose its charge and allows plate D to receive a positive charge. Oscillating the switch between A and B gives an alternating current in the capacitor section of the circuit shown.

Capacitors are used for spark quenching, i.e. to prevent arcing at the contacts of a circuit breaker. In an ignition circuit, self-induction causes a high voltage sufficient to produce a spark across the contacts at the instant they break. Fitting a capacitor in parallel with

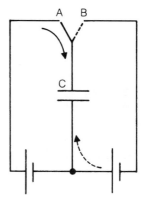

Fig. 1.93 Capacitor subjected to a.c. current

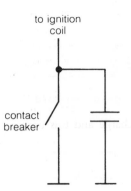

to ignition
coil

contact
breaker

Fig. 1.94 Capacitor in ignition circuit

the contact breaker allows the energy to be momentarily absorbed (Figure 1.94). When the capacitor discharges, the contact gap is too large for arcing to occur.

In many ways the quenching action is similar in principle to the way in which a capacitor is used as a smoothing device in a circuit that is subjected to current surges. In this case the capacitor acts as a buffer to absorb the voltage and current 'peaks' which otherwise might cause damage to circuit components or produce radio interference.

One of the many applications of an RC time constant is an **electronic ignition control module** (see page 206). The timer feature is used to maintain an ignition output that is constant over a wide speed range. One type of breakerless ignition system (type CD) uses a capacitor to store energy until the spark is required. At this point, the energy is suddenly released and a high voltage *capacitor discharge* through the ignition coil gives a high energy spark at the plug.

Capacitor materials Many materials, other than those given on page 37 are used as capacitors in motor vehicle electronic circuits: these include tantalum, ceramic and polyester. Figure 1.95 shows some common types of capacitor.

Capacitors other than the very smallest, are either colour coded, numbered or lettered to show their capacitance. Also in the case of electrolytics the polarity is marked.

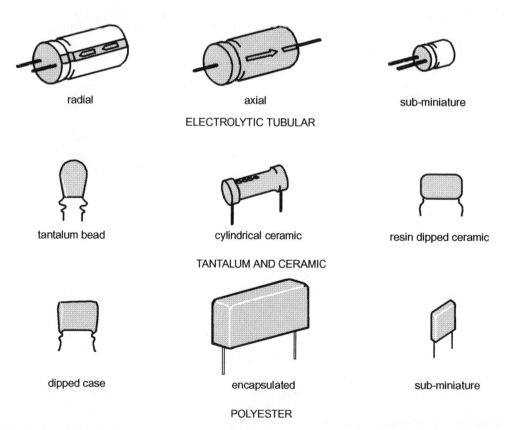

radial   axial   sub-miniature

ELECTROLYTIC TUBULAR

tantalum bead   cylindrical ceramic   resin dipped ceramic

TANTALUM AND CERAMIC

dipped case   encapsulated   sub-miniature

POLYESTER

Fig. 1.95 Types of capacitor

Capacitors in series and parallel When two or more capacitors are connected in series the total capacitance decreases, whereas when they are connected in parallel, the total capacitance increases. This is exactly the opposite to the behaviour of resistors.

When capacitors are connected in parallel, the capacitance of each is added, so:

$$\text{total capacitance} = C_1 + C_2$$

Capacitors in series

$$\text{total capacitance} = \frac{C_1 C_2}{C_1 + C_2}$$

When a 01.1 μF and a 3.3 μF are connected in parallel:

$$\text{total capacitance} = 1.1 + 3.3$$

$$= 4.4 \ \mu F$$

When connected in series:

$$\text{total capacitance} = \frac{1.1 \times 3.3}{1.1 + 3.3} = \frac{3.63}{4.4}$$

$$= 0.825 \ \mu F$$

REMEMBER

Capacitors

- temporarily store electricity
- will not allow d.c. current to flow
- will allow a.c. current to pass
- consist of two plates with a dielectric between
- only the electrolytic type are polarity conscious
- have a charge/discharge time cycle given by $T = RC$

Capacitors in parallel; total capacitance $= C_1 + C_2$

Capacitors in series; total capacitance $= \dfrac{C_1 C_2}{C_1 + C_2}$

Resistors

The resistors used in MV electronics are similar to those used in radio and television equipment and many are used for the same purposes such as voltage dividing, voltage changing and current limiting.

Fig. 1.96 shows the two main groups of resistor, *fixed* and *variable*.

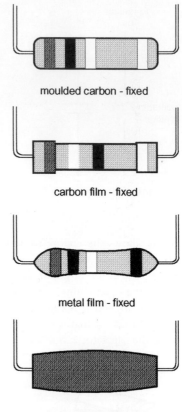

moulded carbon - fixed

carbon film - fixed

metal film - fixed

wirewound (vitreous enamel) - fixed

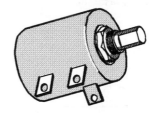

variable resistor - potentiometer

Fig. 1.96 Types of resistor

Fixed resistors The cheapest general-purpose fixed resistors are made of moulded carbon, but where high stability and compactness are important, one of the following types is used:

- *Wirewound*: a resistance wire wound on a ceramic former and coated with either epoxy resin, silicone cement or vitreous enamel.
- *Carbon film*: carbon deposited onto a ceramic rod and the film formed is protected by an epoxy coating.

● *Metal oxide*: tin oxide deposited on a glass or ceramic substrate (carrier) and covered with a protective coating.

Circuits can be made up with several separate resistors or a number of resistors can be grouped together as one to form a very compact unit on a circuit board. Encapsulated in plastic or ceramic, these resistor modules or networks are made of either carbon film or thick film.

Fixed resistors are available in a wide range of values from about 10 Ω up to 1 MΩ. BSI 1852 recommends that a code is used to identify the resistance value (shown in Table 1.4) and tolerance (variation in the stated value).

Resistance value	Code marking
0.47 Ω	R47
1 Ω	1R0
4.7 Ω	4R7
47 Ω	47R
100 Ω	100R
1 k Ω	1K0
10 k Ω	10K
1 M Ω	1M0

Table 1.4 Commonly used resistor values

A letter after the resistance value indicates the tolerance:

$F = \pm1\%$; $G = \pm2\%$; $J = \pm5\%$;
$K = \pm10\%$; $M = \pm20\%$

A resistor marked 6K8F has a resistance value of 6.8 kΩ and tolerance of ±1%.

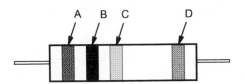

Fig. 1.97 Resistor code markings

Standard colour code   Resistors are identified by a code which normally uses four coloured bands around the resistor. These bands are baked onto the body and coated to give resistance to solvents, abrasion and chipping.

To identify the value and tolerance, the resistor should be positioned with the three bands to the left (Figure 1.97) and reading from left to right, the colour of the three bands indicate the ohmic resistance. The fourth band at the other end gives the tolerance, which is the variation in resistance allowed during manufacture and use. Today many resistors have a tolerance of ±5%, but this is reduced to ±1% when greater precision is needed.

Reference to Table 1.5 shows the colour code.

Example

A resistor is colour coded: red, violet, red and gold. Determine its value and tolerance.

Band A – red has a value of 2
Band B – violet has a value of 7
Band C – red has a value of 2
Band D – gold shows that the tolerance is 5%

Resistor value = 2700 Ω ± 5%
This is written as 2.7 kΩ ± 5% or 2K7J

Colour	A 1st digit	B 2nd digit	C No. of 0's	D tolerance
BLACK	0	0	NONE	–
BROWN	1	1	1	1%
RED	2	2	2	2%
ORANGE	3	3	3	–
YELLOW	4	4	4	–
GREEN	5	5	5	–
BLUE	6	6	6	–
VIOLET	7	7	7	–
GREY	8	8	8	–
WHITE	9	9	–	–
GOLD	–	–	–10	5%
SILVER	–	–	–100	10%
NONE	–	–	–	20%

Table 1.5 Resistor colour code

Preferred values To minimize the number of values, resistors are made in accordance with the *E range* standard. The two most popular ranges are the E12 and E24 (using 12 and 24 values respectively); other ranges are the E6 and E96.

The E12 range is 10, 12, 15, 18, 22, 27, 33, 39, 47, 56, 68 and 82. Since the twelve basic values are also made in sub-multiples (e.g. 1, 0.1, etc) and multiples (e.g. 100, 1K, 100K, 1M, etc), the range is extensive especially when the tolerance overlap is used.

Testing resistors An ohmmeter test should show if the resistance value is within the stated tolerance.

It must be noted that when resistors (and other items such as capacitors) are in a circuit, one end should be disconnected before carrying out the test: this ensures that the instrument is not influenced by other components fitted in parallel sub-circuits.

Variable resistor Also called a *potentiometer* (or POT for short) the resistance can be varied from a low value to its full rated value. The construction may be of the moulded carbon track type or wirewound. They can be designed to be either variable in service or pre-set to trim a circuit to a certain value. They are rated by their maximum resistance and power capacity, e.g. 3 W 100 Ω.

PROGRESS CHECK 1

1. What is the direction of the current for: (a) conventional flow (b) electron flow?

2. What is the difference between: (a) conductor (b) insulator?

3. What is potential? State the unit of potential.

4. Name the force that acts at the source to produce a difference in potential in a circuit.

5. Name the unit of:
(a) potential difference
(b) current
(c) resistance
(d) frequency
(e) power
(f) capacitance.

6. State Ohm's Law in terms of V, I and R.

7. What is the power consumed by a lamp when the rated current and voltage is 2 A and 12 V respectively?

8. Calculate the total and equivalent resistance respectively when two resistors of 2 Ω and 4 Ω are connected: (a) in series (b) in parallel

9. What is the advantage of an earth return system?

10. What is the meaning of (a) open circuit (b) short circuit?

11. How are two magnets arranged to give: (a) a repelling action (b) an attracting force.

12. State the direction of the magnetic flux around:
(a) a permanent magnet
(b) a current carrying conductor

13. How is the right-hand grip rule used to determine the polarity of an electromagnetic field?

14. What is the difference between a solenoid and a relay?

15. What is the effect when a magnet is plunged into a coil of wire?

16. State three factors that govern the e.m.f. induced into a coil of wire.

17. Name the law which states that the direction of the induced current is always such as to oppose the change producing it.

18. What is the difference between mutual induction and self induction?

19. State Fleming's right-hand rule and give its application.

20. What is meant by full wave rectification?

21. What is impedance?

22. What is meant by three-phase?

23. State how eddy currents in an iron core can be minimised?

24. What is meant by turns-ratio as applied to a transformer?

25. State Fleming's left-hand rule and give its application.

26. What produces the force on the armature conductor of a motor?

27. What is Hall effect?

28. State the advantage of a digital multimeter when compared with an analogue type.

29. State four precautions that must be taken when using a multimeter.

30. How is a meter used to measure volt-drop across a switch?

31. What is a Wheatstone Bridge?

32. What is a potentiometer?

33. What is the total capacitance when two capacitors are connected: (a) in series (b) in parallel?

34. State the action of a capacitor in an electrical circuit.

35. What is meant by the expression 'RC time constant' as applied to capacitors?

2 Semiconductors

What is covered in this chapter

→ semiconductor principles
→ diodes: junction, Zener
→ other two-lead devices: LED, LDR, photodiode, thermistor

2.1 Semiconductor principles

Semiconductor materials

A semiconductor is a material which has an electrical resistance value lower than an insulator and higher than a conductor.

To be classified as a conductor or insulator the resistivity is lower than 0.000 000 01 Ωm or higher than 10 000 Ωm respectively.

In addition to the resistivity aspect, semiconductor materials, such as silicon and germanium, have an atomic structure which behaves differently from materials that are good conductors. Earlier (page 2) it was shown that electrical current was produced by the random drift of free electrons. In insulators, and partly in semiconductors, electron drift is limited because there are relatively few free electrons available that are not tightly bound to their atomic 'home'.

Electrons and holes Silicon and germanium have an atomic structure which includes four *valence electrons* in their outermost shell. The name valence is used because the outer electrons bond with other atoms in the structure in addition to the natural bond to their own nucleus (Figure 2.1). At low temperatures the electrons are firmly bonded to their nuclei, but as the temperature is raised, this bond relaxes and some electrons break free. When this happens the loss of an electron leaves a vacant space called a hole (Figure 2.2). The atom is now lacking a negatively-charged electron, so the atom is no longer in a neutrally charged state; instead the creation of a hole gives the atom a positive charge. This is because the positively-charged nucleus is no longer balanced by the negatively-charged electrons.

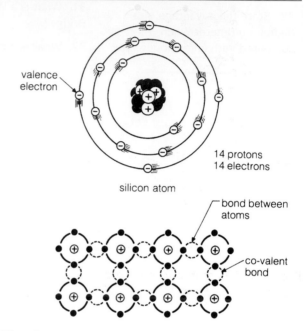

Fig. 2.1 Valence electrons

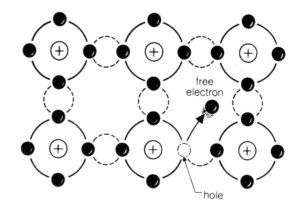

Fig. 2.2 Hole formed by loss of electron

When a hole exists, the positive charge of the atom attracts a valence electron from an adjoining atom and, after transfer has taken place, another hole is formed. This movement of electrons and holes is random: there

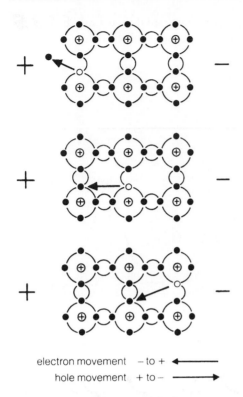

electron movement − to + ⟵
hole movement + to − ⟶

Fig. 2.3 Electron and hole movement under the influence of a p.d.

is no rigid pattern of movement through the semiconductor material at this stage.

Connecting a battery to a semiconductor causes the p.d. to urge all electrons to move in one direction which is towards the positive battery terminal. This electron movement effectively means there is a corresponding 'hole drift' in the opposite direction (Figure 2.3).

Whereas the resistivity of good conductors increases with temperature, the electrical resistance of a semiconductor decreases. This is one way in which a semiconductor can be distinguished from a pure metal.

As the temperature of a pure metal is increased, the vibration of the atoms becomes more violent. This action causes the free electrons to collide more frequently with the atoms blocking their path, so in consequence the resistance to current flow is increased and extra heat is generated.

However, when the temperature of a semiconductor is raised, the increase in thermal energy causes more of the valence electrons to break free from their atomic bonds. These become free electrons and because more current carriers are available, the current flow through the material is increased, i.e. the resistance is decreased.

This *negative temperature coefficient* feature of a semiconductor is useful for temperature sensing. One application is the sensor unit of a cooling-system temperature gauge. This device is called a *thermistor*.

Semiconductor doping Doping a semiconductor means adding impurity atoms to a pure semiconductor crystal.

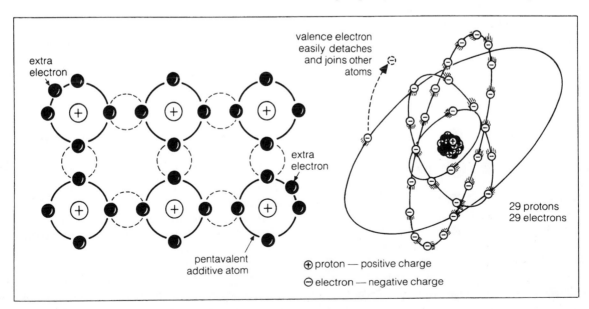

Fig. 2.4 N-type semiconductor doped with arsenic atoms

This alters the behaviour by changing the number of charge carriers (electrons and holes) in the material.

N-type semiconductor This type of semiconductor has a surplus of negatively-charged electrons. It is produced by adding a small trace (about one part in a million) of an impurity such as arsenic to a pure silicon or germanium crystal. Arsenic is a pentavalent element; this means that it has five valence electrons, so when it is added to a semiconductor, the extra electrons are not able to form bonds with the adjoining atoms. Instead, they remain free to drift at random through the crystal and act as extra charge carriers to those that already exist naturally (Figure 2.4).

The name, N-type is short for negative-type. In this case the arsenic is called a *donor* because the impurity gives extra (negatively charged) electrons to the semiconductor.

P-type semiconductor This type is made by adding a trace of an impurity such as boron or indium to a pure crystal of silicon or germanium. The result is that the crystal becomes short of its full complement of electrons so a positive charge is produced; hence the name P-type.

The impurity used is trivalent, i.e. it has only three valence electrons in the outermost shell of its atom. When this is added to a pure semiconductor crystal, a number of holes are formed in the atom because of the incomplete bond between the impurity and the silicon or germanium (Figure 2.5). This feature explains why the impurities are called *acceptors* – they have the effective of robbing the semiconductor of some of its electrons.

A P-type semiconductor in this state may be regarded as a piece of Dutch cheese – full of holes.

2.2 Diodes

P–N junction

When a P- and N-type semiconductor are joined together, the contact region is called a *junction*. At this point the surfaces diffuse together to give a thin region where the electrons and holes penetrate the P- and N-semiconductors respectively (Figure 2.6).

After the initial electron and hole transfer has taken place, the negative charges on the P-side and the positive charges (holes) on the N-side build up to produce a *barrier p.d.* which opposes further diffusion. This occurs without the application of an external p.d. This narrow region at the junction is called the *depletion layer*.

Junction diode Figure 2.6 shows a P–N junction placed in a circuit with a battery. With the battery positive connected to the P semiconductor, the electrons in the N semiconductor readily flow to fill the holes in the P-semiconductor. The P–N junction is said to be *forward biased* in this circuit and this will cause the lamp to illuminate.

Reversing the battery connections applies a *reverse bias* to the P–N junction. Electrons on the P-side are in the minority and since the surplus holes represent positive charges, the conditions will not allow electron flow from P to N at normal battery voltage. Temperature or high voltage affects this basic condition, for if either is increased electrons will be forced across the junction from the P-semiconductor.

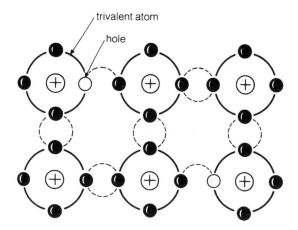

Fig. 2.5 P-type semiconductor

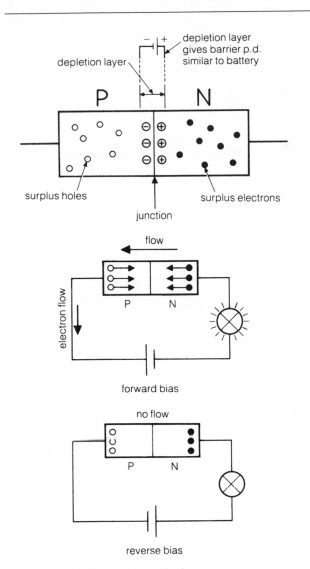

Fig. 2.6 P–N junction diode

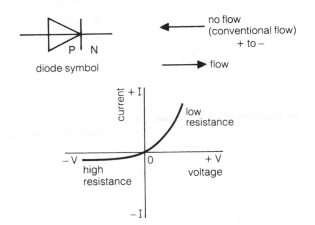

Fig. 2.7 Diode symbol and current flow

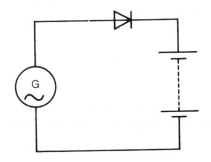

Fig. 2.8 Rectifier action of junction diode

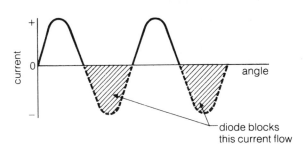

Fig. 2.9 Graph of half-wave rectification of a.c.

The function of the P–N junction describes the basic action of the semiconductor junction diode. The diode symbol and current flow properties are shown in Figure 2.7. (Remember that the convention for current flow is opposite to electron flow.)

Assuming the applied voltage and temperature are not high, the diode will act as a 'one-way valve' and will allow current to flow in one direction only. This feature makes it suitable for use as a *rectifier* (a device for converting a.c. to d.c.) and also in situations where a one-way flow is required (Figure 2.8). Direct current is required for charging a battery so the a.c. generated by an alternator must be rectified.

A single diode in the circuit shown in Figure 2.8 gives *half-wave rectification* of the a.c. generated, but this is wasteful because it loses half of the available energy (Figure 2.9).

To achieve *full-wave rectification* a bridge circuit having four rectifier diodes is needed (Figure 2.10). This circuit ensures that a d.c. flow is obtained irrespective of the direction of current being generated at the source. This type of rectification is used in the alternator circuit.

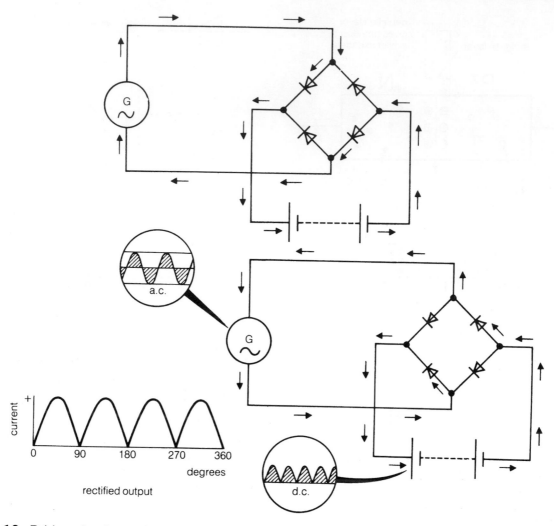

Fig. 2.10 Bridge circuit to give full-wave rectification

Diode characteristic Figure 2.11 shows the current/ voltage characteristic typical of a silicon diode. This shows that when the forward bias (positive voltage applied to the P side of the P–N junction) is less than about 0.6 V, the diode passes very little current, but when the voltage is raised to about 0.7–0.8 V the rate of current increase is high.

When the polarity is reversed, the high impedance characteristic of the diode opposes current flow at normal temperatures and voltages, other than a slight *leakage current*, until it reaches its *breakdown voltage*; this varies from a few volts to many hundreds of volts.

Voltage drop across a diode The actual current in a circuit having a diode and series resistor is difficult to determine without using a load-line (see page 58). For practical purposes it is assumed that the voltage drop across a silicon diode is constant at about 0.6 V. It should be noted that this is different to a resistor: an increase in current flow through a resistor produces a proportional voltage drop as indicated by Ohm's law.

Diode types

Zener diode and avalanche diode Zener discovered that when an increasing reversed-bias p.d. was applied to a junction diode, a point was reached where the diode 'broke down' and allowed current to flow freely (Figure 2.12). This is called the Zener effect. It is due to the high electric field pressure which acts at the junction and causes electrons to break free from their atomic bonds at a particular voltage.

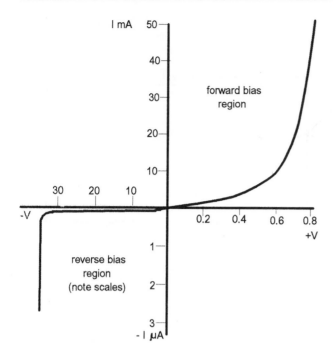

Fig. 2.11 Silicon diode characteristic

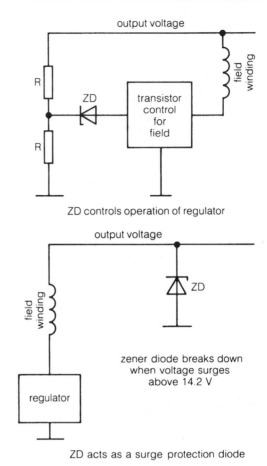

ZD controls operation of regulator

zener diode breaks down
when voltage surges
above 14.2 V

ZD acts as a surge protection diode

Fig. 2.13 Zener-type diode applications

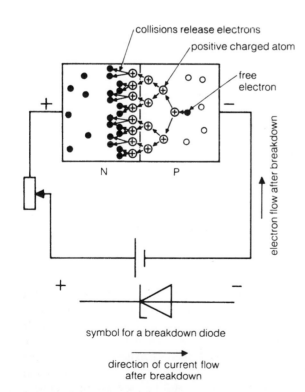

collisions release electrons

positive charged atom

free
electron

electron flow after breakdown

symbol for a breakdown diode

direction of current flow
after breakdown

Fig. 2.12 Zener-type diode

This feature makes the Zener-type diodes particularly suited for use as a voltage-conscious switch in a charging system regulator or as a 'dump device' in a circuit subjected to a voltage surge (Figure 2.13).

The avalanche effect, when the Zener voltage is reached, has resulted in this type being commonly called an 'avalanche diode' but from a scientific viewpoint the Zener diode is different from a true avalanche diode.

Whereas a Zener diode achieves its voltage reference characteristic by 'tunnelling' of the charge carriers through the junction, the avalanche diode achieves the characteristic by producing a physical bulk breakdown across the junction.

Voltage reference diode A diode with a reverse breakdown characteristic below about 4.5 V is a Zener diode and a diode having a 'breakdown voltage' above 4.5 V is generally an avalanche type.

The voltage drop across a diode is constant irrespective of the current it is carrying assuming it is operating within its specified range. This feature also applies to a Zener-type diode so this makes it particularly suitable for applications where a steady voltage is required instead of a varying one. P–N junctions employed to give steady voltages above about 4.5 V are often called *voltage regulator diodes*.

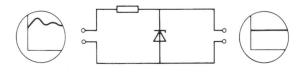

Fig. 2.14 Zener-type diode used as a regulator to stabilize voltage

Figure 2.14 shows the use of an avalanche diode to stabilize the voltage in a circuit. When the input voltage exceeds the diode's breakdown voltage, the diode conducts and 'absorbs' the excess voltage. During this stage, the output voltage remains constant because it represents the potential difference or voltage drop across the diode. This application is shown on page 153.

Diode testing

A test is necessary if it is suspected that a simple diode is failing to perform its 'one-way valve' function.

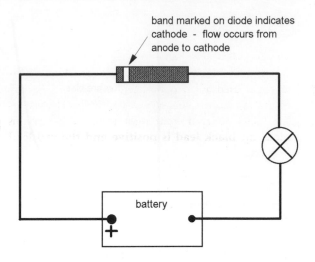

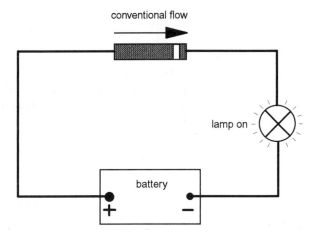

Fig. 2.15 Diode test

REMEMBER

Diodes

- act as a 'one way' valve
- allows electron flow from N to P and opposition to flow from P to N
- are suitable for use as rectifiers i.e. they convert a.c. to d.c.
- can achieve full-wave rectification if four diodes are arranged to form a bridge circuit
- of the Zener-type allow current to flow under reverse bias when a given voltage is applied
- are sometimes called avalanche diodes if they conduct current at a reverse bias above 4.5 V
- of the Zener-type can be used to either protect a circuit against a voltage surge or can be arranged to give a regulated voltage supply
- that emit light are called light emitting diodes (LEDs)

The removal or disconnection of one end of the diode for testing is carried out in a similar manner to that used for other discrete (separate) components. First, the connections are noted, so that the new component can be correctly fitted, and then the solder from the joint is removed with a soldering iron and desoldering tool. Excessive heat will damage semiconductor devices, so pliers or a crocodile clip should be used as a heat shunt.

Many modern multimeters incorporate a diode tester, but if one of these is not available the method shown in Figure 2.15 may be used. The diode is fitted in a circuit with a battery and lamp; these should be selected to ensure that the maximum circuit current is within the diode's capacity.

An ohmmeter can also be used to test a diode. For a good diode the resistance to current flow is:

- low when *forward biased*
- high when *reverse biased*

2.3 Other two-lead devices

Light emitting diode (LED) In 1954 it was discovered that a diode made of gallium phosphide (GaP) emitted a red light when it was forward biased.

Since that time, experiments have shown that the colour of the emitted light can be altered by varying the impurities in the material. LEDs are now commonly available in red, orange, yellow and green (Figure 2.16). In addition, a radiation of near infra-red can be obtained: this is used with a phototransistor as a trigger on some optoelectronic ignition systems.

LEDs have a characteristic similar to a common P–N junction. The normal LED requires a voltage of about 2 V and currents of 10 mA for a red LED and 20 mA for other colours to give a good light output. Up to about 5 V no light is emitted when the diode is reverse biased, but if 5 V is exceeded the LED may be damaged.

LEDs are often used for MV instrumentation systems, so it must be remembered when testing that each

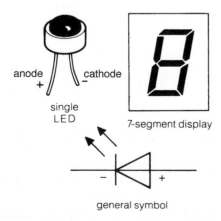

Fig. 2.16 Light emitting diode

LED must have a resistor in series to limit the voltage to 2 V.

For identification purposes, the cathode of a new LED has a short lead.

Light–dependent resistor (LDR) This cadmium sulphide device changes its resistance in response to light energy. Figure 2.17 shows the appearance of an encapulated LDR together with its symbol.

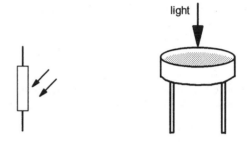

Fig. 2.17 LDR symbol and appearance

As the light intensity passing through the clear end window increases, the resistance increases. In total darkness the resistance of a typical LDR (type NORP–12) is 1 MΩ but this falls to about 400 Ω when the light is bright (1000 lux).

Photodiode This type of silicon junction diode (Figure 2.18) behaves in a similar manner to a LDR. The photodiode is much faster in operation, but it can only carry a current of a few microamperes. Terminated so that it is reverse biased, the leakage current increases proportionally with the incident light, i.e. as the light gets brighter the resistance decreases. The short switching time makes this device suitable for high speed light pulse detection.

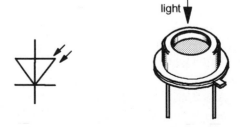

Fig. 2.18 Silicon junction photodiode

The light sensing characteristics of the photodiode and LDR are utilized in MV systems: these include security alarms, automatic systems for parking light operation and self-dipping of headlamp beams.

Thermistor   A thermistor is a resistor that varies its value when the temperature is changed.

Resistance of common metals **increases** with temperature and thermistors having a sensing capsule that responds in a similar way are said to have a *positive temperature coefficient* (PTC). Conversely, a capsule made of a semiconductor material has a resistance which **decreases** with temperature. Such materials have a *negative temperature coefficient* (NTC).

Figure 2.19 shows the symbols and resistance/temperature variation for PTC and NTC thermistors.

Many semiconductor temperature sensors or thermistors are now available shaped as discs, rods, or washers; these are made in the form of beads, glass encapsulated or open. The sensors are combined with other metals and sintered at a temperature of about 1200°C to form a hard ceramic material.

Often a thermistor is fitted in an electronic circuit to compensate for the alteration in resistance values of circuit components brought about by temperature changes.

The NTC type is used to sense temperature in many MV systems: these include the measurement of engine temperature for instrumentation as well as engine

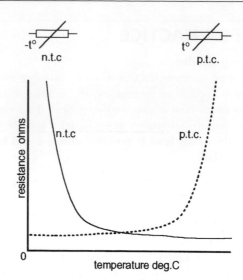

Fig. 2.19 Thermistor characteristic

management. A typical thermistor used to register temperature alters its resistance from 220 Ω to 20 Ω as the temperature increases from 50°C to 115°C.

PROGRESS CHECK 2

1. Does an N-type semiconductor have a surplus of electrons or holes?

2. Name TWO common semiconductor materials.

3. State the direction of drift of electrons and holes through a P–N junction when it is subjected to a p.d.

4. State the direction of electron flow through a forward-biased P–N junction diode.

5. Draw a bridge circuit having four diodes and show the direction of current through

each diode when a battery is being charged.

6. At what voltage does a silicon junction diode start to pass a reasonable current?

7. State how the volt drop across a silicon junction diode and resistor differs when the current is increased.

8. Draw the symbol for (a) junction diode (b) Zener diode. In each case show the polarity.

9. State TWO functions of a Zener diode.

10. Describe how a junction diode is tested using an ohmmeter.

11. State a typical current and volt drop for a red LED.

12. State the operational difference between a LED and a LDR.

13. State ONE advantage of a photodiode over a LDR.

14. What is the difference between a PTC thermistor and a NTC thermistor?

3 *Transistors*

A transistor is formed when two P–N junctions are placed back to back. Positioned one way gives a P–N–P type and the other way, an N–P–N type transistor. The three parts are named collector (c), base (b) and emitter (e).

Figure 3.1 shows a diagram of a transistor and the symbols which are commonly used. In both types, the very thin base is the 'filling' of the sandwich. The arrow in the symbol points either to, or from, the base and is always placed on the emitter side: it shows the direction of conventional current flow e.g. from P to N.

A transistor can be used as a switch device or amplifier.

Transistors are capable of amplifying a signal so they are called *active components*. Devices such as resistors, capacitors and diodes do not amplify so they are called *passive components*.

3.1 Transistor action

Switching action When an N–P–N transistor is connected in the simple circuit shown in Figure 3.2, no current, other than slight leakage, will pass the transistor from P to N. Electrons can be urged to cross the N–P junction from emitter to base but they will not pass to the collector because the collector has no spare holes for the electrons to fill. The base circuit is used to influence and control the flow of electrons and give the switching action.

When the switch in the base circuit is closed a disturbance occurs at the P–N junction. The very small current in the *base circuit* reduces the junction potential and this allows the electron charge carriers to bridge the P–N base–collector junction. This action 'closes' the transistor switch and allows current to flow freely in the

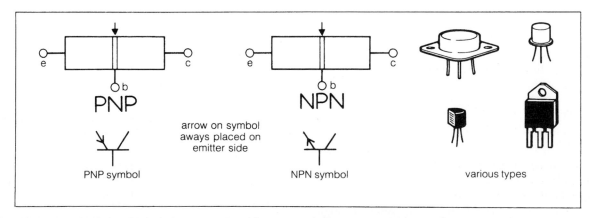

Fig. 3.1 Transistor construction and symbols

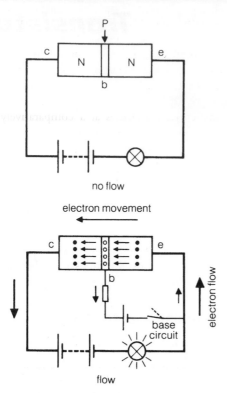

Fig. 3.2 Switching action of transistor

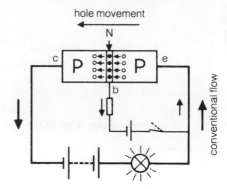

Fig. 3.3 P–N–P transistor

There are two types of transistor:

- *bipolar or junction type*; operation depends on the flow of electrons and holes
- *unipolar or field effect type*; operation depends on the flow of electrons or holes, but not both.

3.2 Bipolar transistors

Transistor switch

Base circuit current can be 'switched' in many ways. In Figure 3.4 a light dependent resistor (LDR) is used: with this it is possible to obtain a very fine control of the base current to utilize the action of a transistor.

When light falls on a LDR, its resistance decreases. In this circuit the LDR controls the base current, so as the LDR is uncovered the base current increases to the point when sufficient light falling on the resistor causes the lamp to illuminate. At first the lamp will be dim

main circuit. In this diagram, this current operates the lamp. (Note: conventional current flow is in the opposite direction to electron flow).

Very little base current is needed to 'switch' the transistor so this feature makes the device suitable for use as an alternative to the electromagnetic relay. This *solid-state* device has no moving parts, is resistant to shock and vibration, is small in size and is electrically efficient. As with other semiconductors, it dislikes heat and is instantly damaged if the battery polarity is reversed: this is because a large electron flow from collector to base destroys the structure of the base.

The circuit for a P–N–P type differs from a circuit for an N–P–N type transistor: a P–N–P type must have its emitter connected to a positive supply. Current flow through a P–N–P type is the opposite to N–P–N (Figure 3.3).

In both types of transistor, the main current flow is controlled by the minute current in the base circuit. No physical movement occurs so the switching action is very rapid.

The N–P–N type operates faster than the P–N–P type: this makes the N–P–N type more suited for high-frequency switching operations.

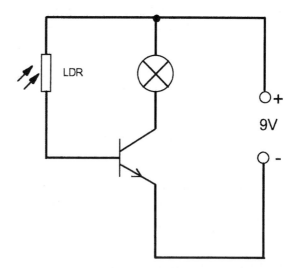

Fig. 3.4 LDR-controlled transistor switch

but this will become brighter as the LDR is uncovered further. Milliammeters placed in the base and collector circuits will show that the base current I_b is much smaller than the collector current I_c. A test shows that a base current of 0.006 mA produces a collector current of 0.6 mA; an increase of 100. This *current gain* can be increased or decreased by changing the type of transistor; gain values can range from about 4 to 800.

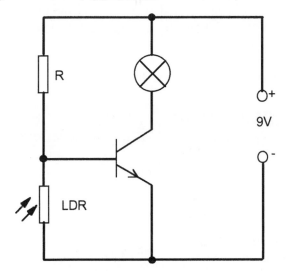

Fig. 3.5 Base voltage controlled by voltage divider

Figure 3.5 shows an alternative position for the LDR. This circuit uses the resistor R and LDR as a voltage divider (potential divider). By altering the ratio of their resistance values, the voltage applied to the transistor base can be varied. Many circuits use this resistor arrangement to control the voltage to transistors and other electronic components.

The effect of the LDR on lamp operation differs from the previous arrangement. In this case the lamp will be switched on when the LDR is covered. When the LDR is exposed to light, the lower resistance causes current to by-pass the transistor. This causes a reduction in the voltage applied to the base so that when it falls below a given value the transistor will switch off and the lamp will go out.

A transistor will be ruined if the polarity is reversed or if the voltage applied to the base is excessive. Once the transistor has switched on, it only requires a very small increase in the base voltage before maximum collector current is reached.

Input characteristics Figure 3.6 shows the relationship between base current and base voltage for a silicon tran-

sistor. This shows that the base current, due to leakage, is negligible below a base voltage of 0.6 V (germanium transistor is about 0.2 V). At this point the base resistance is about 3 kΩ but this drops to about 800Ω when the base current is increased. This drop in resistance means that once the switch-on base voltage of 0.6 V is reached, the current increases at a comparatively high rate.

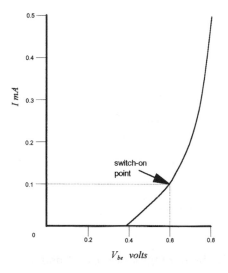

Fig. 3.6 Input characteristics – silicon transistor

Using this graph the resistance value of resistor R can be determined.

Base voltage at switch-on   = 0.6 V

Volt drop across resistor R   = V_R

= supply voltage – switch-on voltage

= 9 – 0.6 = 8.4 volts

Base current at switch-on   = 0.1 mA

Resistor required $\dfrac{V}{I} = \dfrac{8.4}{0.0001}$

= 84 000 Ω

= 84 kΩ

Darlington pair   The limited current gain from a sensitive single transistor means that the collector current is often insufficient to fully activate the load component – the lamp in previous circuits. This problem can be overcome by using two transistors connected so that the output from the first transistor is fed to the base of the second transistor (Figure 3.7). This arrangement is called

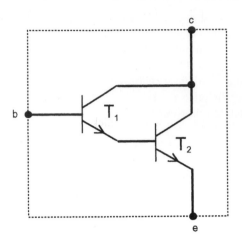

Fig. 3.7 Darlington pair

a Darlington pair and is packaged in a container having three terminals marked b, e and c as though it is a single transistor.

If the gain of transistors T_1 and T_2 is 100 and 20 respectively, the overall gain is $100 \times 20 = 2000$. In this case T_1 is a sensitive transistor having a high gain and low output, whereas the second transistor T_2 has a low gain and high power. By linking the two together, the pair are capable of switching the high currents associated with MV control systems.

Generally the higher the maximum collector current a transistor can handle, the lower is the gain.

Single silicon transistors require a base voltage of about 0.6 V to switch-on, so the voltage required for a Darlington pair is about $2 \times 0.6 = 1.2$ V.

The principles associated with these, and previous switching circuits has many MV applications. Since the switch current is reduced on a transistorised system, a longer life is obtained. Also it is possible to use a micro (very small) switch to replace the original switch. From this it is a small step to replace the normal switch or contact breaker with a system that generates its own electrical signal to trigger (switch on) a transistor to control another circuit; this idea is used in an ignition system.

Heatsink Semiconductor devices are ruined if they are heated. This heat comes from normal operating conditions or from external sources that arise when heating work is carried out in the vicinity of an electronic module. A low power electronic device can normally dissipate through its leads and container the unwanted heat generated from its operation, but a high power device must have intimate contact with a metal heatsink to conduct and radiate the heat away.

Figure 3.8 shows some heatsinks.

REMEMBER

Bipolar transistors

- Have three terminals marked b, e, and c
- Current flow through the collector–emitter is controlled by the current in the base circuit
- A small base current can control a much larger c–e current
- Can be used as a switch or amplifier
- Damaged if base current exceeds a few milli-amperes
- Two connected together so that the output of one is fed to the base of the other is called a Darlington pair
- A Darlington pair is used when a high current has to be switched

Amplification

In addition to the switching function, a transistor can also act as a current and voltage amplifier. This means that small changes in an input signal to a transistor base circuit will produce a proportional change in its collector circuit. This allows a weak a.c. or d.c. signal to be expanded.

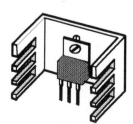
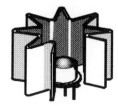

Fig. 3.8 Heatsinks

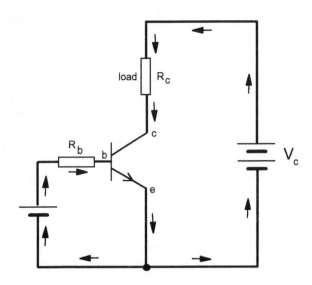

Fig. 3.9 Forward-biased NPN transistor

Type	N–P–N; TO39 package	2N3053
$I_c$max	max collector current	700 mA
P_O	max power at 25°C	5 W
V_{CBO}	collector–base voltage with emitter open	40 V
h_{FE}	gain	50–250
I_C	collector DC current	150 mA
V_{CE}	average DC voltage, collector to emitter	10 V
f_{max}	frequency	100 MHz

Table 3.1 Transistor specification

Output characteristics In addition to the base characteristics shown in Figure 3.6, it is necessary to find out how the output of a transistor varies.

Figure 3.10 shows the relationship between the collector current (I_c) and collector–emitter voltage (V_{CE}) for different base currents (I_b).

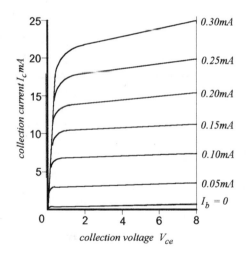

Fig. 3.10 Transistor output characteristic

When the very thin base of an NPN transistor is forward biased as in Figure 3.9, a small base–emitter charge causes a large number of rapidly moving electrons to be swept across the P–N to form the collector current. In this way the transistor amplifies the small voltage and current charges in the base circuit to produce a much larger, but proportional, collector voltage and current. This amplification of *d.c. current gain* (expressed as β) is used to enlarge a weak signal to a strength needed to drive audio and component control systems.

If a base current (I_b) of 0.02 mA produces an emitter current (I_e) of 1.0 mA, the current gain β is calculated as follows:

$$I_c = I_e - I_b$$

$$= 1 - 0.02 \text{ mA} = 0.98 \text{ mA}$$

$$\text{Gain, } \beta = \frac{\text{collector (load) current}}{\text{base current}} = \frac{I_c}{I_b} = \frac{0.98}{0.02} = 49$$

In relation to the emitter current, the base current is very small so for practical purposes:

$$I_c = I_e$$

Many transistors are specially made for amplification; the range offered cover gains from about 20 to 1000. A typical general-purpose transistor such as a 2N3053 type has a specification as shown in Table 3.1. The table shows that a transistor does not have a definite gain value; the manufacturing tolerance can be large.

It will be seen that for a given base current, a change in collector voltage has little effect on the output current; e.g. when the base current is 0.1 mA, the collector output remains about 7.5 mA even though the collector voltage is considerably increased.

The gain of a transistor is calculated at one particular value of the collector–emitter current. Normally this is at the point where the current reaches its maximum, i.e. its *saturation point*.

The actual current that passes through the emitter–collector of a transistor fitted in a simple circuit such as Figure 3.11 depends on the volt drop across the

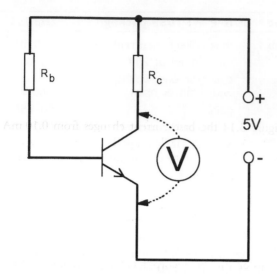

Fig. 3.11 Voltage drop across C–E

collector–emitter. This, in turn, is governed by the collector current so we have two unknown variables that make calculation of current and voltage difficult. One method of overcoming this problem is to employ a graphical solution that uses a *load line*.

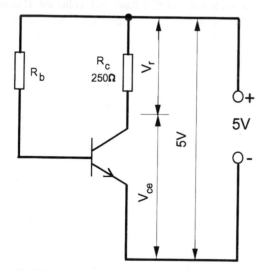

Fig. 3.12 Voltage distribution

Load line   Figure 3.12 shows that the supply voltage is split between the resistor and transistor; this gives:

$$V = V_{CE} + V_R$$

Since $V = IR$

at one particular current:

$$V = V_{CE} + IR$$

This relationship means that a graph of I against V is a straight line; this is called a *load line*.

Two points are needed to draw this line: the point on the voltage axis when $I = 0$ and the point on the current axis obtained from V/R. The load line for the circuit in Figure 3.11 is shown as Figure 3.13. The operating point always falls along this line; e.g. when the circuit is operating at point A, the 5 V supply voltage will be distributed as follows:

voltage across C–E of transistor = 3 V

voltage across resistor = 2 V

When a load line for a circuit is superimposed on the characteristic output curves of a transistor, the current and voltage values can be determined; this gives curves as shown in Figure 3.14.

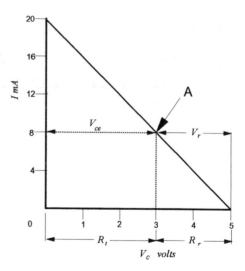

Fig. 3.13 Load line

The *operating range* for this transistor is between the limits A and B. At the *cut-off point*, A, the only current flowing in the circuit is the current–emitter leakage current (I_{CEO}) and since this is only a fraction of a milliampere, there is very little voltage drop across the load resistor R_C, so the collector–emitter drop is nearly equal to the supply voltage.

As the base current (I_B) is increased the operating point moves up the load line to the upper limit B. At this point the current has increased to an extent that the voltage drop across the load resistor is nearly equal to the supply voltage. When this occurs there is little

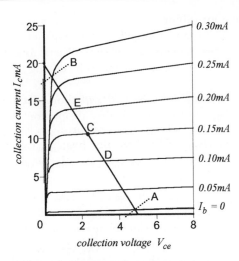

Fig. 3.14 Transistor operating range

voltage available for the collector–emitter so it is said to be *bottomed* or *saturated*.

The d.c. current gain is calculated at the saturation point B so in this example:

$$\text{d.c. current gain} = \frac{\text{steady collector current at B}}{\text{steady base current at B}}$$

$$= \frac{19.0}{0.3} = 63$$

When the transistor is used as a switch the two points A and B are selected for the off–on position. These two regions represent high and low impedance respectively, as achieved with a normal manual switch.

When used as an amplifier the input is connected to the transistor base and the transistor is operated in a mid-range position, e.g. point C in Figure 3.14. The input signal alters the base–emitter voltage, so this will vary the base current. If the input causes the operating region to be between points D and E, the changes in the base and collector currents can be determined.

The *a.c. current gain* is the change in I_c brought about by a change in I_b: this is calculated as follows:

$$\text{a.c. current gain} = \frac{\text{change in collector current}}{\text{change in base current}}$$

$$= \frac{14 - 7}{0.2 - 0.1}$$

$$= \frac{7}{0.1} = 70$$

The voltage gain is given by

$$\text{voltage gain} = \frac{\text{change in output voltage}}{\text{change in input voltage}}$$

$$= \frac{\text{change in } V_{CE}}{\text{change in } V_{BE}}$$

In Figure 3.14 the base current changes from 0.10 mA to 0.20 mA when the collector voltage changes by 2 V. If a base voltage of 0.025 V is required to produce this change in base current,

$$\text{voltage gain} = \frac{2}{0.025} = 80$$

Bipolar transistor circuits

A transistor can be incorporated in a circuit in three different ways. These are

- common emitter
- common collector
- common base

Common emitter The emitter in this circuit is connected to both the base and collector circuits: i.e. the emitter is common to the base and collector (Figure 3.15). This arrangement is often used because high amplification of voltage and current is obtained as shown in Figure 3.10.

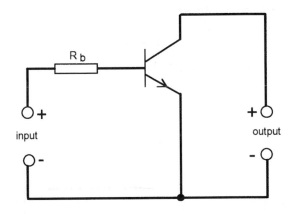

Fig. 3.15 Common emitter

To produce a positive collector voltage, the collector–emitter voltage must be positive. At low collector–emitter voltage V_{ce}, the collector current is low, but once the bend in the output curve (*knee point*) is exceeded, the current remains near-parallel with the base axis of the graph.

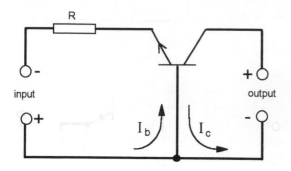

Fig. 3.16 Common base

Common base This connects the base directly with the emitter and collector: i.e. the base is common to both emitter and collector (Figure 3.16).

When a transistor is connected in this way the low current gain (less than 1) of this circuit makes it unsuitable as an amplifier. The forward-biased base–emitter input and reverse-biased collector–base output gives a low and high impedance respectively. This feature makes it suitable for use as an impedance transformer – it matches a low impedance input to a high impedance output circuit.

Common collector A circuit in which the collector is common to the base and collector. This circuit is not used as much as the other two.

3.3 Circuit applications

Transistors form an essential part of many circuits; some common arrangements which form part of various MV systems are considered here.

Voltage amplifier

Figure 3.17 shows a simple voltage amplifier circuit. Its purpose is to intensify a small input signal to a strength sufficient to make it suitable for driving the main system.

The circuit contains two capacitors. From earlier work (page 38) it was seen that a capacitor allows the passage of a.c. but not a steady d.c. current. In this circuit capacitor C_1 permits the input signal to pass but prevents the d.c. flow to the base circuit of the transistor.

For a good gain, the value of resistors R_b and R_L must be fixed to give a base current and collector voltage that permits the transistor to operate around the mid-point of its range (point C in Figure 3.14).

Small a.c. voltage increases and decreases in the input signal are added to, or subtracted from the base voltage of transistor T_1: this change is amplified by the transistor to produce a large collector–emitter voltage at a frequency equal to the input signal. If the value of R_L fails to keep the transistor within its optimum working range, it may operate near the saturation or cut-off points; this will limit the amplification and give *clipping* of the output wave.

Unless precautions are taken when the circuit is designed, changes in the working temperature of the transistor will cause the output to become unstable. An increase in transistor temperature causes more holes and electrons to be produced. As a result more current will flow through it and this will give a further increase in temperature and eventual failure. To avoid this *thermal runaway*, the circuit is designed to include either a *feedback* or *temperature compensation* arrangement.

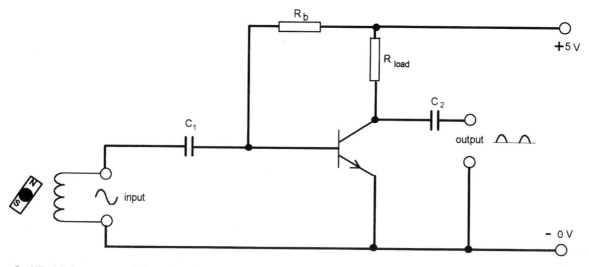

Fig. 3.17 Voltage amplifier circuit

Feedback This circuit arrangement senses any increase or decrease in output and uses the input signal to provide either a negative feedback or positive feedback to control and stabilise the system. Figure 3.18 is an example of negative feedback to stabilise the circuit shown in Figure 3.17.

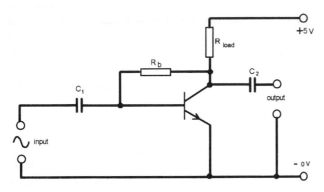

Fig. 3.18 Voltage amplifier with negative

To give minimum distortion, with no input signal, the voltage V_{ce} at the collector should be half the supply voltage V_c. This condition is achieved by setting the value of R_L to give an equal drop.

Increasing the temperature of the transistor will increase the collector current and also increase the voltage drop across R_L. Connecting the base circuit to the collector side of the resistor R_L creates a feedback feature that uses the reduced volt drop across the collector–emitter to adjust the base circuit voltage and keep the collector current constant over a given temperature range.

Temperature compensating resistor The modification of the previous circuit shown in Figure 3.19 uses an additional resistor R_3 in the base–emitter circuit to compensate for the effect of temperature. In this circuit the no-signal base voltage is set by a potential divider, (R_1 and R_2) and the resistor R_3. An increase in collector current due to a rise in temperature gives a larger volt drop across R_3; this gives a lower base voltage and a reduced base current to stabilise the circuit.

The purpose of the capacitor C_2 is to allow the signal output to short circuit resistor R_3; this means that the resistance change due to temperature does not affect the signal.

Time delay circuit
This circuit has been included because it includes some special features.

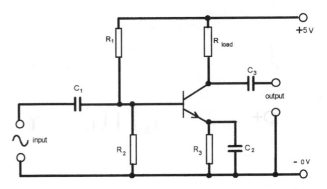

Fig. 3.19 Voltage amplifier with temperature compensating resistor

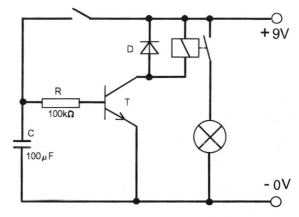

Fig. 3.20 Time delay circuit

Figure 3.20 shows how a capacitor can be used to make a time delay circuit to keep a relay controlled lamp illuminated after the switch has been turned off.

When the switch is closed the voltage applied to the base–emitter causes the transistor to switch on. This allows the collector current to energise the relay, close the contacts and illuminate the lamp. During this time the capacitor is being charged up, so when the switch is opened the energy stored in the capacitor will discharge through the base–emitter and keep the transistor switched on for the time it takes for the capacitor to discharge. The discharge time before the transistor switches off depends on the values of C and R, i.e. it will be governed by the *RC time constant*. Using the values shown in Figure 3.20 a delay time of about 50 s is obtained, but this can be easily altered by changing the value of capacitor C.

In this circuit a reversed biased silicon diode is placed in parallel with the relay winding to absorb the self-induced charge that is generated when the relay current is interrupted. By conducting the reverse polarity charge back through the relay winding, damage to the transistor is avoided. Any electronic circuits that incorporate a coil winding in the system normally use this protection feature.

It is possible to dispense with the relay by using a Darlington pair. This reliable *solid-state* arrangement is very compact and is similar to that used to operate the interior and courtesy lamps on motor vehicles.

Multivibrator

Figure 3.21 shows an astable vibrator circuit. The term astable means that the output is not stable; instead the output current pulses, or surges, in a continuous but consistent wave pattern. The signal generated can be made to give various wave patterns; the common forms are the rectangle and square shapes. These shapes are in common use because they are suitable for many motor vehicle applications such as logic timer circuits (see Chapter 4).

The two transistors and capacitors in Figure 3.21a are coupled together in a way that causes one transistor to switch off when the other is switched on. The automatic switching action produces either a square or rectangular wave at the output taken from across the collector–emitter of one or other of the transistors.

When the circuit is connected to the supply, the vibrating action will start. As a starting point in the operation, consider that T_1 has just switched off and T_2 has just switched on. At this point the voltage on side A of the capacitor C_1 suddenly rises to V_c – an action which causes the voltage on side B to drop below 0 V.

The rapid reversal of potential across C_1 will plunge the base voltage of T_2 to a value well below its operating voltage; as a result T_2 will switch off. This sequence is then repeated by using the charge reversal on capacitor C_2 to operate T_1.

In this circuit the sudden application of a negative charge to the base of the transistors gives a snap action which abruptly cuts off the collector current. This is an example of *positive feedback*; a term used when part, or all, of the output is fed back *in phase* with the input signal to help bring about the required change in output.

The frequency of the multivibrator is controlled by the RC time constant, so if the value of either R or C is reduced the frequency of vibration will increase.

A square wave is formed when the value of R_1C_1 equals R_2C_2 and a rectangular wave in cases where these time constants are not equal. The expression *mark-space ratio* is used to describe the characteristics of a particular wave. '*Mark*' is the on-time and '*space*' the off-time, so if the mark-space ratio is unity, the on-time will equal the off-time.

Reference to Figure 3.21b shows that the output wave is not a perfect square. The rounded corner of the wave is due to the time it takes for the capacitor to reach its charged state. Using a capacitor of higher value increases the build-up time even more, so this can be used if a saw-tooth shaped wave is needed.

The transistor-operated astable multivibrator is a simple way of producing an on/off signal to control a flashing lamp system.

Schmitt trigger

The transistors used in many of the previous circuits did

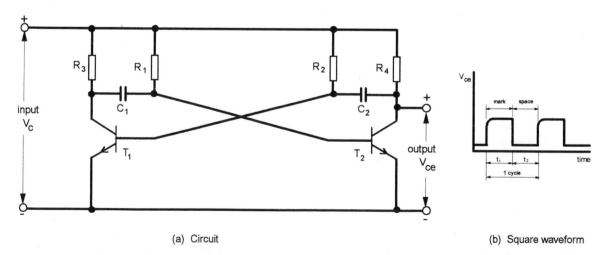

(a) Circuit   (b) Square waveform

Fig. 3.21 Two-transistor astable multivibrator

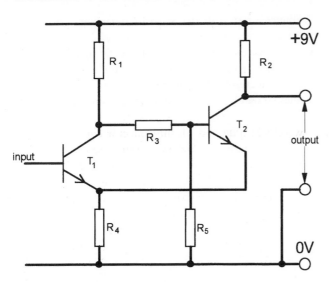

Fig. 3.22 Schmitt trigger

Input voltage	T_1	T_2	Output voltage
Above 3.5 V	switches on	off	high
Below 2.5 V	switches off	on	low

Table 3.2 Schmitt trigger operation

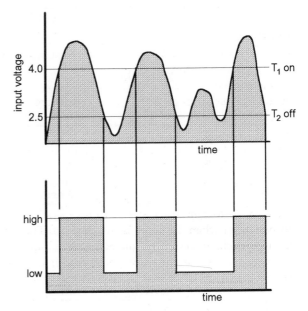

Fig. 3.23 Conversion of an analogue signal to a digital signal

not snap on and off as rapidly as that required by some systems. In these cases a Schmitt trigger, which relies on positive feedback, is used to overcome the problem.

Figure 3.22 shows the circuit layout of a Schmitt trigger. Unlike previous transistor circuits in which the base voltage to switch on the transistor was similar to the switch-off voltage, the Schmitt trigger uses a lower base voltage to switch on the input transistor T_1 than that required to switch it off. This voltage difference overcomes the problem of repeated switching of the transistor between the two states when the base voltage is varied slightly around its operating value.

When T_1 is off and T_2 is on, the collector–emitter current of T_2 passes through the resistor R_4, which is part of the base circuit of T_1. This means that the T_1 base–emitter voltage must be higher than normal to overcome the voltage at R_4 before T_1 can switch on. Using typical values for R_2, R_3 and R_4, a base voltage of about 3.5 V is required to switch on T_1; a voltage much higher than the normal 0.6 V needed for previous circuits. After T_1 has switched on, the base–emitter voltage of T_2 will fall to near-zero and this will cause T_2 to switch off. Any further increase in the T_1 base voltage will have the effect of driving T_1 on more strongly and T_2 off more strongly.

When T_2 is switched off, the voltage drop across resistor R_5 lowers the base voltage applied to T_2, so it will remain switched off until the input voltage has fallen to below about 2.5 V.

The operation of a typical Schmitt trigger is summarised in Table 3.2.

The table shows that when the amplitude of an input pulse exceeds about 3.5 V the Schmitt trigger switches on, also when the pulse falls below about 2.5 V it switches off. This feature has many uses on motor vehicles. Besides giving a snap switching action it can also be used to convert an analogue signal to a digital signal (Figure 3.23).

Transistor testing

In the MV industry, it is often uneconomic (often impossible) to repair electronic control units; normally the module is either scrapped or returned to the manufacturer for repair. In some cases the unit is sealed with a special compound that is dangerous to health if disturbed.

To cover the odd occasions where repairs can be carried out, some basic tests are outlined for your information.

The simplest way of testing a discrete bipolar transistor on or off the circuit board is to use a special tester. Alternatively the transistor can be removed and tested either with an ohmmeter or by using a test circuit.

For all tests, especially the ohmmeter, you must remember that the transistor will be ruined if the current, voltage and power ratings are exceeded.

Test	Result
red to base and black to collector red to base and black to emitter	low resistance
reversed connections on the above terminals connections of either polarity between collector and emitter	high resistance

Table 3.3 Testing NPN transistors

Test	Result
black to base and red to collector black to base and red to emitter	low resistance
reversed connections on the above terminals connections of either polarity between collector and emitter	high resistance

Table 3.4 Testing PNP transistors

REMEMBER

Bipolar transistor

- is formed by placing two PN junctions back-to-back
- is made from silicon or germanium
- is made as a NPN or PNP type
- acts as a switch or amplifier
- has three parts: collector, emitter and base
- is switched on when the base is activated
- of the silicon type has a switch-on voltage of 0.6–0.8 V
- is damaged if the base current is excessive
- symbols have an arrow on the emitter which always points away from positive
- having a gain of 100 means a collector current 100 times greater than the base current

Ohmmeter test   When an analogue meter is used for resistance measurement, the meter leads have to be reversed to give the correct polarity i.e. the red lead is connected to the black terminal at the meter and vice versa. The results for a good transistor are shown in Tables 3.3 and 3.4.

Test circuit   Figure 3.24 shows circuits for testing NPN and PNP transistors. For good transistors a reading of 6 V with the switch open and 0.0 V to 0.5 V with the switch closed should be obtained. The test requires a high grade voltmeter that has an internal resistance at least ten times greater than 4.7 kΩ.

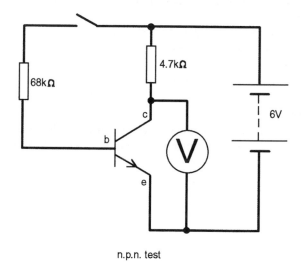

n.p.n. test

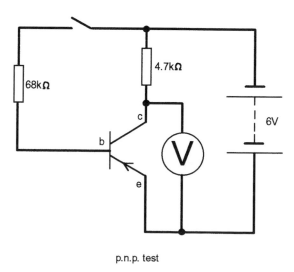

p.n.p. test

Fig. 3.24 Transistor test circuits

Phototransistor

A phototransistor is a photodiode combined with an amplifier. A *photodiode* is a junction diode that is sensitive to light. Reverse biasing the diode causes minority carriers to flow in the circuit and this occurs when the diode is shielded from the light. Exposing the diode to light energy produces more electron–hole pairs which pass the junction and increase the current flow.

A phototransistor has the base connected to the emitter via a resistor and when light falls on the emitter side, electron–hole pairs are formed in the base. The base current produced by this action is amplified by the transistor to give a larger collector current.

An optoelectronic transistor as described can be obtained to suit a given light frequency band. Also they can be supplied to sense electromagnetic radiation waves approaching the infrared (IR) wavelength. An IR phototransistor is used with a LED as a trigger for optoelectronic ignition systems. Another use is for a light-sensing unit in an automatic control system for switching on the parking lights of a vehicle when it gets dark.

Thyristor

This family of semiconductor devices is a development of the transistor, but whereas the transistor has two P–N junctions, the thyristor has three.

The common type of thyristor is called a *reverse blocking triode* or a *silicon-controlled rectifier* (SCR). The term triode indicates that it has three electrodes or connections; these are anode, cathode and gate.

The main feature of a SCR is its switching action. Applying a small trigger current to the gate switches on the thyristor and this causes current to flow from the anode to the cathode. Once this main current starts to flow the interruption of the gate current has no effect. Only when the anode-to-cathode voltage is reduced to zero or its polarity is changed is the thyristor switched off.

This feature makes the thyristor useful in circuits such as a CD ignition system where a small trigger current of short duration is all that is needed to start the flow of a large current.

The operation of a silicon P–N–P–N device is similar to two interconnected transistors as shown in Figure 3.25. When voltage is applied to the anode no current will flow to the cathode because both T_1 and T_2 are switched off. Applying a voltage of similar polarity to the gate will switch on T_2 and as a result T_1 will also switch on. Current flow from the collector of T_1 to the base of T_2 will now keep T_2 switched on even if the gate current is discontinued.

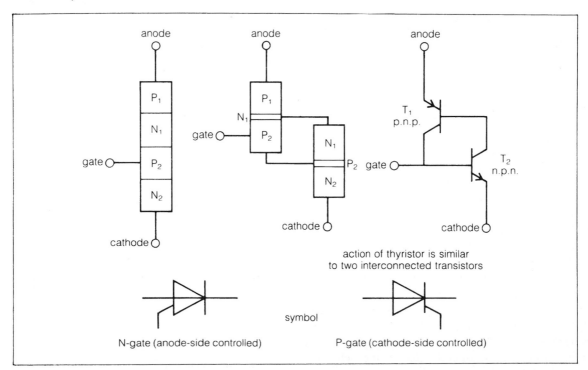

Fig. 3.25 The thyristor construction and symbols

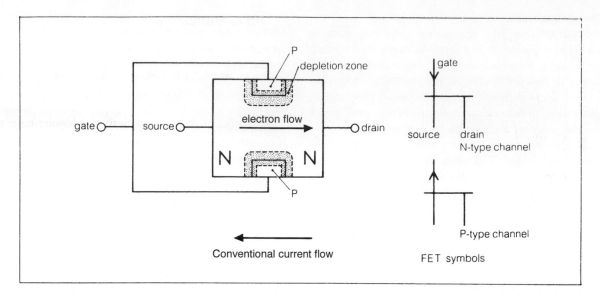

Fig. 3.26 Field-effect transistor (JFET)

3.4 Unipolar transistors

A transistor is called unipolar when it involves only one type of charge carrier such as the majority type. Bipolar transistors, as shown previously, involve the drift of majority and minority carriers through the base region.

Field-effect transistor

One type of unipolar transistor is the field–effect transistor; Figure 3.26 shows an N-channel *junction field–effect transistor* (JFET).

This type of transistor has a P-type silicon region known as a *gate* grown into the sides of a N-type silicon *channel*. The channel is connected to a *drain* (collector) and *source* (emitter). The depletion layer around the P-type gate gives a reverse bias so the gate is negatively biased with respect to the source.

Electrons acting as majority carriers flow from the source to the drain; the rate of flow is limited by the voltage applied to the gate, i.e. as the gate voltage with reference to the source is increased, the electron flow from the source is increased, the electron flow from the source to the drain is reduced. When a sufficiently high gate voltage is applied, the flow between the source and gate ceases altogether.

Control of the main current is achieved by altering the depletion zone around the P-type semiconductor. Raising the gate voltage increases the depletion region and this reduces the width of the channel through which current can flow from the drain to the source (Figure 3.27a). When the gate voltage is increased to extend

the depletion zone across the channel, a *pinch–off* condition is obtained; at this stage the drain current is cut off (Figure 3.27b).

A pinch–off is also obtained when the drain–source voltage V_{DS} is greater than the difference between the pinch–off voltage V_p and the gate source voltage V_{GS}. Under this condition the drain current is not cut off; instead it is forced to flow through the combined

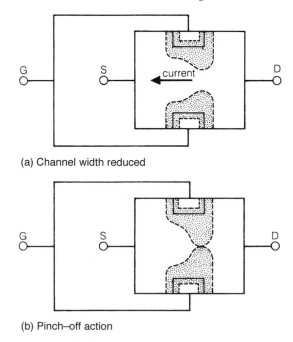

(a) Channel width reduced

(b) Pinch–off action

Fig. 3.27 JFET action

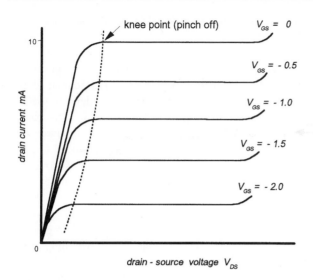

Fig. 3.28 JFET characteristic curves

depletion layer: this gives a near-constant drain current over a wide V_{DS} range.

The characteristic curves for a N-type channel JFET are shown in Figure 3.28. These curves show that for a set V_{DS} an increase in the negatively biased gate–source voltage gives a reduced drain current.

When V_{DS} is greater than the knee point, but less than the junction breakdown, the output current is independent of V_{DS}, so for a given V_{GS} the current is near constant.

Compared with bipolar types, field-effect transistors, in either discrete or integrated form, are preferred because they have a:

- lower switching current
- lower power requirement
- higher input impedance
- higher frequency response.

These advantages, especially the low heat output resulting from the power requirement, make field-effect transistors very suitable for use in integrated circuits. The superior thermal characteristics allow many thousands of them to be fitted on the very small silicon chips used in computers and electronic control units.

Metal oxide semiconductor transistor (MOST)

This type has been developed from the FET. It has an input resistance greater than $10^{12}\,\Omega$ and a gate current that is much lower than the control current for a bipolar transistor. These advantages show why metal oxide semiconductor transistors are now used extensively for circuits involving amplification.

A MOST is formed by diffusing two P+ regions into the side of a N-type silicon crystal (Figure 3.29). The surface is then covered with an insulating layer of silicon dioxide. Holes are made in the insulating material to allow the source and drain to be connected to the P+ regions. On top of the silicon dioxide a gate electrode is deposited; this is a thin metal film which is positioned so that it bridges the N-region between the source and drain.

When a negative charge is applied to the gate, positive charges (holes) are attracted to the N-region adjacent to the gate. This builds up an *inversion layer* which forms a P-type channel between the two P+ regions to provide a path for the electrons to flow from the source to the drain. As the gate voltage is increased, the channel gets deeper so this allows a larger current to flow.

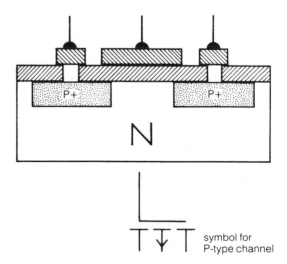

Fig. 3.29 MOST transistor or insulated gate field effect transistor (IGFET)

This type of MOST gives a current flow which increases with the gate voltage so it is said to operate in the *enhancement mode*; types which give a decrease in current for an increase in gate voltage operate in the *depletion mode*.

Both the JFET and MOST devices are made in N-channel and P-channel forms.

3.5 Microelectronics

Since the introduction of the transistor in the early 1950s rapid progress has been made to miniaturize components and circuits so as to save space, speed up operation and reduce costs.

Two basic circuit technologies are used in microelectronics; these are *film (thick and thin)* and *semiconductor integrated circuits* (bipolar and MOST). Circuits which combine the two technologies are called *hybrid circuits*.

Capacitors, conductors, resistors, diodes and transistors can all be made in film form on a small chip of silicon. The semiconductor integrated circuit (IC) was introduced in 1956 and since that time improved production techniques have developed the IC from *small-scale integration* (SSI) through *large-scale integration* (LSI) to the period today where *very large-scale integration* (VLSI) is used. The VLSI type of microcircuitry has over a million devices accommodated on a chip of silicon having an area of only a few square millimetres.

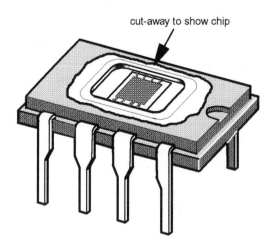

cut-away to show chip

Fig. 3.30 8-pin integrated circuit

Figure 3.30 shows an 8-pin CMOS integrated circuit chip.

Complementary metal oxide semiconductor (CMOS)

The CMOS (pronounced see-moss) family of ICs was introduced in 1968. Its low power consumption and small size soon made this type of chip a popular choice for electronic control units and logic devices used in microprocessors. Using both P-channel and N-channel enhancement MOSFETs, the IC will operate with an input current as small as 10 pico ampere (1 pA = 10^{-12} A) over a wide supply voltage range (0 to 16 V).

A typical IC contains transistors, diodes, resistors and capacitors; these are interconnected to make a circuit that performs a given task in the operation of electronic units such as amplifiers, memory units, regulators, timers, system drivers and high speed switching duties for logic work.

Normally an electronic control unit contains a number of ICs. These are fitted in position by pressing the pins of the IC into a connector mounted on a base-panel called a *motherboard*.

GOOD PRACTICE

Integrated circuit chips:

- A new CMOS integrated circuit should not be removed from its anti-static carrier until the chip is to be fitted
- Anti-static precautions should be taken to avoid damaging the chip during assembly, test or removal

Removal of IC chips The very high input impedance of the CMOS family of semiconductor components and its associated low power consumption, means that static electrical charges can easily build up when the unit is switched off or when the chip is removed from the motherboard. When in use with the power switched on, CMOS integrated circuits use a buffered input to protect them against static voltages, but this does not function if the IC is separated from its circuit board, especially when its pins are touched and charged with static electricity from a human body. A simple precaution is to equalise the static charge by touching the metal chassis of the electronic control unit before starting work.

During manufacture, the following methods are used to avoid static build-up discharge:

- earthed arm bands are worn
- equipment is properly earthed
- earthed bench having a copper surface.

To avoid problems with static, the leads of an IC should always be in contact with a conductive material except when it is being tested or used.

3.6 Semiconductor circuit calculations

Component testing requires a clear knowledge of circuit behaviour, especially voltage distribution and current flow through the various legs of a circuit.

Normally multimeter tests in the MV repair industry are confined to comparatively simple electronic networks: the more elaborate control unit and systems are checked with dedicated test equipment recommended by the manufacturer. However in many instances this specialised equipment only diagnoses a fault in a particular part of the circuit; it does not pinpoint the actual fault. At this stage a multimeter in skilled hands takes over.

Semiconductor circuit problems
The following examples supplement those given in Chapter 1.

Example 1

Figure 3.31 shows a circuit with test meters attached. If the reading on V_2 is 3 V, calculate readings on (i) voltmeter V_1; (ii) ammeter A.

(i) Assuming the resistance of the meters and wiring is negligible:

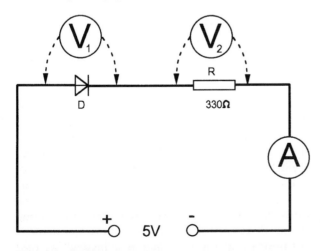

Fig. 3.31 Example circuit

Supply voltage $= V_1 + V_2$

$$5 = V_1 + 3$$

$$V_1 = 2\ V$$

(ii) Voltage drop across R is 3 volts

$$I = \frac{V}{R} \quad (V = IR)$$

$$= \frac{3}{330} = 0.009\ A \text{ or } 9\ mA$$

Reading on meter A = 9 mA

Example 2

In Figure 3.31, state the readings at V_1 and V_2 when the polarity of the 5 V supply is reversed.

The LED would oppose current flow, so no current will flow in the circuit.

Reading on A $= 0$

Readings on $V_1 = 5\ V$

$$V_2 = 0\ V$$

Example 3

In Figure 3.31, calculate the reading on A when the supply voltage is increased to 6 V.

Volt drop across the LED will remain constant at 2 V, so

$$V_2 = 6 - 2 = 4\ V$$

Resistor R will remain at 330 Ω so

current through resistor $= \dfrac{V}{R} = \dfrac{4}{330}$

$$= 0.012\ A \text{ or } 12\ mA$$

Example 4

Figure 3.32 shows a circuit containing two identical diodes. Calculate the reading on the ammeter A when: (i) the circuit is serviceable; (ii) diode D_2 is shorted-out.

(i) When the circuit is as shown:

Volt drop over both diodes $= 0.6 + 0.6$
$$= 1.2\ V$$

Volt drop across the resistor R $= 5 - 1.2$
$$= 3.8\ V$$

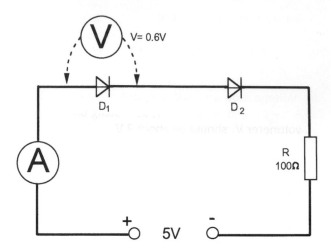

Fig. 3.32 Example circuit

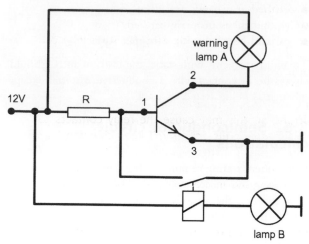

Fig. 3.33 Example circuit

Current through resistor R:

$$I = \frac{V}{R} = \frac{3.8}{100} = 0.038 = 38 \text{ mA}$$

The reading on ammeter A is 38 mA.

(ii) When diode D_2 is shorted out, volt drop across D_1 will still be 0.6 V, because it is unaffected by current.

Volt drop across R = 5 − 0.6 = 4.4 V

Therefore, current through R:

$$I = \frac{V}{R} = \frac{4.4}{100} = 0.044 \ A = 44 \text{ mA}$$

The reading on ammeter A is 44 mA.

Example 5
Figure 3.33 shows a silicon transistor in a lamp monitoring circuit. State why the resistor R is required in the circuit.

The resistor reduces the current in the base circuit of the transistor by lowering the voltage applied to the transistor. Failure of the transistor will result if the voltage is greater than that specified.

Example 6
In Figure 3.33, the lamp B is illuminated. State the reading on a high grade voltmeter when it is connected to (i) terminals 1 and 3; (ii) terminals 2 and 3.

When lamp B is illuminated, the relay will close the switch: this action will short out the transistor base and cause the transistor to switch off. Therefore

Voltage across 1 and 3 = 0

Voltage across 2 and 3 = 12 V

Example 7
In Figure 3.33, if the lamp B is open-circuited, state the reading obtained when the voltmeter is connected to (i) terminals 1 and 3; (ii) terminals 2 and 3.

No current will be flowing through lamp B, so the relay switch contacts will be open. The transistor will be receiving its full base current and will be switched on. Therefore

Voltage across 1 and 3 = 0.6 to 0.8 V

Voltage across 2 and 3 = 0

Example 8
If a voltmeter connected to terminals 1 and 3 reads 12 V in Figure 3.33 when lamp B is open circuit, state ONE fault that could cause this incorrect reading.

A reading of 12 V indicates that there is no current passing through the base circuit of the transistor. This means that the transistor is defective, i.e. the base–emitter circuit is open.

Example 9

In Figure 3.33 another lamp of similar rating is connected in series with lamp B. State why this could prevent correct operation of the warning lamp A.

The two lamps in series will halve the relay current, so this may cause the relay contacts to remain open. This action will keep the transistor switched on and the warning lamp A illuminated when the lamps are on. (In practice a reed switch would be used in place of the relay, see page 94.)

Example 10

Figure 3.34 shows an optoelectronic sensing circuit with test voltmeters connected. Name items A and B. Describe how A and B operate to turn C off.

Item A is a LED and item B is a phototransistor: this is a photodiode combined with an amplifier that is sensitive to light. When light is allowed to pass from the LED to the phototransistor B, the transistor is switched on. The easy current path through the collector–emitter of transistor B causes the voltage applied to the base of transistor C to fall below 0.6 V; this causes it to switch-off.

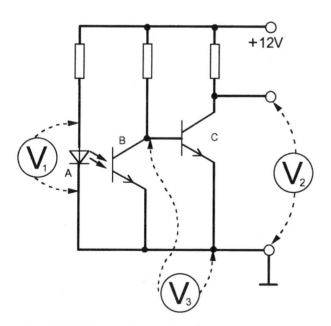

Fig. 3.34 Example circuit

Example 11

In Figure 3.34, state (i) a typical reading for voltmeter V_1; (ii) the reading on voltmeter V_1 when item A is open-circuited.

(i)   Voltage needed to give a good illumination from a normal LED is about 2 V, so reading on voltmeter V_1 should be about 2 V.

(ii) When item A is open circuit, no current will flow in this part of the circuit. As a result the series resistor will not drop the voltage and full supply voltage will appear at the LED. Reading on voltmeter V_1 will be about 12 V.

Example 12

In Figure 3.34, state a reading on V_2 when item C is (i) switched on; (ii) switched off.

(i)   The voltmeter is set to measure the collector–emitter voltage of transistor C. When the transistor is switched on reading at V_2 is about 0 V.

(ii) When the transistor is switched off, reading at V_2 is about 12 V.

Example 13

In Figure 3.34, if the voltmeter V_2 reads 12 V and voltmeter V_3 reads 0.7 V, state ONE fault that these readings indicate.

The transistor should switch on at 0.6 V, so the reading at V_2 should be about 0 V. Since it is 12 V it shows that the transistor has not switched on so it is defective.

PROGRESS CHECK 3

1. State the difference between an active and a passive component.

2. State the difference between a bipolar and unipolar transistor.

3. State the base voltage required to switch on a bipolar transistor made of (a) silicon; (b) germanium.

4. State ONE advantage of using a Darlington pair over a single bipolar transistor.

5. Show, by means of a diagram, the circuit of a Darlington pair.

6. Name ONE motor vehicle system that uses a Darlington pair.

7. A transistor has a current gain of 51. For a base current of 1 mA, calculate: (a) collector current; (b) emitter current.

8. A single bipolar transistor is fitted in a simple switching circuit. State the transistor operating condition when V_{CE} is: (a) 0 V (b) supply voltage.

9. Name the line that is superimposed on the output characteristic curves to indicate the limit of the operating range of a transistor.

10. A single transistor, used in an amplification circuit, is operated at its bottomed or saturated limit. State the V_{CE}.

11. Common–emitter is one type of transistor circuit connection. Name the TWO other circuits.

12. State the purpose of negative feedback as applied to an amplification circuit having one transistor.

13. State the relevance of the term RC time constant as applied to a time delay circuit.

14. Is positive or negative feedback used in a multivibrator circuit?

15. State ONE use of a Schmitt trigger.

16. A thyristor has three connections: anode, cathode and gate. How is the anode–cathode current triggered?

17. State TWO advantages of a FET over a bipolar type transistor.

18. A JFET is operating within its working range. For a given gate current, state the effect on the drain current of varying the drain–source voltage (V_{DS}).

19. How does the input resistance of a MOSFET compare with a bipolar type transistor?

20. What special precautions must be taken before working on an electronic circuit or control unit that uses CMOS integrated circuits?

4 Digital circuit principles

What is covered in this chapter

→ digital signals
→ logic circuits and gates
→ single gates
→ integrated logic circuits
→ logic testers: analysers, probes, pulsers

There are three basic types of electrical signal: variable or linear; pulse or trigger and fixed-level or digital.

Most electrical signals or measurements are continuous but variable quantities and are called *analogue* or *linear* quantities. For example, an instrument that uses a needle to sweep across a fixed scale is called an analogue type. Similarly this term can be applied to any sensor or part that provides a continuous signal that can change by small amounts. (See Figure 4.1.)

Pulse or *trigger* signals are used in timing or switching circuits.

4.1 Digital signals

Many of the electronic units fitted to motor vehicles operate by means of digital signals which pass around the system. These signals transmit data from one part of the system to another by means of a digital code.

Digital quantities are expressed in fixed levels as whole numbers, so when applied to an instrument, the read-out can only alter when the value has changed by a set amount. A digital clock is an example of this type of measurement. If the unit of time used is the minute, then only when time has advances by one full minute does the read-out change.

It is usual to base a digital quantity on two numbers only, 0 and 1; this is called a *binary system*. A simple switch is a binary device because it has only two positions; on and off, or 1 and 0.

Electronic circuits using binary input and output signals are relatively cheap to produce. By combining a large number of digital two-level circuits it is possible to make a computer. Digital signals in this form can be stored in a memory bank for use at a later time.

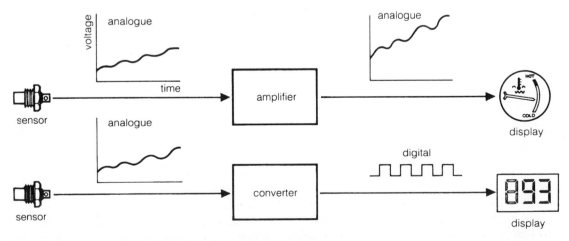

Fig. 4.1 Temperature measuring systems: analogue and digital

	128	64	32	16	8	4	2	1	Denary digit (base 10)
	2^7	2^6	2^5	2^4	2^3	2^2	2^1	2^0	Binary digit (base 2)
	8	7	6	5	4	3	2	1	Bit sequence
Denary number									
0	0	0	0	0	0	0	0	0	
1	0	0	0	0	0	0	0	1	
2	0	0	0	0	0	0	1	0	
3	0	0	0	0	0	0	1	1	
4	0	0	0	0	0	1	0	0	
5	0	0	0	0	0	1	0	1	
6	0	0	0	0	0	1	1	0	
7	0	0	0	0	0	1	1	1	
8	0	0	0	0	1	0	0	0	
9	0	0	0	0	1	0	0	1	
10	0	0	0	0	1	0	1	0	
11	0	0	0	0	1	0	1	1	
12	0	0	0	0	1	1	0	0	
13	0	0	0	0	1	1	0	1	Binary number or code
14	0	0	0	0	1	1	1	0	
15	0	0	0	0	1	1	1	1	
16	0	0	0	1	0	0	0	0	
17	0	0	0	1	0	0	0	1	
18	0	0	0	1	0	0	1	0	
19	0	0	0	1	0	0	1	1	
20	0	0	0	1	0	1	0	0	
21	0	0	0	1	0	1	0	1	
22	0	0	0	1	0	1	1	0	
23	0	0	0	1	0	1	1	1	
24	0	0	0	1	1	0	0	0	
25	0	0	0	1	1	0	0	1	
26	0	0	0	1	1	0	1	0	
27	0	0	0	1	1	0	1	1	
255	1	1	1	1	1	1	1	1	

Table 4.1 Binary and denary tables

Binary and denary numbers

Numbers in everyday use are based in *denary* notation; this uses the ten digits between 0 and 9. *Binary* notation is based on two digits 0 and 1 with each extra digit representing a 'power of 2'. Hence a binary number of 1 1 1 1 is:

$$1 \times 2^3 + 1 \times 2^2 + 1 \times 2^1 + 1 \times 2^0$$

This represents a denary number of $8 + 4 + 2 + 1 = 15$ as shown in Table 4.1.

Logic circuits

Binary notation allows any denary number to be represented by the digits 0 and 1. Electrical circuits which respond to signals based on these two digits are called binary or logic circuits. These circuits respond to two levels of voltage signals; the voltage needed to operate at these two levels is called the *logic level*.

Commonly, the levels used are:

logic 0   0–0.8 V   (low state)

logic 1   2.4–5.0 V   (high state)

Digital electronic control units, used in conjunction with an analogue sensor, incorporate an analogue-to-digital (A/D) converter to change the signal to the binary form required for the logic circuit. Figure 4.1 shows an analogue signal produced by a sensor and the digital signal given after conversion.

When an analogue voltage exceeds 2.4 V, the high-state digital signal is reached and this is held until the voltage drops below the logic level required to switch it back to the low state (Figure 4.2)

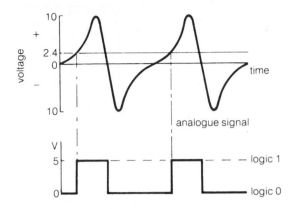

Fig. 4.2 Analogue and digital signals

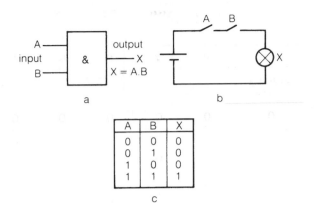

Fig. 4.3 AND gate

Since a digital signal has only two states or levels, it is much easier to transmit, process and store than an analogue signal.

> ## REMEMBER
>
> - Everyday numbers such as 256 are called denary and are based on the number 10 (0–9)
> - Binary notation is based on the number 2 (0,1)
> - Binary code is 0 and 1
> - Powers of 2 are:
> $2^5 = 32$; $2^4 = 16$; $2^3 = 8$; $2^2 = 4$; $2^1 = 2$; $2^0 = 1$
> - Binary code 111 is $2^2 + 2^1 + 2^0 = 4 + 2 + 1 = 7$
> - Denary number 27 has a binary number of:
>   11011
> $= 2^4 + 2^3 + 0 + 2^1 + 2^0$
> - Binary 0 is logic 0 (low state) = 0–0.8 V
>   Binary 1 is logic 1 (high state) = 2.4–5.0 V

4.2 Logic circuits and gates

A logic gate is a device or circuit that operates with certain combinations of digital signals. It gives a digital or binary output signal in response to one or more input signals. Each circuit or gate combines the input signals in different ways.

There are three basic logic gates; the AND circuit or gate, OR gate and NOT gate. From these basic gates can be constructed the NAND gate (NOT AND) and NOR gate (NOT OR).

Many logic gates are used in electronic control units that incorporate electronic counters, controllers, memory units or maths processors; the digital computer has thousands of logic gates in its construction.

The AND gate The simplest AND gate shown in Figure 4.3 has two inputs (A and B) and one output (X). It is designed to produce a digital output of logic level 1 only when all inputs are at logic 1. In all other conditions the output will be at the low level or state, namely logic 0.

Operation of the AND gate is analogous to the simple electric circuit as shown in Figure 4.3(b). Representing the inputs by the operation of the two switches, it will be seen that the lamp will light only when both switches are closed: the light (X) becomes 'active' only when A and B are 'active'.

The logic levels at A, B and X can be represented by a *truth table* (Figure 4.3c); this allows the various input states to be indicated. An alternative method of showing the behaviour of a gate is to use *Boolean algebra*; in the case of the AND gate the expression is:

$$X = A \cdot B$$

The OR gate Figure 4.4 shows the symbol for a two-input OR gate. To produce an output of logic 1 from this type of gate requires only one of the inputs to be set at logic 1, i.e. a high state output occurs when one or both input levels are set to a high state. The Boolean expression for an OR gate is

$$X = A + B$$

The equivalent electrical circuit that produces this action is shown in Figure 4.4(b). This shows that the lamp will operate whenever one or more of the switches are activated, as shown in the truth table Figure 4.4(c).

The NOT gate The NOT gate is a single input/output device called an *inverter* because it changes the logic level

$$X = A \cdot B$$

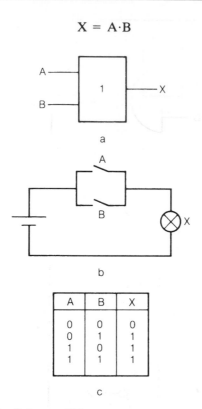

a

b

A	B	X
0	0	0
0	1	1
1	0	1
1	1	1

c

Fig. 4.4 2-input OR gate

as the signal pulse passes through the gate. When the input is logic 0, the output is logic 1 and vice versa (Figure 4.5).

The logical symbol $\overline{A}$ is read and spoken as 'not A'.

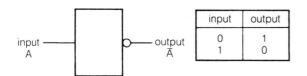

input	output
0	1
1	0

Fig. 4.5 NOT gate

The NAND and NOR gates Other logic functions can be obtained by combining the AND and OR gates with a NOT gate; this produces a NAND (NOT AND) and NOR (NOT OR) gate respectively.

The symbols and truth tables for these gates are shown in Figure 4.6.

In both cases the small circle is the schematic symbol for NOT. The effect of adding the NOT function to the basic AND and OR gates is to invert the output.

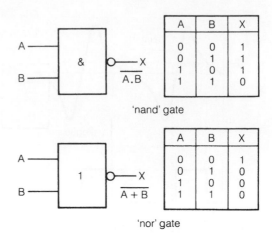

'nand' gate

A	B	X
0	0	1
0	1	1
1	0	1
1	1	0

'nor' gate

A	B	X
0	0	1
0	1	0
1	0	0
1	1	0

Fig. 4.6 NAND and NOR gates

Logic symbols and diagrams

Many electronic circuits used for vehicles' components are American-based so circuit diagrams often show symbols that differ from those recommended by BSI. The main variations are shown in Figure 4.7.

4.3 Single gates

A simple application of a gate is used for an instrument warning system that is intended to illuminate a lamp whenever either the brake pads are worn to their limit or the fluid level is low (Figure 4.8).

REMEMBER

Logic gates:

- The basic logic gates are: AND, OR, NOT
- The gates derived from the basic gates are: NAND, NOR
- AND gate: similar to two switches in series
- AND gate: outputs logic 1 only when both inputs are set to logic 1
- OR gate: similar to two switches in parallel
- OR gate: outputs logic 1 when either one or both inputs are set to logic 1
- NOT gate: inverts signal; it outputs logic 1 when input is logic 1 and vice versa
- NAND gate: combines NOT and AND gates
- NOR gate: combines NOT and OR gates

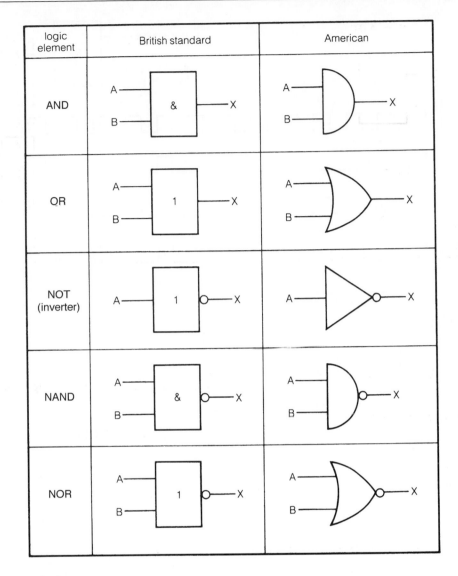

Fig. 4.7 Gate symbols

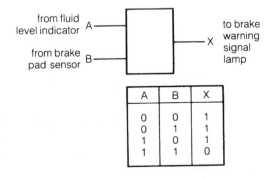

A	B	X
0	0	1
0	1	1
1	0	1
1	1	0

Fig. 4.8 Gate applications using loss of signal (logic level 0) to operate warning lamp (logic level 1)

If the logic 0 represents the dangerous condition in each case, and logic 1 is the output signal needed to operate the warning lamp, then by constructing a truth table it will be seen that a NAND gate is the type required for this application

Another example of a single gate is a case where counting is necessary to obtain the speed of a given component such as a driving shaft.

Figure 4.9 shows this application which uses an AND gate with two inputs A and B. A clock pulse having a constant frequency is applied to A and a square wave pulse, given by a sensor positioned close to the rotating shaft, is applied to B.

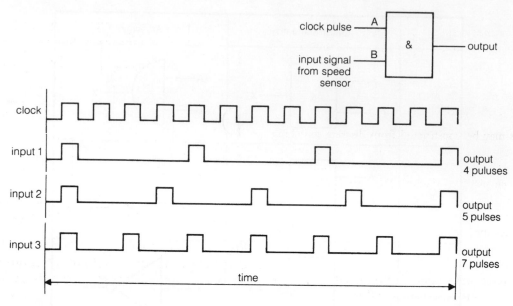

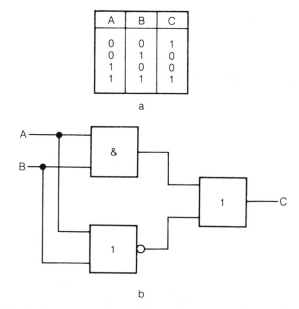

Fig. 4.9 Applications of an AND gate showing three input signal conditions of speed

Comparing the clock pulse with the pulse form labelled (1) shows that in a given time interval the logic gate will output four pulses i.e. when both inputs are at a high state at the same time. As the shaft speed is increased, the number of output pulses from the gate increases, so this can be used to indicate the shaft speed on an appropriate digital meter.

In this case the clock pulse is used as a reference signal to enable the varying frequency pulses from the sensor to be counted against a set time interval.

Clock signals are used to control many electronic units involving logic gates. Usually the clock signal is obtained from a *quartz crystal-controlled oscillator*; this produces a stable square wave of frequency 3.2768 MHz (3 276 800 oscillations per second).

Combinational logic

In the majority of applications, more than one logic gate is needed to produce a given output signal. When more than one gate is used as a single system the term *combinational logic* is used to describe the system.

As an example of this system, suppose a logic circuit is required to compare two inputs to give an output of logic 1 when the inputs are equal (high or low state). After constructing a truth table for this set of conditions (Figure 4.10(a)), it will be seen that a circuit similar to that shown in Figure 4.10(b) is needed.

This combined gate is used in a computer for example when it has to compare the data held in its memory unit with a data signal that is transmitted from a sensor. After comparing the two signals, the gate indicates at its output when the two inputs are equal.

It is possible that any combinational logic system can be made by using just one type of gate for the complete circuit. Either NAND or NOR gates may be used; such

A	B	C
0	0	1
0	1	0
1	0	0
1	1	1

a

Fig. 4.10 Combination logic example

systems are called *universal NAND logic* and *universal NOR logic* systems respectively. This arrangement gives a cheaper layout and minimizes the risk of incorrect assembly.

4.4 Integrated logic circuits

Logic gates may be constructed from discrete switching transistors, diodes, resistors and capacitors. An integrated circuit consists of a number of gates which are formed upon a single piece of silicon. The first IC logic gate was made in 1959 when a transistor and resistor were formed on a single *silicon chip*.

Nowadays these chips are in common use and form 'building bricks' to construct computers and electronic control units.

Logic circuits and systems formed on an IC chip use combinations of diodes, resistors and transistors. These make logic families which are fabricated as:

(a) transistor–transistor logic (TTL)
(b) emitter–coupled logic (ECL)
(c) complementary metal oxide silicon logic (CMOS)

Transistor–transistor logic TTL circuits are widely used in cheap integrated circuits and cover a large range of logic functions. The power consumed is about 40 mW per gate and its speed of switching (*propagation delay*) is about 9 ns (nanoseconds). It has a good *noise margin*; this means that it resists changing its logic state when small spurious voltages are induced into the data transmission line.

Figure 4.11 shows an IC having quad 2-input NAND gates.

Emitter–coupled logic These ECL arrays have a faster switching time than the TTL but they consume more power and are therefore more expensive.

Complementary metal-oxide semiconductor logic The CMOS family is often used in systems having a large number of gates because it consumes very low power (about 0.001 mW per gate). The noise margin is high but it has a slow *switching speed* (about 30 ns). Also it is susceptible to damage from static charges so special care must be exercised when handling this type of IC

MOSFET-type transistors are used for CMOS gates, so this is why the power consumption is low. CMOS units are often fitted to electronic-type instrumentation systems.

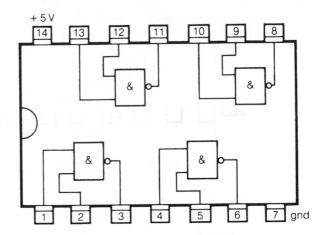

Fig. 4.11 7400 TTL quad 2-input NAND gates showing input and output connections for each gate and common supply terminals

Bistable logic circuits

Some integrated circuits use a *bistable* or *flip-flop circuit* to 'remember' a pulse condition that was previously applied to the inputs. The device can be set to remember the two states, 0 and 1, so this makes it suitable to use as a counter memory store in a computer.

A simple toggle switch is the electrical equivalent to a bistable logic device (Figure 4.12). When the switch is moved to position A, it remains stable in this position until it is moved to position B; the switch is said to flip-flop between the two states.

Gates whose response to the inputs depends on the previous signals applied to the inputs, give a logic behaviour called *sequential logic*.

R–S flip-flop The reset–set (R–S) bistable is made by interconnecting two NOR gates to two NAND gates (Figure 4.13).

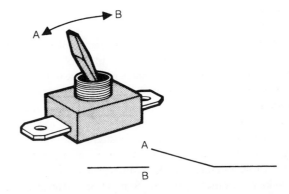

Fig. 4.12 Toggle switch as a bistable device

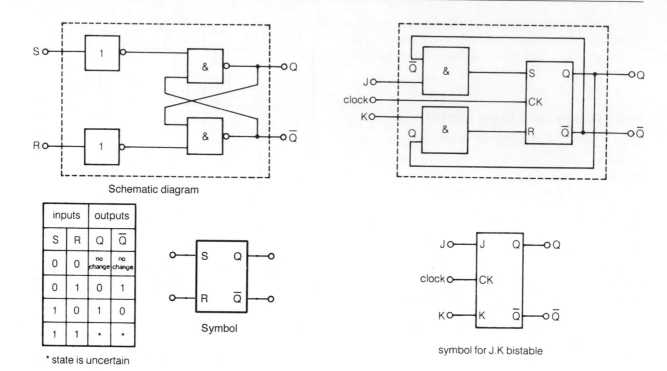

Schematic diagram

inputs		outputs	
S	R	Q	$\overline{Q}$
0	0	no change	no change
0	1	0	1
1	0	1	0
1	1	*	*

* state is uncertain

Symbol

Fig. 4.13 R–S flip-flop and truth table

symbol for J.K bistable

Fig. 4.14 J–K bistable

The truth table for the NAND gates shows that when logic 1 is applied to S (set input), the output at Q is logic 1; it will remain in that high state even after S is changed to logic 0. This shows that the high state of S is *latched* into the state of Q.

Only when R is changed to logic 1 and S goes back to logic 0 is Q unlatched; this *resets* the latch and returns the gate to its original condition.

When R and S are set so that they are both at logic 1, the two gates *buck* each other and the final state of the flip-flop is uncertain; this indeterminate state is not permitted so the external circuit is designed to avoid this condition.

J–K flip-flop A J–K bistable operates similarly to an R–S type but incorporates two extra AND gates to overcome the indeterminate state produced when both inputs of the R–S are set to logic 1 (Figure 4.14).

When either input is changed so that logic 1 is then applied to both J and K, the flip-flop changes its output to a state opposite to that which existed before the input change.

The J–K bistable shown in Figure 4.14 is based on a clocked version of the R–S flip-flop. This gives a synchronized action whereby the flip-flop can only

change its state at a time when a clock pulse is applied to the bistable.

A number of integrated circuits incorporating bistables are used on motor vehicles. Often these integrated circuits are based on a CMOS construction and contain four or six latches with a common reset feature.

Electric counters and registers

An electric counter is a logic system for counting digital pulse signals such as those supplied from a transducer for sensing either movement of a given part or physical conditions such as temperature or pressure.

The output from the counter may be used for instrumentation purposes or for controlling the operating mechanism of systems such as ignition timing control and fuel metering.

Often the signal generated by a sensor is of analogue form so this must be converted by an analogue/digital (A/D) converter to a pulse shape required for a logic circuit. A typical pulse shaping device is a *Schmitt trigger* and the layout shown in Figure 4.15 shows the functional role of the trigger when it is used for tachometer operation.

Counters use binary notation to represent the number of pulses measured in a given time. The digital signals given at the outputs from a counter indicate the

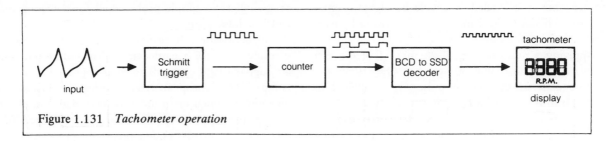

Figure 1.131 *Tachometer operation*

Fig. 4.15 Tachometer operation

logic state of the various signal lines. These signals are passed to a decoder which converts the binary *coded decimal* (BCD) to a *seven-segment display* (SSD). This decodes the signals by using combinational logic circuits and arranges the appropriate LED segments to illuminate in response to the incoming pulses.

Divide-by-two counter When a logic 1 pulse is applied to the J–K bistable shown in Figure 4.16(a), an output of logic 1 will be triggered by the negative-going edge of the clock pulse (Figure 4.16(b)). This logic 1 output pulse is held until the next clock signal negative edge toggles the bistable back to its original setting.

In this case the bistable is triggered by the negative edge of the clock pulse but it is also possible to trigger the bistable at other times as shown by the types represented by the symbols in Figure 4.16(c).

Using a bistable as a counter in this way enables the pulse wave frequency to be halved; this is called a divide-by-two counter. A single bistable performs this division in a control unit of a fuel injection system (see page 228)

Ripple-through counter Cascading a number of bistables in the form as shown in Figure 4.17 and utilizing the output of one bistable to clock the next bistable makes a multistage counter. The three-stage binary

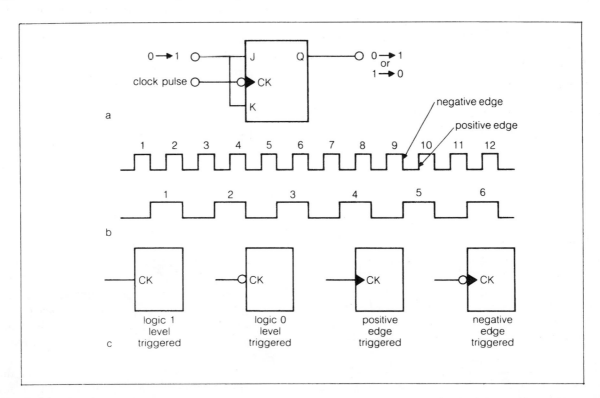

Fig. 4.16 Clock response

counter shown is called a divide-by-eight counter because each stage added increases the division by two; hence three bistables gives $2 \times 2 \times 2 = 8$.

Applying a pulse of logic 1 to input J of the first bistable A gives an output of logic 1 at Q_A. When the negative edge of the output pulse Q_A is applied to bistable B, this second bistable toggles and outputs logic 1 at Q_B. In a similar way, the output from B acts as a clock pulse for C and this causes C to output logic 1 after eight pulses have been applied to the first bistable A, i.e. the waveform produced will have a frequency of one-eighth that of the input pulse.

The term *ripple-through* or *asynchronous counter* is used because each bistable operates the next bistable in the chain. In view of the propagation delay of each bistable there is a short time delay between the original clock signal and the output from the last bistable.

This delay can be overcome by applying a clock pulse to each bistable so that they all operate at the same time; such high frequency counters are called *synchronous counters*.

By using more bistables it is possible to obtain any division required and by rearranging the circuits, *down counters* and *reversible counters* can be formed.

The bistable layouts as described can be used to store binary codes for use at a later time. When the storage is temporary, the system is called a *register* but if the data is to be held for a longer time, it is called a *memory*.

4.5 Logic testers

Equipment available for testing and customising logic circuits range from sophisticated logic analysers and programmers to simple probes used for detecting high and low logic states.

In the motor vehicle field, logic analysers are often specially made for a particular MV manufacturer; these are supplied (and charged) to their approved dealers. A comparatively cheap analyser consists of a hand-held instrument, which often incorporates a digital display to register the test result. The tester is connected to a conveniently situated circuit break-out point.

The more advanced high performance analysers, often used in conjunction with an external computer, have a search and compare facility that allows data, stored in an on-board computer on the vehicle, to be down-loaded and analysed against a reference memory.

Logic probe For about £70 a logic probe can be purchased which is a useful tool for diagnostic work on logic circuits. The model shown in Figure 4.18 is designed for use on TTL and CMOS digital circuitry.

When connected to a suitable supply (e.g. for TTL 4.7–30 V; for CMOS 5–18 V) the probe can be used to sense pulses of short duration and identify whether they are low (0) or high (1). These states are indicated by green and red LEDs to show low and high respectively. Each tester is supplied with various detachable probes such as a spring hook, insulated tip and IC test adapter.

Often a logic probe is used in conjunction with a *logic pulser*. This tester produces a short electrical charge at its tip to imitate high or low digital pulses. A typical TTL/CMOS pulser has a three-position switch to enable the operator to select either single pulse, four pulses or a continuous train of pulses. Since narrow a.c. coupled pulses are produced by the tester, ICs will not be damaged if it is used as recommended.

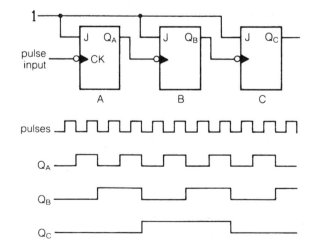

Fig. 4.17 Multistage counter

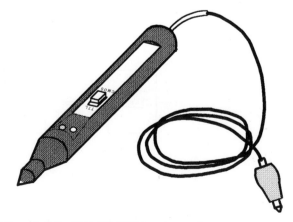

Fig. 4.18 TTL/CMOS logic probe

PROGRESS CHECK 4

1. Show, by means of a sketch: (a) analogue signal; (b) digital signal.

2. On which numbers is the binary code based?

3. Convert the denery number 15 to a binary number.

4. State a typical voltage for: (a) logic 0; and (b) logic 1.

5. State the purpose of an A/D converter.

6. Name the THREE basic logic gates.

7. Name TWO gates that are derived from the basic gates.

8. Construct truth tables for the three basic gates.

9. Name the basic gate in which the signal is inverted.

10. Draw BS and American symbols for the three basic gates.

11. State how a quartz crystal-controlled oscillator is used to measure the speed of a shaft.

12. What is meant by the term combinational logic?

13. One type of gate is often used to make a combination logic system. Name the gate.

14. Write the full meaning of: (a) TTL; (b) ECL; (c) CMOS.

15. State the alternative name for a bistable network of gates.

16. State the operational difference between an R–S bistable and a J–K bistable.

17. State the purpose of a Schmitt trigger in a digital counting system.

18. Name the counter which cascades a number of bistables.

19. Name the tester which is used on digital circuits to identify low and high state pulses.

20. Name the tester which supplies digital pulses to an IC to check it is serviceable.

What is covered in this chapter

➡ types of sensor
➡ pressure sensing
➡ position and level sensing
➡ flow sensing
➡ temperature sensing
➡ gas sensing
➡ knock sensing

An electrical control unit is in many ways similar to a human brain. It *senses signals* or messages from various sources and after processing the information, it either *instructs an actuator* to perform some physical action or it stores the data away in its memory for use at some time in the future.

5.1 Types of sensors

Electronic sensors perform the information-gathering role in an MV system. Each sensor feeds the electronic control unit (ECU) with information that relates to some particular mechanical action or thermal effect (Figure 5.1).

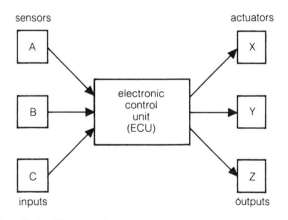

Fig. 5.1 Electronic system

A sensor, or *transducer* as it is called when it gives an output signal proportional to the physical quantity it is measuring, converts the physical actions it notices into either an analogue or digital electrical signal. A temperature switch is a simple type of sensor; it opens or closes to signal when a specific setting has taken place.

The number of sensors required to control a system efficiently depends on the factors that affect the operation of the system, e.g. a simple ignition system shown in Figure 5.2 has three sensors to measure crankshaft position, engine speed and manifold depression; these provide signals to the ECU to enable it to time the spark to occur at the correct instant. Each sensor measures one item only. When greater accuracy of spark timing is required other variables must be measured; these may include the engine temperature and the degree of knock produced during the combustion process. Extra sensors are needed to signal the changes that take place in these areas.

Sensors can be separated into two main classes; these are:

● active or self-generating
● passive or modulating.

The passive type requires an external energy source to drive it and the sensor acts only as an energy controller.

Cost normally influences the accuracy and reliability of a sensor, so a typical general-purpose sensor used for a vehicle system has an accuracy of only about 2–5% and a moderate life cycle. In cases where this error is unacceptable such as pollution control, a more accurate sensor must be used. Since cost is associated with volume, the manufacturers of vehicles are often able to use a higher quality sensor than that which is possible in cases where the demand is limited.

Signal output to the ECU should relate closely to the physical quantity the sensor is intended to measure. Once the signal has been transmitted, no amount of signal processing can improve the original data accuracy, so if control precision is expected, the sensor

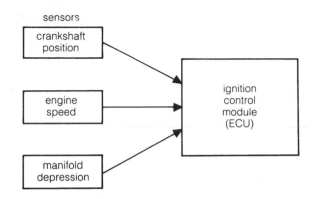

sensors

crankshaft position

engine speed

manifold depression

ignition control module (ECU)

Fig. 5.2 Sensors for ignition system

quality must be high. One method of achieving an accurate signal is to use an 'intelligent' or 'smart' sensor; this type incorporates a microcomputer to correct for systematic errors. A type in which the microcomputer deals only with random errors is named a 'soft' sensor.

Normally the sensor used to perform a specific task has to fulfil the requirements of cost, size, power consumption and compatibility with other electronic circuits.

REMEMBER

Sensors:

- gather information and send it as an electrical signal to a processor unit such as an ECU
- are called transducers when they give an output signal proportional to the physical input messages they receive
- are either active or passive
- of the active type generate their own energy
- of the passive type use their physical inputs to alter the electrical supply signals they receive
- are called smart types when they have an integral microprocessor to correct false or weak input signals

In this book there are many cases where electronic sensing devices are used. At this stage is it necessary to summarize some of the main types. Further descriptions of the sensor applications are given where the full system is covered.

Sensors are used on vehicles to measure various things; these include:

- pressure
- position and level
- flow sensing
- temperature measurement
- gas composition
- knock.

5.2 Pressure sensing

Engine oil pressure The engine oil pressure switch was one of the first sensors to be used on motor vehicles. A pressure switch sensor signals when a certain pressure is reached or it initiates a warning message when the pressure drops below a given point. Using a more costly transducer for oil pressure indication gives an output signal, of digital or analogue form, that is proportional to the pressure. This signal can be processed to indicate to the driver the actual pressure reading.

Engine load The extent of the load on the engine at a given instant is required by the management systems responsible for ignition timing, fuel metering, emission control and automatic transmission operation. In a spark-ignition engine the induction manifold pressure changes with the load and for many years this pressure variation has been used to control the vacuum unit incorporated in the ignition distributor. When the engine is lightly loaded the manifold absolute pressure (MAP) is low, i.e. a high depression exists in the manifold. Opening the throttle to maintain a given speed and provide sufficient output power to overcome the load acting against the engine causes the MAP to rise. This pressure change is both reliable and convenient to use, so modern vehicles utilize this feature to signal the degree of engine loading to the systems that require the information.

Manifold depression is created by the pumping action of the pistons. Since the induction stroke in one cylinder is restricted to one stroke in four, the pressure in the manifold is far from constant. Although the pressure pulsations of the pumping strokes reduce as the number of cylinders and engine speed are increased, the pressure wave variation is still large and must be damped or filtered before it is allowed to act on the MAP sensor. Generally this is achieved by using a small orifice between the manifold and the chamber into which the sensor is fitted (Figure 5.3).

Types of pressure sensor

Manufacturers have a large range of sensors from which they can select the type that suits the particular application. The range includes:

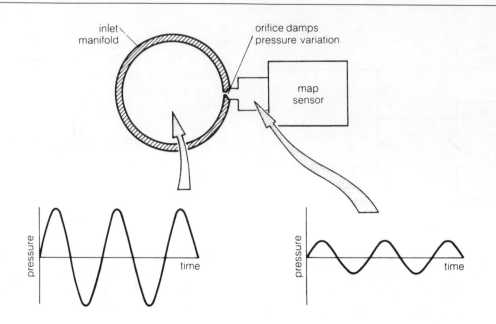

Fig. 5.3 Use of an orifice to filter pressure waves

- variable resistor/potentiometer
- variable inductance
- variable differential transformer
- strain gauge and piezo resistive
- capacitor capsule.

Many of these sensors require an aneroid that responds to pressure changes for driving the electronic sensor.

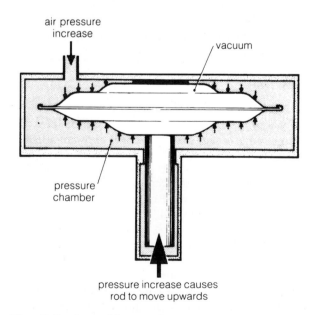

Fig. 5.4 Aneroid capsule

Aneroid pressure capsule An aneroid is a flexible metal box exhausted of air. It is designed to contract and expand as the external air pressure is varied. Figure 5.4 shows an aneroid capsule formed by placing two thin metal diaphragms together and joining them under vacuum conditions.

When the capsule is subjected to a positive pressure such as that given by the atmosphere, the walls of the aneroid are forced inwards. This principle is used in an aneroid–type barometer; in this case a mechanical linkage from the centre of the capsule to a pointer registers the atmospheric pressure.

MAP can be measured by connecting the pressure chamber around the aneroid to the inlet manifold of the engine. As manifold pressure changes, the aneroid moves the operating rod inwards or outwards to relate an increase or decrease in pressure respectively. By careful shaping of the aneroid, the relationship between rod movement and manifold pressure can be made linear (Figure 5.5).

Conversion from mechanical movement of the aneroid to an electrical output signal is carried out in various ways. These include:

- variable resistor/potentiometer
- variable inductance
- variable differential transformer

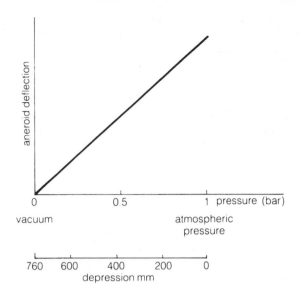

Fig. 5.5 Linear movement of aneroid

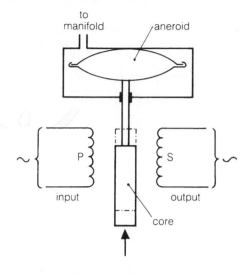

Fig. 5.7 Variable inductance sensor

Variable resistor–potentiometer sensor When a wiper contact blade is rubbed over a resistance material, it acts as a divider of the voltage that is applied to the potentiometer resistor. In the circuit shown in Figure 5.6 a drop in air pressure causes the wiper blade to move towards the earthed end of the resistor; this reduces the output voltage signal. In order to obtain reasonable sensitivity, a comparatively large movement of the wiper blade must be provided.

Variable inductance sensor
When an a.c. current from an oscillator is passed through a primary coil as shown in Figure 5.7, mutual

induction causes an output voltage to be given at the secondary coil (see page 20).

The extent of this output voltage depends on the concentration of magnetic flux, so when an iron core is moved towards the centre of the two coil windings, the output signal is increased.

In this sensor the position of the iron core relative to the windings is controlled by an aneroid. As the pressure is decreased, the expansion of the aneroid moves the iron core towards the centre of the coil windings; this causes the output signal to increase.

A smooth analogue signal is normally required from the sensor so the a.c. output from the secondary is converted and amplified to meet this need.

Variable differential transformer The basic construction of the sensor is similar to the variable inductance type except two output windings are used instead of one (Figure 5.8).

As before, an a.c. current of the order to 10 kHz is applied to the primary winding and this induces a voltage in both secondary windings. These windings are positioned so that they give an equal voltage output when the core is centrally situated. By winding the two output coils in opposite directions the two coil outputs will cancel each other out when the core is in the central position; in this position the sensor output will be zero.

Movement of the core from the central position causes the output from one coil to be greater than that from the other, so the difference in voltage gives an output signal appropriate to the distance the core is moved.

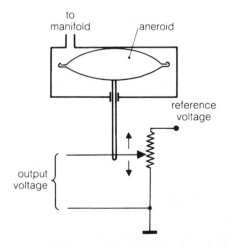

Fig. 5.6 Variable resistor pressure sensor

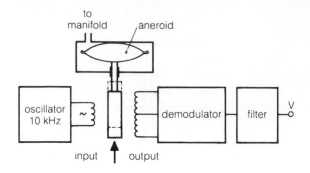

Fig. 5.8 Variable differential transformer

Signal processing, by a demodulator and filter, gives a d.c. output voltage which is normally arranged to be proportional to the manifold pressure. When this is achieved the sensor is called a *linear variable differential transformer* (LVDT).

Strain gauge pressure sensor When a material is strained, a change in length occurs which gives a change in resistance. Early designs of strain gauge has a fine wire filament, but nowadays solid-state semiconductors are used to provide a low-cost and compact sensor.

Figure 5.9 shows a strain gauge pressure sensor. This is built around a silicon chip about 3 mm square which

is formed into a thin diaphragm of thickness about 250 μm (0.25 mm) at the outer edges and about 25 μm at the centre. The chip is sandwiched between two silicon dioxide layers into which is formed four sensing resistors positioned along the edges of the silicon diaphragm. Connection to the resistors is by metal bonding pads formed at each corner of the sensor.

Air pressure sensing requires a vacuum chamber and in this case, the bonding of a Pyrex plate to one face of the chip under vacuum conditions forms the chamber.

The strain gauge is set in a container which is normally connected by a rubber pipe to a region where pressure measurement is to be made.

When the air pressure is varied, the silicon chip deflects; this alters the length of each resistor. By arranging the resistors in a certain manner, two resistors are made to increase their value while the other two decrease they resistance by an equal amount. This resistance change due to pressure, or piezo-resistivity, is harnessed by using a Wheatstone Bridge circuit to give an output signal proportional to the pressure (Figure 5.10).

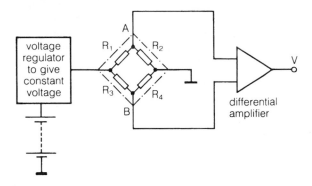

Fig. 5.10 Strain gauge circuit using Wheatstone bridge

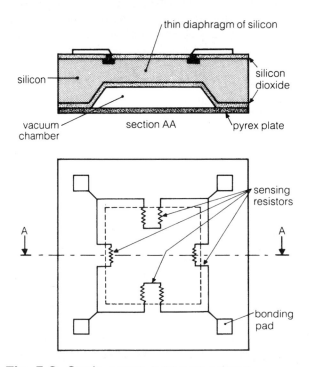

Fig. 5.9 Strain gauge pressure sensor

The four resistors in the strain gauge form the four arms of the bridge. This resistor array is supplied with a constant voltage and the bridge is calibrated so that it is balanced when the strain gauges are undeflected. When pressure is increased, R_1 and R_4 increase resistance and R_2 and R_3 decrease a similar amount. This unbalances the bridge and gives a difference in potential at AB which provides an output signal which is proportional to the pressure.

Using resistors in this form compensates for temperature change. Any increase in resistance due to heat affects all resistors equally, so the bridge balance is maintained over a wide temperature range.

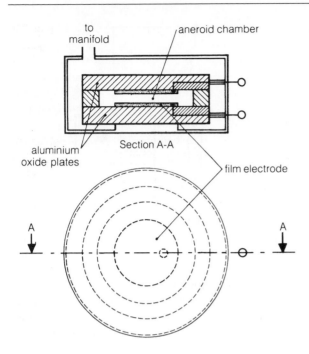

Fig. 5.11 Capacitor-capsule pressure sensor

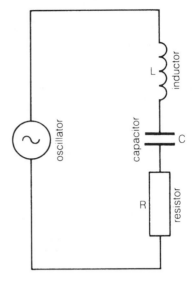

Fig. 5.12 Series resonant circuit

Capacitor–capsule MAP sensor A capacitor consists of two plates separated by a dielectric. Capacitance is varied by altering the distance between the plates, so this feature can be utilized in a pressure sensor.

The basic construction of a capacitor-capsule sensor is shown in Figure 5.11. It consists of two aluminium oxide plates which are coated on the inner surfaces with a film electrode and a lead is connected to each electrode.

The two plates are held apart by an insulation material shaped in the form of a flat washer to provide an aneroid chamber at the centre. The capsule is placed in a container which is connected by a pipe to the pressure source.

Operation of the unit is achieved by using the change in pressure that is communicated to the sensor; this pressure change deflects the plates and alters the distance between the two electrodes.

Signal processing for capacitor-capsule MAP sensor
Change in capacitance caused by alteration in the manifold absolute pressure (MAP) is made to generate an output voltage signal by using various circuit arrangements. One method of signal processing is to use a series resonant circuit (Figure 5.12).

In this arrangement a change in capacitance is made to alter the phase of the frequency produced by an oscillator.

The main circuit consists of an inductor, resistor and sensor capacitor; these are supplied with an a.c. current from an oscillator.

The output from the oscillator gives a normal a.c. waveform, therefore the voltage and current peaks occur at the same time. When the current is supplied to either an inductor or capacitor, the wave patterns are changed. Compared with the voltage peak, an inductor retards the current peak by ¼ cycle and a capacitor advances the current peak by ¼ cycle. These phase alterations are caused by self-inductance by the inductor and charge–discharge action by the capacitor.

At one particular frequency called the *resonance frequency*, the discharge time of the inductor balances the time required for the capacitor to charge. At this frequency the oscillation of the current between the inductor and capacitor is at a maximum, so the voltage of the circuit is high. This feature has been used for many years to amplify radio waves received by an aerial; in this case a variable capacitor is used to 'tune' the circuit to the resonance frequency.

Figure 5.13 shows two voltage pick-up points in an LCR series circuit. Voltage V_1 is the supply or reference voltage and V_2 registers the p.d. across the resistor R. Voltage at V_2 is proportional to the current in the circuit.

At the resonance frequency the peak voltage at CD occurs at the same instant as the voltage at BD, so the voltage across the resistor is in-phase with the reference voltage. At this frequency the phases coincide because

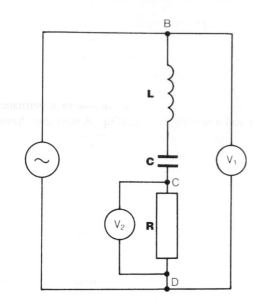

Fig. 5.13 LCR series circuit

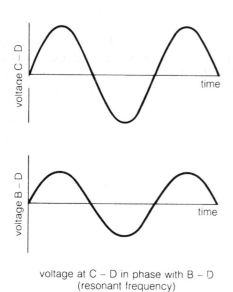

voltage at C – D in phase with B – D
(resonant frequency)

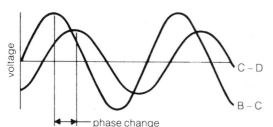

Fig. 5.14 Phase change of V_1 and V_2 due to change in capacitance of LCR circuit in Fig. 5.13.

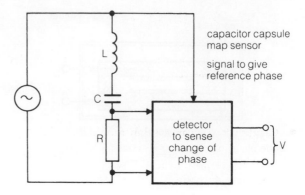

Fig. 5.15 LCR circuit for capacitor type MAP sensor

the ¼ cycle retard in current by the inductor equals the ¼ cycle advance given by the capacitor.

When the capacitance is altered, the circuit will cease to resonate so the current will decrease. Also the time at which maximum current flow through the resistor becomes out-of-phase with the voltage at V_1. Since V_2 depends on the current passing through R, the phase change produced by the alteration in capacitance is shown by the time difference between the voltage peaks at CD and BD (Figure 5.14).

Figure 5.15 shows an LCR series circuit used for a MAP sensor. In this case the frequency and circuit components are tuned to resonate at standard atmospheric pressure. When the pressure is varied, the change in phase between the resistor p.d. and the reference p.d. is measured by a phase detector; this generates an output signal proportional to the change in manifold pressure.

REMEMBER

Aneroid sensor capsule:

● is a thin metal box that flexes when the external pressure is changed
● of the MAP type measures manifold absolute pressure
● is translated into an electrical signal by using the capsule movement to operate
  (a) variable resistor
  (b) variable inductance arrangement
  (c) variable differential transformer
  (d) strain gauge network
  (e) capacitance system

5.3 Position and level sensing

This group of *proximity sensors* is designed to signal either a given position of a mechanical component or the level of a liquid in a reservoir.

The many applications of these position sensors include:

- Crankshaft angular position for timing of the ignition and injection systems
- Crankshaft movement for computation of engine speed for engine management and tachometer operation
- Throttle position for fuel injection and automatic transmission systems
- Gearbox output shaft movement for speedometer, odometer and trip computer operation
- Axle to body position for indication of axle loading
- Maximum wear of brake friction material
- Door position for 'door ajar' indication
- Road wheel movement for anti-skid systems.

Sensing of liquid levels is needed for the monitoring of the vehicle condition. The levels checked by these sensors include: engine oil, coolant, fuel, brake and window washer reservoirs.

Position sensing

The types of sensor used on vehicles are:

- Magnetic – variable reluctance
- Magnetic – d.c.-excited inductive
- Magnetic – Hall effect
- Magnetic – reed switch
- Optical and fibre-optics
- Capacitance

Magnetic–variable reluctance This type of position sensor is very robust and can be applied to a crankshaft, camshaft or distributor drive shaft to signal a given position of a shaft for ignition and fuel timing purposes or for measurement of engine speed.

The sensor in Figure 5.16 consists of a permanent magnet and a sensing coil winding. A steel disc, having a series of cut-away portions, is attached to the driving shaft and is set so that the disc passes between the poles of the magnet.

Reluctance is the term used in magnetic 'circuits' to indicate the circuit's resistance to the 'passage' of a magnetic flux. Placing a ferrous metal between the poles of a magnet makes it easier for the flux to link the two poles; this low reluctance path gives a high magnetic-field intensity.

Turning the reluctor disc to bring the cut-away portion of the discs between the magnetic poles considerably increases the reluctance of the magnetic circuit. As the permeability of air is much greater than that of the steel, the difficult flux path through the air gives a field of low intensity.

In simple terms the reluctor disc is like a water tap – it controls the 'flow' of flux around the magnetic circuit. When the disc protruding tab is between the magnetic poles, the 'tap' is open, but when the cut-away portion is in place, the tap is closed.

The sensing signal is generated by the *changes* which occur in the magnetic flux intensity. When the magnetic flux either increases or decreases, an e.m.f. is inducted into the coil winding. Since the magnitude of the e.m.f. is proportional to the rate of change of the magnetic flux, the faster the change, the greater is the e.m.f., i.e. when the reluctor disc is stationary, no output is obtained. This means that when the variable reluctor

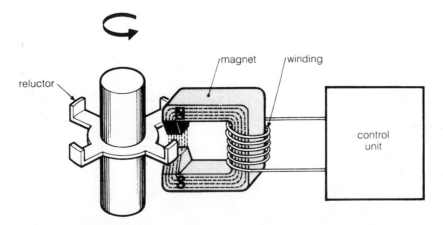

Fig. 5.16 Variable reluctance sensor

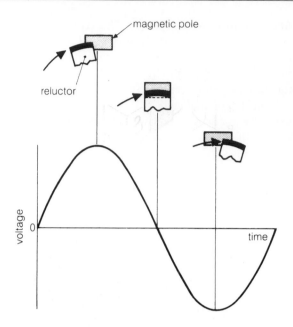

Fig. 5.17 Waveform as reluctor tab moves through magnetic flux

unit is used as an ignition sensor the engine timing cannot be set statically.

Figure 5.17 shows the waveform produced as the reluctor tab is passed through the magnet pole. As the reluctor approaches the pole the e.m.f. builds up to a maximum. When the reluctor tab reaches a point where it is aligned with the pole such that the flux is at its maximum, the e.m.f. is zero; at this point the rate of change of magnetic flux is zero. After this point has been passed, the magnetic flux decays and an e.m.f. of opposite polarity is generated.

The actual shape of the a.c. pulse wave produced by the sensor depends on the shape of the magnetic pole and reluctor. In general the wave resembles that shown in Figure 5.17.

Two crankshaft position sensors are shown in Figure 5.18. Flywheel applications use either a ferromagnetic pin or a partially machined-away tooth to trigger the sensor pulse. Typical peak-to-peak outputs for this type varies from zero when stationary to about 200 V when the peripheral speed of the flywheel is 60 m/s.

A notch cut in the pulley is another way of varying the reluctance. On both position sensors shown the lobe centre line corresponds to the point where the positive pulse half-wave changes to the negative half-wave.

This type of sensor has many advantages: it is robust; it can easily be adapted to use the engine flywheel teeth; needs no exciting voltage or amplifier; operates over a wide temperature range and has a long life. These advantages show why the variable reluctance sensor is often used.

Magnetic – d.c.-excited inductive sensors The disadvantage of low output as given from a variable reluctor sensor is overcome by using a d.c.-excited inductive sensor. This passive type uses direct current to excite a field magnet to give a suitable minimum output voltage such as 2 V peak-to-peak irrespective of the operating frequency.

Figure 5.19 shows the principle of this type of sensor. It consists of a W-shaped iron core with a field core wound around the centre leg of the core. The spacing of the other legs is arranged to bridge the teeth of the rotating ferromagnetic member. In the example shown, the flywheel teeth provide the paths for the flux.

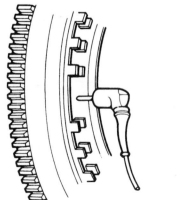

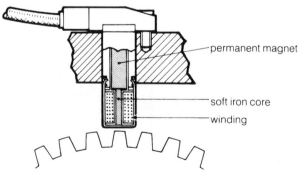

Fig. 5.18 Crankshaft position sensors

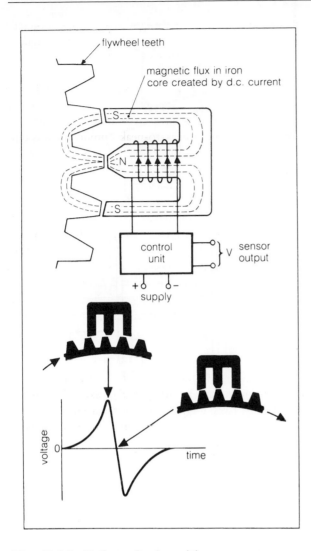

Fig. 5.19 D.C.-excited position sensors

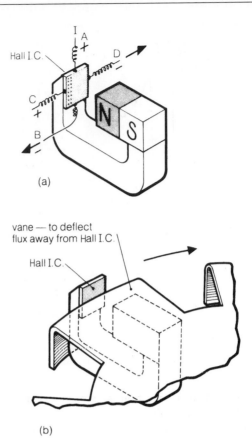

Fig. 5.20 Hall-effect sensor

Unless precautions are taken, the generation of eddy currents causes the pulse peaks to alter in respect to the position of the rotating member. This 'phase shift' problem is minimised in this design by using a ferrite material for the magnetic core. A typical phase shift is given as 0.3° over a speed range of 0–6000 rev/min.

Operation of the sensor is achieved by exciting the field magnet with direct current from a control unit. This unit varies the current to give a constant voltage pulse. At low speeds the exciting current is comparatively large, but as the speed is increased the current is reduced.

As the flywheel teeth pass the legs of the iron core, the change in the reluctor path varies the magnetic field

intensity and as a result it produces an a.c. pulse in the field winding. This pulse is detected by the control unit which processes it to provide the output signal.

Sensors of this type are often used in conjunction with diagnostic test equipment for measurement of ignition and fuel-injection settings.

Magnetic – Hall effect This passive sensor is often used in an ignition distributor as an alternative to the contact points of a Kettering system. For its operation it needs a supply current and this feature enables it to detect zero movement. For this reason it is also used for many other position- and speed-sensing applications.

The Hall generator, as it is often called, utilises the principle whereby a voltage is generated across a plate carrying an electrical current when the plate is exposed to a magnetic flux.

The Hall effect is shown in Figure 5.20(a). This shows a wafer of semiconductor material placed in a magnetic field and supplied with constant current I across the wafer from A to B. Under the influence of

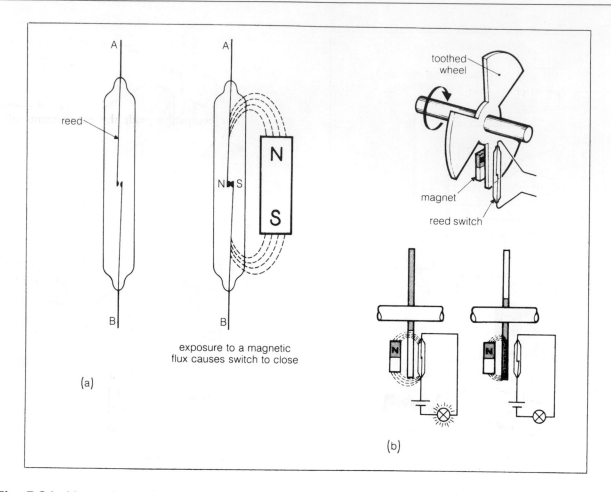

Fig. 5.21 Magnetic-reed switch

a magnetic flux, the electron flow of the current I is deflected as it passes through the semiconductor; this causes a potential difference across the plate in the direction CD. This difference in voltage across the plate is called the *Hall voltage*.

Alteration of the magnetic field strength varies the Hall voltage; the stronger the field the higher the voltage.

Although the Hall voltage is limited to a few millivolts, the incorporation of the semiconductor wafer into an integrated circuit (Hall IC) enables the voltage to be amplified sufficiently to give a comparatively strong output signal.

The sensing feature is achieved by using mechanical means to vary the field strength. One method is to use a rotating vane to act as a switch for controlling the magnetic flux (Figure 5.20(b)). When the vane is in the air gap between the magnet and the Hall IC, the

magnetic field is diverted away from the wafer. This 'switches off' the Hall voltage and signals the position of the shaft controlling the vane.

When used as an ignition timing sensor, ignition occurs when the Hall IC is switched on, i.e. at the point when the vane leaves the air gap and the Hall voltage is re-established.

Magnetic – reed switch   A reed switch consists of two or more contacts mounted in a glass vial to exclude contaminates. The vial is evacuated of air or filled with an inert gas to reduce damage by arcing.

When used as a position or proximity sensor the switch is operated by a permanent magnet. Exposing the reeds of the switch to a magnetic flux causes each reed to take up the polarity of the magnetic pole nearest to it. Since the reed polarities are opposite, they will be attracted together (Figure 5.21(a)). This will close the switch and allow the flow of current to create the sensor pulse.

Although it is possible to operate the reed by using a magnet attached to a rotating shaft, it is more common to keep the magnet stationary and use a mechanical means such as a toothed wheel to divert the flux away from the reed when the switch is to be opened (Figure 5.21(b)).

The reed switch is used for many applications; it can sense shaft position for fuel injection, road wheel movement for speedometer operation and it provides a simple means of indicating a liquid level.

Optical Optoelectronic sensors can be used to signal a shaft position. When used in conjunction with fibre-optics, the numerous advantages suggest that this system will be used extensively in the future.

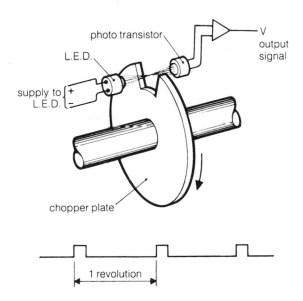

Fig. 5.22 Optoelectronic sensor

The principle is shown in Figure 5.22. A LED light source is positioned opposite a phototransistor; a chopper plate, in the form of a disc, is attached to the moving shaft. A slot or hole in the disc allows the light to pass to the phototransistor at the instant when the slot is aligned with the LED: at this point it signals the position of the shaft.

Although this description suggests a visual form of light radiation, the system often uses light frequencies outside the vision of the human eye. The LED fitted generally has a frequency which falls within the range infra-red to ultra-violet.

Voltage applied to the LED is set to give a photo-transistor output which is sufficient after amplification to signal the ECU. In a case where a TTL logic circuit is used, the typical output voltages will be 2.4 V (high level) and 0.2 V (low level).

A square-wave pulse is given by this type of sensor; this makes it compatible with the requirements of a digital system.

One drawback of this type is the need to maintain the lens of the emitter and receiver in a clean condition. Dirt on the surfaces reduces the sensor output so periodic attention to this task is necessary.

Since the sensor is passive, it has the capability of detecting zero motion.

Fibre-optics system Limited space in the vicinity of the sensor sometimes prevents the fitting of a normal type of optical sensor. This drawback can be overcome by using two fibre-optic strands to transmit the light signal from the LED to the phototransistor (Figure 5.23).

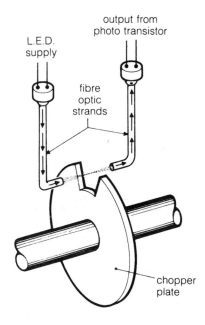

Fig. 5.23 Fibre-optics sensor system

This light-transmission system offers many advantages for motor vehicles; these include:

- space saving
- rate of data transmission is very high
- extra safety because fibre-optic cables do not carry an electrical current
- can be used in hostile regions

- do not suffer 'noise' problems (i.e. electrical charges are not induced from surrounding electrical equipment).

Capacitance This type of sensor uses a toothed wheel to form either a plate or the dielectric of a capacitor. Its operation relies on the following principle.

If a parallel-plate capacitor is charged to a given value the voltage across the plate will:

- increase as the distance between the plates increases
- decrease if a dielectric is used instead of air between the plates.

Capacitive sensors can be designed to utilise one or other of these two features; they can be excited by a.c. or d.c. means.

Figure 5.24(a) shows a sensor which produces a signal by varying the distance between the plates; this is achieved by rotating a toothed wheel. Since the plate and the toothed wheel are electrically charged, the movement of the wheel has the effect of changing the distance between the plates. In the case of a d.c.-excited sensor, this change in voltage provides a pulse which is processed to give the required output.

The alternative construction uses a dielectric wheel (Figure 5.24(b)). Rotation of the wheel between the

two charged plates varies the voltage across the plates to give the pulse.

This arrangement can be used for a high rotational speed but when used at a lower speed, and for detecting zero motion, the difficulty of maintaining the plates in a clean state and at a constant electrical charge makes this type of sensor less attractive than many other types.

When the sensor is a.c. excited, the capacitor forms part of an oscillator circuit. Changes in capacitance due to movement of the toothed wheel result in a change in the frequency (Figure 5.24(c)). To detect high-speed movement, a high frequency must be used but this often causes *interference* with radios and in-car telephones unless the sensor system is adequately screened. Because the screening affects the capacitance of the sensor system, the associated circuitry of the sensor must be situated as close as possible to the sensor. Often lack of space makes this difficult. (See also page 89 for a typical application of another type of capacitor sensor.)

Throttle position sensor Often this type of sensor is a potentiometer (pot); this is a variable resistance which is used as a means for altering electrical potential. One of the simplest arrangements is a variable resistor as shown in Figure 5.25. In this case the throttle is connected to a contact blade which wipes across a resistor coil. As the

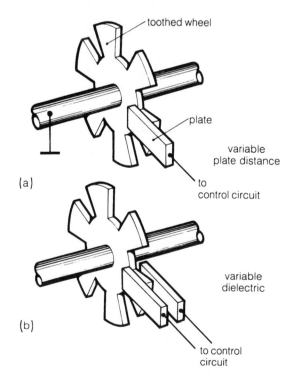

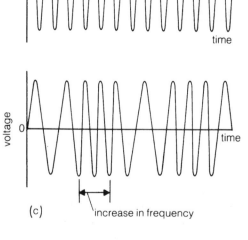

Fig. 5.24 Parallel-plate capacitor

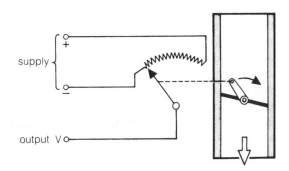

Fig. 5.25 Throttle position sensor

throttle is opened the number of resistor coils in the circuit is reduced. This alters the voltage and potential of the output in relation to 'earth'.

An improved accuracy and a longer life is obtained by using alternative resistor materials to wire. Figure 5.26 shows a typical sensor with two pairs of contact blades; one pair acts as the main potentiometer, the other pair acts as a microswitch to signal the throttle-closed position. A constant voltage of 5 V is applied to the sensor. As the contact blades slide along the resistor in accordance with the opening of the throttle valve, the output voltage increases proportionally. This linear signal is transmitted to the ECU.

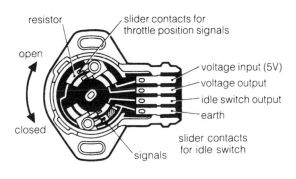

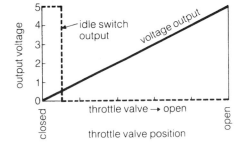

Fig. 5.26 Throttle position potentiometer

Level sensing

Electrical measurement of fluid levels requires the fitting of a sensor in the reservoir, sump or container of the system being monitored. A position-type sensor is normally utilized for this function; some applications are shown on page 320.

REMEMBER

Position sensors:

- magnetic–variable reluctance type uses a permanent magnet, sensing coil and some arrangement to vary the magnetic reluctance
- magnetic–d.c.–excited type is supplied with a d.c. low voltage current which changes to an a.c. pulse when the sensor's reluctor path is varied
- magnetic–Hall effect type has a semiconductor IC placed between the poles of a magnet and a moving metallic vane that diverts the magnetic flux away from the IC to switch off the Hall voltage
- magnetic–reed switch type has a glass vial containing two contacts that operate when they are placed close to a magnet
- optical type operates when a gap in a rotating vane allows light from an LED to fall on a photo-transistor
- capacitance type changes the frequency of its oscillation circuit by using a toothed wheel to form either a plate or a dielectric of a capacitor

5.4 Flow sensing

Measurement of fluid flow in a motor vehicle is needed in two cases:

- air flow for fuel metering as in fuel-injection systems
- fuel flow for computation of fuel consumption and associated information.

Air flow sensors

Full electronic systems for petrol injection use air-measurement sensors such as:

- hot wire
- flap type
- aneroid MAP.

Hot-wire measurement of air mass A hot-wire air-mass meter relies on the cooling effect of air as it passes over a heated wire. If this wire is heated by passing a constant current through it, then the temperature of the wire will fall as the air flow is increased.

Similarly if a hot wire is kept at a constant temperature, then the amount of current required to maintain this temperature will be governed by the air flow; the larger the air flow, the greater the current.

Both the constant-current and constant-temperature methods use electronic means to measure the temperature. Generally this is achieved by utilising the change in resistance which occurs when the temperature is changed.

Hot-wire systems take into account changes in air density. This is particularly important at different altitudes. Atmospheric pressure decreases with altitude, so in an area situated well above sea level, the air mass supplied for a given throttle opening is reduced considerably. Unless this feature is taken into account, the richer mixture received by the engine would cause high exhaust gas pollution.

Figure 5.27 (a) shows the construction of a hot-wire of diameter 0.070 mm, which is exposed to air which passes through a tube situated in the air intake. Figure 5.27(b) shows that the wire is connected into a Wheatstone bridge circuit, (see page 34). A power amplifier, situated where the galvanometer is placed in a bridge circuit, controls the current supplied to the four arms of the bridge. When a signal shows that the bridge is unbalanced, the amplifier adjusts the heating current to restore the bridge to a balanced state.

Operation of the sensor is based on the constant-temperature principle. When air is passing at a constant rate, the supply current holds the hot-wire at a given temperature; consequently the bridge is maintained in a balanced state. Any increase in air flow cools the hot-wire and causes its resistance to decrease. This unbalances the bridge and as a result causes the amplifier to increase the heating current until the original temperature is restored. This increase in the heating current causes a higher voltage drop across R_1, so by measuring

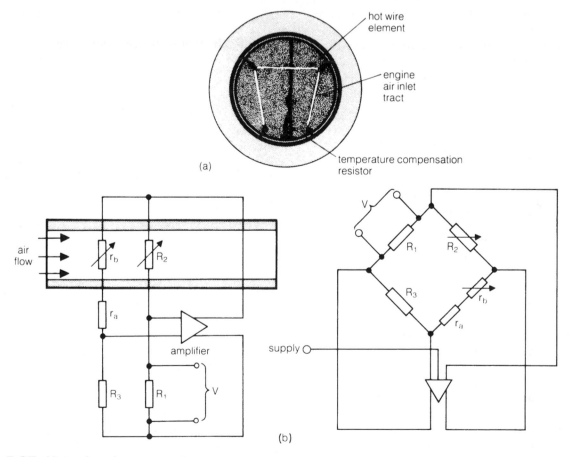

Fig. 5.27 Hot-wire air-mass meter

this drop across a precision resistor placed at R_1 a sensor output signal is obtained. The signal shows the heating current but it also indicates the mass of air flowing through the meter.

By relating the hot-wire sensor signal to values stored in a 'look-up' table in the ECUs memory, the computer can determine the amount of fuel that needs to be injected to give the required air/fuel ratio.

Any alteration in the temperature of the intake air causes the bridge to become unbalanced, so a compensating resistor wire r_b is placed in the air stream adjacent to the hot wire.

Resistance change of the hot wire is measured by using a Wheatstone Bridge circuit. Careful selection of the diameter of a hot-wire ensures that the time taken for the system to respond to changes in air flow is limited to a few milliseconds. This length of time overcomes the air pulsation problem due to the irregular flow through the air intake, especially when the engine is running at low speed under full load.

The temperature of the 'cold-wire' compensating resistor acts as a 'standard'. In operation the amplifier keeps the hot-wire at 100°C above the temperature of the cold-wire.

Heat radiation from a hot-wire is decreased when the wire becomes dirty, so to avoid this problem, the ECU is programmed to burn off the dirt by heating the wire to a higher-than-normal temperature for one second every time the engine is switched off.

A development of the hot-wire system is the *hot-film air-mass sensor*. In this arrangement the wire is replaced by a heated film having integral resistors for air flow measurement and temperature compensation. It is claimed that this system is more robust and reliable than the hot-wire.

Flap-type air-flow meter This system senses the air-flow rate by measuring the angle of deflection of a flap or vane. Mechanical movement of the flap is translated to an electrical analogue signal by a potentiometer ((Figure 5.28).

The sensing flap, placed in the air tract, is spring loaded to oppose the force given by the air flow. Flap pulsations, caused by the irregular air flow, are damped by a small air chamber adjacent to the flap.

The flap moves a slider of a thick-film type potentiometer which provides a voltage signal; this increases as the flap is opened. Using a thick-film resistor minimizes the effect of temperature changes and by varying the resistance of each resistor segment of the potentiometer, a linear relationship can be obtained

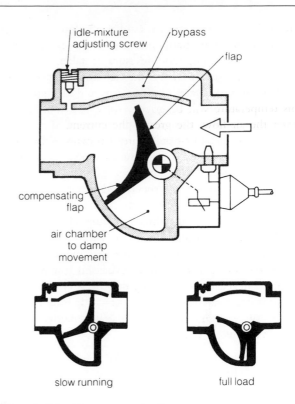

Fig. 5.28 Flap-type air flow meter

between the sensor's output voltage and the fuel to be injected.

When the throttle is opened and the air flow is increased, the greater force given by the air opens the flap. This allows air to spill past the flap until a balance is reached between the air force and the flap spring force. As the flap moves to this position, the higher voltage output signal to the ECU results in the injection of a larger quantity of fuel.

The vane-type air flow sensor only measures the volume of air; it does not take into account any changes in density or temperature. In most cases this is not a problem but other sensors can be fitted to correct for these variables.

Manifold absolute pressure (MAP) sensors Zero on the absolute scale is where pressure ceases to exist; at this point a complete vacuum is formed. Standard pressure of the atmosphere is 1 bar of 101.3 kilopascals when expressed as an absolute pressure.

During the induction stroke of an engine, the pressure in the induction manifold falls below atmospheric pressure; a typical value for an engine operating under light load at 1000 rev/min is 0.4 bar absolute. Relating this value to atmospheric pressure (often called *gauge pressure* when atmospheric pressure is taken as zero) shows that the 'suction' effect on the air by the pumping action of the engine piston has lowered the pressure by 0.6 bar.

A pressure lower than atmospheric is called a *depression*; this term is used in preference to 'vacuum' because a vacuum suggests that no pressure exists whatsoever.

MAP is affected by a number of things; the two main variables are engine speed and throttle opening. Under ideal conditions where the manifold and piston have no air leaks and the throttle is fully closed, a very large depression approaching a vacuum is formed. In practice this is not possible and the maximum obtained is only about 0.17 bar absolute. Even this low pressure can be achieved only when the throttle is closed as the engine is decelerated from a high speed. During normal loading of the engine, the MAP varies between the following limits:

(1) *High speed, light load* Low MAP (high depression), e.g. 0.4 bar;
(2) *Low speed, heavy load* High MAP (low depression), e.g. 0 bar.

Aneroid MAP sensor   The quantity of air flowing through a duct can be measured by knowing:

● the pressure difference across a given orifice (or restriction such as a throttle valve in an engine air intake)
● the area of the orifice.

Assuming a constant air temperature, humidity and pressure, the manifold absolute pressure, as measured by an aneroid MAP sensor, relates to the quantity of air that is entering the engine.

Quantity of air flowing due to pressure difference depends on throttle opening, so the throttle must be fitted with a transducer to signal the extent that the throttle valve is opened. Normally a potentiometer is used as a throttle position sensor.

The MAP sensor used in this application is a pressure type as described on page 85.

Fuel flow sensor

A trip computer, as fitted to many modern vehicles, has the facility to calculate fuel consumption. This feature requires an input signal that indicates the quantity of fuel used by the engine in a given time.

One type of fuel line transducer has a fuel-driven turbine which rotates the chopper plate of an optical sensor unit.

5.5   Temperature sensing

A number of sensors are used on a vehicle to measure temperature. These include:

● engine temperature for ignition, fuel metering and instrumentation
● air intake temperature for fuel metering and vaporization control
● ambient conditions for driving safety
● exhaust temperature for fuel metering.

The majority of temperature sensors use a thermistor, but there are occasions where a thermocouple is used.

Thermistor sensor   This type normally consists of a brass bulb, which is in contact with the substance it is sensing. The bulb contains a capsule called a thermistor.

Resistance of common metals increases with temperature and thermistors which have a sensing capsule that responds in this way are said to have a *positive temperature coefficient* (PTC).

Conversely, a capsule made of a semiconductor material has a resistance which decreases with temperature. These materials, of which silicon is the most common, have a *negative temperature coefficient* (NTC).

Figure 5.29 shows the construction and resistance variation with temperature of a typical sensor as fitted into an engine block to measure the coolant temperature. In addition to temperature measurement the thermistor is often used in an electronics circuit to safeguard

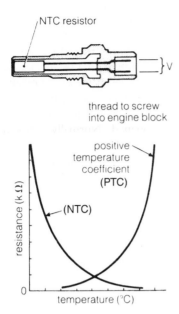

NTC resistor

thread to screw
into engine block

resistance (k Ω)

positive
temperature
coefficient
(PTC)

(NTC)

0

temperature (°C)

Fig. 5.29 Thermistor sensor characteristics

semiconductor devices when the circuit components are cold. It compensates for temperature to keep the circuit 'in tune'.

Thermocouple   The thermistor is excellent for measuring temperature up to about 200°C, but above this temperature a thermocouple is normally used.

The principle of a thermocouple is shown in Figure 5.30. It consists of two wires of dissimilar material joined together and connected to a galvanometer. When the hot junction is heated, an e.m.f. is generated which is registered by the galvanometer. Up to a given temperature, which depends on the metals used (250°C for copper–iron), the current increases with an increase in the temperature difference between the hot and cold ends of the wires. Indication of temperature is achieved by scaling the galvanometer accordingly.

This effect was discovered by Seebeck in 1822. He showed that *thermoelectric currents* are obtained from a pair

of metals when their junctions are maintained at different temperatures.

A thermocouple can be made by joining two metals from: antimony, iron, zinc, lead, copper and platinum. Current will flow from the higher to the lower in this list across the cold junction.

Nowadays other metals and alloys are used for a thermocouple, e.g. nickel–chromium/nickel–aluminium alloys are used for the wires of a common type of thermocouple. This type is suitable for a temperature range 0–1100°C such as exists in an engine exhaust system.

Measurement of exhaust gas temperature is necessary when an oxygen sensor is used.

REMEMBER

Thermistor

- is used for measuring a temperature up to about 200°C
- has a semiconductor capsule that has either a PTC or NTC characteristic
- the NTC type decreases its resistance with increase in temperature

Thermocouple

- is used for measuring a high temperature
- is made by joining two dissimilar metal wires to form a connection called a hot junction
- generates an e.m.f. when the hot junction is heated

5.6   Gas sensing

Oxygen sensing

The detection of oxygen in the gas exhausted from an engine provides a useful means for controlling the air/fuel mixture. Oxygen in the exhaust indicates that the air/fuel ratio is weak, whereas the absence of oxygen shows that the mixture is rich and exhaust gas pollution of the atmosphere is taking place.

A sensor designed to signal when combustion in an engine cylinder completely burns the fuel (i.e. that the air/fuel mixture delivered to the engine is chemically correct) enables the engine management system to operate effectively irrespective of the mechanical state of the engine. The gas detector used to provide this signal is called a *Lambda sensor* (Figure 5.31).

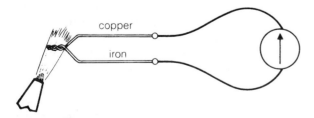

copper

iron

Fig. 5.30 Thermocouple

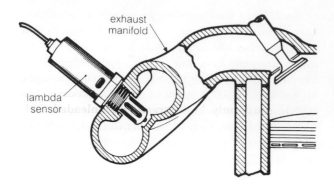

Fig. 5.31 Lambda sensor

Lambda sensor This type of exhaust gas oxygen (EGO) sensor normally uses zirconium oxide (ZrO_2) for its active material. Figure 5.32(a) shows the basic construction of an EGO sensor.

It consists of a thimble-shaped portion of ZrO_2 covered with two thin and porous platinum electrodes. The internal electrode is in contact with air in the centre of the dome and the outer electrode is placed so that it is in contact with exhaust gas. Extra protection against gas erosion is given by covering the outer electrode with a porous alumina ceramic coating through which the gas can penetrate.

The operation of the sensor is similar to a galvanic battery cell; in the case of the sensor the ZrO_2 acts as the electrolyte. At high temperatures this electrolyte becomes conductive so if the two plates are in contact with different amounts of oxygen, then a small voltage will be generated across the two plates. This action is produced because oxygen atoms carry two free electrons so this means that the atom carries a negative charge. The ZrO_2 attracts oxygen ions with the result that negative charges build up on the surface of

the ZrO_2 adjacent to the platinum electrode (Figure 5.32(b)).

When the sensor is exposed to exhaust gas, a greater concentration of oxygen on the air side of the ZrO_2 causes this side to have a greater number of negative charges. In consequence a potential difference is built up across the plates which will depend on the difference in oxygen levels. It will be about 1 V when the engine is operated on a enriched air/fuel mixture but this will drop abruptly at the point where the air/fuel ratio is chemically correct, i.e. at the stoichiometric point. In the weak zone beyond this point, the p.d. across the sensor will remain near constant at about 50 mV (Figure 5.33).

The time taken for the sensor to respond decreases as the temperature is increased. Common types in use

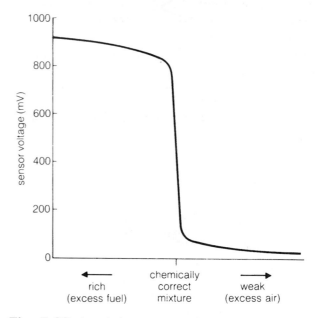

Fig. 5.33 Lambda sensor output voltage

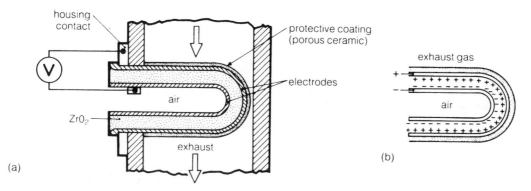

Fig. 5.32 Lambda sensor operation

become operational above about 300°C and have a response time of less than 200 ms. The point on the air/fuel ratio scale at which the abrupt voltage change occurs is not affected by the temperature, but temperature produces a small change in the voltage; a drop of about 200 mV occurs when the temperature is altered from 500 to 1000°C.

An exhaust gas contains gases other than oxygen so these have to be neutralized by conversion to avoid affecting the action of the ZrO_2; this duty is performed by the platinum plates. These plates are porous, so the unwanted gas passing through the platinum is oxidized by the catalytic action of the platinum. (A catalyst is a material which produces a chemical action without undergoing any change itself.)

The catalytic action of the platinum will be prevented if lead is present in the gas, so where catalytic converters are used to oxidize exhaust products **the vehicle must only be operated on unleaded fuel**. If this requirement is met, then the sensor has a life in excess of 50 000 km.

5.7 Knock sensing

The main purpose of a knock sensor is to detect combustion knock (detonation) in an engine combustion chamber.

Combustion knock This fault occurs when the gas charge in one part of the combustion chamber ignites spontaneously instead of burning gradually. The region of the chamber where this explosive action takes place is normally the zone farthest away from the sparking plug; the charge in this region is called the *end gas*. Combustion knock, or *detonation* as it is often called,

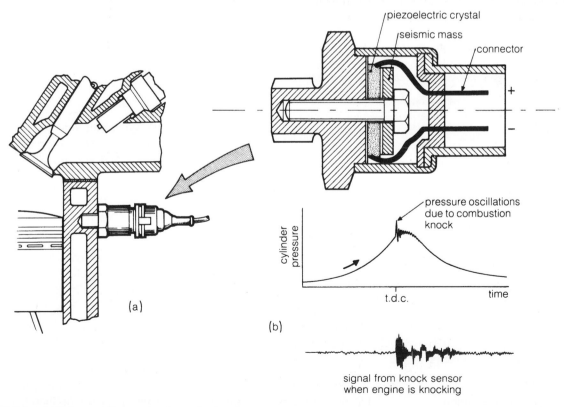

Fig. 5.34 Accelerometer-type knock sensor

generates high-intensity pressure waves which can be heard as a noise called *pinking*.

Severe combustion knock not only subjects the engine to high pressure; it also raises the temperature of the metal in the region of the end gas to a point sufficient to melt the piston crown.

Over-advance of the ignition timing is one of the main causes of combustion knock. Since maximum engine power requires the timing to be set to an angle just below the point where knock is initiated, any slight change in operating conditions can easily take the engine into the knock range and cause extensive damage. In the past, this risk was reduced by setting the ignition advance well below the point where knock might occur.

Principle of a knock sensor A knock sensor has to detect vibrations from combustion knock in the frequency range 1–10 kHz. When severe knock occurs in the combustion chamber, the transference of pressure waves through the cylinder block causes the metal particles to be accelerated to and fro. The accelerometer-type knock sensor detects this oscillatory motion by using a piezoceramic semiconductor. This sensor is similar to the type used for measuring pressure which is described on page 88. Pressure on the semiconductor generates a small electrical charge and this is used to provide the signal current.

Figure 5.34(a) shows the basic construction of a

REMEMBER

Knock sensor:

- is fitted to an engine cylinder block adjacent to the combustion chamber
- detects combustion knock (detonation)
- uses a piezoceramic semiconductor
- outputs an analogue signal that 'tells' the ECU to gradually reduce the ignition timing advance until the detected knock is eliminated

knock sensor. The body is screwed into the side of the cylinder block and the piezoelectric crystal is clamped by a seismic mass which tunes the sensor to the required frequency range.

When an oscillation of the form shown in Figure 5.34(b) is applied to the sensor body, the sound waves vary the compression of the crystal; this causes a small e.m.f. of the order of 20 mV/g to be generated

The small analogue signal current produced by the sensor when the engine is knocking is transmitted to the ECU. After filtering to remove the unwanted waves, the signal is then averaged and converted to a digital form to represent the knock/no-knock conditions. Whenever a digital pulse is sensed by a logic circuit, the system responds by reducing the spark timing advance.

PROGRESS CHECK 5

1. What is a transducer?

2. State the purpose of a sensor.

3. State the difference between an active and a passive sensor.

4. What is a smart-type sensor?

5. List FOUR types of pressure sensor.

6. Describe the operation of an aneroid pressure capsule.

7. What is meant by MAP as applied to pressure sensors?

8. List SIX motor vehicle applications of a position sensor.

9. The variable reluctor is one type of position sensor. List FOUR other types.

10. State how a reluctor is used to signal a given position.

11. Name the passive type position sensor that uses a semiconductor chip and a metal vane to divert the flux away from the chip when an output voltage is not required.

12. State the construction and operation of a reed switch.

13. Hot-wire is one type of flow sensor. Name TWO other types.

14. State ONE motor vehicle application of a flow sensor.

15. State the principle of a hot-wire flow sensor.

16. What method is used on a hot-wire sensor to compensate for changes in airflow temperature?

17. State the operating difference between an NTC thermistor and a PTC type.

18. What is meant by hot junction as applied to a thermocouple?

19. State the purpose of a Lambda sensor.

20. What action is taken by an ECU when signals from a knock meter indicate that severe pressure oscillations are occurring?

6 *Actuators*

What is covered in this chapter

→ linear solenoids
→ linear motors
→ rotary actuators
→ stepper motors

Actuators interpret, communicate and implement motion; they produce mechanical motion when commanded by an electrical signal. Two types of electric actuator are:

(1) linear
(2) rotary.

Most automotive components require a linear operating force, i.e. a force that moves the device in a straight line. This motion can be produced by a linear solenoid or a linear motor.

6.1 Linear solenoids

A simple solenoid consists of a bobbin that holds a coil of thin copper wire which is enamelled to insulate the coils from each other (Figure 6.1(a)). A soft iron armature or plunger, of diameter sufficient to permit axial movement, slides into the bobbin when the coil is energized (see page 18). A spring is normally used to return the plunger when the current is switched off.

When the solenoid is energized for long periods, the current consumption is reduced by using two coils; a closing coil and a holding coil (Figure 6.1(b)). Closing the switch supplies current to both coils until the plunger nears the end of its travel. At this point a pair of contacts are opened to disconnect from the circuit the powerful closing coil; this leaves the holding coil to retain the plunger in position.

Linear movement in both directions can be produced by using two coils, A and B, placed end-to-end (Figure 6.2). When B is energized the plunger moves to the

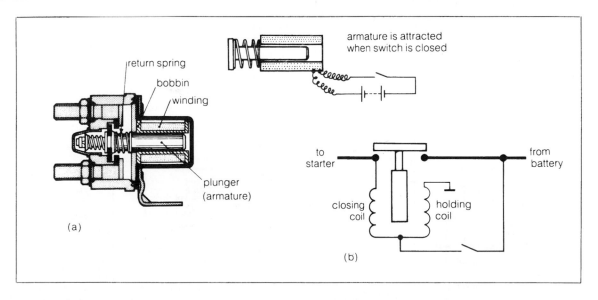

Fig. 6.1 Solenoid

105

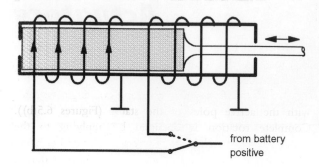

Fig. 6.2 Double-acting solenoid

right and when coil A is energized the plunger is returned. Double-coil solenoids are used on some central door-locking systems.

A solenoid can produce large forces and give a rapid operation but has the disadvantage that the stroke is limited to about 8 mm. This limitation arises because the force on the plunger is proportional to the square of the distance between the plunger and the pole piece. As a result of this, the force decreases considerably when the air gap is increased. Often the solenoid plunger is connected to an extension arm or lever to make it suitable for the application.

6.2 Linear motors

At first sight this appears to be similar to a solenoid; the difference is that the linear d.c. motor uses a powerful permanent magnet to increase the magnetic action. In view of this, a near-constant force over a longer stroke is achieved.

Two main types of linear motor, shown in Figure 6.3 are:

● Moving winding
● Moving magnet (moving field)

Moving winding This has a fixed magnet around which is fitted a hollow armature and coil winding. When a d.c. current is supplied to the coil, the armature is either pushed outwards or pulled inwards, depending on the direction of the current.

Moving field This type of motor has a static field winding and a moveable magnet to provide the actuating force. As before, the direction of motion is governed by the polarity of the supply. The stroke (distance moved in one direction) is limited to half the length of the magnet; to be effective the width of the coil winding should equal the stroke.

An alternative design uses two coils wound in opposite directions. In this case one coil moves the magnet one way and the other moves the magnet the other way. This double-coil system overcomes the need for changing the polarity.

6.3 Rotary actuators

The conventional permanent-magnet d.c. motor, as used originally for windscreen wipers, is still the most common type used to actuate vehicle systems such as washers, fuel pumps, windows, seats, sunshine roofs and radio antennae.

Since the motor is compact, a high speed is needed for it to generate sufficient power. This tends to reduce reliability and means that the motor requires a gearbox to adapt speed and increase torque. Cost and weight of the gearbox are important, so a plastic material is generally used for the gears even though a plastic gear is weaker than metal. Friction is a problem and this is not helped where the motion has to be changed from rotary to reciprocating by means of a flexible rack. Nevertheless, the rotary motion together with its mechanical linkage gives a long-stroke action demanded by many automotive components.

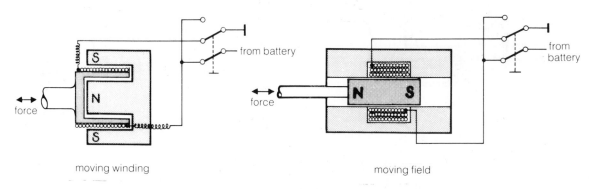

moving winding   moving field

Fig. 6.3 Linear motors

6.4 Stepper motors

The introduction of digital electronic units in automotive control systems has been accompanied by the use of special actuators called stepper motors; these respond to electrical pulse signals. The motor is used to move a mechanical control unit in accordance to the messages it receives from the electronic 'brain'.

Figure 6.4 shows a control system which is based on three main stages: the actuator is part of the final stage. For precise control, the system requires a motor that moves through set angles in either direction. The type of motor used governs the smallest step angle through which it can move; typical angles used are: 1.8°, 2.5°, 3.75°, 7.5°, 15° and 30°.

Stepper motors are made in three versions:

- Permanent magnet (PM)
- Variable reluctance (VR)
- Hybrid

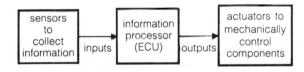

Fig. 6.4 Electronic control system

Permanent-magnet stepper motor The principle of this type is shown in Figure 6.5 (a); in this case the active rotor is a two-pole permanent magnet. The stator has two pairs of independent windings AA_1 and BB_1 through which current may be passed in either direction to make the rotor turn through 90° steps.

When current is passed to phase winding BB_1, the magnetic laws of attraction and repulsion align the rotor with the active poles of the stator (Figures 6.5(b)). Complete rotation is obtained by applying to the motor four electrical pulses of suitable polarity. Direction of rotation depends on the polarity of the stator during the first pulse, e.g. if the current direction in Figure 6.5(b) is reversed, the rotor will move in a clockwise direction.

Altering the frequency of step pulses applied to the stator varies the speed of rotation; also by controlling the number of pulses a given angular displacement can be obtained.

By increasing the number of rotor and stator poles, the step angle (°) can be reduced; this is calculated so:

$$\text{step angle} = \frac{360}{\text{number of step positions}}$$

Each winding has two possible current-flow directions so the number of step positions will always be an even number. Permanent-magnet motors are generally available with basic step angles between 7.5° and 120°.

One advantage of this type of stepper motor is that the magnet holds the rotor in place when the stator is

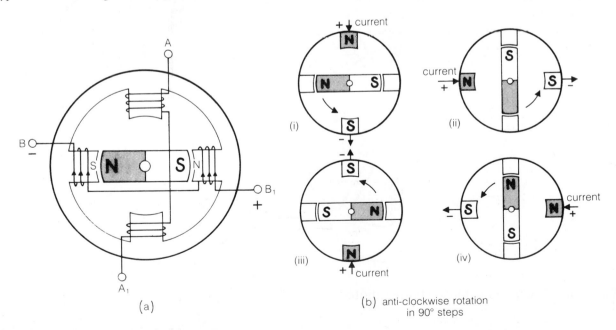

(a)

(b) anti-clockwise rotation in 90° steps

Fig. 6.5 Permanent-magnet stepper motor

not energized; this is called *detent torque* and not all stepper motors have this feature. Disadvantages include high inertia and the fall-off of performance due to changes in magnetic strength.

Variable-reluctance stepper motor This type has a soft-iron rotor with radial teeth and a wound stator having more poles than the rotor. Figure 6.6 (a) shows a simplified layout of a three-phase, 15° step-angle motor; this has eight rotor teeth and twelve stator poles around which the current flows in one direction only.

The number of step positions (N) is calculated so:

$$N = \frac{SR}{S - R}$$

where S = the number of slots in stator and R = number of slots in rotor.

In this case

$$N = \frac{8 \times 12}{12 - 8} = \frac{96}{4} = 24$$

So:

$$\text{step angle} = \frac{360}{24} = 15°$$

Figure 6.6 (b) shows the winding arrangement for phase 1.

When a current flows through one phase of the stator windings, the rotor aligns itself to give the shortest magnetic path, i.e. the path of minimum reluctance. In each step position, the rotor aligns with four stator poles so this gives the motor greater power.

An angular movement of one step from the position shown in Figure 6.6(a) is obtained by energizing either phase 2 or phase 3 depending on the required direction. For a clockwise motion the phases would be energized in the order: 3, 2, 1, 3, 2, 1. The angle turned by the rotor by these six current pulses is 90° and the time for the total movement is governed by the time taken by the control circuit to energize the windings sufficient to move the rotor to the next step.

This type of motor is obtainable with step angles between 1.8° and 15°. It has a fast response because of its low rotor inertia and has a fast stepping rate. As it has no detent torque it is prone to oscillate and resonate unless it is damped externally.

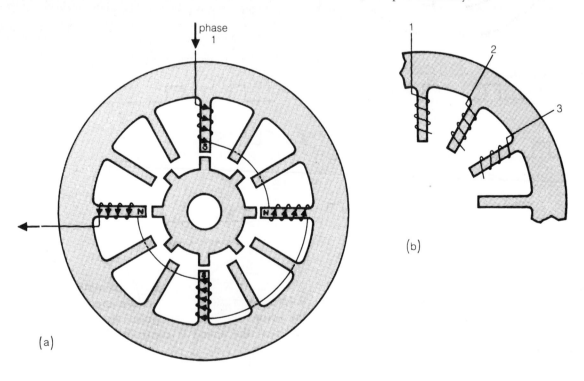

(a)

(b)

Fig. 6.6 Variable-reluctance stepper motor

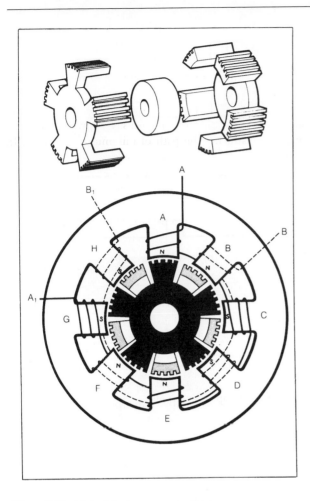

Fig. 6.7 Hybrid stepper motor

Hybrid stepper motor   As the name suggests this type is a combination of the PM and VR types. Figure 6.7 shows that in this type the rotor is constructed in a manner similar to that used in an alternator. A permanent magnet, with its poles coaxial with the shaft, is sandwiched between two iron claws having teeth which form two sets of poles.

The stator has eight main poles which are cut to form small teeth on the surface adjacent to the rotor.

The operation is similar to the PM type; the rotor aligns itself so that the magnetic reluctance is lowest.

The hybrid stepper motor has stepping angles as low as 0.9°, a high torque and the ability to operate at high stepping rates. Disadvantages of this type of motor include high rotor inertia and the risk of resonance at some speeds.

Stepper motor control   All three types of stepper motor respond to digital signals. The direction of current flow through the appropriate stator winding governs the direction of rotor movement and the speed at which the pulse signals are supplied controls the speed of rotor movement.

Taking the PM type as an example, Figure 6.8 (a) shows the pulses that are applied to turn the rotor. Note that the pulses do not overlap and that the speed is controlled by the pulse frequency.

Figure 6.8 (b) shows the pulse pattern needed to move the rotor forward through three steps (270°) and then reverse it to its original position.

The input to the drive circuit, normally from a logic signal source, has a low power so this has to be amplified to a relatively high power to drive the motor.

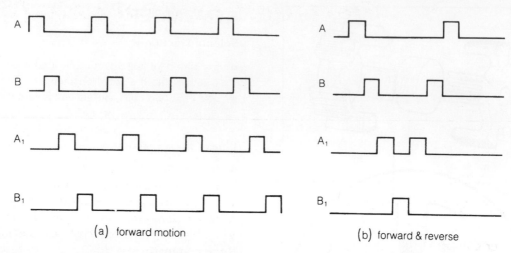

(a) forward motion   (b) forward & reverse

Fig. 6.8 Pulse signals to control stepper motor

PROGRESS CHECK 6

1. State how a linear solenoid can be made to move in both directions.

2. Why do some linear solenoids use a *closing coil* and a *holding coil*?

3. What is the difference between a *linear solenoid* and a *linear motor*?

4. A moving field type of linear motor has two coils that are wound in opposite directions. State the purpose of this.

5. State TWO applications of a rotary actuator.

6. What type of signals, analogue or digital, are used to drive a stepper motor?

7. A permanent magnet (PM) is a type of stepper motor. Name ONE other type.

8. How many poles are needed on the rotor of a PM-type stepper motor to give a step angle of 90°?

9. What method is used on a PM-type stepper motor to produce full rotation in a clockwise direction?

10 Show how a series of pulse signals produce forward motion of a stepper motor.

7 Electronic control unit (ECU)

What is covered in this chapter

➡ microprocessor control
➡ computer control

In this book there are many references to an *electronic control unit* or ECU; this is the brain of an electronic system. After receiving signals from various sensors placed around the vehicles, the ECU compares each with a code stored in its memory; it then takes action as dictated by a set of instructions programmed into it when it was made.

The complexity of the design of ECU is governed by the duties it has to perform; in a modest decision-making system it consists of a simple transistorised circuit, but in a more complicated system it needs the capabilities of an expensive modern computer. In addition to its ability to perform arithmetical and logical functions, a computer-based system used on a vehicle has to perform other functions such as long- and short-term storage of data and an in-built facility to process information so that it can take the appropriate action. In this case the computer is built around a central processor unit called a *microprocessor*.

7.1 The microprocessor

The microprocessor was introduced by the American semiconductor company Intel in 1971 when the company was developing a large-scale integrated circuit for a calculator. To meet the specification would have required a very expensive dedicated 'large scale integration' circuit; this would have had limited application. Instead the company divided the *hardware* circuit into two: one part processed the data and the other part functioned as a memory unit. These two parts required only an instruction program (*software*), for storage in the memory, that applied to the particular application; this meant that the hardware could be used for many other

purposes. This breakthrough prepared the way for large volume production that followed, making the microprocessor a low-cost common part of many machines that required a control device which had to follow either a fixed or variable program.

Because of the way the microprocessor performs this 'thinking' process, it is sometimes called an 'electronic brain'.

The microprocessor acts as a *central processing unit* (CPU) for a computer. This unit is formed on a single silicon chip and its duty is to initiate all actions that take place in the computer; in some cases it also controls the action taking place.

The microprocessor operates on a digital system and uses either high- or low-voltage levels to transmit messages from one part to another. It is common to use the binary symbols 1 and 0 to represent high- and low-voltage levels respectively. Since the microprocessor can recognise only these two levels of signal, the program that dictates its method of operation must be coded in terms of 1's and 0's, i.e. *binary notation*.

Numbers in everyday use are based on the *denary system* of ten digits, 0 to 9. Binary notation is based on two digits and extra digits represent 'powers of 2'. A binary number of 1 1 1 1 is:

$$1 \times 2^3 + 1 \times 2^2 + 1 \times 2^1 + 1 \times 2^0$$

This value represents a denary number of 8 + 4 + 2 + 1 or 15. Other examples are shown in Table 4.1 on page 74.

Eight binary digits can be used by a microprocessor to represent denary numbers, so by referring to page 74 and inserting 0's to fill the spaces, the binary code 0 0 0 1 1 0 1 1 represents the denary number 27 in eight digits.

Each binary digit is called a *bit* and a group of eight bits is called a *byte*.

In the past most microprocessors accepted input data and process instructions at the rate of 8 bits at a time, so programs instructions for these were made up in this grouping. Nowadays microprocessors are also available in 16-bit and 32-bit formats, so when high speed processing is required, these higher cost formats are used.

The CPU has to work in a sequential fashion so each operation must take place very quickly and at the correct time. This is achieved by supplying the CPU with electrical pulses from a crystal-controlled clock that has a frequency of several megahertz.

Data storage

The CPU has the facility to store instructions temporarily while it is processing other data. Information being processed is held in storage 'bins' called *registers*; these are similar in principle to a Parts Store in a garage. Data is first separated and then stored in the appropriate register until required by the particular processing unit.

Microprocessors receive instructions in the form of binary digits that are made up into *words* of one or more bytes. When signals such as 00011011 have to be stored, the register is set to hold each word in one 'bin', and others 'bins' are used to store other words.

Figure 7.1 shows the registers incorporated in a CPU. The *programme counter* is the main register and its duty is to record the location, in the memory store, of the instructions that the CPU has to follow. As a given time when the instruction is required, the CPU *fetches* the data from the memory and *executes* the instruction according to the information given to it in the form of a program.

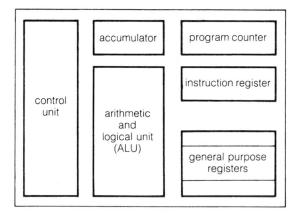

Fig. 7.1 Block diagram of the parts of a microprocessor

Data processing and control

As the name suggests the *arithmetic and logical unit* (ALU) processes information relating to any arithmetic and

logical functions that are needed. All data supplied to the CPU requiring addition or subtraction of binary words is directed to the ALU. Storage of data that is being used by the ALU during the processing operation is retained in a temporary store called an *accumulator*.

The command unit that directs the processing operation is performed by a *control unit*; this arranges the movement of data between the sections of the computer and provides the appropriate control signals to activate the parts that actually process the data.

REMEMBER

Microprocessor:

- acts as the brain of a computer
- houses a central processing unit (CPU)
- consists of:
  (a) a control unit
  (b) an arithmetic and logical unit (ALU)
  (c) special-purpose storage registers such as program counter, accumulator and instruction register

---

7.2   Computers

A computer consists of a *microprocessor*, *extra memory units* and a section to handle *input and output signals*. These units are interconnected by a *bus system* which forms a multilane highway or channel for the transmission of information – *data transmission*.

In the past a computer was enormous, but manufacturing improvements over the past twenty years have now made it possible for a complete computer to be made on a very small integrated silicon chip; this is called a *microcomputer*. This development offers the designer a very small and fast acting device that has the capacity to monitor the working of many vehicle components, compare this information with the data programmed into its memory and then take the appropriate action. The effective way that the computer undertakes these duties, together with its low cost and good reliability, make is an attractive unit to use for the control of many MV systems, especially those relating to engine ignition and fuel management.

Microcomputer components

Most microcomputers used on cars operate according to set instructions programmed into the unit when it is

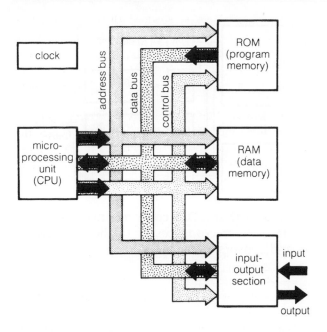

Fig. 7.2 Sections of a microcomputer

Data bus: Normally eight wires that carry data in both directions between the computer parts.

Address bus: This carries the *data address* in the form of a binary code from the CPU to the memory. The signal carried by this bus identifies the actual place in the memory where a given item of information is stored. The bus usually has sixteen wires and signals pass in one direction only.

Control bus: Signals in this bus control the functions of the computer; they select the units required and determine the direction of data movement at a given time. The terms *reading* and *writing* apply to the direction of data movement. Reading means that data is passing to the CPU for action; writing shows that data is being delivered from the CPU for storage and future action.

Operating memory A memory consists of a number of separate cells which store data bits in a binary form so that they can be read by the microprocessor when it is required at a later time. The capacity of a memory is expressed as the number of cells or the total number of bits it can store at any one time, e.g. 64, 256, 512, 1024, etc. (When converted to bytes these capacities are expressed as 8, 32, 64, 128.)

To enable the microprocessor to perform in a set way, it must be given a description of the tasks it has to carry out. The description is known as the *software* and it is conveyed to the microcomputer by a *program*; this is a list of instruction bytes that is held in a *program store* within the memory unit.

The memory unit is separated into two parts; one part stores the program for the CPU and the other holds the information data either as an input to the CPU or as an output from the computer.

Dedicated memory A computer dedicated to perform only one function, such as the control of a simple fuel system of an engine, only needs fixed built-in instructions that never need altering. A memory for this application is called a *read only memory* (ROM). In this case the CPU will not be able to 'write' to it, so the memory is part of the hardware of the computer.

A ROM memory is a non-volatile device; this means that the information remains in the memory the whole time, even when the computer is switched off. Different types of ROM unit are available; two types are the PROM and the EPROM.

A *programmed ROM* (PROM) has its data fixed in it when the memory is manufactured whereas an *erasable programmable ROM* (EPROM) has a memory that can

made. Unlike the normal 'domestic' computer, the dedicated unit fitted on a vehicle generally receives its input signals from various transducers and sensors rather than from instructions given via a keyboard.

The three main components of a vehicle microcomputer are shown in Figure 7.2. This system consists of a microprocessor, memory section and input/output section.

Clock signal Movement of data between the various sections is controlled by a time pulse given by a system clock; this is given by a quartz crystal that oscillates at a high frequency such as 3.072 MHz. When a voltage pulse of the clock is applied simultaneously to two parts of the computer, then data is free to pass between the two parts. Other parts of the computer will be inactive unless their contents are 'unlocked' at the same instant by a similar time pulse. This system of data control and movement allows the various computer sections to be interconnected together in a simple manner by a series of parallel wires called a *bus*. These common wires act as highways for the instructions to pass between the various parts.

Bus system These highways are multilane and in some cases are arranged to give a one-way flow.

A microcomputer bus is divided into three sections which are named according to the signals they carry:

be altered to suit the application. The latter type is particularly suitable for vehicle equipment manufacturers because it is cheaper for them to buy a quantity of standard chips rather than purchase a smaller number of special chips.

A typical EPROM contains a number of cells which are either charged with electrons or left empty to represent the two binary states. When programming or re-programming is necessary, the existing memory is first erased by shining ultra-violet light through a quartz window on the top of the device. After erasing the contents, the device is then connected to a PROM programmer for insertion of the new data.

Temporary memory   Some vehicle computers have to process and then temporarily retain a larger quantity of information than that which can be held in the micro-processor. In these cases, an extra memory called a *random access memory* (RAM) is used. This is a volatile device so any data stored in the memory is lost when the power supply is switched off.

On most vehicles a computer retains information relating to service intervals and any faults it has detected in its own systems or those covered by the VCM layout. This data is held in a RAM unit and to ensure that the information is not lost, the unit has a constant source of power. A separate battery is not always used, so if the battery of the vehicles has to be disconnected, the appropriate instrument readings should be taken before the data is lost. In these cases provision is made to enable the reading to be reset so that the driver knows when a particular service is needed. In future, this feature will be very common.

Peripheral devices

Various peripherals are connected to a microcomputer to enable it to communicate with other components. These *interface units* act as input or output devices; they either supply information to the computer or act in a given manner according to the logic signals that are given out.

Signal processing   Monitoring of vehicle component functions is carried out by *transducers*. These peripheral devices convert physical qualities and quantities into electrical voltages. In cases where the transducer emits a voltage of analogue form, the signal must be converted to a digital form before it enters the computer. This is carried out by a small IC interface unit called an *analogue-to-digital converter* (ADC). In a similar way, a system requiring a supply of an analogue signal would need a

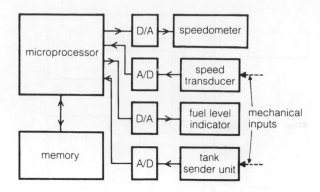

Fig. 7.3 A/D and D/A converter devices to interface the microprocessor to the transducers and sensors

D to A converter placed between the computer and the output system.

When an on-board 'calculator-type' computer is fitted for the driver to obtain vehicle performance such as fuel consumption, the input and output peripherals include a keyboard and display unit.

Automotive microcomputers are normally fitted with a number of transducers and sensors.

Figure 7.3 shows a part of an instrumentation system covering a speedometer and fuel level indicator.

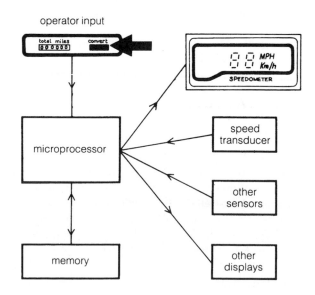

Fig. 7.4 Interrupt applied to speedometer system

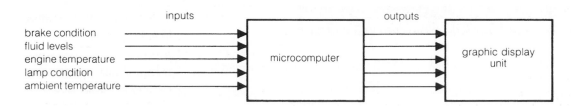

inputs

brake condition
fluid levels
engine temperature
lamp condition
ambient temperature

microcomputer

outputs

graphic display unit

Fig. 7.5 System control example

Signal monitoring   When many sensors are fitted the computer is made to *poll* each one in turn; this allows each signal to be monitored and processed and sent to the instrument panel before moving on to work on the information sent from the next sensor in the polling order. An alternative method allows the computer to continue to perform its routine tasks until a transducer signals a change; at this time the transducer *interrupts* the operation of the computer.

Figure 7.4 shows how an interrupt is applied to a speedometer system. This layout uses a keyboard to give an input signal to the computer when the driver wishes to change the read-out from mile/h to km/h or vice versa. When this new input is keyed-in, an interrupt senses the change from logic level 0 to 1, or 1 to 0, given by the keyboard; this causes the program to change to suit the new requirement. During the interrupt period the signal data from the transducer are stored in the RAM unit. When the program change is complete the data are supplied to update the panel readout.

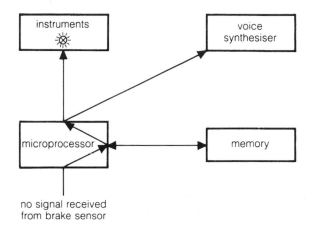

instruments

voice synthesiser

microprocessor

memory

no signal received from brake sensor

Fig. 7.6 Warning sequence

REMEMBER

Microcomputer:

- consists of a CPU, data memory (RAM), program memory (ROM), buses and an input/output section
- RAM is a *random access memory* unit
- ROM is a *read only memory* unit
- data stored in a RAM is lost when the vehicle battery is disconnected, unless an internal battery is fitted in the computer

---

System control

Signals supplied to the computer from various sensors placed around the vehicle provide the input information (Figure 7.5). After comparing these input signals with a stored program of instructions in the memory, the microprocessor performs the required duty, e.g. checking a brake monitoring unit. When the brakes are in good condition, a current is supplied from the sensor in the brake pad; this signal is stored in the memory unit when the computer is manufactured. At given intervals when the car is in use, the microprocessor checks the current from the brake sensors and compares it with the data stored in the memory. If the two signals are similar, the microprocessor takes no further action, but if the input signal does not correspond with the stored information, then it issues a warning command to the instrument panel. Also at this time it may be instructed to send a signal to a voice synthesizer to warn the driver of the detected fault (Figure 7.6.)

PROGRESS CHECK 7

1. Name the main part of an ECU.

2. Name the part in an ECU that acts as the CPU.

3. Name FOUR parts of a microprocessor.

4. State the duty performed by the ALU.

5. Name THREE parts of a computer.

6. State the purpose of a computer bus.

7. State the TWO memory units in a microcomputer.

8. State the effect on the memory units when the vehicle battery is disconnected.

9. State why EPROM units are used on some vehicles.

10. What is the purpose of an A/D converter?

Part B

Applications

8

Batteries

What is covered in this chapter

→ battery types
→ lead–acid high-maintenance type
→ lead–acid low maintenance type
→ lead–acid maintenance-free type
→ charging and maintenance of lead–acid batteries
→ nickel–alkaline batteries
→ small batteries

8.1 Battery types

A battery is required to supply electrical energy to meet the electrical load requirements when the engine is not running. It must 'store' electrical energy and then deliver this energy when it is needed at a later time.

A battery fitted to a vehicle fulfils its storage role by an electrochemical process: the energy delivered by an electrical current produces a chemical change in the battery discharges. Current supplied to a battery is called a *charge* whereas the output from a battery is called a *discharge*.

Primary and secondary batteries

Many years ago it was discovered that when two dissimilar metals were placed close together and immersed in an acid solution, an e.m.f. was produced. (Today this effect can be demonstrated by placing two coins made of different metals in a lemon. If a millivoltmeter is connected across the two coins the meter will register a p.d. In this case the acid juice conducts the electrical charges called *ions* from one plate to the other.) A liquid solution which conducts an electrical charge is called an *electrolyte*.

After a short time the surface condition of the plates of a simple battery causes the p.d. to reduce to a low value and in this state the battery is classed as *discharged*. Recharging has no effect on this type of battery so it is discarded. A battery which cannot be 'reversed' is called a *primary battery*: a standard torch battery is an example of a primary battery.

When a battery enables the chemical process to be reversed after discharge, i.e. it can be charged and discharged, it is called a *secondary battery* or *accumulator*: this type is used on motor vehicles.

Types of secondary battery

Secondary batteries are classified by the materials used to form the plates and the electrolyte into which the plates are immersed. There are two main types used on motor vehicles:

(1) lead–acid
(2) nickel–alkaline.

Lead–acid This type is used on the majority of vehicles because it is relatively cheap and performs well over a long period of time. Unfortunately all batteries are heavy, so until some new construction is discovered it is expected that the lead–acid will remain in common use.

For many years the basic construction of a lead–acid type has remained unchanged, but alterations have been introduced to minimize the periodic maintenance needed to keep the battery in good condition. The original basic type is called a *conventional* battery; later designs are named *low-maintenance* and *maintenance-free*. The name given to each type indicates the work needed to service the battery.

Nickel–alkaline As the name suggests this type is a non-acid battery which uses nickel as a plate material. It is more expensive and larger in size than a lead–acid type, but it is more able to withstand heavy discharge currents without damage. Batteries of this type have a very long life so they are used in situations where reliability over a long period of time is a prime consideration.

8.2 Lead–acid 'high maintenance' type

The lead–acid battery is the most popular type used on motor vehicles. It is capable of supplying the large current of several hundred amps demanded by a starter motor, has a life of four years or more and is relatively inexpensive. In the past it suffered the disadvantages of size, weight and the need for periodic attention, but today these drawbacks have been minimized.

The battery consists of a container which houses a number of cells of 2 V nominal voltage that are connected in series by lead bars to give the required voltage (Figure 8.1). Three cells are used in a 6 V battery and six cells for the common 12 V unit. Normally the connecting bars are internal.

A moulded cover seals the cells and a removable plug allows the cells to be topped-up with distilled water and also exposes the electrolyte for testing purposes. A small vent hole in the plug allows for the escape of gas.

Electrolyte Dilute sulphuric acid (H_2SO_4) forms the electrolyte in which the plates are immersed.

Cell action and construction

When a battery is fully charged and ready for use the positive plates comprise lead peroxide (PbO_2) and the negative plates are spongy lead (Pb).

As the battery discharges through an external circuit, the sulphuric acid reacts with the plates and this changes both plate materials to lead sulphate ($PbSO_4$). The loss of sulphate from the electrolyte to the plates during the discharge process decreases the density of the electrolyte (i.e. reduces the specific gravity), so this feature enables the state of charge to be assessed by using a *hydrometer*.

To charge a battery requires a d.c. supply at a potential sufficient to force an adequate current through the battery in a direction opposite to the direction of the discharge current. To achieve this, the positive terminal

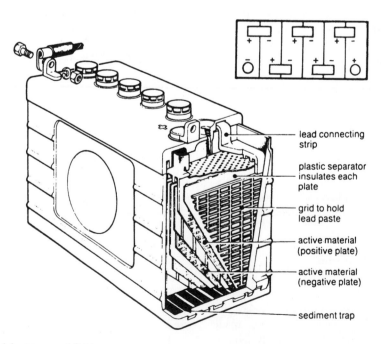

lead connecting strip

plastic separator insulates each plate

grid to hold lead paste

active material (positive plate)

active material (negative plate)

sediment trap

Fig. 8.1 Lead–acid battery; 12 V

of the battery charger must be connected to the battery positive terminal.

During the charging period the plate materials will return to their original forms and the electrolyte density will increase. When the process is complete, i.e. when the battery is fully charged, the continuance of the charge current will lead to excessive gassing of the cell. The gas consists of hydrogen and oxygen, a **highly explosive** mixture, so a naked flame or electric spark must not be produced in the vicinity of a battery at any time.

A cut-away view is shown in Figure 8.1. This basic construction is still used on many vehicles.

SAFE PRACTICE

A lead–acid battery:

- when fully charged gives off hydrogen and oxygen which is highly explosive
- is filled with sulphuric acid – a highly corrosive substance which must NEVER come into contact with any part of a human body
- has plates made of lead – a toxic material which must not be handled

---

Plates and separators   The cell is made up of two sets of lead plates, positive and negative, which are placed alternately and separated by an insulating, porous material such as porous polythene or glass fibre. Each plate consists of a lattice-type grid of *lead–antimony* alloy into which is pressed the active material. This is a lead oxide paste electrically formed into lead peroxide (positive and chocolate brown in colour) and spongy lead (negative and grey in colour).

The surface area of the plates governs the maximum discharge current that can be supplied for a given time, so in order to give maximum output, each cell contains a number of thin plates, each set connected in parallel. Connections within a cell in this manner do not affect the cell voltage.

Container   The case is made of translucent polypropylene or of a black hard rubber composition. Recesses are formed in the bottom of each cell to collect active material that falls from the plates. This space prevents the material from bridging and short circuiting the plates.

The charge and discharge process is shown diagrammatically in Figure 8.2.

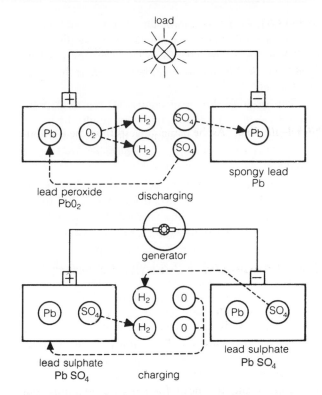

Fig. 8.2 Charge and discharge action

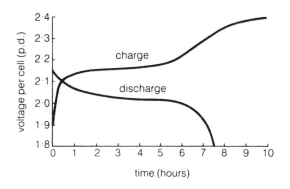

Fig. 8.3 Battery voltage

Voltage variation   Figure 8.3 shows that when a battery is taken off charge, the terminal p.d. is about 2.4 V per cell. This quickly drops to about 2.1 V as the concentrated acid in the pores of the plates diffuses out into the electrolyte.

During discharge at a low rate the cell voltage remains at about 2.0 V for the major part of the discharge period.

Towards the end of this period, the p.d. falls more rapidly until a voltage of 1.8 V is reached, which is the fully discharged condition. This limit should not be exceeded because excessive sulphation causes the growth of large lead sulphate crystals and a battery in this condition is difficult to reconvert when recharging is carried out.

The readings shown in Figure 8.3 represent potential difference (p.d.), so to active these results the battery, or charger, must be supplying a normal discharge, or charge current at the time the voltmeter readings are taken.

Terminal p.d. during the charging process rises towards the end of the period from about 2.1 V to over 2.4 V when the cell is fully charged, but the p.d. soon falls to about 2.1 V when the charge current is stopped.

The rise in p.d. when the battery approaches its fully charged state is used to signal the battery condition to the vehicle's charging system. Setting the regulator to limit the maximum generator output p.d. to 14.2 V for six cells ensures that the battery cannot be overcharged. When the cell voltage reaches about 2.4 V (i.e. $^{14.2}\!/_6$) the p.d. of the generator will equal the p.d. of the battery (14.2–14.6 V), so no current will pass to the battery.

Electrolyte density Electrolyte resistance and, in consequence, internal resistance, rises outside the relative density limits 1.100–1.300, so these values represent the range in which a battery should operate. Furthermore, a density higher than 1.300 would cause the plates to be attacked by the acid.

Figure 8.4 shows the electrolyte density as the battery state-of-charge changes. Values vary slightly for different makes of battery, but the following table gives a set of typical values:

Fully charged: 1.280
Half charged: 1.200
Fully discharged: 1.150

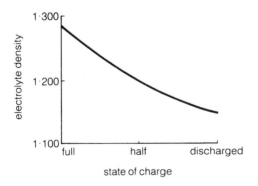

Fig. 8.4 Graph shows variation in density of electrolyte

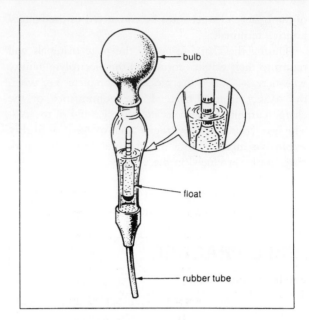

Fig. 8.5 Hydrometer

These values represent the 'strength' of the electrolyte. This is measured by comparing the mass of a given volume of electrolyte with the mass of an equal volume of pure water. The ratio obtained is termed *specific gravity* (sp. gr.) and is measured by an instrument called a *hydrometer* (Figure 8.5).

The reading shown in the diagram is 1.250 and this indicates that the electrolyte is 1¼ times as heavy as pure water. For simplicity, the decimal point is often omitted in speech; in this example the specific gravity is stated as 'twelve fifty'.

The electrolyte expands when the electrolyte temperature is increased, so this must be taken into account if accuracy is required. A temperature of 15°C (60°F) is the standard temperature, so to obtain a true value a correction factor of 0.002 is deducted from the hydrometer reading for every 2°C fall below 15°C and 0.002 is added for every 3°C rise above 15°C.

Freezing of electrolyte The freezing point of the electrolyte depends on the state of charge, i.e. it depends on the electrolyte density. When the density decreases, the acid strength falls, so the freezing point rises as the electrolyte composition moves towards a pure water state. In consequence, the electrolyte of a discharged battery will freeze at a higher temperature than a fully charged battery.

Capacity The capacity of a battery is expressed in *ampere-hours* (Ah). This represents the current that a

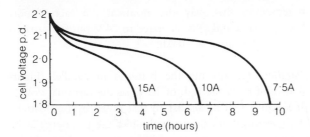

Fig. 8.6 Battery discharge curves

battery will deliver for a given time; it is generally based on a time of 10 hours or in some cases 20 hours; e.g. a battery capacity of 38 Ah, based on a 10-hour rate, should supply a steady current of 3.8 A for 10 hours, at a temperature of 25°C, before the cell voltage becomes 1.8 V (the voltage of a discharged cell).

When the capacity is based on the 20-hour rate, its stated capacity is about 10–20% higher than the capacity given by the 10-hour rate. This increase in capacity is achieved because a lower discharge current is used for the 20-hour rate. The effect of the rate of discharge on the battery voltage is shown in Figure 8.6. This graph shows that the battery capacity reduces considerably as the current is increased.

Under engine-starting conditions, the current used is several hundred amperes so the time that a 38 Ah battery can supply this high current may be considerably less than the calculated time.

Capacity of a battery is governed by the weight of active material in the plates so batteries having many plates of large size have a large capacity. A small-capacity battery may have only five plates (three negative, two positive) per cell, whereas large units may have more than thirty plates per cell.

Capacity reduces as the temperature decreases, so this is an important factor to consider when choosing a battery for low temperatures operation.

Reserve capacity Nowadays the ampere-hour capacity rating has limited appeal; the reserve capacity rating has taken its place. This rating indicates the time in minutes that a battery will deliver a current of 25 A at 25°C before the cell voltage drops to 1.75 V.

The standard current of 25 A represents the average discharge on a vehicle if the charging system should fail. The reserve capacity indicates the time that a battery will keep the vehicle in operation assuming the electrical load is normal, and the battery is fully charged at the start.

A typical value for the reserve capacity of a 40 Ah battery is 45 minutes.

Internal resistance If the voltage could be measured at the source of the energy, i.e. at the plate surface, the voltage obtained would be the electromotive force. This would be the same as the open circuit voltage measured at the terminals. When current flows from a battery, the resistance of the parts within the battery causes the terminal voltage to fall. In view of this, the p.d. of a battery is less than the e.m.f.

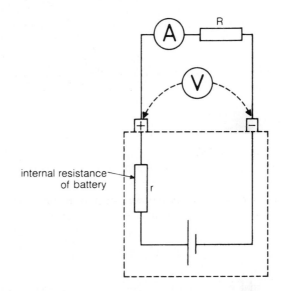

Fig. 8.7 Method for finding internal resistance

The internal resistance can be found by the method shown in Figure 8.7. A voltmeter of high resistance is connected across the battery and an ammeter is used to measure the current, I, that flows through the external resistor R. The internal resistance 'r' is found by using Ohm's law. V is the open circuit voltage of the battery.

$$V = IR$$

In this case there are effectively two resistors in series, so:

$$V = I(R + r)$$

$$\therefore R + r = \frac{V}{I}$$

So internal resistance $r = \dfrac{V}{I} - R$

The lead–acid battery has a low internal resistance so the comparatively high terminal p.d. makes it attractive for vehicle use. Nevertheless the internal resistance causes the battery to become warm and the potential to drop from say 12.6 V when a high discharge current has to be supplied, e.g. a current of 200 A causes a voltage drop of 1 volt:

$$V = IR$$

$$11.6 = 200R$$

therefore $\quad\quad R = 0.058\ \Omega$

but $\quad\quad r = \dfrac{V}{I} - R$

therefore $\quad\quad r = \dfrac{12.6}{200} - R$

$$= 0.063 - 0.058$$

$$= 0.005\ \Omega$$

i.e. the internal resistance for a typical battery is $0.005\ \Omega$. Any increase in the resistance proportionally increases the voltage drop.

Internal resistance is the sum of various resistances; these include the following:

- Plates – an increase in plate area decreases the resistance. When a battery is old, a decrease in the effective plate area increases the resistance.
- Internal connections – these are large in section to improve the current flow.
- Electrolyte – the resistance increases when the temperature is decreased and also when the acid strength is reduced, i.e. when the battery becomes discharged.

Connecting batteries in series and parallel

Occasions arise when two or more batteries are connected together to give a series of parallel arrangement.

Series Figure 8.8 shows two 12 V batteries A and B connected in series with the negative terminal of A joined to the positive terminal of battery B. Joined

together in this way the nominal p.d. across both batteries (at x and y) is increased to 24 V but the capacity remains the same at 40 Ah.

Parallel Connecting the batteries in parallel (Figure 8.9) reinforced the p.d. of 12 V, so the terminal voltage at x and y will be similar to that given by one battery. This arrangement however doubles the plate area available so the capacity available is increased to 80 Ah. The aim behind this battery arrangement is to increase the capacity of the system. No matter how many batteries are connected in parallel, the voltage remains the same.

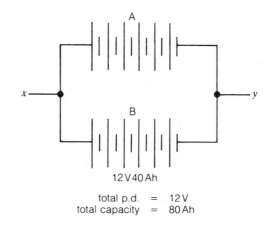

total p.d. = 12 V
total capacity = 80 Ah

Fig. 8.9 Batteries in parallel

Fig. 8.8 Batteries in series

REMEMBER

Lead–acid 'high maintenance' type:

- in a charged state has a *lead-peroxide* (Pb_2) positive plate and a *spongy lead* (Pb) negative plate
- in a discharged state the plates are *lead-sulphate* ($PbSO_4$)
- has an electrolyte of diluted sulphuric acid (H_2SO_4) and a relative density range of 1.150 (fully discharged) to 1.280 (fully charged)
- cell p.d. rises to about 2.4 V at the end of the charging period
- has a capacity expressed in *ampere-hours* (Ah) or given as a *reserve capacity*

8.3 Lead–acid low-maintenance type

Improved materials and new constructional techniques have reduced or eliminated the need for a battery to be recharged or topped-up periodically with distilled water to replace losses due to gassing. New-style batteries which do not need this maintenance task are attractive to the vehicle owner for obvious reasons.

Use of these batteries has been made possible by the improved control of the charging rate, especially the voltage output, given by an alternator system as compared with a dynamo system.

Gassing has been reduced by changing the grid material from lead–antimony alloy to an alloy of *lead–calcium*.

As the name suggests the low maintenance type (shown in Figure 8.10) requires less maintenance than the previous type. Under normal temperature operation and suitable charger conditions, the electrolyte level needs to be checked only once per year, or at vehicle service intervals.

Other than grid material, the construction of a low-maintenance type is similar to a conventional battery. The grid alloy contains a low proportion of antimony.

8.4 Lead–acid maintenance-free type

This type differs in several respects from a conventional battery: the most significant feature is that the battery is sealed (except for a very small vent hole) and requires no service attention other than to be kept clean.

Figure 8.11 shows a Delco–Remy Freedom battery which first appeared in America in 1971. It is claimed that in addition to being maintenance-free, this battery offers better cold weather starting power and improved resistance to heat and vibration damage.

The Freedom battery manufacturer has eliminated antimony from the plate grids and this has reduced overcharge, water usage, thermal runaway and self-discharge problems. *Thermal runaway* is a condition which occurs in a battery when the battery operating temperature is high or when faulty regulation of the charging system is combined with a rising electrolyte temperature. *Overcharge* is the major cause of gassing in a conventional battery. A Freedom battery uses lead calcium (Pb–Ca) for the grid material so with the assistance of the inherently higher e.m.f. given by this construction, as it approaches full-charge, it is possible to reduce water consumption during overcharge conditions. There is

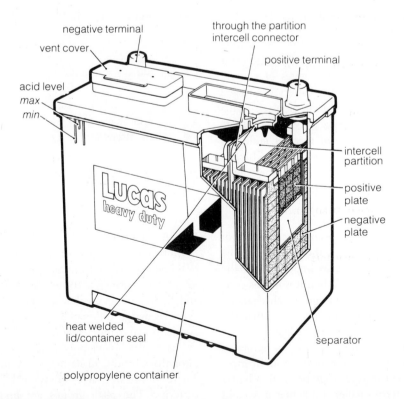

Fig. 8.10 Low-maintenance battery

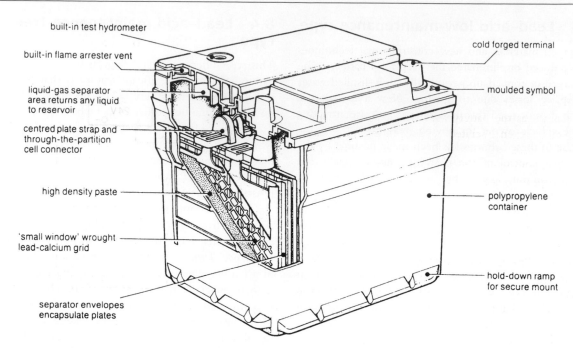

built-in test hydrometer

built-in flame arrester vent

liquid-gas separator
area returns any liquid
to reservoir

centred plate strap and
through-the-partition
cell connector

high density paste

'small window' wrought
lead-calcium grid

separator envelopes
encapsulate plates

cold forged terminal

moulded symbol

polypropylene
container

hold-down ramp
for secure mount

Fig. 8.11 Maintenance-free battery (*Delco–Remy Freedom*)

still some gassing, so a gas reservoir is formed in the container to collect any acid spray and return it to the main electrolyte mass.

This make of battery incorporates a built-in, temperature-compensated hydrometer to indicate the relative density and level of the electrolyte. The indicator displays various colours to show the states of charge. A green-coloured ball shows that the battery is charged and serviceable, whereas a green/black or black signal indicates that recharging is necessary. When a light-yellow signal appears it indicates an internal fault and when this is evident the battery must not be charged or tested. Also when the battery is in this state the engine must not be started with jump-leads. Instead the vehicle should be fitted with a new battery and the alternator should be checked for correct operation.

If the battery is discharged to a point where it cannot crank the engine, and in consequence the engine has to be started by other means, then it will be impossible for the alternator to recharge the battery. When it is in this condition the battery must be removed and bench-charged, because the voltage needed to restore it is higher than the output given by the charging system of the vehicle.

Other design improvements include strengthened grid supports, sealed terminal connections and stronger retention supports. These features together with a better efficiency make this battery smaller and lighter in weight than older type batteries.

REMEMBER

Maintenance-free batteries:

- use lead–calcium (PbCa) for the grid material to reduce *gassing*
- should not be *fast-charged*
- must be removed from the vehicle for recharging when a fault has caused the battery to become fully discharged
- when internal fault indicated by a yellow signal **must not** be charged, tested or used with jump leads to start the engine

VRLA batteries

A more recent innovation is the *valve regulated lead–acid* (VRLA) battery. This maintenance-free battery uses the *recombination* principle to reduce the formation of oxygen and hydrogen when the battery is being charged. The essential design differences between this battery and the conventional maintenance-free battery are the following.

Each plate is wrapped with a glass microfibre separator that absorbs, in its pores, all the liquid electrolyte. There is no free acid in the cell as in conventional batteries. The plate groups are under compression in the cells. There is a slight excess of negative capacity.

The battery is totally sealed, other than a small pressure relief valve set to open if the battery is abused.

The combination of those features – microfibre separator, no free electrolyte, plate group compression, excess negative capacity, and elevated pressure – allow electrolytic water loss to be suppressed by the following mechanism: as the battery approaches its fully charged state, the oxygen liberated at the positive plate passes through the separator to the negative plate. In the presence of sulphuric acid the oxygen reacts with the lead of the negative plate to form lead sulphate.

$$2Pb + O_2 + 2H_2SO_2 \rightarrow 2PbSO_4 + 2H_2O$$

As a result of this action the negative plate never reaches the potential for hydrogen to be released so no water is lost. Since no free oxygen or hydrogen are produced, it is possible to totally seal the battery.

Because the VRLA battery contains less acid than the conventional battery, it is smaller in volume and lighter in weight. Because is has lower resistance separators it can deliver a higher cold cranking current. Because there are no dangerous emissions from the battery the vehicle designer has more freedom in deciding where to locate the battery on the vehicle.

These features make the VRLA battery attractive to both user and the original equipment manufacturer.

8.5 Charging and maintenance of lead–acid batteries

Battery charging

Charging of a battery on a vehicle is performed by a generator. This provides a d.c. current at a voltage sufficient to overcome both the back-e.m.f. and the internal resistance of the battery.

External battery chargers are used when it is inconvenient to use the vehicle generator. External chargers may be divided into the following categories.

Bench charger Fitted in a well-ventilated, divided-off section of the workshop, this type is generally fixed to the wall above a charging bench. Batteries are connected to the charger either individually or in a balanced series–parallel arrangement. In Figure 8.12 it is seen that the '+' terminals of the batteries are connected to the charger '+'. By setting the output at a nominal 24 V, the total output current from the charger takes three paths; the current flow through any branch of the circuit depends on the state-of-charge of the batteries in that branch.

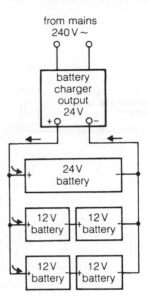

Fig. 8.12 Bench charging

Since the charger is operated from a 230 V a.c. mains supply, the charger must incorporate a *transformer* to step-down the voltage to suit the battery, and a *rectifier* to convert a.c. to d.c. By arranging to connect the diodes or metal plates in the rectifier in a particular way, it is possible to obtain full-wave rectification (see page 23). In Figure 8.13 the transformer only has one voltage output, but when additional tappings of the transformer secondary coil are provided, other outputs can be obtained (Figure 8.14). Although the transformer output

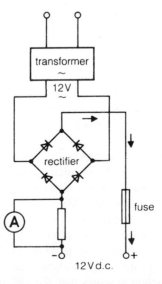

Fig. 8.13 Layout of battery charger

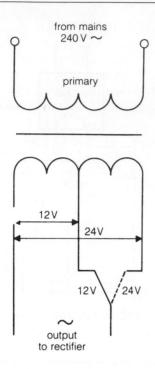

Fig. 8.14 Battery charger transformer

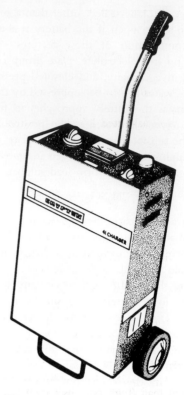

Fig. 8.15 Battery charger (Crypton)

is marked with the nominal battery voltage, e.g. 12 V, the actual output must be higher than that given by a fully charged battery.

A *constant-voltage* charger gives a voltage output equivalent to the voltage of a fully charged battery, e.g. 14.4 V for a 12 V battery. When a discharged battery is connected to the charger, the initial charge current is high, but this gradually falls until it is practically zero. The batteries are normally connected in parallel with this type of charger.

A *constant-current* charger has special switching features which allow, by manual or automatic means, the current to be controlled at a constant rate. A typical rate recommended for a battery is $\frac{1}{10}$ of the ampere-hour capacity, so a 80 Ah battery should be charged at 8 A.

Fast chargers This transportable type of charger enables a battery, but NOT maintenance-free types, to be recharged in about 30–60 minutes to meet workshop requirements. Figure 8.15 shows this type of charger.

Initially the current flow is about 50 A, so special protection devices are incorporated to taper-off the current as it charges to prevent the battery being damaged by overheating. A thermostat is fitted to stop the charge when it senses that the electrolyte temperature exceeds 45°C.

An additional feature of a fast charger is the supply of an extra high current to a discharged battery which enables the engine to be started.

Trickle chargers This type is intended for use in a car-owner's garage. It provides a small charge current of about 2–4 A to enable the battery to be maintained in a fully charged state in cases where the vehicle is used only infrequently.

Extended trickle charging is detrimental because the battery is overcharged.

Battery tests
Personal safety must be observed when batteries are handled or tested. A fully equipped medical kit, including eye-wash facilities, should be available and protective clothing worn. Acid splashes in the eye should be treated immediately with plenty of clean water and medical attention should be sought as soon as possible. Acid on the skin should be washed off with water and neutralized with sodium bicarbonate solution. Acid splashes on clothing must be treated with an alkali, such as ammonia, if holes are to be avoided.

SAFE PRACTICE

Battery terminals should be removed and re-fitted as follows:

- earth terminal removed FIRST when disconnecting
- earth terminal fitted LAST when reconnecting

A safety hazard exists during or after battery charging due to the emission of potentially explosive hydrogen gas. Any testing involving production of sparks, e.g. electrical load test, must not be performed until the gas has dispersed from the cell. A similar hazard occurs when a battery is fitted on to a vehicle immediately after the battery has been removed from a charging plant.

Charging should only be carried-out in a well-ventilated area.

There are three basic checks which are performed on a conventional battery. These are:

- Visual inspection
- Relative density (specific gravity) check
- Electrical load (high rate discharge) test

The first indication that a battery is approaching the end of its life occurs normally when the starter motor is operated on a cold morning. Under these severe conditions the output from a good battery is less than its maximum so this is the time that a battery fault becomes evident.

Assuming that the battery condition is the cause of the starting fault, then the following procedure is used to confirm the diagnosis.

Visual inspection The battery is checked for terminal corrosion, cracks and for leakage of acid. A white powdery corrosion of metal parts in the vicinity of the battery indicates a past leakage of acid. This should be investigated and the corrosion neutralized by washing the affected parts in ammoniated water. After all traces of acid have been removed the metal parts should be painted, preferably with acid-resistant paint.

Evidence of bulging of the container or cover suggests that the plates have deformed and this generally means that the battery capacity has decreased. Distortion of the container can occur after excessive overcharging.

Battery life depends on the use of a battery and on the maintenance given to the battery. Under normal conditions a typical life is about 4 years.

If the initial checks are satisfactory then the fluid level in the cells should be checked. After ensuring that no naked flame is present, the vent caps are opened and the level checked. If the plates are not covered by electrolyte, then top-up with distilled water. After topping-up, the battery should be charged for about 15 minutes at 15–25 A to mix the electrolyte before testing the battery.

Relative density check A specific gravity check of the electrolyte with a hydrometer indicates the state-of-charge. A fully-charged battery in a serviceable condition should give a reading of at least 1.270 with a variation between cells of not more than 50 points (0.050).

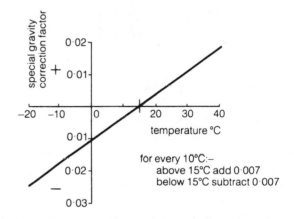

Fig. 8.16 Specific gravity correction

This result relates to the sp. gr. at a temperature of 15°C (60°F). When greater accuracy is required, the graph (Figure 8.16) may be used to find the value which is either added or deducted from the reading at different ambient temperatures.

Table 8.1 shows typical results of a hydrometer test.

Reading	Variation	Action
1.270	less than 0.050	Battery in good condition; confirm with drop test
1.190	less than 0.050	Discharged battery; recharge for 10 hours at the battery's bench charge rate and retest
Some cells less than 1.200	more than 0.100	Battery should be scrapped

Table 8.1 Results of hydrometer testing

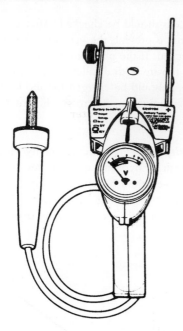

Fig. 8.17 High-rate discharge tester

Electrical load test This is also called a *high-rate discharge test* and *drop test*. It is a severe test and should be performed only on a charged battery, i.e. a battery having a sp. gr. higher than 1.200.

The test simulates the electrical load demanded from a battery during the starting of an engine under cold winter conditions. For this reason, the test should not be extended beyond the time recommended: this is normally about 15 seconds.

The tester (Figure 8.17) consists of a voltmeter and a low-resistance strip which is connected across the battery. The resistance value, and in consequence the current load, can be adjusted to suit the battery being tested. A load of half the SAE cold cranking current for the battery is recommended. This figure can normally be found on a label on the battery.

The voltmeter indicates the battery p.d. while it is supplying the high current. The voltage given by a good battery varies with the capacity and temperature of the battery. A serviceable battery should give at least 9.6 V for 15 seconds.

A decrease in temperature reduces these values, e.g. when the temperature changes from about 20°C to −20°C the voltage reduces by 1 V.

If a charged battery does not maintain the specific voltage for a given time, the battery is unserviceable. In some cases it may be seen that the electrolyte 'boils' in some cells during this test. 'Boiling' is a vigorous reaction which occurs in a faulty cell: this condition should not be confused with the 'gassing' which occurs when a battery on charge approaches full charge.

Cold-cranking test This test indicates the ability of a battery to supply a high current when the battery is exposed to a low temperature. It represents the conditions experienced by the battery during an engine-start in winter. The Society of Automotive Engineers test defines the current in amperes that a battery can deliver for 30 seconds at a temperature of −18°C (0°F) and still maintain a terminal voltage of 1.2 V per cell.

A battery having a rating of 360/60 has a cold cranking current of 360 A and a reserve capacity of 60 minutes.

Self-discharge test When a battery is left unused for a period of time, a small discharge takes place. This is due to internal chemical action and external leakage caused by a small current flow between the two terminals when moisture and dirt are present on the battery cover.

A normal self-discharge is about 1–2% of the ampere-hour capacity per week, but if this rate is exceeded it indicates an internal fault.

Maintenance-free batteries have a smaller self-discharge rate due to the absence of antimony. Since gassing is reduced the external surface of the battery is kept drier and cleaner.

Capacity tests The ampere-hour capacity test and reserve capacity test have been described on pages 120–121.

During the life of a battery, active material becomes dislodged from the grids and this falls into the sediment trap at the base of the cell. The reduction in plate area caused by this decreases the capacity in proportion.

Another factor affecting capacity is *sulphation*. This is a hard white crystalline form of lead sulphate which forms on the plate and acts as a resistance to the passage of charge and discharge currents. Its presence can be detected when the battery is charged because the voltage required to overcome the internal resistance will be in excess of 16 V.

Sulphation is caused when the battery is:

● left discharged for a long period of time
● discharged past its normal limit
● used with a low electrolyte level.

Mild sulphation can be overcome by prolonged charging at low rate, but it is more economical to replace the battery.

Charge rate for conventional batteries It is recommended that the charge current should be ⅒ of the ampere-hour capacity of the battery. Charging at this rate should continue until the sp. gr. values remain constant for three successive hourly readings and all cells are gassing freely.

During charging, the electrolyte should be maintained at the indicated level by topping-up with distilled water.

It takes about 12 hours to recharge a battery at the normal rate from a sp. gr. of 1.190 to its fully-charged state.

Battery replacement

Conventional batteries are supplied as new in the following forms:

- charged and filled ready for use
- dry-charged.

Dry-charged batteries This form has the plates in a charged state but the cells contain no electrolyte. After the battery has attained room temperature it is filled, to the indicated level, with sulphuric acid diluted to give a sp. gr. of 1.260 at 15.5°C (60°F). The battery is allowed to stand for 20 minutes. After this time, the temperature and sp. gr. are measured. Assuming the temperature has not risen by more than 6°C (10°F) or the sp. gr. has not dropped by more than 0.010, then the battery is ready for use. If either the temperature of sp. gr. readings are outside the limit, then the battery should be recharged at the normal rate.

Electrolyte preparation

Sulphuric acid is normally supplied as a concentrated solution of sp. gr. 1.840 in a large carboy. Special care must be exercised when diluting the acid to the strength required.

Suitable protective clothing and goggles must be worn and the vessel used for the mixing should be either glass or earthenware. The acid must be added slowly to the water because mixing in the opposite way causes a violent reaction. (N.B. the 'A' and 'W' are in alphabetical order).

To obtain a final sp. gr. of 1.260, 1 part of acid at (1.840 sp. gr.) is added to 3.2 parts of distilled water, by volume.

In countries where average temperatures are normally above 26°C, an acid strength of 1.240 is used for filling a battery: this strength is obtained by mixing 1 volume of acid to 3.5 volumes of distilled water. The

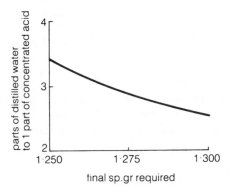

Fig. 8.18 Graph shows water required to dilute concentrated acid (by volume)

graph (Figure 8.18) shows the quantity of water required to obtain a given sp. gr. value.

Attention to low-maintenance batteries The low water loss of a low-maintenance battery means that an electrolyte level check need only be performed every 12 months or at vehicle service intervals if these are more frequent.

In other respects this type of battery is treated in a similar way to a conventional battery.

Attention to maintenance-free batteries If the battery is sealed, no topping-up can be carried out. A normal visual inspection is necessary for cracks and corrosion and where an indicator is provided, a sp. gr. check is made. When the battery is fully charged the built-in hydrometer displays a green dot but when the area is dark recharging is necessary.

Testing for state-of-charge

A voltmeter can be used to ascertain the state-of-charge. The method used on the vehicle is:

(1) Switch on headlamps for 30 s to remove the 'surface charge'

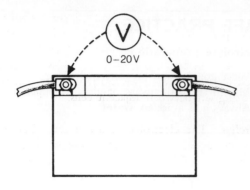

Fig. 8.19 Battery test for state-of-charge

(2) Switch off lamps and any external loads on the battery such as courtesy door lights.
(3) Measure voltage across the battery as shown in Figure 8.19.

Electrical load test   This may be carried out in a manner similar to that used with conventional batteries.

Charging a maintenance-free battery off the vehicle
Because the battery cannot be topped up it is necessary to charge it in such a way that water is not electrolysed i.e. the charging voltage is kept below the gassing voltage. The battery manufacturer's recommendations should be carefully adhered to.

Typical voltage values are:

Less than 12.2 V: deeply discharged
12.2–12.5 V: partially discharged
Greater than 12.5 V: fully discharged

General battery faults
Table 8.2 gives some typical faults relating to batteries.

Most battery faults become apparent at a time when winter is approaching. The extra demand on the battery results in sluggish operation of the starter motor. The remedy is to apply the basic fault diagnosis sequence:

● visual inspection
● state-of-charge test (recharge if necessary)
● load test.

The result of this test sequence will confirm whether or not the battery has reached the end of its useful life.

Fault	Cause
Undercharging	● Low alternator output, perhaps due to a slipping drive belt ● Excessive drain on the battery, which may be due to a short circuit ● Faulty alternator regulator ● Terminal corrosion
Overcharging (excessive gassing)	● Defective cell in battery ● Faulty alternator regulator
Low battery capacity	● Internal or external short circuit ● Sulphation ● Loss of active material from plates ● Low electrolyte level ● Incorrect electrolyte strength ● Terminal corrosion

Table 8.2 Battery faults

Battery terminals
Various types of connector are shown in Figure 8.20.

Terminal corrosion   This creates a high resistance which can cause the battery to be suspected of being faulty. If a terminal is coated with a white powder or green-white soft paste then this should be removed by immersing the terminal lug in ammonia solution or soda dissolved in water.

After cleaning both contacting surfaces the terminals should be coated with petroleum jelly and tightened securely.

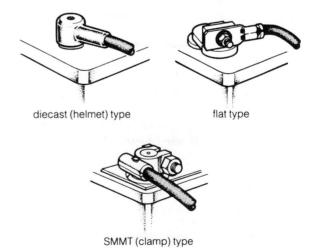

Fig. 8.20 Battery connectors

8.6 Nickel–alkaline

The nickel-alkaline battery is a strong, long-life battery which withstands greater abuse than a lead–acid type but it is more bulky and expensive.

There are two main types of nickel–alkaline battery. The types are classified by their plate material; nickel–cadmium (Ni–Cd) – often referred to as 'Nicad' – and nickel–iron (Ni–Fe). The latter type, often called a 'Nife' battery, is less suitable for automobile use so it is not considered in this book.

Nickel–cadmium battery

Figure 8.21 shows a 'cut-open' view of one cell. Both positive and negative plates are made of a nickel-plated steel frame into which are spot-welded a number of flat-section perforated tubes, also made of nickel-plated steel. In the positive plates the tubes are filled with powdered nickel hydroxide and in the negative plates with cadmium oxide.

The plates have lugs by which they are attached to collecting bars to each of which a terminal pillar is also fixed. The plates are assembled into sets in which the negative plates are interleaved between positive plates with ebonite rods between the plates to prevent electrical contact between them.

In what might be called the traditional construction, each cell is enclosed in a nickel-plated steel container having welded seams. The terminal pillars pass through rubber gland rings in the cell lid and are secured by nuts. Each cell has a combined filler cup and vent cap.

An appropriate number of cells is assembled to make up a battery, five cells being used for a nominal 6 V battery, nine for a 12 V and eighteen for a 24 V. Since the steel containers are in electrical contact with the positive plates they must not be allowed to touch one another in the battery crate. Each cell has two suspension bosses welded on opposite sides by which they are located in tough rubber sockets in the wooden crates, gaps being left between adjacent cells.

Electrolyte The electrolyte is a solution of potassium hydroxide (caustic potash, KOH) diluted with distilled water to a specific gravity of about 1.200. The density does not change with the state of charge because it does not chemically combine with the plate material. Instead the electrolyte acts as a conductor for the electrical current and allows oxygen to pass from the negative plates during charge and return during discharge.

Charge and discharge During the charging process the positive plates become oxidized while the negative plates are deoxidized (reduced) from cadmium oxide to spongy cadmium. When the battery is discharged the reverse action takes place. The cell voltage during the charge–discharge cycle varies from about 1.4 V to a minimum of 1.0 V.

Since the active-plate material does not chemically combine with any element in the electrolyte, there is virtually no self-discharge. Therefore the battery can 'stand' for long periods in either the charged or discharged state without causing damage to the battery.

Maintenance of nickel–cadmium–alkaline batteries

Electrolyte Periodically the electrolyte level in the cells should be checked. If the level is below that which is recommended then the cells should be topped-up with pure *distilled water*. Great care must be taken to ensure that no trace of acid is allowed to contaminate the cells, so all **equipment used for lead–acid batteries must not be used on nickel–alkaline batteries**.

The electrolyte deteriorates with age, so about every four years the electrolyte should be completely changed. When a hydrometer shows that the relative density has fallen to about 1.160 changing is necessary. The ageing process quickens if the electrolyte is exposed to air, therefore the cell vents must be kept closed except when the level is being checked.

In the UK, the electrolyte is supplied in liquid form but for use overseas it is supplied in solid form and must be dissolved in pure distilled water. In both solid and liquid forms the electrolyte must be handled with extreme care and must not be allowed to come into contact with clothing or the skin. It will cause severe

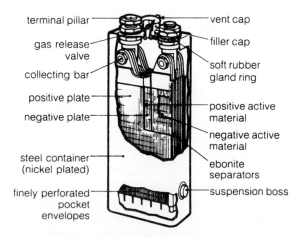

terminal pillar
gas release valve
collecting bar
positive plate
negative plate
steel container (nickel plated)
finely perforated pocket envelopes

vent cap
filler cap
soft rubber gland ring
positive active material
negative active material
ebonite separators
suspension boss

Fig. 8.21 Nickel–cadmium battery

burns on the skin which should be covered immediately with boracic powder. (A supply of boracic powder should always be available whenever electrolyte is being handled.) Prevention being better than cure, it is recommended that goggles and rubber gloves be worn.

Battery tests There is no simple test for the state of charge of a nickel–cadmium–alkaline battery; neither the cell voltage nor the relative density of the electrolyte give any useful information. In vehicle applications, advantage is taken of the fact that the battery cannot be damaged by over-charging so one should ensure that the charging rate is sufficiently high to provide ample charging. This can be checked by examining the battery from time to time immediately after the vehicle has been running: if the cells are found to be gassing it can be taken as an indication that the state of charge of the battery is being satisfactorily maintained. A further check is the need for topping-up. A reasonable consumption of distilled water is the best indication that the battery is being kept properly charged. Excessive consumption indicates overcharging.

No satisfactory high-rate discharge tester is available for this type of battery, chiefly due to the difficulty of obtaining an adequate area of contact with the steel cell terminals.

General attention The battery should be kept clean and dry and periodically the terminals should be cleaned, fully tightened and lightly smeared with petroleum jelly.

Plastic and wood cell containers should be inspected for damage from fuel oil and hydraulic fluid and the containers should be checked to ensure that no metal objects bridge the metal cells.

The battery should not be discharged below a cell voltage of 1.0 V.

8.7 Small batteries

Batteries are used to operate portable test equipment and remote controllers. Also very small batteries are made to provide back-up power to retain the data in the RAM computer memory at times when the main battery is disconnected. The main types of 'dry' battery are covered here.

Zinc–carbon type This type of cell has been used for many years for low current domestic items such as torches and toys (Figure 8.22). The cell consists of a zinc case (negative), a rod of carbon (positive) in manganese dioxide and an electrolyte of ammonium chloride. The

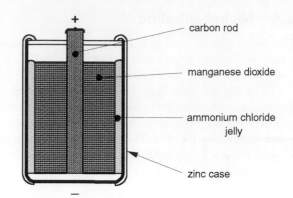

Fig. 8.22 Zinc–carbon battery

e.m.f. is 1.5 V per cell and the capacity is governed by its physical size. Normally the battery is discarded when it is exhausted.

In many industrial applications a *zinc–chloride* battery is often used instead of a zinc–carbon type because of its higher energy content.

Alkaline–manganese Compared with other non-rechargeable batteries, this type can supply a larger maximum current and has a significantly higher capacity.

This steel-cased battery has a zinc negative electrode, a manganese dioxide positive electrode and an alkali electrolyte of potassium hydroxide. The e.m.f. is 1.5 V per cell.

Nickel–cadmium rechargeable This type has a nickel positive electrode, a cadmium negative electrode and a potassium hydroxide electrolyte. Made in many standard and non-standard sizes it is claimed that it can supply a high discharge current and accept over 700 full charge/discharge cycles. A constant current must be used to charge these cells. The e.m.f. is only 1.2 V per cell so this must be taken into account when using it in place of a non-rechargeable battery.

Some nickel–cadmium batteries are specially made for mounting on a printed circuit board (PCB) to support volatile memory systems and other standby applications. These compact batteries incorporate a resistor/diode charging circuit.

Other types of battery Modern electronic systems use many different shapes, sizes and plate combinations, so it is essential to use the type recommended for a given application. In addition to those already covered in this chapter, other types are made which include:

- lithium
- lithium thionyl chloride
- lithium manganese dioxide
- nickel metal hydride
- silver oxide and mercury oxide.

PROGRESS CHECK 8

1. List THREE safety precautions associated with lead–acid batteries.

2. For each of the following name TWO batteries that are classified as:
(a) primary
(b) secondary.

3. State the relative density of the electrolyte of a lead–acid battery when it is:
(a) fully charged
(b) fully discharged.

4. Draw a graph to show how the cell p.d. of a lead–acid battery changes during charging.

5. The cold-cranking capacity and reserve capacity of a battery is given as 360/60. State how these values are determined.

6. What constructional feature of a maintenance-free battery minimizes gassing?

7. State why gas vented from a battery increases the rate that it self-discharges.

8. What method is used on a maintenance-free battery to indicate that it is:
(a) charged;
(b) discharged;
(c) dangerous to charge?

9. State FOUR causes of low battery capacity.

10. State FOUR types of small dry battery.

9 *Vehicle circuits and systems*

What is covered in this chapter

→ electrical circuits
→ cables
→ terminals and connectors
→ circuit protection
→ remote switching and multiplexing
→ fault diagnosis

9.1 Electrical circuits

In bygone days a wiring diagram for a vehicle consisted of a few lines to link the battery with two or three electrical components. How things have changed! Today circuit diagrams are so involved that they have to be divided into separate systems and spread over a number of pages of a manufacturer's repair manual. Every day sees the introduction of more electrical components and gadgets, each one needing its own switch control, supply cables and, in many cases, monitoring devices to signal the driver when the system is malfunctioning.

To simplify a rather frightening circuit layout, a vehicle electrical system is divided into separate circuits. This helps the technician understand the interconnection and working of each part − two essentials needed before any fault finding work is commenced.

Vehicle electrical systems
Figure 9.1 shows some of the electrical systems that form part of a modern vehicle.

Battery and charging system   The battery provides the electrical energy to the other systems when the engine

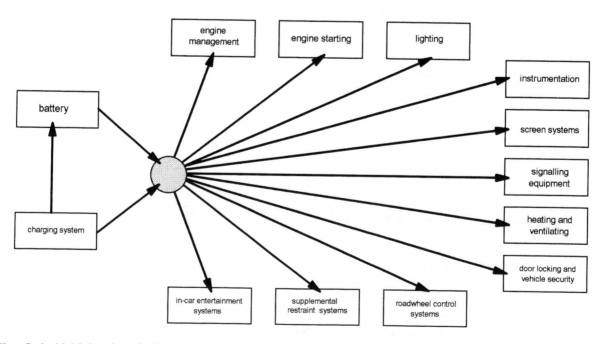

Fig. 9.1 Vehicle electrical systems

is not running, but once the engine is operational, the energy demands are provided by the charging system.

Engine management   In the past, ignition and fuelling systems were separate, but nowadays sophisticated electronic control arrangements are used to integrate the two systems in order to meet stringent emission regulations.

Starting system   In early days of the motor car the engine was started by manual cranking with a starting handle. This time has long gone; today the driver only has to turn a key to operate the electric starting motor. This action cranks the engine and automatically sets the ignition and fuel mixture ratio to suit the engine and ambient conditions. This feature relieves the driver of many worries, but when a fault occurs, the technician's task of mentally separating an integrated system is more difficult unless the job is thought out systematically.

Lighting system   The law requires all vehicles to be fitted with a specified range of lights. These show its presence and also allows the driver to see where the vehicle is going. All driving lights must be positioned to avoid dazzling oncoming drivers and for the same reason the headlamps must have some arrangement for dipping the main beam.

Instrumentation system   The vehicle must have a speedometer and other instrument lamps to signal to the driver the operation and any malfunction of essential systems such as directional indicators, main beam warning, reversing lamps (if manually switched), brake system including the anti-lock braking system (ABS), and engine management.

Screen systems   This covers windscreen wipers and washers, heating of rear window and external mirrors and in some cases the heating of the windscreen.

Signalling equipment   By law all vehicles must be fitted with directional indicators and an audible warning system (horn).

Heating and ventilation   Today occupants require the interior of the vehicle to be supplied with fresh air at a comfortable temperature. To fully satisfy this requirement on more expensive vehicles, an efficient air conditioning system is needed to either heat or cool the air, filter out the pollutants and control the humidity.

Door locking and vehicle security   Electrically operated door locks, central locking systems and security devices such as burglar alarms and engine immobilisers all form part of a modern vehicle.

Roadwheel control system   These electronically operated anti-skid systems include anti-lock braking and traction control; this minimizes wheel spin during acceleration. Often the two systems are integrated.

Driver restraint system   The fitment of air bags to protect front seat occupants is law in some countries; in others it is a selling feature. The air bag is 'exploded' by means of an electronic control that senses rapid deceleration when the vehicle is subjected to sudden impact. Electronic control is also used on seat belts; some systems have warning devices to signal when the belt is not used, others have a belt restraint arrangement which tightens the belt when the vehicle is involved in a collision.

In-car entertainment (ICE)   Most modern vehicles are fitted with a standard radio and multi-speaker array. In addition to this basic layout, many vehicles today are fitted with tape players, CD systems, TV for rear seat passengers and elaborate sound reproduction arrangements.

The wide range of equipment now available to the motorist has enticed into the motor industry many specialist dealers who concentrate solely on the sale and repair of audio equipment.

Electrical circuits and electronic systems

Having identified some of the main circuits and systems it is possible to break down each system into its appropriate circuit. These are considered in separate chapters in this book.

The word 'electronic' tends to be used when any circuit or system is fitted with a semiconductor device. Widespread use of these devices in vehicle electrics means that the term 'electronic' is often over-used to the extent of causing confusion. This even occurs when it is used to describe control systems such a engine fuelling, gearbox, steering etc. In these, and many other cases, the components are only controlled by electronics, the main mechanism is still mechanical or electromechanical.

9.2 Cables

Each main electrical component requires a source of energy and a circuit around which electricity can flow.

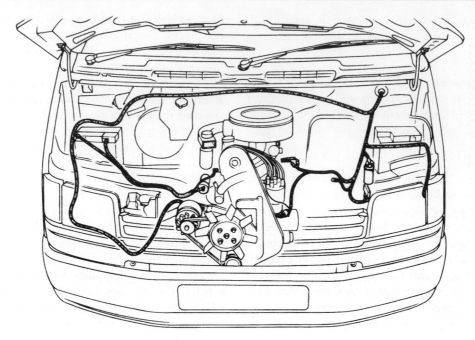

Fig. 9.2 Engine cable loom or harness

The supply cable is called a *feed wire* and the cable from the component to the battery is termed the *return*; normally the vehicle frame acts as the return. The various electrical components must be connected to the electrical supply by cables having a low resistance. Copper cables, stranded to give good flexibility, are used to connect components that are remotely situated.

Where several cables run together they are formed into a *harness* or *loom*. Depending on their application and operating environment, harnesses are finished in a number of different ways. For in-saloon applications, space taping or spiral taping may be used since the physical environment is kind. Behind the fascia, the harnesses can be protected with fabric or soft foam tapes in order to prevent squeaks and rattles when contacting the surrounding trim.

Under the bonnet, body harness is fully taped and engine harnesses are often protected by convoluted plastic tubing. This provides a high degree of abrasion resistance as well as shielding the cables from direct heat sources such as catalysts and turbochargers.

To obtain maximum protection, the cables only leave the loom at the point where each component is situated (Figure 9.2).

The quoted size of a cable refers to the *wire diameter* and *number of strands*. If the cable size is too small for either its length or the current it has to carry, then it will produce a voltage drop. This will affect the performance of the particular item of equipment it is supplying, e.g. lights will not give their maximum illumination and starting motors will turn slower than normal.

Operating temperature of a cable is affected by its resistance and by its ability to radiate its heat to the air.

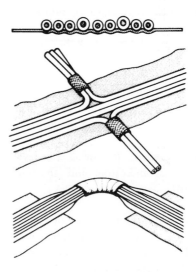

Fig. 9.3 Cables placed side by side (*Lucas Rists*)

Conductor size No. of strands/ diam. (mm)	Maximum current rating (ampere)	Application
9/0.30	5.75	Lightly loaded circuits
14/0.30	8.75	Ignition circuits, side and tail lamps, general body wiring
28/0.30	17.5	Headlamps, horns, heated rear windows
65/0.30	35	Ammeter circuit
120/0.30	60	Alternator charging circuit (heavy duty)

Table 9.1 Cable ratings and applications

This means that the current density (current per unit of area) of cables bound in a loom is far less than individual cables surrounded by air.

An alternative multicable arrangement is obtained by placing the cables side by side and welding the cable coverings to a flat strip of plastic material (Figure 9.3). This construction is easier to accommodate in narrow places and also gives better heat dissipation.

The current is to be carried by an appropriate-sized cable: this means that different-sized cables are needed since minimum weight is essential. Most cables, other than thick starter cables, have a strand diameter of 0.30 mm. Table 9.1 gives a general guide for cables of average length.

When a defective cable has to be renewed, it should be replaced by a cable of similar size. If a new circuit is to be installed, the maximum current load should be estimated in order to determine the cable size. Assuming the length is not exceptional, a maximum current of 0.5 A per 0.30 mm strand is suggested.

Cable covering In the past, cotton and rubber were used to insulate the conductor, but in Europe, these have been superseded by PVC plastic. (In the USA polythene insulation is widely used).

Special automotive-grade PVC-based polymers have been developed to allow the material to operate at temperatures of 105°C or more, compared with 70°C maximum for standard PVC insulators.

A PVC covering does not require the copper to be tinned as was required with rubber if chemical action was to be avoided. The PVC has a good resistance to petrol and oil. Although it is non-combustible, it gives off dangerous fumes when heated.

Cable coding

Cables forming part of a loom or complicated circuit are difficult to trace. To aid the identification, the PVC covering is coloured. Unfortunately, the *colour code* varies with countries, so the specific code used on a particular vehicle depends on the home of the parent company.

It is recommended by the British Standards Institution (BSI) that vehicles made in the UK should have a cable code which corresponds with the standard AU7.

Most wiring diagrams are shown in black and white, so a letter code is used on the diagram to identify the colours. Table 9.2 shows some of the main colours used for principal circuits.

Circuit wiring	BSI colour	Letter code (British)	Letter code (DIN)
Earth wire from component to earth tag	black	B	SW
Ignition switched fused supply, e.g. instrument, indicators, brake and reverse lights	green	G	GN
Battery supply from fusible link box	brown	N	BR
Fused permanent supply, e.g. interior lamps, radio cassette, clock	purple	P	VI
Fused supply, e.g. side lamps, interior illumination	red	R	RT
Fused supply, e.g. central door locking	slate (grey)	S	GR
Fused supply, e.g. headlamps	blue	U	BL
Ignition switched supply to passenger compartment fusebox	white	W	WS

Table 9.2 Wire colour code examples

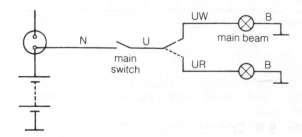

Fig. 9.4 Colour coding: British system

In addition to the base colour, some cables have a thin tracer line running along the cable. The colour of this tracer identifies the part of the circuit occupied by the cable (Figure 9.4), e.g. a cable shown as UW has a blue base colour and a white tracer.

In view of the different standards used by manufacturers, it is wise to consult the wiring diagram for the vehicle whenever a particular cable or circuit has to be identified.

Circuit numbering   In addition to colour coding, some manufacturers use numbers to identify the circuits as recommended by the German DIN Standard. Table 9.3 shows the main numbers used.

Circuit No.	Application
1	Ignition, earth side of coil
4	Ignition, h.t. output
15	Ignition, feed (unfused)
30	Feed from battery
31	Earth
51	Alternator output
54	Ignition, feed (fused)
56	Headlamps
58	Side/tail lamps
75	Accessories

Table 9.3 Number coding: DIN system

Printed wiring and circuits
A printed circuit board (PCB), used instead of a number of interconnected cables, provides a more compact and reliable circuit arrangement. It is particularly suited for instrument panels and component subassemblies found in electronic control units (Figure 9.5).

The material used for a circuit board has an insulated base onto which is bonded a thin layer of copper. After printing the circuit image on the copper, the board is then immersed in acid. This removes the unwanted copper and leaves a number of conductors in the shape

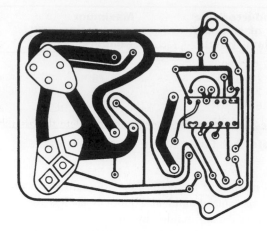

Fig. 9.5 Printed circuit board for a wiper control showing copper conductors

of the circuit image. These provide soldered connections for the component parts. In the case of many PCBs such as an instrument panel, the circuit board is connected to the various cables by means of a multipin plug and socket arrangement.

The copper image forming the printed circuit is very thin (about 40 microns or less), so it must be handled carefully and should not be subjected to a heavy current.

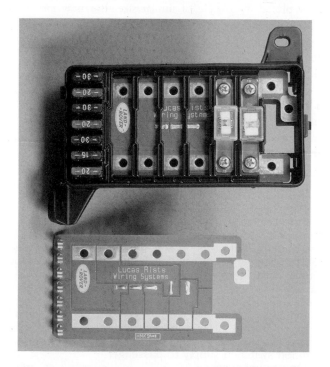

Fig. 9.6 PCB fusebox fitted with 7 Autofuses and 2 Pacific fuses (*Lucas Rists*)

Accidental breakage of the copper foil can be repaired provided the minimum amount of heat is used.

A recent development of printed circuits is their use in fuse boxes. In these applications a much thicker copper track is used (up to 400 microns) and these are capable of handling several tens of amperes, depending on the track widths. Connectors and fuse clips are soldered to the PCB in order to complete the assembly (Figure 9.6).

9.3 Terminals and connectors

Cables are attached to components via terminals and joined together by connectors.

Terminals

Fork and eyelet terminals and Lucar-type blades shown in Figure 9.7 are still found on vehicles, but their use, other than for earth connections, is rapidly being superseded by more advanced connector systems.

A suitable crimping tool (Figure 9.8) should be used to fit these terminals: they should be soundly joined to the copper core and must be secured to the insulation covering to resist breakage due to vibration. A terminal should be protected from moisture since this can cause corrosion and give a high resistance.

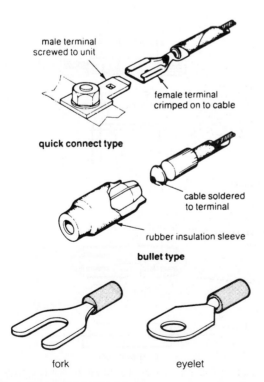

Fig. 9.7 Single terminals

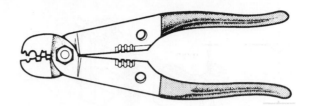

Fig. 9.8 Crimping tool for fitting terminals

Connectors

In order to meet vehicle owner's expectations for reliable electrical systems, the designs of connector systems have changed rapidly in the recent past.

Previously familiar components such as 'bullets' and Lucar-type terminals have all but disappeared and they have been replaced by higher technology connector families using round pin or flat blade components.

This change has been prompted by the rapid growth of electronics on vehicles. In many cases, circuits operate at levels of a few milliamperes and in these circumstances leakage paths (due to damp ingress), electrolytic and fretting corrosion have become much more significant issues than was the case with older designs and higher circuit currents.

Connectors for these circuits are generally sealed using either diaphragm or annular sealing elements, and their terminals are often selectively gold plated in the contact interface area.

Perhaps the most graphic example of the requirements of vehicle systems on their connections concerns airbags. Here, connections must be able to pass very low diagnostic currents for maybe in excess of 20 years with no change in their volt-drop characteristics, yet should the airbag be triggered, the tens of amperes needed to fire the squibs must be handled with absolute reliability. Anything less than a totally predictable performance of such connectors in critical circuits could cause concern over product liability.

Many of these sophisticated connector systems are much less able to tolerate abuse than the more traditional types, and they can easily be damaged by inexpert 'probing' during fault finding procedures. Similarly, their sealing systems can be rendered inoperative with the resulting water ingress causing unusual and confusing fault conditions as the various low-current circuits are effectively short-circuited together.

Modern connector families feature a variety of latching systems such as *positive-mate* and *throw-apart* to ensure that the connections are fully made. They also feature clips to enable their retention to the body and

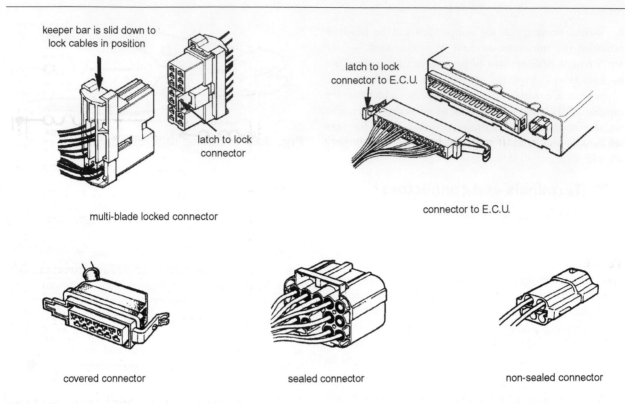

Fig. 9.9 Cable connectors

trim to eliminate rattles and reduce strain on the cables and sealing systems.

Figure 9.9 shows a range of modern connections.

9.4 Circuit protection

Without circuit protection, a short circuit will allow a higher than normal current to flow from the electrical supply. This excess current heats the cable, melts the cable insulation and may cause a fire. Assuming the short circuit is less severe, the continuous current drain soon discharges the battery. A circuit protection device, such as a suitable fuse or thermal circuit breaker, reduces the risk of these problems

Fuses Fuses are made in different forms as shown in Figure 9.10; the glass cartridge is the oldest type. This type consists of a short length of tinned wire connected at both ends to metal caps and enclosed in a glass cylinder. A strip of paper, colour coded and marked with the fuse rating, is placed close to the wire. Different ratings are available to suit the various circuits. When the current exceeds the rating, the fuse 'blows', i.e. the wire melts, the paper is scorched and the circuit is broken.

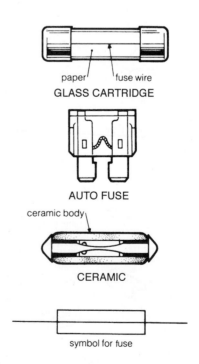

Fig. 9.10 Types of fuses

Some fuses, such as a ceramic type, are rated according to the continuous current that can be carried by the fuse; this is normally half the current required to melt the fuse.

The most common type of fuse used today is the *autofuse* (ATO) fuse. These fast-acting blade-type fuses are available in a range of capacities from 5 A up to 30 A, and they are differentiated by the colour of their moulded bodies (Table 9.4).

Colour	Current rating (A)
violet	3
tan	5
brown	7.5
red	10
blue	15
yellow	20
clear	25
green	30

Table 9.4 ATO fuse colour code

The advantage of the Autofuse-type over other types is that their 'blowing' performance is much more consistent and thus they can be 'sized' to suit various cable ratings without the need to over-specify cable cross-sectional area.

Autofuses are also available in 'mini' (half the size of a conventional type) and 'maxi' versions in ratings of over 60 A.

Fuses are either centrally mounted on a fuseboard or placed in a separate fuse holder 'in-line' to individually protect a component, e.g. a radio.

Some vehicles have a *fusible link* soldered into the main battery lead from the battery. This heavy duty fuse 'melts' and reduces the risk of fire if an accident causes the main cable to short to earth. Figure 9.11 shows the layout of a fuseboard which contains duty fusible links, rated between 30 A and 60 A, and a series of normal fuses.

Because the 'blowing' characteristic of a fusible link is difficult to control, some manufacturers are replacing the link with high current 'Pacific' fuses; these have ratings of up to 120 A (see Figure 9.6).

When a fuse 'blows', it should be replaced with a fuse of a similar rating. If the second fuse fails immediately, then the circuit should be checked to locate the short circuit.

Many faults are caused due to poor cable mounting or lack of protection at points where the cable passes through holes in metal parts of the vehicle.

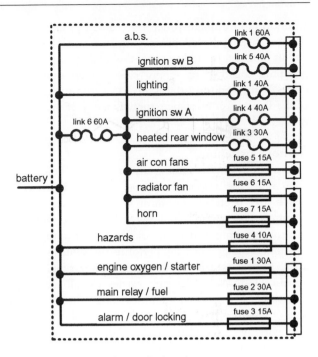

Fig. 9.11 Fuseboard circuit

Some circuits, such as a lighting system, need more than one fuse, because if the fuse 'blows' the system is put out of action. To avoid this problem a lighting circuit has a separate fuse for each headlamp.

Thermal circuit breakers These use a bi-metallic strip to control a pair of contacts in the main circuit. At times when there is a current overload, the strip heats up and bends; this opens the contacts and temporarily interrupts the circuit. The comparatively costly device fits into a fuse holder in a similar way to an Autofuse.

When a thermal circuit breaker is used in a lighting system, a short circuit will cause the light to go off and on repeatedly, so the driver should be able to bring the vehicle to rest safely. Some companies claim that this device is superior to a system that uses separate fuses for each lamp.

9.5 Remote switching and multiplexing

The number of electrical units and the need for monitoring systems have increased, so this has meant that the number of cables has increased to carry these signals and feeds. Although these cables are tied together to form a compact harness, the bulk, and weight of the looms and connectors makes accommodation difficult, especially in the driver's control area. In the past, areas around the instrument panel have caused problems, but this has been relieved partially by the use of printed circuit boards. In addition to the bulk problem, the grouping together of supply cables often causes the cables at the centre of the loom to overheat; as a result of the increase in resistance, the efficiency of the system is lowered.

Remote switching

One method of overcoming the problem of bulky *cable looms* is to use a *remote switching* system. This system, which has been in use during recent years, uses a common power cable and numerous signal cables to control switching devices mounted adjacent to the actuator unit. A relay normally performs the switching duty so all the relays can use the same power supply. The signal cable to each relay only carries a small current so the cables can be smaller than those originally used. This type of system is often used for electric windows, heated rear windows and other systems that consume high power (Figure 9.12).

Multiplexing

In the twenty years since remote switching was introduced, the electrical content of motor vehicles has increased dramatically. Functions once restricted to the

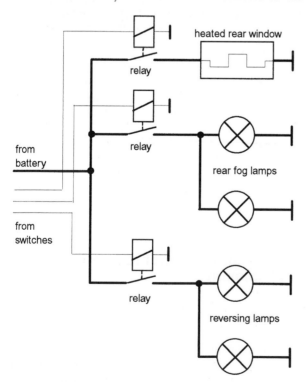

Fig. 9.12 Remote switching

luxury end of the market, such as central locking, electric windows, electric mirrors are now found on the most basic models.

Since this trend is expected to continue, engineers are forced to devise an alternative to the conventional wiring system; *multiplexing* is one such technique.

From the mid-1990's many vehicles use this completely fresh approach to vehicle wiring. This change is hastened by the commitment of some governments (e.g. France) to a policy on automotive electronics that states that from 1995 all cars must have a multiplexed bus interface for low speed diagnostics. After the '*intelligent wiring*' system is introduced on up-market models, it is claimed that the weight saving will give a much improved fuel consumption.

Basic principle A muliplex system has a large supply cable running around the vehicle, to which is connected, by relays, the lamps, actuators and motors that make up the electrical equipment for the vehicle body. Switching of these units is achieved by transmitting a coded digital signal, either electrical or optical, around a second cable called a bus using a similar principle to that employed in a computer (see page 113).

Fitted adjacent to each consumer unit is a *decoder*, a device that recognizes when a given data signal is being transmitted along the bus. On receipt of the message by the decoder following the recognition of its call-up code, a relay is operated by the decoder as instructed and the consumer unit is actuated.

A single *data bus* is used to carry messages for a number of units, so a time allocation system is utilized to ensure that each unit has exclusive use of the bus during its time slot. A separate slot is provided for each unit; this process for dividing the time is called *time division multiplexing* (MUX).

When the driver closes a switch to operate a particular unit, an *encoder unit*, controlled by a microprocessor, sends a series of binary voltage pulses along the bus: an initial code in the form of an *address* to enable the decoder to recognize its 'call sign' followed by a command to instruct the unit to perform a set function.

Suppose the driver wishes to heat the rear window. After closing the switch on the control panel, the microprocessor transmits a coded signal through the bus during its time slot and the decoder responds by energising the relay controlling the current flow to the heater element. The coded signal is repeated many times a second until the driver switches-off the heater. This causes a change in the command signal with the result

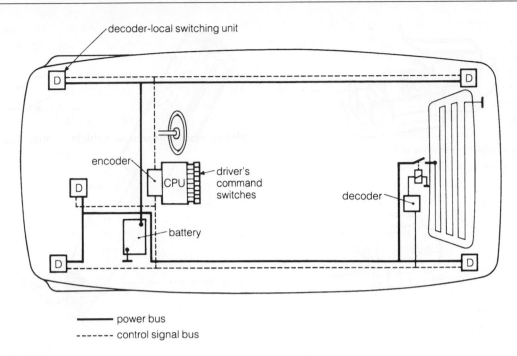

Fig. 9.13 Multiplex control system

that the decoder de-energises the relay and opens the heater circuit.

The signal current needed to operate this system is very low (about 10 mA), so good circuit connections are needed. Furthermore, precautions must be taken to reduce *electrical noise* in the line, since this can alter the digital pulse signals in a manner that affects the operation of the system.

Multiplex systems that use fibre-optics to carry the signal data are being developed for automotive use. A fibre-optic is a thin strand of light-conducting glass through which digital light signals can be transmitted. This method of data transmission is unaffected by electrical fields especially those radiated from the HT ignition system.

For more information on multiplexing see pages 329 and 399.

9.6 Fault diagnosis

Once the section of a circuit has been identified as the region in which a fault has developed, a detailed examination of the fuses, external cables and connectors should be carried out. If this initial inspection fails to show the cause, then meter tests as recommended by the manufacturer should be carried out at points that are readily accessible. An intermittent failure is the most difficult fault to isolate. Since this type of fault is often due to a poor contact at one of the connectors, it is wise to attempt to locate the defect without separating the connectors.

Typical procedure

Consider the case of an unwanted intermittent resistance at the blade of the terminal 1 in Figure 9.14 (a). Pulling the connectors off the lamp holder will, in this case, effect a temporary cure, but if a multimeter test is carried out before the connector is separated, the actual location of the resistance can be pinpointed and a permanent repair can be made. The sequence of tests should be to measure:

- supply voltage by using probes inserted to the back of both connectors, Figure 9.14(b);
- voltage at terminal blades on lamp side of connector, Figure 9.14(c);
- voltage drop across each connector, which will show a volt drop in excess of 0.2 V (in this case) across the defective terminal 1, Figure 9.14(d).

Having located the connector with the unwanted resistance, the connector should be disconnected and the terminal blade cleaned by using the method recommended by the manufacturer. These methods range

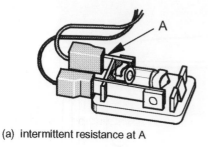

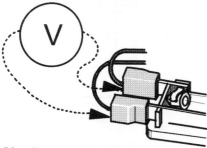

(a) intermittent resistance at A

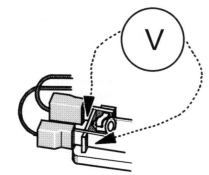

(b) voltage supply to unit

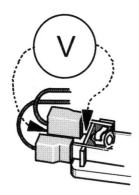

(c) voltage on lamp side of connectors

(d) voltage drop across connector

Fig. 9.14 Use of voltmeter to locate resistance

from using an ink eraser to spraying the surfaces with a special contact cleaning fluid. **Emery cloth should not be used** for two reasons; it removes the contact

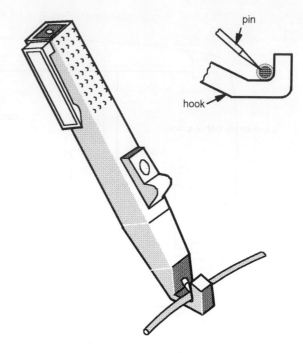

Fig. 9.15 Hook and pin probe

surface and is likely to create a short-circuit due to the electrical conductivity of the particles removed. In cases where sealed multipin connectors are used, sometimes it is recommended that the pins are smeared with a special *contact grease* to aid fitting. **Ordinary grease should not be used**.

Sealed multipin plugs are more difficult to test because the moulded cover should not be removed to test-probe the back of the plug. In these situations a special hook and pin probe can be used (Figure 9.15).

After identifying the cable and separating it from the others, the probe is inserted through the insulation to allow the pin to make contact with the wire.

REMEMBER

Fault diagnosis:

- clearly establish the symptoms, especially the vehicle operating conditions at the time the defect showed up, i.e. what, where and when.
- distinguish the system that may be defective
- identify possible faults in the various parts of the circuit of the system
- make sure there is a good supply and then test the circuit to pin-point the cause of the fault

PROGRESS CHECK 9

1. Name TEN circuits which form part of a vehicle electrical system.

2. State how cables are classified.

3 State the purpose of a thin tracer line used on a cable.

4 State an alternative to colour coding for identification of a cable in a circuit diagram.

5 State ONE advantage of a PCB over earlier constructions.

6 State the reason why connector pins of analogue sensor cables are often gold plated.

7 Two fuses, one glass cartridge and the other ceramic, are rated at 25 A. State why one of these fuses can carry a greater current before it 'blows'.

8 State ONE purpose of a fusible link.

9 What method is used on a remote switching system to control the main current to the consumer unit?

10 What method is used on a multiplex system to signal the switching action?

10 Generation of electric energy

What is covered in this chapter

→ charging-circuit principles
→ alternator
→ external tests on alternator
→ internal tests on alternator

A large amount of electrical energy is required to drive the numerous electrical systems contained in a vehicle. The battery will supply this energy for a short time, but when the battery is exhausted the engine will come to rest and the electrical systems will cease to function.

To overcome this problem a charging system is provided to fulfil the needs of the various systems and maintain the battery in a charged state. This ensures that when the engine is stationary, the battery can meet reasonable electrical demands for a time which is governed by the size of the battery. Since a larger capacity battery means greater weight, the modern battery must be kept as small as possible; this places greater demands on the charging system.

10.1 Charging-circuit principles

As time progresses, more and more electrically operated devices are fitted to a vehicle, so the charging system now has to provide a much greater output. In addition to giving a high maximum output, the modern generator has to be made more efficient and lighter in weight. In the early 1960s these requirements forced the manufacturers to change from a dynamo to an alternator.

Charging systems

On page 18 it was shown how an e.m.f. can be generated by moving either the conductor or the field relative to each other. The parts that are moved, or fixed, give the main difference between the two types of generator, namely:

- Dynamo – magnetic field is fixed and the conductor is moved.
- Alternator – conductor is fixed and the magnetic field is moved.

The name 'alternator' implies that the dynamo generates direct current, but this is not so. Both machines generate alternating current, and in each case some form of rectifier is needed to produce the d.c. current required for charging the battery.

Figure 10.1 shows the main components for both types of charging system.

Dynamo

Basically the dynamo consists of a conductor coil which is rotated in magnetic flux. The coil is wound around a soft iron armature and on the end of this is mounted a pulley which received a drive from a vee-belt driven by the engine crankshaft. Although some dynamos use a permanent magnet to provide the magnetic flux, most vehicle units use electromagnets because the strength of these magnets can be easily varied to restrict the dynamo output.

Rectification in a dynamo system is performed by a commutator – a cylindrical part, made up of copper segments, that is fitted to the end of the armature. Two carbon brushes rub on the commutator to collect the armature output current; one brush is joined to the main output terminals (often marked 'D' in the circuit diagrams).

Most dynamos, such as the one shown in Figure 10.2, have a small terminal (often marked 'F') situated adjacent to the main terminal. One end of the field coil, which is shunt wound in relation to the armature winding, is connected to this small terminal; the other end of the coil is connected to the casing. The output of the dynamo depends on the current supplied to the field winding, i.e. the output depends on the strength of the magnetic flux.

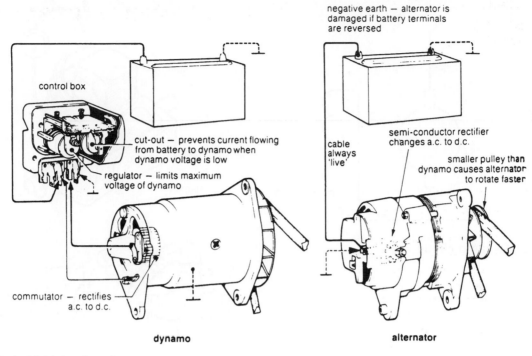

Fig. 10.1 Vehicle charging systems

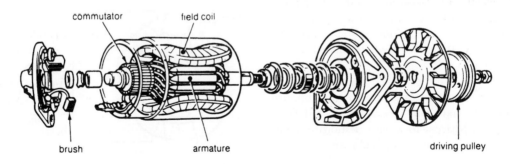

Fig. 10.2 Dynamo

The circuit diagram of a shunt-wound dynamo is shown in Figure 10.3.

Control box   The control box for a dynamo is mounted remote from the dynamo and houses the cut-out and regulator.

Cut-out   The cut-out is an electromechanical relay which allows current to flow from the dynamo to the battery, but not vice versa. This action prevents current from flowing from the battery to the dynamo when the dynamo is stationary or when the dynamo p.d. is less than the p.d. of the battery. A faulty cut-out would cause the dynamo to act as a motor and if this occurs current conveyed by the cables soon causes the cables to become red-hot.

Regulator   The regulator controls the dynamo output to suit the state of charge of the battery. It also prevents damage to the dynamo, especially at high rotational speeds, by limiting the output to a safe figure. When the battery is fully charged, its voltage is about 14 V, so by setting the regulator to limit the charge voltage to this figure, overcharging of the battery is prevented.

Once the engine is in operation the electrical energy is supplied by the dynamo, so voltage control of the

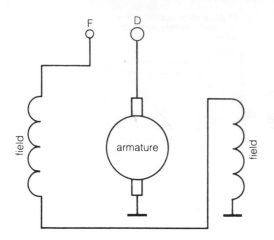

Fig. 10.3 Dynamo circuit

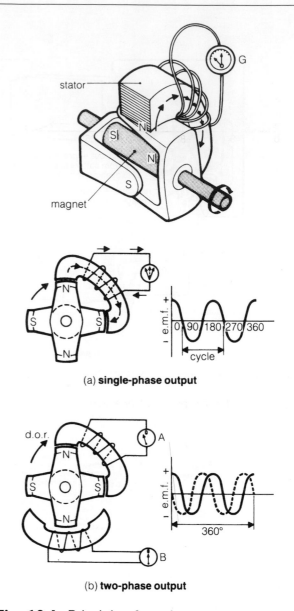

(a) **single-phase output**

(b) **two-phase output**

Fig. 10.4 Principle of an alternator

dynamo is necessary if the vehicle's equipment, rated to operate at a given voltage such as 12 V, is not to be damaged.

Regulation is obtained by using electromechanically controlled contacts to interrupt the field current. These contacts vibrate at a near-constant rate and control the current by varying the closed/open period of each vibration cycle.

Often two regulators are fitted side by side; one controls the voltage, the other limits the current.

Alternator

The principle of an alternator is shown, in simplified form, in Figure 10.4(a). This shows a shaft and four-pole magnet fitted adjacent to a *stator* (stationary member) around which is wound a conductor coil. This winding is connected to form a simple circuit and in the diagram a galvanometer is included to show output.

Rotation of the magnet generates an e.m.f. in the stator winding and since the North and South poles present themselves to the stator in alternate order, the current produced will be a.c.

Output increases as the speed of rotation increases, but when the rate of change in current exceeds a certain value, self-inductance will retard the growth of current in relation to the increase in speed. This is fortunate because it causes the current to peak at a set speed and as a result gives protection to the machine against damage due to current overload.

Adding another stator winding in the position shown in Figure 10.4(b) gives two independent outputs as shown by the graph of e.m.f. Stator winding B gives an output which is 45° out-of-phase to winding A; this

double-curve pattern is called *two-phase output*. Similarly if another stator is added and all three are spaced out around a multipole magnet, then a *three-phase output* is obtained (Figure 10.5). Due to the increase in the number of magnetic poles, each cycle will be shorter, therefore one revolution of the shaft will produce a large number of a.c. cycles (see page 22).

Rectification of the current is performed by semi-conductor diodes. A single diode, as shown in Figure 10.6, gives *half-wave rectification* and since half the output is lost a more efficient means is needed. One method

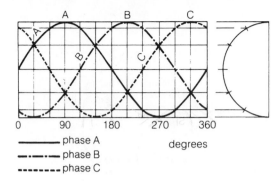

phase A
phase B
phase C

degrees

Fig. 10.5 Three-phase output

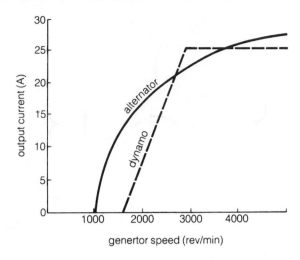

Fig. 10.7 Comparison of outputs

that is used for bench-type battery chargers (see page 125) is shown in Figure 2.10; this uses four diodes formed into a *bridge circuit*, described on page 48).

Fig. 10.6 Half-wave rectification

Arrangement of the diodes ensures that the current flow, in each direction, is channelled through the appropriate diodes to give a unidirectional flow through the battery, i.e. *full-wave rectification*.

Besides acting as rectifiers, the diodes also serve another purpose; they prevent current flow from the battery to the alternator when the battery p.d. is higher than the alternator p.d. This feature overcomes the need for a cut-out in the charging circuit.

Output voltage control is needed to prevent the voltage exceeding a given maximum; otherwise this would cause overcharging of the battery and also damage the electrical devices in other circuits. Output control is achieved by using an electromagnet instead of a permanent magnet for the field. Current to the field winding is governed by a regulator: some systems use an externally mounted 'bobbin' type regulator; this has vibrating contacts similar to that used with a dynamo. Today most alternators are fitted with microelectronic solid-state regulators; these control the output accurately to 14.2 ± 0.2 V.

Advantages of an alternator Compared with a commutator-type generator (dynamo), the alternator has the following advantages:

Higher output. Rotating parts are more robust so a higher speed of rotation can be allowed; this is achieved by using a drive pulley of smaller diameter. Although extra output at high speed is needed, the improvement at low engine speed is more significant because of the time spent at this speed when the vehicle is operated in congested traffic situations (Figure 10.7).

Lower weight and more compact. The constructional features and improved efficiency allows the required output energy to be given by a smaller unit.

Less maintenance. Output current is not conducted through a commutator and brushes, so breakdown due to brush wear or surface contamination is eliminated.

More precise output control. The use of a solid-state regulator enables the maximum output limits to be reduced. This permits the use of maintenance-free batteries and other electronic systems which would otherwise be damaged by excessive voltage.

Requires no cut-out. Rectifier diodes also serve the same purpose as a cut-out.

10.2   The alternator

The many advantages of this type of generator has meant that since the late 60s most vehicles have been fitted with an alternator. Although many different designs are in use, the basic principle of each is similar.

Construction
Figure 10.8 shows an exploded view of a typical alternator. This alternator is a 3-phase, 12-pole machine

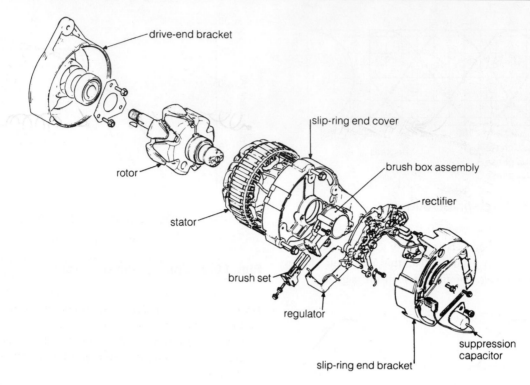

Fig. 10.8 Exploded view of alternator

which incorporates a rectifier and microelectronic regulator.

The lightweight aluminium alloy casing of the alternator contains the following:

- rotor to form the magnetic poles;
- stator to carry the windings in which the current is generated;
- rectifier pack to convert a.c. to d.c.;
- regulator to limit the output voltage.

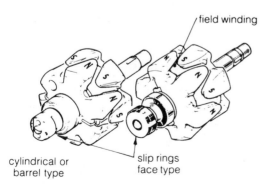

Fig. 10.9 Rotor construction

Rotor This consists of a field winding that is wound around an iron core and pressed on to a shaft. At each end of the core is placed an iron claw to form 12 magnetic poles; one claw has 6 fingers to give N poles and the fingers on the other claw form S poles (Figure 10.9)

The magnetic excitation winding is made by two carbon brushes which rub on two copper slip rings. Two types of brush arrangement are in use, namely:

- Cylindrical or barrel type. Two slip rings placed side by side.
- Face type. The two brushes are fitted coaxially with the shaft.

The rotor is belt-driven from the crankshaft through a vee-pulley and Woodruff-type key. Since alternators are suitable for speeds of up to 15 000 rev/min, and because the belt tension must be high to prevent slip when a large current output is being produced, ball bearings are needed to support the rotor. These bearings are packed with lubricant and sealed for life.

Forced ventilation of air through the machine is essential to cool the semiconductor devices and prevent the windings overheating. Air movement for this

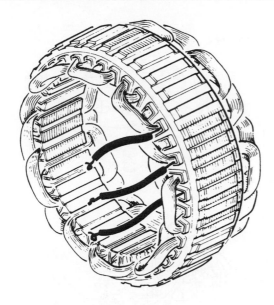

Fig. 10.10 Stator construction

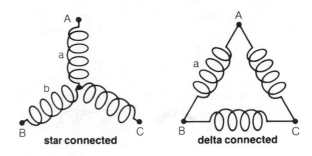

Fig. 10.11 Stator windings

Voltage output from star = 1.732 × voltage output from delta-wound machine

Although the output from the star arrangement is obtained mainly from two windings, the total e.m.f. is not doubled because only one winding can be positioned at any one time at the point of maximum magnetic flux, hence the value 1.732, i.e. $\sqrt{3}$.

The energy generated for both arrangements at a given speed is equal, so a comparison of current outputs shows that:

Current output from delta = 1.732 × current output from star-wound machine

The star arrangement is used on the majority of alternators for light cars, but where higher current output is needed, the delta-wound stator is preferred.

On some special designs of heavy-duty alternators, the operator can alter the stator windings from star to delta when a large output current is needed.

Rectifier Although some alternators use an external plate-type selenium rectifier, most machines use

ventilation is achieved by a centrifugal fan fitted adjacent to the pulley.

Stator This is a laminated soft–iron member attached rigidly to the casing that carries three sets of stator windings (Figure 10.10). The coils of comparatively heavy-gauge enamelled copper wire forming the stator are arranged so that separate a.c. waveforms are induced in each winding as they are cut by the changing magnetic flux.

There are two ways in which the three sets of windings can be interconnected; they are:

(1) star
(2) delta.

Figure 10.11 shows both forms of stator windings. In the *star connection*, one end of each winding connects to the other two windings and the output current is supplied from the ends A, B, and C. The *delta connection* method is named after the Greek letter 'Δ'; the output is again taken from points A, B and C.

The main operational difference between the two arrangements is in the magnitude of the output. In the star arrangement the voltage between A and B (or two other output points) is the sum of the e.m.f. induced into windings 'a' and 'b', whereas the voltage from the delta arrangement is limited to the e.m.f. induced in winding 'a' only. For a given speed and flux density:

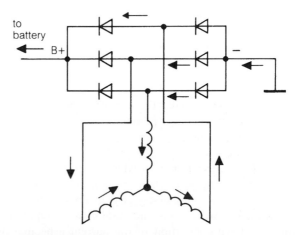

Fig. 10.12 Rectifier circuit

semiconductor diodes which are arranged to form a bridge network (see page 48). For a 3-phase output, 6 diodes are needed to give full-wave rectification and these are arranged as shown in Figure 10.12. The diodes act as 'one-way valves' so the current generated in any winding will always pass to the battery via the terminal marked 'B+'. Since a complete circuit is needed to give this d.c. current flow, the appropriate earth diode (the negative diode in this case) is fitted to pass current from 'earth' to the active windings.

The action of the diodes can be verified by inserting two arrows adjacent to any two of the stator winding shown in Figure 10.12. Irrespective of the position and direction of the arrows, it will always be possible to trace the circuit between earth and 'B+'.

Besides the rectifying function, the diodes also prevent flow of current from the battery when the alternator output p.d. is less than the battery p.d. Therefore the diodes overcome the need for a cut-out as is required in a dynamo charging system.

Figure 10.13 shows alternative constructions used to mount the rectifier diodes. In all cases the semiconductors must be kept cool, so it is usual to mount the diodes in an aluminium alloy block or plate called a *heatsink* (see page 56). Air pumped through the machine cools this as well as other internal parts.

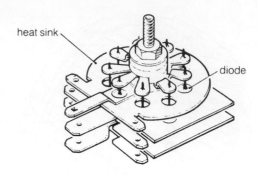

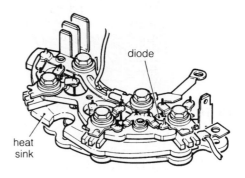

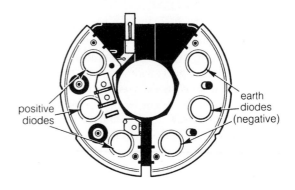

Fig. 10.13 Alternative locations for rectifier diodes

GOOD PRACTICE

Alternator B+ terminal

It must be noted that the cable connected to B+ is *live* when the alternator is stationary. Prior to starting work on the alternator, either disconnect the battery earth terminal or, if loss of power causes a computer problem, take some other suitable precaution.

Field excitation Unlike the dynamo, there is insufficient residual magnetism present in the magnetic poles to start the charging process, so a battery is used to initially excite, or activate, the field magnets.

Early alternator systems used a field relay to connect the battery to the field when the ignition was switched on. This *battery excited* system has given way to a *self-excited* system, which uses three *field diodes* to supply the rotor field with a portion of the current generated by the alternator (Figure 10.14).

Although the self-excited machine supplies the field current when the alternator is charging, it is not able to provide the initial current to energize the field to start the charging process. This is achieved in a simple manner by utilizing the charge-warning lamp; in this way the warning lamp sub-circuit fulfils two duties; it provides a signal to warn the driver when the system is not functioning and also supplies the initial field current.

When the engine is to be started, the ignition is switched on; this connects the lamp to the battery and makes a circuit through the field to earth. At this stage

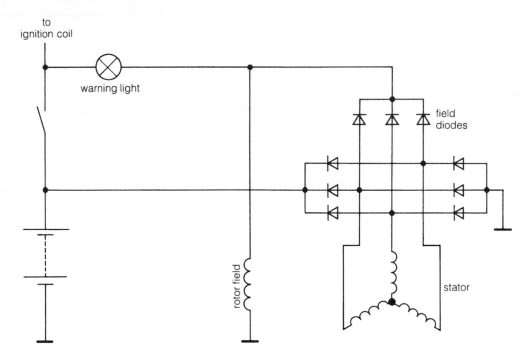

Fig. 10.14 Self-excited field system – 9 diodes

the lamp is illuminated and the field is excited to the extent controlled by the wattage of the lamp; a typical lamp size is 12 V, 2.2 W.

As the alternator speed is raised, the p.d. on the output side of the field diodes is increased. This gradually reduces the voltage applied to the lamp so the light slowly fades and eventually goes out when the output voltage of the alternator equals the battery voltage; i.e. when the alternator 'cuts-in' and starts to charge. When this happens the field diodes will be providing all the field current. The cutting-in speed, which is normally about 1000 rev/min, depends on the field current so if an earlier cutting-in speed is desired, the wattage of the lamp should be increased.

In view of the dual role fulfilled by the warning lamp, it will be apparent that if the lamp filament is broken, the alternator will not charge.

Figure 10.14 shows the rectifier and field diode arrangement used in a Lucas ACR-type alternator. The cable from the charge indicator light connects with the 'IND' terminal on the alternator which is, in turn, joined to the '+' side of the field.

Regulator Output voltage from an alternator must be limited to prevent the battery from being overcharged and to protect the electrical equipment from excessive voltage. On a 12 V Lucas machine the regulator sets the alternator voltage to a maximum of 14.2 V.

Since this voltage corresponds to a fully-charged battery, the alternator must be made to vary its charging current to suit the state-of-charge of the battery.

Control of the field current is achieved by fitting a regulator on one side (earth for Lucas alternators) of the rotor field (Figure 10.15). The regulator uses a power transistor to act as a field-switching device; the current flow is controlled by the proportion of time that the switch is closed in relation to its open period. When the alternator is below 14.2 V the switch is closed, but at the maximum voltage the switch operates and keeps the output voltage at 14.2 V irrespective of the current being generated.

Surge protection diode Breakdown of the main transistor in a regulator occurs if the alternator is charging and a poor connection, or similar fault, causes the voltage to suddenly increase. To avoid this damage to the regulator, a surge protection diode is sometimes fitted between the 'IND' lead and earth. This avalanche diode conducts when the surge voltage exceeds a given value. Failure of this diode, in a manner that causes it to continually conduct, shorts out the field and prevents the alternator from charging.

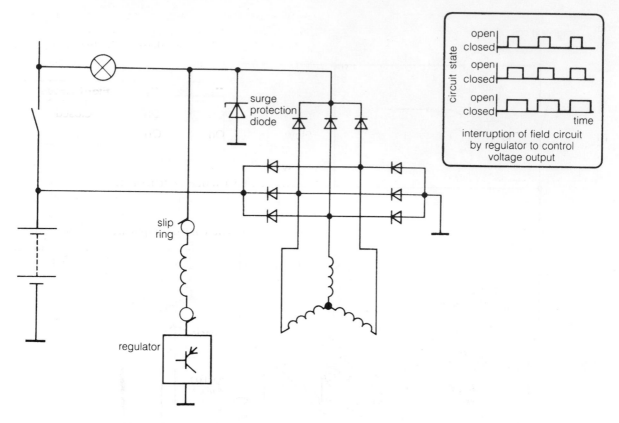

Fig. 10.15 Regulator control of field current and surge protection

Regulator construction Early alternators used a remotely situated regulator which used either vibrating contact or solid-state switches to control the field current. Today British vehicles use a microelectronic regulator that is housed within the alternator body. This type is either connected by short leads or push-on terminals to the alternator.

The principle of a regulator is shown by the simplified circuit shown in Figure 10.16. This circuit is built around a Zener diode, ZD (see page 48). This type of diode will not conduct any appreciable current until a given voltage is reached; at this point it conducts freely. By using this characteristic, the Zener diode senses when output voltage limitation is needed. When the given voltage is reached the diode conducts and activates the field-switching transistor. The Zener diode used operates at a voltage less than 14.2 V, so resistors R_1 and R_2 are fitted to reduce the voltage applied to the Zener diode.

As in similar electronic control systems, more than one transistor is used; this enables a very small current supplied by the Zener diode to be amplified by the driver transistors to a current sufficient to operate the robust power transistor which switches the full field current.

When alternator output voltage is low, current flows from 'B+' through resistor R_3 to the base of T_2 and then to earth. Current passing through the base circuit of T_2 switches on the transistor and causes the field 'F' to be linked to earth. During this phase, a strong magnetic field is obtained.

As the output voltage reaches 14.2 V the diode conducts and passes the current to the base of T_1 and

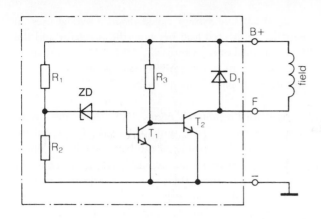

Fig. 10.16 Simplified circuit of a transistorized voltage regulator

allows current to flow freely through T_1 from R_3 with the result that the base of T_2 is robbed of current; T_2 is switched-off and current through the field winding is interrupted. This sequence is summarized as follows:

ZD	T_1	T_2	Field circuit
No flow	Off	On	Closed
Flow	On	Off	Open

When the output voltage falls below its operating value, the Zener diode switches back to a non-conductive state; this switches the transistors to re-establish the field circuit. The process continues in rapid succession to give a constant voltage output from the machine.

The diode D_1, fitted across the field winding, prevents a high voltage being applied to T_2 when the

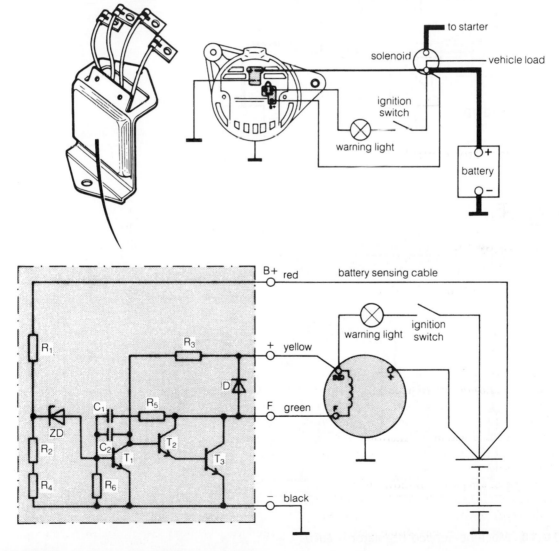

Fig. 10.17 Battery-sensed regulator – *Lucas*

field is suddenly interrupted by the rapid switching of T_2.

Voltage-sensing circuits

Since the alternator is remotely positioned in the circuit away from the battery, the take-off points for the supplies to other circuits means that the energy delivered to other equipment alters the p.d. sensed by the regulator situated in the alternator. To overcome this problem, a separate direct lead is sometimes taken from the battery to enable the regulator to sense, without voltage disturbance, the battery p.d.; this system is called *battery sensing*.

An alternative system called *machine sensing* uses an internally connected lead between the regulator and the 'IND' terminal of the alternator. This system limits alternator output to the regulated voltage irrespective of external loads placed on the battery.

Battery-sensed regulator   Figure 10.17 shows the circuit for an alternator fitted with a Lucas 8TR regulator connected to give sensing of the battery voltage. Three transistors are used in this regulator which operates in a way similar to the system shown in Figure 10.16.

In this system the cable connected between the battery and the regulator terminal 'B+' acts as the sensing

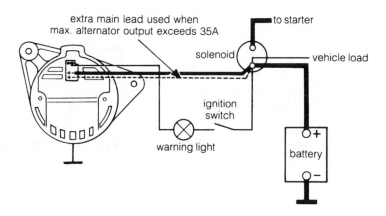

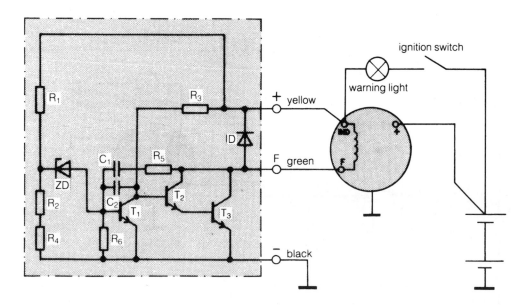

Fig. 10.18 Machine-sensed regulator – *Lucas*

lead. Voltage applied to 'B+' signals the point at which the Zener diode starts to conduct.

Machine-sensed regulator When a Lucas 8TR was used for this layout, the regulator had a circuit similar to Figure 10.17, except the regulator lead 'B+' was internally connected to the '+' terminal. This arrangement sensed the voltage given at the 'IND' end of the field winding. The regulator had three leads; '+' (yellow), 'F' (green) and '−' (black).

Later designs of a regulator, e.g. Lucas 14TR, used a Darlington amplifier to perform the heavy-duty switching of the field winding. Figure 10.18 shows a typical machine-sensed circuit.

Two additional resistors R_3 and R_6 and two capacitors C_1 and C_2 are shown. This sub-circuit allows the regulator to oscillate at a frequency controlled by the internal time-constant given by the charge–discharge action of the capacitors; this ensures that the transistor T_3 is rapidly switched on and off. Output voltage control by the regulator is obtained by the modulation of the mark–space ratio, i.e. the ratio between the closed and open periods (Figure 10.15).

The adoption of spade connectors in Lucas-type regulator 16TR–21TR improves reliability by eliminating interconnecting cables; this forms an 'integral' circuit with stator and field systems.

Lucas alternators The Lucas A-range alternator uses machine-voltage sensing and gives a regulated voltage of 14.2 ± 0.2 V.

An option makes provision for fault diagnosis by providing a positive indication of loss of output due to:

- open-circuit field/worn brushes
- open-circuit regulator

REMEMBER

Regulator:

- is built around a Zener diode
- uses transistors to switch the field to earth
- is connected to the earth side of the field
- is set to 14.2 V – the voltage of a fully-charged battery
- is called battery-sensed when a separate cable, fitted between the battery and regulator, is used to signal battery voltage
- is protected from sudden voltage surges by a surge protection diode

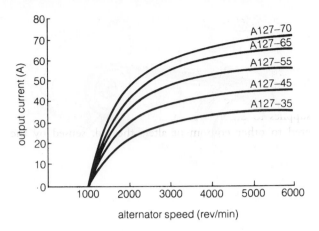

Fig. 10.19 Alternator – Lucas A127

- open-circuit output cable
- broken drive belt
- overcharge through faulty regulator.

Output from an A127 type alternator is shown in Figure 10.19.

10.3 External tests on alternator

Very little maintenance is required on a modern alternator other than a check of the tension and condition of the driving belt at 10 000 km (6000 miles) and a brush check at 65 000 km (40 000miles). At times when an under-bonnet check is being made for general security of all items, the alternator mounting and cable condition should be examined.

Fault diagnosis
Equipment needed for testing a charging system on the vehicle should include:

- D.C. moving-coil voltmeter, 0–20 V;
- D.C. moving-coil ammeter, 5–0–100 A.

No-charge or low-charge Many different types of charging system are used so the following is intended to outline the basis method for diagnosing a fault.

(1) *Battery test.* The battery should be tested as described on page 126.

(2) *Drive belt.* The condition and tension should be checked and adjusted as shown in Figure 10.20.

(3) *Visual check.* All cables and connections should be checked for security.

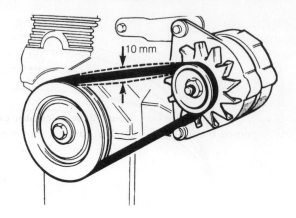

Fig. 10.20 Belt drive tension

(4) *Cable continuity*. The connector is removed from the alternator, the ignition switched on and the p.d. checked at each of the leads (Figure 10.21). No voltage at any one lead indicates an open circuit. In the case of the 'IND' lead, the charging light bulb may be defective.

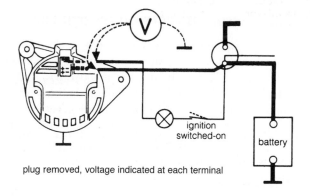

Fig. 10.21 Check for cable continuity

(5) *Alternator output*. Maximum output will not be supplied if the battery is fully charged, so switch on all loads (excluding wipers) for about one minute. With the ammeter securely connected in series with the output lead(s), the engine is run-up to about 3000 rev/min (Figure 10.22). The output should not be less than the manufacturer's specification, e.g. Lucas alternators:

15ACR − 25A	*20ACR − 60A*
16ACR − 30A	*23ACR − 50A*
18ACR − 40A	*25ACR − 60A*

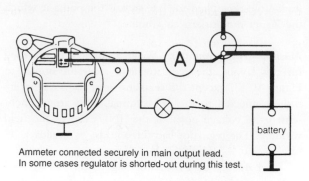

Ammeter connected securely in main output lead.
In some cases regulator is shorted-out during this test.

Fig. 10.22 Check for maximum output

Lucas A-range alternators are classified by their output rating, e.g.

$$A127–35 − 35 A \qquad A127–45 − 45 A$$

If the output is considerably less than the specified value, the alternator should be removed and examined. Prior to removing the unit, the output test should be repeated with the surge protection diode (if fitted) disconnected; this test will show if the diode is defective.

(6) *Voltage drop of external circuit*. A voltmeter is connected across the insulated output cables(s) from alternator to battery. With all loads on (except wipers) the engine is run-up to about 3000 rev/min and the reading is noted. If the voltage drop exceeds 0.5 V on any alternator charging system (English and foreign) it indicates a high resistance in that line (Figure 10.23). Sometimes a similar check is made on the earth line to ensure the voltage drop is 0–0.25 V.

(7) *Regulator operation*. A voltmeter is placed across the battery and an ammeter is connected *in series* with the

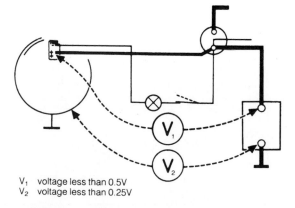

V_1 voltage less than 0.5V
V_2 voltage less than 0.25V

Fig. 10.23 Voltage drop of external circuit

main output lead(s) (Figure 10.24). The engine is run at about 3000 rev/min until the ammeter shows a charging current of less than 10 A. When this occurs the voltmeter should show a reading of 13.6–14.4 V if the regulator is serviceable.

Foreign alternators The service manual should be consulted when testing a charging system fitted to an imported vehicle. Where this is difficult to obtain, Table 10.1 may be used as a general guide in conjunction with the previously described tests.

CRO tests on an alternator Faults in an alternator can be diagnosed by using a CRO. The patterns shown on the screen will enable the operator to pin-point the fault (Figure 10.25).

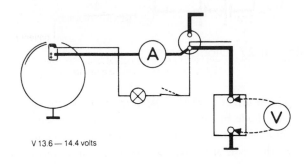

V 13.6 — 14.4 volts

Fig. 10.24 Regulator check

Fig. 10.25 CRO alternator test

	French	German	Italian	Japanese	Significance of reading
General features	9 diode Ext. regulator	6 or 9 diode Int. or ext. regulators	6 or 9 diode Ext. regulator	6 diode Int. or ext. regulators	
TEST 4 Cable continuity	Battery voltage at all leads (except earthing leads)				No reading indicates open circuit in that lead
TEST 5 Alternator output	'Exc' lead and output lead are shorted together during test	If low output is obtained with ext. reg., short 'B+' and 'DF' together to cut out regulator	Output '30' and field '67' are shorted together during test	Output 'B' and field 'F' are shorted together during test	Output current should be as stated. No output or low output indicates that alternator should be removed
TEST 6 Voltage drop	Maximum drop on insulated line should be less than 0.5 V				High reading indicates presence of resistance in that line
TEST 7 Regulator check	13.8–13.2 V	Int. reg.: 13.7–14.5 V Ext. reg.: 13.9–14.8 V	13.9–14.5 V	Colt Honda }13.5–14.5 V Mazda Toyota 13.8–14.8 V Datsun 14.3–15.3 V	Suspect reg. If lower or higher

Table 10.1 Foreign alternators

10.4 Internal tests on alternator

Electrical tests are conducted on the:

- diode pack
- rotor field
- stator windings.

The following description applies to alternators in general, but the specific values given apply to a type similar to Bosch type K1–35A.

Diode pack Prior to testing, the diode connections must be unsoldered from the stator windings. Heat from the soldering iron must be prevented from passing to the diode by using a pair of pliers as a heat sink (Figure 10.26).

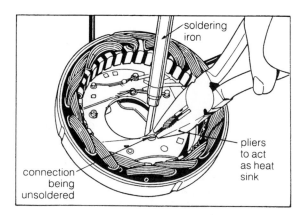

Fig. 10.26 Protection of diodes

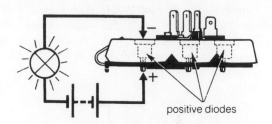

Fig. 10.27 Diode tests

The leads of a 12 V, 5 W test lamp are connected to each diode in turn; when the current flows through the diode in one direction the lamp should light but when the leads are reversed the lamp should not light (Figure 10.27).

Rotor field The field is checked for:

- resistance
- insulation.

To measure the resistance, the leads of an ohmmeter are applied to the slip rings. A typical resistance is 3.4 Ω (Figure 10.28).

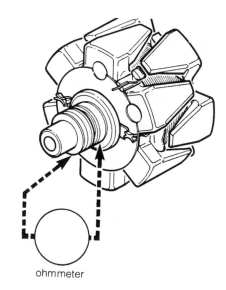

Fig. 10.28 Rotor field resistance test

Insulation is checked by the use of a 110 V (a.c.) supply fitted with a 15 W lamp. The test prods are applied to the iron pole and one slip ring. Insulation is defective if the lamp illuminates (Figure 10.29).

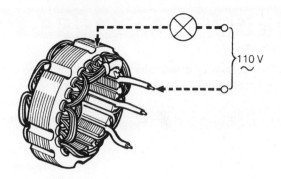

Fig. 10.31 Stator insulation test

Stator windings The leads of an ohmmeter are applied to two of the three leads of the stator and the resistance is measured. One of the ohmmeter leads is then transferred to the remaining stator leads and the resistance is measured again. Both results should be equal and the resistance should be as specified by the manufacturers; a typical value is $0.09\ \Omega$ (Figure 10.30).

Insulation is checked in a way similar to the rotor; the tester should show good insulation between the winding and the iron laminations (Figure 10.31).

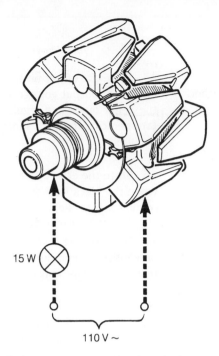

Fig. 10.29 Rotor test for insulation

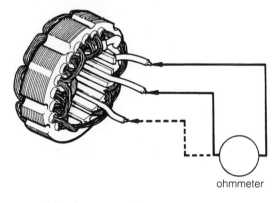

Fig. 10.30 Stator resistance test

PROGRESS CHECK 10

The following questions relate to an alternator

1. What is meant by three-phase output and how is it obtained?

2. What method is used to rectify the current?

3. State the purpose of the winding on the rotor.

4. Which part is driven?

5. State why a slack drive belt causes a low output.

6. How many sets of winding are wound on the stator?

7. State why an open-circuited rectifier diode lowers the output.

8. What method is used to cool a rectifier pack?

9. A system uses a separate cable to sense battery voltage. State why this cable should not be used to supply add-on electrical devices

10. The connector plug is removed from an alternator and the ignition is switched on. What voltage should be obtained between the alternator end of the IND lead and earth when:
(a) system is serviceable;
(b) indicator lamp is open-circuited?

11. State the effect on the battery if a regulator fault causes the voltage to be:
(a) 12 V; (b) 16 V.

12. An alternator will not charge when the charge warning lamp has failed. State the reason for this.

13. State the precautions that should be taken when using jump-start leads to avoid a voltage surge at the alternator.

14. The alternator will not charge following a voltage surge. State the diode which is most probably defective.

15. State the effect on the maximum output voltage when the Zener diode in a regulator is:
(a) open circuited; (b) short circuited.

16. State the effect on output when the black lead on the regulator is broken.

17. Describe the test, and precautions taken during the test, to measure maximum current output.

18. Draw the CRO pattern obtained from a serviceable alternator.

19. A rotor field test is carried out on a dismantled alternator. Name TWO other tests.

20. Describe the TWO tests that should be carried on a rotor winding.

11 Combustion and ignition

Before a manufacturer can sell a new model, a vehicle of the type must be tested in a laboratory and a certificate granted by the appropriate authority to show that all exhaust emissions from the vehicle are within the statutory limits. Various aspects of combustion influence performance.

11.1 Combustion process

Normal combustion in a petrol engine
Under normal conditions the compressed air mixture is ignited by a sparking plug and a flame, originating from the vicinity of the plug electrodes, progresses across the combustion chamber at a regular rate (Figure 11.1). Although the combustion process is completed in a fraction of a second, the pressure caused by the heat of the burning gas rises steadily to give a smooth start to the power stroke.

Power output and economy depend on the flame speed; this can be varied by altering the following:

● *Compression ratio.* A high flame speed is obtained when the fuel and air particles are closely packed together: this occurs when the compression ratio is high or when the engine inhales a large volume of petrol–air mixture (i.e. when the volumetric efficiency is high).

● *Air/fuel ratio.* The highest flame speed and highest power is obtained from a ratio which is slightly richer than the chemically correct figure of 15 parts of air

to 1 part of petrol. When the mixture is weakened from the ratio that gives highest power, the flame speed decreases considerably.

● *Ignition timing.* The maximum gas pressure developed during combustion should occur about 12° after top dead centre (t.d.c). Since it takes a comparatively long time for the burning gas to build up to its maximum pressure, the spark must be timed to occur well before t.d.c. If the timing of the spark is too early (over-advanced), a very rapid burning

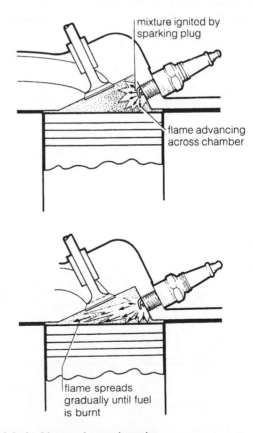

Fig. 11.1 Normal combustion

163

takes place which is similar to an explosion; this can damage the engine. Conversely a late spark (over-retarded) causes a very slow burning and this results in low engine power and poor economy. Accurate timing of the spark is essential if good engine performance and a low exhaust emission is desired.

- *Degree of turbulence.* Air movement in the chamber increases the flame speed.
- *Quantity of exhaust gas present in the chamber.* Any exhaust gas that is combined with the new mixture slows down the burning and this lowers the maximum combustion temperature. In high-performance engines it is sometimes necessary to recirculate back some of the exhaust gas in order to reduce pollution from the exhaust gas.

Combustion in a diesel engine The compression-ignition (CI) engine has no sparking plug to initiate combustion. Instead, an injector is used to spray fuel oil into the combustion chamber just before the piston reaches t.d.c. at the end of the compression stroke. Because the compression ratio of a CI engine is much higher than that used with a petrol engine, the heat generated by the high compression of the air is sufficient to ignite the fuel oil as it is sprayed into the chamber.

A special provision must be made when a cold CI engine is to be started. This is necessary because the low temperature of the cylinders absorbs the heat generated by the compression of the air; the result is that the injected fuel oil will not ignite. One way of overcoming this problem is to fit a heater plug in the combustion chamber (Figure 11.2). This device is an electrically heated bulb or wire filament which glows red-hot when

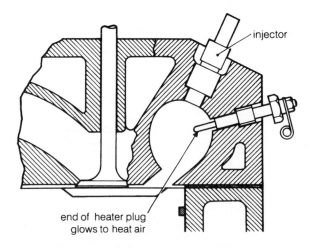

Fig. 11.2 Diesel heater plug

in use. Prior to starting a cold engine, the heater plugs are switched on manually or automatically for a few seconds to raise the temperature of the air in the cylinder.

Combustion faults – spark-ignition engines

Two combustion faults associated with a petrol engine are:

- combustion knock (often called detonation)
- pre-ignition

Both faults reduce engine power and if they are allowed to continue for a long period of time, they can seriously damage the engine.

Combustion knock (detonation) To obtain good engine power, a high flame speed is necessary, since the quicker the fuel burns, the higher will be the temperature of the gas. This requirement suggests that the factors controlling flame speed should be set so as to give the highest speed, but when this is attempted various combustion faults develop. To illustrate this problem, consider an engine which has a provision for varying the compression ratio. As the compression pressure is increased, the flame speed is also increased, but when a certain compression is reached, the flame speed suddenly rises to a figure which equals the speed of sound. No longer is the fuel burnt in a progressive manner; instead the petrol–air mixture explodes to give a condition called *detonation*. The compression pressure at which detonation occurs depends on may factors; these include the grade of petrol used and the type of combustion chamber.

Examination of the combustion process prior to the onset of this severe detonation would show that a portion of the petrol–air mixture remote from the sparking plug (i.e. the end gas) would not be performing in the normal way. Instead, this pocket of gas, which has been compressed and heated by the gas already burnt, will spontaneously ignite and cause a rapid build up of pressure and noise. This condition is called *combustion knock*.

Although detonation and combustion knock are two different combustion faults, the general effects are similar. For this reason the two conditions are often grouped together. In both cases they occur *after the spark*.

Effects of detonation and knock depend on the severity of the condition, but the main results are:

- pinking – a sound produced by the high-pressure waves; the noise described by some people as a 'metallic tapping sound' and by others as the 'sound of fat frying in a pan'.

- shock loading of engine components.
- local overheating – piston crowns can be melted.
- reduced engine-power.

These effects show that detonation and knock should be avoided, and if this is to be achieved attention must be given to the items that promote detonation. The main factors are:

- *Compression pressure and grade of petrol.* The compression ratio is linked to the fuel used; engines having high compression ratio generally require a fuel having a high octane number.
- *Air/fuel ratio.* Weak mixtures are prone to detonate.
- *Combustion chamber type.* The degree of turbulence and provision for cooling of the end-gas have a great bearing on the compression ratio which is used.
- *Ignition timing.* An over-advanced ignition promotes detonation.
- *Engine temperature.* Overheated components increase the risk of detonation.

Pre-ignition This condition applies when the petrol–air charge in the cylinder is fired by a red-hot particle before it is ignited by the sparking plug. The incandescent objects may be a carbon deposit or any protruding component which forms a part of the combustion chamber. Pre-ignition always occurs *before the spark* and is an undesirable condition which can lead to detonation, melting of the piston crown and other forms of damage. Normally pre-ignition gives a considerable reduction in the engine's power output and is often accompanied by the sound of 'pinking'.

Pre-ignition of a charge produces a situation where the rising piston is compressing a gas that is attempting to expand. This results in a considerable increase in gas pressure and combustion temperature.

Running-on An engine which continues to run after the ignition is switched off is caused by the petrol–air charge being ignited by a 'hot spot', such as a sparking plug, valve or carbon deposit, that glows and fires the charge at about t.d.c. Cooling system faults and excessive carbon deposits are often responsible for this condition.

Weak mixtures used on modern engines to obtain a low exhaust emission of pollutant gases cause the various parts within the combustion chamber to operate at a higher temperature than that used in the past. Running-on in these engines is avoided by fitting a special device to starve the engine of fuel when the ignition is switched-off. One system uses a solenoid valve to close the slow-running petrol jet in the carburettor and another arrangement has an electrically-operated valve which allows air to by-pass the carburettor and enter the manifold.

Combustion and fuel requirements

To obtain good burning, the fuel must be mechanically broken up (atomized) as it leaves the carburettor and be vaporized to form a gas as it passes through the warm intake manifold. Furthermore the petrol should have a sufficiently high octane rating to avoid detonation and be metered to give a suitable air/fuel ratio to meet the engine conditions. An incorrect ratio causes problems as shown in Table 11.1

Fault	Effect	Symptom
Rich mixture	Incomplete combustion	1. Black smoke from exhaust 2. High exhaust pollution
	Slow burning	1. Low power output 2. High fuel consumption
	Sparking plugs soon soot-up	1. Misfiring 2. Poor starting
Weak mixture	Slow burning	1. Low power output 2. High fuel consumption 3. Overheating
	Detonation	1. Pinking (excessive knocking) 2. Low power and if condition persists will give blue smoke from exhaust showing piston failure

Table 11.1 Effects of incorrect mixture strengths

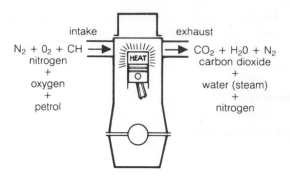

Fig. 11.3 Chemical changes – correct mixture

Exhaust-gas composition

Clean air is made up of nitrogen and oxygen; petrol consists of carbon and hydrogen. When air and petrol are mixed together in the correct chemical proportions and ignited, the resulting combustion liberates heat and changes the chemical structure to form carbon dioxide and water (Figure 11.3).

A rich mixture, as produced when the ratio is less than 15:1 by mass, has insufficient air to give complete combustion, so some of the fuel particles are exhausted before they have been fully burnt. This forms a poisonous gas called *carbon monoxide* (CO) and legislation exists to limit the amount of CO that is exhausted from a modern engine.

Equipment as shown in Figure 11.4 analyses the exhaust gas to check that the various systems are operating correctly and that the pollutants are within the legal limits. On older type engines the analyser is also used to set the air/fuel ratio to give good combustion and a 'clean' exhaust.

REMEMBER

Incorrect ignition timing can cause:

- overheating
- combustion knock (detonation), which is the ignition of the charge *after* the spark – emits a *pinking* sound
- pre-ignition, which is ignition *before* the spark
- undesirable exhaust products
- low power
- poor economy
- difficult starting

11.2 Non-electronic ignition systems

Engines using petrol as a fuel require a spark to start the combustion process; the timing of the spark is critical if maximum power and economy are required.

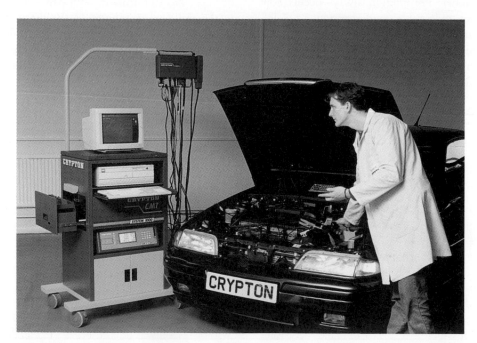

Fig. 11.4 Exhaust gas analysis

History of the internal combustion engine shows that the jump-spark system used today was gradually developed through the stages of hot wire, break-spark and trembler coil, with each step showing a definite improvement over its predecessor.

There are two jump-spark ignition generator systems in use today; they are the *battery-coil* and the *magneto*, the latter confined mainly to the small engines used on motor cycles and lawn mowers.

Ignition requirements

The number of sparks required depends on the type of engine; two-stroke engines require one spark per cylinder per revolution of the crank, whereas four-stroke engines need only one spark per cylinder for every other revolution.

The conditions inside the cylinder at the time of ignition govern the voltage required to produce a spark. Whereas it needs only a few hundred volts to make a spark jump across a plug gap of 0.6 mm (0.024 in), the voltage rises to over 8 kV when the pressure is raised to represent cylinder conditions. Today most ignition systems are capable of supplying a voltage in excess of 28 kV.

Although this high voltage can be produced, it does not mean that the system always operates at this voltage. The voltage produced is only that needed to make a spark jump the spark gap. Since engine conditions such as compression pressure and fuel mixture change with speed and engine load, the voltage needed by the plug varies from about 10 kV during cruising to over 20 kV when the engine is being accelerated. This difference in voltage requirement shows up when an ignition fault is present. Although the engine may perform well when it is under light load, the demand for either high power or high speed is answered by a poor response from the engine because the ignition system will not give the high voltage required.

In addition to the voltage aspect, the spark produced at the sparking plug electrodes must also have sufficient energy to produce a spark of very high temperature and enough heat to initiate the burning of the fuel droplets situated between the plug electrodes. A normal mixture in a warm engine needs about 0.1 mJ of energy per spark, but this has to be increased considerably during cold starting or when the engine is operated on a weaker-than-normal mixture as is the case when good economy and low emission are required.

Widening the sparking plug gap to meet these operating conditions increases both the energy and the voltage outputs, but as the output is raised, an increase in erosion wear at the sparking plug electrodes and distributor components is caused as well as placing extra stress on the ignition coil.

The duration of the spark in milliseconds is an indication of the energy content of a spark; a typical time is 1 ms (0.001 second).

Coil ignition system

This battery–inductive ignition system was introduced by C.F. Kettering of Delco in 1908 but it was not until the mid-1920s that it was commercially accepted as a successor to the magneto.

Up to that time very few vehicles needed a battery, so the magneto was used because it was a self-contained ignition generator. With the introduction of electric lighting, a battery then had to be carried. This step, together with the difficult starting characteristics of the magneto-ignited engine, brought about a change to the battery–inductive system which is commonly known as coil ignition.

Coil ignition circuits Figure 11.5 shows the main details of a coil ignition circuit. The heart of the system is the ignition coil; this transforms the low-tension (l.t.) 12 V supply given by the battery to the high-tension (h.t.) voltage needed to produce a spark at the sparking plug.

The coil has two windings, a primary and a secondary: these names are also used to identify the two circuits which make up the complete system. Primary is the *l.t. circuit* supplied by the battery and secondary is the *h.t. circuit* that incorporates the distributor and sparking plugs. Each circuit must be complete to give current flow, so the end of the secondary winding in the coil is earthed. This is achieved by connecting the winding either to an l.t. coil terminal (normally the negative) or to an additional coil terminal that is linked by an external cable to earth. The latter arrangement is needed on a vehicle that uses an insulated return (IR) system, so this type of coil is called an *IR coil* to distinguish it from the common earth return (ER) type.

Interruption of the primary d.c. current for the induction of the h.t. voltage into the secondary winding, is made by the contact breaker at the instant the spark is required. Precise timing of the spark is achieved only if the break in the primary circuit is sudden, so to avoid arcing at this critical stage a capacitor is fitted across the contact breaker terminals.

The principles of mutual induction and the transformer are described on pages 20 and 25. These

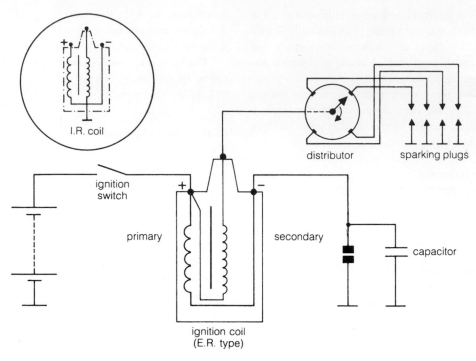

Fig. 11.5 Coil ignition system

principles are used in the operation of a coil ignition system and at this stage only the basic operation is considered.

Ignition circuit operation When the ignition switch and contact breaker are both closed, a current of about 3 A flows through the primary circuit. Passage of this current through the primary winding of the coil creates a strong magnetic flux around the winding. At the appropriate time, the contact breaker is opened by a cam driven at the same speed as the engine camshaft, i.e. half crankshaft speed. The breakage of the primary circuit gives a sudden collapse of the magnetic flux in the coil and causes an e.m.f. to be mutually induced into the secondary winding. The secondary winding has about 60 times as many turns as the primary winding, so the transformer action, combined with the effect of the self-induced voltage in the primary, steps up the voltage to that required to produce a spark at the plug. If the coil were 100% efficient the output energy would equal the input energy. In this case the increase in the secondary voltage is accompanied by a proportional decrease in the current.

By connecting the secondary winding to the negative l.t. coil terminal, the primary and secondary windings will be arranged in series with each other when the contact breaker is open. This connection, called the *auto-transformer connection*, allows the self-induced e.m.f. in the primary to be added to the mutually-induced e.m.f. in the secondary to give a higher output.

In a single-cylinder engine, the h.t. current is conveyed by a highly-insulated lead direct to the sparking plug, but when the system is used on a multi-cylinder engine, a distributor is needed to allocate the h.t. current to the appropriate sparking plug. In effect, the distributor is a h.t. rotary switch that consists of a distributor and a rotor arm, which revolves at camshaft speed. The plug leads are connected, in the firing order of the cylinders, to brass electrodes in the cap and a lead from the coil tower makes contact with a carbon brush that rubs on a brass blade forming part of the rotor arm.

An automatic advance mechanism alters the timing of the spark to suit the engine speed and load. This mechanism is situated adjacent to the contact breaker and it alters the spark timing by moving both the cam and the baseplate on which the contact breaker is mounted.

The unit that incorporates the distributor, contact breaker and automatic advance mechanism is commonly called the *ignition distributor*.

Coil ignition components

Ignition coil   Sometimes the ignition coil is called a pulse generator because it provides an h.t. output only where a spark is required. Figure 11.6 shows in exploded form the constructional details of a coil. At the centre is a laminated iron core around which is wound a secondary winding of about 20 000 turns of thin enamelled wire of diameter 0.06 mm. Over this winding, and separated from it by layers of varnished paper, is placed the primary winding. For a 12 V system this consists of about 350 turns of enamel-covered wire of diameter 0.5 mm. Varnished paper is placed between each layer of wire to improve the insulation.

A slotted iron sheath is placed inside the aluminium case to localize the magnetic flux and the winding assembly is held clear of the case by a porcelain insulator support and a plastic moulded, air-sealed cover. Low-tension terminals in the cover are connected to the ends of the primary winding. The secondary winding is connected to the coil tower which is made remote from the l.t. terminals to reduce the risk of the h.t. current flashing over to earth or tracking across the cover when moisture is present.

Flash-over   occurs when the voltage required for the h.t. current to jump to earth outside the cylinder is lower than the voltage needed to produce a spark inside the cylinder. *Tracking* is the term used when the h.t. current takes an alternative path to earth over the surface of an insulator instead of sparking at the plug: the spark path taken by the current burns the surface and leaves a deposit which then acts as a conductor. To avoid tracking, the insulator surfaces should be clean and non-porous.

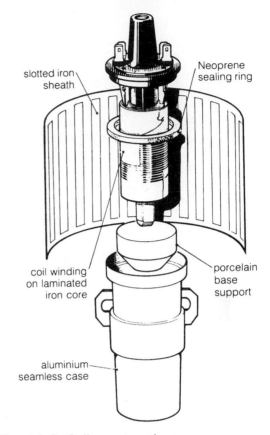

Fig. 11.6   Coil construction

The windings of most coils are immersed in oil. This improves insulation, overcomes the corona effect (faint glow of light around the coil) and reduces moisture problems. In addition, the oil improves cooling of the primary winding especially when the ignition is accidently left switched on for a long period with the engine stationary.

Contact breaker   This cam-actuated switch acts as a *trigger* to signal when an h.t. impulse must be applied to the sparking plug. The cam revolves at half crankshaft speed, so in one revolution of the cam all cylinders are fired.

For 4-stroke engines, the numbers of lobes on the cam are:

4 cylinders: 4 lobes
6 cylinders: 6 lobes
8 cylinders: 8 lobes

Figure 11.7 shows the layout of a contact breaker assembly for a 4-cylinder, 4-stroke engine. The two contacts, or *points* as they are often called, are made of

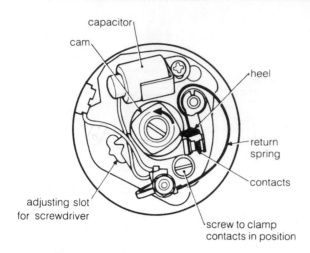

Fig. 11.7 Contact breaker assembly

tungsten–steel alloy: this metal resists the electrical burning action that occurs when the contacts are parted. One of the contacts is fixed to the baseplate and the other is attached to a plastic block which rubs on the cam face. A stainless-steel strip spring pushes the heel of the block firmly on to the cam, holds the contacts closed when the heel is free from the cam lobe and also acts as a conductor for the current.

The cam in Figure 11.7 is positioned at a point where the contacts are just opening; this represents the instant that the spark occurs. Further rotation of the cam opens the contacts wider up to the point where the gap is the greatest. In this position the gap can be checked with a feeler gauge; a typical gap is 0.38 mm (0.015 in).

When the distributor assembly is positioned to give the correct sparking timing, an alteration to the contact gap will change the timing; e.g. a smaller gap causes the cam to strike the contact heel later so the spark is retarded.

Examination of a contact breaker that has been in long service shows that the metal from one contact has vaporized and has been transferred to the other contact (Figure 11.8). The crater normally occurs on the positive side, but this is reversed when a smaller capacitor

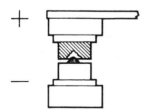

Fig. 11.8 Pitting and piling of contacts

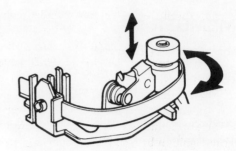

Fig. 11.9 Sliding contact type of contact breaker

has been used. Electrical burning blackens the contact face; this is an oxide that is resistant to current so when the contacts reach this stage they should be changed.

Various methods are used to overcome the crater and burning problems. One method uses a contact, on the positive side, that has a hole formed in the centre.

Another method uses a *sliding contact* as shown in Figure 11.9. In this design the operational movement of the base plate causes the smaller contact to move across the other contact. This wiping action has a cleaning effect; it is claimed that the reduction in the pitting of the contact increases the life to 40 000 km (25 000 miles).

Dwell Figure 11.10 shows the angle formed by the closed–open period for a 4-cylinder engine is 90°. This phase angle, or firing angle, depends on the number of engine cylinders. The phase angle is 360/(number of cylinders), so a 6-cylinder cam has an angle of 60°, and for 8 cylinders the angle is 45°.

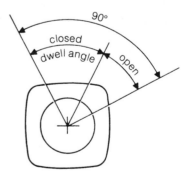

Fig. 11.10 Dwell angle

The angle moved by the cam during the *contact-closed period* is the *dwell angle* (or cam angle). An instrument called a *dwell meter* is used to measure the angle and since this method takes the reading whilst the engine is running, a more accurate result is obtained.

A typical dwell angle for a 4-cylinder engine is 54 ± 5°, but the angle depends on the type of distributor and the number of engine cylinders. When the contact gap is set to give the correct dwell angle, the gap measurement (in mm) should be within the specified limits, but this will not be so if the unit is worn.

When the contact gap is increased, the dwell angle is decreased. Furthermore, a decrease in the dwell angle advances the ignition by a similar amount, e.g. reducing the dwell angle from 54° to 51° will advance the ignition by 3°. The affect of dwell on the ignition timing emphasizes the need for the dwell on each cam lobe to be equal; if this is not so, the timing variation between cylinders will make the engine run erratically.

Sometimes the dwell is stated as *percentage dwell*. In this case the dwell angle is related to the phase angle. To find the percentage dwell the following equation is used:

$$\text{percentage dwell} = \frac{\text{dwell angle}}{\text{phase angle}} \times 100$$

A dwell angle of 54° for a 4-cylinder engine has a percentage dwell of 60%. This is obtained from:

$$\text{percentage dwell} = \frac{54}{90} \times 100 = 60\%$$

Capacitor   The importance of a capacitor, or *condenser*, can be seen when it is disconnected and the action of the contact breaker is observed: as the cam is rotated, severe arcing takes place at the contacts. When the contacts are opened, an induced e.m.f. of over 400 V generated in the primary circuit causes a spark to jump across the contacts as they initially part. The passage of this induced current, in the form of a spark across the contacts, results in a gradual fall in the primary current instead of a sudden fall that is needed. Besides affecting the speed of collapse of the magnetic flux, arcing quickly destroys the surface of the contacts. Therefore the duty of a capacitor is to minimize arcing and as a result speed up the collapse of the magnetic flux. Details of a capacitor are given on page 39.

A capacitor fitted in an ignition circuit acts as a 'buffer' device. When the contacts have just parted the capacitor gives the surge current an alternative path to take, so instead of jumping the small contact gap, the current flows into the capacitor and charges it up. After a fraction of a second the capacitor discharges, but by this time the contact gap is too wide for the spark to jump across.

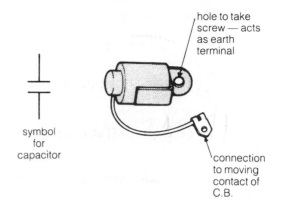

Fig. 11.11 Capacitor or condenser

Figure 11.11 shows a cylindrical-type capacitor commonly used with a coil-ignition system. It consists of two rolled-up sheets of metallized paper separated from each other by a dielectric insulator. The earthed aluminium alloy container is joined to one of the sheets and an insulated terminal, attached to a 'pig tail', is connected to the other sheet. A typical capacity is about 0.2 μF.

The capacitor is connected in parallel with the contact breaker and is positioned close to the breaker to minimize inductance and resistance of the lead.

Automatic advance mechanism
Precise timing of the spark is essential if maximum power and economy are to be obtained. If the spark occurs at the incorrect time in relation to the piston position, then problems will occur such as: overheating, pinking, piston damage and exhaust pollution.

These problems are overcome when the spark timing allows the maximum cylinder pressure to always occur about 12° after t.d.c.

A certain time elapses between the production of the spark and maximum cylinder pressure. For a given engine this '*burn time*' is affected by the air/fuel ratio and by the compression pressure; the latter is governed by the throttle opening.

Timing the spark to suit the speed   Taking into account the pressure and mixture factors, it is possible to 'time the spark' to give the required pressure at the correct instant, but this timing will only be suitable for one particular speed. At a faster speed, the crankshaft will move through a larger angle during the burn-time, so the spark must be made to occur earlier, i.e. the ignition has to be advanced.

A simple example of the *ignition advance* requirement is shown in Figure 11.12(a). For this engine the burn time is 0.004 s, so at 1000 rev/min the spark timing is 10° before t.d.c. Maximum pressure is at 12° after t.d.c. At this speed the total burning period is 22°.

Assuming the burn time is constant at 0.004 s, then the angle moved by the crankshaft and the spark advance is as follows:

Speed (rev/min)	Angle during burn	Advance from TDC
1000	22°	10°
2000	44°	32°
3000	66°	54°

Figure 11.12(b) shows the spark timing for a speed of 2000 rev/min.

In practice the burn time does not remain constant, so taking the variation into account gives a spark advance requirement as shown in Figure 11.12(c).

Figure 11.13 shows one type of speed-sensitive centrifugal advance mechanism. Although a number of different constructions are made, the basic principle of operation is the same. The rolling contact type shown consists of two flyweights that are pivoted on a base-plate, which is driven by the distributor spindle. A contoured face on the driving side of each flyweight acts against the cam plate on to which is secured the contact breaker cam. This cam bears on the drive spindle but does not receive a direct drive from it: instead the cam is driven via the flyweights. Two tension springs, situated between the base plate and the cam plate, hold the cam plate firmly against the flyweights. The strength of the springs determines the movement of the flyweights in relation to the centrifugal force generated at a given speed.

When the engine speed is raised, the increase in centrifugal force on the flyweights overcomes the resisting force of the springs and causes the flyweights to move outwards. As this occurs, the part rotation of the flyweights moves the cam plate forward in relation to the base plate and causes the cam to open the points earlier. This action gives a progressive advance to match the increase in speed up to the point where the full travel of the flyweight is reached.

Altering either the spring strength or the contour of the flyweight changes the angle of advance for a given speed.

The maximum advance for a typical mechanical advance mechanism is about 46 crankshaft degrees.

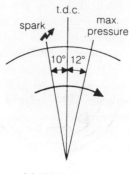

(a) 1000 rev/min

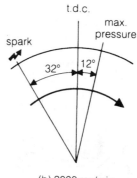

(b) 2000 rev/min

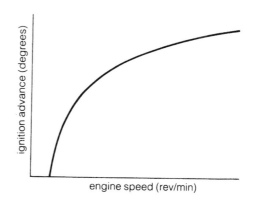

(c) ignition advance requirement

Fig. 11.12 Ignition advance

Figure 11.14 shows the relationship between advance and speed.

Some advance mechanisms use unequal strength springs and Figure 11.15 shows this type. The strong spring is slack on its post and the weaker spring is under

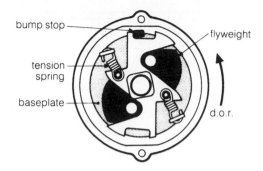

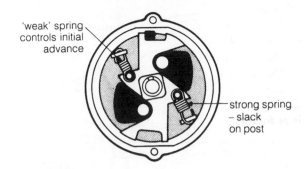

Fig. 11.15 Centrifugal advance unit fitted with unequal strength springs

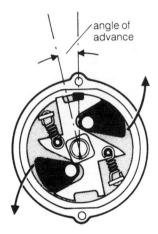

Fig. 11.13 Speed-sensitive centrifugal advance

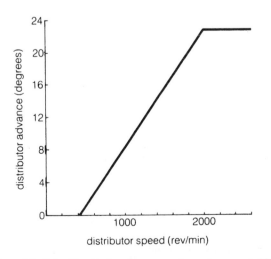

Fig. 11.14 Typical advance given by centrifugal advance mechanism

tension. This arrangement relies on the weaker spring only to resist outward movement of the flyweights until an engine speed of about 1000 rev/min is reached; above this speed both springs come into operation. A unit constructed in this way provides a large rate of advance up to 1000 rev/min and a smaller rate of advance beyond this speed.

Timing the spark to suit the load For economy reasons some carburettors supply a slightly weakened mixture when the engine operates under light load, i.e. when the vehicle is 'cruising'. Because a weak mixture burns slower than the correct mixture, extra advance of the spark is needed. The depression in the induction manifold varies with the load placed on the engine so the manifold is used by the advance mechanism and carburettor to sense the cruise condition. A high depression (low absolute pressure) exists when the engine load is light, but when it is under heavy load, the depression is very low; i.e. the pressure is just below atmospheric.

Manifold depression (low pressure), or to use the common (but technically incorrect) term 'vacuum', is used to operate a spring-loaded diaphragm to control the timing of the spark. This load-sensitive *vacuum control* operates independently from the centrifugal control mechanism.

Figure 11.16 shows a typical *vacuum advance* unit which gives an advance of about 13 crankshaft degrees. The diaphragm chamber is mounted on the side of the distributor unit and a rubber pipe connects the chamber with the induction manifold. A small vent on the non-vacuum side of the diaphragm allows atmospheric pressure to act on that side. A linkage connects the diaphragm to the contact breaker baseplate, which is allowed to part-rotate in relation to the distributor body. To advance the spark the baseplate is moved in

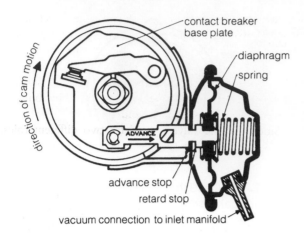

Fig. 11.16 Operation of vacuum control

a direction **opposite to cam rotation**, i.e. the contact breaker heel is moved towards the cam lobe.

No advance should be given by the vacuum advance unit when the engine is idling even though the manifold depression is very high. This is achieved by connecting the vacuum pipe to the carburettor in the vicinity of the throttle but slightly biased towards the air intake. As the throttle is nearly closed at idling, the manifold depression is prevented from acting on the advance unit (Fig. 11.17).

At small throttle openings, maximum depression acts on the diaphragm, so the pressure difference on the diaphragm moves it against the resistance of the spring

---

REMEMBER

Increasing the contact breaker gap:

- decreases the dwell angle
- advances the ignition timing

Capacitor:

- is fitted in parallel with the contact breaker
- increases life of contact breaker by reducing arching
- accelerates collapse of the coil's magnetic field

Automatic advance:

- alters the spark timing to ensure that maximum cylinder pressure always occurs at 12° after t.d.c.
- of the centrifugal type is speed sensitive
- of the vacuum type is load sensitive

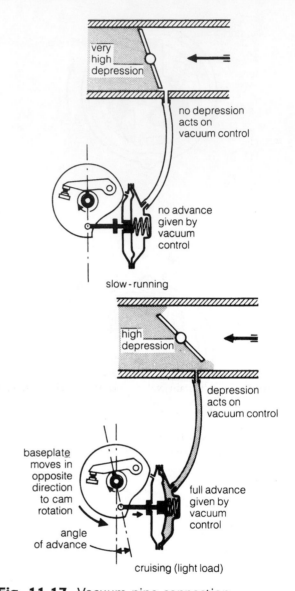

Fig. 11.17 Vacuum pipe connection

and advances the ignition. At other throttle openings, the reduced depression will give an appropriate advance to suit the cylinder conditions.

When the vehicle is cruising, a sudden opening of the throttle will immediately destroy the manifold depression. This is fortunate because the vacuum advance will retard the ignition and counteract the tendency for the engine to pink under these heavy conditions. Figure 11.18 shows the advance given by the vacuum advance unit.

Various additions are made to a basic vacuum advance system to satisfy the *exhaust emission regulations*

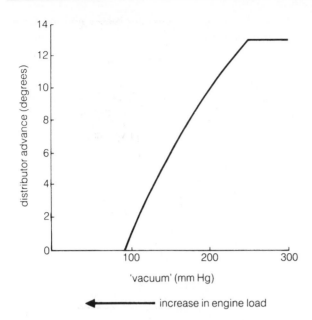

Fig. 11.18 Typical advance given by vacuum advance unit

in force in various countries. Two of these additions are the spark delay/sustain valve and the dual-diaphragm unit.

Spark delay/sustain valve This dual-purpose valve can be fitted in one of two ways to suit a given engine.

The item shown diagrammatically in Figure 11.19 has a one-way valve and a by-pass bleed orifice. It is fitted in the rubber pipe between the vacuum advance unit and the carburettor.

When pipe A is joined to the carburettor the device is a *spark delay valve*. This improves driveability and reduces emissions by delaying the full ignition advances until the air/fuel mixture has stabilized. On some cars the device is called a *spark control system*.

When pipe B is connected to the carburettor the device becomes a *spark sustain valve*. Connected in this way the valve maintains vacuum advance for a short time after the throttle has been operated. Although the valve has little effect on the performance of a warm engine, a considerable improvement in driveability is noticed when the engine is cold.

Since the one valve is used for two different roles, it is essential to fit the valve so that it operates in the manner intended.

Dual-diaphragm vacuum control This arrangement is used to give an improvement in exhaust emission. It gives extra retardation when the engine decelerates with a closed throttle and when it is idling.

Emission at the idling speed is improved by setting the throttle so that it is opened wider than normal and then the dual-diaphragm is used to retard the ignition

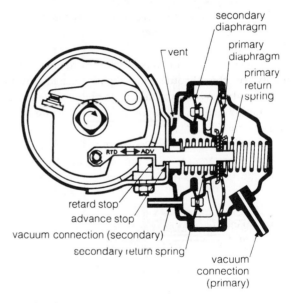

Fig. 11.20 Dual diaphragm vacuum

so as to offset the increase in speed. The unit shown in Figure 11.20 has a second diaphragm which controls the stop that limits the retardation movement of the first diaphragm. Manifold pressure, at a point far away from the carburettor throttle, is used to sense the idling condition and a rubber pipe connects this point in the manifold with the second diaphragm chamber.

When the engine is idling, the high depression acting on the second diaphragm moves the stop to the left (Figure 11.21 a). In this condition no depression acts

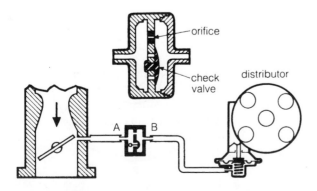

Fig. 11.19 Spark delay valve

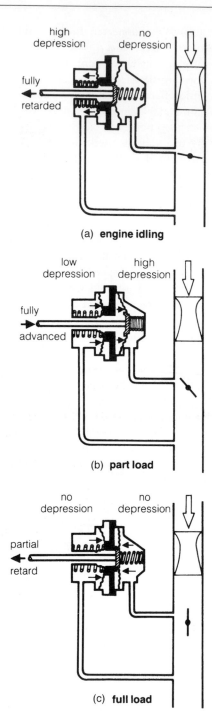

(a) **engine idling**

(b) **part load**

(c) **full load**

Fig. 11.21 Dual diaphragm vacuum

Figure 11.21 (b) shows the diaphragm position when the throttle is opened more than one quarter. In this position, the primary diaphragm gives maximum advance.

In Figure 11.21 (c) the throttle is shown full open and a low depression acts in both chambers. Both diaphragms are in the returned position and the strong secondary spring is pushing the movable stop to the right. When held in this position, the primary diaphragm makes the spark occur earlier compared with the 'idling-timing', but since the engine speed is high, the centrifugal advance system will be providing the main control.

Rotor and distributor cap

The sparking plugs of a multicylinder engine must be connected to the secondary winding of the coil when the cylinder is set for firing. The distributor fulfils this task by using a revolving *rotor arm* to transmit the h.t. impulse to the appropriate fixed *electrode* in the cap. When the rotor arm tip is adjacent to the cap electrode, the h.t. voltage causes a spark to jump across the small *air gap*. Each electrode is connected to a highly-insulated cable which conveys the current to the sparking plugs.

Figure 11.22 shows a plan view of the distributor layout. The rotor arm is a press fit on a boss formed on the contact breaker cam. A positive drive, at half crankshaft speed, is achieved by engaging a projection of the rotor with a slot in the driving boss. Electrical contact between the centre king-lead terminal and the brass rotor blade is made by either a spring-loaded carbon brush or a strip spring attached to the rotor arm.

on the main diaphragm so the primary return spring holds the primary diaphragm against the movable stop which is set so that extra retardation of the spark is obtained.

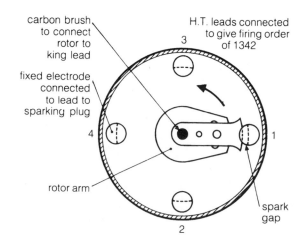

Fig. 11.22 Distributor: plan view

On some rotor arms, the electrode end of the blade is extended towards the next electrode in the direction of rotation. Use of this feature reduces the risk of the engine running backwards. If the crankshaft starts to move backwards, the rotor discharges the h.t. current to a plug of a cylinder which has its piston situated in the region of b.d.c. instead of the firing position.

The *distributor cap* is made of a brittle, antitracking, phenolic material that is moulded around the fixed electrodes and cable connections.

The cap is normally secured by quick-action spring clips and provision is made to prevent entry of dust and water. Sparking produces the corrosive gases nitric oxide and ozone, some form of ventilation or shielding is provided to prevent the gases causing damage to metal surfaces.

Ignition distributor Figure 11.23 shows a distributor which houses the contact breaker, mechanical and

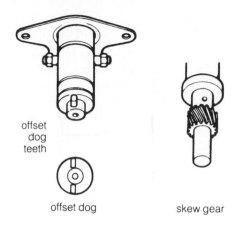

Fig. 11.24 Distributor drives

vacuum advance mechanisms and the actual h.t. distributor. The shaft is supported in two sintered-iron bearings and the drive from the camshaft, at half crankshaft speed, is by a helical skew gear or by an offset male dog (Figure 11.24).

The distributor is secured to the engine by a plate and clamp, clamp bolt or body flange. Provision is made to enable the distributor body to be partly rotated for timing purposes. Rotation against the direction of rotation advances the ignition.

High-tension cables

In the past, a rubber-covered, multistrand, copper lead was commonly used. But with the advent of plastics, the rubber is often replaced by PVC, since this material gives better protection from oil and water but is less effective than rubber where high temperatures are experienced. Whatever material is used, great care must be taken to prevent the h.t. current shorting to earth.

Each lead should be kept clear of all low-voltage cables and other h.t. leads because mutual induction can cause problems. Any leakage path will reduce the voltage applied to the sparking plug, so cold-starting difficulties can be expected if the voltage applied to the plug is low due to loss of current.

Also moisture can be very troublesome if the leads are porous or when water comes into contact with the coil, distributor cap or sparking plugs. In these cases an aerosol-applied silicone spray can be used to repel the moisture. These sprays are extremely effective for dispersing moisture and for sealing against moisture.

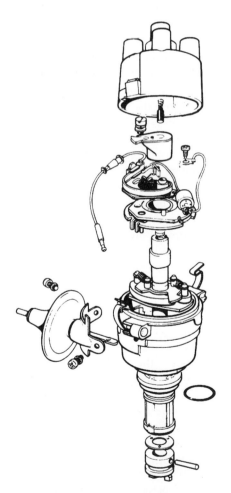

Fig. 11.23 Distributor assembly

Radio-frequency energy is produced by an ignition system and the energy radiated from a metallic h.t. cable causes serious *interference* to television and radio receivers even when they are situated at a considerable distance from the vehicle. Legislation has been introduced to limit this interference and in order to meet this requirement, the electrical resistance of the h.t. circuit has been increased. This resistance, which reduces the capacity current that discharges each time a plug fires, is obtained by using a special *suppression cable* for all h.t. leads. It consists of a core of graphite-impregnated, stranded and woven rayon or silk, which is insulated by a PVC or Neoprene covering. Special connectors are needed to join the non-metallic cable core to the terminal of the component.

The resistance of a typical cable is about 13 000–26 000 Ω per metre. Engine performance is not affected if the cable resistance is within the limits recommended. Moreover by limiting the discharge current, burning of the distributor and sparking plug electrodes is reduced.

Ballast resistor

A ballast resistor fitted in the primary circuit can fulfil two purposes; these are:

- To improve cold starting
- To reduce the variation in coil output with respect to speed.

Cold-start ballast resistor In the past the drop in battery p.d. that occurs when an engine is being cranked by the starting motor on a cold morning lowers the coil voltage below that needed to produce a spark at the plug. Under low-temperature conditions the performances of the battery, starting motor and ignition systems are all far from their best, and this deficiency occurs at a time when the ignition requirement is very high.

A low voltage applied to a coil during starting motor operation shows up in a number of ways. In one case the engine will not start while the starting motor is operating, but it starts easily when it is 'bump-started'. Similarly, some engines will not start until the starter switch is released; at that instant the momentum of the crankshaft gives sufficient movement to allow the engine to fire.

Although these situations are not frequent nowadays, it highlights the need for the driver to limit the duration of time that the starter switch is operated. Beyond a period of about 5 seconds, the voltage output from many batteries falls considerably, whereas if the starter

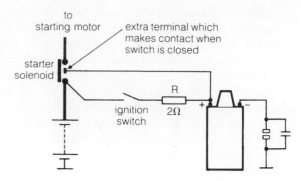

Fig. 11.25 Cold-start ballast resistor

switch is released after a short time and is not re-applied for a few seconds, the battery will then have chance to recover.

Many cold-starting problems have been overcome by the fitting of a ballast resistor, or by using a resistive cable between the battery and the ignition coil. In Figure 11.25 a ballast resistor is shown: this is a $2\,\Omega$ resistor connected in series with the ignition switch and a 7.5 V coil.

When the current flow in the circuit is 2.25 A, the voltage drop across the resistor is 4.5 V, so the p.d. applied to the coil is 7.5 V. By designing a coil to suit this voltage (or some other voltage as dictated by the ballast resistor used), the secondary output is kept within the limits required by the engine.

The improvement in the cold starting of the engine is achieved by fitting an extra cable in parallel with the ballast resistor. The ends of this cable are connected to an additional terminal on the starter solenoid switch and the ignition coil. When the starter solenoid is operated, current will be supplied to the coil. Since this current by-passes the ballast resistor, full battery voltage, even though it may be only 10 V at this time, is applied to the coil. Whereas the output from a conventional 12 V would be poor during engine-cranking by the starter, the higher-than-normal voltage applied to a 7.5 V coil will actually boost the output to meet the ignition requirement at this time.

Output control ballast resistor

It takes a comparatively long time after the contact breaker has closed for the primary current to build up to its maximum. Figure 11.26 shows the growth time for a typical ignition coil and in this case a time of about 0.01 s is required before the maximum primary current is obtained.

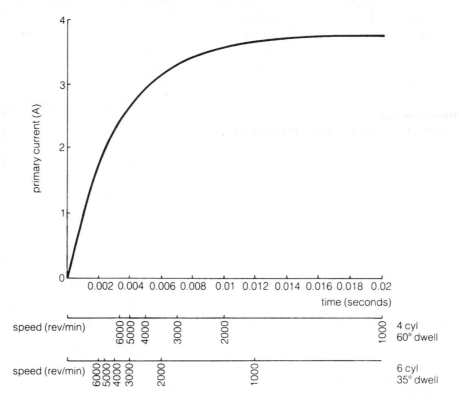

Fig. 11.26 Growth time for primary circuit

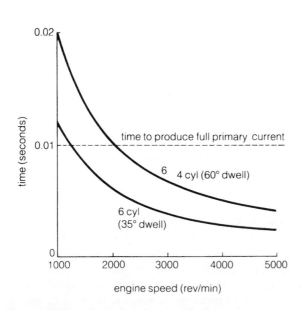

Fig. 11.27 Variation in dwell time

Current flow starts when the contact breaker closes and continues to build up during the dwell period. Although the dwell angle should remain constant with speed, the dwell time in seconds shortens. When the dwell time is less than about 0.01 second for this coil, the primary current is no longer capable of reaching its maximum, consequently the output from the coil gradually falls when the speed is increased beyond this point.

Figure 11.27 shows the variation in dwell time for 4- and 6-cylinder engines. If the dwell time for a particular speed and engine is read from this graph, it is possible to use Figure 11.26 to ascertain the primary current at that speed.

These graphs show that an engine having 6 or more cylinders suffers a gradual fall-off in coil output when the speed is increased. Fitting an *output control ballast resistor* in series with the primary circuit compensates for this variation in output.

The *iron-wire resistor* has a high-temperature coefficient such that the 'hot' resistance is about three times as great as the 'cold' resistance. Temperature of the resistor depends on the current passing through it, so when the engine is running at low speed, the long dwell time causes the resistor to run hot; as a result, the average current in the primary is reduced. This allows the coil to run cooler and also reduces the ill effects of spark erosion due to high voltage.

Similarly, the natural drop in primary current as the engine speed is increased allows the ballast resistor to run cooler. This causes its resistance value to fall and as a result increases the primary current to offset the fall-off due to speed.

A ballast resistor of this type has a cold value of about $0.25\ \Omega$. The resistor can be fitted either internally in the coil or externally in the circuit.

Low-inductance ignition coil

Current growth in the primary winding of a coil is restricted by the coil's self-inductance. As the primary current gradually increases, self-inductance in the winding produces a back-e.m.f. which opposes any change in the current. This opposition to current growth is increased as the number of turns on the primary winding is increased.

Engines having a large number of cylinders, especially 8-cylinder units, need a coil which gives a quicker growth than a conventional coil, so a high-output coil, called a *low-inductance coil* is often fitted to these engines. Since the primary winding of a low-inductance coil has fewer turns and therefore the wire is shorter in length, the current flowing when the engine is in its stalled condition is about three times as great. Naturally the erosion wear, due to this high current, on a conventional contact breaker is severe, so the low-inductance coil is often fitted in conjunction with a transistorized breaker system.

Twin contact breaker

The short dwell time associated with high-speed operation of 8-cylinder engines can be improved by using twin contact breakers. This system reduces the time that the primary circuit is broken because it arranges for one set of contacts to 'make' the circuit immediately after the spark has occurred.

In the twin contact arrangement shown in Figure 11.28 the contact set A is connected in parallel with contact set B. Mounted in this way, the circuit is interrupted only when both contacts are opened simultaneously. As soon as contact set A opens to give a spark at the plug, the other set closes and starts the build-up of the primary current.

The introduction of transistorized systems has made the twin contact arrangement obsolete.

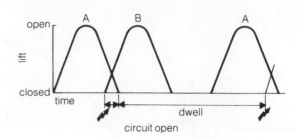

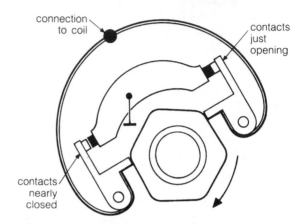

Fig. 11.28 Twin contact breakers

Magneto ignition

A magneto is a self-contained unit which generates its own electricity and at the right time steps up the voltage to give a spark at the plug. A magneto has two advantages over a coil ignition system: it does not require a battery and the voltage output improves as the engine speed is increased.

Its main disadvantage is its low performance at cranking speed. This drawback has made the coil ignition system universal for cars, but the magneto is still used on small engines such as motor cycles, mowers, etc.

Rotating-magnet magneto   Small engines have used this type of magneto since improved magnetic materials were introduced as permanent magnets.

A flywheel magneto has the magnet cast into a nonferrous flywheel, hence it is classified as a rotating magnet type. Figure 11.29 shows the basic construction.

In this design a laminated soft-iron armature containing the coil windings, is stationary, and a cam formed on the flywheel hub operates a contact breaker.

Rotation of the magnet with the flywheel causes an alternating magnetic flux to pass through the armature.

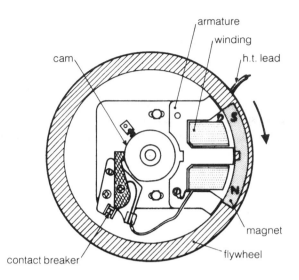

Fig. 11.29 Rotating magnet magneto

Having generated its own primary current, the magneto transforms the low voltage to a voltage sufficient to produce a spark at the plug. This is achieved by using a circuit as shown in Figure 11.30. It consists of a contact breaker and two windings, a primary and a secondary, interconnected similar to that used in a coil ignition circuit but without a battery. A capacitor is used to speed up the collapse of the magnetic flux which it does by reducing arcing at the contacts.

A complete circuit is required for the primary current to build up to its maximum, so during this period the contact breaker is kept closed. Just before the primary starts to fall in order to build up in the other direction, the contact breaker is opened. This interruption mutually induces a high voltage into the secondary winding which is connected to the sparking plug.

Many magnetos have a safety spark-gap which is used to protect the insulation of the magneto coil when either a plug lead becomes disconnected or the h.t. is open-circuited.

As the primary coil is wound on this armature, a current is induced into the coil every time a change occurs in the magnetic flux. Movement of the magnet across the complete armature will give a full reversal of the flux, so an alternating current is generated which peaks every time the flux reversal occurs.

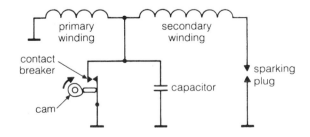

Fig. 11.30 Circuit of magneto

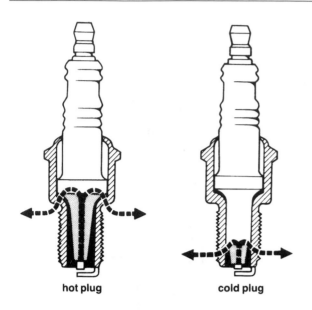

hot plug   **cold plug**

Fig. 11.35 Sparking plug heat range

At the other end of the heat range is the cold (or hard) plug. This plug has good thermal conductivity and is used in engines that have a high power output for their size.

Manufacturers offer a range of plugs, so it is possible to match the heat range of a plug to the engine.

REMEMBER

Sparking plug operating temperature:

- is between 350°C and 900°C
- depends on:
  (a) insulator nose length
  (b) projection of insulator
  (c) bore diameter
  (d) material

General rule for heat range

- Hot plug for a cold engine
- Cold plug for a hot engine

Electrode features

A conventional plug uses nickel alloy for the electrodes to give resistance to corrosive attack by combustion products or erosion from high-voltage discharges. In engines where corrosion and erosion are severe, a special material, such as platinum, is sometimes used.

Both electrodes must be robust to withstand vibration from combustion effects and also they must be correctly shaped to allow a spark to be produced with minimum voltage (Figure 11.36 (a)). Under normal conditions, erosion eats away the electrodes, so after a period of time the earth electrode becomes pointed in shape (Figure 11.36 (b)): in this state it requires a higher voltage to produce a spark.

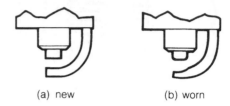

(a) new   (b) worn

Fig. 11.36 Electrode shape and wear

Between the period of the maintenance checks, the increase in the voltage requirement of the plug is accompanied by a general deterioration in the output voltage of the ignition generator system. Unless regular attention is given, the system will fail: most probably this will show up when attempting to start the engine on a cold, damp day.

A typical sparking plug gap is 0.6 mm (0.024 in), but wider gaps are sometimes used for engines which run on a mixture weaker than normal. These mixtures are more difficult to ignite so a higher voltage is required.

An *auxiliary gap* (or booster gap) is used on some types. This series gap is formed between the terminal and the end of the electrode. Its purpose is to reduce the build-up of carbon on the insulator nose and so improve the plug performance when the engine is operated at low power for a considerable time.

The introduction of an extra series gap in the circuit raises the h.t. voltage and as a result causes the spark to jump the gap rather than short along any dirt or carbon on the insulator.

This is similar to the method used in the past to restore normal sparking from a plug that has been fouled by petrol. The plug lead is held, by suitably-insulated tongs, about 6 mm from the plug terminal and the engine is started. After a short time the plug begins to operate normally.

Copper-cored electrode Increasing the insulator nose length reduces the risk of carbon fouling when the vehicle is operated on short journeys, but when a high vehicle speed is maintained for a long period, the spark plug seriously overheats.

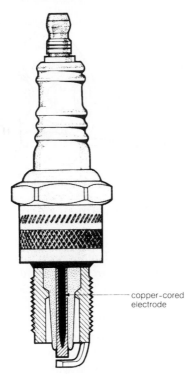

Fig. 11.37 Copper-cored electrode sparking plug

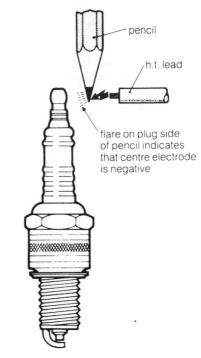

pencil

h.t. lead

flare on plug side of pencil indicates that centre electrode is negative

Fig. 11.38 Pencil test to determine polarity

This temperature problem can be overcome by using expensive electrode materials such as platinum, iridium, silver or gold-palladium, but a cheaper alternative is to use copper-cored electrodes to improve thermal conductivity (Figure 11.37).

Electrode polarity A lower voltage is needed to produce a spark at the plug when the centre electrode is negative in relation to the h.t. circuit polarity. A hot surface emits electrons and since the centre electrode is the hotter of the two, the natural flow of electrons is from the centre electrode to the earth electrode. If the circuit is connected to give this direction of flow, then the natural flow of electrons will aid, rather than oppose, the electron movement given by the ignition coil.

The direction of electron flow in the secondary depends on the polarity of the primary windings. Nowadays the l.t. terminals on most coils are marked (+) and (−) to indicate the connections required to give a 'negative spark'.

Electronic diagnostic equipment is able to test the coil's polarity, but if this equipment is not available, a pencil test can be carried out (Figure 11.38).]

Inspection of a plug which has been in use for a long time shows that more erosion occurs on the earth electrode when the centre electrode is negative.

11.4 Maintenance of non-electronic systems

In the past, complete or partial failure of an ignition system was the most common cause of breakdowns. Many of these failures could have been prevented if the recommended maintenance had been carried out at the appropriate time.

Many manufacturers recommend that the ignition system is checked every 10 000 km (6000 miles). At this time the following tasks are performed.

● Contact breaker replaced and adjusted.
● Sparking plugs cleaned and tested.
● Wiring is checked for condition and security.
● Dirt and moisture is removed from the coil and any other surface which is exposed to h.t. charges.
● Lubrication of the cam face and also the moving parts of the automatic advance system.

Contact breaker

Constant use over a period of time causes burning of the contact surfaces which increases the electrical resistance. In addition pitting and piling of the contacts alters the gap: this changes both the dwell angle and the ignition timing.

Failure to service the contacts will lead to poor engine performance, high fuel consumption and difficult starting, especially when the engine is cold. Low available secondary voltage, combined with incorrect timing of the spark, will also raise the exhaust emission levels.

The condition of the contacts can be ascertained by measuring the voltage drop across the contacts **when the contacts are fully closed**.

Often this test includes the wiring from the coil to the contact breaker. To check this, the voltmeter is connected to earth and to the l.t. coil terminal (normally marked '−') which is connected by a lead to the contact breaker.

The voltage drop allowable varies with the make of distributor; typical maximum limiting values are:

Ducellier and Delco:	0.25 V
Lucas, Bosch and most other types:	0.35 V
Ford Motorcraft	
− without tachometer:	0.4 V
− with tachometer connected:	0.6 V

Nowadays it is rare that the contact points are cleared or reground; instead a new contact set is fitted at the appropriate time. This task is simplified by the use of 'quick-fit' assemblies that are held in place and adjusted by only one screw. With all types, attention is needed to ensure that the insulated lead from the coil makes contact with the strip spring attached to the movable contact, but it must not make contact with the casing.

The correct contact gap is set by using a feeler gauge or dwell meter.

Feeler gauge method This is shown being used in Figure 11.39. The cam is rotated until the **contacts are full open** and the gap is checked with a *clean* feeler gauge. A typical gap is 0.35–0.412 mm (0.014–0.016 in): this is obtained by slightly slackening the contact set clamp screw and moving the contact plate until the correct setting is obtained. Generally a niche is cut in the plate to enable a screwdriver to lever the plate in the required direction.

After tightening the contact adjusting screw and checking the gap, a smear of high melting point grease is applied to the cam face before refitting the rotor arm and distributor cap.

The correct gap is essential because an incorrect gap causes the following faults:

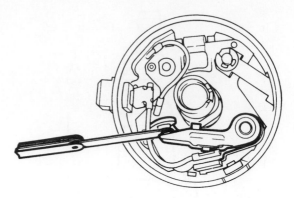

Fig. 11.39 Adjustment of contact breaker gap

(1) *Gap too wide*. Timing is advanced and the time for the primary current to build-up is reduced
(2) *Gap too narrow*. Timing is retarded

Dwell meter method This takes into account the wear on the distributor bushes and cam eccentricity. This wear causes the cam to take up a different position when it is in motion compared with the static condition used for the feeler gauge adjustment.

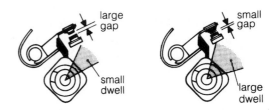

Fig. 11.40 Dwell

Dwell is expressed either as an angle or as a percentage; it indicates the time that the contacts are *closed* (Figure 11.40). For a 4-cylinder engine, a typical dwell angle is $54° \pm 5°$, i.e. $49°$–$59°$. A dwell angle of $54°$ gives a percentage dwell of $54/90 = 60\%$. This means that the contacts are closed for 60% and open for 40% during the phase in which the spark for one cylinder is being produced.

A dwell meter is similar to a voltmeter, so when it is connected between the contact-breaker lead and earth, it measures the average voltage. Since the voltage fluctuates as the contacts quickly open and close, the instrument needle dampling system is made to give a steady reading (Figure 11.41). The reading obtained will depend on the ratio between the open and closed periods.

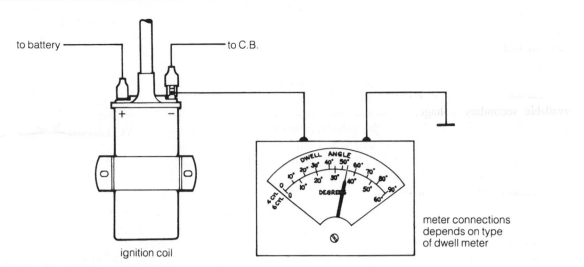

Fig. 11.41 Dwell measurement

Dwell measurement is taken when the engine is slow-running. If the reading is incorrect, the dwell meter can be used while the engine is being cranked with the starting motor and the contacts are being adjusted.

Contact gap and dwell are interrelated: a larger gap causes the contacts to open earlier, so this gives a shorter dwell.

Similarly, dwell-angle alteration changes the spark timing; a dwell angle change from 54° to 59° causes the spark to occur 5° later.

Spindle wear and other drive defects can be diagnosed by observing the change in dwell angle as the speed is increased from 1000 rev/min to 3000 rev/min. Normally the *dwell variation* should be less than 3°.

Sparking plugs In the past it was recommended that plugs were serviced and/or replaced at 16 000 km (10 000 mile) intervals. Today, the use of electronic ignition, precise fuel mixture control and improved engine design has more than doubled this service interval and considerably extended plug life.

The following servicing procedure is included to cover the older type engines.

After being used for a long period of time, erosion causes the plug gap to increase, and carbon, oil or petrol additive deposits on the internal surfaces decrease the plug's resistance to misfire.

Any shunt path to earth decreases the energy available for the spark, so this results in poor engine performance, especially power and economy, at times when maximum energy is required.

Alteration of the spark gap varies the voltage supplied by the coil for a given compression pressure. The effects are:

Gap too small. Low-voltage spark which may be insufficient to fully ignite the air/fuel mixture. This shows up when cold-starting, slow-running and when the engine is cruising with a weakened mixture.
Gap too wide. High-voltage spark which may demand more voltage than that produced by the coil. Consequently high-speed and cold-starting performances are poor, and erosion of the distributor and sparking-plug electrodes will be severe.

Before removing the plugs the h.t. leads should be removed by withdrawing the connectors rather than pulling on the leads. Plug removal is achieved by using a suitable plug socket and care must be exercised to avoid cracking the ceramic insulator.

Cleaning is performed normally by sand-blasting, followed by air-blasting to remove all particles of sand from the interior of the plug. Deposits on the electrodes at the spark gap are removed by a contact file and afterwards the gap should be reset to the recommended value by bending the earth electrode. A wire-type feeler gauge allows more accurate setting of the gap because a flat feeler blade does not allow for the contour of the earth electrode when erosion has occurred.

Attention should be given to cleaning all sand from the threads and deposits from the external surface of the insulator.

Testing is carried out normally in a chamber that

allows the air pressure to be varied while the plug is supplied with an h.t. current at a predetermined maximum voltage. This voltage is set to give good regular sparking by a new plug up to a given pressure.

The plug is screwed into the chamber and left finger-tight to allow slight escape of air so as to improve ionization. After clipping on the h.t. test lead, the switch is operated and the air pressure is gradually increased. Sparking is observed through a window in the chamber and the pressure registered on the gauge is noted. A good plug should give regular sparking at the electrodes up to the set pressure.

Manual cleaning by a wire brush is a poor substitute for a sand-blast. Care must be taken when using a brush to avoid damaging the insulator, but sufficient pressure must be applied to remove all deposits.

Inspection of the plug prior to cleaning often acts as a guide to the state of tune of the engine. Figure 11.42 shows the appearance for the following conditions:

- *Normal.* The core nose is lightly coated with a grey-brown deposit and the electrode is not unduly eroded. Typical erosion wear causes the gap to increase by about 0.016 mm per 1000 km (0.001 in/ 1000 miles).
- *Carbon fouling.* A matt black sooty appearance which can cause the h.t. charge to short to earth without jumping the spark gap. This deposit originates from an over-rich mixture; also it occurs when the vehicle is engaged on short journeys that require the repeated use of the choke as well as other

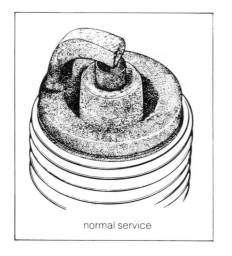
normal service

carbon fouling

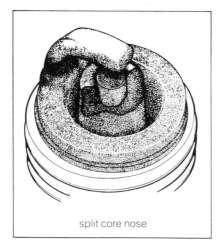
split core nose

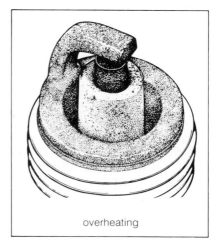
overheating

Fig. 11.42 Sparking plug condition

conditions that cause the engine to operate below its normal running temperature.

- *Split core nose.* Initially a hair-line crack appears which soon causes a part of the insulator to break away. This failure is often promoted by detonation.
- *Overheating.* Insulator is white, the electrodes have glazed appearance and carbon deposit is minimal. This condition can be caused by any factor which gives overheating of the combustion chamber. Plug temperature increases with ignition advance so if over advance is given, plug failure will result. A plug in this condition should be discarded and the cause rectified.

When refitting a plug to the engine the correct torque should be applied especially with plugs having a taper seat.

Ignition timing

The need for correct timing cannot be over-emphasized, since incorrect spark timing can cause many problems as stated previously in this book (page 165).

When a distributor unit is refitted to an engine the following method may be used assuming the detailed manufacturer's instructions are unavailable.

(1) Set No. 1 piston to t.d.c. 'compression'.
(2) Connect the drive so that the **contacts are just opening** when the rotor arm is pointing to the distributor segment 'feeding' No. 1 cylinder. (The contact position may be found by using a lamp as shown in Figure 11.43).
(3) Fit h.t. leads to distributor in the order that the cylinders fire.
(4) Start engine and make final adjustments with a timing light.

This method is sometimes called *static timing* and manufacturers often quote the crankshaft position at which the spark should occur when the timing is set in this way, e.g. a static timing of 4° indicates that when the crankshaft is set to 4° before t.d.c. the test lamp should show that the contact points have just opened.

Stroboscopic timing

A strobe-type timing light gives a sudden flash of light at the instant the spark occurs. The high-intensity, short-duration flash is triggered by the h.t. impulse from No. 1 plug lead. When the lamp is held close to the member that carries the timing marks, the instantaneous flash illuminates the marks and 'freezes' the motion to enable the spark timing to be ascertained (Fig. 11.44).

To set the timing, the recommended advance at a certain speed should be known, e.g. advance is 10° at 900 rev/min with the vacuum pipe disconnected. This example requires the engine speed to be set to 900 rev/min, the vacuum advance pipe disconnected and

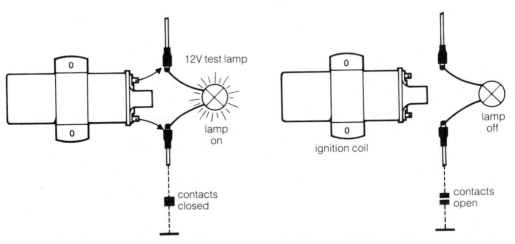

Fig. 11.43 Use of test lamp to determine where contact breaker opens

Fig. 11.44 Stroboscopic timing

the mark on the crankshaft pulley (or flywheel) should then show an advance of 10° when the timing is correct. If the timing is incorrect, the distributor clamp should be slackened and the distributor body rotated until the correct setting is obtained. Slight rotation of the distributor body in the same direction as the movement of the rotor arm retards the ignition. When the timing is correct, the distributor must be clamped securely, the timing rechecked and the vacuum pipe reconnected.

A development of this method allows the automatic advance mechanism to be tested. Special timing lights are available which incorporate a control to make the flash occur a set time after the spark is produced. The extent of this delay is indicated to the operator by an analogue-type meter or digital read-out.

A development of this method allows the automatic advance mechanism to be tested. Special timing lights are available which incorporate a control to make the

---

SAFE PRACTICE

Timing light:

● strobe effect gives impression that fan and other moving parts are stationary – don't be deceived!

Rotating parts:

● can entangle hair and loose clothing – KEEP CLEAR and wear suitable protective clothing.

---

flash occur a set time after the spark is produced. The extent of this delay is indicated to the operator by an analogue-type meter or digital read-out.

After setting the normal timing, the engine speed is raised through set increments. At each speed the timing-light control is altered to make the original timing marks coincide: the angle of advance is shown on the meter.

Ignition circuit testing

If an engine fitted with a conventional ignition system fails to start, the following checks can be made to test the operation of the system.

Test 1: Visual check Check all cables and connectors for security and ensure that the battery is in good condition.

Test 2: Coil output Remove king lead from the distributor cap, fit extension (e.g. centre electrode from old sparking plug) and hold lead with insulated pliers so that the end of the extension is about 6 mm from a good earth such as the engine block (Figure 11.45). Switch on ignition and crank the engine. If a good spark is obtained, then the fault, if present, is in the secondary circuit beyond the coil h.t. lead, so proceed to Test 7.

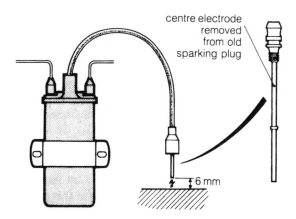

Fig. 11.45 Coil output test

Test 3: Contact breaker If no spark, or a poor spark from the coil h.t. is evident, then examine the contact breaker for the condition of the surfaces and the gap setting. The surface condition is best checked with a voltmeter, but a 12 V, 3 W test lamp can also be used in parallel with the contacts: the lamp should go out when the contact close.

Test 4: Primary circuit A high resistance in the primary circuit can be pin-pointed by measuring the p.d. at

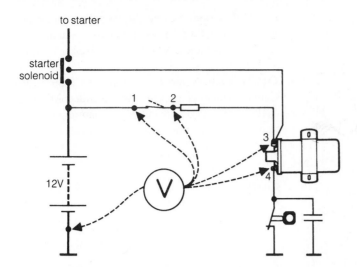

contact breaker closed		
voltmeter position	voltage without ballast resistor	voltage with ballast resistor
1	12	12
2	12	12
3	12	5–6
4	0	0

Fig. 11.46 Voltmeter checks on primary circuit

various parts of the circuit (Figure 11.46). This test requires the **contact breaker closed**, so that current flows in the circuit. Unless the contacts are set in this position, the voltage at the points 1–4 in Figure 11.46 will correspond to the battery e.m.f. unless the circuit is completely broken at some point between 1 and 4.

Test 5: Capacitor Unless special test equipment is available, the capacitor condition is assessed by substituting a test capacitor. Failing this, the contact breaker can be observed when the engine is cranked with the distributor cap removed so as to assess the degree of arcing. If arcing is severe, the capacitor should be changed.

Test 6: Ignition coil The resistance of each winding can be checked by an ohmmeter. Typical values for a conventional coil are:

- Primary winding: 1.2–1.4 Ω
- Secondary winding: 5–9 kΩ

A visual inspection of the insulated surfaces should be made for signs of tracking. Breakdown of insulation, internal and external, often shows up when the coil is 'loaded'.

Test 7: HT leads The coil h.t. lead is reconnected and the h.t. lead is removed from the sparking plug. An extension is fitted to the end of the lead and the extension is held about 6 mm from a good earth while the engine is cranked.

If a good spark is obtained, then the sparking plugs should be suspected. When no spark is obtained, the h.t. circuit between the coil and the sparking plug should be tested.

Test 8: Rotor arm The coil king lead is held about 3 mm from the rotor arm blade and the engine is rotated or the contacts are opened manually with an insulated screwdriver. If regular sparking occurs, then the insulation of the rotor arm is defective.

Test 9: Distributor cap The cap is examined visually for cracks and signs of tracking: this is a thin carbon line which allows the h.t. current to take an easier path than that required. Tracking can cause misfiring, but normally the engine will start with the cap in this condition.

If the weather is damp, then h.t. leads should be checked at a very early stage in the test program. Moisture causes the electrical charge to 'leak' to another lead or directly to earth, so to prevent this, the h.t. leads should be sprayed with a moisture repellent or they should be separated from one another.

Complete breakdown of the king lead will prevent the engine from starting whereas a similar failure of a plug lead will cause regular misfiring under load or poor engine performance in general. An ohmmeter should be used to check the resistance of the h.t. leads, which, in the case of a supression lead, will have a value of 13 000–26 000 Ω/metre.

Diagnostic equipment – engine analysers

The need for quick and accurate diagnosis of engine faults makes it necessary for the automotive engineer to possess and use modern electronic equipment. This

REMEMBER

Contact breaker:

- voltdrop indicates condition
- set with a dwell meter or feeler gauge
- dwell angle is the number of degrees that the contacts are *closed*
- dwell angle is about 57° for a 4-cylinder engine
- spindle wear is indicated by the *dwell variation* (should be less than 3°)

Sparking plug:

- gap too small shows up on cold-starting, slow-running and when cruising
- gap too wide shows up on cold-starting and at high speed.
- tested outside the engine must be subjected to pressure

Ignition timing:

- must be correct to:
  (a) avoid engine damage
  (b) achieve good power and economy
  (c) minimize pollution
- is checked with a strobe light to ascertain:
  (a) spark timing
  (b) operation of the automatic advance system

Simple circuit testing:

- *Coil output* – checked by holding king lead with insulated pliers about 6 mm from good earth
- *Contact breaker* – checked with test lamp or voltmeter across contacts; readings should be:
  (a) contacts open – 12 V
  (b) contacts closed – less than 0.4 V
- *Low tension* – with ignition switched on and contacts closed, voltmeter reading between battery side of coil and earth should be about 12 V (less ballast resistor voltage)

- Oscilloscopes for the display of test patterns.
- Computers which test the engine systems and display the results on a VDU (visual display unit).

Oscilloscope Figure 11.47 shows a Crypton Diagnostic Centre which comprises a cathode-ray oscilloscope (CRO) together with analogue and digital meters for testing and adjusting, where necessary:

- ignition circuits and components;
- spark timing;
- relative output from cylinders (cylinder balance);
- CO emission from exhaust;
- electrical equipment involving the use of basic test meters.

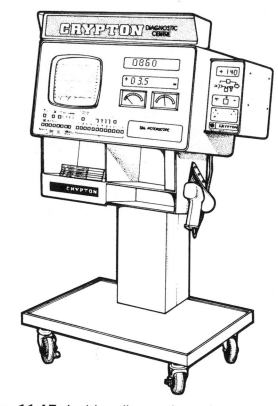

Fig. 11.47 Ignition diagnostic equipment

equipment has been designed to pin-point common and obscure faults in the engine and associated systems, and, where necessary, provide the vehicle operator with detailed information on the condition of the engine.

A number of analysers are available and these can be divided broadly into two main categories:

CRO display The pattern formed on the screen is obtained by a spot of light which sweeps horizontally across the screen in step with the engine speed. Each time a given sparking plug fires, the spot is made to return to the left-hand side of the screen. As the phosphorus coating on the inside of the cathode-ray tube retains the image for a short-time, the human eye sees a continuous line formed on the screen instead of a moving spot of light.

Vertical deflection of the line corresponds with the voltage sensed at a given point in the ignition system. Switches are provided to select various display and scales and voltage pick-up points in the circuit; these enable the operator to analyse the complete process of ignition.

In this form the CRO is a high-speed voltmeter. Whereas the sluggish movement of an analogue meter needle only gives a mean value of the voltage; a CRO shows the actual voltage at all stages of the operating cycle.

Before using a CRO to examine ignition patterns, the primary circuit is normally tested with a voltmeter to eliminate the effects of basic circuit faults from the patterns.

Primary pattern The trace shown in Figure 11.48 represents an ignition system in good order. It shows the voltage variation in the primary circuit for the production of one spark.

At point (1) the contacts open and self-induction causes the voltage to increase. The oscillations at (2) are due to the charge–discharge action of the capacitor. A good capacitor should give four or five oscillations at this stage.

After the rise in the voltage at point (3) at the end of the sparking period, the energy remaining in the primary winding is dissipated. This phase (4) should produce four or five oscillations as the energy fades away.

At point (5) the contacts close and the trace should show a clean line joining the two horizontal lines. Although preliminary tests should pin-point a dirty

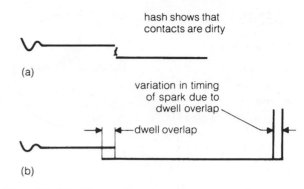

Fig. 11.49 Part of primary pattern; diagram shows two common faults

contact condition, the CRO will show up this condition as a 'hash' at the point where the contacts close (Figure 11.49(a)).

When the patterns for each cylinder are superimposed on the original trace, no large separation in the patterns should be seen. However if the cam or spindle is worn, the dwell angles will vary: this will appear as shown in Figure 11.49(b) and is called *dwell overlap*.

The need for greater accuracy of dwell measurement has meant that most modern analysers now incorporate a digital meter to show the *dwell angle*. Furthermore, these modern units can measure the *individual dwell* given by each cam lobe. Having ascertained each dwell angle, the operator can subtract the smallest angle from the largest angle to find the dwell overlap.

Secondary patterns Figure 11.50(a) shows a normal pattern which represents the voltage variation in the secondary circuit. The opening of the contacts at (1) causes the voltage to rise until a spark is produced: the

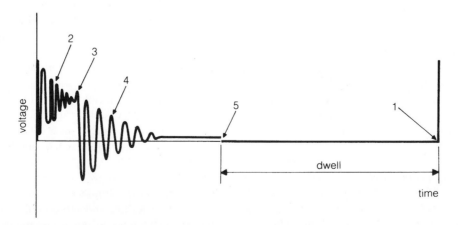

Fig. 11.48 CRO pattern; primary circuit

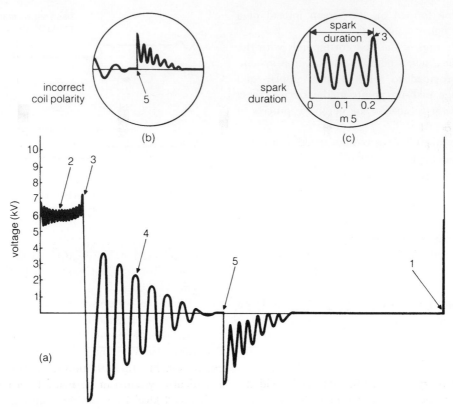

Fig. 11.50 CRO pattern; secondary circuit

voltage during the sparking process is shown at (2). When sparking ceases, the voltage rises (point 3) and this is followed by the dissipation of energy in the secondary winding. As this occurs, the oscillating voltage will give four or five surges before dying away.

At point (5) the closure of the contacts and the start of the current flow in the primary winding mutually induces a small e.m.f. into the secondary winding.

If the pattern at point (5) is inverted (Figure 11.50(b)) it indicates that the coil polarity is incorrect. This is corrected by changing over the l.t. coil connections.

Faulty coil windings and poor h.t. leads give an unstable pattern and broken trace respectively.

Most modern analysers enable the length of the spark line to be measured in milliseconds (Figure 11.50(c)). Conventional systems have a spark line of length 0.75–1.5 ms.

Secondary pattern, parade order Secondary output is shown by presenting each secondary trace, side by side; to ease the measurement the vertical trace lines are broadened (Figure 11.51). Normally the pattern is displayed in the order that the sparking plugs are fired.

This trace shows clearly the voltage needed initially to fire each sparking plug. If conditions are normal, the height of each of the prominent verticals is similar. A vertical scale, which can be set at a maximum of either 20 kV or 40 kV is provided to measure the voltage applied to each plug. At 1000 rev/min the voltage should be 8–14 kV, but if the variation exceeds 3 kV, the cause should be investigated.

The performance of the sparking plugs under load can be assessed by snapping the throttle open. During this test, the voltage should increase to about 16 kV.

Maximum voltage output of the coil is measured by using insulated pliers to remove the h.t. lead from the sparking plug and to hold it clear of the engine. During this test the 40 kV scale is selected, because most coils fitted to British vehicles since 1970 give a maximum output of at least 28 kV when supplied with a 14 V input.

Engine diagnostic computer To meet modern demands for accurate testing and efficient fault diagnosis, many engine analysers now use a computer. Information is displayed on a VDU and the incorporation of a printer

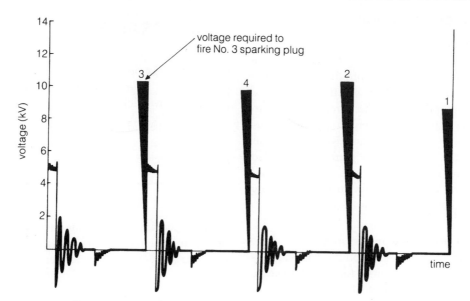

Fig. 11.51 CRO patterns: secondary, parade order

enables the customer to be given a report on the condition of the engine.

Detachable memory pods (EPROM) are provided to store data which include: test procedure for instructional needs, printer commands for laying out the header information on the customer's report form, and the specifications for the engines to be tested.

Access to the engine data allows the computer to make a comparison between actual and specified values of a particular system so that it can pin-point any faults.

When set to an 'automatic mode' the computer guides the operator through the test program; this makes it a simple task to carry out a 'health-check' of the basic engine systems. Identification of the cause of a fault in a particular system can be made by a person having a higher skill level by using the computer in its 'manual mode'; in this setting the computer works to the instructions given by the operator.

Ignition patterns of the form associated with conventional CROs are not displayed; instead values, such as maximum ignition voltages, are shown as a bar chart (Figure 11.52).

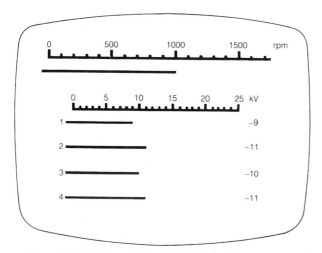

Fig. 11.52 Bar chart display

REMEMBER

Cathode ray oscilloscope (CRO):

- is a high speed voltmeter that shows voltage at a given instant
- displays traces to show primary and secondary voltages
- primary pattern shows:
  (a) condition of the coil primary, capacitor and contact breaker
  (b) dwell angle, overlap and variation
- secondary pattern shows:
  (a) condition of coil secondary, h.t. leads and sparking plugs
  (b) coil polarity
  (c) cylinder conditions, e.g. variation in cylinder compressions and air-fuel mixture strength

11.5 Electronic ignition

Since 1960, new requirements for ignition systems have been made that could not be met by the conventional inductive ignition system. The introduction of new exhaust emission criteria in 1965 and the demand for improved fuel economy in 1975, has forced designers to turn to electronics to provide a system to satisfy the statutory requirements for a vehicle. Legislative requirements and driver demand for better engine performance, added to the manufacturer's need to offer a more sophisticated vehicle to counter a competitor's product all show why electronic innovation in this field is taking place.

Drawbacks of a non-electronic system

The basic principle of a non-electronic inductive ignition system has remained unchanged for over sixty years, but it is unable to meet present and future needs as regards energy output and contact breaker performance.

Whereas an ignition output of 10–15 kV was sufficient in earlier days, the modern high-speed engine demands an output of 15–30 kV to ignite the weaker mixtures needed to give good economy and emission. To achieve this progression a low-inductive coil (see page 180) is often fitted, but because the current through this coil is much higher than a normal coil, the erosive wear of the contact breaker is unacceptable.

This reason alone suggests a need for an electronic replacement for the mechanical breaker, but other drawbacks of the breaker show why it should be superseded. These are:

- Ignition varies from specification as the speed is varied. This is due to (a) *wear* at the contact heel, cam and spindle and erosion of the contact faces; (b) *contact bounce* and the inability of the heel to follow the cam at high speed.
- Adverse effect on the *dwell time* for the coil current due to dwell angle variation.
- Frequent *servicing* is necessary.

Although many of these breaker drawbacks affect the energy output of the coil, the variation of the spark timing between service intervals has meant that engines fitted with mechanical breakers cannot meet current emission regulations in force in many parts of the world. When statutory requirements insist that exhaust emission levels must be maintained for 80 000 km (50 000 miles), manufacturers have turned away from the mechanical breaker to alternative systems which do not suffer the aforementioned drawbacks. Electronic systems fill this requirement.

SAFE PRACTICE

It must be appreciated that the voltage output from electronic ignition systems, *even from the l.t. circuit terminals and cables*, is far greater than that developed from a conventional system used in the past.

A shock received from any live ignition component can prove fatal, so use extra care when working on electronic ignition systems.

The following descriptions cover the basic principles of the main ignition systems used during the period from the start of the change-over to the present day.

Breaker-triggered systems

Transistor-assisted contacts (TAC)

This system uses a normal mechanical breaker to 'drive' a transistor which controls the current in the primary circuit. By using a very small breaker current, erosion of the contacts is eliminated and, as a result, the cleaner contact faces maintain good coil output; it also gives accurate spark timing for a much longer period. The use of a low inductive coil and ballast resistor with this system, allows the benefits of this type of coil to be obtained without suffering the ill-effects of excessive contact arcing produced by the high primary figure.

Figure 11.53 shows the basic principle of a breaker-triggered, inductive, semiconductor ignition system. In this system, a transistor performs the duty originally undertaken by the contact breaker, namely to act as a power switch to 'make and break' the primary circuit. The transistor (as described on page 54) in this circuit acts as a relay which is operated by the current supplied by a cam-operated control switch; hence the term 'breaker-triggered'.

When the contact breaker is closed, a small control current passes through the base–emitter of the transistor. This switches on the collector–emitter circuit of the transistor and allows full current to flow through the primary circuit to give energization of the coil. At this stage current flow in the control circuit and transistor base is governed by the total and relative values of the resistors R_1 and R_2. Values are chosen to give a control current of about 0.3 A, because this small current will not overload the breaker but is sufficient to give a self-cleaning action of the contact surfaces.

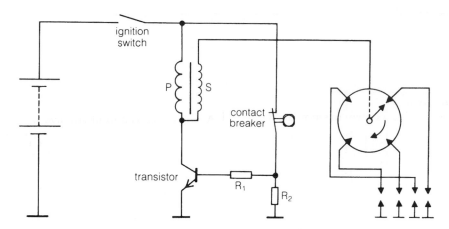

Fig. 11.53 TAC ignition system

At the instant the spark is required, the cam opens the contact breaker to interrupt the base circuit: this causes the transistor to switch off. As the primary circuit is suddenly broken, a high voltage is induced into the secondary to give a spark at the plug. This sequence is repeated to give the appropriate number of sparks per cam revolution (Figure 11.54).

Compared with a non-transistorized system, the TAC arrangement gives a quicker break of the circuit and, in consequence, a more rapid collapse of the magnetic flux. Since secondary output depends on the speed of collapse of the flux, a high h.t. voltage is obtained from the TAC system.

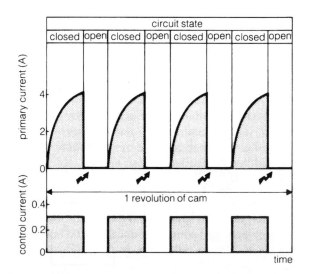

Fig. 11.54 Primary current control (4-cylinder engine)

With the exception of the extra control module containing the power transistor, the other units of this ignition system are similar to those used with a non-electronic system.

Although the basic circuit shown in Figure 11.53 illustrates the principle of a TAC system, extra refinements are needed to protect the semiconductors from overload due to self-induction and to minimize ratio interference. In addition it will be seen that the circuit shown is unsuitable for use with a conventional contact breaker that has a fixed-earth contact. To overcome this problem an additional transistor is used (Figure 11.55).

In this layout the transistor T_1 is fitted in series with the contact breaker in the control circuit and its duty is to act as a driver for the power transistor T_2. As in the previous systems, resistors are fitted to limit the base current in T_1 and T_2 as well as the contact breaker current.

When the contact breaker is closed a small current flows in the control circuit. Most of this current passes through R_1, but a very small proportion is passed through the base of T_1 which causes the transistor to switch on. This sensitive transistor then supplies a current to the base of the power transistor T_2 and causes this transistor to switch on. When this happens, the collector–emitter of T_2 conducts and completes the primary circuit to allow the build-up of magnetic flux in the coil.

At the time of the spark, the contact breaker is opened; this interrupts the current in the control circuit and base circuit of T_1. With T_1 switched off the current is cut off from the base of T_2, so this causes T_2 to switch off and break the primary circuit.

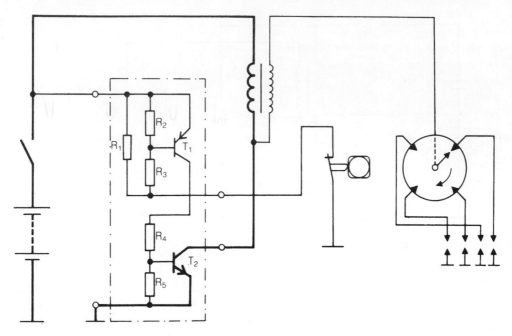

Fig. 11.55 TAC with driver and power transistors

The power transistor T_2 must be robust to handle the large current and high voltage due to self-induction. These conditions are particularly severe when a low-inductance coil is used, especially when the engine is being started. In this case a current of about 9 A built up in the primary circuit during normal operation can increase to about 16 A when cold-starting. As a conventional breaker can handle a maximum of only 5 A, the high currents associated with this type of coil can be switched effectively only by electronic means. Even so, this high load would reduce the reliability of a normal power transistor so a special dual-transistor called a *Darlington amplifier* is used (see page 56).

Breakerless systems

Replacing the mechanical contact breaker with an electronic switch gives the following advantages:

- Accurate spark timing achieved throughout the speed range.
- No contacts to erode and wear. This eliminates maintenance in respect of constant replacement, dwell adjustment and setting of the spark timing. Furthermore, the timing remains correct for a very long period.
- Build–up time for the ignition coil can be varied by altering the dwell period to suit the conditions. This gives a higher energy output from the coil at high

speed without the risk of h.t. erosion at low speed.
- No bouncing of contacts at high speed to rob the coil of its primary current.

Figure 11.56 shows the main layout of a breakerless, electronic ignition system. The distributor unit is similar to a non-electronic unit with the exception that the contact breaker is replaced by an electronic switch called a *pulse generator*. As the name suggests, this device generates an electrical pulse to signal when the spark is required. This action is similar to the trigger of a gun – when the trigger is operated the coil fires its h.t. charge.

The duty of the *solid-state control module* is to make-and-break electronically the primary current for the ignition coil. To do this, it must amplify and process the

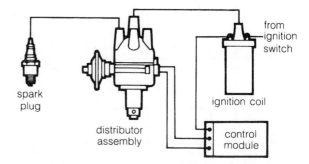

Fig. 11.56 Layout of breakerless electronic system

signals received from the pulse generator. In addition to the switching duty, the control module senses the engine speed from the pulse frequency and uses this information to vary the dwell time to suit the engine speed.

Pulse generator

The three main types of pulse generator are:

(1) Inductive
(2) Hall generator
(3) Optical.

Inductive type   Figure 11.57 shows one type of inductive pulse generator. The permanent magnet and inductive winding are fixed to the base plate and an iron trigger wheel is driven by the distributor shaft. The number of teeth formed on the trigger wheel or reluctor matches the number of engine cylinders. When a tooth is positioned close to the soft iron stator core, the magnetic path is completed and this gives a flux flow as shown in the diagram. When the trigger wheel is moved away from the position shown, the air gap between the stator core and the trigger tooth is increased. This larger gap increases the magnetic resistance or reluctance, so the flux in the magnetic circuit is decreased.

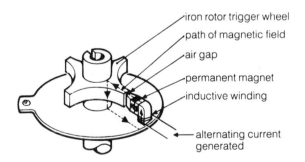

Fig. 11.57 Inductive pulse generator

Generation of an e.m.f. in the inductive winding fitted around the iron stator core occurs as a result of the *change* in the magnetic flux, so maximum voltage is induced when the rate of change in flux is greatest. This occurs just before, and just after, the point where the trigger tooth is closest to the stator core.

Figure 11.58 shows the variation in voltage as the trigger wheel is moved through one revolution. This shows that the build-up of flux gives a positive peak and the decay of flux gives a negative peak. In the trigger position of greatest flux, no e.m.f. is induced into the winding. It is this mid-point of change between

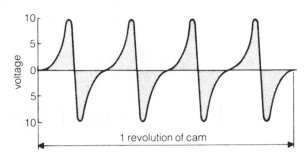

Fig. 11.58 Voltage output from pulse generator

the positive and negative pulses that is used to signal that the spark is required.

Rotational speed of the trigger wheel governs the rate of change of the flux, so the output of the pulse generator varies from about 0.5 V to 100 V. This voltage variation, combined with the frequency change, acts as sensing signals that can be used by the control module for purposes other than spark triggering.

The size of the air gap varies the reluctance of the magnetic circuit, so the output voltage depends on the size of the air gap. Due to the magnetic effect, the gap is checked with a non-magnetic feeler gauge, e.g. a plastic gauge.

A Bosch pulse generator operates on a similar principle but uses a different construction (Figure 11.59). This type uses a circular disc magnet with the two flat faces acting as the N and S poles. On the top face of the magnet is placed a soft iron circular pole piece; this has fingers bent upwards to form four stator poles in the case of a 4-cylinder engine. A similar number of teeth formed on the trigger wheel make a path for the flux to pass to the carrying plate that supports the magnet. The inductive coil is wound concentrically with the spindle and the complete assembly forms a symmetrical unit that is resistant to vibration and spindle wear.

Some manufacturers do not use a conventional distributor. Citroën uses a single metal slug called a target that is bolted on the periphery of the flywheel and a target sensor mounted on the clutch housing (Figure 11.60). The target sensor comprises an inductive winding arranged around a magnetic core and set so that the core is 1 mm ± 0.5 mm from the slug when No. 1 piston is just before t.d.c.

The voltage output is similar to other pulse generators with the exception that in this case the control module (computer) receives only one signal pulse per revolution.

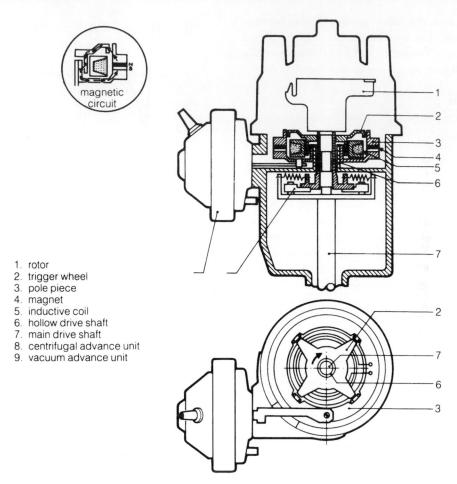

1. rotor
2. trigger wheel
3. pole piece
4. magnet
5. inductive coil
6. hollow drive shaft
7. main drive shaft
8. centrifugal advance unit
9. vacuum advance unit

Fig. 11.59 Pulse generator – Bosch

For control purposes, Citroën fit a second target sensor, of identical construction to the other sensor, adjacent to the starter ring teeth on the flywheel. This sensor signals the passage of each flywheel tooth so that the computer can count the teeth and determine the engine speed; this sets the ignition advance to suit the conditions.

Hall generator The operation of this type of pulse generator is based on the Hall effect as described on page 27.

When a chip of semiconductor material, carrying a signal current across it, is exposed to a magnetic field, a small voltage called the Hall voltage is generated between the chip edges at 90° to the path taken by the signal current.

Changing the magnetic field strength alters the Hall voltage, so this effect can be used as a switching device to vary the Hall current and trigger the ignition point.

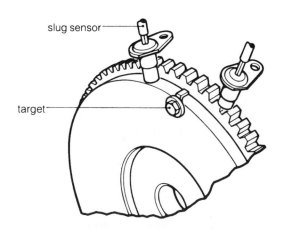

Fig. 11.60 Pulse generator – Citroën

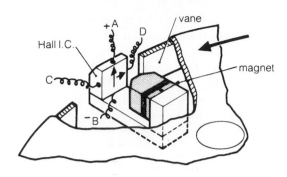

Fig. 11.61 Hall-effect pulse generator

The principle is shown in Figure 11.61 A semiconductor chip retained in a ceramic support, has four electrical connections; an input signal current is supplied to AB and an output Hall current is delivered from CD. Opposite to the chip, and separated by an air gap, a permanent magnet is situated.

Switching is performed by vanes on a trigger wheel which is driven by the distributor spindle. When the metal vane is clear of the air gap, the chip is exposed to the magnetic flux and the Hall voltage is applied to

CD: at this stage the switch is turned on and current flows in the CD circuit.

Moving the vane into the air gap between the magnet and the chip blocks and diverts the magnetic flux away from the chip: this causes the Hall voltage to drop to zero. When the vane is in this flux-blocking position, the switch is off; i.e. no Hall current flows in the CD circuit (other than slight leakage current).

The control module used with this system switches on the primary current for the ignition coil when the pulse generator's trigger vane is passing through the air gap. Therefore the dwell period is governed by the angular spacing of the vanes; the smaller the space between the vanes the greater is the time that the primary circuit is closed. This closed period is terminated and the spark is produced at the instant when the Hall switch is closed, i.e. **the spark occurs when the vane leaves the air gap**.

Figure 11.62 shows the layout of a Hall generator used in a Bosch distributor. The semiconductor chip in this model is incorporated in an integrated circuit which also performs the duties of pulse shaping, pulse amplification and voltage stabilization. The number of vanes on the trigger wheel equals the number of engine cylinders. In this design the trigger wheel and the rotor arms form one integral part.

A three-core cable connects the Hall generator with the control module; the leads are signal input, Hall output and earth.

Figure 11.63 shows the general shape of the wave produced when the chopper vane is rotated. In this case the 4-bladed chopper screens the Hall chip for 63° periods of vane movement, i.e. 70% of the 90° cycle. At a given point during this screening period, the control module will start to energize the ignition coil primary in preparation for the spark that occurs when the vane leaves the gap. A capacitor in the module alters this starting point to vary the dwell to suit the engine speed.

Optical pulse generator This system senses the spark point by using a shutter to interrupt a light beam

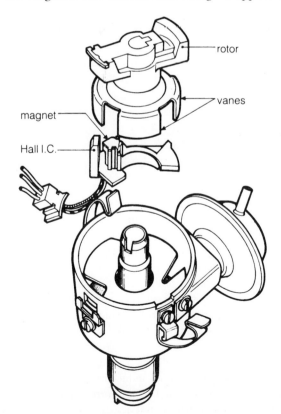

Fig. 11.62 Hall generator – Bosch

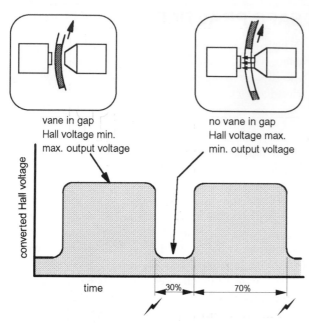

Fig. 11.63 Hall generator output

projected by a light-emitting diode (LED) on to a phototransistor (see pages 5 and 65).

Figure 11.64 shows the principle of this type of trigger. An invisible light, at a frequency close to infra-red, is emitted by a gallium arsenide semiconductor diode and its beam is focused by a hemispherical lens to a width at the chopping point of about 1.25 mm (0.05 in). A steel chopper, having blades to suit the number of cylinders and dwell period, is attached to the distributor spindle; this controls the time periods that the light falls on the silicon phototransistor detector. This transistor forms the first part of a Darlington amplifier which builds up the signal and includes a means of

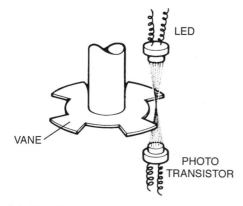

Fig. 11.64 Optical pulse generator

preventing timing change due to variation in line voltage or due to dirt accumulation on the lens.

The signal sent by the generator to the control module switches on the current for the coil primary so when the chopper cuts the beam the primary circuit is broken and a spark is produced at the plug.

This optoelectrical method of triggering was developed for the Lumenition system.

Control modules

The control module, or trigger box, is responsible for switching the current of the primary winding of the ignition coil in accordance with the signal received from the pulse generator.

Two control systems in use are:

(1) Inductive storage
(2) Capacity discharge

REMEMBER

Pulse generators:

- produce a signal to trigger the spark
- are used to sense the speed of rotation
- are either inductive, Hall generator or optical types
- of the inductive type have two leads including earth
- of the inductive type signal a spark when a tooth on the reluctor trigger wheel lines-up with its magnet
- of the Hall type have three leads including earth
- of the Hall type signal a spark when a vane leaves the Hall I.C. chip.

Inductive storage This system uses a primary circuit layout similar to the Kettering system except that a robust power transistor in the control module 'makes-and-breaks' the primary circuit instead of using a contact breaker.

A typical control module has four important semi-conductor stages which perform the duties of pulse shape, dwell period control, voltage stabilization and primary switching (Figure 11.65).

Pulse shaping The full line in Fig. 11.66 represents the output voltage from an inductive-type pulse generator when it is connected to a control module circuit. It should be noted that the full negative wave is achieved only when the generator is tested on open circuit.

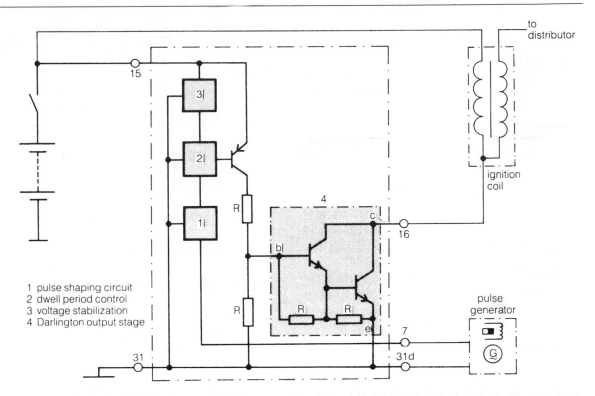

Fig. 11.65 Inductive storage control module

1 pulse shaping circuit
2 dwell period control
3 voltage stabilization
4 Darlington output stage

After feeding the a.c. signal to the trigger circuit stage, the pulse is shaped into a d.c. rectangular form as shown in Figure 11.66. The width of the rectangular pulse depends on the duration of the pulse output from the generator, but the height of the rectangle, or the current output from the trigger circuits, is independent of engine speed.

Dwell period control and voltage stablization This stage normally varies the dwell period by altering the start of the dwell period. Secondary output is reduced when the dwell period is decreased, so by means of this control feature, the period of time that current flows through the primary winding of the coil is altered to suit the engine speed.

The voltage supplied to this resistor–capacitor (RC) network must not vary, even though the supply voltage to the control module alters due to changes in charging output and consumer loads. This control duty is performed by a voltage stabilization section of the module.

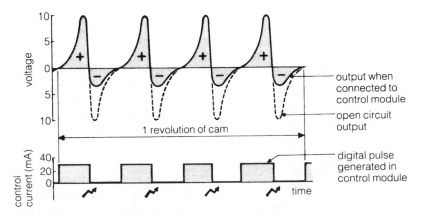

Fig. 11.66 Pulse shaping

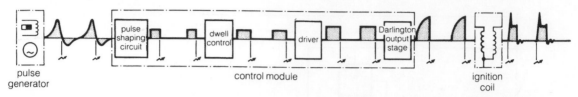

Fig. 11.67 Pulse processing

Primary switching Switch control of the primary circuit current is normally performed by a Darlington amplifier. Pulse signals received from the dwell period control stage are passed to a driver transistor which acts as a control current amplifier. At the appropriate times, current from the driver is switched on or off to control the heavy-duty power transistor of the Darlington output stage.

Pulse processing Figure 11.67 shows the sequence of events from the time that the original pulse generator's signal is received to the instant of the spark in the cylinder.

The secondary output patterns show the image given when a cathode ray oscilloscope (CRO) is connected to the output of an ignition coil forming part of an electronic ignition system. Vertical and horizontal axes of the CRO pattern represent voltage and time respectively. Figure 11.68 shows the main features of one secondary discharge.

At the instant the primary circuit is broken, the secondary voltage increases until the spark is initiated; when this occurs the voltage needed to sustain the spark

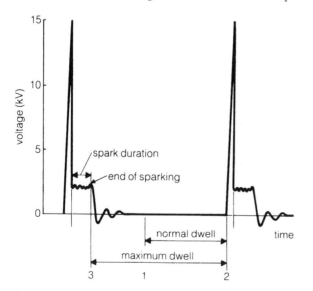

Fig. 11.68 Dwell in relation to secondary voltage

falls until a value is reached which is then maintained until the output energy is no longer sufficient to support the sparking process. At this point the secondary voltage rises slightly; it then falls and oscillates two or three times as the remaining energy is dissipated in the coil.

Secondary output control
Disregarding changes due to mechanical defects, a breaker-triggered system has a constant dwell over the whole speed range. This means that at high speed the dwell period is too short; as a result the secondary output is poor owing to the comparatively low primary current. Use of a low-inductance coil improves the output in the upper speed range, but this type of coil causes erosive wear at the lower end of the speed range. To overcome this problem a *constant energy* system is used. This system uses a high-output coil and is electronically controlled to vary the dwell period to suit all speeds. At low speed the percentage dwell is kept relatively small but it is lengthened progressively as the speed is increased.

Figure 11.68 shows that at low speed the dwell starts at (1) and ends at (2). As the engine speed is increased, the start of the dwell period (i.e. the point at which current starts to flow in the primary winding) is gradually moved towards the extreme limit (3). Any increase in dwell past point (3) reduces the spark duration because this point represents the end of the sparking discharge period.

Figure 11.69 shows the variation in percentage dwell with engine speed. At idling speed the percentage dwell is set large to provide a high-energy spark to limit exhaust gas emissions, but between idling and 4000 rev/min the increase in percentage dwell prevents a reduction in the stored energy. As a result, this gives a near-constant secondary available voltage up to the system's maximum; this is generally about 15 000 sparks/min.

When the system is used on 6- and 8-cylinder engines it is necessary to reduce the percentage dwell at speeds beyond 5000 rev/min. This is because the start of the dwell would otherwise occur before the end of the spark discharge period. To overcome this problem, the control system uses a transistor to switch on the

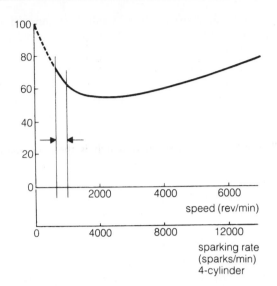

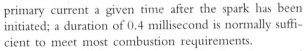

Fig. 11.69 Alteration in dwell to suit engine speed

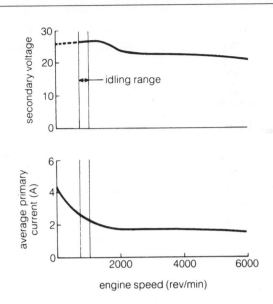

Fig. 11.70 Output from constant energy system

primary current a given time after the spark has been initiated; a duration of 0.4 millisecond is normally sufficient to meet most combustion requirements.

Constant-energy systems using dwell-angle control give an output as shown in Figure 11.70. (The use of the terms 'dwell angle', 'percentage dwell' and 'dwell period' should be noted. In many electronic systems the term 'dwell angle' is inappropriate).

Control module circuit

Having identified the functions performed by a control module, it is now possible to examine a typical circuit.

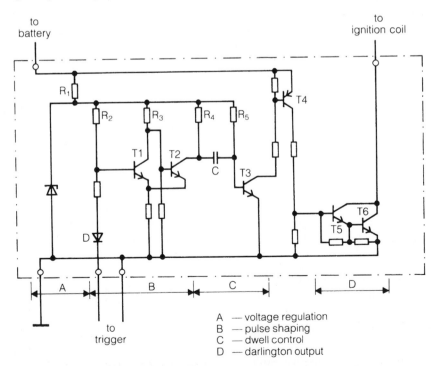

A — voltage regulation
B — pulse shaping
C — dwell control
D — darlington output

Fig. 11.71 Control module circuit (simplified)

Figure 11.71 shows a simplified circuit laid out in a manner to identify the four main sections, A, B, C and D.

A. Voltage regulation Voltage stabilization is performed by the Zener diode (ZD). This ensures that the voltage applied to control sections B and C is kept constant and is not affected by voltage variations that take place in other circuits of the vehicle.

Voltage drop across a diode is constant so this feature is utilized to provide the regulated voltage to drive the control circuit (see page 48).

B. Pulse shaping In the form shown, the two transistors, T_1 and T_2, produce an arrangement called a *Schmitt Trigger*. This is a common method for converting an analogue signal to a digital signal, i.e. an A/D converter for forming a rectangular pulse.

Transistor T_1 is switched on when the pulse generated by the external trigger is of a potential that opposes current flow from the battery to the trigger via the diode D. This causes current to flow through the base-emitter of T_1 which switches on the transistor and diverts current away from the base of T_2. The action of this Schmitt trigger causes T_2 to be 'off' when T_1 is 'on' and vice versa; the voltage at the time of switching is governed by the threshold voltage required to switch on T_1.

In this application the switching of T_1 occurs at a very low threshold voltage so, for practical purposes, the switching is considered to take place at a point when the trigger potential changes from positive to negative.

C. Dwell control Coil primary current flows when the P–N–P transistor T_4 is switched on. This is controlled by T_3 in a way that when T_3 is 'on', T_4 is also 'on'. The switching of T_3 is controlled by the current supplied via R_5 and the state-of-charge of the capacitor C. All the time the capacitor is being charged with current from R_5 no current passes to the base of T_3; during this stage, T_3 is switched off. Only when the capacitor is fully charged will current pass to the base of T_3 and switch it on to start the dwell period, i.e. to initiate current flow in the primary winding of the coil.

The time taken to charge the capacitor dictates the dwell period, so in this case the *R–C Time Constant* is determined by the amount that the capacitor is discharged prior to receiving its charge from R_5.

At low engine speeds, the transistor T_2 will be switched on for a comparatively long time, so this allows the capacitor plate adjacent to T_2 to pass to earth the charge it received from R_4 when T_2 was switched off. At this slow speed, there is sufficient time for the capacitor to fully discharge to a point where the plate potential becomes similar to earth; this causes the capacitor to attract a large charge from R_5 when the transistor T_2 switches 'off'. Since the time taken to provide this charge is long, the switch on point of T_3 will be delayed and a short dwell period will result.

At high speed, the duration that T_2 is switched on is short so this only allows partial discharge of the capacitor. As a result, the time taken to charge the capacitor is shorter and the dwell commences at an earlier point and gives a longer period.

Interruption of the coil primary takes place when T_2 is switched on. This is dictated by the trigger signal so the end of the dwell period always takes place at the same time. At the instant T_2 switches on, the capacitor starts to discharge; this causes T_3 to switch off to trigger the spark.

D. Darlington output A 'Darlington pair' is a common power transistor array used for switching large currents (see page 56). The pair consists of two robust transistors, T_5 and T_6, which are integrally constructed in a metal case having three terminals – base, emitter and collector.

When a forward-biased voltage is applied to the base–emitter circuit of T_5, the transistor is switched on.

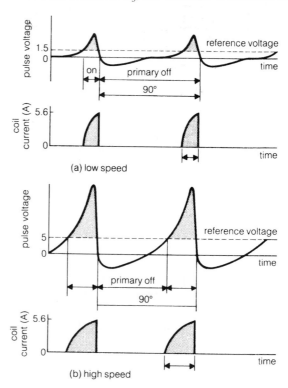

Fig. 11.72 Use of reference voltage to control dwell

This increases the voltage applied to the base of T_6 and when it exceeds the threshold value, this transistor also switches on. When T_5 and T_6 are switched on, the coil primary is energized, but when T_5 is switched off by the switching off of T_4, the primary circuit is broken and a spark is generated.

The switching of transistors is summarized as follows:

Trigger pulse	T_1	T_2	T_3	T_4	Primary	
+	on	off	on	on	on	
						← spark
−	off	on	off	off	off	

To make the system suitable for a vehicle, additional capacitors and diodes are fitted to the circuit shown in Figure 11.71. These extra items prevent damage to the semiconductors from high transient voltage and they also reduce radio interference.

Alternative method of dwell control
Another method of achieving dwell-angle control is to superimpose a reference voltage on to the output signal supplied by the pulse generator (Figure 11.72(a)).

In this system the triggering of the spark at the end of the dwell period occurs at the change-over point between the positive and negative waves, whereas the start of the dwell period is signalled when the pulse voltage exceeds the reference voltage.

At low speed a reference voltage of 1.5 V acts on the dwell-control stage and this rises to 5 V at high speed. Figure 11.72(b) shows that the stronger pulse signal, combined with the higher reference voltage, gives a longer dwell period.

No pulse signal is generated when the engine is stationary, so the dwell control cannot operate. This feature ensures that no current can flow through the coil when the engine is stalled.

Integral module
In this layout the control module is mounted on the side of the distributor assembly and connection is made by a four-pin multi-plug built into the distributor body. External l.t. cables from the distributor are limited to two leads; these connect with the coil and ignition

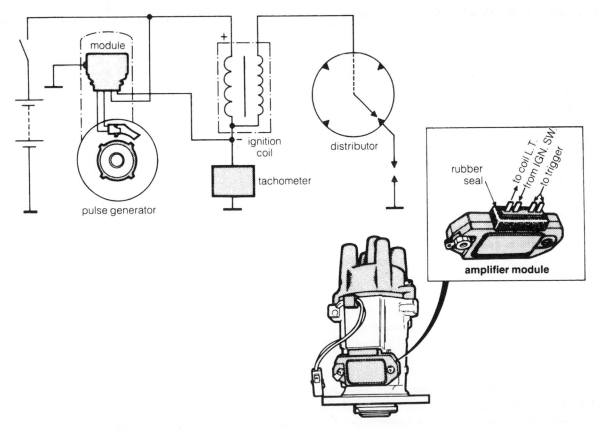

Fig. 11.73 Distributor with integral amplifier

switch (Figure 11.73). A tachometer, connected to the '–' side of the coil, uses the l.t. charge pulses of the coil to sense the engine speed.

When fitted initially, the distributor is accurately timed to the engine and, because it has a breakerless construction, no further check of the timing is necessary when the vehicle is being serviced. Because the 'dwell angle' is governed by the control module, no check or adjustment is necessary.

Honda electronic ignition

This system has an inductive-type pulse generator and a control module called an *igniter* (Figure 11.74).

In this system, the switching of the coil's primary current is performed by two transistors, a driver transistor T_1 and a power transistor T_2. The pulse generator has a *reluctor*, shaped in the form of a saw tooth, to produce the a.c. wave form.

When the ignition switch is closed with the engine stationary, a voltage is applied by R_2 to the base of T_1. This voltage is above the T_1 trigger voltage and, since the resistance of the pulse generator's winding is about 700 Ω, the transistor T_1 will be switched on. At this stage, T_1 conducts current 'A' to earth instead of passing the current to the base of T_2, so T_2 is switched off and the primary circuit is open.

Cranking the engine causes an e.m.f. to be generated by the movement of the reluctor. When the polarity of the generator's e.m.f. at the T_1 end of the winding is negative, the resistor R_2 supplies current which flows through the winding and diode D_1 to earth. At this stage, voltage applied to the base of T_1 is less than the trigger voltage, so T_1 is switched off. Current A from R_3 is now diverted from T_1 to the base of T_2, so T_2 is switched-on and current passes through the primary winding of the ignition coil.

When the e.m.f. from the pulse generator is reversed, the combined effect of the voltage from R_2 and the e.m.f. from the pulse generator triggers T_1. This causes T_1 to switch on, T_2 to switch off to interrupt the primary current and give a spark at the plug.

Zener diodes ZD_1 and ZD_2, fitted at each end of the primary winding, conduct to earth the high-voltage oscillatory currents caused by self-induction. These diodes protect both transistors from high-voltage charges.

Constant energy system

Although many of the systems previously described offered some degree of spark energy control, the limits are too wide for modern low-inductance coils. The quick build-up of primary current, achieved by using a primary winding with a very low resistance (less than 1 Ω), makes the low inductance coil attractive for an electronic system. One drawback of this coil is the high current flow at low engine speeds; this damages the system unless a current-limiter is used.

A modern circuit provides *current regulation* and uses a *dwell-angle closed-loop control system* to minimize the variation in output energy.

Closed loop control is a term used to describe a *voltage feedback* arrangement in which an output is controlled by using a monitoring signal from the output to regulate the input (see page 61). This is similar to a system managed by a human being; e.g. when a constant engine power output is required, the driver has to sense any changes in power and then alter the throttle setting to compensate for the change. In this case of an ignition system, a constant primary current is needed, so when an increase in this current (output) is detected, the input voltage is lowered and vice versa.

Figure 11.75 shows how the primary current is regulated by a voltage feedback system. Primary circuit switching and current flow is controlled by a Darlington pair and the voltage drop across a current sensing resistor provides the feedback signal. The resistor is in series with the primary winding of the ignition coil, so the feedback voltage (as shown by the voltmeter) is proportional to the current. When the current exceeds its rated value, the high feedback voltage signals the system to reduce the input voltage to the Darlington pair; this decreases the collector–emitter current which drops the feedback voltage and causes the loop sensing cycle to start again.

Figure 11.76 (page 210) shows how feedback is used to give closed-loop control for Hall-effect and inductive pulse generators.

Current regulation is achieved by comparing the feedback voltage with a standard reference voltage. When the two voltages are not equal, a signal is passed to the driver of the Darlington pair; this directs it to alter the input.

The closed-loop dwell-angle control system uses the same feedback voltage, but in this case it directs the signal to the dwell control stage. By comparing the sensed voltage with the frequency of the pulse generator (engine speed), the dwell controller can find out whether the coil current is too high or too low. It then makes the necessary dwell-angle alteration to make the primary current correct for the engine speed.

The continuous monitoring of current and dwell gives a closed-loop control system that maintains the output within the design limits.

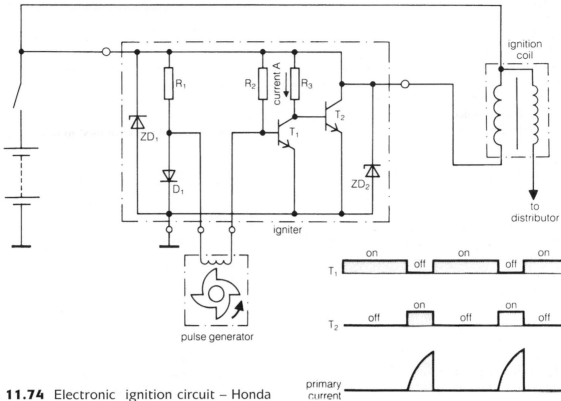

Fig. 11.74 Electronic ignition circuit – Honda

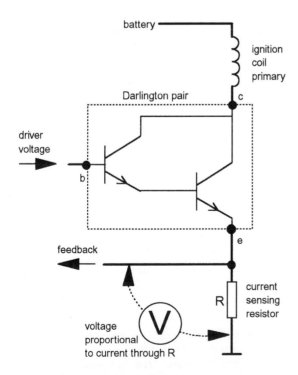

Fig. 11.75 Voltage feedback control

Dwell-angle control senses engine speed, so this characteristic can be used to interrupt the supply to the ignition coil when the engine is stationary.

Digital electronic ignition
A description of this and other systems is covered on page 255.

Capacity discharge (CD)
The module of this system stores electrical energy of high voltage in a capacitor until the trigger releases the charge to the primary winding of a coil. In this system the coil is a *pulse transformer* instead of being an energy-storage device as is normal (Figure 11.77).

To obtain a voltage of about 400 V for the capacitor, the battery current is first delivered to an *inverter* (to change d.c. to a.c.) and then it is passed to a *transformer* to raise the voltage. When the spark is required, the trigger releases the energy to the coil primary winding by 'firing' a *thyristor* (a type of transistor switch which, once triggered, continues to pass current through the

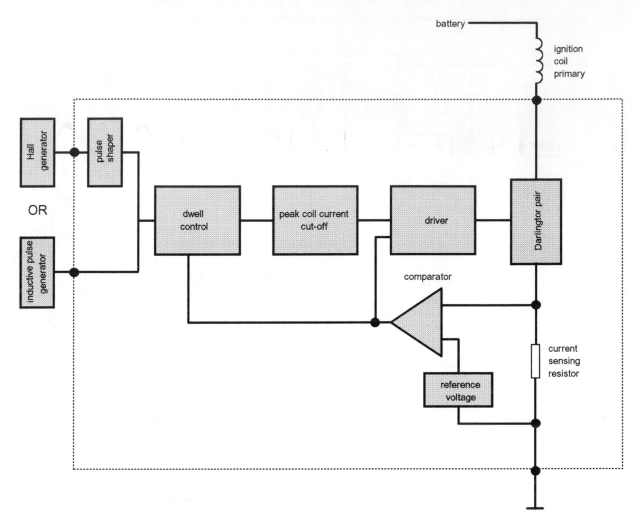

Fig. 11.76 Layout of constant energy system

switch even after the trigger current has ceased). Sudden discharge of the high-voltage energy to the primary winding causes a rapid build-up in the magnetic flux of the coil and induces a voltage in excess of 40 kV in the secondary circuit to give a high-intensity, short-duration spark.

Although the CD system is particularly suited to high-performance engines, a spark duration of about 0.1 ms given by this system is normally too short to ignite reliably the weaker petrol–air mixtures used with many modern engines.

Advantages of a CD system are:

- High secondary voltage reserve.
- Input current and output available voltage are constant over a wide speed range.

- Fast build-up of output voltage. Since the speed of build-up is about ten times faster than the inductive type of electronic ignition, the CD system reduces the risk of the h.t. current shorting to earth via a fouled plug insulator or taking some path other than the plug electrodes.

To offset the problem of the short spark duration, advantage is sometimes taken of the high secondary output by increasing the sparking plug gap to give a larger spark.

Although the system can be triggered by a mechanical breaker, the advantages of a pulse generator, using either inductive or Hall effect, makes this type more attractive. The a.c. signal from the generator is applied to a pulse-shaping control circuit which converts the

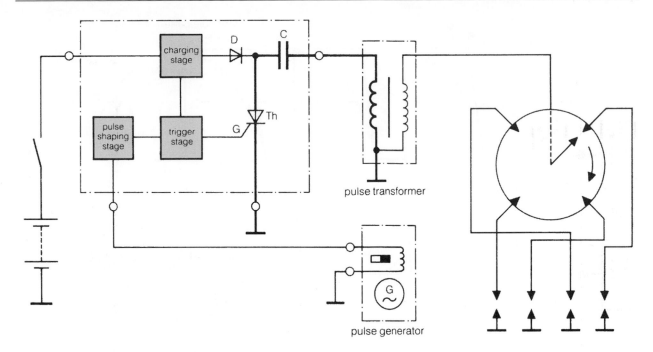

Fig. 11.77 Capacity discharge electronic ignition layout

signal into a rectified rectangular pulse and then changes it to a triangular trigger pulse to 'fire' the thyristor when the spark is required (see page 63).

Charging of the 1 μF capacitor by the charging stage to a voltage of about 400 V is performed by a voltage transformer which gives either a single- or multi-pulse output. In both cases a diode is fitted between the charging stage and the capacitor to prevent the current flowing back from the capacitor.

Single-pulse charging of the capacitor is preferred because it enables the build-up to maximum voltage to be achieved in about 0.3 ms, whereas the oscillatory charge given by the multipulse is much slower (Figure 11.78). This short charge-up time overcomes the need for 'dwell-angle' control because the charge time of a CD system is independent of engine speed. Since the primary winding of the ignition transformer (coil) always receives a similar energy discharge from the capacitor, the secondary available voltage is constant throughout the speed range (Figure 11.79).

Although the external appearance of an ignition transformer of a CD system is similar to a normal ignition coil, the internal construction is quite different. Besides being more robust to withstand higher electrical and thermal stresses, the inductance of the primary winding is only about 10% of that of a normal coil.

Since its impedence is only about 50 kΩ, the CD coil will readily accept the energy discharged from the capacitor. In view of this, the rise in secondary voltage is ten times faster. It is this feature that reduces the risk of misfiring due to the presence of h.t. shunts, i.e. leakage paths such as a fouled sparking plug, which has a resistance of 0.2–1.0 MΩ.

As the ignition transformer and capacitor form an electrically tuned circuit, it is necessary to fit the recommended type of transformer when replacement is required. Although a standard coil used in place of an ignition transformer will operate without damaging the system, many of the advantages of a CD system are lost. Conversely, if an ignition transformer is used with a non-CD system, damage to control module and transformer will occur immediately the 'system' is used.

The CD principle is also used in some small engines as fitted to motor cycles, lawn mowers, etc. A battery is not used in these cases, so the energy needed by the CD system is generated by a magneto.

11.6 Maintenance of electronic systems

In some systems (e.g. CD systems) a high-voltage charge is still stored when the ignition is switched off.

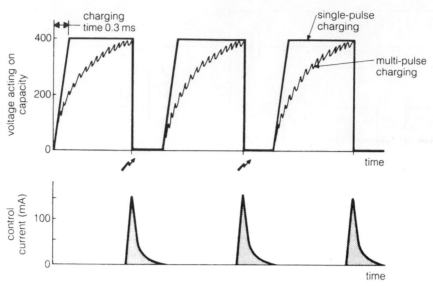

Fig. 11.78 Capacitor charging

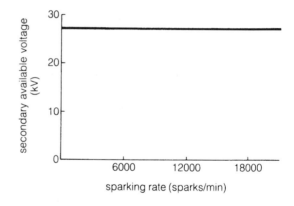

Fig. 11.79 Secondary output from CD system

REMEMBER

Electronic control modules:

- are also called amplifiers and ignitors
- are made as *inductive storage* or *capacity discharge* types
- have four main stages:
  (a) pulse shaping
  (b) dwell control
  (c) voltage stabilization
  (d) Darlington pair output
- use a *Schmitt trigger* to shape pulse
- set the dwell period by using a *resistor–capacitor* arrangement
- use a *Zener diode* for voltage stablization
- switch the primary current of the coil with a *Darlington pair*
- are called *constant energy* when the dwell period is varied to give uniform h.t. energy to sparking plug irrespective of speed.
- use a *closed-loop* feedback system to give a precise, constant output energy
- of the capacity discharge (CD) type use a *pulse transformer* to give a voltage output in excess of 40 kV
- of the CD type use a *thyristor* to trigger the spark

Many different systems are in use, so the manufacturer's service manual should be consulted for the specific service and test information, and safety precautions.

General maintenance

Very little routine maintenance is necessary because checks on dwell angle and spark timing are not required. Also sparking plug service intervals are extended with these systems. When the distributor is timed initially by the manufacturer, a mark is stamped on the flange to indicate its correct position.

SAFE PRACTICE

Extra care must be exercised when checking and testing breakerless systems to avoid receiving a fatal electric shock

GOOD PRACTICE

Damage will occur to the control module if the engine is cranked and the king lead is set so that the gap it too large for the spark to jump to earth

When a mechanical advance system is used, lubrication should be provided at the appropriate time. During this service operation, a timing light may be used to check the operation of the mechanism.

Ignition circuit testing

If an engine fails to start, the following basic checks are made to most systems before conducting detailed tests on the control module and pulse generator.

(1) *Visual check.* Check all cables and connectors for security and ensure that the battery is in good condition.
(2) *Coil output.* Remove king lead from distributor cap, fit extension and hold with insulated pliers so that the end of the extension is about 6 mm from the engine block.

Switch on ignition and crank the engine. A good spark indicates that the fault is beyond the coil h.t. lead: in this case proceed as with a non-electronic system.

If a coil output test shows that the system is defective, the full circuit should be checked. There are many types of breakerless system, so the makers' instructions should be consulted where possible. The following description is included to show the general principles.

Inductive storage with inductive pulse generator

Test 1: Amplifier static test   With the ignition switched on and the engine stationary, voltage readings are taken at points A, B, C and D as shown in Figure 11.80.

Test 2: Amplifier switching test   The engine is cranked and the voltage between battery '+' and coil '−' is measured (Figure 11.81).The voltage should increase when the engine is cranked.

Test 3: Pulse generator coil resistance (pick-up resistance)
The pick-up leads from the pulse generator are disconnected at the harness connector and the resistance of the pick-up coil is measured with an ohmmeter. The

resistance value depends on the application (a typical value is $2\text{–}5\ \text{k}\Omega$). If the reading is incorrect, the pick-up is assumed to be faulty, but if the resistance is between the limits, the control module should be changed.

It will be necessary to remove an integral type of control module from the distributor to carry out this test.

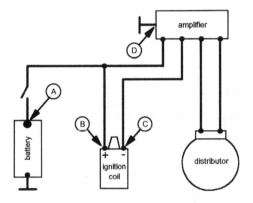

Static test		
Correct reading	A	more than 11.5 V
	B	less than 1 V below A
	C	less than 1 V below A
	D	less than 0.1 V
Battery discharged	A	less than 11.5 V
	B	correct
	C	correct
	D	correct
Defective switch and/or wiring	A	correct
	B	more than 1 V below A
	C	more than 1 V below A
	D	correct
Defective coil or amplifier	A	correct
	B	correct
	C	more than 1 V below A
	D	correct
Poor amplifier earth	A	correct
	B	correct
	C	correct
	D	more than 0.1 V

Fig. 11.80 Test 1

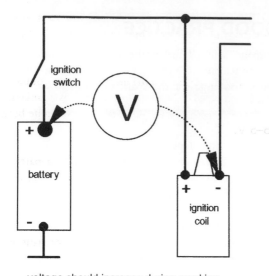

voltage should increase during cranking

Fig. 11.81 Test 2

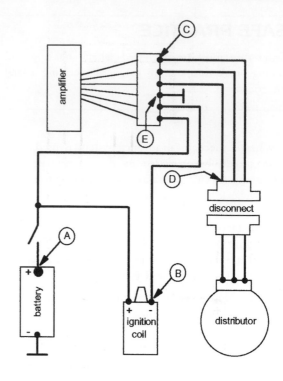

Test 4: Pulse generator gap If the reluctor pick-up has been disturbed for any reason, the reluctor gap should be checked. The gap depends on the engine type, but a typical gap is 0.2–0.4 mm (0.008–0.016 in). A plastic feeler gauge blade is used for this test (Figure 11.82).

Test 5: Other components The remaining parts of the system are checked in a manner similar to that used for a non-electronic system.

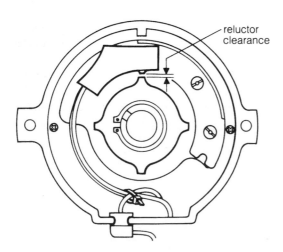

Fig. 11.82 Pulse generator gap

Static test		Hall generator
Correct reading	A	more than 11.5 V
	B	less than 2 V
	C	less than 1 V below A
	D	less than 2.5 V below A
	E	less than 0.1 V
Battery discharged	A	less than 11.5 V
	B	correct
	C	correct
	D	correct
	E	correct
Defective amplifier	A	correct
	B	more than 2 V
	C	more than 1 V below A or correct
	D	more than 2.5 V below A or correct
	E	correct
Defective switch and/or wiring	A	correct
	B	correct
	C	more than 1 V below A
	D	more than 2.5 V below A or correct
	E	correct
Defective amplifier	A	correct
	B	correct
	C	correct
	D	more than 2.5 V below A
	E	correct
Poor amplifier earth	A	correct
	B	correct
	C	correct
	D	correct
	E	more than 0.1 V

Fig. 11.83 Test 1

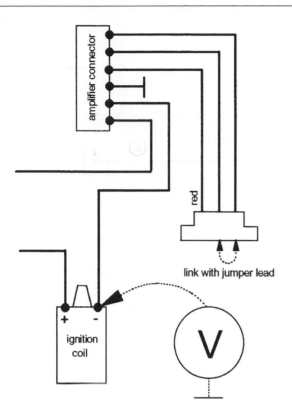

link with jumper lead

voltage should be more than 1V below
battery voltage

Fig. 11.84 Test 2

Hall-effect pulse generator

Test 1: Amplifier static test With the ignition switched
on, the engine stationary and the Hall generator plug
disconnected, voltage readings are taken at points A, B,
C, D and E as shown in Figure 11.83.

Test 2: Amplifier static test The Hall generator plug
is lined as shown in Figure 11.84 and the voltage is
checked at the '−' terminal of the coil. If the voltage
is more than 1 V below battery voltage, check the coil
and if this is serviceable replace the amplifier.

Test 3: Rotor vane earthing An ohmmeter is connected
between the chopper vane and earth. The resistance
should be less than 50 Ω

Test 4: Amplifier switching test A voltmeter is
connected to coil '−' and the engine is cranked. The
voltage should fluctuate and show a mean value between
2.5–5 V.

Test 5: Other components The remaining parts of the
system are checked in a manner similar to that used for
a non-electronic system.

Constant energy system

An example of the tests made on a constant energy
system are shown in Figure 11.85.

Engine management systems

See page 271 for tests on ignition units that are
controlled by an engine management system.

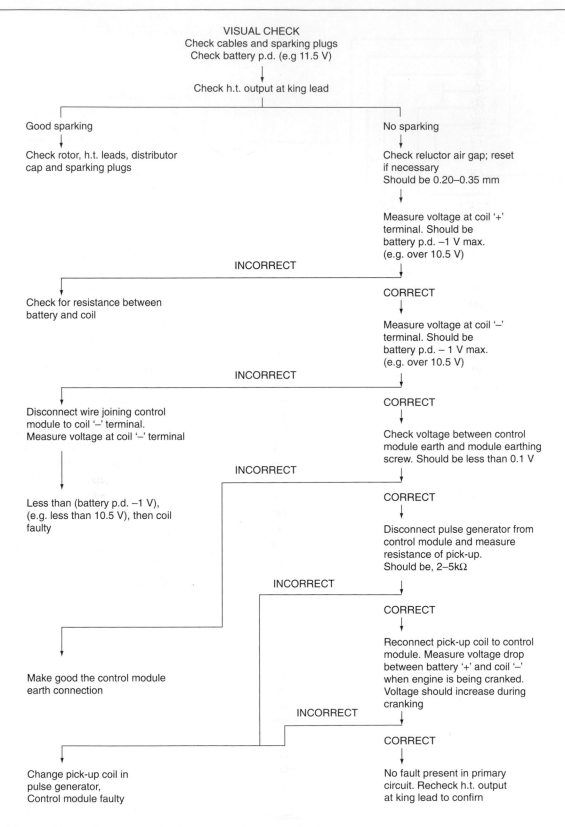

Fig. 11.85 Fault diagnosis chart: constant-energy ignition

PROGRESS CHECK 11

1. What is the difference between *pre-ignition* and *combustion knock?*

2. State THREE effects on an engine of severe combustion knock.

3. State FIVE adverse effects of incorrect ignition timing.

4. What voltage is required to produce a spark in an engine when it is operated under (a) light load; (b) full load?

5. The dwell angle is set too large on a Kettering-type system. State the effect of this on (a) primary current; (b) maximum available secondary voltage.

6. A capacitor fitted to a Kettering-type system has a lower capacitance than recommended. State how this will affect (a) collapse of magnetic flux; (b) contact breaker life.

7. For utmost power the maximum cylinder pressure should occur at 12° after t.d.c. State THREE factors that govern the angle of spark advance.

8. Which one of the undesirable exhaust gases is reduced when the angle of spark advance is decreased?

9. State the purpose of a cold-start ballast resistor.

10. Low-inductance ignition coils are fitted on modern engines. Describe how these coils improve engine performance.

11. State THREE plug features that control the operating temperature of a sparking plug.

12. The sparking plug gap is set to 1.0 mm instead of 0.6 mm as recommended. State the effect of this on a non-electronic system.

13. A voltage test is being carried out on a non-electronic ignition system to locate a high resistance. State why the contact breaker must be closed during this test.

14. State one merit of a CRO for ignition fault diagnosis.

Questions 15 to 30 relate to electronic ignition systems

15. State the features of an electronic system that improve: (a) reliability; (b) exhaust emission; (c) engine power output.

16. Name TWO types of (a) pulse generator; (b) control module.

17. Which type of pulse generator gives an output that rises with engine speed?

18. One pulse generator gives a rectangular wave output. Show, by means of a diagram, the output and indicate the point at which the spark occurs.

19. One type of pulse generator is connected to the control module by three leads. Name the type.

20. Name the FOUR main stages in a control module.

21. What method is used in a control module to (a) shape the pulse; (b) switch the primary current?

22. State why the dwell period does not remain constant over the speed range.

23. What method is used in a module to control the dwell period?

24. What is meant by the term *constant energy* as applied to an ignition control module?

25. What is a closed-loop system?

26. State how voltage feedback is used to control primary current.

27. How is the h.t. voltage obtained in a CD system?

28. Why is it necessary to take extra safety precautions when working on a CD system?

29. During an ignition test the king lead is held close to a good earth. State the effect on the system if the gap is (a) 1 mm; (b) 20 mm.

30. An amplifier static test is being carried out. Name the system which requires the operator to disconnect the pulse generator from the amplifier in order to carry out the test.

12

Engine fuelling

What is covered in this chapter

→ metering requirements
→ electronic carburettor
→ types of petrol injection
→ pressure-sensed PI systems
→ direct air-flow systems
→ single-point injection
→ maintenance of PI systems
→ diesel fuel pump control

Over the past few years, a general tightening of emission limits together with the need for an engine to keep within these limits, without adjustment, for a set period of time, has forced manufacturers to adopt more precise systems of fuel management. Over the years gradual changes, achieved at comparatively low cost to the engine and carburettor, were needed to keep in step with the exhaust emission regulations in force at that time. By the early 1990's the very strict emission limits laid down by the European Union (EU) made it necessary to adopt a more sensitive fuel system – a requirement satisfied by using electronic devices to sense the operating conditions and control the fuel accordingly. Initially this system of control was used on a carburettor, but today most vehicles have some form of positive fuel injection system that is called *petrol injection*, or *jetronic* if it is of German origin. Even with these sophisticated arrangements, the exhaust emission is still considered by the legislators to be dirty, so current regulations require a *catalytic converter* to be fitted in the exhaust system.

12.1 Metering requirements

Air/fuel mixture control

Under ideal conditions the air/fuel ratio is 15:1 (by weight). This proportion is called the *chemically correct ratio* because when this air/fuel mixture is ignited, it burns completely to form carbon dioxide (CO_2) and water (H_2O).

When a richer mixture such as 12:1 is supplied to an engine, the fuel consumption is increased. Also undesirable products such as carbon monoxide (CO), nitrogen oxides (NO_x) and unburnt fuel (HC) are exhausted from the engine.

Less pollution of the atmosphere occurs when the engine is operated on a weaker mixture, e.g. 17:1. Although slightly weaker mixtures also give the best economy, the power output is not so good. In addition, a weak or lean mixture is more difficult to ignite, is prone to detonate (i.e. cause combustion knock), and since it burns slower, is more likely to overheat the engine.

With the many problems associated with weak mixtures, the need for its use might well be questioned. However, the overriding reason for its use is the need for the engine to conform to the stringent statutory regulations that exist in many parts of the world in respect of exhaust pollution and fuel economy.

All spark-ignition engines must be supplied with an air/fuel mixture that is correctly calibrated and thoroughly mixed. This must be accurately controlled to give good economy, high power and an exhaust pollution level that is within the legal requirements for the country in which the vehicle is to operate.

REMEMBER

An air/petrol mixture supplied to an engine cylinder is:

- normally in the proportion of 15 parts of air to 1 part of petrol
- burnt to give the minimum amount of CO, NO_x and HC in the exhaust
- thoroughly mixed to give complete combustion

218

12.2 Electronic carburettor

Electronic actuation is used to control various carburettor functions; these include:

Cold-starting mixture. Automatic 'choke' control
Speed control. Slow-running speed adjustment to allow for temperature variation of the engine and ambient (outside) conditions.
Fuel cut-off. Improves economy and emissions by cutting off the fuel both on overrun and when the engine is switched off. Without this cut-off many lean-burn engines would continue to run due to 'dieseling'.
Mixture control. Varies the air fuel ratio to suit the conditions.

SU carburettor

The electronically controlled SU carburettor used by the Rover Group and shown in Figure 12.1 satisfied emission standards up to the early 1990's. This carburettor used electronics to control:

● slow running speed when the engine is warm;
● fuel cut-off when the vehicle is 'coasted';
● anti run-on when the ignition is switched-off;

● mixture regulation over the full speed range;
● cold-start mixture.

In the past, cold-start systems that used mechanically-operated automatic chokes often lacked sensitivity due to the limitations of the sensor system. This resulted in unreliable operation, high emissions and poor fuel consumption, especially when the vehicle was used on short journeys.

To overcome this problem, many electronic carburettors used an auxiliary starting carburettor controlled from an ECU. This unit used data supplied from ambient and engine coolant temperature sensors to actuate, often by means of a stepper motor, the mixture and slow running systems.

Fixed-choke carburettors Stringent emission regulations in Germany and the United States caused some vehicle manufacturers in these countries to use electronically controlled fixed-choke carburettors before moving on to full PI systems. In the UK a comparatively cheap PI system was used during this period rather than the electronically controlled fixed-choke carburettor.

In most electronic carburettors, the basic layout resembles a simple carburettor with the final adjustment

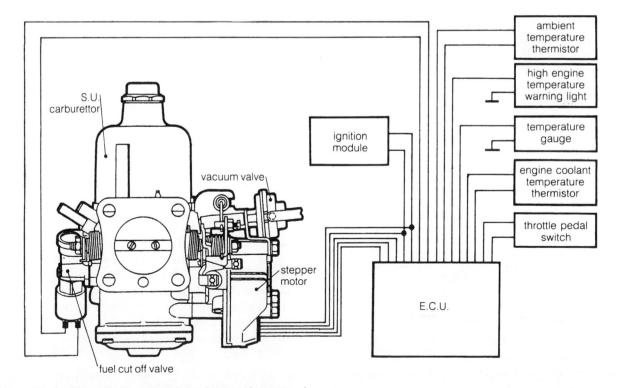

Fig. 12.1 SU carburettor with electronic control

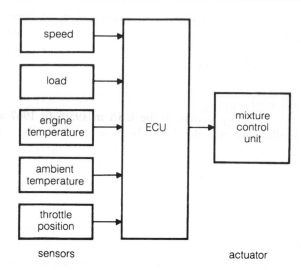

Fig. 12.2 Mixture control system

of the air/fuel ratio dictated by an ECU. The output from the ECU controls a separate metering system; this supplements the fuel provided by the basic system and gives an air/fuel ratio to suit the conditions as sensed by the various transducers. The main sensing system signals the engine speed and load. In addition, electronic carburettors have extra transducers to sense other important variables that affect the air/fuel ratio requirements (Figure 12.2).

Generally the ECU is a computer which is preprogrammed with the mixture requirements for a particular engine. Engine tests during development of the engine determine the air/fuel ratio needed to suit the various operating conditions; this data is then entered and locked into its memory. When the engine is in

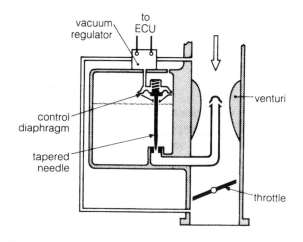

Fig. 12.3 Electronic carburettor – tapered needle control

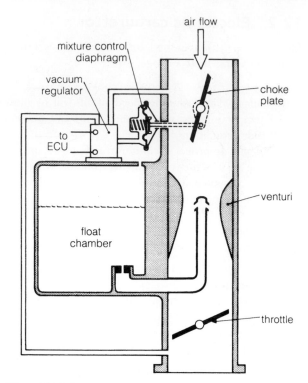

Fig. 12.4 Electronic carburettor – choke plate control

normal operation, the computer relates the input information to its stored data; it then gives the carburettor an output signal which instructs the metering system to provide a given air/fuel ratio.

Digital or analogue output signals are converted by a vacuum regulator or stepper motor respectively to physically control the rate of flow of fuel. Various arrangements are used; one system in the use controls the flow by a *tapered needle* (Figure 12.3). Another system uses the *choke plate* to vary the depression in the venturi (Figure 12.4).

12.3 Types of petrol injection

Electronic control of a fuel injection system provides precise metering of the air/fuel mixture to suit the wide range of conditions under which an engine operates. The sensitivity of an electronic control system gives high engine power and good economy while maintaining a pollution-free exhaust.

Petrol injection systems can be divided into two main groups:

- *Multipoint injection*: separate injectors for each cylinder.

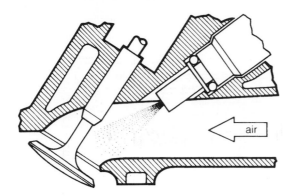

Fig. 12.5 Downstream injection

- *Throttle body injection*: one injector only that discharges fuel into the air stream at the point used by a carburettor.

Multipoint injection systems

Multipoint systems have one injector per cylinder situated to give a fuel spray into the air stream at a point just before it enters the cylinder. Injection of fuel at this point ensures that each cylinder receives its full share of fuel, so equal power output from the cylinders is achieved.

Overlap of induction strokes of adjacent cylinders supplied by a carburettor causes some cylinders to rob other cylinders of their full charge. This induction robbery drawback is minimized by a multipoint fuel-injection system so an improved all-round engine performance is obtained. Unfortunately, the multipoint system is more expensive than a system which uses either a carburettor or throttle body injection.

Injection of the petrol takes place in the induction manifold. Normally the fuel spray is directed towards the inlet valve as shown in Figure 12.5. This *downstream injection* spray is produced by a pressure of about 2 bar (30 lbf/in²) which is either 'timed' or 'continuous'. The former method gives an intermittent spray from injectors which open at least once every cycle whereas the continuous method delivers a constant stream of fuel at a rate proportional to the quantity of air that is entering the engine.

Multipoint systems are controlled by either mechanical or electronic means. The former uses a mechanical system to measure the air and fuel, whereas the latter measures, meters and injects the fuel by electronic means.

Most modern mechanical systems need some form of electronic control to make the system sensitive to changes in temperature and pressure, so this need, together with electrical operation of the pump, makes the system very different from early types that were completely mechanical.

Electronic systems The first fully-electronic system was introduced by Bendix in the USA in 1950. In 1967 a similar unit was developed by Bosch and fitted to a Volkswagen car. Since that time, electronic injection has become the common system for many luxury and sport-type cars. With the greater emphasis placed on cleaner exhaust products, the electronic system is now used in the popular car market.

A number of different types of fully-electronic system is in use. The main difference between them is the way in which the air flow is measured; the two main systems are:

- indirect or pressure-sensed airflow
- direct air-flow measurement.

12.4 Pressure-sensed PI systems

This system uses a manifold absolute pressure (MAP) sensor to measure the manifold depression. Signals from the MAP sensor are passed to the ECU and, after taking into account the data received from other sensors, the ECU signals the injector to open for a set time; this is proportional to the quantity of air that the engine is receiving.

System elements

Figure 12.6 shows a simplified layout of a pressure-sensed system: this is included to show the basic principles of this type of control. The layout shown is similar to an early system used by Bosch, which they called D-Jetronic (the D stood for *druck*; the German word for pressure).

In this layout the quantity of air induced into the engine depends on the manifold pressure and the throttle opening. These two variables are measured by a MAP sensor and a throttle position switch respectively.

The electrical control system performs two duties: it signals the start of injection and determines how long the injector is to stay open. The latter controls the quantity of fuel to be mixed with the air charge, so the duration increases as engine speed, or load, is increased.

Commencement of injection is triggered by either a switch in the ignition distributor or a sensor situated

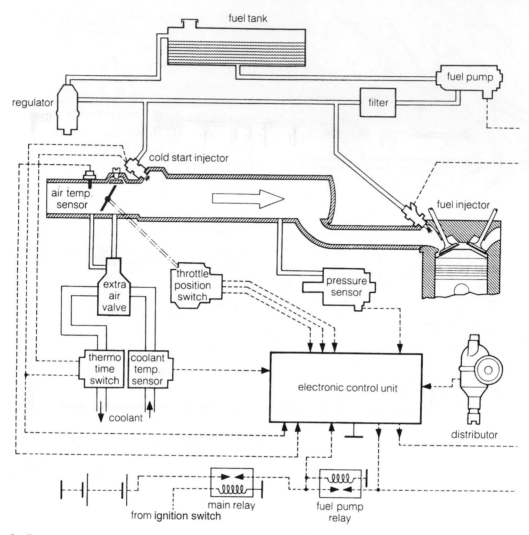

Fig. 12.6 Pressure-sensed electronic system for fuel injection

adjacent to the flywheel. For 6-cylinder engines, the injectors are operated in sets of three, i.e. three injectors spray at the same time.

An example of a modern pressure-sensed system is shown on page 267.

12.5 Direct air-flow systems

Systems using this principle normally use solenoid-operated injector valves; these have a variable opening time to suit engine speed and load conditions.

Bosch L-Jetronic

This was one of the first designs to use electronic sensing of the airflow. In this case the 'L' stands for *Luft* which is the German word for 'air'.

Measurement of air flow is obtained by using a:

- vane or flap
- hot wire.

The principles of these two sensors are described on page 98.

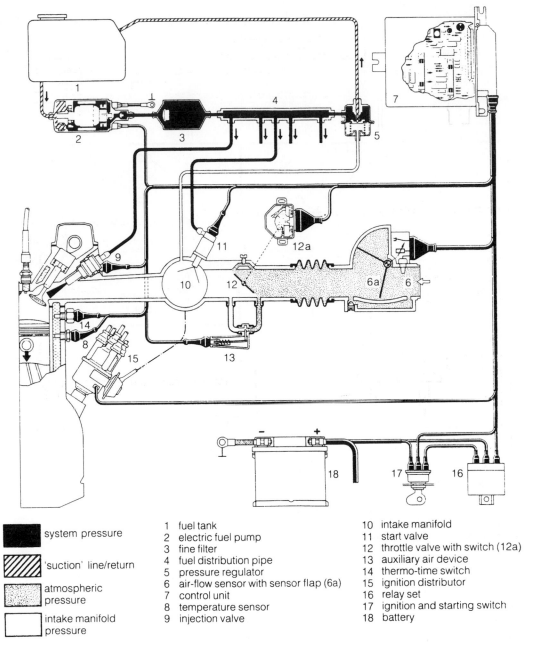

■ system pressure	1 fuel tank	10 intake manifold
	2 electric fuel pump	11 start valve
▨ 'suction' line/return	3 fine filter	12 throttle valve with switch (12a)
	4 fuel distribution pipe	13 auxiliary air device
▨ atmospheric pressure	5 pressure regulator	14 thermo-time switch
	6 air-flow sensor with sensor flap (6a)	15 ignition distributor
□ intake manifold pressure	7 control unit	16 relay set
	8 temperature sensor	17 ignition and starting switch
	9 injection valve	18 battery

Fig. 12.7 Vane or flap metering (*Bosch LE-Jetronic*)

Vane or flap metering Figure 12.7 shows the layout of a system similar to a Bosch L-Jetronic. Fuel pressure, produced by an electrically-driven fuel pump, is maintained constant at 2 bar by a pressure regulator.

Injector valves, connected in parallel and positioned close to the engine inlet valves, are activated one per crankshaft revolution. The period of injection is computed by an ECU by using the data supplied from the various sensors. On this system each pulse of the injector delivers half of the total required for the cycle.

During cold-start and warm-up conditions, the cold lubricating oil produces a greater drag, so to compensate for this an *auxiliary air valve* allows a small quantity of air to by-pass the throttle. This action is similar to the fast–idle feature provided in a carburettor.

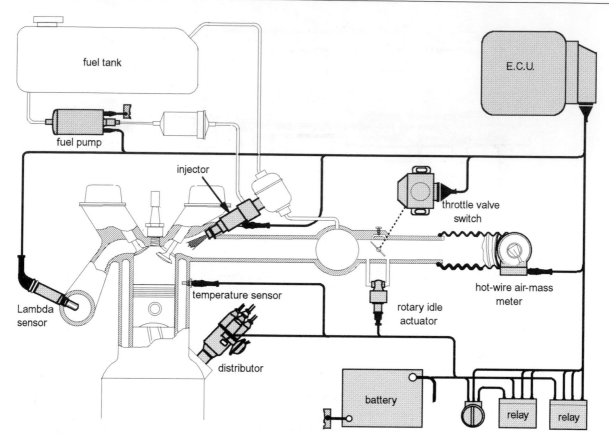

Fig. 12.8 Hot-wire metering (*Lucas EFI and Bosch LH*)

Air flow to an engine is irregular, so this causes pulsations which make it difficult for the air-flow sensor to measure the flow accurately. To minimize this problem the induction manifolds of fuel-injected systems incorporate a *plenum (air) chamber*. A volume of about 0.8–1.2 of the engine capacity is normally sufficient to damp the pulsations and smooth the air flow.

Hot-wire metering The Lucas EFI and the Bosch LH-Jetronic use this principle. Both types have a similar layout to the previous arrangement, but in the system shown in Figure 12.8, an improvement in engine performance is claimed by using a hot-wire air mass sensor (see page 98). This type of sensor measures air mass directly, so the signal transmitted to the ECU will not need further correction for changes in density and temperature of the intake air.

Hot-wire systems are in common use so this system is described in greater detail. The layout can be divided into two main sections:

- fuel system
- electronic control.

Fuel system

The purpose of a fuel-supply system is to provide the injector with adequate fuel at a pressure sufficient to allow the injector to give good atomization (this means that fuel is mechanically broken up into fine particles).

The layout shown in Figure 12.9 includes the following parts.

Pump This is normally a roller-type pump driven by a permanent-magnet electric motor (Figure 12.10). Rotation of the pump moves the rollers outwards and seals the spaces between the rotor and casing. As the fuel is carried around with the rotor, the combination of the rotor movement and the decrease in volume causes an increase in pressure.

Fuel from the pump passes through the motor; this aids cooling. Although sparks are generated in the

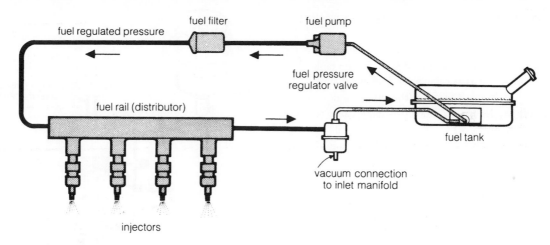

Fig. 12.9 Fuel system

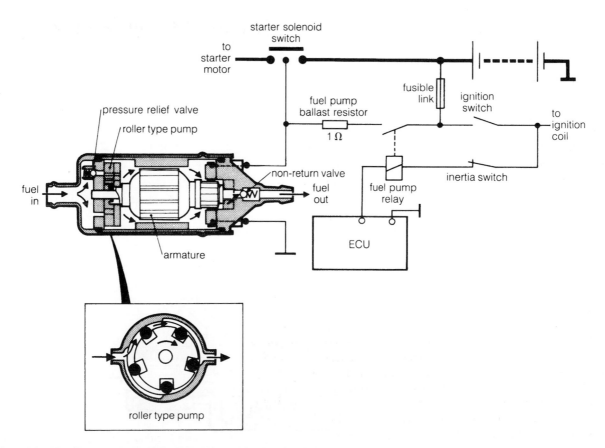

Fig. 12.10 Fuel pump and electrical supply circuit

motor, combustion does not occur because insufficient oxygen is present.

The pump is designed to supply more fuel than is needed; excess fuel is recirculated back to the tank. This feature reduces the risk of vapour-lock problems.

Two ball-valves are fitted in the pump: a non-return valve at the outlet and a pressure-relief valve to limit the maximum pressure.

The pump is controlled by the ECU via a fuel pump relay. Supply to the pump is taken through a ballast resistor which drops the voltage to 7 V. This resistor is shorted out when the engine is being cranked to compensate for the lower battery voltage.

On switching on the ignition, the pump motor runs for a short time to fully pressurize the system. After this initial period the pump is stopped until the engine is cranked.

For safety reasons an inertia switch is fitted in the supply line to the pump relay. This switch opens if it is jolted so, in the event of a collision, the pump ceases to operate. The switch can be reset by pushing down a protruding plunger.

Fuel pressure regulator This controls the operating pressure of the system and is set to maintain a constant pressure difference (e.g. 2.5 bar or 36 ibf/in²) above the manifold pressure irrespective of the throttle opening. It consists of a spring-loaded diaphragm and ball-valve (Figure 12.11).

Manifold pressure depression depends on throttle opening, i.e. engine load, so when the opening is small the depression encourages more fuel to leave the injector. To compensate for this, the fuel system operating pressure is lowered when the manifold depression increases. This is achieved by connecting one side of the regulator to the induction manifold. At times when the engine is operated under a light load, the

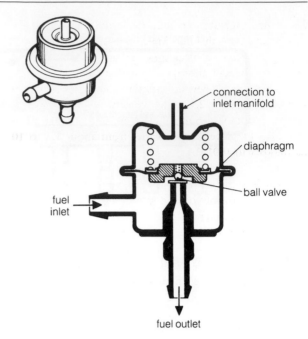

Fig. 12.11 Pressure regulator

regulator valve is slightly opened and the pressure is reduced.

The pressure controlled by the regulator is as follows.

Engine condition	Manifold depression	Typical operating pressures
idling	large	1.8 bar (26 lbf/in²)
full throttle	slight	2.5 bar (36 lbf/in²)

Injectors The duty of an injector is to deliver a finely-atomized spray into the throat of the inlet port. In addition, the injector must vary the quantity of fuel to suit

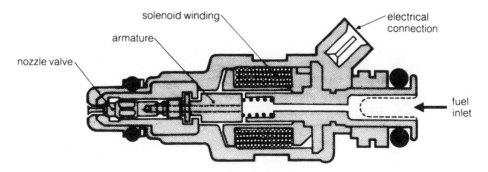

Fig. 12.12 Fuel injector

the engine operating conditions; this is achieved by varying the time that the injector is open.

The required conical spray pattern is obtained by pumping the fuel through a pintle-type nozzle. Fuel flow takes place when the nozzle valve is opened by a solenoid (Figure 12.12). Movement of the valve is limited to about 0.15 mm (0.006 in) and the period of time that the valve is open varies from about 1.5 to 10 ms (0.0015 to 0.01 s).

This variation in opening time alters the amount of fuel that is supplied to each cylinder per cycle. Open time depends mainly on the rate of air flow and engine speed, but engine temperature and fuel temperature also have a bearing on the amount that needs to be delivered.

All injectors are electrically connected in parallel, so for 4- and 6-cylinder engines they all open and close at the same time. When the engine is warm, this opening normally occurs once every other revolution.

When the engine is cold-started extra fuel must be injected; this is provided by increasing the frequency of injections.

Injector opening is obtained by using a solenoid winding of resistance about 16 Ω. This solenoid over-comes a return spring which is fitted to hold the nozzle against its seat when it is closed.

Electronic control

The control system of a fuel-injection system must arrange for the correct quantity of fuel to be injected at the right time. To meet this requirement, the quantity of air entering the system, together with the engine crankshaft position, must be measured accurately. The quantity of air entering the engine dictates the amount of fuel needed and the crankshaft position, acting on pulses from the ignition coil, signals when injection should commence.

The brain of the control system shown in Figure 12.13 is the ECU.

Electronic control unit During recent years, advances made in ECU technology have made it possible for the ECU microprocessor to accurately match the requirements of the engine. This means that the operating performance of a modern system depends largely on the quality of the peripheral component, namely the accuracy and efficiency of the various sensors and actuators (particularly the former) which are the input, and output, to the ECU.

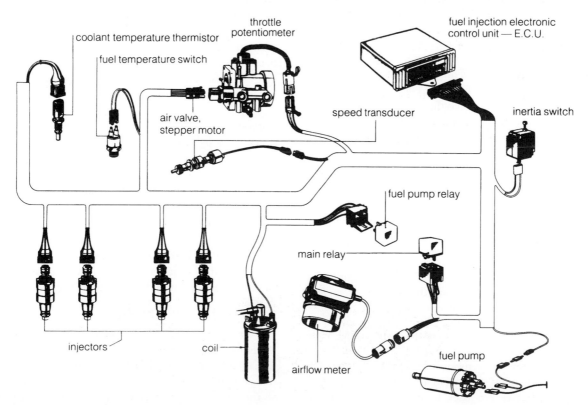

Fig. 12.13 Electronic fuel injection (*Rover*)

Normally the ECU consists of a number of integrated circuits and many hybrid modules containing various semiconductors which are all mounted on one or two printed circuit boards. Input and output signals are communicated by a wiring harness that is connected to the ECU by a multipin connector.

The ECU computer unit interprets the data received from the sensors and, after calculating the duration of the injection time, it signals this message, together with the time of opening, to the injectors.

Many designs of electronic fuel-injection system work on an analogue computing principle. These use electrical signals which are variable so the memory capacity of such a system is limited. In consequence, it is suitable only for engines with a relatively simple fuelling requirement.

Digital control More recent developments use digital control units. These allow quite complex fuelling needs to be stored in a micro-sized silicon chip. One system uses a 5 mm square chip containing about 5000 transistors as a part of its control circuitry.

The digital units process information at two levels only by sensing the presence or absence of a voltage pulse, so greater stability is achieved compared with analogue ECUs with less drift especially when a change in temperature occurs.

Most digital ECU units store the fuelling requirements in a digital memory pictorially represented by a three-dimensional map. This gives a standard injection pulse length for 16 different engine speeds and 8 different engine loads. Once the standard pulse has been determined, it is then modified to take into account the conditions that exist at that time, namely coolant and air temperatures. Correction must also be made for battery voltage, because the action of the injector depends on the voltage applied to it.

Many different control units are in use; the following description covers the basic principles of a Bosch ECU as fitted to L-Jetronic systems.

ECU operation

The block diagram of the ECU shown in Figure 12.14 has five sections for processing the pulse so as to make it suitable for operating the injector.

Pulse-shaping This circuit converts the signal sensed from the ignition coil's l.t. to a rectangular form. The circuit incorporates a monostable multivibrator. This 'switch' changes its state from level 0 to 1 on receipt of a signal, but reverts back to its original state 0 after a fixed time.

Frequency divider Located on the same chip as the pulse shaper, the frequency divider converts the number of pulses given by the input signal to one per crankshaft revolution. A 4-cylinder engine has 4 ignition pulses per 2 revolutions, so the frequency divider halves the input frequency. In a similar way 6-cylinder and 8-cylinder engines have to be divided by 3 and 4 respectively.

The frequency divider uses a bi-stable multivibrator or flip-flop; this circuit rests in one or other of its two levels or states, 0 or 1, and requires a pulse to switch it from one state to the other.

Division-control multivibrator This circuit determines the standard injection pulse by using input signals of:

- engine speed, from the frequency divider;
- air flow, from the air-flow sensor.

Since this pulse duration is proportional to the air flow during the induction stroke, the air flow must be divided by the engine speed. The charge–discharge action of a capacitor is used to perform this division.

Multiplier stage Standard pulses, appropriate to the engine speed and air flow are modified in duration by this stage to take into account the actual engine conditions. Signals from the temperature and throttle sensors allow the circuit to calculate a correction factor which is used to multiply and lengthen the standard pulse; this gives a pulse duration suitable for conditions such as warm-up and full load.

Output stage Further modification of the pulse duration is needed to compensate for changes in battery voltage, since any change affects the injector opening time. The pulse voltage is then amplified to enable a current of about 1.5 A to be produced for energization of the injector solenoid. This final stage is performed by a Darlington driver circuit (see page 56).

Control of the injector current is achieved by using either a *ballast resistor* in series with each valve, or a *current regulation* arrangement that provides a large current to open the injector and a smaller *holding current* to keep it open.

Ballast resistor control Figure 12.15(a) shows four injectors, each controlled with a ballast resistor to limit the total current to about 6 A. The actual injection differs slightly from the rectangular pulse signal produced at the output stage; this variation is due to the time delay in the build up and decay of the pulse signal and

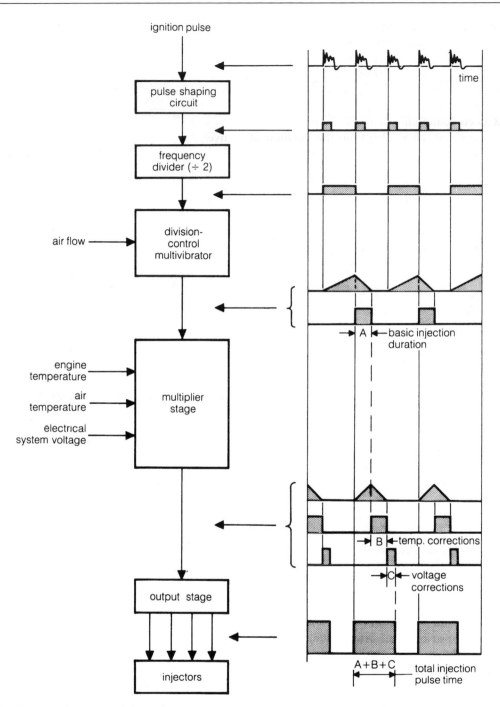

Fig. 12.14 Electronic control functions

mechanical factors. The delay periods for opening and closing are called *response delay* and *drop-out delay* respectively.

Figure 12.15(b) shows that without ballast resistors the total current required is too high for the Darlington driver. Even with ballast resistors, two final stage units are needed if more than four injectors have to be driven.

Current regulation This arrangement overcomes the need for an external ballast resistor to limit the injector

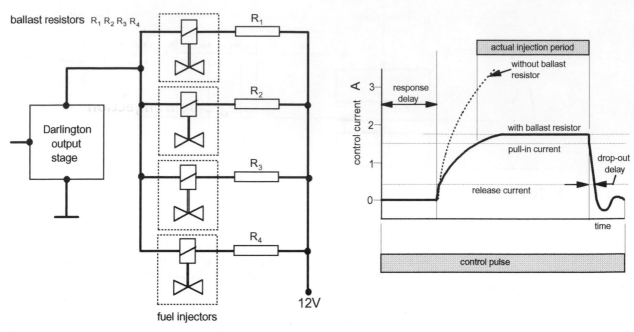

Fig. 12.15 Ballast resistors to limit injection current

current. It uses a current regulator in the ECU to provide a high current to open the injector and a smaller holding current to keep it open for the required period (Figure 12.16). The opening current of about 1.7 A per injector gives a short response time and the lower holding current of 0.5 A reduces the loading on the output stage. This feature simplifies the external circuit and also allows up to 12 injectors to be switched from one output stage.

Other features
In addition to the above basic functions, an ECU fitted to a modern injection system incorporates extra control circuits to include:

- cranking enrichment
- after-start enrichment
- hot-start enrichment
- acceleration enrichment/deceleration weakening
- full-load enrichment
- over-run fuel cut-off
- idle-speed control.

Cranking enrichment When the engine is rotated at cranking speed, the ECU provides double the number of injection pulses to satisfy cold-start conditions.

After-start enrichment The ECU provides extra fuel by extending the injection pulse duration for a given time after the engine has been started. This feature is provided for all engine temperatures but the enrichment period is much shortened when the engine is hot.

Hot-start enrichment When the fuel in the fuel rail (gallery) is very hot, the ECU lengthens the pulse duration to compensate for the change in fuel density.

Acceleration enrichment/deceleration weakening Signals from the throttle potentiometer and air-flow sensor indicate when the engine is accelerating or decelerating. Under these conditions, the ECU enrichens or weakens the mixture accordingly by increasing or decreasing the pulse respectively.

Full-load enrichment Slight enrichment is required when the engine is put under full load. When the sensors indicate this condition, the ECU lengthens the pulse duration.

Over-run fuel cut-off The ECU cuts off the fuel so as to improve economy and exhaust emissions when the following conditions are sensed:

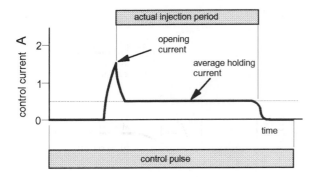

Fig. 12.16 Current regulation control of injector current

- engine speed is above 1500 rev/min;
- throttle is closed;
- coolant temperature is above 25–30°C.

Idle-speed control   Idle speed is controlled by a stepper motor energized by pulses supplied from the ECU. A valve moved by the motor varies the quantity of air that is allowed to by-pass the throttle valve.

The main engine sensors provide the main signals for this feature but extra data is required when the

> ## REMEMBER
>
> **A multipoint direct air-flow PI system:**
>
> - has one injector per cylinder
> - measures air flow with either a vane or hot-wire sensor
> - using a vane measures volume of air
> - using a hot-wire sensor does not have to be corrected for changes in air density and temperature
> - has a plenum chamber to damp air pulsation
> - uses a regulator in the fuel line to control pressure
> - uses an injection pressure of about 2 bar
> - has an inertia switch to stop the pump in an emergency
> - has all injectors solenoid valves connected in parallel
> - controls engine power by altering the length of injection pulses
> - has an ECU which processes the input signal through the stages: pulse shaping, frequency divider, multivibrator, multiplier and output

vehicle is fitted with an automatic gearbox and/or air conditioning. Idle speed must be increased if the gearbox is set in 'drive' or if the air-conditioning unit is 'switched on' Other fuel injection systems are shown on page 264.

12.6   Single-point injection

Throttle body injection

A single-point injection system provides a comparatively simple replacement for a carburettor.

Replacing a carburettor with this system gives the advantages:

- More accurate metering of the fuel and air since electronic control is used.
- Better atomization of the fuel over the speed range, especially at part-load.

These advantages result in good economy and less pollution from the exhaust. Furthermore the control system can easily be programmed to include fuel cut-off and enrichment requirements. Also, it can take into account signals from other sources which have some influence on the air/fuel ratio requirements.

Figure 12.17 shows the layout of an early design of throttle body injection. This shows a single solenoid-operated injector situated centrally in the air intake. It is supplied by a pressurized fuel system similar to that used in a multi-point layout.

Injected fuel is directed into a venturi-shaped region around the throttle, so the increased air speed at this point is used to further break up the fuel.

Air flow is measured by a flap or hot-wire sensor. On this housing is mounted the ECU so a compact layout is obtained. Since the ECU contains a microcomputer it can easily process data from additional sensors other than the throttle and temperature units shown.

> ## REMEMBER
>
> **Single-point injection:**
>
> - is also called throttle body injection
> - has one fuel injector positioned in a similar place in the induction manifold as a carburettor
> - has an electronic control system similar to a multipoint fuel injection system
> - achieves many of the advantages of a multipoint system but at a lower cost

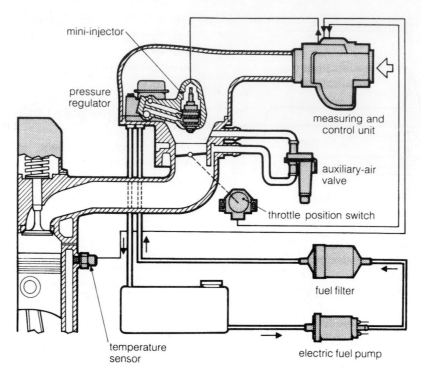

Fig. 12.17 Throttle body injection

Working in conjunction with these sensors the ECU varies the fuel flow to give deceleration cut-off and enrichment during cold-start warm-up, acceleration and full-load operation.

When the engine is cold, fast idle of the engine is provided by an auxiliary air valve.

It is claimed that this single-point injection system is capable of giving the same metering accuracy and long-term stability as a multi-point injection system.

A later design of this type of injection is shown on page 267.

12.7 Maintenance of PI systems

In the past, the ECU was unjustly blamed for many fuel system faults and this produced many costly, inefficient repairs. This situation arose because many repairers did not have either the test equipment or staff to undertake work in this new field: as a result the public formed the opinion that the reliability of electronic components was very poor. Statistics showed that about 30% of ECUs returned to the manufacturer for testing were serviceable, so in those days many vehicle owners were faced with unnecessary bills. Looking at this statistic in another way shows that 70% of the returned units were

defective, so the manufacturers must accept some responsibility for the bad reliability record.

Fortunately, all factors that contributed to this poor record have improved: component quality and reliability is far better; special test equipment has been purchased; and electronic knowledge is on the increase. These changes were necessary because many repairers realized that modern electronic systems could not be serviced without suitable equipment and competent staff.

General maintenance
The periodic maintenance of a fuel system involves checking the system for security of electrical connections and fuel lines. When this check is carried out, an inspection should be made for fuel leaks.

Fuel-injection systems incorporate a fuel filter so this must be changed at the appropriate time, e.g. every 48 months or 80 000 km. Direction of fuel flow through the filter is important so it should be fitted as indicated by the arrow on the filter casing.

Carburettor systems
Manufacturers provide a test sequence for checking the electronic operation of the carburettor. Often these tests involve the use of a multimeter.

The following summary illustrates the method of checking a unit such as an electronically controlled carburettor.

(1) Initial check After completing a check of the basic engine systems, the coolant thermistor is then disconnected; in this state the panel should register a hot engine.

A cold engine is then simulated by connecting the thermistor cable to earth. This action should cause the stepper motor to operate through its full travel; the throttle jack should also move.

(2) Stepper motor Five cables are connected to the stepper motor: one common feed and five returns. Using a multimeter between the common feed, and each of the other cables in turn, should show a given resistance, e.g. 12–15 Ω.

(3) Coolant temperature thermistor The bulb is placed in water and the temperature is raised. Using an ohmmeter, the resistance is checked at given temperature and the results are compared with the specification. Typical values are:

Temperature (°C)	Resistance (Ω)
20	2350–2650
40	1050–1250
60	550–650
80	300–360

(4) Ambient air temperature sensor This NTC thermistor is checked in a way similar to the coolant thermistor. Resistance values are compared against a table of values.

(5) Fuel cut-off solenoid This normally has a resistance of 20–25 Ω and is operated at battery voltage. After checking that the resistance is correct, the harness is disconnected and voltage is applied to the solenoid; a click should be heard as it energizes.

Fuel-injection systems
Before carrying out specific tests on a fuel-injection system, basic engine checks, such as plugs, timing, etc., should be made to ensure that these items are serviceable.

For safety reasons, it should be noted that any test involving the disconnection of a fuel line must take into account that the line is pressurized to the extent of about 2 bar.

As in the case of many other electronic components, items such as ECUs can easily be damaged by workshop test equipment (and personnel), so care must be exercised when testing any part connected to an ECU.

Full diagnostic tests of a fuel-injection system normally require the use of specialized test equipment. Without this equipment, tests are limited to items which can be checked with a multimeter. By incorporating the appropriate meters and switches in a dedicated test unit, it is possible to cover the numerous checks in a shorter time. This leads to quicker and more accurate fault diagnosis.

Test equipment Many manufacturers offer a range of portable test equipment for checking the operation of PI systems to aid fault diagnosis. One comparatively cheap tester, developed for the a hot-wire EFI system, is shown in Figure 12.18. The *Fast-Check tester* is plugged into the main connector at the ECU and the result of each test is signalled by a LED. This type of tester is simple to use, but it can only be used on one PI system, i.e. it is **dedicated to one vehicle model**. One problem with this tester is that repeated removal of ECU

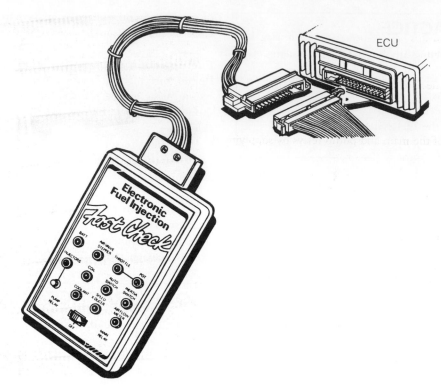

Fig. 12.18 Electronic fuel injection tester

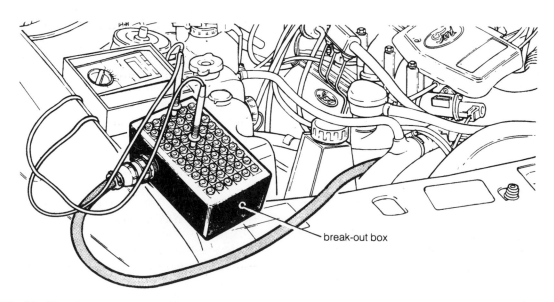

Fig. 12.19 Break-out box (*Ford*)

connectors damages the pins; as a result a high resistance occurs and this creates other faults. For this reason modern ECU control system have a separate connector for the hookup of diagnostic test equipment.

The Fast-Check tester is connected to the 25-pin main harness plug that is normally joined to the ECU. The test sequence covers the following:

- Operation of the main and pump relays by supplying each relay, in turn, with a current.
- Indication by LED of battery voltage, air valve stepper motor circuit resistance, throttle pot circuit, supply from ignition coil, automatic transmission inhibitor switch, inertia switch, coolant sensor, road-speed transducer and air flow meter resistance.
- Injector operation by supplying current to each injector in turn.
- Pump operation.

Results given by this Fast-Check pin-point the area of the system that if faulty. More detailed tests can then be made.

In addition to the electronic checks, other tests are made to the hydraulic system to determine the fuel pressure and the correct functioning of the injectors.

Break-out box Completely shielded connectors are necessary to protect against corrosion, but this shielding often makes multimeter testing difficult even when the probes are inserted at the back of the plug. To minimize this problem, the Ford Motor Company developed a central test unit called a *break-out box* (Figure 12.19).

This box has 60 sockets and a provision for the connection of these sockets to the multiplug which normally fits into the ECU.

Tests conducted with the aid of this box cover many sub-sections. Its use minimizes the problems of connecting test equipment to the wrong pin and making ineffective connections to the test meters.

Each socket is numbered, so, when used in conjunction with a fault-diagnosis chart, the testing procedure is simplified. As with many other tests of electronic equipment, great care must be taken when using a multimeter to measure resistance. This is because the current supplied by the meter can damage many of the components in an electronic control unit.

Multimeter tests

Fault diagnosis without using dedicated equipment is time consuming, but with the aid of a good digital multimeter and circuit diagram it is possible to pin-point

Fig. 12.20 Use of multimeter (*Fluke*)

the cause of a particular problem (Figure 12.20) This technique is still needed when elaborate equipment is used, because in many cases it only indicates the faulty sub-circuit and not the actual defect in this circuit.

Most electronic units are now fairly reliable, so a diagnostic test must start with an examination of all cables and connectors that link the units in the suspect sub-circuit.

Ensure that all connectors are secure and bearing in mind that many faults in the past were due to bad contacts, it is suggested that each plug is wriggled to improve its conductivity.

Fault diagnosis by substitution can be very costly because a defect in another part of the circuit may, and often does, destroy the newly fitted unit. This is similar to the case where a cable shorts to earth and blows a fuse – you know how long the new fuse lasts!

Tests should be carried out in a methodical manner; start at the source and proceed through the circuit to build up a clear picture of the operation of each part of the circuit. Repair operations should begin by finding out from the driver all the symptoms before starting on a costly repair that may be unnecessary. Information gained will indicate the suspect area, so tests of this

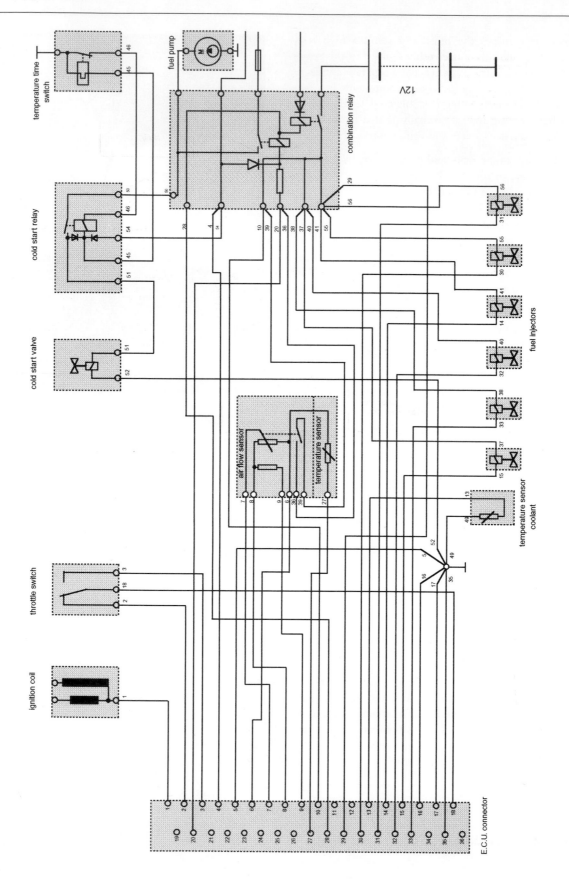

Fig. 12.21 Fuel injection circuit diagram (*Bosch L-Jetronic*)

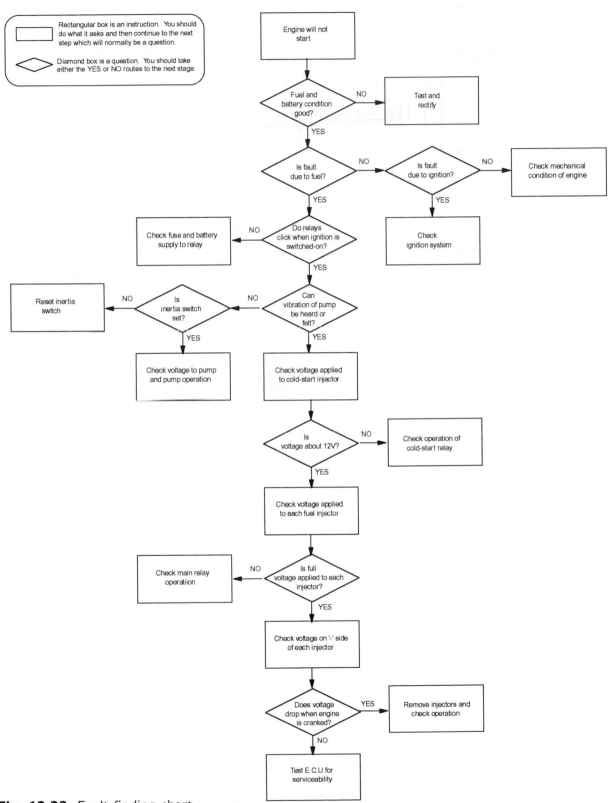

Fig. 12.22 Fault finding chart

region will be a starting point. In many ways this verbal analysis is similar to that used by dedicated equipment: the test computer scans all sub-circuits until it recognizes that a part of the system is defective.

In the absence of special equipment, knowledge of the circuit is essential. A wiring diagram, similar to that shown in Figure 12.21, is a vital aid. In addition to indicating cable terminations, it also enables you to estimate the voltage at each point, e.g. the voltage on both terminals of the injector will be about 12 V (the e.m.f. of the battery) when the ignition is switched on and the engine is stationary. Using numbered terminals on a circuit diagram makes interpretation and testing much easier, especially when the number is stamped on the actual unit.

Previously it was stated that circuit testing must follow a logical pattern, so in the absence of detailed guidance instructions, the tester should plan the tests in a sequence similar to the example shown by the flow chart in Figure 12.22. A few moments spent on planning will not only save time and money, it will result in an effective repair.

Further tests on petrol injection systems are described on page 271.

GOOD PRACTICE

Multimeter tests on petrol injection systems should:

- be made in a logical sequence
- be made with a good quality digital meter
- start at the power source where possible
- NOT be carried out until you are satisfied that all connectors and cables are securely fitted
- NOT involve the separation of any connector, especially cables carrying a sensor signal, unless it forms part of the test
- NOT involve resistance tests on any units that may be damaged by the meter current

---

12.8 Diesel fuel pump control

Compression-ignition (CI) engine principles
Before dealing with the electronic control of fuel pumps, it is necessary to revise some facts about this type of engine. In the past the CI engine, or diesel-engine as it is commonly called, had the following features:

- an unrestricted supply of air was delivered via the induction manifold to the engine;
- power output was controlled by the quantity of fuel injected at high pressure directly into the engine cylinder;
- the engine had no throttle valve – the accelerator pedal was directly connected to the fuel pump;
- maximum engine power was reached when smoke started to appear in the exhaust;
- the exhaust gas still contained a large quantity of oxygen even when smoke was being emitted;
- when a turbocharger was used to force more air into the cylinders, extra fuel could be injected before smoke was emitted which gave more power,
- high combustion temperatures produced NO_x when the boost pressure was excessive.

Emission problems In the past, the emission of black smoke was regulated because visibility was impaired. Recent studies have shown that pollutants from diesel-type engines are also hazardous to health, so emission laws now apply to this type of engine. New engines designed for sale in the EU must have exhaust gas levels below those shown in Table 12.1. (The limits apply to all new designs after 1995 and current designs after October 1996).

Gram per installed kw-hour limits			
CO	HC	NOx	Particulates (when abov
85kW)			
4.0	1.1	7.0	0.15

Table 12.1 Exhaust gas limits in the EU

Whereas emission levels in spark-ignition engines are monitored by using an oxygen sensor as the main feedback in a closed-loop system, the excess oxygen in the exhaust of a diesel engine rules out this method of fuel control. Instead a system is needed to regulate the quantity of fuel, set the injection timing and control the amount of oxygen that is allowed to enter the cylinder: this is achieved by using an electronic control system in conjunction with a conventional catalytic converter.

There are various designs of electronic fuel control for diesel engines; the following system is based on a Bosch rotary pump.

SAFE PRACTICE

Diesel fuel:

- should not be handled
- can damage skin so gloves or a barrier cream should be used when hands are likely to come into contact with the fuel

Diesel injection pressures:

- are very high – fuel can penetrate skin, so no part of the human body should be exposed to fuel spray discharged from an injector
- can damage eyes unless eye protection is used

Diesel fuel spray:

- can damage lungs if inhaled

Electronic diesel control system (EDC)

This closed-loop system in Figure 12.23 is similar to that used on Rover light vehicles. Electronic sensors and actuators control:

- fuel quantity
- start of injection
- quantity of exhaust gas recirculated
- turbocharger boost.

Fuel injection pump The pumping element of the pump is similar in principle to that used in a conventional Bosch rotary pump. Fuel delivery is changed by moving a *control spool* axially along the pumping plunger and injection timing is varied by rotating a roller follower assembly by fuel pressure supplied by a vane-type transfer pump. A mechanical governor is not needed with the electronic control system because this function is fulfilled by the ECU.

The main electronic items on an EDC pump are:

- servo control unit to vary the fuel quantity;
- potentiometer sensor to signal the position of the servo control unit;
- solenoid-operated valve to control the start of injection.

Fuel quantity Figure 12.24 shows the principle of a quantity servo control unit. Mounted at the lower end

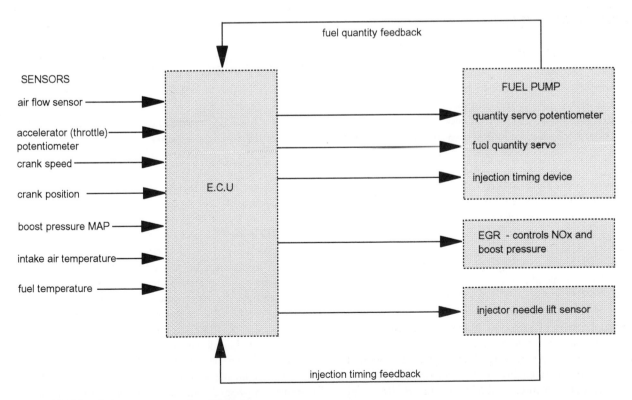

Fig. 12.23 Primary control system

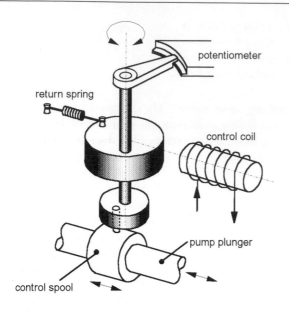

Fig. 12.24 Quantity servo control unit with potentiometer

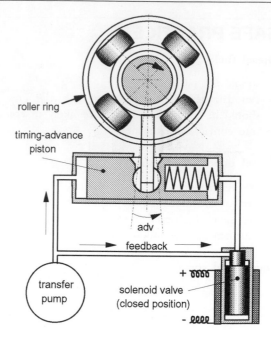

Fig. 12.25 Injection timing control unit

of the control shaft is an offset pin which engages with the control spool. Rotation of the shaft moves the control spool axially along the pumping plunger; this movement alters the quantity of fuel that the pump delivers.

Rotation of the control shaft is achieved by a magnetic actuator: this consists of an eccentrically mounted armature positioned between two poles of an electromagnet. A return spring pulls the armature towards the *no-fuel* position. When the electromagnet is fully energized, the armature rotates through an angle of about 60° to the *maximum fuel* position.

Quantity servo potentiometer Mounted at the top end of the control shaft is a rotary potentiometer; this senses and signals by means of rising voltage output the position of the pump control spool as it moves to increase the fuel. This feedback allows the ECU to vary the servo current in order to set the control spool in the desired position.

Start of injection solenoid valve In a non-electronic pump, the start of injection is advanced as the speed is increased by using a hydraulic piston to rotate a roller carrier in relation to a cam drive plate. The hydraulic pressure that operates this automatic advance mechanism is provided by an internal transfer pump. As the engine speed rises, the transfer pump pressure increases. This

causes the auto-advance piston to move against its spring and rotate the roller carrier.

The start of injection is controlled by the pressure acting on the auto-advance mechanism, so this feature is used as an actuator in an electronic pump to vary the point of injection to suit the operating conditions. Control of the pressure is achieved by inserting a solenoid valve in the fluid line between the transfer pump and the operating cylinder (Figure 12.25).

The valve has a *modulating action*; this means that it oscillates between the open and closed positions. Energizing the solenoid at a frequency of about 50 Hz, and changing the *mark–space ratio* (see page 62), the operating pressure needed to correctly time the injection can be set by the ECU.

Needle lift sensor Injection timing is very important if low emission is to be achieved with good engine performance. This cannot be attained unless factors such as fuel viscosity and general wear of components are taken into account. An electronic system overcomes these problems by using a sensor on one of the injectors to signal when the injector needle starts to lift. This provides a feedback signal to give a *closed-loop control system*.

The needle lift sensor is a coil mounted around an cylindrically-shaped armature formed on the end of the injector needle (Figure 12.26).

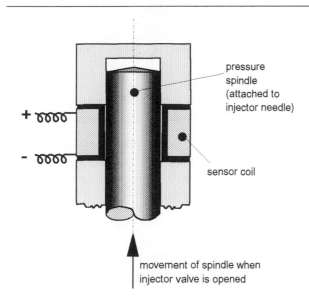

pressure
spindle
(attached to
injector needle)

+

-

sensor coil

movement of spindle when
injector valve is opened

Fig. 12.26 Needle lift sensor

Energized with a d.c. current from the ECU, the coil produces a constant magnetic flux when the armature is stationary. At the time of injection, movement of the armature produces a change in the path of the magnetic flux; as a result the voltage of the d.c. supply is momentarily altered. This signal disturbance occurs when the needle starts to lift, so the feedback signal to the ECU registers the precise time when injection commences. Using this information the ECU compares the timing point with the updated, mapped value and, if necessary, makes a timing correction by altering the signal transmitted to **the start of injection solenoid**. Repeating the monitoring cycle many times a second provides close control of fuel quantity and timing.

Drive by wire throttle control The EDC system has no mechanical linkage between the accelerator pedal and the pump. In this system movement of the pedal is communicated to the ECU by a voltage signal produced from a *potentiometer*. This throttle position sensor uses a thick film type of potentiometer which operates in conjunction with a *sender switch*. When the pedal is raised the switch is open, but after the pedal has moved the potentiometer more than 9° the switch closes. This

switch action is used by the ECU to check the circuit, implement idle speed control and activate the over-run fuel shut-off setting.

Movement of the accelerator pedal causes the sensor voltage to rise and fall during acceleration and deceleration respectively. Interpretation by the ECU of the accelerator movement allows it to calculate the fuelling requirements to obtain the desired engine response within the operating limits.

Electronic control is more precise and sensitive than a mechanical governor, especially at times when the engine has a tendency to surge.

Safety features are incorporated in the control system to continually monitor the operation of the throttle position sensor. If any electrical fault is detected, the system is programmed to be fail-safe.

Mass air-flow sensor This *hot-film sensor* is fitted in the air intake to measure the mass of air that is entering the engine (see page 98). After receiving this signal, the ECU is able to assess the combustion conditions and, at times when NO_x emission is likely to occur, the ECU activates the *exhaust gas recirculation (EGR) valve*. This allows exhaust gases to enter the inlet manifold and cylinder; this gas dilution slows down the burning process and lowers the maximum combustion temperature.

Secondary control

To further refine the operation of a diesel-type engine, the EDC system uses other sensors and electrical controls. The additional sensors are:

● MAP sensor – to measure turbocharger boost pressure;
● coolant temperature sensor;
● intake air temperature sensor;
● fuel temperature sensor;
● vehicle speed sensor.

Controls and auxiliary fittings include:

● glowplug control;
● fuel shut-off solenoid – shuts off the fuel if the ECU detects a major fault;
● burglar alarm;
● engine warning lamp and diagnostic connector.

PROGRESS CHECK 12

1. List the undesirable exhaust products that are limited by statutory regulations.

2. State FOUR carburettor systems that are electronically controlled.

Questions 3–18 relate to PI systems

3. State the main difference between multipoint injection and throttle body injection.

4. State a typical injection pressure.

5. State the effect of a defective MAP sensor on engine power, economy and emissions.

6. An extra-air valve (auxiliary air device) sticks in the hot-engine position. When will this defect be apparent?

7. What information is supplied to an ECU by a flap-type sensor fitted in an induction manifold?

8. Name the device that cuts off the fuel pump in the event of vehicle impact.

9. The wire of a hot-wire sensor breaks and opens the sensor circuit. State the effect of this on engine performance.

10. When the engine is being cranked, the voltage applied to the pump is higher than when the engine is running. Describe how this feature is achieved.

11. The Darlington pair fitted in an ECU fails to operate. State the effect of this on the injection process.

12. An open circuit occurs in one resistor of a ballast resistor control arrangement fitted in the injector circuit. State the effect of this on: (a) engine performance (b) exhaust emission.

13. Name the injector control system which supplies a higher valve opening current than the holding current.

14. State TWO ways in which a rich mixture is provided for cold starting.

15. What method is used to time the commencement of injection?

16. Fuel is cut off during over-run. Name TWO sensor signals which determine when this cut-off takes effect.

17. Comparing single-point with multipoint injection, state ONE advantage and ONE disadvantage.

18 What problems occur if multipin connectors are separated more than necessary?

Questions 19 and 20 relate to an EDC system

19. Name the fuel control actuators and sensors that are activated when the accelerator pedal is depressed.

20. Describe the electrical actions that take place in the fuel pump when the ECU signals the pump to increase the fuel quantity.

13

Engine management

The behaviour of a large family of mechanical components is difficult to investigate when the whole assembly is complete, because each part responds in a different way to a given change. To simplify this study the assembly is split up into smaller sections; this allows the function of each part to be analysed. When this study has been completed, it is possible to see the effect, or interaction, of individual parts on the complete system

13.1 Engine systems

A system is a collection of interacting parts. When these parts are linked together they perform a particular function. This function may be complete in itself or it may form just a part of a larger system. Conversely, a system may be divided into a number of smaller systems, i.e. a number of sub-sections.

In the case of an engine, ignition arrangements and fuel supply layouts are two examples of systems. Along with other parts they form a larger system, namely the engine or power system. A carburettor and a distributor are examples of sub-systems. In many ways the division of a major unit into systems is similar to a family structure. Human beings are grouped into families which, in turn, are assembled or divided into nations or individuals respectively.

System function and performance

An examination of a system often involves two separate studies; an analysis to determine its *function* and a study of its behaviour to ascertain its *performance*.

A functional study is known as a *qualitative analysis* because it establishes the basic qualities of a system and indicates the role that each part of the system fulfils. The manner in which the system performs its given duty, and the effectiveness of a given system in respect to its performance, is called a *quantitative analysis*.

Whereas a qualitative study gives the basic information about the fundamental duties performed by each main part of a system, the quantitative analysis is concerned with the 'filling-in' of the operational details and the measurement of the effectiveness of its operation.

A qualitative analysis of an electronic ignition system is shown in Figure 13.1. Representation of the main parts by blocks in this diagram allows the function performed by each part to be shown. This block diagram layout is a simple method commonly used in electronics to show the arrangement of the various sub-systems and the paths taken by the control signals as they pass through the system.

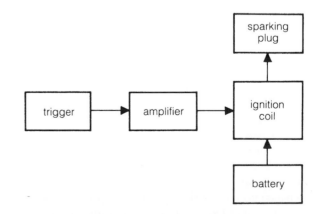

Fig. 13.1 Electronic ignition system (qualitative analysis)

A quantitative analysis involving a component's performance is often expressed in the form of a mathematical equation. By comparing the equations of alternative parts, designers are able to make an accurate, non-subjective judgement which helps to select the most suitable system or part for a particular application.

System modelling

The idea of using mathematical equations to represent the performance of individual parts can be extended to the complete system. When mathematics is used in this way, the equation covering the particular system or subsection is called a *mathematical model*.

Combining the models and supplying the mathematical data of individual models to a computer enables the designer to observe the overall performance. In addition to this important feature, the system's response can be determined when any part of the system is altered.

A modern electronic system has to operate over a wide range of conditions, so with the aid of this modelling facility, it is possible to vary the signal from each part and observe the result of the change on the complete system. These modern design aids enable the designer to predict accurately the performance of a major system well before it is put into production. This allows numerous modifications to be tried to see if it is possible to improve the performance or establish a simpler and cheaper system. Prior to the use of the computer for this purpose, the introduction of a new system required a program of practical tests on the actual components; this took many hours.

Control systems

A control system is an arrangement which directs the operation of a main system.

The commands given by the control system should ensure that the main system performs according to a given *program*. This program will have been devised to achieve a given *performance*; in the case of a power unit, this may be the production of a given power, the achievement of a set economy or the limitation of a given exhaust product.

To achieve a set program within the parameters of the control system's scope, the system must be able to respond quickly and accurately to changes in the operating conditions, maintain a stable control and be able to separate valid input signals from those that are induced into the sensing lines by electrical disturbances, i.e. the system should have 'noise immunity'.

The two main systems of control are:

- open-loop
- closed-loop.

Open-loop control

This type of control sends commands to the main system but does not have the ability to check or monitor the actual output of the main system (Figure 13.2).

Fig. 13.2 Open-loop control

Assuming the main system is an engine, then once a control signal has been delivered, the engine will produce its output, but this output will not always be the same if the engine operating conditions alter, e.g. if the engine control system does not take into account an ambient condition such as air temperature, then any variation in this condition will alter the power output and will not be corrected by the control system.

Although an open-loop control system is suitable for many applications, it cannot be used where the engine has to operate within narrow limits such as the case where exhaust emissions must be controlled closely to meet environmental legislation requirements.

Open-loop controls are still commonly used for fuel supply and ignition systems. In these applications the fuel mixture and ignition timing setting are arranged so that they follow independent programs. Ideally any change in the air/fuel ratio should be accompanied by an alteration in the timing, but in many cases this is not so. Consequently, the engine performance is lower than expected, economy is poor and a high exhaust emission results. To overcome this problem, many new vehicles now use closed-loop control systems.

Closed-loop control
This is similar to an open-loop system but has one very important addition; it has a means for measuring the output and feeding back a signal to allow a comparison to be made between the command signal and the system's output.

Figure 13.3 shows the principle of a closed-loop system. In this diagram the feedback signal from the output sensor is passed back to the input where it is compared by use of an error amplifier. This intensifies and processes the signal to allow it to be compared with the input command. If the output differs from that commanded by the input, the command signal is altered until the required output is obtained.

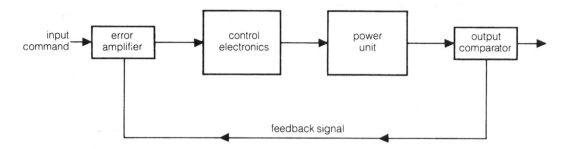

Fig. 13.3 Closed-loop control

When this control system is applied to an engine, the feedback facility allows any variation in the output to be corrected. This provides a more accurate and stable output than is possible with an open-loop system. Furthermore the system can be made to respond quickly and correct for any changes in the operation conditions. If these conditions are not compensated, then the output would be much different from that intended; in some cases this incorrect condition can result in extensive damage to the engine.

Two forms of closed-loop control are:

- proportional control
- limit cycle control.

A *closed-loop proportional control system* uses a sensor in the output to generate a signal proportional to the output; therefore the magnitude of the feedback signal indicates the system's output.

A *closed-loop limit cycle control system* uses the feedback to signal when a given limit is exceeded. The output sensor is inoperative during the normal operating range, but when a preset limit is exceeded, the feedback circuit passes a signal back to the input; this allows an alteration to be made to the command input.

This type of control has a number of automotive applications, e.g. combustion knock and fuel control.

13.2 Engine mapping

Open-loop digital systems store ignition-timing and fuel-mixture data in a memory unit of a ECU. The data stored in the individual cells of the computer's memory can be represented graphically by a *characteristic map*. Information for this 'graph' is obtained by carrying out a series of tests on the engine; the program for these tests is called *engine mapping*.

These tests measure the performance and investigate the effects of each variable that has some bearing on the output of the engine. When the effects are known, the settings that give the best performance can be determined and noted.

A dynamometer is an essential item for these tests since it can be programmed to simulate road conditions. The engine is loaded by means of this 'brake' and the torque, power output, economy, and emissions are measured against speed and other factors that have some effect on the engine output (Figure 13.4).

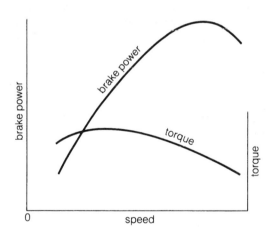

Fig. 13.4 Engine characteristic, full load test (throttle full open)

Engine maps
Performance curves plotted by hand or by computer show graphically the behaviour of the engine when it is subjected to changes in the following:

- speed
- load (throttle opening)
- ignition timing
- air/fuel ratio
- engine and ambient temperatures.

The performance curves derived from the tests are called engine *maps*. Some of the more important maps are included here.

Torque v. consumption loop This map is obtained by varying the air/fuel ratio and measuring the fuel consumption and torque output for each setting. Speed is kept constant during each test so a series of tests is needed to cover the engine operating range.

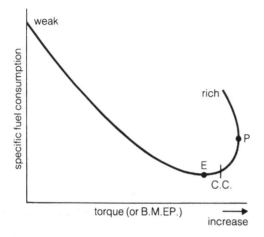

Fig. 13.5 Torque/consumption loop

Figure 13.5 shows a characteristic 'fish-hook' shaped map which is obtained when the engine is operated under full-load. On the *y*-axis (vertical axis) the specific fuel consumption (SFC) is plotted; these values are obtained from

$$SFC = \frac{fuel\ consumption\ (kg/h)}{brake\ power\ (kW)}$$

The specific fuel consumption indicates the quantity of fuel that is needed to produce one unit of power.

The map shows that when the engine is run on a weak mixture, the SFC is high and the torque output is low. As the mixture is enriched, the consumption falls to a point E where maximum economy is achieved. Enriching the mixture past this point gives an increase in torque but at the expense of fuel; maximum torque and power occurs at point P. It will be seen that the chemically correct (C.C.) ratio of 15:1 gives neither maximum torque nor maximum economy; to achieve these outputs, the mixture must be slightly enriched and slightly weakened respectively.

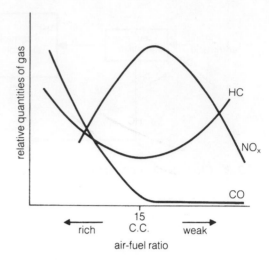

Fig. 13.6 Exhaust emissions

Exhaust emission v. air/fuel ratio Before exhaust emission regulations were introduced, the mixture supplied was based on the air/fuel ratios required to give either maximum power or maximum economy. Unfortunately the 12–15% enrichment from the C.C. ratio to give maximum power also gives a high emission of health-damaging exhaust gases such as carbon monoxide (CO), hydrocarbons (HC) and nitrogen oxide (NO_2).

Figure 13.6 shows the relationship between the formation of undesirable gases and the air/fuel ratio. This map shows the need to avoid operating the engine on an enriched mixture if exhaust pollution is to be kept to a minimum. Comparing the results shown in Figure 13.6 with Figure 13.5 indicates that 'lean-burn' engines designed to operate with minimum exhaust pollution suffer a considerable increase in consumption and decrease in power if the air/fuel ratio is weakened beyond the economy point E. The tolerance is very small, so close control of fuel metering is needed if satisfactory output, combined with freedom from engine damage, is to be achieved.

Spark timing and engine performance The general effects of varying the spark timing are well known. Maximum power over the speed range is achieved when the spark is timed so that maximum gas pressure occurs at 12° after t.d.c. Reducing the spark advance for a set engine speed reduces the power, increases the consumption and, as a result of the slower burning mixture, overheats the engine. An over-advanced spark also gives poor performance but in addition is likely to

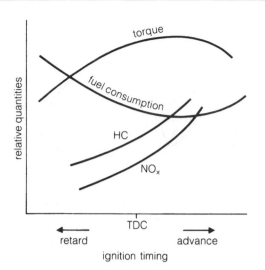

Fig. 13.7 Effect of varying ignition timing

cause combustion knock (detonation) which quickly damages pistons and causes a high level of noise due to 'pinking'.

In addition to these effects, spark timing also alters the exhaust products. Figure 13.7 shows a map obtained from running an engine at one set speed and load, and altering the ignition timing. This map allows the best setting of the spark to be determined.

Factors affecting spark timing   Spark timing to achieve a set power depends on three main factors:

- *Speed.* As the speed increases, the crank moves through a larger angle in the time taken for the gas to burn.
- *Load.* As the load is increased, the throttle has to be opened a larger amount to maintain a set speed. This increases the gas filling of the cylinder and as a result of the higher compression pressure, the flame rate is increased and the gas burns quicker.
- *Air/fuel ratio.* A weaker mixture takes longer to burn than the C.C. ratio.

By using a series of maps the effects of these three factors can be determined; as a result the optimum timing can be established. The following is a summary of the timing requirements. The spark timing advance is increased when the:

- engine speed is increased;
- air/fuel ratio is weakened.

The spark timing advance is decreased when the:

- engine load is increased;
- exhaust emission of HC and/or NO_x is too high.

Fuel mixture requirements are allied to engine load because when the engine is under light load, or if

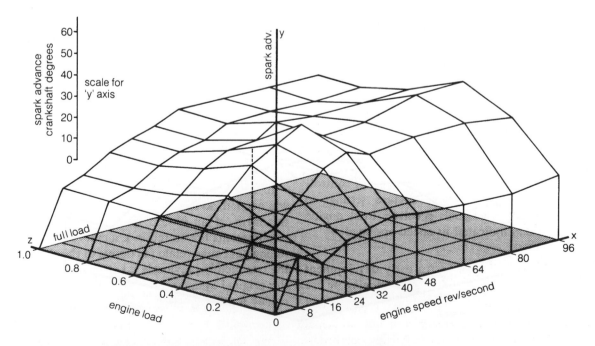

Fig. 13.8 Typical three-dimensional spark advance map (simplified)

the vehicle is 'cruising', a weaker mixture is supplied for economy purposes. Conversely, a full-load condition indicates that high engine power is needed, so a stronger mixture has to be provided by the fuel system.

Since the air/fuel ratio is dictated by the load on the engine, the spark timing need only be responsive to load and speed. For this reason most timing maps are based on these two variables.

REMEMBER

Timing of the spark, relative to t.d.c. depends on:

- engine speed
- load on engine (throttle opening)
- air/fuel ratio
- composition of exhaust gas

Three-dimensional maps

After performing a series of engine tests at different loads to determine the optimum angle of advance with respect to speed, a large number of maps is obtained. The number can be reduced to one by using the three-dimensional form as shown in Figure 13.8. The three axes of the map x, y and z represent engine speed, spark advance and load respectively. Accuracy of the timing requirement is dependent on the number of tests used

to construct the map. In the simple map shown, a total of 60 timing settings is used.

To determine the spark advance for a speed of 32 rev/s (1920 rev/min) and a half-load condition, the 32 point on the x-axis is located and the line from this point is followed until it intersects the half-load line; at this intersection the height of the map indicates the advance. In this case the angle is 52° (Figure 13.9).

Fuel mixture map A three-dimensional map is used to show the fuel requirements of an engine. In this case the three factors are: speed (x), air/fuel ratio (y) and load (z). Plotting these on the appropriate axis indicates the air/fuel ratio that is needed to suit the conditions of speed and load (Figure 13.10).

This map is often called a 'lambda' map. The term *lambda* is the name of the Greek letter 'L'. The symbol λ is used when the mixture is chemically correct, or to use a more technical term, the stoichiometric ratio. At this ratio:

$$\lambda = \frac{\text{Supplied quantity of air}}{\text{Theoretical air requirement}} = 1$$

When the 'excess air factor' represented by the symbol λ is less than 1, there is insufficient air for combustion, i.e. the mixture is rich. Conversely when λ is more than 1, there is excess air; the mixture is weak.

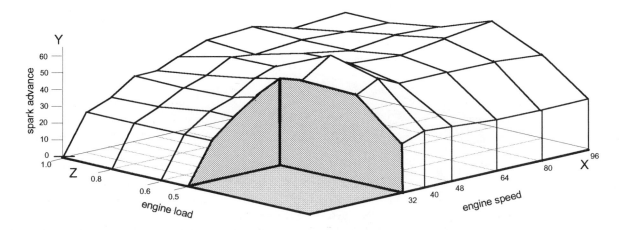

Fig. 13.9 Graph shows spark temp for engine running at 32 rev/s under half-load

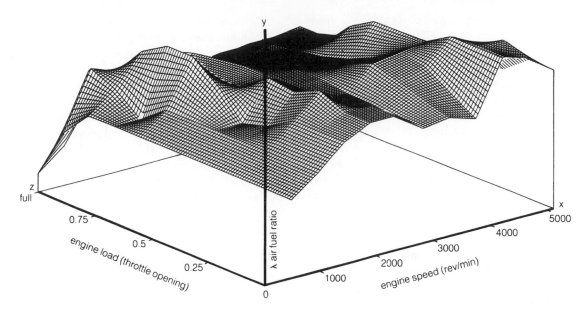

Fig. 13.10 Fuel mixture map

To summarize:

$\lambda = 0.95$ mixture rich
$\lambda = 1.00$ mixture correct
$\lambda = 1.05$ mixture weak

REMEMBER

A three-dimensional map plots engine speed and engine load to indicate:

- spark advance
- air/fuel ratio

Lambda value:

- indicates air/fuel ratio
- is 1.0 when quality of air supplied is equal to the air needed to completely burn the fuel
- less than 1.0 indicates a rich mixture
- less than 1.0 causes the exhaust gas to contain a high level of undesirable CO and HC pollutants

---

13.3   Open-loop control

Control arrangements based on the open-loop principle have been in common use since the engine was first introduced many years ago.

Prior to about 1935 the driver had the job of acting as a 'feedback' system, because in addition to manipulating the main controls, he also had to adjust the ignition timing and set the air/fuel mixture. This demanded considerable skill since it involved the setting of the ignition to a point where the engine was just knock-free and keeping the mixture at the point where it was just rich enough to develop maximum power. In later years, these driver duties were taken over by open-loop systems. These automatically controlled the ignition and fuel mixture settings in accordance with signals received from engine sources that indicated its speed and load.

Open-loop ignition and fuel systems are described in detail in Chapters 11 and 12.

Ignition timing control

An early development was the introduction of automatic timing by use of a centrifugal timer. This speed-sensitive unit advanced the spark to ensure that maximum cylinder pressure was maintained at about 12° after t.d.c. over the full speed range.

This type of automatic control assumes that the burn-time between spark and maximum pressure remains constant in time. Weakening the air/fuel mixture makes this burn-time longer, so when economy carburettors came into use in the late 1930s, the weaker mixture delivered by this type of carburettor during part-load operation required a larger advance than that given by the centrifugal timer. This was provided by a load-sensitive vacuum control unit. The spring-loaded diaphragm used the manifold depression to sense engine load and since the carburettor also used this source for the same purpose, the actions of the ignition timing control and the carburettor were harmonized.

In later years greater precision of the timing was needed, so electronics were used. This took the form of an ECU in which the timing requirements are stored in a memory unit. The timing data must relate the timing of the spark to the two factors previously taken into account by the original systems, namely engine speed and engine load (Fig. 13.11).

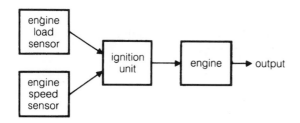

Fig. 13.11 Ignition timing system

The modern open-loop system is a large improvement over earlier designs, but one drawback is that it has to assume that the engine is in the same condition as that used when the memory was programmed. When this is not so, the timing given by the look-up table in the ECU will be unsuitable for the engine; as a result, emission, economy and power will all suffer.

Fuel-mixture control

Development of the constant-choke carburettor brought about mixture-compensation systems to correct for enrichment of mixture with increase in load/speed; this was followed by economy systems which weakened the mixture during part-load operation.

Methods for improving mixture distribution and poor atomization at low speeds received considerable attention from carburettor manufacturers, but the benefits of fuel injection with respect to these problems did not become attractive until stricter emission controls were introduced.

Both carburettor and fuel-injection systems must be capable of sensing engine load and engine speed, so these factors must be measured by the main sensing system. Mechanical and electronic sensing systems suffer the same drawback as the ignition unit; they can only follow the program introduced when the engine is made. Variable factors such as air leaks past the pistons, valve guides, throttle spindles, etc. are not taken into account, so output will suffer. The introduction of more sensors improves the situation and in this area, electronic systems can take into account many more variables than those used with mechanical systems.

Combined ignition and fuel-supply systems Previous studies show that both the ignition timing and fuel-supply systems requires sensors to measure engine speed and engine load. Duplication of the basic sensors and control electronics is uneconomic, so in many cases the two systems are combined to form a single Engine Management System.

Combination of the two systems allows other sensing signals to be used jointly by ignition and fuel systems so greater precision of control is possible. These additional peripheral devices include the measurement of ambient and engine temperatures and other factors that affect the operation of the engine (Figure 13.12).

Use of engine maps

To achieve precise control of an engine that has no means for feeding back output data, the control system must be programmed with very accurate information relating to the setting that is required for each condi-

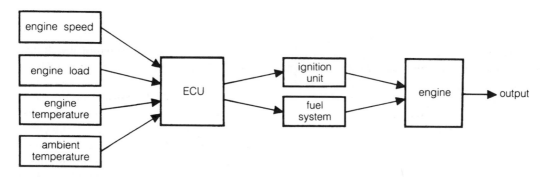

Fig. 13.12 Combined ignition and fuel system

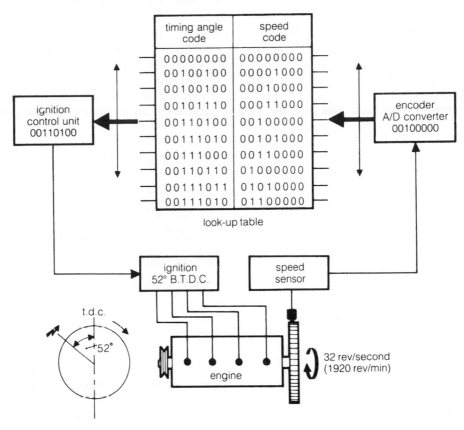

timing angle code	speed code
00000000	00000000
00100100	00001000
00100100	00010000
00101110	00011000
00110100	00100000
00111010	00101000
00111000	00110000
00110110	01000000
00111011	01010000
00111010	01100000

Fig. 13.13 Spark timing look-up table

tion under which the engine is expected to operate. This program should ensure that the input command produces the expected engine response.

Control maps compiled during the engine development stage show the settings of the main systems in relation to the variables which affect the particular systems. The control data indicted by the maps is programmed permanently into the computer's memory unit.

The computer uses the stored data in various ways; one way is to operate the computer so that it calculates the ignition and fuel mixture settings each time the speed or load conditions change. This computation may take as long as 100 ms to perform and since this operation may have to be repeated at 50 ms intervals, a quicker method is needed. This is achieved by using *look-up tables*.

Look-up tables A look-up table is a list of related values stored in the memory unit of a computer. This table relates the output settings given by the computer to the input signals received from a given sensor.

The principle used by a computer when it is performing this duty is easier to understand by considering the example of the spark-timing look-up table as shown in Figure 13.13; this has been constructed from the engine map illustrated in Figure 13.8. To simplify the example, only the speed factor is considered at this stage.

Assuming the engine is running at 32 rev/s (1920 rev/min), the appropriate sensor signals this speed to the ECU. After entering the computer the signal initially is converted by an encoder into the 8-bit digital form 00100000; this is the binary code for the number 32. The code is then stored in one of the registers of the CPU and the memory is searched until a similar code is recognized. When the search has been completed and the result verified, the memory unit then issues another binary code such as 00110100. This is the code that the computer has been programmed to write whenever it reads the code 00100000, i.e. the matching value in its look-up table. The 8-bit code is the spark timing instruction to the ignition control unit, so, after it has been deciphered, the control unit sets the spark to occur at 52° before t.d.c.

Although this example is limited to a table of 10 values, a modern computer has a much larger table.

In addition to the spark advance/speed table, extra look-up tables covering other variables are stored in the memory unit. Spark advance depends mainly on load and speed, so the advance given in the 'load look-up table' must be added to the value given by the 'speed look-up table'. This calculation is performed by the computer very quickly because it involves only the addition of the values given by the look-up tables.

To obtain this method of control, development must progress through the following steps:

(1) Mapping of the prototype engine to determine the best settings.
(2) Construction of maps to show graphically the required settings to suit the varying operating conditions.
(3) Programming the computer's look-up tables with the data contained in the maps.
(4) Testing the engine to verify that the computer is giving out control instructions in accordance with the requirements.

Detailed maps To achieve the best possible engine performance, the various maps should closely follow the requirements of the engine. This involves the use of maps with many more reference points than those used in Figure 13.8 (page 247) and the fitting of an engine management computer that has a memory unit of sufficient capacity to store the detailed look-up tables. An example of a detailed map is shown in Figure 13.14.

REMEMBER

A computer-controlled open-loop system:

- does not monitor the output
- sets ignition and fuel supply from data stored in *look-up tables* programmed into the memory unit
- has *look-up tables* derived from three-dimensional maps
- uses signals from air and engine temperature sensors to modify memory output values

13.4   Closed-loop control

The accuracy of setting the ignition timing and metering the fuel in an open-loop system is as good as the

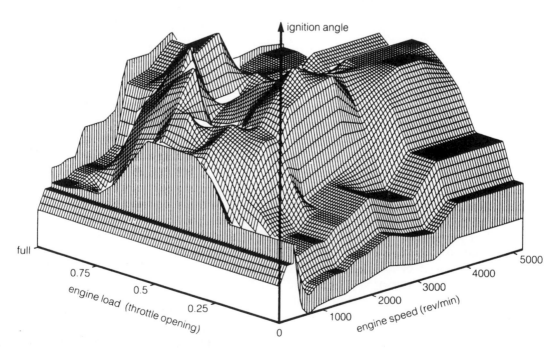

Fig. 13.14 Detailed map for electronic spark advance

mechanical condition of the engine and the program for the control function. Systems using the open-loop principle can only follow a program set-up after testing a prototype engine in a first-class mechanical condition. If the engine is not in a similar condition then the timing and fuel settings will be incorrect. This problem can be illustrated by highlighting the problem of setting the ignition timing of an older type engine with the aid of a strobe light. Although the timing may be set to the angle recommended by the manufacturer, it may not be the ideal setting for the actual engine being tuned.

These problems can be minimized by using a closed-loop control system. This system can be applied independently to manage ignition and fuel metering or can be combined to give a *full engine management system*.

Ignition control

The correct ignition timing for an engine is where combustion is just free from knock. On modern engines this setting cannot be obtained accurately without special equipment; this is because knock occurs before it can be detected by the human ear. Many factors affect the maximum spark advance that can be used before the onset of knock; these include:

- mechanical condition of engine
- compression ratio
- octane rating of fuel
- volumetric efficiency
- throttle opening
- shape of combustion chamber
- air/fuel ratio
- engine temperature
- carbon deposits.

To program for all these variables would require a very sophisticated open-loop system having many sensors together with an elaborate map containing a very large number of ignition angles. This is not possible so a simpler map is used for normal open-loop systems; this map gives suitable ignition angles to meet general needs but maintains a margin of safety to keep the engine free from knock and damage.

Knock control   This safety margin can be reduced with the result that better power and improved emissions can be obtained if a sensitive knock-control system is used. With this closed-loop control system the feedback signal generated by the knock sensor is used to adjust the spark timing so that combustion in the chamber is set to be just knock-free.

It has long been known that a large spark-advance is needed to obtain maximum power and economy from an engine, but when the spark is over-advanced, combustion knock will occur. Knock should be avoided for two reasons: the sound is undesirable; also it is likely that knock will cause engine damage particularly when it occurs when the engine is under heavy load.

Modern lean-burn engines are prone to knock, so when the ignition advance is programmed into a memory unit, a margin of safety is maintained to keep the engine knock-free. In view of this, the advance angle is set considerably less than the ideal. Even so, the engine still enters the knock region if an inferior grade of fuel is used or when engine wear alters the spark-advance requirement.

This can be overcome by using a *knock limiter* to slightly retard the ignition at the first sign of detonation. Engine protection given by this device allows the use of a larger spark-advance than is normal, so an improvement in engine performance is achieved. The difference in the spark-advance given by an electronic unit with spark control, and a conventional mechanical system is shown in Figure 13.15. This graph shows how an electronic system can be made to match more closely the ideal requirement.

A knock-control system, as shown in Figure 13.16, consists of a sensor, evaluation circuit, control circuit and an actuator. The *knock sensor* is mounted on a part of the engine that allows it to detect sound waves transmitted through the engine structure when detonation takes place. A piezo-ceramic disc is the active

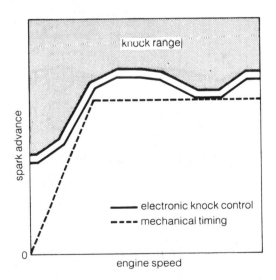

Fig. 13.15 Graph shows advantage of knock control

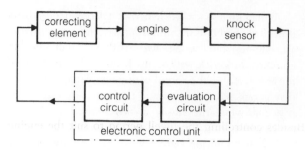

Fig. 13.16 Knock-control system

component of the sound-transducer sensor. This delivers a small voltage signal when it is triggered by mechanical oscillations. (See page 103 for construction and operation of knock sensor).

Initially the timing is set by using the data contained in the characteristic map. This basic timing setting is then advanced by the ECU until the knock sensor detects a given degree of knock. When the sensor signals that the engine is knocking, the timing advance is reduced in steps of 1.5 crankshaft degrees until the sensor indicates that the engine is knock-free. The continual repetition of this sequence ensures that the timing for each individual cylinder is maintained at the optimum angle (Figure 13.17).

The analogue signal from the sensor is filtered in a bandpass filter and fed to an integrator. After A/D conversion the signal flow is split up with one branch leading to the reference signal processing stage; the refer-

ence signal generated is the mean value of the previous power strokes. The actual signal is compared in a comparator; this furnishes information about the presence or absence of engine knock for each cylinder. When knock is detected, the control circuit retards the spark in accordance with a given program.

The knock-control system incorporates a safety circuit which recognizes malfunctions of the system. At times when a fault is detected, a warning light on the instrument panel is activated and the ignition timing advance is reduced sufficiently to prevent damage to the engine.

Closed-loop dwell-angle control

This feature is used to ensure that the correct primary current is achieved under conditions of differing battery voltage, engine speed and temperature.

This is particularly important when the engine is cold-started, because at this time the voltage applied to the coil is much lower than normal. To allow for this, a longer time must be allowed for the primary current to build up, i.e. the dwell must be lengthened. Conversely, if the dwell angle is set electronically at too large an angle, then power loss and heating of the ignition system is experienced.

Like other closed-loop systems, the dwell-angle control circuit uses a feedback circuit to signal when the primary current exceeds a predetermined value. When the signal is passed to the dwell-angle control section, the dwell angle is reduced accordingly.

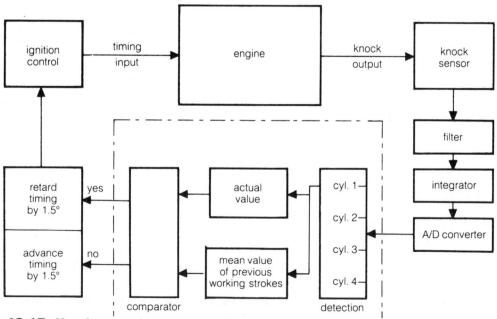

Fig. 13.17 Knock-control system

REMEMBER

Knock-control sensor:

- keeps ignition advance just below the point where knock occurs
- is the output sensor of a closed-loop system for controlling ignition timing
- allows a greater ignition advance than an open-loop control system.
- detects the presence of knock by a piezo-ceramic disc
- transmits an analogue voltage signal when it detects mechanical oscillation
- defects are recognized by the ECU which reduces the advance to a safe value and normally activates a warning lamp on the instrument panel.

13.5 Digital closed-loop ignition control

This system provides the next step in the evolution from the breakerless arrangements first used on vehicles in the late 1970s.

After a time, moving parts in a conventional distributor drive begin to wear and when any slackness in the drive affects spark timing, some of the advantages of a breakerless electronic system are lost. The timing variation due to component wear, together with the introduction of more stringent emission and fuel-economy regulations, has forced many manufacturers to use a distributor assembly and ignition control unit which satisfies the following requirements:

- To provide an optimum spark timing to suit all load and speed conditions. In particular, it must provide a high degree of advance at light load.
- To give a constant energy output over the full speed range as needed by lean-burn engines.
- To be able to give a spark timing which allows the engine to operate just clear of the detonation region.

These requirements are achieved by using a solid-state, digital-control unit to perform the duties undertaken originally by the mechanical advance mechanism; i.e. an electronic system replaces the centrifugal and vacuum control units used in a distributor for the last 50 years.

Microelectronic memories in which the stored data cannot be changed are called *Read-Only Memories*

(ROMs). Sometimes the manufacturer wishes to buy a standard memory chip and then program it to suit a given application: this is called a EPROM (an Erasable Programable ROM) and is used when the number of units required is limited.

Electronic spark advance (ESA)

Besides controlling the dwell period to suit the engine speed, this unit also varies, by electronic means, the angle of advance. A memory chip is programmed with data obtained from prototype engine tests to give the optimum advance needed for the best performance in respect of power, economy, acceleration and emission.

Two main factors dictate the angle of advance; they are speed and engine load. Figure 13.8 (page 247) shows a typical map of spark advance that is programmed into a memory chip. It is normally shown as a three-dimensional 'graph' having three axes, x, y and z, representing speed, advance and engine load respectively.

Angle of advance is the 'contour height' from the axis or base of the map to the intersection point obtained from set conditions of speed and engine load. For each step of speed and load, the map shows the spark advance that should be given.

A typical control grid is sub-divided into 16 throttle positions (engine load) and 16 engine speed positions, thus providing 16×16 or 256 memory calibration points. On more expensive systems an additional computer program allows each one of these points to give even more control of the timing.

The single-chip minicomputer fitted in the control module needs three basic input signals to allow it to search its memory so that it can trigger the spark at the correct time. These signals relate to engine speed, position of the engine crankshaft, and engine load, which can be sensed by the manifold depression or throttle position. Normally analogue sensors search out this information and then transmit the electrical signals to the control module. After the signal has been processed, it is converted to a digital form by an analogue/digital (A/D) converter.

Figure 13.18 shows an alternative method for displaying data stored in a memory unit; the two axes represent the digital signals needed to indicate the correct angle of advance for the engine. For example, when the digital signals received from the speed and load sensors are 3 up and 2 across, the memory output will read 33. After this memory output has been processed, the spark will be triggered 33° in advance of the time when the crank angle sensor sends its reference signal.

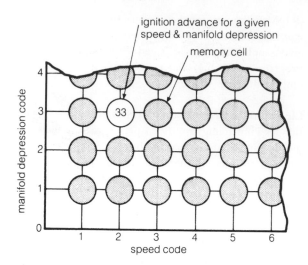

Fig. 13.18 Storage of ignition advance data

This advance setting is called up after each revolution of the engine, so when the sensors detect a slight change in either the speed or engine load, a suitable alteration in the spark timing is made.

Fig. 13.19 shows a first generation digital electronic system. An ESA unit can be made as a discrete (separate) or hybrid module. Hybrid systems lend themselves particularly well to mass production and since they fulfil

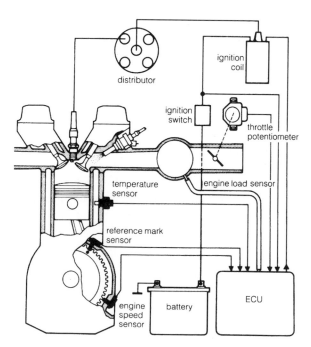

Fig. 13.19 First generation digital electronic system

other duties besides ignition control, the cost, weight and size are all reduced. In the hybrid system the conductors, contact surfaces and resistors are printed, but most semiconductors and capacitors are soldered in place.

The ESA system uses two speed-based inductive sensors which are mounted either in the distributor, or, if greater precision is required, fitted adjacent to the flywheel teeth. One of these sensors monitors engine speed and the other provides a given reference mark, such as 10° before t.d.c., for the firing impulse.

Engine load can be sensed by a throttle potentiometer or by an inlet manifold pressure transducer such as a silicon strain gauge type.

Extra sensors may be added to this basic system to refine further the operation of the electronic control unit (ECU). These additions often include special transducers to signal the engine temperature and detect the onset of combustion knock (detonation).

A safety circuit is built into the system to protect the engine in the event of a cable break, sensor failure or evaluation circuit fault. To cover these situations, the spark is retarded and an instrument light comes on to warn the driver that a fault is present.

When a knock-control system is used on a turbo-charged engine, it can also be arranged to control the turbo-charger boost. When the sensor detects detonation, the spark-advance is quickly reduced to take the engine out of the knock region. This is followed by the charging pressure being reduced by the opening of the waste gate valve. When this slower-acting control has taken effect, the spark-advance is restored to its optimum setting.

Figure 13.20 shows a digital system called *programmed ignition* (PI).

Distributorless electronic ignition
Modern ignition systems have eliminated the need for a mechanically operated contract breaker and automatic advance mechanism so the demand for a bulky distributor unit is questionable. Since the only duty that remains is to distribute h.t. energy to the sparking plug in the correct firing order, other methods have been developed to take the place of the cumbersome rotor and distributor unit.

One distributorless system uses one h.t. ignition coil for every two cylinders, so a 4-cylinder engine has two coils. Whereas an ordinary coil has one end of its secondary winding connected to the primary, a distributorless system has its secondary winding connected to two sparking plugs, one at each end of the winding

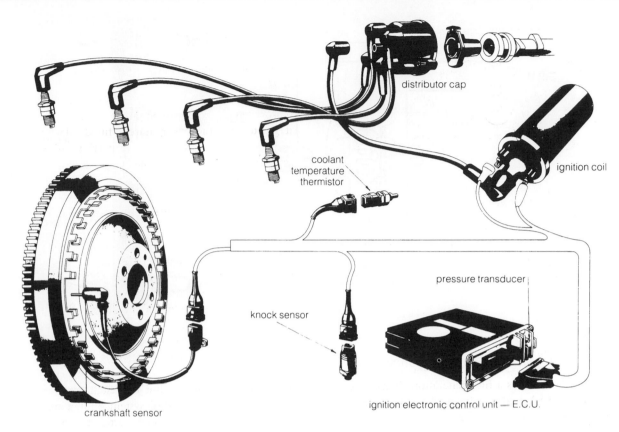

Fig. 13.20 Programmed ignition system

(Figure 13.21). Manufacturers use various names for this system; these include *wasted spark, all electronic ignition* (ALI), as well as other abbreviations; many of these help to confuse an outsider until the system is recognized and placed in its general category.

Compared to past methods, a distributorless system has the following advantages:

● less electromagnet radio interference, particularly at the higher frequencies, which was caused on earlier systems by the unscreened 2 kV spark at the rotor gap;
● less noise because sparking is eliminated;
● no moving parts to wear;
● fewer cables.

Figure 13.22 shows the layout of a *wasted-spark system* suitable for a 4-cylinder engine. This is a good descriptive name for the system, because the spark in the cylinder that has just completed its exhaust stroke is not used for combustion; its only purpose is to complete the h.t. circuit path for its companion sparking plug. The low cylinder pressure at the end of the exhaust

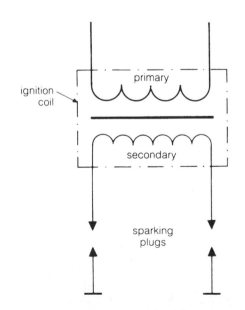

Fig. 13.21 Distributorless ignition system

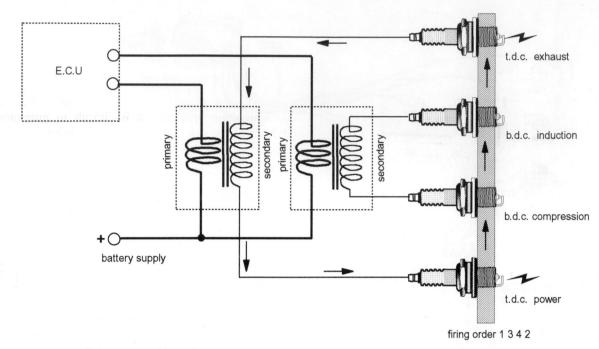

t.d.c. exhaust

b.d.c. induction

b.d.c. compression

t.d.c. power

firing order 1 3 4 2

Fig. 13.22 Wasted-spark ignition system

stroke means that the voltage required to produce a spark in this cylinder is less than required at the rotor of the old systems.

The reverse direction of current through one of the two plugs is not ideal, but the slightly higher voltage that is needed for this is well within the capability of the system. Nevertheless, the phasing of the ignition coil should be arranged to give an equal build-up time for each coil. For a 4-cylinder engine this is achieved by linking plugs 1 and 4 to one coil and 2 and 3 to the other coil; both coils being of the *double-spark type* having a sparking plug connected to each end of the secondary winding.

Engines with an odd number of cylinders have a separate *single-spark coil* for each sparking plug. This type of coil provides one spark per revolution for 2-stroke engines and one spark every other revolution for 4-stroke engines. In the latter case the firing sequence is controlled by a camshaft sensor.

Some systems use a *four-spark coil* that has two primary windings and one secondary winding; this is connected to the plugs through high voltage diodes (Figure 13.23). Since the two primaries are wound in the same direction, the opposite polarity of each winding produces a reversing h.t. current which is controlled by the diodes to fire two plugs. When the polarity of the secondary at point B in Figure 13.23 is positive, for

example, Nos. 1 and 4 diodes will conduct and produce a spark at Nos. 1 and 4 plugs; at this instant the diodes at 2 and 3 block the current.

Ignition coils Coils used on double-spark and four-spark systems are made wider than a regular coil to accommodate the two h.t. towers and other connections (Figure 13.24). An externally mounted iron core makes the coil more compact and also provides a securing point for the plastic moulded coil body. For cooling purposes the coil is filled with oil.

Distributorless systems are controlled by an ECU in a similar way to other digital layouts.

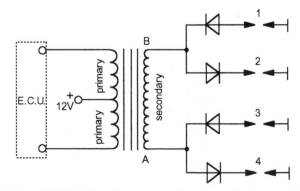

Fig. 13.23 Diode control for h.t. distribution

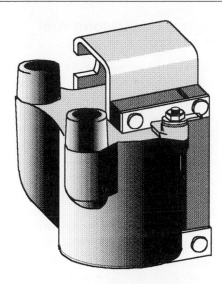

Fig. 13.24 Ignition coil for distributorless system

Coil-on-plug direct ignition system

High tension leads have caused problems over the years, such as:

- short-circuiting of h.t. current either to earth or to leads connected to cylinders having a lower gas pressure;
- mutual induction to other h.t. leads and delicate sensor circuits;

- leakage due to damp operating conditions;
- radio and TV interference;
- suppression difficulties;
- conductivity and security of cables especially when routed in close proximity to a hot exhaust:

Although modern designs of cable have minimized the effects of these problems, it is difficult to guarantee reliability to the standard required by current and future emission regulations. As a consequence, some manufacturers have eliminated all h.t. leads on their engine by making the sparking plug and ignition coil an integral unit. Each coil-plug unit needs only two low tension connections, one to supply battery voltage and the other to provide the ECU trigger signal.

This arrangement means that the problems listed above are overcome, the only drawbacks being the size of the unit and the extra cost.

Saab Trionic engine management system

The Saab company has pioneered many systems such as turbo-charging that are now regarded as standard, so their new system must be carefully considered.

The Saab Trionic system is built around a 32-bit Motorola central processor, which is a large step forward from the 16-bit and old 8-bit processors used in the past. The term 32-bit indicates the rate at which the computer can handle and process data; 8-bit data

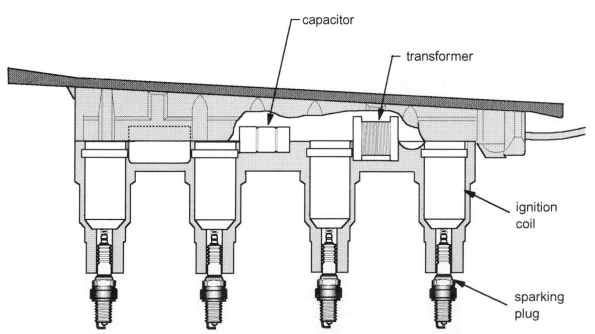

Fig. 13.25 Integral coil and sparking plug assembly (*Saab*)

processing is much slower than the others so the time taken for a computer to react to any changes in the operating conditions is that much longer. The new processor, which was developed for the American market, can carry out 2 million calculations a second, or produce enough data to fill an office binder each half metre at a steady 50 mile/h. The company claim that in its current form the Trionic system meets American emissions standards by a comfortable margin.

In addition to the new processor, the Trionic system uses a coil-on-plug direct ignition capacity discharge system that also doubles as a knock sensor (Figure 13.25). A low voltage (80 V) is applied across the sparking plug electrodes after the main firing impulse and measurement of the flow of ions (electrically charged atoms) gives an early and precise warning of the onset of knock. This measurement is taken in each cylinder so greater control over knock is achieved.

In addition to the ignition function, the management system also controls fuel injection and turbo boost pressure. This integration, together with the 32-bit processor, overcomes the need for the system to revert to standard reference settings during changes in engine operation. Instead the speed of the computer allows spark timing and injection changes to be made during these transient conditions. The company state the system can sense these changes during the injection period and make any correction before the injection pulse has terminated.

REMEMBER

Closed-loop ignition control system:

- uses a knock meter to monitor output
- is fitted with an ECU that is programmed to give standard settings
- advances the ignition over the standard until a knock signal is received
- is set to give a basic timing, such as 10° advance, when the ECU detects a system fault – this is called a *limp home mode*
- using a *wasted-spark* arrangement connects two sparking plugs in series – each pair of plugs has its own ignition coil
- using a *coil-on-plug* arrangement has no high tension leads
- using a 32-bit central processor performs calculations at a much faster rate than the old 8-bit processor

13.6 Digital closed-loop fuel injection control

The need for a closed-loop fuel control system was originally highlighted in the USA when the Environmental Protection Agency (EPA) introduced the *Clean Air Act* in the early 1970's. This stipulated that vehicles produced in 1975 had to reduce pollution levels by about 90%. Now in the 1990's the European Union (EU) has followed this lead and each year sees a general tightening of the regulations. Directives to Member States by the EU lays down the timetable for vehicle emission limits that must be met for all new vehicles.

In the UK the gradual tightening of the statutory emission limits scheduled for the 1990's meant that the open-loop fuel control systems could no longer satisfy the requirements. At an early stage petrol injection replaced the carburettor and a catalytic converter had to be fitted in the exhaust to meet the law. This law states that spark-ignition engines require a three-way converter to oxidise CO, HC and NO_x to the required levels. Fitting the converter had a knock-on effect because this unit is only effective when the exhaust gas is a product of a near-correct air-fuel mixture. Means had to be found to sense and signal to a control system any changes in the combustion process that is caused by incorrect fuelling. To achieve this condition a *closed-loop control system* is adopted: this system uses a *Lambda oxygen sensor* fitted in the exhaust to provide *feedback* information about gas content to an ECU.

Lambda sensor

The Lambda sensor is an oxygen sensor which produces a voltage pulse when no oxygen is present in the exhaust gas; this occurs only when the air/fuel ratio is on the rich side of stoichiometry (the chemically correct ratio).

The system layout is shown in Figure 13.26. This diagram shows the feedback circuit through which the digital pulse signal is conveyed when no oxygen is present in the exhaust gas. The principle of the Lambda exhaust gas oxygen (EGO) sensor is described on page 101.

When the sensor signals that the oxygen content is below a certain limit, a voltage pulse from the EGO sensor commands the fuel system to decrease the fuel supply so as to weaken the mixture. Shortly after this fuel alteration the EGO sensor will detect that oxygen is present in the gas; this will cause its voltage output to fall and as a result the output from the sensor will change to zero. When the controller discovers that the feedback signal has ceased, it instructs the fuel system

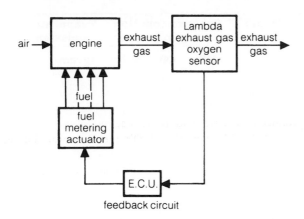

Fig. 13.26 Closed-loop fuel control system

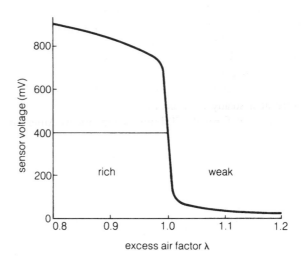

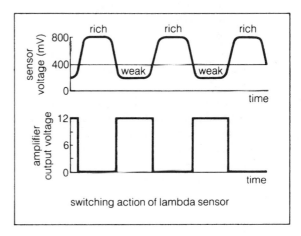

Fig. 13.27 Operation of Lambda sensors

to enrich the mixture. Mixture control is obtained by oscillating the mixture between the rich and weak limits; in this way the controller is able to keep the air/fuel ratio within a mixture range that is near correct. Since modern sensors are capable of working to a very small tolerance with respect to the air/fuel ratio, the risk of severe exhaust emission is considerably reduced; a limit of 0.05 from the required value of 15:1 is typical for many sensors.

Figure 13.27 shows the voltage variation when the air/fuel ratio is varied. The abrupt change in voltage between the point where the excess air factor (λ) is greater than 1.0 to the point where λ is less than 1.0 in the region where the voltage pulse is produced for use as an output signal. This signal gives a limit-control type of cycle so the EGO sensor may be considered as a switch which opens and closes to signify weak and rich mixtures respectively, i.e. the EGO gives a digital output with the two states, 0 and 1 used to identify the weak and rich mixtures.

Since this control system is expected to operate very fast, the arrangement used for mixture adjustment must respond to electronic control signals without delay; this can be achieved by using either an electronic carburettor or fuel-injection system.

The EGO sensor does not function efficiently below about 300°C, so when the exhaust temperature transducer detects that the mean temperature of the exhaust gas is below this minimum temperature, the engine control system is switched to the open-loop mode. This mode is used during cold-starting, when the engine is idling, and at times when the control system detects a fault in the EGO sensor circuit.

During acceleration and deceleration an engine has to operate outside the range of the EGO sensor.

At these times other sensors signal the engine condition and, in response to these signals, older type ECUs select the open-loop mode until steady conditions are re-established. The EGO sensor will only operate satisfactorily with lead-free fuel.

Heated Lambda sensor Internally heating the sensor gives more accurate mixture control when the exhaust temperature is below 300°C. This occurs during cold-starting and when the engine is operated at part-load for long periods.

The heating feature also allows the sensor to be mounted farther away from the engine. It is claimed that the cooler position gives this type a life in excess of 100 000 km. This is an improvement, because a sensor mounted close to an engine is exposed to a temperature in excess of its rated maximum (850°C), during long periods of full-load operation.

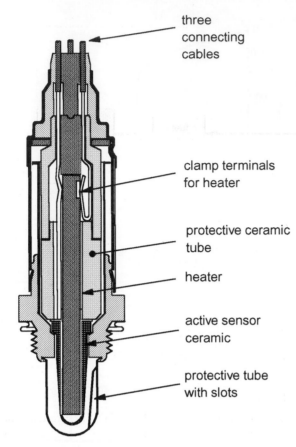

three
connecting
cables

clamp terminals
for heater

protective ceramic
tube

heater

active sensor
ceramic

protective tube
with slots

Fig. 13.28 Heated Lambda sensor

Model year	Exhaust emission g/mile			Evaporative emissions
	HC	**CO**	**NOx**	**(gram/test)**
1967 (pre-control)	15	90	6.2	6.2
1970	4.1	34	--	--
1973	3	28	3.1	2
1977	1.5	15	2	2
1981	0.41	3.4	1	2
1994–1998	0.25	3.4	0.4	(New procedures)
California 1994–2003				
TLEV	0.125	3.4	0.4	
LEV	0.075	3.4	0.2	
ULEV	0.04	1.7	0.2	
ZEV	0	0	0	

Table 13.1 Emission levels

Notes LEV = low emission vehicle; T=transitional; U = ultra; z = zero (electric)

Figure 13.28 shows the construction of a heated EGO sensor. The centrally positioned electric heating element, supplied with energy from an ECU, heats the inner surface of the active sensor ceramic. When cold-starting the heater brings the sensor up to its working temperature in about 30 s.

Engine control

Besides meeting the rising tide of emission legislation (Table 13.1), the modern vehicle must perform much better than its predecessors.

A potential purchaser expects the power unit to:

● develop high power for its size
● be cheap to operate
● accelerate briskly
● have good driveability over its speed range
● run smoothly at all speeds
● slow-run evenly without stalling
● start easily when cold and hot
● have a low initial cost.

A modern electronic system allows the engine to achieve these features, but in order to do so, the ECU has to be supplied with far more information than in the past. With these extra inputs the ECU is then able to process the data and decide on the actions that must be taken to achieve the programmed objectives.

Figure 13.29 shows some of the data inputs needed to operate a modern closed-loop control system. If a powerful computer is fitted, the information can be processed quickly: this will overcome the need for the control system to operate on fixed values during changes of engine load or speed.

In the past the ignition and fuel systems were each controlled separately with their own computers; as a result some inputs were shared. This duplication was necessary because the low-powered computers used in those days took a comparatively long time to process the total data. On some luxury vehicles, more than ten computers were fitted. The need for shared common inputs, bulky and complex interlinking cables and difficult siting of each computer resulted in poor reliability and slow response times. These early configurations proved that reliability is compromised both by using too many connectors and by parting them unnecessarily.

Integrated closed-loop control systems

These systems are used on modern vehicles and some of the different arrangements are considered here.

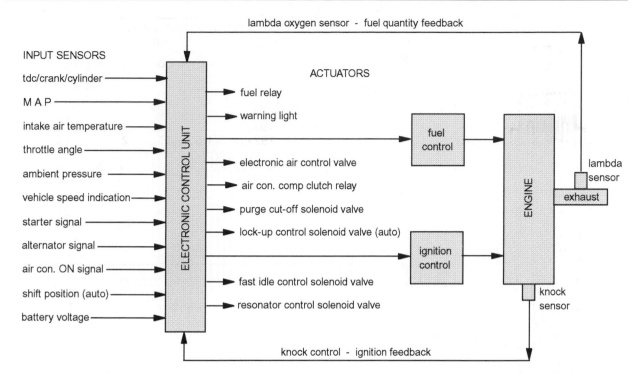

Fig. 13.29 Data flow paths

Hot–wire sensing   Figure 13.30 shows a system similar to that used on Ford Zeta engines. This arrangement uses an *Electronic engine control* (EEC) unit to manage the ignition and fuel systems. It also incorporates a distributorless high tension supply system, self-test fault diagnosis and idle speed control facilities to compensate for changes in the engine load caused by external factors such as: air conditioning, power steering, alternator, clutch pedal actuation and neutral gear selection.

Compared with earlier arrangements, the new management system has a more powerful ECU. This consists of more than a dozen integrated circuits with over 80 000 transistors. The ECU module incorporates:

- a 66% larger memory to store extra calibration data, more advanced mathematical control features (algorithms) and diagnostic information;
- a 20% faster controller clock to process information and issue commands more quickly;
- more input/output ports (16 instead of 12) to access more variables and export additional instructions.

The system can also handle all the environmental monitoring and fault storage data required for a dealer's diagnostic equipment.

Fuel is injected through a 4-hole injector in a sequential pattern that is timed to coincide with the opening of each inlet valve. This intermittent spray method of fuel injection is now becoming commonplace, because it produces lower emissions.

An ECU used with a *sequential electronic fuel injection* (SEFI) system needs an input to signal when each inlet valve is open; this is in addition to a crankshaft sensor, which, in this system, uses depressions cast into the rear flywheel face to signal engine speed and piston position.

Pressure-sensed system   In the past many manufacturers, especially Japanese, used a pressure-sensed engine management system. Based on the principle that the engine is a calibrated air pump, the volume of air that passes the throttle is governed by the difference in air pressure on each side of the restriction, i.e. between the air intake and the induction manifold. This pressure difference is measured with a MAP sensor.

Signals from this sensor do not take account of the density, so to calculate the mass of air entering the engine, the ECU must be 'told' the temperature at each side of the throttle; two sensors signal this information.

In a similar way the density of the fuel varies with temperature, so by fitting a temperature sensor in the fuel line close to the injectors, the ECU is able to calculate the mass of fuel and set the length of injection pulse to satisfy the expression:

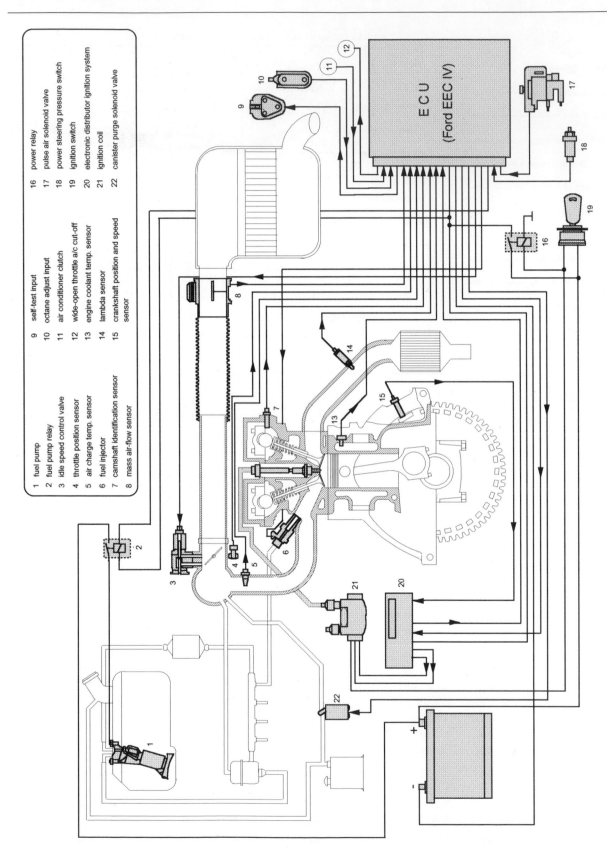

1	fuel pump	9	self-test input	16	power relay
2	fuel pump relay	10	octane adjust input	17	pulse air solenoid valve
3	idle speed control valve	11	air conditioner clutch	18	power steering pressure switch
4	throttle position sensor	12	wide-open throttle a/c cut-off	19	ignition switch
5	air charge temp. sensor	13	engine coolant temp. sensor	20	electronic distributor ignition system
6	fuel injector	14	lambda sensor	21	ignition coil
7	camshaft identification sensor	15	crankshaft position and speed	22	canister purge solenoid valve
8	mass air-flow sensor		sensor		

Fig. 13.30 Hot-wire sensing system with distributorless ignition (*Ford Zeta*)

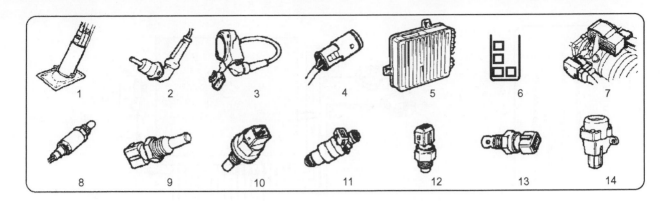

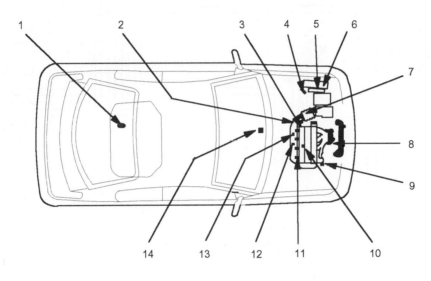

1	fuel pump	8	oxygen sensor
2	crankshaft sensor	9	coolant temperature sensor
3	camshaft sensor	10	knock sensor
4	diagnostic connector	11	fuel injector
5	E.C.U.	12	fuel temperature sensor
6	relays; fuel pump, main and oxygen sensor	13	intake air temperature sensor
7	stepper motor and throttle potentiometer	14	inertia switch

Fig. 13.31 Component locations – Rover MEMs system

$$\text{air/fuel ratio} = \frac{\text{mass of air}}{\text{mass of fuel}}$$

Figure 13.31 shows an ignition and fuel layout similar to a *modular engine management system* (MEMS) used on some Rover cars. This type of diagram is often found in a service manual and is useful when a particular part needs to be located.

In this system, a rubber pipe connects the manifold to a MAP sensor mounted inside the ECU: this is placed in a cool part of the engine compartment behind the battery.

Operation of the system starts when the ECU receives manifold pressure, speed and throttle position signals. These allow the processor to search the ROM memory for the basic fuel and ignition settings. These

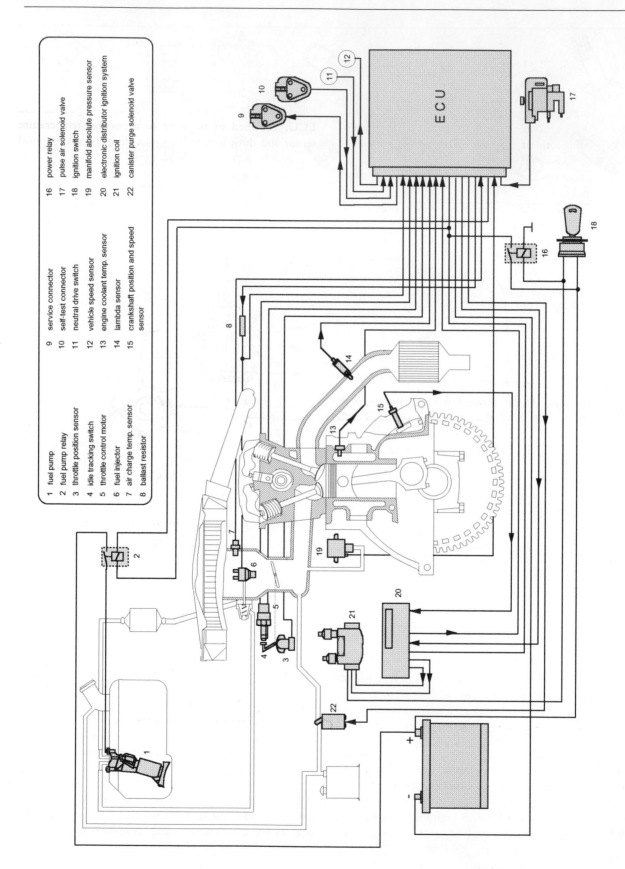

1 fuel pump
2 fuel pump relay
3 throttle position sensor
4 idle tracking switch
5 throttle control motor
6 fuel injector
7 air charge temp. sensor
8 ballast resistor

9 service connector
10 self-test connector
11 neutral drive switch
12 vehicle speed sensor
13 engine coolant temp. sensor
14 lambda sensor
15 crankshaft position and speed
   sensor

16 power relay
17 pulse air solenoid valve
18 ignition switch
19 manifold absolute pressure sensor
20 electronic distributor ignition system
21 ignition coil
22 canister purge solenoid valve

Fig. 13.32 Layout of a single-point injection system (*Rover*)

values are then modified to take into account the feedback and secondary signals. When these corrections are completed, the ECU sets the length of injection pulse together with the ignition and fuel timing.

As is usual with modern systems, the ECU has a separate diagnostic connector to enable the record of any intermittent faults stored in its memory to be downloaded. If the computer detects a fault when the vehicle is in use, a *back-up (limp home) program* comes into operation; this allows the vehicle to be driven but at a reduced performance level.

Engine idling speed is set electronically by using special test equipment. If a situation arises that causes the speed to change, the ECU signals a stepper motor to alter the position of the throttle. This alteration is sensed by the MAP sensor, which results in the ignition timing and fuel delivery being changed to suit the new conditions. The effectiveness of this compensation can be seen when an engine has a defect such as a faulty sparking plug. In the past this would soon be noticed by the vibration, but with modern systems the ECU attempts to hide the fault by resetting the idling speed.

All injectors, except those fitted to engines with turbos, are arranged to spray simultaneously. Turbo applications and later models operate sequentially; this can be identified by the extra sensor fitted to the camshaft.

Besides catering for basic engine needs, the extra power of a modern ECU allows it to perform other duties. These include:

- fuel cut-off when the vehicle is coasted;
- over-speed fuel cut-off to protect the engine when maximum speed is reached;
- immobilization of the system unless it receives a coded signal from an anti-theft device.

Single-point injection

Modern systems that use one injector to direct its spray into a throttle body are generally controlled in a similar manner to a multipoint system. Compactness and the comparatively low cost of a single-point layout makes the system attractive for use on smaller engines.

Closed-loop control Figure 13.32 shows a pressure-sensed closed-loop system arranged around an ECU. This receives primary signals from a crankshaft sensor, an in-built MAP sensor and a throttle potentiometer; together these register t.d.c. position, speed, engine load and throttle position. An oxygen sensor monitors the

engine output and using this feedback signal in conjunction with data received from other sensors, the ECU computes the ignition timing, injection timing and the length of each injection pulse.

Idling control Ignition advance, as mapped in the ECU, is varied in response to a cooling temperature sensor and throttle switch to provide stable idling, good driveability and low emissions.

Idle and fast-idle speed is maintained by a stepper motor as shown in Figure 13.33. This sensitive control continually makes throttle adjustments during idling, so the ignition timing varies with the speed during this period.

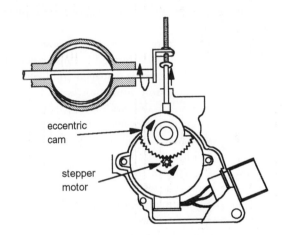

Fig. 13.33 Stepper motor control of idling speed

Coil type A low inductance ignition coil having a primary winding resistance of about $0.75 \, \Omega$ is used to give high spark energy throughout the speed range.

Fuel injection Fuel delivery to, and around, the solenoid-operated injector is by means of an electric pump. This is located in the fuel tank and is supplied with electrical energy from the ECU via a fuel pump relay and inertia switch. The injector sprays fuel when the solenoid is earthed by the ECU; this takes place once per cylinder per cycle, i.e. for a four-cylinder engine twice per crankshaft revolution.

Manifold heating To improve fuel vaporisation during warm-up, the system includes an electrically operated manifold heater; this is controlled by the ECU.

Fuel evaporation As is normal with modern engines, vapour in the fuel tank is collected and stored in a charcoal canister. This is purged with air into the throttle housing, via a solenoid-operated purge valve, at times when it can be accepted without affecting the performance of either the engine or catalyst. When the engine temperature is above 70°C and the speed is over 1500 rev/min, the valve repeatedly opens and closes, provided the manifold pressure is below 30 kPa.

Turbo boost control of spark-ignition engines

It is well know that a turbocharger is an exhaust-driven air pump used to force air into the engine cylinders instead of relying on atmospheric pressure. Whereas manifold pressure of a normal aspirated engine is slightly below atmospheric, in a turbocharged engine the pressure is greater; the increase above atmospheric is called *boost*.

Engine power and torque rises as the boost pressure is increased, but this must be limited because when the boost is too high, the engine is damaged and high NO_x emissions will occur. Boost limitation is achieved by allowing some of the exhaust gas to by-pass the turbo through a port opened by a valve called a *waste gate*.

The flap-type gate is operated by a pneumatic cylinder connected by a hose to the induction manifold at a point on the engine side of the throttle. When the maximum boost is reached, the pressure overcomes a spring in the pneumatic cylinder and the gate is opened. In the past this was the only method used to limit boost pressure, but current emission regulations have meant that a more precise electronic control system is necessary.

Figure 13.34 shows a pneumatically operated waste gate that is actuated by a boost control valve. This solenoid valve is fed from the main relay and earthed by the ECU at times when the valve is to operate.

13.7 On-board diagnosis (OBD)

Over the past twenty years engine management systems have kept pace with legislation introduced locally to limit vehicle emissions. History shows that European regulations have followed the lead given by the United States (especially the State of California), so this has allowed European manufacturers three or four years grace to develop their products to satisfy future EU legislation. Although the EU sets minimum standards for emission limits, each country is entitled to tighten these limits; e.g. Sweden who adopts US regulations in

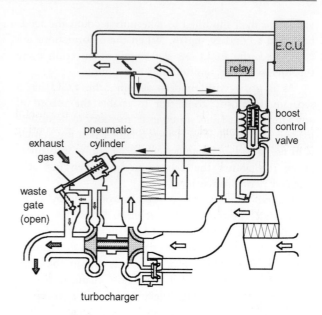

Fig. 13.34 Electronic control of turbo waste-gate

full. Also some manufacturers use strict emission limits to standardize and rationalize their products to minimize export problems.

Since 1992 emission regulations in the USA have been covered by the *Clean Air Act* (CAA). Under this Act, the *California Air Resources Board (CARB)* and the *Environmental Protection Agency* (EPA) introduced one aspect of emission control legislation that has been noted by many countries outside the US. This new law required all vehicles manufactured after 1993 to have an *on-board diagnosis* (OBD) facility. In addition, the new law (called *OBD I*) specified new test cycles, laid down performance periods and up-dated emission limits. In 1996 the second generation of OBD came into effect: called *OBD II* this regulation is persuading many European manufacturers to update their engine management systems to match the essential requirements of this Law.

Requirements of OBD II

Besides giving detailed specifications for emission controls, components and drive cycles, the CAA regulation OBD II requires:

- electronic monitoring of the exhaust system;
- indication of emission-related malfunctions by a warning lamp;
- rapid heating of the catalyst to reduce pollutant emissions in the warm-up phase;

- optimization of the engine management system in conjunction with an *evaporative emission control* (EVAP);
- CO emission limit maintained for 5 years/80 000 km;
- provision of a standard diagnostic plug.

Introduction of OBD is intended to extend the useful life of emissions-related components by preventing potentially damaging faults from going unnoticed (hence the warning lamp requirement). Also the need for the system to adapt fuel and ignition settings to compensate for any defect, ensures that the exhaust emissions are kept within the specified limits.

Since engine management now relies on electronic systems, radical modification of the ECU and control arrangement was needed to implement basic OBD requirements. Although management systems used at present provide limp-home and self-diagnosis features as a convenience for the driver and technician, the level of these facilities is well below that required for OBD. Some of the main changes required are considered at this stage.

Component defect On many current systems the total or partial failure of a vital sensor activates the *limp-home* or *limited operating strategy* (termed LOS by Ford) facility. This program makes the ECU disregard any signal from a defective sensor and, in its place, substitutes a standard signal. Over the last few years, the capability of the ECU to operate with a system fault has improved to the extent that the driver sometimes finds it difficult to recognize that the engine has a defect, especially when a warning lamp is not fitted. Continuous operation in the limp-home mode causes high emissions and destroys the catalytic converter.

More precise and regular monitoring of the system is required for OBD. Continuous checking and comparison of one set of sensors against others in the system show if each part is performing satisfactorily. The measure of air flow is a typical example of this cross-check feature.

One management system having a hot-wire air-mass meter compares the flow through this meter with the value calculated from the throttle valve opening and engine speed. If the results do not compare, the system performs a plausibility check to ascertain which one is faulty. Only after this check is made, is action taken and the fault code generated.

Combustion defects Cylinder faults such as *misfiring*, are difficult to detect and this is compounded when the

oxygen sensor signal associated with combustion faults is wrongly suspected of being faulty. As a result the ECU substitutes a standard signal with damaging consequences; in addition it creates and stores a fault code in its memory which can be misunderstood by a technician when the vehicle is repaired.

Special means are required by OBD to detect faults such as misfiring. One method is to monitor the rotation of the crankshaft from ignition-point to ignition-point. When the monitoring system detects an unequal time interval, the fuel supply to the defective cylinder is cut off; as a result harmful emissions are prevented and converter damage is avoided.

Catalytic converter defects Harmful emissions will be exhausted if the converter is ineffective. An OBD system monitors this component by using two Lambda sensors, one fitted upstream (on the engine side of the converter) and the other downstream. The upstream sensor performs its normal duty whilst the downstream sensor monitors the performance of both the converter and the upstream Lambda sensor.

When the signal pattern from both sensors is similar, it shows that the converter is defective; this condition prompts the ECU to activate the driver's warning lamp.

The sensitivity of the upstream sensor deteriorates if it is exposed to excessive heat for a considerable period of time; this condition is detected by comparing the frequency patterns of the two sensors. When the ECU detects from the wave comparison and other sensor plausibility checks that the performance of the main sensor is outside the accepted limits, the limp-home facility and warning lamp systems are activated.

Other emission-related defects New management systems designed to meet OBD requirements incorporate extra monitoring facilities to those previously outlined. These include:

- *fuel supply* – to check that the air/fuel mixture does not deviate from stoichiometric for a long period of time;
- *secondary air injection* – to ensure that air is supplied to the converter only at times when the catalytic converter is below its operating temperature;
- *exhaust gas recirculation* (EGR) – to verify that the system is functioning correctly;
- *fuel tank emissions* – to check the canister purge system.

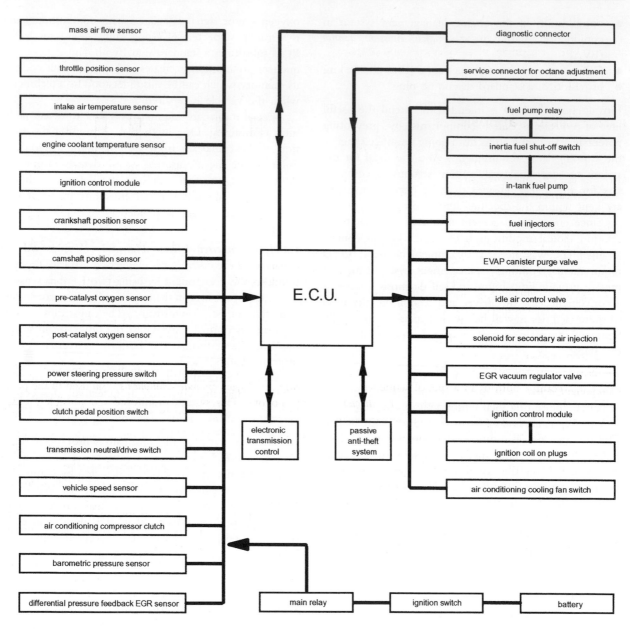

Fig. 13.35 Engine management system with OBD

Management systems

Figure 13.35 shows a typical layout of a system designed to meet the United States OBD II regulations. Systems such as the Bosch Motronic M5 and Ford EEC V are already in use in the UK ahead of any future EU legislation.

Other than the addition of the second Lambda sensor, the general appearance of OBD II systems does not differ greatly from pre-OBD systems, but the operation is far more involved. All sensors are built to a higher specification and the capability of the ECU is enhanced considerably.

The system shown in Figure 13.35 has a coil-on-plug arrangement to eliminate problems associated with h.t. leads.

Interesting developments are currently taking place to use the spark plug for cylinder sensing purposes; knock sensing is already being used by Saab (see page

259); another system uses the crown of the piston as an earth electrode. With this system it is claimed that ionisation between a single plug electrode and a piston crown provides a monitoring system for detecting cylinder misfires and other combustion faults.

13.8 Fault diagnosis

Sometimes vehicle performance does not warn the driver of the existence of an engine management fault. At these times the illumination of a 'check engine' light on the instrument panel is intended to alert the driver to the problem and suggest that expert attention should be sought as soon as possible.

When the ignition is switched on, the 'check engine' lamp should illuminate for about three seconds whilst the circuit is being monitored. After this initial lamp and system test, the light should go out. If this is not so, it indicates that the computer has detected a system fault, the details of which are stored in the RAM memory unit in code form. Access to this code is obtained in various ways; it may involve monitoring two terminals in the system or by operating two or more fascia control buttons in a special sequence.

When the system has been accessed, the *diagnostic trouble codes* (DTC) stored in the computer RAM memory will activate the 'check-engine' light; this assumes the battery has not been disconnected in the interval since the original defect was detected.

Any loss of data due to an interruption in the supply is avoided if the computer incorporates a small battery to maintain its volatile memory unit. If such a battery is not fitted, it is advisable to connect an external battery to the cigar lighter socket to retain the RAM data whilst the main battery is disconnected.

Lamp flash codes
The flash code diagnosis system used depends on the date of manufacture on the vehicle; one system interrogates the computer memory by connecting a test lamp

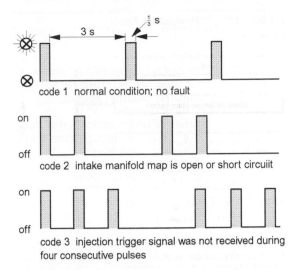

code 1 normal condition; no fault

code 2 intake manifold map is open or short circuit

code 3 injection trigger signal was not received during four consecutive pulses

Fig. 13.36 Fault diagnosis by lamp signal

to the ECU: another uses a LED fitted to the case of the ECU. Today the diagnostic codes are accessed by the instrument panel lamp.

The flash code principle can be shown by considering the *Toyota computer-controlled system* used in the past by Toyota. This system monitored ten possible faults, five of these were capable of producing an engine stall, so in these cases the 'check engine' lamp was illuminated. When a specified test terminal is short-circuited, any fault sensed by the computer from the time that the RAM was last activated causes the panel lamp to flash intermittently in a coded manner. Reference to the manufacturer's service manual allows the coded message to be translated. Figure 13.36 shows three examples of lamp behaviour.

Modern management systems use more sophisticated flash codes to communicate the contents of the RAM memory. These systems allow DTC's to be read from the 'check engine' lamp. When the ignition is switched on the code follows the lamp test. Flash codes can be repeated until the memory has been cleared. This is

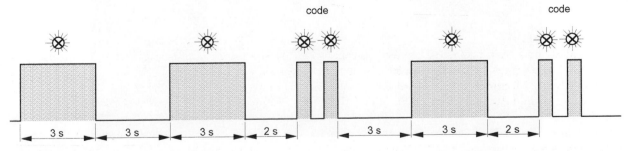

Fig. 13.37 Example of flash code

Number of flashes	Probable fault
2	MAP sensor
3	Intake air temperature sensor
4	Coolant temperature sensor
5	Throttle position sensor
6	Oxygen sensor
7	Adaptation (modification of fuel setting) including connection of sensors and hoses
8	EVAP canister purge valve
9	Control module, internal fault

Table 13.2 Toyota flash code

achieved either by using special test equipment or by removing the main supply fuse to the ECU for the recommended time, e.g. five minutes.

Figure 13.37 shows another example of flash code signals given by the 'check engine' lamp when the ignition is switched on. In this case the lamp behaves as follows:

- lights–up and stays on for 3 seconds
- goes out for 3 seconds
- lights–up and stays on for 3 seconds
- goes out for 2 seconds to indicate flash code is to follow

- flash code which consists of a number of brief flashes, each of duration 0.4 second
- goes out for 3 seconds
- lights–up and stays on for 3 seconds
- flash code repeated

Figure 13.37 shows a code having two flashes, so by referring to Table 13.2, the fault area can be identified and further tests can then be made to pinpoint the cause.

These examples show that there are many ways to signal a fault by a flash code, so reference should be made to manufacturer's literature to interpret the code used on a given model.

Although a flash code is a useful diagnostic tool, it must be remembered that a fault in one sensor circuit can affect other parts of the system. When this happens the flash code may give misleading information; a particular code does not always mean that a component is defective.

Special test equipment for fault diagnosis
To improve and speed up fault diagnosis, special test equipment has been developed. Most vehicle manufacturers specify the diagnostic equipment that their dealer network must purchase and use. These dedicated units

Fig. 13.38 Rover Group Testbook

range from sophisticated computers to comparatively cheap hand-held code readers. In this country manufacturer's test figures are not readily available to non-franchised dealers, so if such a dealer undertakes work on different makes of vehicle, it is often necessary for the company to purchase a suitable engine analyser from a general equipment supplier.

The following items of test equipment have been specially designed for franchised dealers linked to one manufacturer. No attempt is made to describe in detail the manner in which each item is used; this information is given either in the restricted technical literature or displayed on the screen of the equipment.

The Rover Group Testbook This is a sophisticated system built around a 486SX, 25 MHz, 120 Mbyte laptop computer having a touch screen and CD-ROM drive (Figure 13.38).

When used with its associated software, *Testbook* offers features that include:

- *Engine analyser and diagnostic search*. Gives access to the various ECUs on the vehicle via the serial interface connection and vehicle diagnostic plug, and allows fault codes to be downloaded and displayed on the VDU screen. Also it acts as a signal generator to emulate data associated with sensor and actuator operation
- *Toolbox*. This provides and displays on its backlit LCD screen, multirange meters for voltmeter, ohmmeter and ammeter tests
- *Technical information support*. Gives immediate access to the latest service information, product manuals, technical data, schematics, wiring diagrams and other repair documents
- *Interactive training*. At a touch of the screen this provides training programmes for technicians.

With the aid of simple operating instructions displayed on the screen, the technician is able to systematically interrogate and test the vehicle's management systems, diagnose faults and make tuning adjustments. At any time during its use, the data displayed on the screen can be printed for record purposes.

Since *Testbook* uses a CD input, the base unit can be programmed to interface with other manufacturer's equipment to allow the dealer to undertake work on non-Rover Group vehicles.

The scope of *Testbook* can be upgrading by adding dedicated modules to carry out more detailed tests such as engine analysis, and MOT tests for emission and diesel smoke.

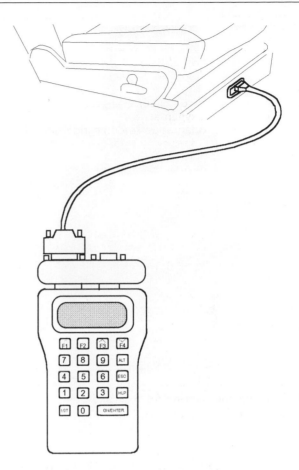

Fig. 13.39 Scan tool

Dedicated hand-held scanner Some vehicle manufacturers, such as Saab, recommend that their dealers use a portable tester, similar to the *scan tool* shown in Figure 13.39.

This is a dedicated multipurpose test instrument that is designed to interface with the on-board computer via a special 10-pin diagnostic plug fitted on the vehicle.

When used with the appropriate adapters, two-way communication with the ECU is obtained. The instrument has a keyboard and alphanumeric LCD display (see page 324) to allow the operator to select the test program, key-in data and observe test results; these are temporarily retained in the instrument's RAM memory. In addition to its test functions, the scan tool is able to interrogate the on-board computer to provide information on part number, program version, engine variant and serial number.

When used as a code reader, the scan tool shows a range of fault codes much larger than that given by the 'check engine' lamp. Once the fault code is displayed,

Fig. 13.40 Computer analyser (*Sun Electric (UK) Ltd*)

Sun computer analyser This top-of-the-range piece of equipment shown in Figure 13.40 is built around a 486SX computer platform having a 130 Mbyte hard drive, 4 Mbyte RAM memory, floppy disc drive, large colour monitor and standard keyboard. Other features and options include an approved 4-gas exhaust analyser, 24-pin printer, CD-ROM kit, mouse and remote control unit; these make the analyser suitable for testing and adjusting 2- and 4-stroke engines with 2 to 12 cylinders.

The unit offers the technician in-depth problem solving, fingertip reference and scope functions in a powerful computer that can be updated and expanded by loading floppy disc or CD software programs to cover new models and testing techniques.

Scope patterns show the performance of the commonly used sensors, injector behaviour and ignition outputs of conventional, wasted-spark, transistorized and full electronic systems.

The equipment is supported by software that guides the technician through a wide range of diagnostic tests, and emission checks recommended for a particular make and model of vehicle.

reference to the manufacturer's manual shows the additional tests that should be made to pinpoint the cause. They may require a particular input signal to the ECU, or some electrical test normally performed by a multimeter; these functions, together with vacuum and pressure measurement, are performed by the one instrument.

General engine analysers

In this country non-franchised dealers, and companies undertaking work on 'foreign' vehicles, are often unable to gain access to dedicated test equipment and technical data issued by some vehicle manufacturers. Without this support, repair work and accurate fault diagnosis is impossible unless alternative equipment and technical test data can be purchased from 'outside' sources. This need is filled by companies such as Sun Electric (UK) Ltd., who manufacture a complete range of vehicle test equipment suitable for detailed fault diagnosis and engine adjustment.

Fig. 13.41 Portable data link (*Sun Electric (UK) Ltd*)

Sun portable data link (PDL) The PDL instrument, shown in Figure 13.41, is a hand-held tool similar to the scan tool described on page 273. One major difference is that the PDL has provision to accept slot-in modules to make it suitable for a wide range of makes and models.

The LCD-type screen has a 40 character wide, 8-line display with a graphic capacity to show test results in a variety of formats including bargraph; also instructions, illustrated with pictures and symbols, can be displayed to guide the operator through the test sequences.

Using the appropriate adapter cable to connect with the diagnostic plug of an on-board computer, the unit is able to record in its memory, about 30 s of data associated with the operation of the ECU. The unit can be triggered either manually, or by the initiation of a fault code; after storing the data it can be displayed on the screen or exported to a printer.

The PDL unit can also act as an *electronic screwdriver* on management systems that alter engine settings (idle speed, CO, etc.) by electronic means.

On vehicles that have no diagnostic plug, the ECU multiplug is removed and a *break-out box* (BOB) is

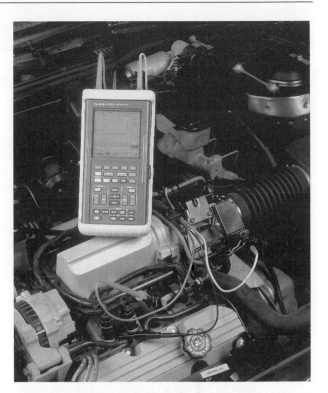

Fig. 13.42 Hand-held oscilloscope (Fluke)

connected in parallel with the main cable. When connected to a PDL unit, all signals going to, and coming from, the ECU can be monitored simultaneously; as a result the overall picture of system behaviour can be obtained for analysis.

Sun Automotive Information System (SAIS)

To overcome the lack of technical information available to non-franchasised dealers, the Sun Electric company produces a SAIS software package.

This can be used on a 386 (and above) personal computer having a CD-ROM drive. The software disc covers many vehicle models and contains topics such as test data, maintenance schedules and repair information.

By using a CD format, the information can be easily updated when new models are introduced.

Scopemeter®

Figure 13.42 shows a Fluke digital multimeter that is combined with an oscilloscope. This hand-held meter allows wave patterns of components, such as fuel injectors, to be displayed and examined when the system is in operation.

The Scopemeter incorporates many functions including a large memory.

REMEMBER

CLOSED-LOOP FUEL CONTROL SYSTEMS

Lambda sensor:

- monitors output
- detects oxygen in the exhaust
- produces an output voltage when no oxygen is present in the exhaust gas
- produces an output voltage when the air/fuel ratio is rich
- is damaged by lead in a fuel
- is electrically heated to allow it to operate when cold-starting and during extended part-load use

Fuel system:

- has an ECU that integrates ignition and fuelling requirements
- uses either single-point or multipoint injection
- injectors normally operate intermittently either in groups or sequentially in the firing order
- normally cuts off the fuel when the engine is coasted, overspeeded or is subjected to impact
- turbochargers have a waste gate valve controlled by an ECU to limit manifold boost

PROGRESS CHECK 13

1. State the advantage of a closed-loop control system for engine management over an open-loop system.

2. State the difference between proportional control and limit control as applied to a closed-loop system.

3. What is meant by mapping as applied to an ECU?

4. Why is a three-dimensional map required to plot ignition advance?

5. A Lambda sensor shows that the air/fuel mixture is correct. State the stoichiometric ratio for this mixture condition.

6. An engine, fitted with a single Lambda sensor, develops an injector fault. What values are used by the ECU to allow the engine to operate under limp-home conditions?

7. What is the purpose of a look-up table as applied to an ECU?

8. An engine has a closed-loop control system. What arrangement is used to provide feedback data on: a) ignition timing; b) fuel mixture strength?

9. Name two components of a conventional ignition system that are not needed for a wasted-spark system.

10. On some wasted-spark systems, two sparking plugs operate simultaneously. State why ignition only occurs in one cylinder.

11. State why the oxygen sensor on modern engines are normally electrically heated.

12. What method is used to measure air flow on an engine management system that does not use hot-wire or flap-type sensors?

13. Name the method used to electronically control turbocharger boost pressure.

14. Write in full the abbreviation OBD.

15. List FOUR requirements specified in OBD II.

16. Why does the limp-home facility used on UK vehicles in the early 1990s not comply with OBD II?

17. Why are two oxygen sensors required to comply with OBD II?

18. Describe how a flash code should be used to diagnose component defects.

19. What provision is made on modern electronic systems to enable fault codes to be read?

20. State why modern engine analysers normally use CD-ROM software.

14 *Starting-motor systems*

What is covered in this chapter

- ➡ types of light vehicle motors
- ➡ circuits for light vehicle motors
- ➡ light vehicle starting-motor drive mechanisms
- ➡ heavy vehicle motors
- ➡ maintenance and fault diagnosis

A starting motor converts electrical energy supplied from the battery into mechanical power. The system must supply sufficient power to enable an engine to be cranked, i.e. turned over, at a speed of about 100 rev/min so as to atomize the fuel and compress the air/fuel mixture sufficient to start the engine. In addition, the speed must be adequate to allow the momentum of the moving parts to 'carry' the engine over from one firing stroke to the next.

Power requirements

The power needed to attain a suitable speed depends on the size and type of engine and on the ambient conditions. Whereas a normal start of a warm 1½ litre engine requires a power of about 1.2 kW, this is increased to about 4 kW on a cold morning in winter.

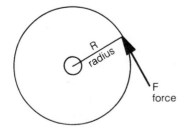

$$\text{torque} = \text{force} \times \text{radius}$$
$$T = F \times R$$

Fig. 14.1 Torque is the product of force and radius

Power is the product of torque and speed. By definition *torque* is a turning moment and is the force exerted at a given radius (Figure 14.1). A starting motor pinion driving an engine flywheel must exert sufficient torque to provide *breakaway*, i.e. initially move, the engine and then accelerate it to the cranking speed.

To provide high power, the motor circuit must be of low resistance to enable a current of up to 500 A to flow freely. The cables and switches must withstand the large load and the motor must be capable of converting the energy in an efficient manner. Naturally a starting system will not function properly unless the battery can provide the high current that is demanded. Similarly the battery p.d. should not fall excessively as this will affect the motor speed.

14.1 Types of light vehicle motors

Motor vehicles use a d.c. motor which is based on the principle described on page 26. In the past, motors with electromagnetic field systems have been popular, but improved permanent magnet materials have enabled the construction of lightweight, and more compact starting motors.

Starting motors have field windings connected in series or series–parallel with the main circuit and armature. Since a series-wound motor is capable of producing a high torque at low speed, it is particularly suitable as an engine-starting motor.

Series motor

This type of motor has the thick field coils arranged in series with the armature windings and all current that passes to the armature also goes through the field: this gives the strongest possible field.

Figure 14.2 shows a diagram of a simple series motor. When the switch is closed, the combined effect of the current in the armature and field windings distorts the

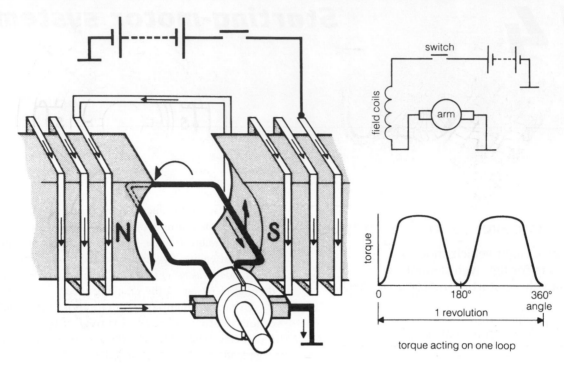

Fig. 14.2 Principle of a series wound motor

magnetic flux; this generates a torque that pushes the armature away from the field pole.

Constant rotation and a steady torque is required, so a number of armature conductor coils are needed: these coils are set in slots around a laminated soft-iron core. The end of each coil is soldered to a copper commutator segment which is insulated from the adjacent segments by mica (Figure 14.3). Armature conductors are made in the form of thick copper strips to provide a high current flow.

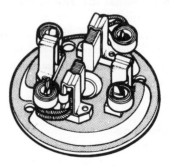

Fig. 14.4 Brush springs

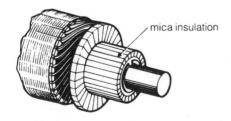

Fig. 14.3 Commutator

Comparatively hard brushes, often of a composition of carbon and copper, are used and these are pressed against the commutator by springs of a spiral shape (Figure 14.4).

Using a normal armature and commutator allows the brushes to 'feed' the armature conductor that is positioned where the field flux is most dense. When this conductor is pushed away, another conductor takes its place. By using a number of conductors, a near-uniform rotation is obtained. A typical armature has about 30 slots for conductors: the larger the number of slots, the smoother the motion.

Fig. 14.5 shows the construction of the field coils. These are made of copper or aluminium alloy and are wound in a direction which produces 'N' and 'S' poles. Each coil is bound with tape to provide insulation.

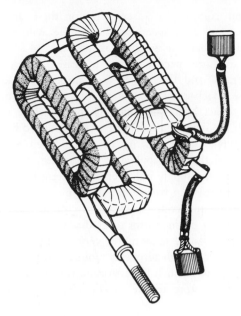

Fig. 14.5 Field coil construction

In the case of the two-pole field coils shown in Figure 14.5, one end of the coil is connected to a brush and the other end is attached to the starter supply terminal.

By using more poles a more powerful motor is obtained. Figure 14.6 shows a 2-brush, 4-pole motor in which the total magnet strength of the series-wound field is doubled because the current is made to form other field paths. The polarity of the poles is N–S–N–S and the diagram shows how the yoke forms a part of the magnetic circuit.

As the motor is in use for only short periods of time, plain, oil-impregnated sintered bronze brushes are suitable for the armature bearings.

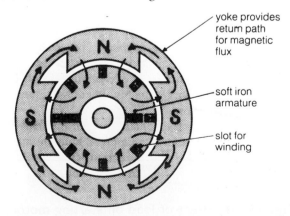

yoke provides return path for magnetic flux

soft iron armature

slot for winding

Fig. 14.6 A 4-pole, 2-brush motor

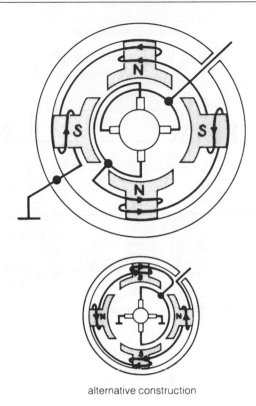

alternative construction

Fig. 14.7 Series wound motor

A 4-pole, 4-brush series motor is shown in Figure 14.7. In this design the current from the field is fed to the two insulated brushes, so the reduced brush resistance allows more current to flow. Current is the same throughout the circuit, so two other insulated brushes must also be fitted.

Some Lucas starting motors, which use this field-and-brush arrangement, have a 'wave-wound' field system and a 'face-type' commutator (Figure 14.8). This modern design is more compact and is cheaper to manufacture.

Series-parallel motor Figure 14.9 shows a series-parallel motor. This has the field coils in series with the armature but connects the two pairs of field coils in parallel. Current flowing to the armature divides as it enters the motor; half passes through one pair of field coils and the remainder flows to the other pair.

A lower field resistance is achieved with this arrangement, so the motor can handle more current and give a higher torque output.

Characteristics of a series motor Torque output of a motor is directly proportional to the product of magnetic

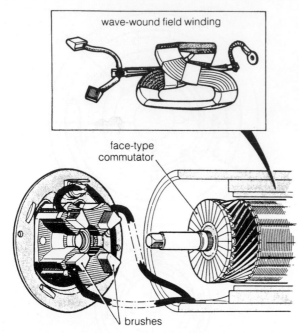

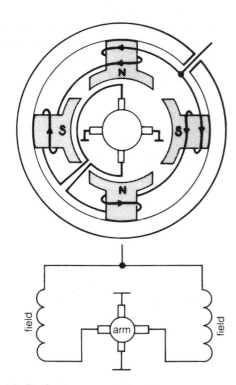

Fig. 14.8 Wave-wound field and face-type commutator

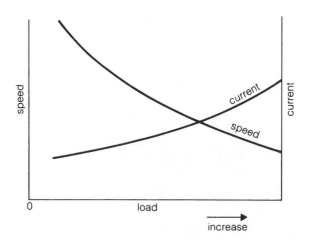

Fig. 14.9 Series-parallel motor

flux and current. In a series motor these are at a maximum at zero speed so the torque will be at a maximum when the armature is 'locked'.

As armature speed is slowly increased, a *back-e.m.f.* is generated and this causes the current to gradually decrease. Back-e.m.f. is due to the tendency of the motor to act as a generator. As the armature moves through the magnetic flux, an e.m.f. is induced into the conductors. As the polarity of the induced e.m.f. is opposite to the p.d. applied to the motor, the e.m.f. acts against the supply p.d., hence the term back-e.m.f.

The increase in back-e.m.f. with increase in speed, and in consequence the decrease in current, causes the torque output of the motor to gradually fall. This characteristic makes the series motor very suitable for engine starting. A very high torque is required to give engine breakaway but a much lower torque is needed to overcome the resisting torque of the engine at cranking speed.

Speed of a motor varies inversely as the field strength, i.e. when the field strength is decreased the armature speed is increased. Figure 14.10 shows the effect of load on a series motor. Under a heavy load the field is saturated and no large variation in speed occurs with slight alteration in load, but when the load is considerably reduced, the rise in the back-e.m.f. causes the magnetic flux to diminish: this results in a rise in the motor speed.

The graph shows that a series motor will over-speed if it is allowed to run free without load: this may cause serious damage to the motor.

The efficiency of a starting motor is between the limits 50–70%.

Fig. 14.10 Effect of load on starting motor

14.2 Circuits for light vehicle motors

Ideally the battery should be situated as close as possible to the motor to minimize voltage drop of the cables. A thick cable such as 37/0.90 is used and a solenoid is fitted to act as a remote-controlled switch to limit the length of the main cable.

Although an insulated-return system is sometimes used, the earth-return arrangement shown in Figure 14.11 is the most common. Since the circuit may have to carry a current of up to 500 A, it is essential that all connections are clean and secure and that the earth-bonding strap joining the engine to the vehicle body is in good condition.

Solenoid   The solenoid shown in Figure 14.11 is a single-coil, single-stage type which can be operated only after the ignition has been switched on. In the past, an independent starter switch was used but it is now common practice to combine the starter and ignition switches: by turning one key both switches can be operated.

The solenoid has copper contacts of adequate area, which are brought together in one stage when the solenoid is energized. When the starter switch is released, a spring returns the solenoid plunger and the contacts are opened.

A two-coil, single-stage type, shown in Figure 14.12, has two windings connected in parallel. When the switch is operated both windings are energized, but as soon as the contacts close, the closing coil is short-

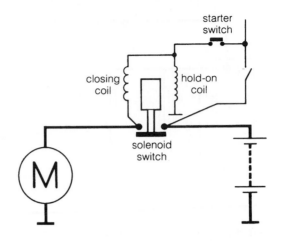

Fig. 14.12 Two-coil, single-stage solenoid

circuited. At this stage, the comparatively small current needed by the hold-on coil is sufficient to hold the solenoid plunger in the closed position.

Vehicles fitted with an automatic transmission require an additional switch in the solenoid switch circuit. This extra switch, called an *inhibitor switch* (or *neutral safety switch*), is set to open and prevents starter operation when a gear is selected.

Starting motor immobilization   A modern anti-theft unit fitted as original equipment normally works in conjunction with the engine management system. In addition to immobilizing the ignition system, these units also isolate the starting motor when the ignition key is removed.

Figure 14.13 shows an example of a circuit that incorporates an anti-theft and engine immobilization control unit. In this double-fused circuit the external relay is energized when the combined ignition/starter switch is closed to complete the circuit to earth through the anti-theft alarm.

14.3 Light vehicle starting-motor drive mechanisms

On the majority of vehicles the flywheel is fitted with a ring gear and this meshes with a pinion that is driven by the armature of the motor.

Gear ratio

The ratio of the flywheel gear and the starter pinion is governed by the characteristics of the motor. Figure 14.14 shows a typical output for a motor and in this case the maximum power is developed when the motor

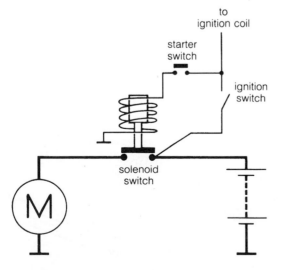

Fig. 14.11 Starting-motor solenoid

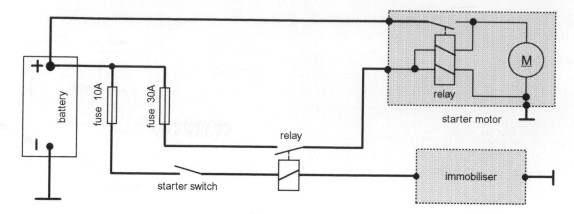

Fig. 14.13 Starter circuit with anti-theft alarm

speed is 1000 rev/min. Assuming the cranking speed required is 100 rev/min, then the ratio needed for this motor is given by:

$$\text{ratio} = \frac{\text{motor speed}}{\text{cranking speed}} = \frac{1000}{100} = 10:1$$

Normally the pinion has about 9 teeth so the number of teeth on the flywheel is set to give the appropriate ratio; in this case 90 teeth.

Pinion engagement

The pinion is meshed with the flywheel only when the starting motor is operated. Engagement can be made in one of two ways:

● inertia engagement
● pre-engagement.

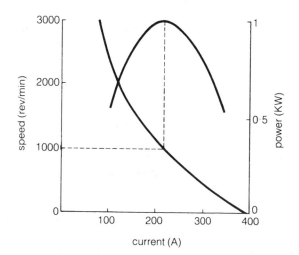

Fig. 14.14 Motor performance

Inertia engagement Inertia is the natural tendency of a body to resist any change to its velocity. In the case of a starting motor, the inertia of a pinion is utilized to move the pinion along its shaft (i.e. to move it axially) and slide it into mesh with a flywheel gear. When the pinion becomes fully engaged, the rotation of the pinion drives the flywheel.

Figure 14.15 shows the main features of a Lucas 'S' type inertia drive. The pinion is mounted on a helical screwed sleeve that is splined to the armature spindle and retained by a strong compression spring.

When the motor is operated, the combined effect of the sudden rotation of the armature and the inertia of the pinion causes the pinion to move along the helical sleeve in a direction towards the motor. During this movement, the pinion slides into mesh with the flywheel teeth aided by the chamfer on the teeth. The sudden shock as the pinion starts to drive is cushioned by the large compression spring. While the pinion is driving, the reaction to the variable resisting torque of

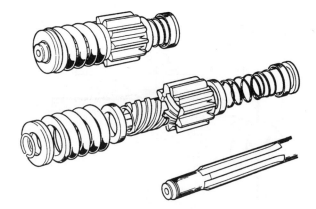

Fig. 14.15 Lucas 'S' type inertia drive

the engine causes the helical sleeve to move axially. This movement is absorbed by the spring so the shocks are damped.

When the engine starts, the speed of the flywheel throws the pinion along the helical sleeve to disengage the drive. This ejection is quite rapid so the large compression spring is again used to cushion the shock as the pinion hits its stop.

The nominal distance between the pinion and the flywheel teeth for the drive shown in Figure 14.15 is only about 4 mm, so a thin wire retaining spring is fitted to prevent the pinion vibrating along the helix and touching the flywheel when the engine is running.

Movement of the pinion for engagement is either towards the motor (inboard type) or away from the motor (outboard). The pinion, fitted to the commonly used inboard arrangement, is close to the motor when it is driving so the bending stress in the shaft is less than that given by the outboard type.

An alternative type of inertia drive is the Lucas 'Eclipse' shown in Figure 14.16. This type is similar to the Bendix drive commonly used on American vehicles.

Inertia action is the same as that used in Figure 14.15 but one difference is that the Bendix type uses the main spring to transmit the drive from the armature shaft to the helical sleeve. In addition to the torsional load, the spring also acts as a cushion to absorb the shocks of engagement and disengagement.

An engine that has a small flywheel requires a small pinion to give the required gear ratio. In this case the pinion is mounted on a barrel which has a suitable mass and diameter to give sufficient inertia for engagement. A Lucas 'SB' barrel-type drive is shown in Figure 14.17.

All inertia-type drives rely on the pinion sliding on the helical sleeve. This is not possible if the sleeve is

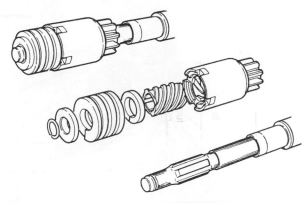

Fig. 14.17 Lucas barrel-type drive

lubricated with normal engine oil because the wet surface collects dust from within the clutch housing. One recommended lubricant is Molykiron (SAE5), but if this type of lubricant is not available then the helix should be left in a dry state after cleaning.

Pre-engaged drive   This type was originally introduced for diesel engines, but nowadays it is used on many petrol engines.

The pinion engagement is performed by an electrical solenoid which is integral with the starting motor. In addition to its mechanical engagement role, the solenoid acts as a relay switch to delay the passage of the full motor current until the pinion has fully meshed with the flywheel. When the engine fires, the pinion does not eject until the driver releases the switch. This feature overcomes the problem of premature ejection of the pinion during isolated firing stroke. Better starting and reduced wear of the flywheel teeth is therefore achieved.

After the engine has started, overspeeding of the motor is avoided by using a unidirectional (overrunning) clutch between the pinion and the armature.

Figure 14.18 shows the constructional details of one type of pre-engaged motor. A solenoid plunger is connected to an operating lever, which is pivoted to the casing at its centre and forked at its lower end to engage with a guide ring. This ring acts against the unidirectional roller clutch and pinion. Helical splines, formed on the armature shaft, engage with the driving part of the unidirectional clutch. These splines cause the pinion to rotate slightly when the clutch and pinion are moved axially. A strong return spring in the solenoid holds the lever and pinion in the disengaged position.

When the starter switch is operated, the two-coil solenoid winding becomes energized and the plunger is

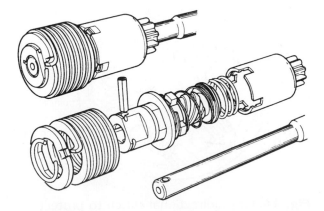

Fig. 14.16 Lucas Eclipse-type drive

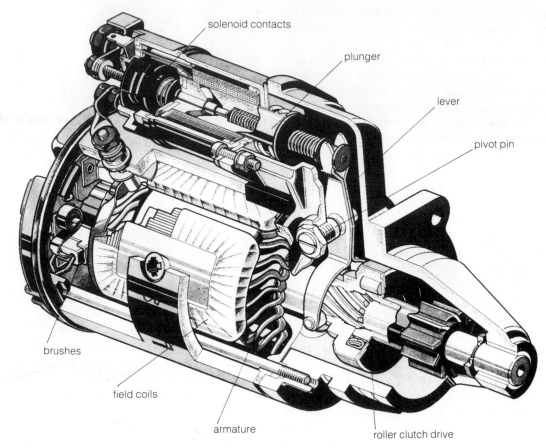

Fig. 14.18 Pre-engaged starting motor (Lucas M50)

drawn into the core. This initial action causes the lower end of the operating lever to move the guide ring and pinion assembly towards the flywheel teeth. This movement, aided by the slight rotation of the pinion, normally gives full meshing of the gears. After this initial action, extra travel of the solenoid plunger causes the main contacts to close: this connects the battery to the motor.

Drive from the armature is transmitted to the unidirectional clutch and pinion by helical splines.

Sometimes the initial movement causes the pinion teeth to butt against the flywheel teeth and this prevents full engagement. When this occurs, a spring in the linkage flexes and allows the solenoid plunger to operate the main switch. As soon as the armature and pinion start to move, the teeth engage and the meshing spring pushes the pinion to its driving position.

After the engine has fired, the pinion speed will exceed the armature speed. If the motor is still in use, the rollers in the unidirectional clutch will exceed the armature speed. If the motor is still in use, the rollers

in the unidirectional clutch will be unlocked and the clutch will slip to protect the motor (Figure 14.19).

Release of the starter switch de-energizes the solenoid and allows the return spring to open the switch

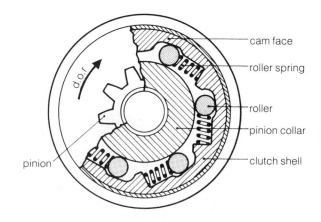

Fig. 14.19 Unidirectional clutch to protect motor

contacts. This occurs well before the pinion disengages and so avoids overspeeding of the motor. Further movement of the plunger causes the operating level to fully withdraw the pinion from the flywheel.

Armature braking After disengagement there is a tendency for a large armature and pinion assembly to continue to rotate due to its momentum. On some starting motors this is prevented by using a disc brake (Figure 14.20). The driving part of the unidirectional

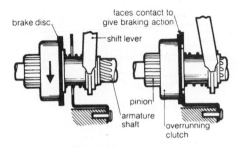

Fig. 14.20 Armature brake

clutch is designed to rub against a part of the casing when the pinion has fully returned. This device minimizes noise and tooth wear which would otherwise occur if the starter was operated before the components had come to rest.

Low-power indexing As applied to starting motors, indexing means the lining-up of the pinion and flywheel teeth to allow full engagement before maximum power is supplied by the motor.

Low-power indexing is used on Lucas M50 starting motors. These motors have a two-stage solenoid that enables one field winding to be energized before the other field windings come into operation. The low-powered initial rotation of the pinion reduces the problem of tooth abutment.

Pinion setting A pinion of an inertia drive should have the correct out-of-mesh clearance so that it does not contact the flywheel before it starts to revolve. Lucas 'S' type drives should have a clearance of about 3 mm.

On some pre-engaged motors, an adjustable pivot pin for the operating lever allows the pinion to be set in the correct position. After energizing the solenoid from a 6 V supply, the pin is adjusted until the recommended clearance is obtained between the pinion and end housing.

Permanent-magnet motor

A significant improvement in the performance-to-weight ratio is achieved by using a permanent-magnet field system. Used in conjunction with a planetary gear reduction drive, this type of motor is very compact and is suitable for use as a starting motor for a car engine.

Figure 14.21 shows the basic construction of a permanent-magnet motor. This type uses a planetary gear train made of a new plastic–steel material. The sun gear is attached to the armature and the output is taken from the three planets which revolve around the inside of a fixed ring gear.

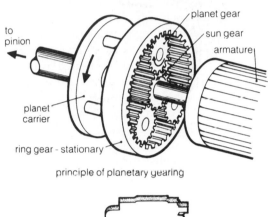

principle of planetary gearing

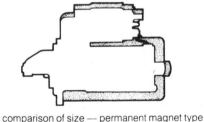

comparison of size — permanent magnet type and conventional type motor

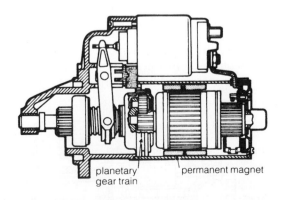

Fig. 14.21 Permanent-magnet starting motor (Bosch type)

14.4 Heavy vehicle motors

An engine having a capacity of more than 3 litres needs a starting motor of considerable power, especially if the engine is a compression-ignition (CI) type. This type of engine must be cranked at a speed of at least 100 rev/min to initiate combustion, whereas a petrol engine will usually start if it is rotated at about 50–75 rev/min.

The CI engine always draws in a full charge of air and has a very high compression ratio, so the maximum torque required to drive the engine over 'compression' is greater than a petrol engine. Having passed top dead centre (t.d.c.) the high pressure in the cylinder accelerates the piston rapidly, so this causes both the rotational speed and the resisting torque loading on the starting motor to vary considerably.

To obtain high starting power many vehicles use a 24 V system. For a given electrical power requirement, the doubling of the voltage, compared with a light vehicle's 12 V system, reduces the current by half. Without the extra 12 V, the current load on the battery and starter circuit would be exceptionally high, especially on a cold morning in winter.

Another problem experienced with large engines is the high torque required to overcome breakaway and inertia of the heavy parts. It needs a strong drive system and the pinion of this system must be fully engaged before full power is applied to the motor.

Two types of motor and drive system are used; these are:

- axial (sliding armature)
- coaxial (sliding gear).

Axial (sliding armature) starting motor
The main features of this type are its size and robust construction. Engagement of the pinion to the flywheel is obtained by arranging the complete armature assembly to slide axially through the motor casing. Figure 14.22 shows a simplified construction.

The motor is shown in the rest position and in this state the armature is held by a spring so that it is offset

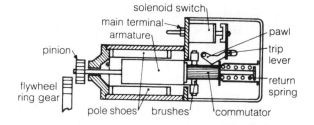

Fig. 14.22 Construction of axial starter

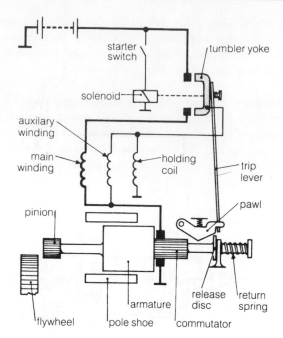

Fig. 14.23 Circuit of axial motor

to the field poles. When the field is energized, the armature is pulled to the left and the pinion is slid into engagement with the flywheel.

Figure 14.23 shows the electrical circuit which incorporates three field windings. The main winding is the usual thick-section, low-resistance winding and is connected, in series, to the armature. The auxiliary winding is wound with thinner wire and has a relatively high resistance; it is also connected in series with the armature but in parallel with the main winding. The holding winding is also a high-resistance winding but is connected in parallel with the armature as well as with the other windings.

The starter is operated through a two-stage solenoid switch, mounted on the starter, and is energized by the driver's switch in the cab. When the switch is operated, the first pair of contacts closes but the second pair is held open by a pawl which engages in a slot in the trip lever. Only when the pinion is near fully engaged does the pawl allow the second pair of contacts to meet.

Figure 14.24 shows the operation of this type of motor. In Figure 14.24(a) the first pair of contacts has been closed which energizes the auxiliary windings, holding windings and armature. This action causes the armature to rotate slowly and move axially to a position where it is central to the field poles. At the same time, the pinion is slid into mesh with the flywheel gear.

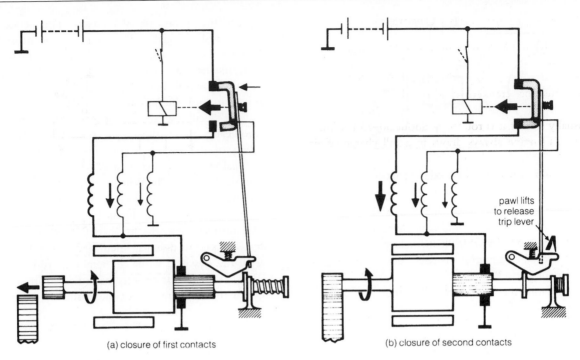

(a) closure of first contacts   (b) closure of second contacts

pawl lifts
to release
trip lever

Fig. 14.24 Action of axial motor

When the pinion is near to full engagement, the release disc on the armature strikes the pawl and causes the trip lever to close the second pair of contacts (Figure 14.24(b)). Current now flows through the main windings, which allows the motor to develop its full torque.

As cranking speed increases, back-e.m.f. causes the current through the main and auxiliary windings to decrease, especially when the engine fires spasmodically but does not actually start. In this condition, the magnetic strength in the main and auxiliary windings is insufficient to oppose the armature return spring and hold the pinion in full engagement. This is prevented by the holding winding because the current in this winding is not affected by the back-e.m.f. generated by the rotating armature.

After the pinion has de-meshed and the armature has returned, the momentum of the rotating mass tends to keep the armature rotating. This is resisted by the 'generator effect' produced by the interaction of the holding winding and the armature. This electrical reaction to the armature 'brakes' the armature and quickly brings it to rest to enable the driver to re-engage the starter without damage to the gear teeth.

The pinion is connected to the armature shaft through a small multiplate clutch. This serves two functions:

- It is arranged to slip if the torque applied to it exceeds a pre-determined limiting value, thus safeguarding the starter from damage should the engine backfire.
- It is arranged to disengage when the engine starts and drives the pinion faster than the armature, thus preventing the armature being damaged by excessive speed.

Coaxial (sliding gear) starting motor

Lucas CAV can offer this type of motor in 12 V or 24 V versions as an alternative to the axial type, whereas Bosch use it for the heavy end of their range.

As with the axial starting motor, this type moves the pinion into engagement under reduced power and only when it is fully meshed is full power applied. The main difference is in the way the pinion is slid into mesh with the flywheel. Instead of the whole armature assembly moving axially, the pinion only is made to slide into mesh by a solenoid mounted in a housing co-axially with the shaft.

Figure 14.25 shows the main details of the circuit of a coaxial starting motor. The main terminal is connected directly to the battery and the terminal marked 'sol' is connected to the battery via a starter switch in the cab. When this switch is operated, the two-stage solenoid is energized, which moves the pinion

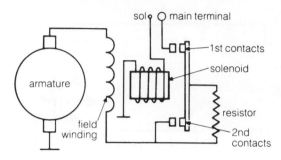

Fig.14.25 Circuit of coaxial starter

into mesh and at the same time closes the first set of contacts, the second set being kept open by a trip lever. At this state, current to the main field is limited by the resistor, so the armature rotates slowly during the engagement period.

Just before the fully-meshed position is reached, a lever trips the second set of contacts. This action by-passes the resistor, gives full current to the main field and allows the motor to produce its maximum torque.

The mechanical details of one type of Lucas CAV motor are shown in Figure 14.26. This design uses four steel balls to lock the pinion sleeve to the shaft to avoid premature ejection of the pinion when the engine fires spasmodically. When the engine starts normally, over-speeding of the motor is prevented by utilizing the centrifugal effect on a set of steel balls positioned adjacent to the locking balls. When a given speed is reached, the outward force on the balls moves the locking collar and allows the pinion to disengage.

A return spring at the flywheel end of the armature shaft assists pinion disengagement and holds the pinion clear of the flywheel while the engine is running.

Bosch sliding-gear motors have the main solenoid placed at the opposite end of the motor to the pinion.

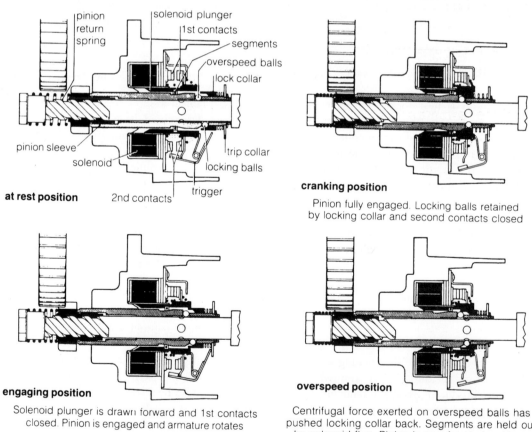

at rest position

cranking position

Pinion fully engaged. Locking balls retained by locking collar and second contacts closed

engaging position

Solenoid plunger is drawn forward and 1st contacts closed. Pinion is engaged and armature rotates

overspeed position

Centrifugal force exerted on overspeed balls has pushed locking collar back. Segments are held out by solenoid flux. Pinion is now free to be driven out of engagement.

Fig. 14.26 Action of coaxial starter

This solenoid keeps the pinion in full engagement until the driver releases the starter switch. Drive from the armature to the pinion is transmitted by a multidisc clutch. In addition to its torque-limiting duty, this clutch also prevents overspeeding by releasing the plates and slipping when the engine starts and overruns the motor.

Some motors use a shunt field winding to limit the no-load speed and others have a brake winding which comes into action when the driver releases the starter switch.

REMEMBER

A starting motor:

- has either a *series* or a *series-parallel* wound field
- can be damaged if it is allowed to run free
- is placed close to the battery to minimize voltage drop across the supply cables
- pinion is normally pre-engaged to reduce shock of gear impact
- of the *axial* or *coaxial* type is used on heavy vehicles

14.5 Maintenance and fault diagnosis

The most important part of a starting system is the battery; if this is not in first-class condition, then the speed will be low and the duration of cranking will be limited. It should be noted that a fault attributed to a battery may be due to other factors such as: a defective charging system, a short to earth in another system, or overload of the battery due to driving or seasonal conditions.

Attention to warning instruments and observation of the engine's starting performance, enables the driver to recognize the initial conditions that soon develop into a major fault.

As a very large current has to be provided by a battery to the starting motor, a drop in the battery p.d. occurs. When this drop is excessive, the ignition system is 'robbed' and the voltage output of the coil may then be insufficient to give a suitable spark at the plugs, although the starting motor is still functioning, albeit at a low speed. This condition can be confirmed when an engine cannot be started with the motor, but can be started easily by 'bump-starting' (rolling the vehicle in top gear and suddenly releasing the clutch). Normally this problem is associated with a battery fault, but on many modern engines the problem is overcome by fitting a cold-start ballast resistor in the ignition supply lead. In addition to the resistor lead, a separate lead is fitted between a terminal on the starter solenoid and the ignition coil; this lead allows the resistor to be by-passed when the starter is operated (see page 178).

Maintenance

Routine attention should be given to the battery, especially the terminals. All terminals and connectors in the starter circuit should be clean and secure.

Fault diagnosis

If the likely defects of each part of the system are considered, together with the possible symptoms given by each defect, then it is possible to reverse the order and, as a result, the electrician should be able to offer a probable cause of a particular fault.

The parts of the system which cause the main problems, and the possible faults are:

- *battery*: low state of charge or defective;
- *terminals*: high resistance due to corrosion or slackness;
- *cables*: broken or partially broken, especially the earth-bonding strap between the engine and frame;
- *solenoid*: dirty contacts or faulty connection between windings and terminals;
- *starter switch*: high resistance at contacts or broken cables;
- *motor*: brushes not bedding or dirty commutator;
- *pinion*: not meshing or jammed due to a worn flywheel ring gear.

These faults are incorporated in Table 14.1. The second column suggests some initial checks which should be made to enable the actual cause to be diagnosed. Location of the precise cause often requires the use of test equipment.

A starting motor that seizes the engine when the motor is operated indicates that the teeth on the flywheel have worn to the extent that they allow the gears to jam together as they attempt to mesh.

An engine always comes to rest at the start of one of the compression strokes, so the flywheel becomes burred due to pinion entry in these positions. The number of places that wear occurs around the circumference depends on the number of cylinders of the engine, e.g.:

4-cylinder engine = 2 places
6-cylinder engine = 3 places
8-cylinder engine = 4 places

Symptom	Result of initial check	Possible cause
Low cranking speed	Lights dim when starter switch is operated	1. Discharged or defective battery 2. Poor connections between battery and solenoid 3 Tight engine
Starter does not operate	No lights or lights go out when starter is operated	1. Discharged or defective battery 2. Poor connections between battery and solenoid or between battery and earth 3. Severe short circuit to earth in starting motor
	Solenoid 'clicks' when starter switch is operated; lights unaffected	1. Poor connection between solenoid and motor 2. Broken or insecure earthstrap 3. Defective solenoid 4. Defective motor – most probably commutator or brushes
	No 'click' from solenoid; lights unaffected	1. Defective solenoid 2. Defective starter switch 3. Poor connections between starter switch and solenoid 4. Defective inhibitor switch (auto. transmission)
	Repeating 'clicking' from solenoid; lights unaffected	1. Broken holding coil in solenoid
	Repeated 'clicking' from solenoid; lights dim	1. Discharged or defective battery
	Lights dim when starter is operated and engine has seized	1. Pinion teeth jammed in flywheel 2. Engine has seized due to engine problem
Starter 'whines' but piniondoes not engage		1. Dirt on helix (inertia drive) 2. Defective pinion engagement system (pre-engaged)

Table 14.1 Fault diagnosis

Whereas in the past a spanner was used to wind-out the pinion after it had jammed, on a modern unit it is necessary to slacken-off the securing bolts of the motor. In emergency, it is sometimes possible to free a pinion by rocking the car backwards and forwards with top gear engaged **and the ignition off**, but this practice may result in a bent armature spindle.

Most starter-ring gears are held on to the flywheel by an interference fit. When a new gear has to be fitted, the worn gear is removed by drilling a hole in the gear and then splitting the ring with a chisel. The new ring is preheated to the recommended temperature and, while it is still hot, it is tapped into place making sure that the chamfer on the teeth is positioned on the side of pinion entry.

SAFE PRACTICE

Disconnect earth terminal of battery before removing a starting motor from an engine

After motor has been refitted don't forget to re-program all coded units, such as radio, and ECUs

---

Circuit tests

Prior to carrying out these checks, the battery condition should be determined by using a hydrometer and heavy-discharge tester.

The tests shown in Figure 14.27 are made with a multimeter or moving-coil voltmeter (0–20 V range) and all readings are taken **when the engine is being cranked**. To prevent the engine starting, the low-tension ignition circuit should be disconnected or, in the case of a diesel engine, the stop control should be operated.

Although the diagram shows an inertia drive motor, the same method is used on a pre-engaged motor.

Test 1. The meter is connected across the battery and the reading is noted. If the voltage is less than 10 V the battery is suspect.

Tests 2, 3 and 4. Readings taken at the points shown should be similar to test 1. If the reading at point 4 shows a voltage drop greater than 0.5 V, then the cause of the resistance should be investigated.

Test 5. This test measures the voltage drop on the earth side of the circuit. If the reading is greater than 0.25 V then all earth connections should be checked, especially the engine-bonding strap.

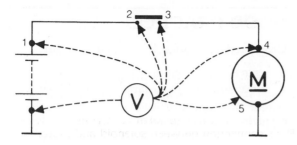

Fig. 14.27 Starting motor circuit tests

A high resistance at any connection point causes a drop in voltage; this can be verified by connecting a voltmeter across the part of the circuit where the resistance is suspected (Figure 14.28). If the voltage applied to the starter is lower than specified, the current will be reduced and this will lower the motor's speed and torque.

Brushes and commutator
If the battery and external circuit are serviceable but the motor fails to operate, then the motor should be removed, dismantled and inspected. The earth terminal of the battery must be disconnected before attempting to remove the motor.

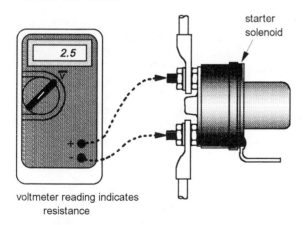

Fig. 14.28 Volt-drop test to locate resistance

Commutator This should be cleaned with a petrol-moistened cloth; any burnt spots can be removed by using fine glass-paper, but not emery cloth.

When a satisfactory surface cannot be obtained, it will be necessary to skim the commutator in a lathe.

Brushgear All brushes must move freely in their boxes, the springs must exert sufficient force and each brush

should not be less than the specified length. For example, in the case of Lucas motors, the minimum length is 9.5 mm and 8 mm for face type and cylindrical commutators respectively.

Fitting new brushes involves the soldering of the brush leads to the appropriate connector points. In the case of aluminium alloy field coils, the old brush lead is cut at a given distance from the field and the new lead is soldered to the old lead.

A brush used on a cylindrical commutator must be bedded-in by using glass-paper to cut the brush to the same contour as the commutator.

Bench testing the motor
A number of tests can be applied to the motor; these include the following:

Light-running test Under free-running conditions on a test stand, the power of the motor can be measured (Figure 14.29). The time taken for this test must be short because the centrifugal effect at the no-load speed can cause damage to the armature windings.

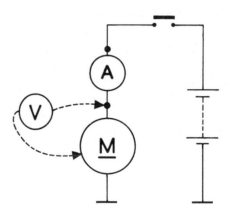

Fig. 14.29 Position of meters for light-

A Lucas 9M90 motor should 'draw' 840 W from a 12 V supply.

Locked-torque test A torque arm is clamped to the pinion and a spring balance is used to measure the force exerted by the motor (Figure 14.30). When the armature is locked the motor produces its maximum torque and consumes its maximum current. Any high resistance in the motor reduces current and as a result the torque is lowered.

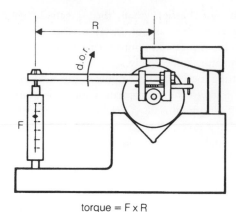

torque = F x R

Fig. 14.30 Locked-torque test

A Lucas 9M90 motor should produce a maximum torque of 12.88 Nm (at 20°C) and 'draw' 3220 W from a 7 V supply.

Running–torque test The torque can be measured by using a dummy flywheel on a special test bench which

GOOD PRACTICE

Unwanted resistance in a starter circuit:

- reduces torque and speed
- is diagnosed by a volt–drop test carried out when the motor is under load
- gives the same symptoms as a defective battery

loads the motor and simulates the resisting torque of an engine. By noting the output torque t (Nm) and speed n (rev/s), the power (W) is obtained from:

$$\text{Power} = 2\pi nt$$

Comparing the output power with the input power allows the efficiency of the motor to be calculated:

$$\text{Efficiency (\%)} = \frac{\text{output power}}{\text{input power}} \times 100$$

PROGRESS CHECK 14

1. Series wound is one type of motor. Name ONE other type.

2. State the duty of an armature in a motor.

3. State why four brushes are used in preference to two.

4. What is meant by back-e.m.f. and how does it relate to current flow through a motor?

5. A solenoid fitted to a light-vehicle starting motor has two windings. State why two windings are used instead of one.

6. Two fuses and an external relay are used on some light-vehicle starting systems. Draw the circuit of this layout and explain the effect of a:

(a) defective external relay;
(b) blown fuse.

7. State the effect on motor operation if the gearing between the motor and engine is either too low or too high.

8. State one reason of failure-to-engage for each of the following types of motor drive:
(a) inertia; (b) pre-engaged.

9. State the purpose of a unidirectional clutch in a motor drive system.

10. State ONE advantage of a permanent magnet motor over a conventional type.

11. One type of heavy vehicle starting motor is called axial. Name ONE other type.

12. Describe the sequence of events which take place in an axial type motor when the starter switch is operated.

13. State the reason why current must be flowing in a circuit when a motor circuit is being drop-tested.

14. Engine flywheel teeth do not wear evenly when an inertia-type drive is used. State the wear pattern of the teeth when the engine has:
(a) 4-cylinders;
(b) 6-cylinders;
(c) 8-cylinders.

15. What information is gained from a locked-torque motor test?

15 *Vehicle lighting systems*

What is covered in this chapter

➡ circuit layout
➡ lamp construction
➡ maintenance and fault diagnosis

Lights are needed on a vehicle to allow the driver to see, and be seen, in conditions of darkness and poor visibility.

Statutory regulations dictate the number, position and specification of many of the external lights fitted to a vehicle. In addition to the *obligatory lights*, vehicle manufacturers and vehicle owners often fit other *supplementary lights* to fulfil other purposes.

15.1 Circuit layout

Lamps are grouped in separate circuits; these include the following:

- *Side and rear lamps* including lamps for the number plate, glove compartment and instrument panel illumination.
- *Main driving lamps* (headlamps) fitted with a dipping facility to prevent approaching drivers being dazzled.
- *Rear fog lamp(s)* for 'guarding' the rear of the vehicle in conditions of poor visibility.
- *Auxiliary driving lamps* including spot lamps for distance illumination and fog lamps that are positioned suitably and designed to reduce the reflected glare from fog.
- *Reversing lamps* to illuminate the road when the vehicle is moving backwards and warn other drivers of the movement.
- *Brake lights* to warn a following driver that the vehicle is slowing down.
- *Interior lights* and courtesy lights on doors.

- *Instrument panel lights* for signalling either the correct operation of a unit, or the presence of a fault in a particular system.

In addition to these lights, directional indicators and hazard warning lights are fitted; these are covered at a later stage in this book.

Circuit arrangements

For maximum illumination the lamps are connected in parallel with each other (see page 9). This arrangement provides various circuit paths for the current so an open circuit in any branch will cause failure in that one branch only; the other lamps will still function normally.

Most vehicle lighting systems use an earth-return circuit; this requires less cable than an insulated return or two-wire system. When the vehicle body is used as an earth, a good clean connection must be made at suitable earthing points on the main body. This earthing lead is essential where the lamp is mounted in a plastic body panel.

Lighting circuit diagrams are drawn in either a *locational* or *compact* theoretical form. The former type shows each component positioned relative to its situation on the vehicle. Although this is useful in showing the location of the various connectors and component parts, it makes the diagram more difficult to trace out a particular circuit path. To minimize this problem, some manufacturers use extra diagrams to show separate parts of the circuit, e.g. the supply system is shown separately. Figure 15.1 shows a simple circuit drawn both ways.

This parallel circuit has the lamps controlled by three switches: *Switch 1* operates the side and rear lamps. It also supplies: *Switch 2* which operates and headlamps, and supplies: *Switch 3* to distribute the current to either the main beam or the dip-beam headlamp bulbs.

Circuit protection
A single fuse, mounted in the main supply cable, protects a circuit in the event of a severe

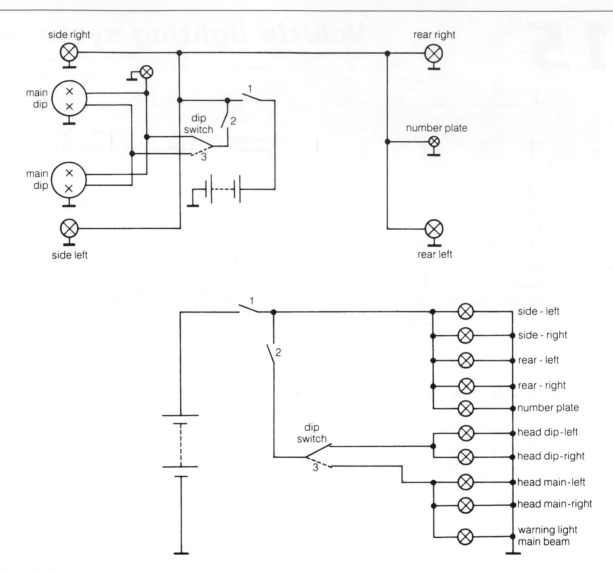

Fig. 15.1 Lighting circuit – simplified

short. This simple protection system cannot be used in the external lighting supply cable because all lights will go out when the fuse fails; a dangerous situation when the vehicle is travelling at speed along a dark road.

To avoid this danger manufacturers either fit separate fuses for each light system, or refrain from fusing the headlamp circuit altogether (Figure 15.2).

The circuit in Figure 15.2 incorporates the following extra features.

Headlamp flash switch This switch enables the driver to signal to other drivers during daylight and avoids the use of the main light switches. The spring-loaded switch operates only when the lever is held in the 'on' position.

Ignition-controlled headlamps Regulations insist that the headlamps should not be used when the engine and vehicle are stationary. This is achieved by using the ignition switch to control the feed to the headlamps. A relay is often used to reduce the current load on the switch.

Auxiliary driving lamps These long-range lamps (spot lamps) are used when the headlamps are set to main beam, but they must be extinguished when other vehicles are approaching. This is achieved by connecting the auxiliary lamps to the main beam branch of the circuit. As the power consumed by these lamps is considerable, the load on the lighting switches is reduced by using a relay to control these lamps.

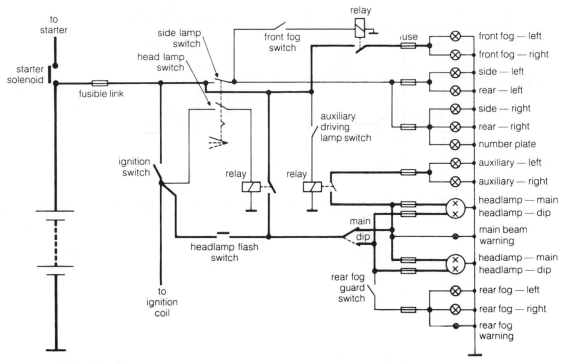

Fig. 15.2 Lighting circuit incorporating fuses and relays

Fog lamps (front) In fog the main headlamps cause glare so by using low-mounted fog lamps this problem is minimized. These twin lamps can be used instead of headlamps so the feed must be taken from the side lamp branch of the circuit.

Rear fog guard The high-intensity fog lamp(s) guard the rear of the vehicle; they must be used only in conditions of poor visibility. To prevent the driver using the lights illegally the feed is taken from either the dipped beam or the front fog lamps. A warning light must be fitted to indicate when the rear fog guard lamp(s) are in use.

Lamp failure indicator Many manufacturers now fit a warning system to inform the driver when a light is not functioning correctly. Often the lamp signal indicator on the instrument panel is a graphical map of the vehicle. On this display sections are illuminated either when the lights are operating normally, or as a signal to warn the driver that a light is 'out'.

In addition to the graphical display unit, a module (sometimes called a 'bulb outage module') is fitted to sense when a specific section of the circuit does not consume the appropriate current. When an open-circuit condition exists, the module triggers a light on the instrument panel to show the driver the actual lamp that is 'out'.

To enable the module to monitor the system, each branch of the circuit passes through the module. Unfortunately, this feature tends to complicate the circuit and also increases the weight and bulk of cable needed for the lighting system. However, its use is defended on grounds of safety.

Most graphical display systems are arranged to illuminate fully for a few seconds after switching-on the ignition; this tests the lights in the graphical display panel and shows that they are functioning correctly. For further details on lamp monitoring systems, see page 316.

Dim-dip lighting devices British vehicles registered after 1 April 1987 must be fitted with dim-dip lighting. This regulation makes it impossible for the vehicle to be driven on side lights alone. The side lights will operate only when the ignition is switched 'off' so they may be regarded as parking lights.

Headlamps can be operated in two dip modes. A dim-dip light of low power is intended for use, without dazzling other road users, in conditions such as well-lit

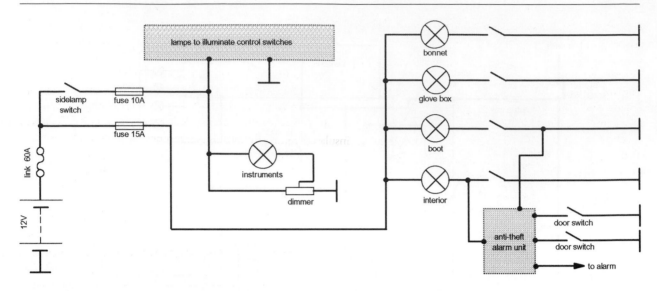

Fig. 15.3 Interior lamp circuit

streets at night or dull weather at twilight. The dip beam of standard intensity is for normal night driving in out-of-town areas.

The regulation requires one pair of headlamps to incorporate a dim-dip device. Compared with the normal dipped beam, the dim-dip light intensity should be:

- 10% (halogen lamps)
- 15% (normal filament lamps).

Anti-theft lamp control Most alarm systems flash the headlamps when the sensing system detects that somebody is tampering with the vehicle. In this situation the headlamps are supplied from a separate multifunction unit which receives its feed direct from an alarm ECU.

Interior lamp circuit In the past the interior lamp circuit consisted of a roof lamp and perhaps two lamps for instrument panel illumination. Today many lamps are used; these are controlled by manual and automatic switches. Figure 15.3 shows an interior lamp circuit of a vehicle fitted with a factory-installed alarm.

Interior circuits can be further refined by incorporating features such as a lamp-out delay device; this gives interior illumination for a short time after the doors are closed. Normally the delay module uses a capacitor to control a transistorized switch (see page 60).

15.2 Lamp construction

Illumination can be obtained from an incandescent filament or from the glow emitted when an electric current is passed through a glass tube containing a special gas. The majority of motor vehicle lamps are filament types but the alternative type is often used on public-service vehicles for interior lighting. These fluorescent lamps have the advantage of a light source that is spread over a large area, so passengers are not subjected to glare and eyestrain.

Light intensity

The intensity of light or luminous intensity is the power to radiate light and produce illumination at a distance. Luminous energy refers to the source of light and its intensity is measured in *candelas* (cd); in the past the unit 'candle power' (c.p.) was used. For practical purposes:

$$1 \text{ cd} = 1 \text{ c.p.}$$

The amount of light that falls on a surface is called the illumination and the intensity of illumination is measured in *lux* or *metre-candles*. A surface illumination of 1 metre-candle or 1 lux is obtained when a lamp of 1 cd is placed 1 m from a vertical screen. When the distance is increased the intensity of illumination decreases; it varies inversely as the square of the distance from the light source. This means that if the distance is doubled, the illumination of the surface on which the light rays fall will be reduced to 1/4 of the original illumination; if the original brightness is required, the power of the lamp must be quadrupled.

Filament lamps

The main details of a lamp are shown in Figure 15.4. Enclosed in a glass container is a tungsten filament that is secured to two support wires; these are normally attached to contacts in a brass cap. Low wattage bulbs, such as those used for side lamps, are normally of the vacuum type. Removal of the air prevents oxidation and vaporization of the filament, and reduces the heat loss. Oxygen in the air causes tungsten deposits to blacken the glass above the filament; also after a very short time the filament burns away.

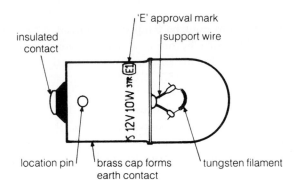

Fig. 15.4 Filament lamp

When operated at the rated voltage, a filament temperature of about 2300°C is reached and a white light is produced. If the lamp is operated at a lower voltage both the temperature and light output will be low. Conversely the operation of a lamp at a higher voltage soon vaporizes the tungsten, blackens the glass and burns-out the filament.

Filaments of larger powered bulbs, such as those used for headlamps, can be made to operate at a higher temperature and give about 40% more light by filling the bulb to a slight pressure with an inert gas such as argon. Heat loss from the filament due to convection movement of the gas is reduced by winding the filament in the form of a helix.

Regulations state that all bulbs used on vehicles must be marked with the letter 'E' and a number that identifies the country where approval was given. This mark indicates that the bulb conforms to the EU standard specified for a given application.

Tungsten–halogen bulbs

During the life of a normal gas-filled bulb, evaporation of a tungsten filament causes the glass to turn black. Although this can be minimized by spreading out the tungsten deposit over a larger glass bulb, the light intensity after a period of time is far from ideal.

The problem has recently been overcome with the introduction of the tungsten–halogen bulb; this type is also called quartz–halogen, quartz–iodine and tungsten–iodine. A much higher output is obtained from these types; efficiency is also maintained for a longer time.

Halogen refers to a group of chemical elements that includes iodine and bromine. When a halogen is added to the gas in a bulb a chemical action takes place which overcomes the evaporation problem. Evaporation of the tungsten still occurs but as the tungsten moves from the hot filament towards the envelope it combines with the halogen and forms a new compound (tungsten halide). This new compound does not deposit itself on the glass envelope; instead the convection movement carries it back to the hot gas region around the filament. Here the tungsten halide splits up and causes the tungsten to redeposit itself back on the filament; the halogen particles released are returned to the gas. This regeneration process not only prevents discolouration of the bulb; it also keeps the filament in a good condition for a much longer time.

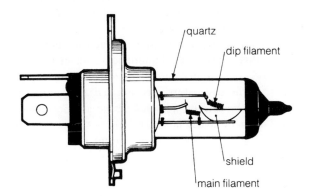

Fig. 15.5 Quartz–halogen lamp bulb

To produce this action, the bulb must be made to operate at a gas temperature higher than the 250°C needed to vaporize the halogen; this is achieved by using a small bulb of quartz. This material can withstand the heat and is sufficiently strong to allow the bulb to be gas filled to a pressure of several bars so as to give a brighter filament for a given life (Figure 15.5).

An added advantage is obtained from the smaller filament needed with this type; it allows more precise focusing than is achieved with the normal bulb.

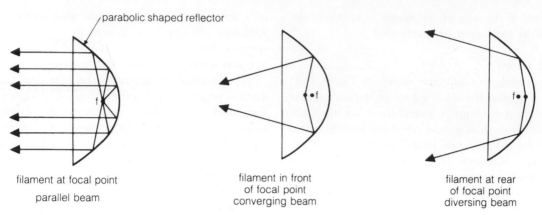

parabolic shaped reflector

filament at focal point
parallel beam

filament in front
of focal point
converging beam

filament at rear
of focal point
diversing beam

Fig. 15.6 Headlamp filament position

Reflector

The function of a headlamp reflector is to redirect the light rays. An ideal reflector gives a beam of light that illuminates the road from far ahead to the region immediately in front of the vehicle.

A normal reflector is shaped in a paraboloid form, highly polished and then coated with a material such as aluminium to give a good reflective surface.

To give good illumination, the lamp filament must be accurately positioned at the *focal point* of the reflector; this allows it to reflect the light rays in the form of a parallel beam (Figure 15.6).

Other positions of the filament put the lamp out-of-focus; this reduces the illumination and, in the case of a diverging beam, may dazzle the drivers of oncoming vehicles. In the past, lamps incorporated a focus adjustment, but nowadays *pre-focus bulbs* have a fitting which sets the filament at the correct place.

Some bulbs are shielded on the lens side to ensure that all light rays are directed back to the reflector.

Lens

A glass lens, moulded to form several prismatic block sections, bends the rays and distributes the light to obtain the required illumination. The design of a headlamp lens pattern attempts to achieve good illumination for both main- and dip-beam positions. The main beam requirement is a long-range penetrating light whereas a dipped light needs a low-level beam that gives a wide light spread just in front of the vehicle and offset to the nearside of the vehicle.

Figure 15.7 shows a typical headlamp lens. This European-type lens design incorporates a region (marked A) to deflect the dip beam towards the left-hand side, if intended for use on UK roads. For Continental touring this lens must be temporarily converted to 'dip to the right' either by fitting a pair of beam deflectors to the lens or by masking-out with tape the region marked 'A' in Figure 15.7.

All lamp lenses must be 'E' marked and have an arrow moulded in the glass to show the dip direction. When two opposing arrows are shown, the lens is suitable for both dip directions; the actual direction is dictated by the position of the bulb.

Dipping facility

The eye takes time to adjust when it moves from a brightly lit area to an area where the light is poor. For the few seconds that it takes the iris of the eye to open, vision is poor. Conversely, movement from a dim to a bright zones reverses the iris movement; the immediate effect is to squint the eye to restrict the sudden burst of light until the iris adjustment has been completed.

Applying this example to night driving shows that an arrangement is needed to prevent a dazzling light beam from entering the driver's eyes. This provision allows the driver's vision to be maintained during, and after, the time that the passing light is directed towards the driver.

Once the eye has adjusted itself to a high level of illumination it finds difficulty in seeing clearly the areas that are dimly lit. For this reason the headlamp design should graduate and distribute the light rays to even-out the illumination rather than concentrate the light in one small region. Also under this distributed pattern, dazzle is less pronounced.

Eye strain results if the eye has repeatedly to adjust to cope with varying illumination levels. This further emphasizes the need for efficient anti-dazzle headlamp arrangements.

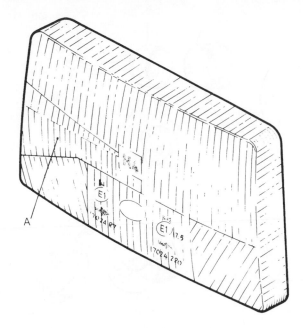

Fig. 15.7 Headlamp lens

The statutory requirements are detailed in the *Road Vehicle Lighting Regulations*. These state that the lighting system must be arranged, so that it is:

'incapable of dazzling any person standing on the same horizontal plane as the vehicle at a greater distance than 25 feet from the lamp whose eye level is not less than 3ft 6in above the plane.'

Nowadays the dip facility is achieved by redirecting the rays downwards and towards the near-side; this is obtained by using a bifocal, *twin-filament* bulb which has the dip filament either offset to the focal point of the reflector or shielded (Figure 15.8).

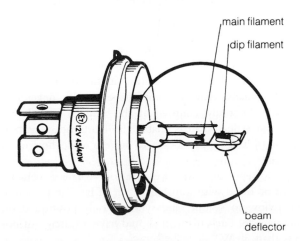

Fig. 15.8 Twin-filament bulb

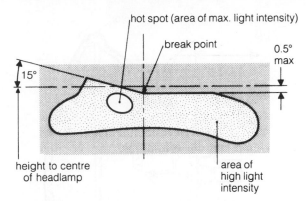

Fig. 15.9 Light pattern from European-type headlamp, dipped beam; left dip

When these bulbs are combined with a modern lens as fitted to European-type lamps, the light pattern, as projected on to a vertical screen, gives an asymmetrical image with a sharp cut-off as shown in Figure 15.9. The dimensions shown indicate the legal requirements, so to meet this regulation adjusters must be provided for horizontal and vertical alignment.

Sealed beam

In the past a headlamp was made up of separate parts and this made it difficult to locate the filament at the focal point. Also the efficiency deteriorated severely when dust and moisture settled on the reflector after entering the lamp through various gaps between the lens and reflector.

The designers of the sealed beam lamp unit overcame these problems by producing a one-piece sealed glass unit that incorporated the lens and aluminized reflector. Two tungsten filaments for the main and dip beams are precisely positioned at the correct points and the complete lamp is filled with an inert gas. Because the bulb has no independent glass envelope, tungsten deposits are spread over a very large area, so the light efficiency of this unit remains high for a long period of time (Figure 15.10).

Although this type of lamp is a great advance over earlier designs, the sealed beam unit has two disadvantages: it is more costly to replace when the filament fails; also sudden light failure occurs when the lens becomes cracked. In some countries a secondary glass screen is used to improve the aerodynamic line and give extra protection to the lamp lens.

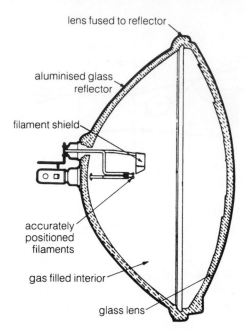

Fig. 15.10 Sealed beam light unit

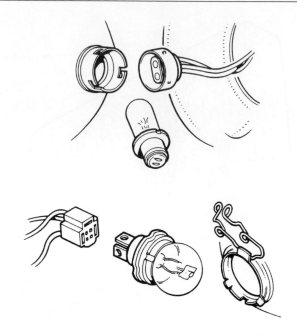

Fig. 15.11 Bulb types used in European headlamp

Four-headlamp system

Optically it is difficult to produce a single lens and reflector unit that gives an illumination to satisfy both main and dip conditions.

To overcome this drawback some manufacturers use four headlamps: two for long-distance illumination and two for lighting the area immediately in front of the car. Each one of the outer lamps has two filaments; a dip filament situated at the focal point to give good light distribution and a second filament positioned away from the focal point to provide near-illumination for main-beam lighting. When the lamps are dipped the inner lamps giving long distance illumination are switched off.

For accommodation reasons the lamp of a four-headlamp arrangement is smaller than that used on a two-headlamp system.

British–American and European headlamps

Headlamps can be divided broadly into three main categories which can be identified by the lens marking and shape. Identification of the lamp type is necessary because the alignment method differs with each type.

British–American lamps Those having the number '1' or '1a' moulded on the lens, or in some cases no number whatsoever, are checked on main beam. These lamps are always circular in shape, are often of a sealed-beam construction, and have a symmetrical main-beam pattern.

Other British–American lamps having the number '2' moulded on the lens are checked on the dipped, or passing beam.

European headlamps These may be circular, rectangular or trapezoidal in shape and incorporate a prismatic region as shown in Figure 15.7. These lamps normally have the number '2' moulded in the glass as well as the 'E' approval mark. All lamps of this type are checked on the dipped beam when carrying out an alignment test.

This type of lamp has an integral lens and reflector assembly and the bulb is removable (Figure 15.11). This feature allows for variation in the bulb type and enables many different lens shapes to be developed to suit the body contour of the vehicle. The larger lens and reflector areas enable the illumination pattern given by the dipped beam to have a wide horizontal spread.

UK regulations require that four-wheeled vehicles must be fitted with a matched pair of headlamps, white or yellow in colour, and symmetrically positioned on the vehicle. Each filament should have a wattage of not less than 30 W.

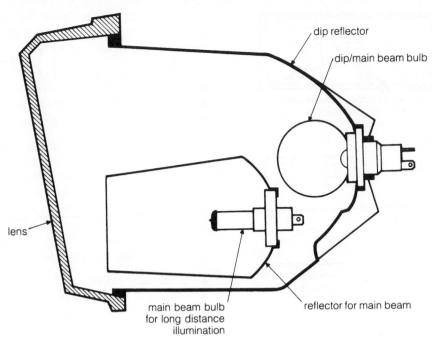

Fig. 15.12 Double-reflector headlamp

Double-reflector headlamp

This highly efficient light source combines two bulbs and two reflectors in one headlamp unit. This makes it possible to meet, with precision, the optic requirements for main and dip beams as well as satisfying the European regulations covering bulb replacement and dazzle.

The Amplilux range of lamps, produced by SEV Marshal, gives out over twice the output of the average conventional headlamp, e.g. the 7-inch quartz–halogen unit produces 70 000 cd compared with 32 000 cd for an average non-iodine unit.

The circular or rectangular lead crystal glass lens and reflector are bonded together to ensure maximum weather protection and constant performance over a long period of time.

Figure 15.12 shows the construction of this type of lamp. In front of the main reflector is a small inset reflector and bulb that provides the main beam. The back of the main-beam reflector is used to screen the lower half of the dip-beam reflector; this gives a sharp horizontal cut-off to the asymmetrical dipped-beam pattern and avoids dazzle. On some lamps a screen (*occulteur*) is placed in front of the dip bulb to stop direct light from the bulb showing above the cut-off axis.

Homofocular headlamps

These headlamps use an advanced design of reflector divided into separate segments with different focal lengths, all sited inside the one light unit (Figure 15.13).

Use of this type of reflector is necessary where low bonnet lines limit the depth and height of the headlamps and where the lens has to be angled to blend with the body contour.

The homofocular reflector features parabolic segments of different focal lengths arranged about the same focal point. This 'stepped' reflector cannot be manufactured in sheet metal; instead the unit is moulded from a plastic material that combines a very smooth surface with resistance to heat that is radiated from halogen bulbs.

Headlamp range adjustment

Vertical alignment of the headlamps is affected by the load distribution; when passengers are carried in the rear seats the vehicle is tilted upwards at the front. This causes the light beams to be aimed higher than normal so that approaching drivers are dazzled; also illumination of the road immediately in front of the car is poor.

On the Audi car this problem is minimized by a headlamp range adjustment system. This provides the driver with a thumbwheel control that enables the light

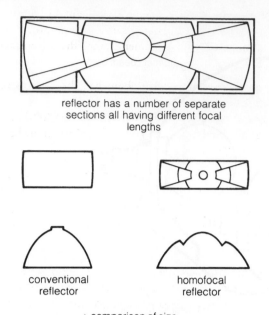

reflector has a number of separate sections all having different focal lengths

conventional reflector

homofocal reflector

comparison of size

Fig. 15.13 Homofocular headlamp

beam to be lowered below the normal position when the rear seats are occupied.

Each reflector is moved by an electric servo-motor which is operated by an electronic control element. This unit senses when the voltage delivered from the driver's control differs from the voltage given by a variable resistor positioned by the movement of the reflector. When the two voltage signals differ, the servo-motor moves until a position is reached where the signal voltages are equal. The control system moves the lamps to the setting selected by the driver.

Other external lamps

Auxiliary driving lamps These lamps are fitted normally to supplement the illumination given by the obligatory lamps; they include fog lamps and long-range driving lamps (spot lamps).

Current regulations should be consulted prior to fitting any lamp; the following is intended to act as a guide. If a pair of auxiliary lamps is fitted then the lenses must NOT be:

- higher than 1200 mm above the ground
- lower than 500 mm from the ground
- more than 400 mm from side of vehicle.

These lamps must have a dipping facility or be capable of being extinguished by the dipping device.

A lamp fitted less than 500 mm from the ground may be used only in conditions of fog or falling snow. Although one front fog lamp is permitted, this can only be used in addition to the headlamps. If glare is to be avoided from the headlamps a second fog lamp is needed. The two fog lamps must be placed:

- at the same height
- equidistant from the centre line of the vehicle
- so that the illuminated area is not more than 400 mm from the outermost part of the vehicle.

Fog lamps have a lens that gives a wide flat-topped beam with a sharp cut-off to illuminate the road immediately in front of the vehicle without causing glare in fog conditions (Figure 15.14).

Fog lamps must not be used when the visibility is in general more than 100 metres.

Driving lamps incorporate a lens that projects a narrow spot beam of high intensity light to illuminate the road well ahead of the vehicle.

Sidelamps UK regulations require a vehicle to carry two white sidelamps each having a wattage of less than 7 W and be visible from a reasonable distance. Since it is now illegal in the UK to drive during the hours of darkness using only the sidelights, the role fulfilled by the sidelamps is now limited to marking the vehicle when it is parked.

On many cars the 'parking' light is incorporated in the headlamp; the bulb often used is a 5 W capless type as shown in Figure 15.15.

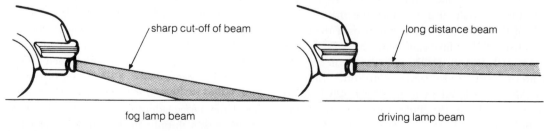

sharp cut-off of beam

long distance beam

fog lamp beam

driving lamp beam

Fig. 15.14 Auxiliary lamp beams

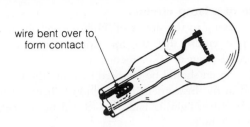

wire bent over to form contact

Fig. 15.15 Capless-type bulb

Rear lamps A car must carry two red 'E' marked rear lamps of a given size and of wattage not less than 5 W. They must be positioned:

- between 1500 mm and 350 mm from the ground
- spaced apart more than 500 mm
- set so that the distance between the edges of the vehicle and the illuminated area is not more than 400 mm.

The red lens must diffuse the light and be 'E' marked to show that it meets the specified standard.

In addition to the rear lamps, a car must be fitted with two red reflectors of approved design.

Stop lamps Two stop lamps each of wattage between 15 and 36 must be fitted. These lamps must illuminate a red diffused, and 'E' marked, lens when the service (foot) brake is applied and be designed to be visible through a given angle.

The lamps must be positioned:

- between 150 mm and 350 mm from the ground
- symmetrically at least 400 mm apart.

Often a single 6/21 W bulb with twin filaments is used to provide rear lamp and stop lamp functions; the bright light given by the 21 W filament is used for the stop lamp.

LED stop lamps One recent development in external lighting is the use of LEDs in place of the conventional incandescent filament lamp bulb. This is possible because the EU have recently changed the wording of the regulations from 'incandescent lamp' to 'light source'.

Since LEDs were first produced commercially by Hewlett-Packard in 1968, their use quickly spread to vehicle systems, in particular instrumentation. Standard LEDs are made in the colours red, amber, yellow and green, so a vehicle lamp requiring any one of these colours can be made. Developments are taking place to make a blue LED; when this is commercially viable, it

will be possible to produce white light by combining the colours red, blue and green (see page 50).

Compared with a filament lamp, the advantages of a LED are:

- quick response – takes about half the time to reach full brilliance;
- good reliability – life is rated over 50 000 hours;
- good durability – absence of a filament makes the LED shock resistant.

The fast response time makes the LED attractive to use as a stop lamp, and although the initial cost is about three times as great as a conventional filament-type, companies such as Volvo feel that this is worth the extra safety.

High-mounted stop lamps Lighting laws in some countries specify that stop lamps must be positioned at the driver's eye level. It is claimed that this location makes the lamps more visible when one vehicle is closely following another. Many countries that specify this lamp siting also require the lighting system to switch on the dipped-beam headlamps when the engine is started.

Side marker lamps Each side of vehicles over a certain length must be fitted with a specified number of lamps to warn drivers of the length of the vehicle.

Number plate The rear number plate must be clearly illuminated by a white light, but the bulb must not be visible from behind the vehicle. The light is connected in parallel with the sidelights.

Rear fog lamps These high-intensity red lamps are used to improve safety in conditions of poor visibility; namely fog, falling snow, heavy rain or road spray. Either one or two lamps must be fitted by the manufacturer on current vehicles and these must be set:

- between 250 mm and 1000 mm from the ground
- more than 100 mm from any stop lamp.

If two lamps are used they must be set symmetrically, or in cases where only one lamp is to be used it must be fitted either on the offside or on the vehicle centre line.

Normally each lamp has a 21 W bulb and a lens of large area; both must be 'E' marked. The circuit must allow the rear fog lamp to be operated by an independent switch and a warning lamp must be fitted to signal to the driver when the rear fog lamp is in operation. Furthermore the circuit must function only when the headlamps, front fog lamps or sidelights are in use. In some cases a fog guard relay coil prevents operation of the rear fog lamps until the front fog lamps are switched on.

Reversing lamps When a reversing lamp is fitted it must conform with the statutory regulations. These state that not more than two lamps may be used and the total wattage per lamp must not exceed 24 W. The white light should be switched automatically by the gearbox and be subject to anti-dazzle requirements. Where automatic switching is not provided, a separate switch, together with a warning lamp, may be used.

Area illuminating lamps When the vehicle is not in motion, a manually positioned white light can be used to illuminate the area, provided it does not cause a hazard to other road users. Originally these special lamps were used for illuminating signposts, but today they have a more general use. Lamps for private use that are made in the colours used by the emergency services are illegal for use on the public highway.

15.3 Maintenance and fault diagnosis

Other than the usual superficial checks for cable security and condition, most items of work occur only when a fault develops. On modern vehicles the graphical display on the instrument panel will warn the driver of a lighting fault.

Failure of a lamp circuit

Initial warning to the driver of 'bulb outage' should be verified to ensure that the monitoring system is not giving a false signal. If an incorrect message is shown, then the circuit should be checked by using the method outlined in the Instrumentation section (Chapter 10) of this book. Most lighting faults are caused by the failure of a fuse or bulb.

Fuse A 'blown' fuse should be replaced with a fuse of the correct rating. If the new fuse blows immediately then the fault must be pin-pointed before fitting another fuse.

Bulb failure The suspected bulb should be removed and replaced with the recommended type. Glass surfaces must not be touched with the fingers, especially the quartz–halogen type, so a clean cloth should be used. Stains on a bulb can be removed by washing in methylated spirit and drying with a lint-free cloth.

Wiring faults If the initial check shows that the bulb and fuse are serviceable, and a visual check of the cables does not reveal the defect, then the circuit should be tested with a voltmeter. Figure 15.16 shows the principle as applied to a simple lighting circuit.

Tests

Test 1 A voltmeter (V_1) is connected across the battery to measure the voltage under lighting load.

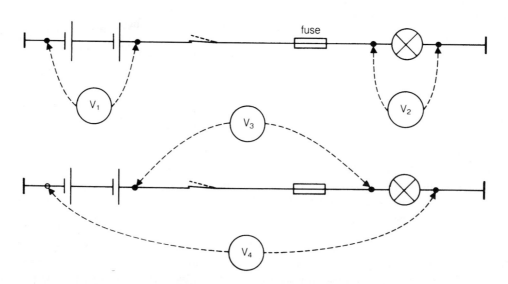

Fig. 15.16 Voltmeter checks on simple lighting circuit

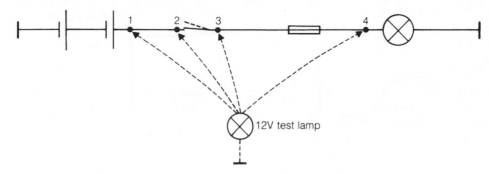

Fig. 15.17 Open-circuit test using a test lamp

Test 2 When the voltmeter (V_2) is placed across the lamp the voltage should be similar to the voltage at Test 1. If a resistance in the circuit causes the reading to differ by more than 10% of the battery voltage, the cause should be investigated by using Tests 3 and 4.

Test 3 Voltmeter V_3 shows the voltage drop on the insulated line. If an excessive drop is shown, the location of the fault can be detected by moving one voltmeter lead along the connection points in the circuit path until a stage is reached where the change in voltage is considerable.

Test 4 With the meter arranged as in V_4, the drop in the earth line is shown. By using a similar technique to Test 3, a high resistance can be located. The total voltage drop from Tests 3 and 4 should be less than 10% of the battery voltage, e.g. less than 1.2 V for a 12 V system.

A quick check for an open-circuit can be made by using a 12 V test lamp (Figure 15.17). A circuit break between points 1 and 4 is easily found. With one side of the lamp connected to a good earth, the break can be located.

Headlamp earth faults If an earth wire from one headlamp is broken, the first impression is that the lamp with the defective earth will not operate. This is not so, because the lamp will earth through the other headlamp via the lamp filaments. Since the three filaments are in series, each filament will glow. For example, when the supply is to the main beam, the filament of the defective lamp's main beam will be in series with the two dipped-beam filaments.

Headlamp alignment

The alignment of headlamps must be correct to meet the requirements of the Law in respect to dazzle and also to provide good illumination for the driver. Headlamp alignment, as well as lamp condition, forms a part of the annual MOT Test.

Although the lamps may be checked by observing the illumination pattern on a vertical screen, most garages use special aligning equipment to achieve a greater accuracy.

Special equipment Figure 15.18 shows one type of optical beam setter. This equipment checks horizontal and vertical aim and enables the lamps to be set accurately. Adjusters are provided at each lamp to alter the setting.

Initially the aligner is set level and positioned parallel with the front of the car. When the lamps are switched on, light rays from the lamp pass through a

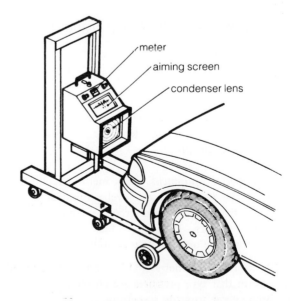

Fig. 15.18 Optical beam setter

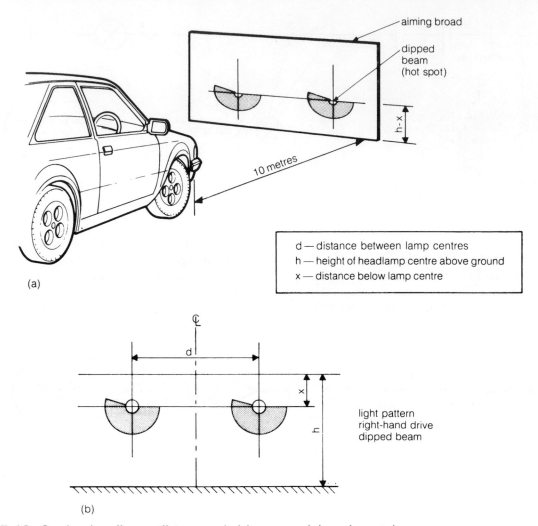

Fig. 15.19 Setting headlamp alignment (without special equipment)

condenser lens and are reflected by a mirror on to a small screen.

Most lamps, other than the British–American type having a symmetrical beam and identified by the number '1' or '1a' moulded on the lens, are set to dip beam when aligning the lamps.

Without special equipment This method requires the vehicle to be positioned on level ground at a given distance in front of a vertical screen set parallel with the headlamps (Figure 15.19(a)). One method recommended for the Ford Escort is as follows:

(1) Position car 10 metres (33 ft) from aiming board.
(2) Ensure that tyre pressures are correct.
(3) Bounce car to settle suspension.
(4) Mark out aiming board as shown in Fig. 15.19(b).

The distance x depends on the vehicle, e.g. Escort saloon, 130 mm.

(5) Mark centres of front windscreen and rear window with wax crayon and position car so that it is aligned with the centre line of the aiming board.
(6) Switch on dipped beam and cover one lamp.
(7) Adjust horizontal and vertical alignment to give light pattern as shown in Figure 15.19(a).

Auxiliary driving lamps can also be aligned by using this method. The beams are deflected downwards a small amount, e.g. the distance x is about 180 mm when measured at 10 metres from the lamp.

Lamp fitting

Care must be taken before and during the fitting of additional lamps to ensure that the system functions

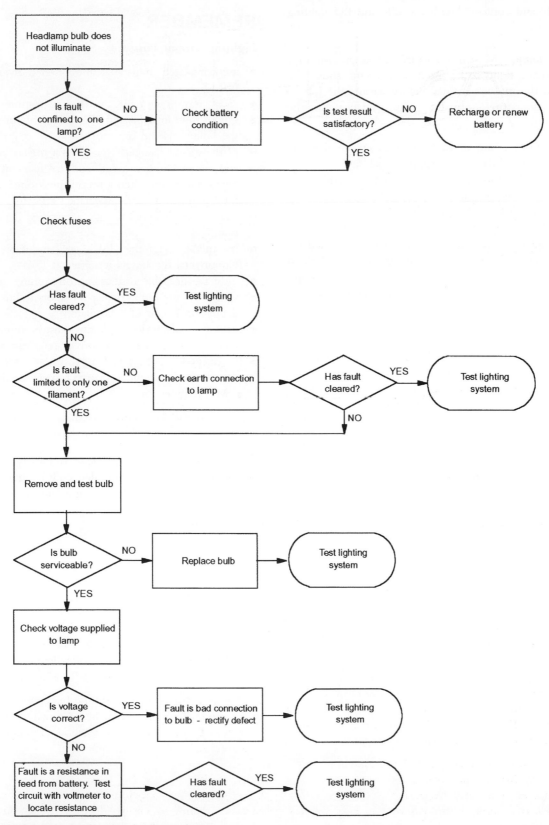

Fig. 15.20 Fault diagnosis flow chart

correctly and conforms with the UK and EU lighting regulations.

Driving lamps Most manufacturers make provision for extra driving lights to be fitted, so reference should be made to the maker's manual before starting the job.

The literature normally gives guidance on the following:

- maximum rating of each lamp to ensure that the extra load is within the supply capability;
- approved lamp designs, including the need for 'E' marked components;
- facia provision for suitable lamp switches;
- regulations regarding lamp siting;
- location of factory-installed connectors intended for the feed and earth of the extra lamps; these link to a fused circuit which, in the case of spot lamps, extinguish when the headlamps are dipped;
- provision for a relay and suitable fuses.

Flowchart

This type of chart shows a logical sequence in which some task, such as fault finding, should be carried out. The system is similar to that used for computer programming; it uses the following three symbols:

- *rectangle*: gives an instruction
- *diamond*: asks a question that normally has either a *yes* or *no* answer
- *ellipse*: indicates that the task can be taken no further or that the job is complete

---

REMEMBER

Lighting circuit lamps:

- are connected in parallel and often individually fused
- must comply with UK and EU regulations
- must show an approved 'E' mark; this includes the bulb, lens and reflector
- of the quartz–halogen type gives a higher output and longer life than a conventional filament type
- give parallel rays when a bulb is positioned at the focal point of a parabolic-shaped reflector
- have a lens designed to give a specified illumination
- if suitable for the UK are unsuitable for Continental use unless modified
- must be incapable of dazzling on-coming drivers
- sometimes use homofocular reflectors to limit the depth and height of a headlamp
- used as auxiliary driving lamps must be fitted and used in accordance with current regulations
- if classified as obligatory lamps are tested for type, condition, alignment and correct operation during a MOT inspection

---

(In flowcharts the term *ellipse* is loosely used to describe a rectangle with rounded ends.) Figure 15.20 shows a flowchart for fault-finding a lamp defect.

PROGRESS CHECK 15

1. List the lamps that must be fitted on a vehicle to satisfy the regulations.

2. State why an ignition-sensed relay is fitted in the headlamp circuit.

3. State the circuit in which the rear fog lamps are wired.

4. State how the circuit is arranged to meet the dim-dip regulations.

5. A quartz–halogen gives a higher candela output than a conventional filament lamp. State what is meant by this expression.

6. What causes glass blackening of a filament lamp?

7. State the position of the lamp filament, in relation to the reflector, to give parallel light rays.

8. A lamp is fitted with a pre-focussed, bi-focal bulb. State the meaning of these two features.

9. State TWO advantages and TWO disadvantages of a sealed beam headlamp compared with a detachable bulb type.

10. A vehicle is fitted with a four-headlamp system. Which lamps are switched-off in the dipped position?

11. State one merit of a homo-focular-type headlamp.

12. State the operational difference between a fog lamp and a spot lamp.

13. State TWO advantages of using a LED stop lamp compared with a filament type.

14. A defective earth is suspected as the reason why a headlamp does not operate. Describe how a meter is used to verify this diagnosis.

15. The earth wire to one of the two headlamps is broken. State the symptom.

16 Instrumentation

What is covered in this chapter

→ basic instrumentation systems
→ vehicle condition monitoring
→ electronic displays
→ maintenance and fault diagnosis

16.1 Instrumentation systems

Only a few years ago the instrument panel consisted of:

● Speedometer incorporating an odometer to register mileage covered;
● Fuel contents gauge;
● Engine temperature gauge;
● Engine oil-pressure gauge or warning light to signal low pressure;
● Signal lights to indicate battery charge (ignition warning light), directional indicator operation and headlamp main beam.

These instruments formed the basic panel and even today they still form the minimum equipment used on 'low-line' models. With the exception of the speedometer, other instruments were electrified at a comparatively early stage to simplify the drive arrangement, save on cost and reduce weight. Today, very few instruments are mechanically operated; even the speedometer is often electrically operated. In addition, numerous other displays and signals have been introduced to provide the driver with information relation to normal operation or malfunction of a vehicle system.

Before considering a sophisticated modern system of instrumentation, the electrical equipment forming a basic panel is covered. The main items of equipment are shown in Figure 16.1.

Fuel contents gauge

In the past the moving-iron cross-coil gauge was commonly used. The gauge unit of this system is mounted in the panel and is similar to a simple ammeter;

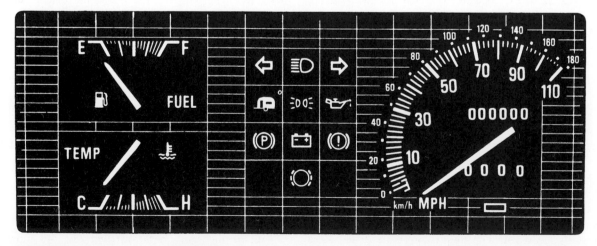

Fig. 16.1 Basic instrument panel

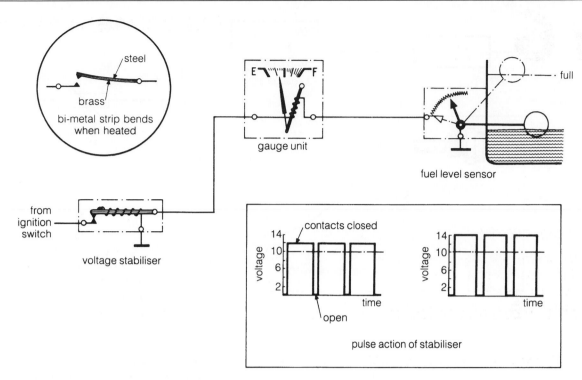

Fig. 16.2 Thermal-type fuel level gauge

the tank unit or transmitter is variable resistor, the sliding arm of which is operated by a float.

Although this type operated immediately the ignition is switched on, surging of the fuel in the tank causes the gauge needle to swing about; as a result the gauge is difficult to read. It was mainly due to this that the thermal, or bi-metal, type was introduced.

Thermal type This system, shown in Figure 16.2, has a gauge unit operated by a bi-metal strip and a variable resistor sensor fitted in the fuel tank. Since voltage affects the current flow through the circuit, to obtain an accurate reading the supply voltage has to be kept constant; this duty is performed by a voltage stabilizer.

The stabilizer shown in Figure 16.2 is a bi-metal type. A heating coil is wound around a *bi-metal strip*, which consists of two metals: brass and steel. When the strip is heated, the strip bends towards the side of the steel due to the brass expanding nearly twice as much as the steel. In the stabilizer, the bending of the strip opens a pair of contacts and interrupts the current flow in the circuit. After cooling for a fraction of a second, the circuit is re-made; this cycle is repeated and a pulse current is provided. The frequency of the digital pulse output is preset to give a heating effect on another

bi-metal strip similar to that produced if a constant voltage is supplied to the circuit. Stabilizers in use generally provide a mean voltage of either 10 V or 7 V.

Instead of a bi-metal stabilizer some vehicles have a solid-state voltage regulator; these use a Zener or avalanche diode in a control circuit to provide the required voltage.

In addition to providing current for the fuel gauge, a stabilizer also supplies the other thermal instruments such as the engine temperature gauge.

The sensor, or transducer, fitted in the fuel tank is operated by a metal or plastic float. Movement of the float arm causes a contact blade to wipe over a wire-wound rheostat. Raising the fuel level moves the blade and decreases the resistance. Later designs of fuel level sensor make more use of plastics and have a laser-trimmed thick-film resistor set on to a ceramic substrate to give greater accuracy and reliability. A typical resistance range is from 19 Ω (full) to 250 Ω (empty).

The gauge unit, or indicator, has a bi-metal strip around which is wound a heater coil. One end of the strip is anchored and the other end is attached to the gauge needle.

When the ignition is switched on, the intermittent current causes the bi-metal strip to heat up to a

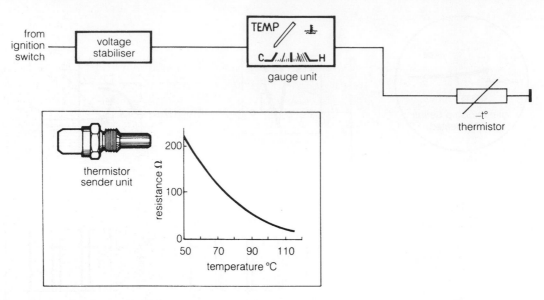

Fig. 16.3 Thermal-type engine temperature gauge

temperature dictated by the resistance of the sensor in the fuel tank. Under full-tank conditions the low resistance of the tank sensor allows each pulse supplied by the stabilizer to give a large current flow so the bi-metal strip in the gauge bends a large amount.

After switching on it takes about two minutes before an accurate reading is obtained; this sluggish action is one advantage of the thermal-type unit.

Care must be taken to avoid an explosion when testing the operation of the system with the sensor unit removed and positioned close to the tank. Sparks generated in a fuel-saturated tank area are safe, but it is highly dangerous to produce sparks where both oxygen and fuel vapour are present.

Engine temperature

The conventional thermal-type gauge used for this instrument is similar to that used to indicate the fuel contents. Gauge reading is affected by supply voltage, so the system is fed via a voltage stabilizer, the same unit as that used to supply the other thermally-operated gauges.

The engine temperature sensor is generally situated in the coolant system on the engine side of the thermostat. Normally the brass bulb in contact with the coolant contains a sensing capsule called a *thermistor*; this semiconductor resistor pellet is thermally sensitive, but varies its resistance in the opposite way to most metals: when the temperature is increased, the resistance is decreased. The thermistor's high *negative temperature*

coefficient (NTC) of resistance causes the resistance to vary from about 220 Ω at 50°C to 20 Ω at 115°C.

The circuit for a bi-metal indicator gauge and thermistor is shown in Figure 16.3. In operation, a rise in engine temperature lowers the thermistor resistance and increases the current passing through the gauge unit; this causes the bi-metal strip to bend more than before. Damage will occur if the thermistor is connected directly to the battery.

Engine oil pressure indication

Nowadays the majority of engines use a signal lamp, or electronic display, to warn the driver of low oil pressure. The types of transducer used to sense engine oil pressure are:

- spring-controlled diaphragm
- thermal
- piezoresistor.

Spring-controlled diaphragm Figure 16.4 shows the principle of this type. It consists of an oil-pressure sensor switch which is controlled by a spring-loaded diaphragm. Under low-pressure conditions the switch is closed and the warning light is 'on', but when the oil pressure is sufficient to move the diaphragm and overcome the spring, the contacts are opened and the light is switched off.

Thermal transducer An indication of the actual oil pressure can be given when a thermal-type indictor is

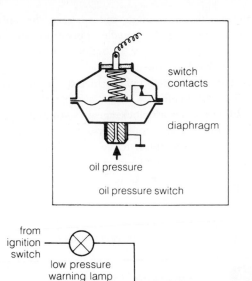

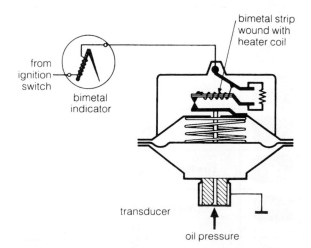

Fig. 16.4 Spring-controlled diaphragm-type oil pressure indicator

used (Figure 16.5). The principle of this type is similar to the thermal fuel contents gauge described previously.

In the construction shown, the pressure on the diaphragm in the transducer holds the contacts closed until the bi-metal strip has been heated sufficient to bend the strip and open the contacts. The heating effect needed to perform this action matches the effect on the bi-metal strip in the indicator, so the needle of the indicator will register the appropriate pressure.

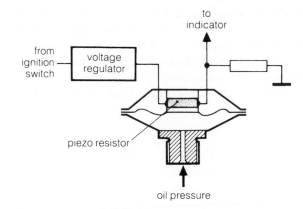

Fig. 16.6 Piezoresistor-type oil pressure transducer

Piezoresistor The term *piezō* is a Greek word for pressure, so this type of transducer is based on the change in resistance which occurs when pressure is applied to a special semiconductor crystal.

By arranging this resistor in the simple circuit shown in Figure 16.6, a voltage change can be detected when the oil pressure drops below a given value. This signal is passed to the panel where it is processed to operate the warning display.

Tachometer

The common type of tachometer in use today uses the pulses generated by the interruption of the ignition primary current to sense the engine speed.

Figure 16.7 shows a typical circuit for an impulse tachometer. Voltage pulses produced at the negative side of the coil by the circuit breaker allow a transistor array in an IC chip in the tachometer to count and then convert the pulses to a steady current; this can be measured by a meter and indicated on a suitably calibrated scale. For example, when a 4-cylinder, 4-stroke engine is operating

Fig. 16.5 Thermal-type pressure tranducer

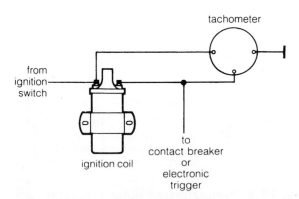

Fig. 16.7 Circuit for tachometer

at 3000 rev/min, there are 6000 voltage pulses per minute or 100 per second: this 100 Hz frequency signals the tachometer to register a reading of 3000 rev/min. Any alteration in the signal frequency produces the appropriate response by the instrument.

Analogue or digital displays are used to indicate speed.

Speedometer

Indication of road speed by electrical means overcomes the need for a cumbersome flexible cable drive which is an essential part of the mechanical system used on cars for many years.

Electric speedometers have been in use for a number of years on many public service vehicles and commercial vehicles. These systems use a permanent-magnet a.c. generator to sense the road speed and a voltmeter, scaled to read 'm.p.h.', as the indicating instrument. Since this type of system senses the speed of rotation of a shaft, an arrangement similar to a tachometer can be used to indicate road speed.

The systems used on modern cars are more compact and less costly than the generator system.

Transistorized pulse generator   The speedometer system uses a transducer to generate a series of pulses that correspond to the movement of the output shaft of the gearbox. The pulse frequency transmitted to the speedometer fitted in the panel indicates the vehicle speed; the number of pulses shows the distance covered.

The transducer has a fixed magnet over which passes a rotating plate. This plate has a series of projections that pass across the magnetic pole to generate the pulse. Drive to the plate from the gearbox output shaft is by means of a short length of conventional speedometer cable.

The weak pulse is amplified within the transducer by a small solid-state circuit having two transistors.

The circuit, shown in Figure 16.8 has a single cable joining the transducer to the speedometer. Pulses are passed through this cable to an IC chip within the speedometer; this chip counts and converts the pulses to an analogue signal. Needle operation of the speedometer is produced by an action similar to that given by a normal voltmeter.

Nowadays the digital pulse generator is normally connected to the main ECU. This compares the input with the ECU processor's clock signal to compute speed in order to provide the control system with information that shows, in addition to vehicle speed, the rate at which the vehicle is accelerating or decelerating. This arrangement allows the ECU to use the vehicle speed

Symbol	Information provided
	Brake warning light
	Turn signal/hazard indicator light (green)
	High beam indicator light (blue)
	Charge warning light
	Door open reminder light
	Hazard warning flasher indicator light
	Low washer fluid warning light
	Oil pressure warning light
	Glow plug indicator light
	Heated rear window indicator light
	Rear fog light indicator light
	Low fuel warning light
	Stop/tail warning light

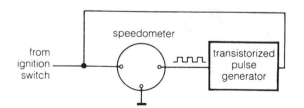

Fig. 16.8 Transistorized pulse generator-type speedometer

Fig. 16.9 Instrument panel symbols

data to control engine management, automatic gear changes and any other system that is speed dependent.

When the speed is displayed digitally on the instrument panel, the driver can select either metric or Imperial units.

Instrument panel symbols
An international standard for instrument symbols has been agreed; the main symbols are shown in Figure 16.9.

16.2 Vehicle condition monitoring (VCM)

In the past, the service state of a vehicle was assessed by inspections; these were made as frequently as every 4800 km (3000 miles). At these intervals, preventative maintenance tasks were performed and checks were carried out to ensure that the vehicle could operate satisfactorily until the next inspection was due.

Against a background of rising servicing cost and inconvenience to the owner by the loss of use of the car, manufacturers gradually extended the service intervals to periods of about 20 000 km (12 000 miles) or more.

During this long period, both in time and distance travelled, fluid levels fall and vital components wear, so to improve safety and avoid breakdown due to system failure, a monitoring system has been developed.

In addition to the monitoring of systems originally checked at a time when the car was being serviced, other areas are now included which hitherto had been the responsibility of the driver, e.g. oil and coolant levels.

The degree of sophistication of the monitoring system depends on the model line. Introduction of VCM generally appears on the 'high-end' models first, but in due course the increased use of VCM parts reduces the price; as a consequence it allows the system to be used on even the 'low-end' models (Figure 16.10).

Some items such as engine oil pressure and temperature, charging, fuel contents, main beam and directional indicators have been monitored for many years. Nowadays the popular middle-range vehicles have additional facilities to monitor and signal when the:

- lighting system is defective due to a bulb or circuit failure;
- brake pads need replacing;
- engine oil level is low;
- fluid levels are low in either the cooling or washer systems;

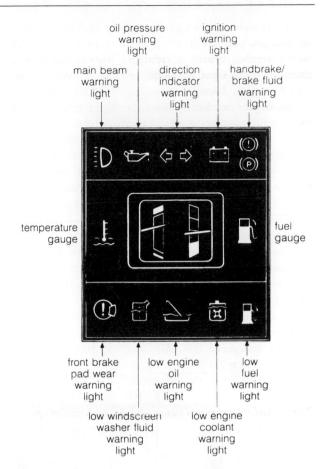

Fig. 16.10 Vehicle condition monitoring

- brake reservoir is low or brake operating system is faulty.

Warning signals, in various colours and patterns, located in a separate and prominent region in the instrument panel, command the driver's attention by indicating the appropriate warning. On some models the monitoring system is up-rated by the incorporation of a voice synthesizer unit; this uses the radio speaker to communicate operating information or give warnings to support the visual displays.

Most VCM systems use an electronic digital unit to process the information received from the various sensors placed around the vehicle. Many sensors act as a switch. When the warning signal of a defect has to be given, the sensor switch alters its state and either gives, or interrupts, a flow of current in that particular branch of the circuit. The change of current flow triggers an electronic switch in the VCM control unit and a warning display illuminates an instrument panel symbol shaped to conform to the international standard.

If the system is to be trusted by the driver, it is necessary to periodically check the various sensor circuits to ensure that the VCM system is serviceable; this is normally carried out when the ignition is switched on. A test current, delivered to each sensor and signal lamp for about five seconds, enables the driver to check that the complete system is functioning correctly.

These additional features show why a simple circuit is incapable of meeting modern requirements. The many duties that have to be performed require the fitting of a microprocessor. As the name suggests, the data supplied to this electronic unit is processed and, when necessary, it gives out an electrical signal to activate a warning device.

The principle of a VCM system can be shown by considering some of the sensor arrangements.

Bulb failure

This safety feature is commonly used on vehicles. The arrangement monitors the main lighting system and also includes directional indicators and stop lamps.

Indication of a bulb filament failure, or circuit defect, is generally signified to the driver by lights on a graphical display panel. This shows a plan view, or map, of the vehicle which includes miniature lights to represent the lamps of the vehicle; these display lights become illuminated when a particular lamp is not functioning correctly. On some systems the panel works in the opposite way; it shows the lamps that are in operation instead of illuminating when a fault is present. In most cases an audible warning or extra light on the main panel is used to initially attract the driver's attention; this warning of a defect allows the driver to refer to the vehicle map to identify the faulty lamp.

Many lamp-failure systems, as well as other monitoring arrangements, use a *reed switch* as a sensor.

Reed switch   A reed switch consists of two or more contacts mounted in a glass vial to exclude contaminates. The vial is evacuated of air, or filled with an inert gas, to reduce damage by arcing.

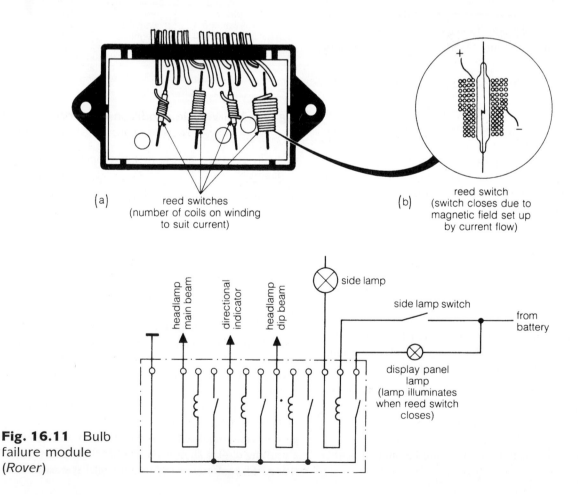

(a)   reed switches
(number of coils on winding
to suit current)

(b)   reed switch
(switch closes due to
magnetic field set up
by current flow)

side lamp

side lamp switch

from battery

headlamp main beam

directional indicator

headlamp dip beam

display panel lamp
(lamp illuminates
when reed switch
closes)

Fig. 16.11 Bulb failure module (*Rover*)

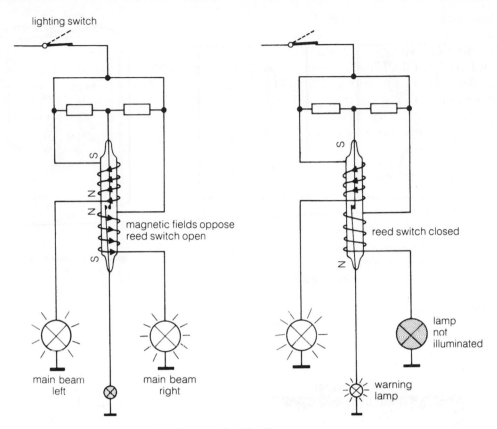

Fig. 16.12 Differential relay bulb failure unit (*Audi*)

In the type shown in Figure 5.21 (page 94) the contacts are open and in this position no current will flow between A and B.

Closure of the switch is achieved by using the magnetic flux produced by a permanent or electro-magnet. When a given magnet flux acts along the axis of the switch, the contacts close. Opening of the contacts is obtained either by moving a magnet away from the reed or by using another magnet or ferrous metal vane to divert the magnetic flux away from the reed. When electromagnetic operation is required, a coil is wound around the switch to create the magnetic field.

Reed switches can also be used for sensing:

● The position of a component part (fuel level indi-cator);
● Speed of movement of a rotating part (speedometer).

Limiting frequency of a reed switch is about 600 Hz, but well before this frequency is reached a contact bounce of duration about 1 ms is evident. Life of the reed depends on the application, but in a typical case is of the order of 10^8 cycles. The electrical load must not exceed the manufacturer's recommendations.

Bulb failure module   Figure 16.11(a) shows a module as used on some Rover cars. Four bulb-failure monitor units are often used: two at the front and two at the rear. Each monitor unit is mounted adjacent to the lamp it is sensing; this eliminates a false signal being sent if a short circuit occurs in the wiring to the lamp.

Each monitor unit consists of a reed switch mounted inside a wire coil (Figure 16.11(b)). The coil is connected in series with the lamp, so when the lamp is operating correctly the magnetic flux produced by the coil closes the reed switch; this passes current to illuminate the appropriate segment of the display panel.

A different construction of reed switch, shown in Figure 16.12, is used on Audi vehicles. This differen-tial relay, a double coil wound around the reed switch, monitors two lamps; each coil provides the current for one lamp.

When the lamps are operating normally, the equal current passing around each coil creates its own magnetic flux. Since the two coils are wound in oppo-site directions, the opposing flux polarities cancel each other out so the reed switch remains open.

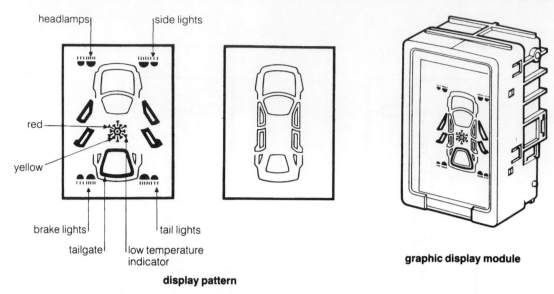

Fig. 16.13 Graphic display unit

Failure of one lamp filament, or fuse, reduces or stops the current flow in one coil, so a magnetic flux is built up which causes the reed contacts to be drawn together. This action occurs because the closed contacts provide a shorter path for the flux through the centre of the coil. Closure of the reed switch contacts allows a current, controlled by a load resistor, to pass to the ECU; this switches on a central warning lamp and activates a speech synthesizer to announce the fault.

Graphic display unit This unit forms a part of the instrument panel, or console, and generally shows a vehicle map that is illuminated by means such as a vacuum fluorescent display. Besides warning the driver of 'bulb outage', the map is often used to indicate other features such as door ajar and low external air temperature.

In the unit shown in Figure 16.13, the snowflake symbol for low air temperature changes colour to highlight critical temperatures of 4°C and 0°C. The whole display requires 18 terminals; 3 are used for ignition voltage, earth and sidelamp supply, and 15 are used to supply the logic signals for triggering the map segments.

Brake lining wear

A sensor set into the brake friction material detects when the friction material reaches the end of its life. This is a useful safety feature and it eliminates the need for periodic inspections to assess the degree of wear of the material.

A simple system in shown in Figure 16.14(a). This has an insulated metal contact, buried into each friction surface, which rubs against the drum or disc when the friction material has worn down to its limit. When contact is made with earth a signal lamp illuminates a symbol on the instrument panel.

This system is cheap, and its reliability is poor. This is because the presence of an open circuit in the system prevents the warning system operating even though the friction material has worn to its limit. This is overcome by using the closed-loop system as shown in Figure 16.14(b).

The loop sensing system has a wire buried in the friction material. This is arranged so that the wire is ground away and cut when the friction material is worn to its limit, e.g. worn to a thickness of less than 2 mm.

The brake sensors are arranged in series with each other and the two cables forming the circuit loop are connected to an ECU. This processor unit is programmed to pass a current to the lamp for about five seconds after switching on the ignition to ensure the system is serviceable.

After the initial check period, the illumination of the warning lamp indicates that a brake inspection is necessary. If a brake check shows that the material is serviceable then tests should be carried out to locate the cause of the open circuit.

When the external circuit is found to be satisfactory, but the lamp still remains 'on', then a fault is present in the ECU; this usually requires replacement.

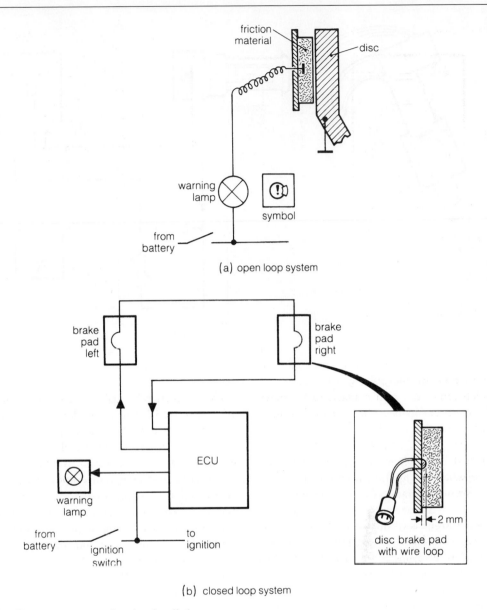

friction material

disc

warning lamp

symbol

from battery

(a) open loop system

brake pad left

brake pad right

ECU

warning lamp

from battery

ignition switch

to ignition

2 mm

disc brake pad with wire loop

(b) closed loop system

Fig. 16.14 Sensor system for brake lining wear

GOOD PRACTICE

Damage to the ECU will occur if current from an ohmmeter is passed to the ECU; this unit should be disconnected when checks are being made to the external circuit.

Engine oil level

One method of sensing the oil level is to use a *'hot-wire dipstick'* (Figure 16.15). In this arrangement, a resistance wire is set inside a hollow plastics moulding, which carries the normal dipstick oil level marks. Two cables from the dipstick are connected, via the main loom, to the ECU.

Operation of the system relies on the increase in resistance of the hot-wire when a small current of about 0.2 A is passed through the wire for about 1.5 s. This

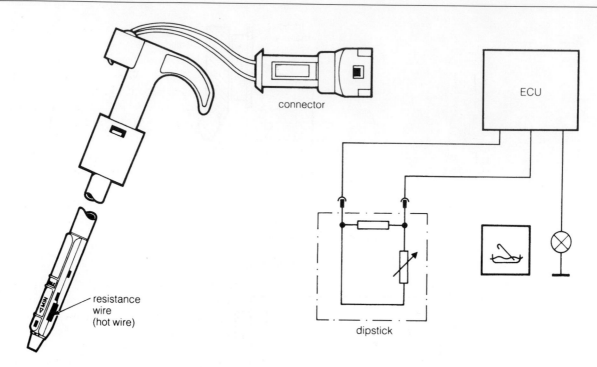

Fig. 16.15 Engine oil level sensor

current is supplied only when the ignition is initially switched on, or when the ignition is switched on after the engine has been inoperative for over 3 minutes.

When the wire is immersed in oil, the heat from the interrogating current is dissipated to the oil, so the temperature of the hot-wire sensor remains constant. But when the oil level drops more than 3 mm below the 'low' mark, the sensor temperature and wire resistance increases. If the resistance during the period of current flow differs from that given when the current is switched off, the ECU activates the warning lamp.

Faulty operation of this sensitive system will occur if a resistance develops in the circuit, e.g. when a pin of a multiplug connector becomes dirty. Manufacturers recommend that before carrying out diagnosis checks, all contact pins are cleaned with a typist's eraser pencil.

It is essential to disconnect the ECU from the sensor circuit before attempting to measure the resistance of the hot-wire; a typical resistance when the dipstick is dry is 7.5–8.5 Ω. Faults in the circuit can be pin-pointed by comparing the resistance at the sensor with the resistance at the pins of the multiplug at its connection point with the ECU (Figure 16.16).

Fluid levels

Most VCM systems monitor the levels in the reservoirs of the cooling, windscreen washer, brake system and fuel tank. Float switches are the cheapest and simplest, but other types of probe sensor are used such as those involving a.c. impedance and hot-wire techniques.

Float switch   The fluid level sensor shown in Figure 16.17(a) (over) is fitted on the side of the fluid reservoir. It consists of a reed switch which is activated by a small permanent magnet fitted in the float.

The display warning signal is illuminated when the fluid level falls to the minimum level; typical settings for a small car are 25% of the washer capacity, 7 litres of fuel in the tank or the low mark on the coolant reservoir. The warning is triggered by a sensor magnet as it moves away from the reed switch. At a given point the reed switch opens; this reduces the current flow in the sensor circuit. When the ECU detects this fall in current it passes a signal to the instrument display panel.

To avoid a false signal due to fluid 'slosh', the ECU is programmed to receive a continuous sensor signal for about 8 seconds before it activates the warning display.

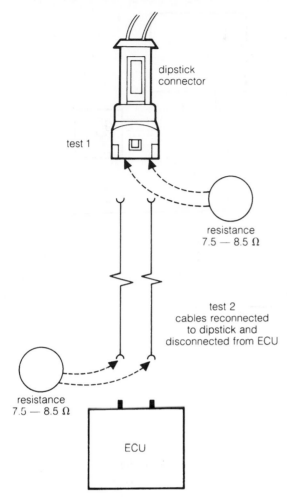

Fig. 16.16 Resistance test of engine oil level sensor circuit

Fail-safe sensing is obtained by fitting a fixed resistor in parallel with the reed switch; this provision enables the sensor circuit to be monitored for short- and open-circuit defects.

Figure 16.17(b) shows an alternative construction for a reed float switch in a coolant reservoir. A ring magnet is set in the float and the reed switch is positioned so that the magnet closes the switch when the minimum level is reached. The path to earth provided by the switch signals the ECU to activate the appropriate warning display.

Low coolant level a.c. probe This a.c. sensor has two flat metal blades that protrude from an insulated boss which is screwed into the coolant reservoir. Two resistors, mounted within the boss, are connected to the blades and to the supply leads which carry a high-frequency a.c. current.

The liquid level is detected by monitoring the impedance of the circuit. When the two blade electrodes are not immersed in liquid, the impedance increases; this raises the a.c. voltage across the sensor terminals and allows the ECU to signal the warning display.

Wiring faults are detected by measuring the resistance across the two resistors; when its value changes, the ECU signals the fault.

A.C. operation overcomes the polarization effects given by d.c. systems and avoids the build up of contaminants on the probe.

Air temperature

Advance warning of the risk of ice on the road allows the driver to adjust speed to suit the conditions.

Sensing of the external air temperature is provided by a special thermistor fitted in a position which is exposed to the air flow (Figure 16.18).

The sensor is mounted in a circuit supplied from the ECU. A typical thermistor unit has a resistance of $1\,\Omega$ at 20°C and a negative temperature resistance coefficient 4.3 %/K (K − absolute temperature in degrees Kelvin).

16.3   Electronic displays

Until about 1980 conventional electromechanical analogue instruments were commonly used to give the driver details about the operation of the vehicle.

Technological advances in solid-state display devices and drive circuits, combined with the application of digital electronic systems for the execution of engine and vehicle control functions, have persuaded many manufacturers to fit a solid-state instrumentation system. This system has the following advantages:

- Faster and more accurate indication.
- No moving parts.
- Layout is more comprehensive and the display is more attractive.
- Improved clarity of display due to the flexibility and format of the display area. Dot matrix, alphanumeric, ISO symbols and bar graphs may be used.
- Greater freedom in display location enables instruments to be sited in the most visible position.
- Panel is easier to accommodate due to its compact form.

Figure 16.19 shows an electronic display.

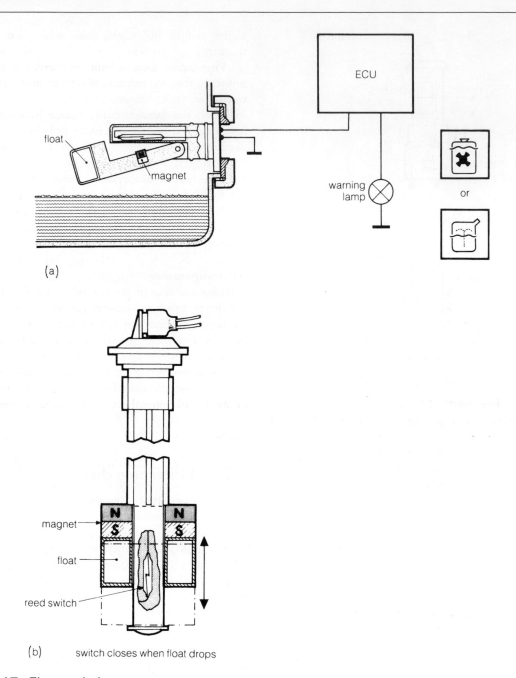

(a)

(b)   switch closes when float drops

Fig. 16.17 Float switch system

Display technologies fall into two groups: *active* and *passive*. An active display emits light whereas a passive reflects the incident light that falls on it. Current electronic display systems include the following:

- light-emitting diode, LED
- vacuum fluorescent display, VFD
- liquid-crystal display, LCD
- d.c. electroluminescence, DCEL
- cathode-ray tube, CRT.

These systems can be arranged to display data in an analogue or digital form. Systems can be designed as a single unit or can be built up from a series of solid-state modules. Often instrumentation layouts use more than one display system, e.g. LED and VFD.

voltage such as 5 V is applied to it (see page 50). Since the forward resistance of an LED is very low, a series resistor must be used to limit the current when there is a risk of the voltage exceeding the normal operating value.

A LED is formed when a diode is combined in a reflective backplate and embedded in a translucent potting material. It is compact, is mechanically robust and has a life in excess of 50 000 hours.

Light radiation patterns are controlled by the encapsulation; if it is transparent the LED functions as a point source with the emitted light restricted to a small angle. When the encapsulation is translucent the light is diffused over a wide angle up to about 80°. Since the encapsulation acts as a lens, the light pattern can be varied to suit the application.

Bar-chart displays Figure 16.20 shows how a series of LEDs can be arranged to produce a bar-chart pattern for a tachometer. The line formed by in-line LEDs can be designed to change colour as the engine speed rises. Common colours are red, orange, yellow and green; these colours are obtained by varying the proportions of arsenic and phosphorus in the diode material.

Seven-segment displays A numeral display based on a simple 'figure-of-eight' is obtained by using seven LED segments (Figure 16.21). With each segment connected to a common earth, the display of a given digit is achieved by applying a voltage to the appropriate

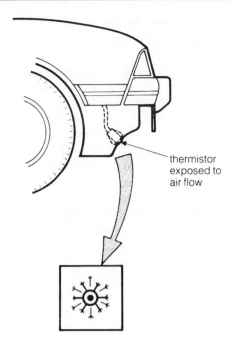

Fig. 16.18 Air temperature sensor

Light-emitting diode (LED)

The widely used LED is one of the simplest forms of display device. In many cases it has displaced the traditional hot-filament lamp used in an instrument panel.

Based on relatively simple modification of a semiconductor diode, the LED gives a pin-point light of high intensity from the semiconductor junction when a

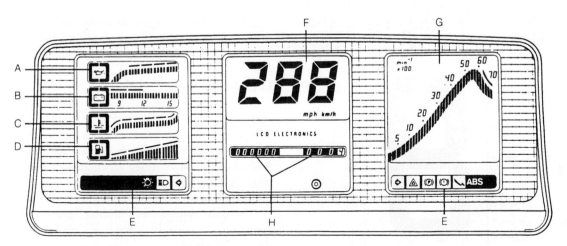

Instrumentation illustrated in check-mode with all functions and warning lights illuminated prior to starting the engine.

A = oil pressure gauge   C = water temperature gauge   E = warning lamps   G = tachometer
B = voltmeter   D = fuel contents gauge   F = speedometer   H = odometers

Fig. 16.19 Electronic display

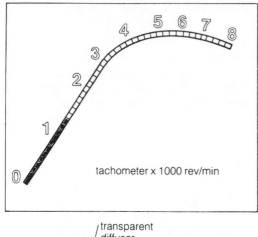

Fig. 16.20 LED display as applied to a tachometer

connections numbered 1 to 7 in the diagram. A series of separate LEDs can be used to form letters of the alphabet; this can display simple messages. An alternative display is to use LEDs to illuminate an *annunciator*: a visual signal to indicate a given situation. These signals can represent complete words or be made to display an ISO-recommended symbol.

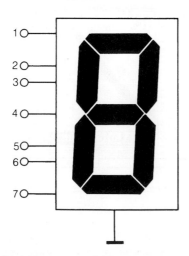

Fig. 16.21 Figure-of-eight display with 7-segment LEDs

Vacuum fluorescent display (VFD)

This active display system has a wider colour range than LEDs and even includes a pleasing blue which is difficult to obtain with LEDs. Its general ruggedness and ease of connection to a drive circuit makes the system suitable for the display of numbers, word patterns and bar graphs.

Figure 16.22 shows a VFD display used for a digital speedometer. The anode of this module has 20 small numeral segments, each one coated with a fluorescent substance and connected to a terminal pin.

The segment is activated when the fluorescent surface is bombarded with electrons. When this happens, the surface glows and the yellow-green light that is emitted illuminates the segment.

Electron movement is caused by arranging the construction in a way similar to that used in a triode valve. It consists of a filament that acts as a cathode to emit electrons, and a grid, which controls and evens-out the flow of electrons to the anode. These parts are all sealed in an air evacuated chamber. This has a flat glass front incorporating a coloured filter to allow the display to be seen in the required colour.

When a current is passed through the thin tungsten filament wires, they heat up to about 600°C and emit negatively-charged electrons. Normally these are attracted to the positively charged control grid, but when a segment of the anode is also given a positive potential by applying a charge of about 5 V to it, some of the electrons pass through the grid and strike the anode; this causes the anode to glow.

The appropriate segments needed to form the various digits are arranged in a way similar to that used in an LED display.

Liquid-crystal display (LCD)

This passive and relatively inexpensive system operates with a low voltage and consumes little power even when a large area is used. Many manufacturers select this for their instrumentation system because the display is not washed out in direct sunlight conditions. It gives a sharp image and by using coloured filters it can be made to present a display in different colours.

The basic system uses reflective light, so when light conditions are poor, back-lighting must be used to make the display visible.

A LCD display utilizes the characteristics of polarized light to produce the image.

Polarized light A ray of light travels in a wave formation similar to that produced when one end of a length

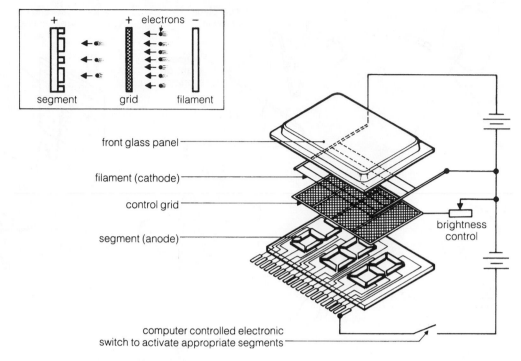

Fig. 16.22 Vacuum fluorescent display

of rope is rapidly moved up and down (Figure 16.23(a)). This action causes a transverse wave, initiated by 'whip' action, to travel along the length of the rope. In the case of light, the velocity of the wave through space is 300 000 km/s.

Normal light comprises a number of waves which vibrate in many different planes. Figure 16.23(b) shows this effect, but for simplicity, only two waves are shown and represented as AA and BB.

If a light ray is passed through a special polarizing filter material such as that used in polaroid-type sunglasses, the filter prevents the majority of waves from passing through it. Only the waves which vibrate in the same plane as the 'axis' of the filter will pass. A similar action results when a rope is passed through a grid having parallel wires (Figure 16.23 (c)).

When vibrations of the light ray are confined to one plane, the resultant light is called *plane polarized light.*

Light rays will not pass through two filters which are 'crossed', i.e. two filters set so that the axis of the second filter is at 90° to the axis of the first filter (Figure 16.23 (d)). This can be demonstrated by holding one pair of polaroid-type sunglasses in front of another pair. By rotating one pair it will be seen that a position is reached where the light is blocked out; this is when the polarizing axes are crossed.

Polarized light in an LCD LCDs are based on a range of strange materials known as liquid crystals; these behave like liquids but have optical properties similar to crystals. In an LCD the long thin nematic (thread-like) molecules forming the liquid crystals are sandwiched between two glass plates. These are placed about 10 μm apart and the crystals are contained in the cell by a perimeter seal. The inner surface of each glass plate is coated with a transparent conductor and polarizing filters, attached to the front and rear of the cell, are set 'crossed' so that their axes are at 90° (Figure 16.24).

A common LCD displays a black character against a light background; this type is called a *twisted nematic* LCD. Crystals of this type rotate the plane of light polarization through 90°, so when a reflective surface is formed on the second polarizer, the light is returned by the same path and a bright image similar to the background is provided.

Applying a voltage of 3–10 V at 50 Hz between the two conductor surfaces causes the electric field to rearrange the molecules; this sets them in a position which prevents the 90° rotation of the polarization plane. When the crystals are set in this condition, light cannot pass to the reflector because it cannot get through the second filter. Since no light is returned, a black

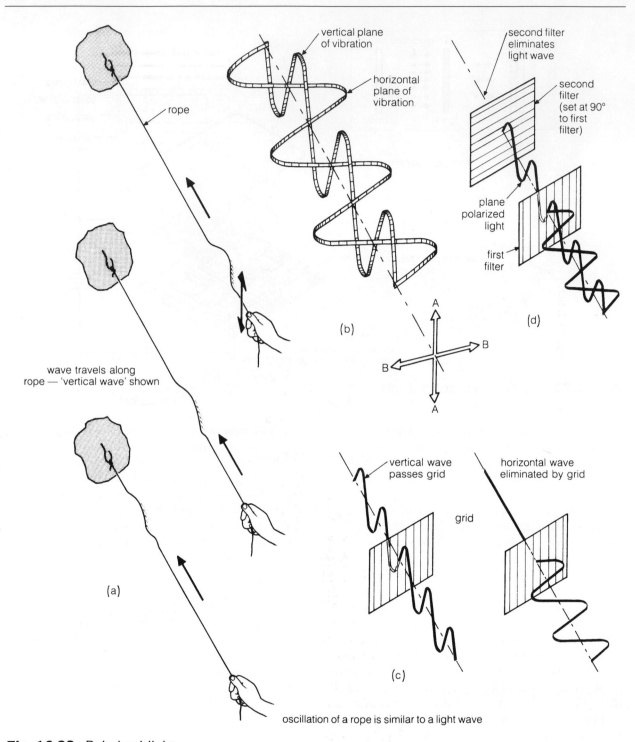

vertical plane of vibration

horizontal plane of vibration

rope

wave travels along rope — 'vertical wave' shown

(a)

oscillation of a rope is similar to a light wave

(b)

second filter eliminates light wave

second filter (set at 90° to first filter)

plane polarized light

first filter

(d)

vertical wave passes grid

horizontal wave eliminated by grid

grid

(c)

Fig. 16.23 Polarized light

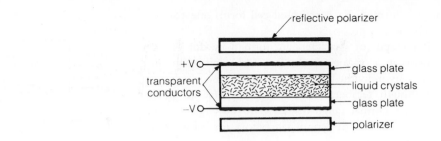

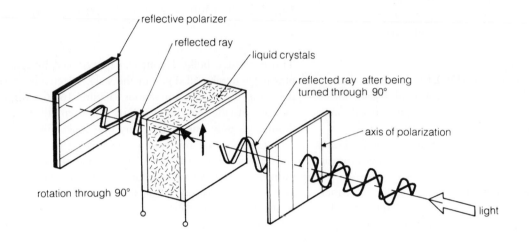

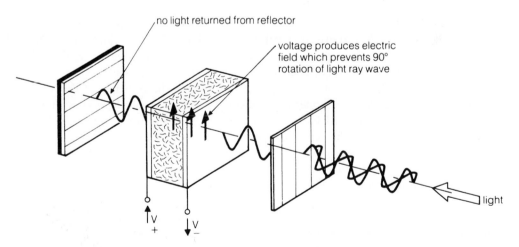

Fig. 16.24 Twisted nematic LCD

image is formed. Each activated cell forms one part of the character.

Bar graphs or characters are formed by dot or bar segments in a manner similar to a LED unit; each cell requires its individual electrical connections.

Although temperature affects the operation of an LCD, the normal range of −20°C to 80°C of a standard twisted nematic type is satisfactory for automotive use.

Coloured backgrounds can be obtained by backlighting and using colour filters. An alternative method is to use the 'guest-host' arrangement in which a dye (guest) is dissolved in the liquid crystal material (host).

DC electroluminescence (DCEL)

An electroluminescent (EL) panel is a solid-state device similar to a LCD cell with the liquid-crystal layer replaced by a zinc sulphide-based compound.

This system has many of the advantages of the LCD; in addition it provides a display by emitting light instead of relying on reflected light.

Many colours can be produced by an EL panel. Operation of the system is by d.c. or a.c.; often the d.c. electroluminescent panel is used to provide back-lighting for a LCD display.

Cathode-ray tube (CRT)

The provision of a single visual display unit (VDU) in the instrument panel enables graphics and other items of driver information, including gauge functions, to be displayed at a comparatively low cost.

The CRT needs a high-voltage supply for its electron beam and it is more fragile and bulky than other displays. Experience gained from the aerospace industry shows that the CRT's brightness, speed of operation, high resolution and simpler driving function makes it very suitable for an instrumentation system.

Driving displays

Electronic display units use numeric read-outs, alphanumeric prompts, quasi-analogue gauge patterns and bar graphs; these signal to the driver various operating conditions and warnings of specific faults.

Irrespective of the type of display, many electrical connections are needed to supply the various rectangular bars or dot images that form the display.

Standard 7-segment displays (Figure 16.25) require seven electrical connections to form one digit so for the display of vehicle speed, a three-digit stack would require 21 connections plus a number of auxiliary lines.

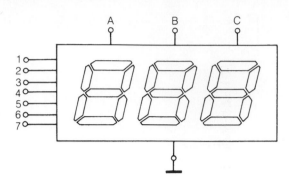

Fig. 16.25 Multiplexing a 7-segment display

This expensive bulky layout can be reduced by multiplexing, whereby all digits in the stack effectively share the same electrical connections (Figure 16.26). Rapid cycling of the driving current between the digits illuminates only one digit at any one time; this cycling action is achieved by making the driving circuit earth each connection A, B and C independently. Since the human eye retains an image for a short time, the impression is gained that each digit is lit continuously. Flicker is avoided by switching each display segment on and off many thousands of times per second.

Data sampling

A computer can deal with only one item of information at any one time, so to handle the numerous items of data being fed to it, the multiplexing technique is often used to separate the various signals. Figure 16.26 shows the principle of this system of sampling. In this diagram the *multiplexer* is shown as a switch (M); this selects the signal source and conveys the data to the computer for processing.

After processing, the signal must be transmitted to the correct display area at the right time. This is achieved by fitting a similar switching device, called a *demultiplexer* (D) to the computer output. Naturally the two 'switches' must be timed to ensure that the display subject matches the appropriate sensor.

The switching time between subsequent signals that are received from given signal sources depends on the rate at which an individual signal varies. Quantities such as fuel contents and coolant temperature change very slowly, whereas vehicle speed and engine speed change rapidly. These differences require some data sources to be sampled more often than others.

In addition to the variable sampling periods, a system must also allow for the longer time needed by the computer to process some items of data which are

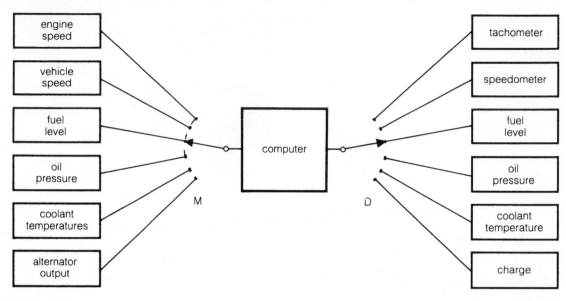

Fig. 16.26 Data sampling by multiplexing

numerous and lengthy in operation; these control functions are programmed into the computer.

System configuration

A typical instrumentation system incorporates analogue displays, on–off warning lamps and digital 7-segment displays. Figure 16.27 shows a configuration of six

instruments involving three types of display that are operated by a computer system. Sensor signals, converted into 8-bit two-level digital codes by the A/D unit, are supplied to the CPU by the multiplexer. After processing, the demultiplexer outputs the signals in an 8-bit or on–off form to drive the appropriate area of the display unit.

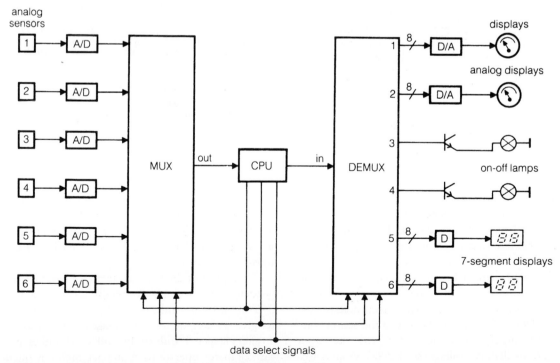

Fig. 16.27 Multiplex system for various displays

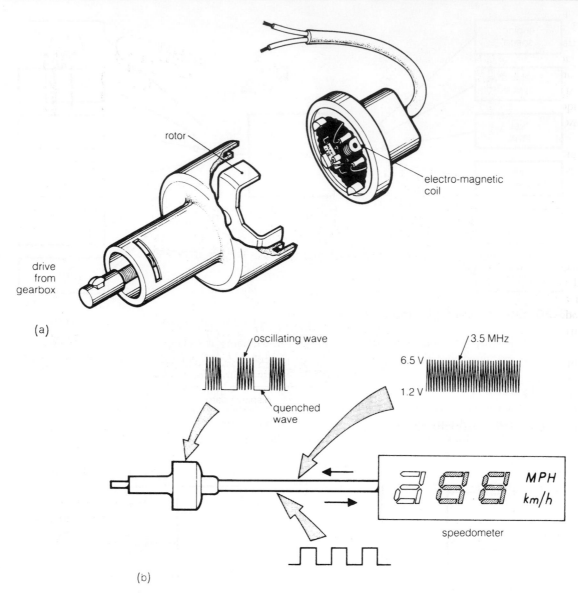

Fig. 16.28 Electronic speedometer

Electronic speedometer

This system can be actuated by a transistorized pulse generator type of sender unit driven by a short length of flexible cable from the gearbox output shaft.

The sensor shown in Figure 16.28(a) consists of an electromagnetic coil, a four-bladed rotor driven from the gearbox, and a solid-state circuit incorporating two transistors. Two cables are connected to the sensor, one gives a 12 V supply from the battery and the other provides an oscillatory voltage of 1.2–6.5 V at a frequency of 3.5 MHz (Figure 16.28(b)).

When the rotor pole passes the electromagnet, the oscillation is quenched and this produces a signal similar to that shown. This is passed to the logic circuit in the instrument panel where it is converted into a signal of square wave form.

The speed of the rotor controls the number of pulses generated per second. A typical application produces 5968.8 pulses per mile which the logic board converts to give an output to the speedometer display unit of 1.6588 Hz per 1 mile/hour and 6151 pulses per mile for odometer operation. A stepper motor is often used to drive the odometer.

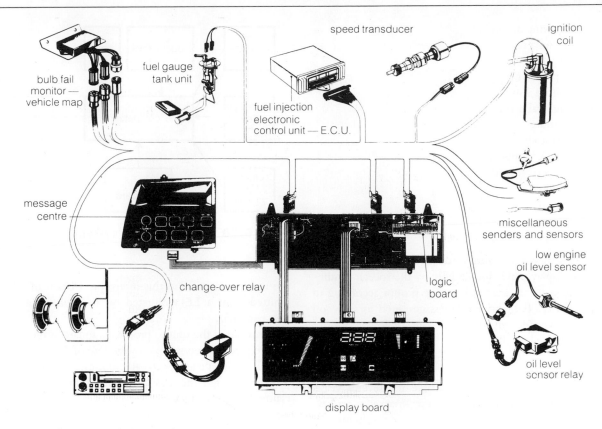

Fig. 16.29 Driver information centre

Speech synthesizer

In addition to the main instrumentation display, some vehicle manufacturers provide a speech synthesizer to convey warning to the driver of critical vehicle operating conditions. This information supplements the normal visual displays and ensures that the driver is made aware of operating problems.

When it is triggered by the onset of a critical operating condition by the main instrumentation motherboard (logic board), the speech synthesizer unit uses the vehicle's audio equipment to announce the warning statement.

Speaker units of audio equipment translate electrical waves into sounds, so by using a computer to generate waves of the required form, it is possible to reproduce human speech. The *phoneme synthesis* technique is one method used. This constructs words from the basic units of sound of a given language. By storing signals that form these sounds in a memory chip, the computer can build up any word, or collection of words, in a manner similar to that used by a human being.

Assuming the memory capacity is adequate, warnings can be stored in several languages, so if the vehicle is supplied to a multi-lingual market, the dealer can select the appropriate language.

Speech processors can be obtained in a single chip form to provide the following basic functions:

(1) *Software-programmable digital filter.* Models a human voice, male or female.
(2) *16K ROM.* Stores the data and program.
(3) *Microprocessor.* Controls the:
    (a) flow of data from the ROM to the digital filter;
    (b) assembly of word strings for linking the speech elements together;
    (c) pitch and amplitude information for the control of the digital filter.
(4) *Pulse width modulation.* Creates a digital signal that can be converted to analogue signal by an external circuit.

Figure 16.29 shows a speech synthesizer module similar to that used on some Rover cars. This unit also incorporates a LCD message centre and a trip computer.

The VCM feature overrides the trip computer and initiates warnings from the following inputs:

- engine temperature
- engine oil pressure
- battery charging
- brake pads worn
- brake fluid low
- parking brake on
- lamp failure
- doors not shut
- outside air temperature
- vehicle servicing due
- low engine oil
- low engine coolant
- low fuel level
- low screen-wash fluid level.

With this model, warnings are given as a text on the message display panel and audibly by the speech synthesizer. Messages are graded into five groups according to their priority; high-priority messages such as 'low oil pressure' override any other message of lower priority being displayed at that time.

Trip computer

Trip computers have been available for several years; they were first introduced as an after-market accessory.

The use of electronic instrumentation systems and their associated sensor signals make it comparatively easy and cheap to use these signals to provide an input for a trip information computer.

In addition to giving the time and date, a typical module can compute:

- average speed
- estimated time of arrival
- fuel used
- instantaneous fuel consumption
- average fuel consumption
- distance to empty fuel tank
- average fuel cost per mile.

Figure 16.30 shows a block diagram of the hardware required to provide a trip information system. Two sensors, in addition to signals for the odometer and clock, are already part of the basic instrumentation system, so a fuel-flow sensor is the only extra part required by the computer.

Fuel-flow sensor

The signal representing fuel flow can be derived from the vehicle's fuel injection system or from a separate transducer fitted in the fuel line.

One type of fuel line transducer has a turbine and a light interrupter. When fuel flows through the unit,

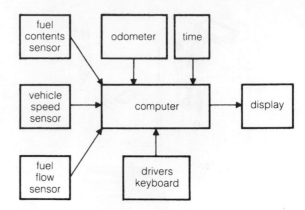

Fig. 16.30 Trip computer system

the turbine rotates and this interrupts a beam of a light emitted from a LED directed on to a phototransistor (see page 65).

This causes the unit to produce a square-wave output at a frequency proportional to the rate of fuel flow. One model in use produces 10 404 pulses per litre of fuel flowing through the transducer; an accuracy of ±3% is claimed.

16.4 Maintenance and fault diagnosis

Maintenance of basic instruments

Most systems can be divided into three sections: sender, wiring loom and instrument unit. When a fault develops, the method of diagnosis is to check out each section in turn.

Sensor check   The sensor or transducer is disconnected from the system and its condition is checked. This is carried out by:

- Checking the insulation and circuit resistance with an ohmmeter. This **instrument must not be used** when the sensor contains solid-state devices because the current supplied by an ohmmeter can cause damage.
- Substituting a test instrument which generates a test signal to simulate the signal given by a good sensor (Figure 16.31). If the indicating unit on the panel functions correctly when the test signal is generated, then the fault is most probably in the sensor. Before fitting a new sensor it is recommended that the original sensor is rechecked: in many cases the fault is due to a bad connection.

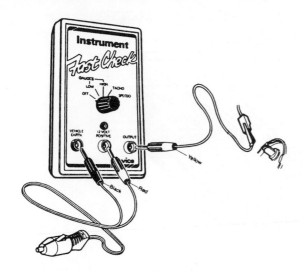

Fig. 16.31 Instrument tester

In the case of thermal-type gauges, a quick check can be made if a jumper lead is used to short out the sender unit for a few seconds. On most instruments this will cause the needle to move towards the maximum position if the gauge unit and circuit are serviceable.

Cable check The purpose of a cable is to transmit messages by passing current along the cable. Any unintentional resistance in the cable, or at a connection point, affects the 'message' received by the instrument, so close attention should be given to this vulnerable section of the circuit.

Although cable resistance can be measured by a standard meter check, most manufacturers recommend that a signal generator test should be applied directly to the instrument end of the cable to isolate faults in the cable.

Instrument check Direct application of the signal generator to the instrument eliminates the remainder of the circuit. If the panel unit fails to respond to this test, then it is concluded that the unit fitted in the panel is faulty. Naturally this conclusion assumes that the test apparatus is serviceable.

Maintenance of electronic displays

At first sight an electronic instrumentation system looks very complicated, but when the layout is considered as a series of separate units, the system becomes easier to understand and simpler to repair. Initially it is necessary to understand the method used to operate the system

before attempting to diagnose apparent faults in the system.

Panel self-tests Many systems incorporate a self-test function whereby the computer performs a check sequence of its main display and speech features. On some systems this check is initiated when two specific keys of the trip computer are pressed simultaneously.

Before applying any test equipment to the system it is recommended that a full test of the panel is carried out.

Need for care Compared with normal electrical equipment, a display panel with its companion logic board, or mother-board, is easily damaged. With replacement costs in the region of £500–£1000, great care must be taken when working on this type of equipment. Fault diagnosis tests should be carried out as recommended by the manufacturer, and unless otherwise stated, **full-battery voltage should not be applied to any of the panel inputs**. In most cases the incorrect use of a test meter such as an ohmmeter, can seriously damage the computer circuits.

Checking the driver information centre

The following description applies to a Rover-type electronic display panel. It is intended that this outline will introduce the reader to some of the main checks. Further study of the manufacturer's literature is necessary before attempting any work on this type of equipment.

Pin connectors

Many models use a number of connectors to link the harness to the panel. The connectors are generally coloured for identification purposes and locking tabs are often used to hold the connectors secure. Pins, and their mating sockets, must not be damaged during the testing operation, especially when meter connections have to be made to the harness. Often damage can be avoided by using a spare connector plug when meter connections have to be made.

Failure of individual segments Setting the panel to its normal static display mode enables various sections of the panel to be checked. Failure of one or two segments to illuminate indicates that the logic board is transmitting the correct pulse signal via the multiplexed circuit, but the symptom shows that the display segments are not functioning correctly. In this case the display panel normally has to be replaced.

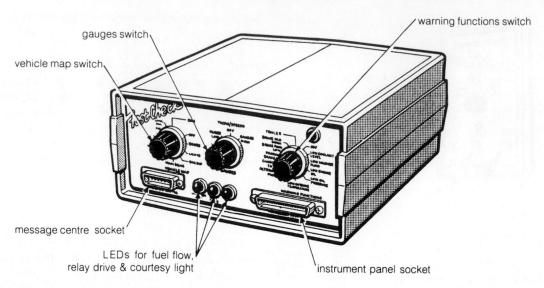

gauges switch

vehicle map switch

warning functions switch

message centre socket

LEDs for fuel flow,
relay drive & courtesy light

instrument panel socket

Fig.16.32 'Fast-Check' tester

Failure of one instrument unit If a unit, such as the temperature gauge, fails to operate, the first check is to examine visually the wiring harness between the sensor and the instrument panel. Assuming this is satisfactory, the next step is to use the appropriate test equipment to locate the fault.

Any fault in the system must be situated in one of three sections, namely: sensor, wiring harness, instrument panel or connectors joining these three sections. To locate this fault, the Rover Company produced 'Fast-Check' testers to simulate the signals produced by the sensors. By substituting these signal generators for the sensors, the remainder of the circuits can be checked (Figure 16.32).

If the display shows the correct reading when the test signal is applied to the system, then the sensor is assumed to be faulty.

When 'no display' is obtained, then the Fast-Check tester is applied direct to the appropriate input socket of the panel. Failure to obtain the correct reading with the tester giving an input at this point shows that the panel is faulty. Conversely, if the tester produces a display, then a fault is present in the harness or connectors.

Computer 'Fast-Check' This tester reproduces the signals of the fuel flow and speed sensors. The operation of the computer and display unit can be verified by using a method similar to that described previously.

LCD instrument tester This tester, which is applied direct to the instrument panel, provides reference input signals for the main panel and message centre, so the operation of the complete driver information centre can be ascertained. This test is used generally to confirm the diagnosis when previous tests have suggested that the panel is faulty.

Dismantling a mother-board
When a part of the instrument panel is found to be faulty and a new part has to be fitted, the complete assembly normally has to be removed. As in the case of other electrical components, the battery should be disconnected before work is commenced.

Separation of the mother-board from the display panel should be carried out in a clean area. Also, precautions should be taken to prevent static electricity from the human body damaging the IC chips; body static can be discharged by periodically touching a known earth point to conduct the charge to ground. In cases where this type of work is common, a static conducting wrist strap and dissipative mat should be used.

Panels should be handled by touching the edges only, and surfaces such as the non-reflective display window and face of the display board should not be fingered.

REMEMBER

Instrument sensor for:

- temperature gauge is normally a thermistor
- oil pressure is often a piezoelectric crystal
- speedometer is often an inductive type

- handbrake application
- engine oil pressure
- door ajar system
- ABS operation
- air bag circuit

VCM systems can monitor:

- fluid levels – engine, coolant, washer, fuel and brake
- battery state and charging system operation
- engine management operation
- operation of lighting system
- engine coolant temperature
- condition of brake pads
- outside air temperature

Electronic instrument panel systems:

- display information by LED, VFD, LCD, DCEL and CRT
- often use LEDs to illuminate an annunciator
- using LCDs operate with polarized light
- uses an A/D unit to convert analogue signals to digital pulses
- sample data by a *multiplexer* and after processing, exports the data by a *demultiplexer*

PROGRESS CHECK 16

1. State the effect on the fuel level reading if the contacts of a thermal-type voltage stabilizer are welded together.

2. State the effect on the temperature gauge if a fault causes the thermistor resistance to remain constant.

3. State TWO methods used to sense engine oil pressure.

4. Name the instrument on the panel that operates by using ignition pulses.

5. Name the instrument on the panel that operates by sensing the rotation of the gearbox output shaft.

6. Describe one method used to monitor bulb failure.

7. State how the circuit of a closed-loop brake lining wear monitor differs from an open-loop system.

8. State the principle of operation of a hot-wire oil level sensor.

9. A coolant level sensor uses a reed switch. Name and describe the part that activates the reed switch when the fluid level falls.

10. How many LED segments are required to produce a figure of eight?

11. What is meant by: data sampling by multiplexing?

12. Which test instrument must NOT be used to test an ECU?

13. A driver observes that some of the VCM warning lamps illuminate for a few seconds when the ignition is switched on. State the reason for this.

14. State the purpose of a signal generator that is used during a check of a VCM system.

15. List TWO precautions that should be taken when dismantling a mother-board of an electronic panel.

17 Screen and window systems

What is covered in this chapter

→ windscreen wipers
→ windscreen washers
→ window winding
→ heated windows
→ door mirrors
→ maintenance and fault diagnosis

17.1 Windscreen wipers

The majority of wipers are operated electrically. Whereas in the past a vehicle was fitted with only one wiper, today it is more common to use two wiper blades for the front windscreen with both blades driven from a single motor. The Law requires the wiper on the driver's side to operate effectively.

Hatchback and fastback-type cars normally have a single-speed wiper and separate washer for the rear window. This is necessary because air flow over the body of cars of this shape cause road spray and dirt to be deposited on the rear window. Some cars in the more expensive range also have wipers fitted to the headlamps.

The force needed to drive a rubber wiper blade across a glass surface is considerable, especially when the blade has to sweep away a large volume of water or snow. Most modern vehicle windscreens have a double curvature, so long articulated wiper blades with the ability to flex to the contour of the glass are needed. Systems often have two wipe speeds to suit the driving conditions and in addition, an intermittent wipe facility is often provided.

Modern requirements for a car wiper motor demand a high-powered quiet unit that operates on a current of 2–4 A. In the past, shunt-wound motors were used but the introduction of powerful magnetic materials during recent years has made the *permanent-magnet motor* the type commonly used today.

Figure 17.1 shows the layout of a typical wiper system. A worm on the armature drives a worm wheel which is connected to a crank to provide the reciprocating action needed to oscillate the wiper blades. The gearing gives the speed reduction and the torque increase needed to drive the wiper blades.

Permanent-magnet type

Figure 17.2 shows the construction of a single-speed motor. The 8-slotted armature is mounted on self-lubricating sintered bushes and two carbon brushes, set 180° apart, rub on an 8-segment commutator normally placed at the driving end. Two strong permanent magnets are bonded with an adhesive to the steel yoke; this is sometimes coated externally with a non-ferrous metal to resist corrosion.

A steel worm formed on the end of the armature drives a worm wheel, made of plastic, at a speed of about 1/10th the speed of the armature. In the motor shown in Figure 17.2 the output drive is by a pinion gear driven directly by the worm wheel. Rubber seals at the joint faces of the motor exclude moisture and a polythene pipe vents the gases formed by arcing at the brushes.

Two-speed operation

This is achieved generally by using an extra brush. This third brush is thinner than the main brushes and is set as shown in Figure 17.3(a).

When the switch supplies current to 'B', a low wipe rate of about 50 wiping cycles per minute is obtained; this is increased to about 70 when the supply is delivered to terminal 'C'. The rise in speed is due to an increase in the current flow through the motor.

When brushes 'A' and 'C' are used fewer armature windings are involved so the lower resistance gives a larger current flow and a higher rotational speed. As the

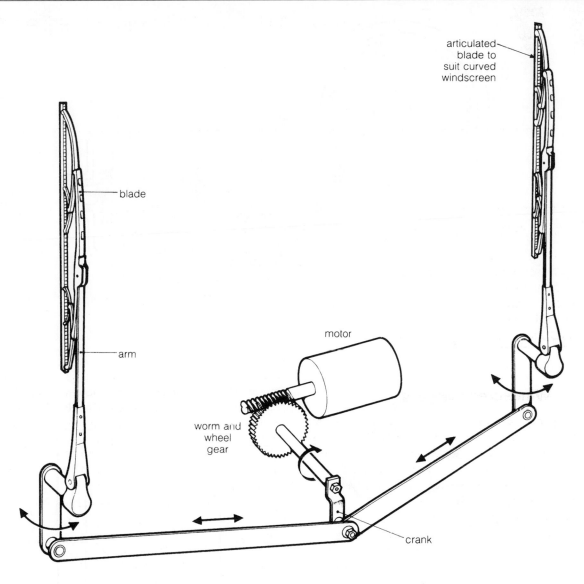

articulated
blade to
suit curved
windscreen

blade

arm

motor

worm and
wheel
gear

crank

Fig. 17.1 Layout of a typical wiper system (simplified link-type drive)

speed is increased a rise in back-e.m.f. reduces the current flow. The shorter armature path between brushes 'A' and 'C' is shown in Figure 17.3(b). Figure 17.3(c) shows the interconnection of the coils of a 'lap wound' type of armature normally used for a wiper motor.

High speed should not be used when there is a heavy load on the wiper blade, e.g. in heavy snow or on a wind-screen which has been swept clear of water and is dry.

Self-switching action When the wiper is not required, the blades should be set so that they are at the end of their wiping stroke. The driver finds it difficult to stop

the blades in this position so a *limit switch* is fitted to achieve this requirement. This automatic switch is controlled by the gearbox of the wiper motor and is arranged to open only when the wiper blades are at one end of their stroke.

Figure 17.4 shows the principle of the limit switch. If the driver switches off the motor in any position other than that shown, the limit switch continues to supply current until the 'park' position is reached.

Even with this switch, the blades do not always come to rest at the correct place owing to the momentum of the moving parts. This problem is overcome by using an action called *regenerative braking*.

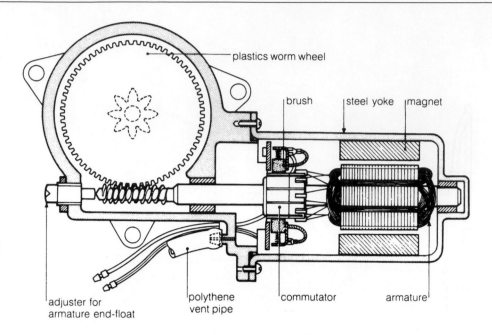

Fig. 17.2 Single-speed motor

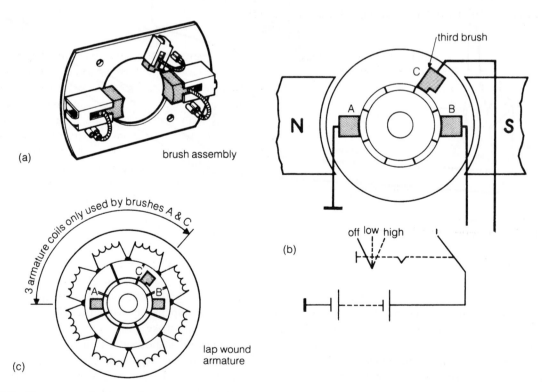

Fig. 17.3 Two-speed operation

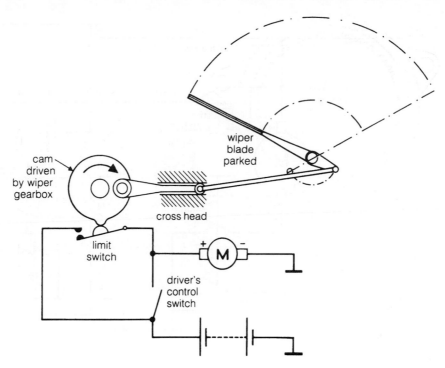

Fig. 17.4 Limit switch to give self-switching action

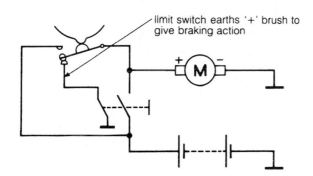

Fig. 17.5 Regenerative braking

When the driver has switched off the motor, another set of contacts on the limit switch is arranged to connect the two main brushes together (Figure 17.5). At this point the current generated by the moving armature creates a load on the armature which gives a braking action and quickly brings the motor to rest.

Intermittent wipe Spray from passing vehicles and light drizzle conditions require the screen to be wiped infrequently, say every few seconds, so most vehicles have a switch position to provide this facility.

To overcome the regenerative braking provision on a permanent magnet-type motor, a current pulse of comparatively long duration is needed to rotate the armature sufficient to move the limit switch from its 'braked' position. Most vehicles use a semiconductor-controlled relay to provide this function; the time period between wipes is governed by the action of a capacitor. This time constant is governed by the resistance–capacitance (RC) of a circuit, so by varying either 'R' or 'C' the interval can be varied to suit the requirement.

Figure 17.6(a) shows one electronic circuit layout which gives an intermittent wipe action.

The diagram shows the two main brushes interconnected through the two switches and relay contacts (1); regenerative braking takes places when the contacts are set in this position.

When current is supplied to terminal A, the relay is energized and the contacts are closed. This connects the negative brush to earth and causes the motor to operate, irrespective of the position of the limit switch.

If at this stage, the supply is disconnected from A, the relay will open and the contacts (1) will close. Since the limit switch is earthed, the motor will continue to operate until the earth contact at the limit switch is broken.

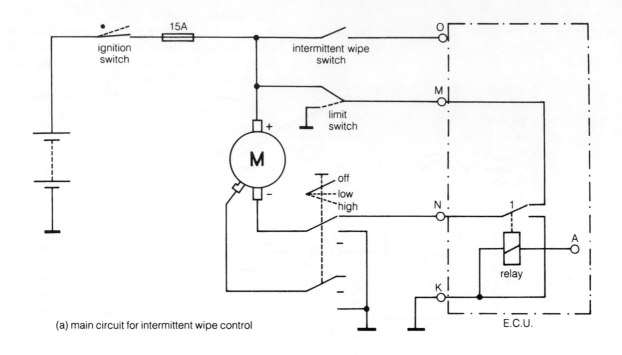

(a) main circuit for intermittent wipe control

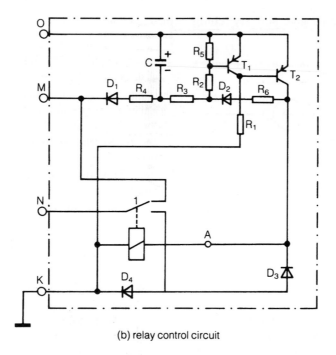

(b) relay control circuit

Fig. 17.6 Intermittent wipe control

The control circuit for the relay is shown in Figure 8.6(b); the operating sequence is commenced from the point where the intermittent wipe switch is closed. The sequence is:

(1) Current flows from the switch through the base of T_2 to earth via R_1. This switches on T_2 to energize the relay and start the motor.

(2) After a time the motor moves the limit switch to the earth position. Current from T_2 will now pass to the limit switch via R_6 and will cause the relay to deactivate; this closes the relay contacts '1' and provides an alternative path from the negative brush to earth. In consequence the motor continues to operate.

(3) When the limit switch makes its earth contact, current passes through the base of T_1; this switches on T_1 and switches off T_2. During this stage the p.d. across the capacitor causes it to charge up.

(4) Further rotation of the motor moves the limit switch to the stop position; this causes the motor to stop abruptly. Current flow through R_4 from T_1 now ceases but T_1 is prevented from switching off by the discharge current from the capacitor. This current gives a flow in the sub-circuit incorporating the base of T_1 together with R_2 and R_3.

(5) It takes about five seconds for the capacitor to release its charge so after that time T_1 will switch off and T_2 will switch on to repeat the cycle.

On some vehicles intervals can be varied to suit the conditions. This provision can be made by fitting a variable resistor control in the capacitor-discharge sub-circuit in place of resistor R_3.

Self-parking wipers On some vehicles the wiper blades are parked off the windscreen. This provision can be achieved by switching the circuit so that after the motor has stopped the current through the armature is reversed. When the brush polarity of a permanent magnet motor is changed, the armature rotates in the opposite direction.

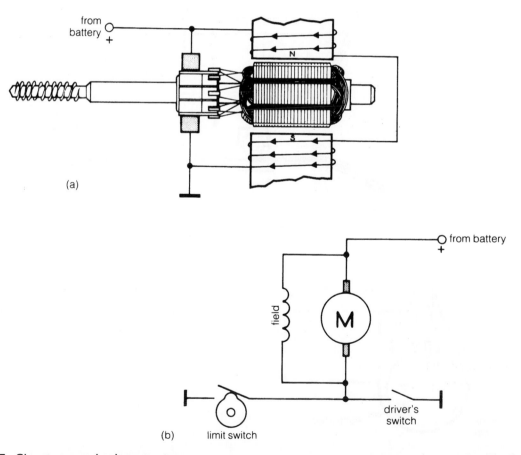

Fig. 17.7 Shunt-wound wiper motor

By arranging the gearbox linkage so that reverse motion extends the wiping stroke, the movement is made to park the wiper blades well away from the glass screen.

Wound motors These are seldom used today in view of the superiority of the permanent magnet type in respect of power, noise, efficiency, cost, reliability and current consumption.

Figure 17.7(a) illustrates the layout of a single-speed motor having a shunt-wound field; Figure 17.7(b) shows the circuit when a limit switch is fitted to provide a self-switching facility.

Two–speed operation Although this could be achieved by switching-in a resistor in the battery feed line, the loss of efficiency due to heat loss at the resistor makes it unsuitable.

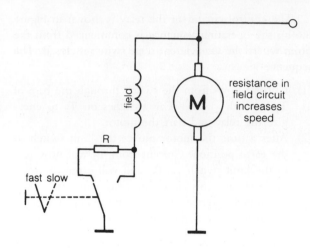

Fig. 17.8 Two-speed wiper motor circuit

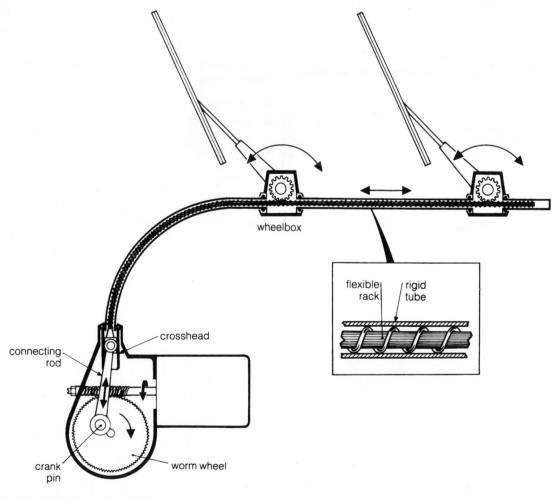

Fig. 17.9 Flexible rack drive

Figure 17.8 shows one arrangement for obtaining a two-speed operation. When 'low-speed' is selected, the current passing through the field winding is divided between the armature and the field.

Moving the switch to 'high-speed' inserts a resistor in the shunt field. This causes a larger current to flow through the armature and this results in an increase in the motor speed.

Overload protection   Under snow or ice conditions the load on a motor becomes excessive; this causes it to slow down or in extreme conditions it stops. A decrease in armature speed reduces back-e.m.f.; this lower opposition allows a large flow of current in the order of 11 A through the motor and leads to overheating and possible damage to the motor.

Protection is normally given by incorporating a thermal switch in series with the supply lead. The switch is controlled by a bi-metallic strip; when the strip is heated by a higher-than-normal current, the contacts are opened.

Mechanical drive systems

For accommodation reasons the motor is situated remote from the wiper blades. This means that a mechanical drive must be used to transfer the motion to the blades. The two main systems used are:

- link
- flexible rack.

Link system   Figure 17.1 (page 337) shows the layout of a link system. This efficient system uses a crank on the output shaft of the motor to reciprocate a transverse link. This drives the levers and partially rotates the shafts on to which the wiper arms are connected. The relative lengths of the levers control the angle of sweep of the wipers. Self-lubricating bushes are normally fitted at each connection.

Flexible rack   This system is more compact and quieter than the link system. Also it allows the motor to be situated in an accessible place, normally under the bonnet.

Figure 17.9 shows a crank pin on a worm wheel driving a rod which connects with, and reciprocates, a flexible rack contained in a rigid tube. The rack is similar to a speedometer cable except that it is wrapped with a wire to form a 'thread'. Drive from the rack to the wiper is by means of a pinion which engages with the rack teeth. Each pinion is held in a wheelbox

(or gearbox), the casing of which is screwed to the rigid tube.

17.2   Windscreen washers

Statutory regulations require that a screen washer must be fitted to clean the driver's side of the windscreen. Today most vehicles fit an electrically-operated pump to supply water or cleaning fluid to two or more jets that spray the windscreen. On some vehicles an extra pump is fitted to supply a headlamp wash system; some of these vehicles are also fitted with headlamp wipers.

The small centrifugal pump is either fitted directly on to the water reservoir or mounted in the hydraulic line. The pump is driven by a permanent-magnet motor controlled by a switch that is often operated from the wiper switch stalk on the steering column (Figure 17.10). The pump is self-priming and is protected by a filter at the inlet. Polythene tubing is used to supply the jets. A typical motor consumes about 3 A and supplies about 0.75 litre/min at a pressure of 0.67 bar (10 lbf/in²).

In the winter, a small quantity of methylated spirit added to the water lowers the freezing temperature.

Various refinements can be embodied in the wash system; these include:

- timer to control the wash period;
- timer programmed to give a controlled wipe/wash action following the touch-operation of the washer switch;

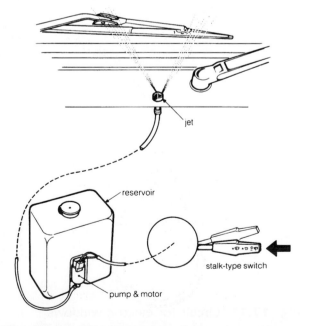

Fig. 17.10 Windscreen washer

- integration of the washer outlets with the wiper blades to eliminate spray problems;
- heating the washer fluid before it is applied to the screen to minimize risk of freezing.

GOOD PRACTICE

Window wiper should not be operated on a dry surface because:

- glass will be scratched by the grit on the blades
- motor will be overloaded

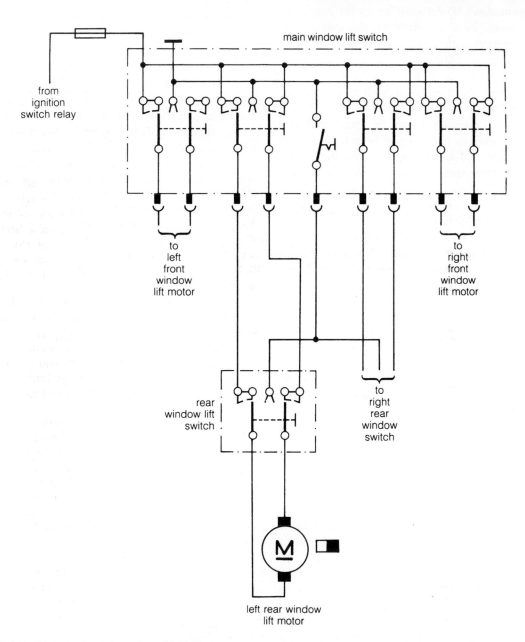

Fig. 17.11 Circuit for electric windows

17.3 Window winding

Electrically-operated windows

Most electric-window applications use a d.c. permanent magnet motor for each window; this is operated via a three-position rocker switch to enable the polarity to be changed to give up-and-down motion of the window. The driver's panel has four main window switches, one for each window, and an isolation switch to disconnect the supply to the rear windows.

Current through the switches and associated cables is reduced by fitting two relays to control the current to each motor; these relays are supplied by a common feed. Since the signal current for a relay is low, the size of cable for this current is considerably smaller than that needed for a direct supply.

Drive between the motor and the window glass is by means of a gearbox; this amplifies the torque sufficient to raise the window which is more difficult to undertake than the downward motion. The output gear of the gearbox drives either a flexible rack or acts directly on to the window winding mechanism similar to a manual system.

One or more thermal cut-out switches are fitted in the circuit, sometimes in the motor, to limit the current in the event of overload. The cut-out is opened if the operating switch is held closed when the window reaches its limit of movement or in a case where ice prevents free movement of the glass. When a main overload switch is fitted it is often a type that requires resetting after the circuit has been exposed to an overload situation.

Figure 17.11 shows a circuit for electric operation of a rear-passenger window; the remainder of the circuit has been omitted for simplicity. The motor in this layout is supplied directly via the ignition switch. The additional rear-window switch enables a passenger to adjust the window, but this control can only be operated when the driver's isolation switch is closed.

Operation of the window by moving the appropriate ganged switch supplies the motor with a current of a suitable polarity to rotate the motor in the required direction.

17.4 Heated windows

Heated rear windows

Most cars are fitted with an electrically heated rear window to clear and/or prevent condensation. Saloon cars that have no rear wiper also use the heater to assist

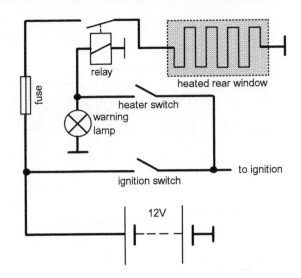

Fig. 17.12 Heated rear window circuit

the clearance of rain drops that cling to the external surface of the rear window and impair visibility.

The heating element consists of a wire or strip element bonded to the interior surface of the glass. Figure 17.12 shows the basic layout of a heated rear window circuit. Effective de-misting of the window requires a high power; this ranges from about 80 W when the element is cold, to about 35 W when it is hot.

Provision of this power to the remotely sited window requires a relay placed close to the heater; this minimizes the voltage drop in the cable and reduces the load on the switch. In addition the extended use of the rear window heater places an extra load on the alternator; by itself this is not great but at times when it is in operation, other systems such as lighting, wipers and interior heaters are also being used.

To remind the driver that the heater is in operation, either a warning lamp is incorporated in the switch or a heater window symbol is displayed on the instrument panel. Battery protection is achieved by operating the heater via the ignition switch. Unintentional use can be further guarded against by fitting either a timer unit or a control that automatically switches off the heater for the driver when the engine is stopped.

Heated windscreens

On some top-of-the-range vehicles, the windscreen has a very thin, transparent coating of metal such as gold. This acts as an electrical conductor to slightly heat the screen to minimize condensation and functions as a defroster.

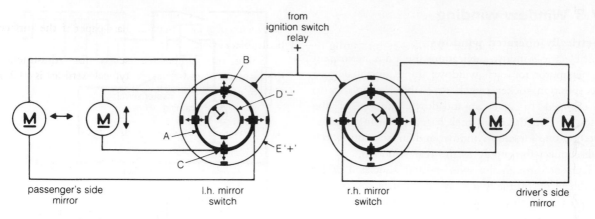

Fig. 17.13 Electrically-operated door mirrors

17.5 Door mirrors

Electrically-operated door mirrors

Adjustment of a door mirror is difficult for the driver, especially the setting of a mirror on the passenger door. This task is made easier by using an electrical control system.

Figure 17.13 shows a system for the control of two mirrors. Each mirror is electrically adjusted by two reversible permanent-magnet motors fitted behind the mirror. One motor controls the vertical tilt of the mirror and the other the horizontal tilt.

Each mirror is set by means of a single switch; this has a stalk with a universal movement to enable single or combined operation of the two motors.

When the switch is depressed to vertically tilt the mirror, the switch cage (A) is moved downwards and the two contacts (B) and (C) make a circuit with the '−' and '+' surfaces, (D) and (E).

Conversely, when the switch stalk is moved upwards, (B) contacts the positive surface and (C) contacts the negative or earth surface. In this switch position, the potential applied to the vertical tilt motor is opposite to that given when the switch was in the previous position. This causes the motor and mirror to move in the opposite direction.

Heated door mirrors

Moisture on mirrors can impair safety, so a heating element placed behind the glass improves the mirror image when driving conditions are poor.

Connecting the mirrors in the same circuit as the heated rear window overcomes the need for a separate switch.

17.6 Maintenance and fault diagnosis

Maintenance of a wiper system

Good clear visibility is essential for safe driving, so for this reason a check on the operation of the driver's wiper and washer is included in the annual MOT test. *Routine maintenance* should cover an inspection of the following.

Wiper blades   Blades should be replaced if the rubber shows signs of cracking, tearing or becoming hard and brittle. The metal part of the blade should be sound and the fixing to the arm must be secure.

A wiper motor must not be operated when the screen is dry; this overloads the motor and also severely scratches the surface of the glass.

Screen   Traffic film can be removed from the screen and wiper blades by using methylated spirit. Polishes containing silicone and wax should not be allowed to contaminate the screen or blade surface.

Wiper arms   These should be checked to ensure that the spring is serviceable and is applying sufficient force (generally about 350 g) to the blade. The arm should not be bent because this can cause the blade to 'chatter' on one stroke.

Wiper faults   Slackness or tightness of the mechanical drive system can cause *noise*. Also noise occurs in the link system when the moving parts contact other parts such as the metal tubing of the screen washer tube.

If a visual inspection fails to locate the noise, then each part should be checked independently. Flexible racks should be checked for tightness by measuring the force required to move the rack through the tube when it is disconnected from the motor and wheelbox; a maximum force of 27 N (6 lbf) is typical.

The tube holding the rack must not be dented or kinked and the radius of any bend should not be less than 230 mm. The rack should be lubricated with a grease such as HMP to give a smooth movement.

Motor faults 'Failure to operate' and 'low operating speed' are two faults that can occur. In both cases a voltmeter check should be made to ensure that the motor is receiving the full battery voltage.

To test the motor *in situ* it is recommended that a pair of test leads is used to supply the motor direct from the battery; a spare wiper motor plug makes this task easier. This test reveals possible faults in the switch and wiring.

After a comparatively long time the brushes wear down and the commutator becomes dirty. On many models brush replacement is necessary when the main brushes are worn to a length of less than 5 mm, or the stepped part of the third brush has worn away. New brushes, complete with springs and plastic mounting plate can normally be obtained.

The commutator should be cleaned with a petrol-moistened rag or a strip of glass-paper if the surface is badly blackened.

Some motors have a screw for adjustment of the armature end-float; a typical setting is 0.2 mm (0.008 in).

Maintenance of heated rear windows

Care must be execised when cleaning the interior side of the rear window to avoid damaging the heater grid.

If the grid fails to heat, the sequence shown in Table 17.1 should be followed until the fault is isolated.

Defective heater grid When the grid is sandwiched in the glass, a new window must be fitted when failure occurs. When the grid is bonded to the inside surface of the glass, a voltmeter is used to locate the break. One lead of the meter is connected to a good earth on the vehicle and the break is found by carefully applying the pointed probe of the meter at different points along the grid.

After marking the break on the outside of the glass, a small break in the grid can be repaired by using a special electrically-conductive adhesive that is specially made for this purpose.

Test	Result – Yes	Result – No
Is the fuse serviceable?	Proceed with test	Replace fuse
Is correct voltage applied to grid?	Check grid for open-circuit	Check circuit continuity and operation of relay

Table 17.1 Test sequence for 'Heated rear window fails to operate'

Test	Result – Yes	Result – No
Do front windows operate?	Check that driver's isolation switch is on	Proceed with test
Is fuse serviceable?	Proceed with test	Replace
Does right-side rear window operate?	Proceed with test	Check continuity from isolation earth switch to rear window switch and check feed to rear window switch
Expose left-hand-side switch: is supply voltage 12 V?	Proceed with test	Check continuity between left- and right-hand switches
Measure output voltage from left-hand switch in up and down mode: is voltage 12 V?	Fault is in relay, limit switch, or motor	Fault is in switch

Table 17.2 Test sequence for 'Left-hand-side rear window fails to close'

Maintenance of electrically-operated windows

This system is normally very reliable; when a fault is reported it is often caused by either a blown fuse or a defective switch contact.

As is normal with most electrical faults, considerable time is saved if the precise symptom is known before starting the job.

If the left-hand-side rear window fails to close, the sequence shown in Table 17.2 should be followed until the fault is isolated.

REMEMBER

Windscreen wipers of the permanent magnet type:

- use a thin *third brush* to obtain high-speed operation
- are stopped at the end of the wiping stroke by a *limit switch*
- use *regenerative braking* to quickly bring the motor to rest
- normally use a *R–C circuit* to provide the intermittent-wipe feature
- are protected against overload by a *thermal switch*
- use either a *link* or *flexible rack* mechanical drive system

Windscreen washers:

- are required by law and are subject to the annual MOT test

- are normally operated by a *permanent magnet* (PM) type motor

Electrically operated windows:

- have one PM motor for each window
- use a PM motor because changing the supply polarity reverses the d.o.r.
- should be fitted with an *overload thermal switch* for safety purposes
- have an *isolation switch* to allow the driver to prevent rear seat operation of the windows

Heated rear windows:

- consume high power
- are relay operated
- have a signal lamp to indicate when the heater is in operation

---

PROGRESS CHECK 17

Questions 1–7 relate to windscreen wipers

1. State TWO reasons why permanent magnet (PM) motors are commonly used today.

2. State the method used in a PM-type motor to provide:
(a) high-speed operation;
(b) low speed operation;
(c) self-switching;
(d) armature braking.

3. What method is used to control the operation of the intermittent-wipe relay?

4. How is two-speed operation

achieved in a wound-type motor?

5. State the purpose of a thermal switch in the supply line.

6. Why should a wiper not be used on a dry screen?

7. A PM-type wiper motor will not operate when the switch is set in the high-speed position. State TWO possible causes of this fault.

8. Name a suitable solution that can be added to the water in a washer reservoir to lower the freezing point.

9. Name the type of actuator used to electrically raise and lower a window.

10. State the method used with 'electric windows' to control the direction of rotation of the actuator.

11. State TWO reasons why a relay is used in a heated rear window circuit.

12. Refer to the test sequence shown in Table 17.2. Draw a flow chart (similar to that shown in Figure 15.20 page 307) for this fault diagnosis routine.

18 Signalling equipment

What is covered in this chapter

→ horns
→ direction indicators
→ maintenance and fault diagnosis

The Law requires a motor vehicle to be fitted with an audible warning device which emits a continuous note that is not too loud or harsh in sound.

The law also requires vehicles made after 1986 to have three lamps on each side that flash simultaneously at the rate of 60–120 flashes per minute. In addition a tell-tale indicator for the driver must be fitted.

18.1 Horns

Most horns are operated electrically and the note is obtained either by magnetically vibrating a diaphragm or by pumping air past a diaphragm into a trumpet.

The note produced should be 'musical' rather than a noise likely to cause annoyance to the public. To give a pleasing and penetrating note two horns are often fitted: one emits a high-pitch note, to overcome traffic noise, and the other a low pitch, to carry over a distance. The *pitch* of a note is its frequency, i.e. the number of oscillations made per second. The unit of frequency is the *hertz* (Hz); one oscillation per second is one hertz.

There are three types of electric horn; they are:

● high frequency
● windtone
● air horn

High-frequency horn (HF) This comparatively cheap type of horn has been in use for many years. An electro-mechanical action vibrates a steel diaphragm at about 300 Hz which causes a tone disc to oscillate at about 2000 Hz. The combined sound produces a highly penetrating note that meets the normal requirements of a horn.

Figure 18.1 shows how the oscillatory movement of the diaphragm is produced by the action of a magnetic field winding on an iron core.

When the horn button is pressed, the closed contacts allow a current of about 4 A to flow around the field coil; this generates a magnetic flux which attracts the armature. After the armature has moved a given distance as set by the adjustment, the contacts are opened; this causes the magnetic field to collapse with the result that the natural spring of the diaphragm returns the armature and closes the contacts. This cycle continues for the period that the horn button is pressed.

Windtone horns This type uses a similar electrical operating system to the HF horn for moving the

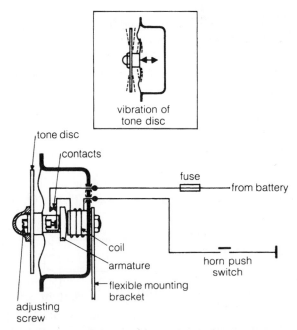

Fig. 18.1 High-frequency horn and circuit

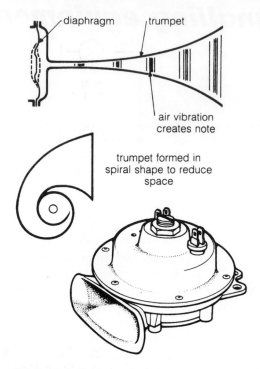

Fig. 18.2 Windtone horn

diaphragm, but instead of oscillating a tone disc, a wind-tone horn vibrates, or resonates, a column of air contained in a trumpet (Figure 18.2). The sound is produced in the trumpet in a manner similar to that used in a wind instrument.

The pitch of the note is governed by the length of trumpet and since the trumpet needs to be fairly long in length, it is often shaped in a spiral form, or like a snail's shell, to conserve space. Normally two horns are fitted to a vehicle; these are harmonically tuned to the interval of a major third.

Horns should be mounted flexibly; this limits the transmission of external shocks that would otherwise affect the quality of the horn note. The majority of horns, especially the windtone types, consume a total current in excess of 10 A, so to prolong the life of the horn switch a relay is generally fitted (Figure 18.3).

Air horns An air horn consists of a trumpet through which air is forced by means of an electrically-driven air pump. Vibration of the air column in the trumpet is initiated by a diaphragm valve positioned at the end of the trumpet.

Operation of the horn switch causes the motor-driven air-compressor pump to discharge air into the pressure chamber in the horn. The air pressure deflects the centre of the diaphragm and this allows some air to escape into the trumpet. As this occurs the slight pressure drop in the chamber closes the diaphragm valve and the cycle is repeated. The rate of vibration of the diaphragm combined with the trumpet length governs the pitch and quality of the note emitted.

18.2   Direction indicators

Pre-warning that the driver intends to turn or overtake is signalled to other road users by the flashing of amber-coloured lights.

Each directional indicator light must be sited so that it is visible through a given angle, the light unit must carry the appropriate 'E' marking for its position and the bulb must be rated at 15–36 W.

Figure 18.4 shows the layout of a typical directional indicator circuit. When the switch is moved to the left or right, current is supplied to the appropriate lamps. Regular interruption of the current to give a flashing light is performed by the flasher unit: this is situated on the battery side of the switch.

If the vehicle breaks down on the highway the driver should be able to warn other drivers by arranging all the directional indicator lamps to flash simultaneously. This *hazard-warning* feature is activated by a separate switch by the driver (Figure 18.5).

There are three types of flasher in common use:

- thermal
- capacitor
- electronic.

Thermal-type flasher This type uses the heating effect of an electric current to bend or extend a metal strip.

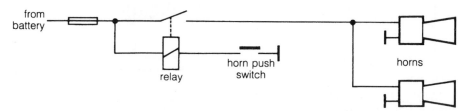

Fig. 18.3 Horn circuit with relay

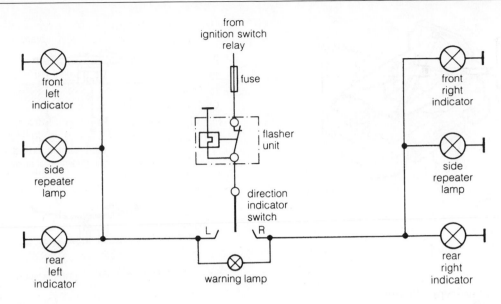

Fig. 18.4 Directional indicator circuit

One type uses two bi-metallic strips; each strip is wound with a heating coil and fitted with a contact. When the switch is operated, the strips bend to open and close the contacts.

Another type of thermal flasher is the vane type. The Lucas 8FL uses a vane construction and this gives a compact, reliable and cheap unit (Figure 18.6). It consists of a rectangular, snap-action, spring-steel vane supported at a point midway along the longer side. A thin metal ribbon, diagonally connected to the corners of the vane, pulls the vane towards the base. A pair of contacts, one on the centre of the ribbon and the other fixed to the base, make the electrical circuit. This flasher unit is fitted in series with the lamps and current to supply these lamps is taken through the metal ribbon, vane and contacts.

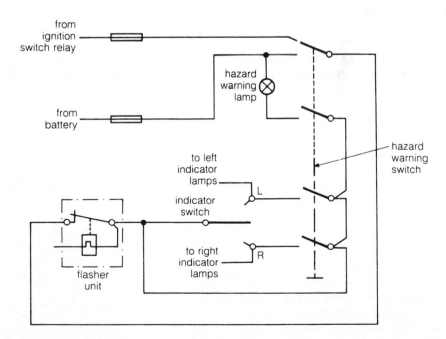

Fig. 18.5 Hazard warning circuit

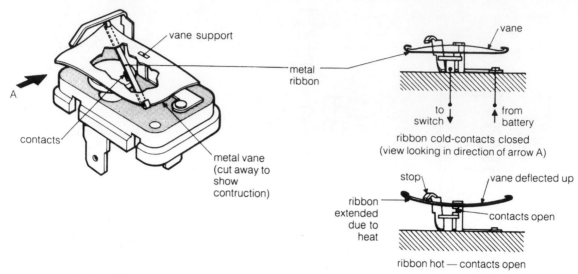

Fig. 18.6 Vane-type flasher

Operation of the directional indicator switch instantly activates the signal lamps. The heating effect of this current on the metal ribbon extends its length and this allows the vane to click upwards to its natural position. This action opens the contacts which breaks the circuit and extinguishes the signal lights. A short time after this action the lack of heating current causes the ribbon to cool and contract; this clicks the vane downwards and once again closes the contacts to repeat the cycle of events.

The time taken to heat the vane depends on the current, so the flash frequency is governed by the lamp load. Failure of one lamp reduces the electrical load so this prevents the vane from operating; as a result the remaining lamps stay on continuously.

Capacitor type Some systems use the timer action of a capacitor while it is performing its charge–discharge cycle to trigger a relay which in turn controls the switching and flashing of the signal lamps. The improved performance of electronic control has resulted in the development of the capacitor type into a new design called an electronic type.

Electronic type Turn-signal flasher units of the electronic type are more efficient than the thermal pulse generator types such as the vane flasher unit. The electronic type meets international standards which include the provision of an audible and visual warning system to signal when a bulb has failed.

Bulb failure in a system fitted with an electronic flasher is indicated by arranging the lamps to flash at twice the normal rate or by using an extra warning lamp.

Many electronic systems work on the principle of an astable multivibrator (see page 62).

The type shown in Figure 18.7 can handle a directional indicator signal load of up to 98 W without altering the flash frequency; in addition it provides a hazard warning signal for many hours of continuous use.

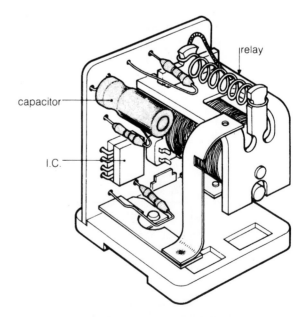

Fig. 18.7 Electronic flasher unit; Lucus FL19

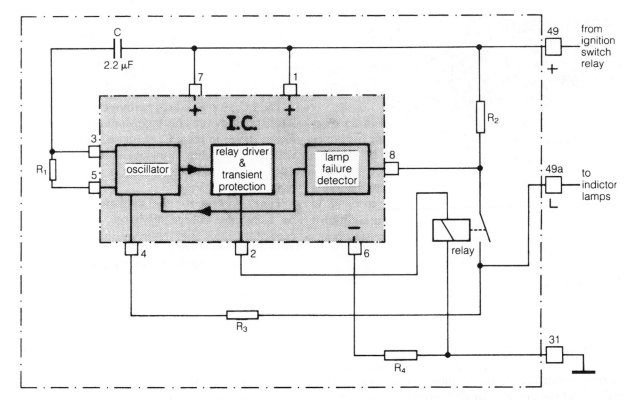

Fig. 18.8 Electronic flasher unit circuit

Electronic flasher units normally use an electro-magnetic relay to control the current to the signal lamps. This method is preferred to transistor switching because in addition to giving an audible signal it is not affected by the high voltage spikes that are generated during the switching operation. Also the relay contacts give very little voltage drop. Compared with the transistor, the drop across the relay contacts is about one-tenth of that of a transistor. Although transistor switching is ideal for high-speed applications, the relay is still preferred when slow-speed, heavy-current switching is required.

The basic construction of a typical flasher unit such a Lucas FL19 consists of a printed circuit board which carries an IC, capacitor, relay and three resistors (Figure 18.8).

The IC chip has three main sections: an oscillator, relay driver and lamp failure detector. A Zener diode in the IC regulates the operating voltage of the chip to ensure that the flash frequency remains constant over a supply voltage range of 10–15 V.

Timer control for the oscillator is achieved by using the charge–discharge action of the capacitor C; this operates in conjunction with the resistor R_1 to give a RC time constant for a flash frequency of 90 per minute

with a 50–50 off–on signal time (see page 38).

Pulses from the oscillator are passed to the relay driver which is a Darlington amplifier; this provides the current pulses to energize the relay coil. Transient protection of the output transistor is achieved by fitting a diode across the collector–emitter of the power transistor; this allows the self-induced charges in the relay coil to bypass the transistor.

The lamp failure detector senses the voltage drop across the resistor R_2. This resistor senses the current passing to the signal lamps via the relay contacts. In the event of a lamp failure, the lower current flow will cause the voltage drop (IR drop) across the resistor to decrease. This reduced voltage will cause the detector to alter the resistance of the RC time element and as a result the frequency of flashing will be doubled.

18.3 Maintenance and fault diagnosis

Horns

Horns are often positioned in an exposed place behind the radiator grill, so special attention is needed to avoid the ingress of moisture.

REMEMBER

Horns:

- are made in three types: high frequency, windtone and air operated
- produce an audible note by vibrating a diaphragm
- of the windtone type use air resonance in a trumpet to produce a note
- of the windtone type consume about twice the current of a high frequency type
- of the air type use a motor-driven pump to generate air pressure

Direction indicator lamp:

- must be 'E' marked
- must flash at the rate of 60–120 flashes per minute
- fitted at the front and rear must be rated at 15–36 W; a typical lamp is 21 W
- is made to flash by using a flasher unit operated by thermal, capacitance or electronic means
- can be controlled by a vane-type thermal flasher
- operation must be signalled to the driver by audible and visual means
- controlled by an electronic flasher uses a relay driven by an astable multivibrator
- failure normally causes the flash rate to alter

Most faults are due to cable and connector problems, so when a fault is present a visual check should be followed by a voltmeter test to determine that the p.d. applied to the horn is correct.

Adjustment After a long period of time the horn contact may require adjustment, so an adjusting screw is provided to alter the contact setting. The position of the screw is varied until the horn consumes the current specified for the particular type; a typical current consumption for a HF horn is 4 A.

Direction indicators

A flasher unit that fails to operate when full voltage is applied to it is identified as being faulty when a substitute unit fitted in the circuit shows that the remainder of the circuit is serviceable.

The common faults are bulb failure and loss of earth at the lamp. These faults are diagnosed by observing the rate of flashing, but the type of flasher governs whether the rate will be slower or faster. Earth problems are often caused by a bad connection of the earth cable and this can normally be detected by a visual check.

Assuming the bulbs are serviceable, a system that does not flash is due to an open circuit in the supply line; this can be pin-pointed by using a voltmeter.

PROGRESS CHECK 18

1. What is the purpose of a tone disc fitted to a high-frequency horn?

2. Why are two horns often fitted to a vehicle?

3. The method used to produce the sound in a windtone horn is different to that used in a high frequency horn. State the main constructional difference.

4. Why are windtone horns flexibly mounted?

5. Why is a relay necessary with a windtone horn?

6. State FOUR legal requirements relating to directional indicators.

7. State the purpose of the metal ribbon and vane in a thermal type flasher.

8. What method is used in an electronic flasher unit to drive the relay?

9. How does the lamp failure detector in an electronic flasher unit increase the flash rate when a bulb filament breaks?

10. What problem will occur in a thermal-type flasher system if the rated power of the lamp is higher than specified?

19

Heating, ventilating and engine cooling

What is covered in this chapter

➡ fan and heater motors
➡ heating and ventilating
➡ electric sun roof
➡ air conditioning
➡ climate control
➡ engine-cooling fan

19.1 Fan and heater motors

Motors used to operate the engine cooling fan and the heating ventilation system are normally of similar construction, in many cases the same model.

The motor normally used is a 2-pole permanent-magnet type having two brushes set at 180°. This type is also used for window operation, seat adjustment and many other general applications. Since this motor must operate in both directions the brushes are positioned at the mean magnetic axis.

Brush position

Poor efficiency and excessive sparking between the brushes and commutator will arise if the angle between the brushes and magnet poles is incorrect. This sparking occurs at the point of commutation, i.e. when the brush contact changes from one commutator segment to the next.

The simplified diagrams (Figure 19.1(a)) shows how the brush position is affected by the armature current.

In Figure 19.1(a) no armature current is flowing and in the diagram the brushes are positioned at 90° to the magnetic axis; this position is called the *geometric neutral axis* (g.n.a.).

When current is supplied to the armature, a secondary field is set up around the conductors and this distorts the main field (Figure 19.1(b)). The distortion

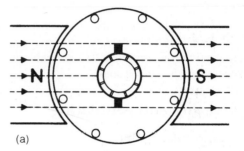

(a)

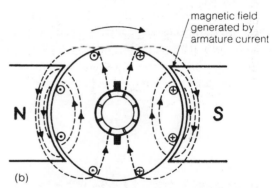

magnetic field generated by armature current

(b)

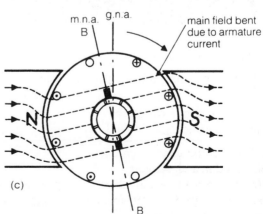

m.n.a. g.n.a.
B

main field bent due to armature current

(c)

B

Fig. 19.1 Brush position

moves the axis of the main field away from some of the armature conductors and this lowers the efficiency of the motor. To overcome this problem the brushes are moved through an angle to a position called the *magnetic neutral axis* (m.n.a.). The position shown in Figure 19.1(c) depends on the magnitude of the current but because the current varies with the speed, the final position is a compromise.

Although the brush position BB is suitable for the direction as shown, a reversal of the armature current to give an opposite direction of rotation requires the brush axis to be moved through an angle in a clockwise direction.

Due to this problem, a reversible motor requires the brushes to be set at the mean of the two m.n.a. positions. Consequently the efficiency of a reversible motor is lower than a unidirectional unit.

19.2   Heating and ventilating

Heating and ventilation fan
Most systems use a centrifugal-type fan to boost the air flow into the interior of the vehicle (Figure 19.2). Variable motor speeds are generally required and this is achieved by changing the voltage applied to the

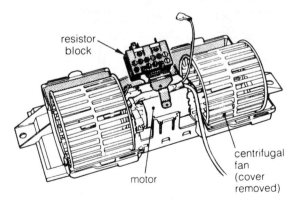

Fig. 19.2 Heating and ventilation fan

motor either by a variable resistor or by a resistor network.

Figure 19.3 shows a circuit for a 3-speed operation. Moving the switch through the three positions – low, high and boost – shorts out a resistor at each stage and steps up the applied voltage.

Maintenance
Each system is fused so this is the first check to make when the system fails to operate. If this is not the cause then a voltmeter check should be made to ensure the battery voltage is applied to the motor when the switch is set to give maximum fan speed.

In the case of a fan motor a quick check of the thermal switch can be made by disconnecting the leads at the switch and earthing the lead from the motor.

19.3   Electric sun roof

Electrically-operated sun roof
Operation of a switch, instead of winding a handle to open/close a sun roof, is safer and more convenient for the driver, so electricity is utilized for this duty on many top-of-the-range cars.

Movement of the roof panel is achieved by a rack that is driven by a pinion gear. This is rotated by a reversible permanent-magnet motor after passing the drive through a gearbox to amplify the torque.

A three-position switch giving open–stop–close positions acts as a 'polarity changer' to give the required rotation of the motor and a relay adjacent to the motor reduces the current carried by the switch.

Often the gearbox incorporates an extra rack to control the switching mechanism. This uses a switch to limit the travel of the roof panel and another switch to insert a resistance in series with the motor to reduce the speed of movement as the roof panel approaches the limits of its travel.

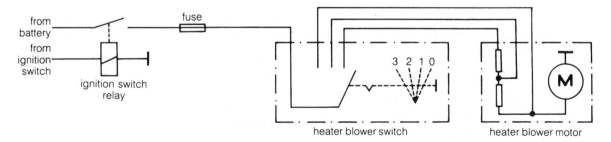

Fig. 19.3 Control circuit for three-speed operation of heating and ventilating fan

19.4 Air conditioning

An air conditioning system provides cool and dehumidified air, fresh or recirculated, to the interior of the vehicle. The cooling effect is obtained by blowing air through a cold evaporator unit to control the temperature of the interior.

Since the construction and operation of an air conditioning system is described in *Fundamentals of Motor Vehicle Technology*, treatment in this chapter is confined to the electrical control system.

Control of a basic system

Figure 19.4 shows the main layout. In this system the temperature of the *evaporator* is controlled by the flow of *refrigerant* (R134a) around the system. This flow is initiated by a belt-driven *compressor* that is engaged to the engine by an electrically-operated clutch in response to a relay-controlled supply signalled from the driver via the engine ECU.

Compressing the refrigerant generates heat; this is dissipated by a *condenser* placed next to the engine radiator. When the air flow through the condenser is insufficient, electrically-driven *cooling fans*, connected in series for normal cooling, come into operation.

Temperature of the evaporator is primarily controlled by a thermostatic expansion valve, but if the evaporator temperature falls low enough for ice to form on the fins, a thermostatic switch, mounted on the fins, will open. This causes the ECU to disengage the compressor clutch.

A pressure switch is fitted to prevent damage to the compressor. This senses the pressure in the line between the condenser and drier and sends a signal to the engine ECU to activate a control circuit when the pressure is:

- *below 2.0 bar* – a drop to this pressure indicates leakage so the electromagnetic clutch disengages the compressor; when pressure rises above 2.4 bar the clutch is re-engaged;

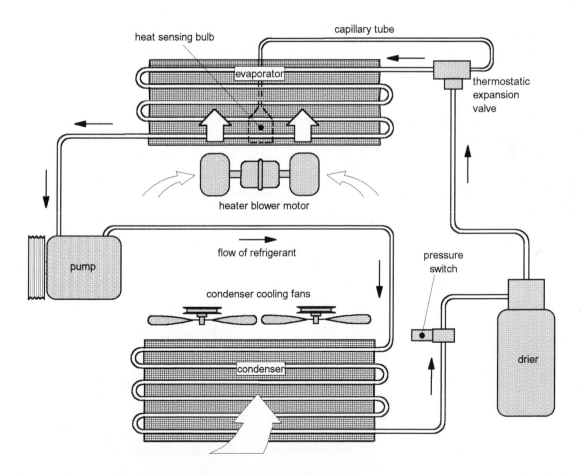

Fig. 19.4 Schematic layout of air conditioning system

- *above 1.9 bar* – cooling is increased by energising relays which connect the two cooling fans in parallel;
- *above 2.7 bar* – if this high pressure is reached with maximum cooling (due to possible blockage) the clutch is disengaged until the pressure drops to 2.1 bar.

ECU control In addition to the basic control of the air conditioning system, the ECU adjusts the idling speed of the engine to compensate for the extra load when the compressor is in use. Also the compressor is disengaged when:

- the vehicle is accelerated with a near-fully-opened throttle;
- the oil temperature in the compressor is very high;
- engine speed exceeds 5000 rev/min. to protect the hoses of the air conditioning system.

Driver controls The air conditioning system works in conjunction with the interior heater controls, so when the system is switched on, the fan, air entry mode, air distribution and temperature, are all operated in the same manner as that used for the heater.

SAFE PRACTICE

Refrigerant R134a is a dangerous substance, so refer to the manufacturer's manual before disconnecting any part of the refrigeration system.

Control circuit The system is normally controlled by the engine ECU because engine adjustments must be made to allow for the extra load on the engine.

Figure 19.5 shows a simplified layout of an air conditioning circuit. Four relays are used in this circuit, one to control the compressor clutch and three to control fan operation. With relays B and C both set in position 1, the two fans are in series, but when the relays are set in position 2, both fans operate at high speed.

19.5 Climate control

Today many luxury category vehicles having air conditioning fitted as original equipment use a system called *climate control* to automatically regulate the temperature, quality and distribution of the air.

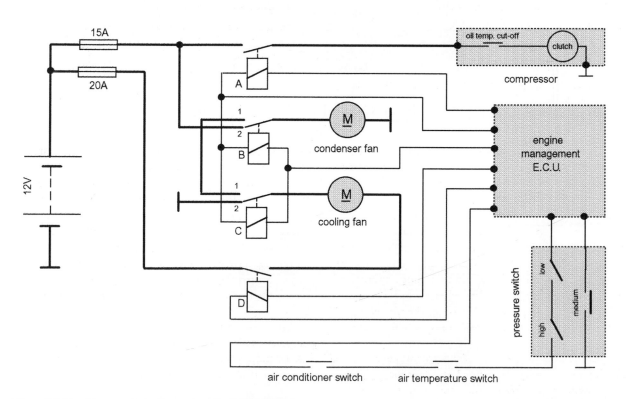

Fig. 19.5 Air conditioning circuit (simplified)

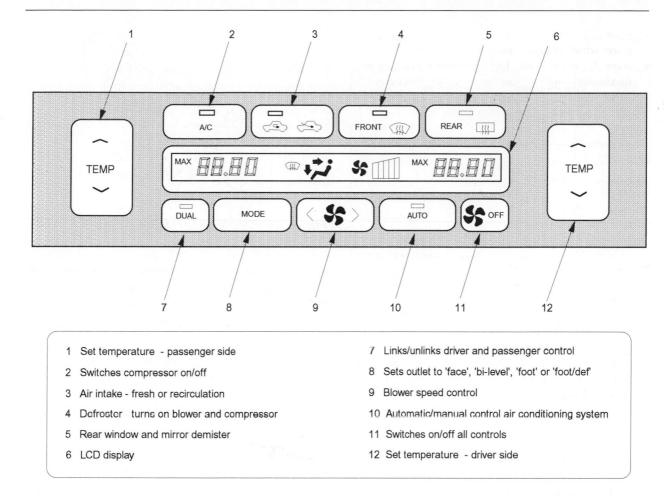

Fig. 19.6 Control panel for climate control

1. Set temperature - passenger side
2. Switches compressor on/off
3. Air intake - fresh or recirculation
4. Defroster turns on blower and compressor
5. Rear window and mirror demister
6. LCD display
7. Links/unlinks driver and passenger control
8. Sets outlet to 'face', 'bi-level', 'foot' or 'foot/def'
9. Blower speed control
10. Automatic/manual control air conditioning system
11. Switches on/off all controls
12. Set temperature - driver side

Once the driver has set the required interior temperature, the climate control ECU regulates the mix of hot and cold air to maintain the target temperature irrespective of the outside temperature.

In addition to the cooling and heating aspects, a modern environmental control system also prevents misting of the window, an annoying problem that occurs on damp, cold days. This is achieved by passing the heated air through the air conditioning evaporator before pumping the air to the vehicle interior.

Air quality is improved by passing the air though a renewable filter; this removes most of the foreign particles.

Figure 19.6 shows a typical control panel. This centrally mounted fascia panel has a number of push button switches to enable the front-seat occupant to program the system to suit their requirements.

Control system Figure 19.7 shows the main parts of an automatic control system. Signals from the temperature monitoring sensors and control panel switches are passed to a processor in an ECU that is normally incorporated in the control panel. After computing any differences between the panel setting and input sensor data, the ECU makes the necessary correction by energising the appropriate actuators. Since this input/output loop monitoring is carried out continuously, it is possible to achieve precise temperature control with this system.

The heat from the sun can quickly alter the interior temperature. This factor is taken into account by fitting one or more photodiode-type sensors behind the windscreen to measure solar radiation.

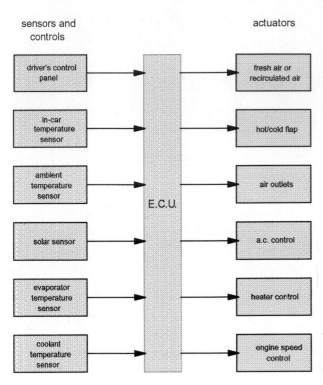

Fig. 19.7 Climate control system

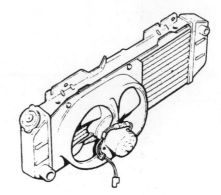

Fig. 19.8 Electric cooling fan

- easy to accommodate, especially for transverse engines;
- close control over engine operating temperature.

Figure 19.8 shows a typical installation. A plastic fan impeller is fitted to the armature shaft of the motor and the assembly is situated to provide the appropriate air movement through the radiator.

The control circuit (Figure 19.9) uses a bimetal-type thermal switch located at the radiator side of the thermostat housing. This switch operates the fan when the coolant temperature reaches about 90°C and switches it off when the temperature drops to about 85°C. In the layout shown, the current for the motor is supplied from an ignition switch relay. This relay energizes when the ignition is switched on.

Fault diagnosis

Since the system is complex, the ECU has a self-diagnosis facility. The diagnostic checks are processed by pressing certain control buttons in a given sequence. Any faults, including any that are stored in the memory unit, are then displayed as a code on the LCD control panel.

19.6 Engine cooling fan

A cooling fan driven by an electric motor instead of a belt gives the advantages:

- energy saving – fan can be switched off when not needed;

SAFE PRACTICE

Use care when working in the vicinity of engine cooling fans; they can operate without warning even after the engine has been switched off

---

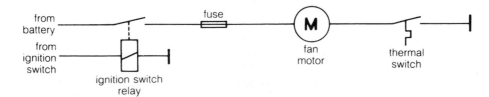

Fig. 19.9 Control circuit for engine cooling fan

REMEMBER

Fan motors:

- are normally 2-pole permanent-magnet type
- have brushes set in the magnetic neutral axis
- can be driven at different speeds by switching-in resistors

Air conditioning:

- system has a compressor, condenser and evaporator
- condenser radiates heat from the refrigerant
- evaporator absorbs heat from the air
- refrigerant used on modern vehicles is R134a
- refrigerant must not contact human skin
- cooling fans are connected in series for slow-speed operation
- system operation affects engine operation such as idling speed

Climate control:

- is a system that automatically regulates temperature, quality and distribution of the air
- has a separate ECU to regulate air temperature
- system has sensors for ambient temperature, interior temperature and solar radiation
- can incorporate separate controls for driver and passenger to alter local temperature
- normally has a self-diagnosing facility

Engine cooling fan:

- only operates when the engine reaches a given temperature
- is controlled by a thermal switch or by a signal from the engine ECU

PROGRESS CHECK 19

1. Why are brushes for a fan motor not positioned in the *geometric* neutral axis?

2. State ONE method used on heating fan motors to give 3-speed operation.

Questions 3–8 relate to air conditioning

3. State the purpose of:
(a) compressor; (b) condenser;
(c) evaporator.

4. What method is used on a 2-fan condenser system to obtain two different fan speeds?

5. State the purpose of the triple pressure switch.

6. What electrical method is used to engage the compressor to the engine?

7. State the symptom of a defective compressor relay.

8. What alterations are made to engine settings by the ECU when the air conditioning system is in use?

Questions 9 and 10 relate to climate control

9. State the merits of the system.

10. State the type of sensor that is used to measure solar radiation.

20 *Door locking and vehicle security*

What is covered in this chapter

→ central door locking
→ engine immobilisers
→ security alarm systems

20.1 Central door locking

A typical door-locking system allows all doors, including the tailgate or boot, to be locked simultaneously when the driver's door lock is activated. On the turn of a key, or operation of the driver's door-lock button, the electrical system energizes all the locking activators fitted adjacent to the door locks. Unlocking the door has a similar effect except the locking actuators are moved in the opposite direction. Both for convenience and safety reasons, mechanical latches allow each door to be unlocked manually from inside the car.

Various actuator systems are used to provide the mechanical locking action; these include:

* electromagnetic
* pneumatic.

Electromagnet systems
The electrical methods used for actuating door-lock mechanism are electromagnet solenoids, linear motors and permanent magnet rotary motors. In each case the reversing action is achieved by changing the polarity.

Solenoid system Activation of a solenoid-operated locking system consumes a large current during the time that the locking mechanism is in action. In order to minimize this time, door-locking circuits incorporate a timing feature; this normally utilizes the charge or discharge action of a capacitor. After a given time interval, the current to the locking mechanism is discontinued and this represents the normal locked or unlocked condition.

One arrangement uses two relays: one for locking and the other for unlocking the doors. These relays are controlled by a transistorized switching circuit, which is timed by the charge–discharge action of a capacitor to give a current pulse length sufficient to activate the locks (Figure 20.1).

An alternative arrangement uses the discharge current from a previously charged capacitor to energize the relay. When the door key is turned and the appropriate switch is closed by the key movement, the capacitor releases its charge through the relay coil. After the capacitor has been fully discharged the relay opens and the system goes out of action (Figure 20.2).

Figure 20.3 shows a solenoid-type actuator for operating a door lock.

External circuit The layout of the complete circuit is shown in Figure 20.4 (page 365). In this case the driver's door switch operates the locks on four other doors.

Rotary motor system The permanent magnet motor gives a quieter and slower action than a solenoid actuator. The system normally has a reversible motor fitted to each door lock, but in some cases a unidirectional motor and crank arrangement is used. Reciprocation of the crank produces the *lock* and *unlock* action, so by opening a limit switch at the end of the stroke, the required lock setting is obtained. This arrangement simplifies both the switch construction and cable layout.

Reversible actuators fitted to modern vehicles are often linked into the security alarm system and provide extra security by using a second motor in each door to provide a double-lock feature. Figure 20.5 (page 366) shows a simplified layout for a 2-doored car having these features.

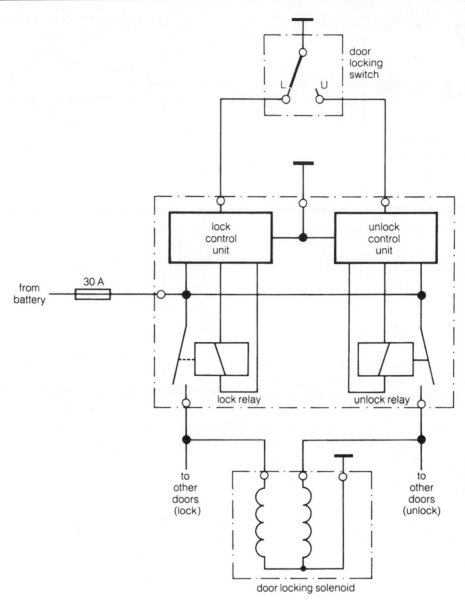

Fig. 20.1 Central door-locking circuit; transistorized control

Pneumatically operated system

This very quiet system uses a small pneumatic actuator in each door and an air pump, normally fitted in the boot, to provide 'pressure' to lock and 'vacuum' to unlock the doors. A reversible electric motor drives the pump; forward rotation makes it a compressor and backwards movement a vacuum pump.

Polarity of the permanent magnet motor governs the direction of rotation, so a change-over control switch similar to that fitted in Figure 20.5 is used.

A timer arrangement, normally capacitor controlled, interrupts the battery supply when sufficient time has been given for full operation of the lock mechanism.

Small-bore plastic tubing connects the pump with the pneumatic actuators, so any problem relating to the locking action of a single door is normally a non-electrical fault.

Maintenance

Faults in actuator circuits should be diagnosed by using

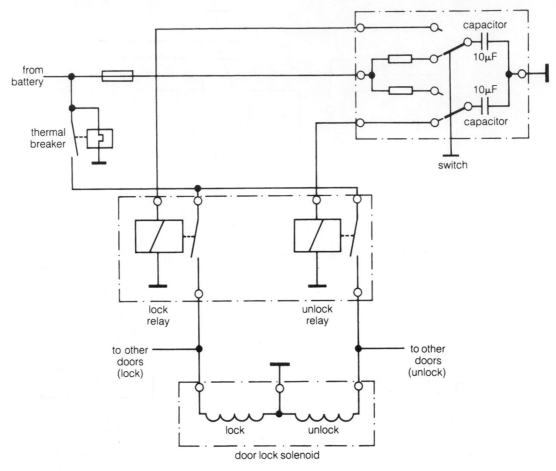

Fig. 20.2 Central door-locking circuit; capacitor control

a systematic approach. A system such as a central door-locking arrangement, should be initially checked to isolate the fault to a particular area before the trim is removed to expose the locking mechanism. Many manufacturers suggest that a table is compiled to show the results obtained from the door-lock switching action. This table should then be used to compare the results with the fault-finding chart normally shown in the manufacturer's service manual.

As with most 'black-box' components, it is essential to refer to the circuit diagram or an appropriate fault diagnosis chart before applying either full battery voltage or an ohmmeter to a particular cable or test pin. Expensive components are soon damaged if haphazard testing is carried out; this is important especially if the unit contains delicate semiconductors or ICs that are designed to operate at a voltage well below that of the battery.

An example of a check-out sequence as applied to a system similar to that shown in Figure 20.4 is as follows.

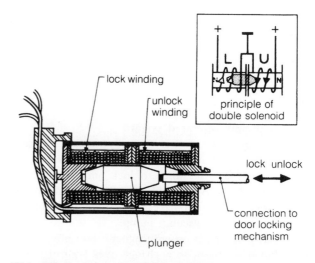

Fig. 20.3 Door-locking actuator

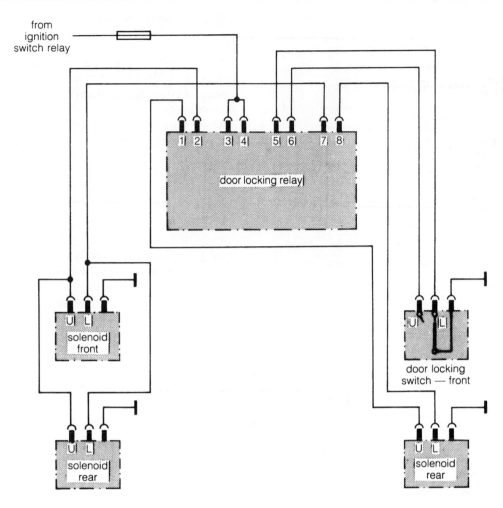

Fig. 20.4 Central door-locking – external circuit

For 'all locks fail to operate', this suggests that the fault is due to:

- no power to the relay unit
- defective switch
- faulty relay unit.

Each one of these possible faults should be tested to narrow-down the actual cause. The following method can be used:

(1) After checking the circuit breaker, the input voltage applied to the relay unit pins 3 and 4 should be checked.

(2) Assuming the supply is good, then a jumper lead should be used to connect pin 5 to earth to repro-duce the switch action; this will prove if the switch section of the circuit is faulty.

(3) Having ascertained that the input and switch are satisfactory, the output voltage, at one of the pins 1, 2, 7 or 8, should be measured when the switch is operated. If battery voltage is not shown at the instant the switch is closed, then the relay is defective and should be changed.

This description can be reduced considerably by using a fault diagnosis chart as shown in Figure 20.6. Since the path followed through the chart is controlled by the result given by a particular test, then the need to read other test data is avoided. For this reason the use of charts has become commonplace for fault diagnosis of electronic equipment.

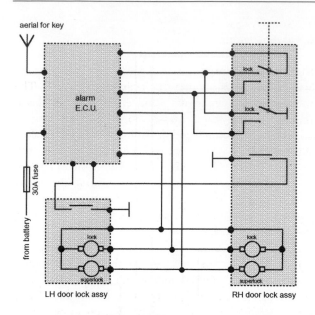

aerial for key

alarm
E.C.U.

30A fuse

from battery

lock

lock

LH door lock assy

lock
superlock

RH door lock assy

lock
superlock

Fig. 20.5 Lock system for a two-door car fitted with alarm and rotary actuators

20.2 Engine immobilisers

Manufacturers of vehicles, and potential owners, now appreciate the advantage of having a theft deterrent system fitted at the time when the vehicle is built. This change of policy has been encouraged by the introduction of electronically controlled engine management systems. These systems provide a platform that can be easily linked in to a security alarm sensing complex to prevent engine operation at times when the owner wishes to secure the vehicle. The term *'engine immobilizer'* is normally used when the vehicle has a factory-installed system.

When the immobilizer is activated (armed), any attempt to gain entry to the vehicle, open the boot or bonnet, or remove the battery terminal alerts a separate alarm control unit; a typical system then carries out a plausibility check. If this suggests either illegal entry or unauthorised tampering, the horns are sounded and headlamps flashed for a given time; normally about a minute.

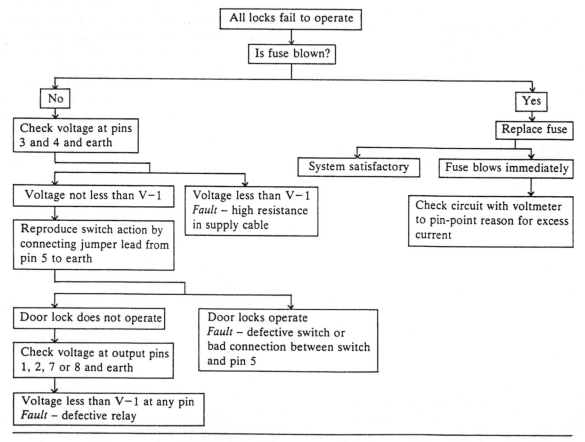

Fig. 20.6 Fault diagnosis chart – central door-locking system (V = battery voltage)

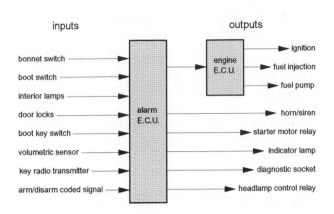

Fig. 20.7 Immobilizer system layout

A thief gaining entry by breaking any window glass is detected if the interior of the vehicle is protected by movement sensors such as infra-red or ultrasonic types.

Figure 20.7 shows some of the sensors used to guard the vehicle. These inputs to the ECU signal when the system needs to raise the alarm. Disconnection of the main battery supply is countered by incorporating in the alarm ECU a separate battery.

If, for any reason these protection systems are beaten, the armed immobilizer will prevent engine operation due to the isolation of the systems controlling:

- ignition
- fuel pump
- fuel injection
- starting motor

System activation

Various methods are used to activate the alarm. The simplest method is to use a hidden switch, but this is unsuitable for systems having movement detectors; in these cases the arming and disarming is delayed to allow the driver to get in and out without sounding the alarm.

Most systems use a LED mounted on the dashboard to indicate that the system is armed. A door key incorporating either an infra-red or radio transmitter is a convenient method for locking the doors and arming the security system by *remote control*.

Infra-red   In this system, pressing a button on the door key, or on a small transmitter unit on the key ring, causes digital infra-red light signals to be emitted. These are received by an optical sensing unit on some part of the car. The principle is similar to that used to control a domestic TV.

Radio control   In this system, pressing the button on the key produces a weak radio wave that is received by the car's antenna; this is normally the element of the car's heated rear window. Powered by a small lithium battery, each transmitter has its own code.

Figure 20.8 shows the layout of a system that uses a high frequency carrier wave (e.g. 41 MHz) and a frequency-modulated (FM) circuit to transmit a digital signal.

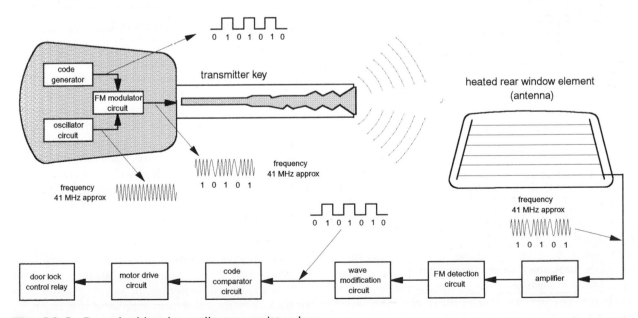

Fig. 20.8 Door locking by radio transmitter key

20.3 Security alarm systems

Owners of motor vehicles that are not fitted with a factory-installed immobilizer system have a wide choice of alarm systems available to them if they wish to make their vehicle more secure. These systems range from comparatively low-cost basic units for the DIY market, to highly sophisticated professionally-installed systems that make it very difficult for the thief to steal or tamper with the vehicle without causing great disturbance.

Types of alarm

Alarm systems use different methods to protect the vehicle; these include:

- *Voltage drop or current drain* – monitors the level of power used when the vehicle is parked; when this power is increased the alarm is triggered.
- *Direct earth contact* – senses by door, bonnet and boot switches when an earth contact is made; this direct switch action triggers the alarm.
- *Infra-red* – interruption of an invisible infra-red light beam transmitted from one side of the car to a receiver fitted on the other side triggers the alarm.
- *Ultrasonic* – floods the interior of the vehicle with an ultrasonic signal that reflects from all surfaces (including glass). Any change in the signal strength received by an ultrasonic sensor triggers the alarm.
- *Shock sensor* – triggers the alarm when the vehicle is moved or disturbed.
- *Level reference monitor* – used to protect the wheels, this sensor monitors the angle at which the vehicle is parked. It triggers the alarm if this angle is changed in any plane more than a given amount (e.g. 2°) in three seconds.

Although an ultrasonic system offers a high level of security and is effective against breakage of glass, it does have one disadvantage: it is extremely sensitive to air movements. This means that it cannot be used on soft-top cars; also precautions must be taken to avoid draught from air vents. This problem can be overcome by using a microwave system. For safety reasons, any alarm system that uses ultrasonic or hyper-frequency sensors must comply with BS 6803.

Insurance rating

The high rate of crime relating to vehicles has made insurance companies aware of the importance of security. Many companies offer significant discounts if a recognized system is installed. Furthermore, some classes of vehicle will not be offered cover unless the car is fitted with an approved alarm system.

To determine which systems are acceptable, the insurance companies use their research centre at Thatcham. If the alarm is approved they are classified as follows:

Category 1. Offers immobilization and alarm functions appropriate to high risk vehicles.

Category 2 Offers immobilization but gives no protection against the theft of items from the vehicle.

Approved alarm system The system shown in Figure 20.8 is a *Category 1* alarm manufactured by Cobra Car Alarms. The items shown include a 125 dB siren, alarm ECU, ultrasonic sensor, automatic window closer and radio keys that have a random code to protect against a thief having a code scanner. This system provides the driver with a wide range of security features.

Fig. 20.9 Alarm components (*Cobra*)

At this time there is no specific Transport Law in the UK to restrict the time that a vehicle alarm siren or horn can operate. However manufacturers of alarm systems use a protocol that limits the duration of the alarm signal to about one minute. Following this period the system resets itself; if it still detects that the vehicle is insecure, the alarm will sound again after a set time. If any door is open the cycling will continue until the battery is exhausted, but if the disturbance is detected by a volumetric sensor, the alarm/reset program is limited to about 10 cycles.

Vehicle tracker system

In addition to the normal security alarm, this system also fits a radio transmitter on the vehicle to allow it to be tracked by the equipment supplier if it is stolen.

REMEMBER

Central door locking systems:

- use solenoid, linear motor and rotary actuators
- often use a capacitor to provide the energy for door locking
- using rotary motors or pneumatic actuators are quiet in action
- sometimes have a double-lock to improve security

Engine immobilizer systems:

- use the engine ECU to prevent engine operation
- are normally armed by a door key or remote controller
- having a radio transmitter use the rear window heater as an antenna
- have a time delay switching arrangement if movement detectors are fitted
- having a radio transmitter use a FM signal around 41 MHz

Security alarm systems:

- detect door movement by *voltage drop* or *direct earth* sensors
- detect movement inside the vehicle by *infra-red*, *ultrasonic* or *microwave* sensors
- can incorporate *shock* and *tilt* sensors
- having ultrasonic sensors are not used on soft-top cars
- are classified for insurance purposes by Thatcham
- using a radio key can be uprated by using a *random code*
- using an audible warning system will operate for a limited time only
- of the *tracker-type* are fitted with a radio transmitter

PROGRESS CHECK 20

Questions 1–5 relate to door locking systems

1. Name TWO types of electro-magnetic actuator.

2. State the purpose of using a capacitor in the actuator circuit.

3. The locking actuator provides two-way movement. State how this is achieved in: a) a linear actuator; b) a rotary actuator.

4. Name ONE locking method that provides a comparatively quiet, slow action.

5. The fuse controlling the locking system blows when all doors are locked. State how the driver: a) gains entry to the vehicle; b) exits the vehicle.

Questions 6–10 relate to security systems

6. Name three engine systems that will not function when the immobilizer is armed.

7. Name ONE method that senses the breakage of glass.

8. Describe the operation of a radio-controlled key.

9. State TWO methods that are used to detect when a door is opened to make an illegal entry into the vehicle.

10. What is meant by the expression: *category 1 alarm system*?

21 *Road wheel control systems*

What is covered in this chapter

➡ cruise control
➡ anti-lock braking system (ABS)
➡ automatic transmission control
➡ traction control

21.1 Cruise control

Holding the vehicle at a near-constant speed for a long period while cruising on a road such as a motorway is very tiring for the driver. This task can be made easier and less fatiguing if an electronic system is used to control the throttle opening to keep the vehicle speed constant even though the resistance acting against the vehicle may vary due to changes in the wind or road gradient.

Nowadays a *cruise control system* is fitted as original or optional equipment to a number of vehicles. Although various layouts are used, the functional role of the main components in each system is similar.

Basic system
The principle of a typical closed-loop cruise control system is shown by the block diagram in Figure 21.1.

The brain of the system is the control unit; this has two inputs: the command speed signal, set by the driver to indicate the desired speed of the vehicle, and the feedback signal, which signifies the actual speed of the vehicle.

When the feedback signal shows that the vehicle speed is different to the command speed, the control unit transmits a signal to the actuator. This adjusts the throttle of the fuel system in a direction which quickly restores the vehicle's speed to that specified by the driver.

On all vehicles there is a delay between the opening of the throttle and the alteration in vehicle speed. A cruise control system incorporates in its circuitry a feature to take this into account. This reduces the severe oscillation in speed which would otherwise occur when the system attempts to equalize the actual speed with the command speed.

Special attention to safety is needed to ensure that the driver can quickly and automatically override the cruise system when the vehicle has to be braked. This is achieved by fitting a switch on the brake pedal that cuts off the electrical supply to the control system.

A similar switch is fitted to the clutch pedal of vehicles fitted with manual transmission systems to prevent over-revving of the engine when a gear is changed. This would occur due to the drop in road speed and the

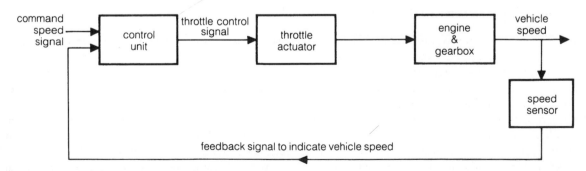

Fig. 21.1 Cruise control system

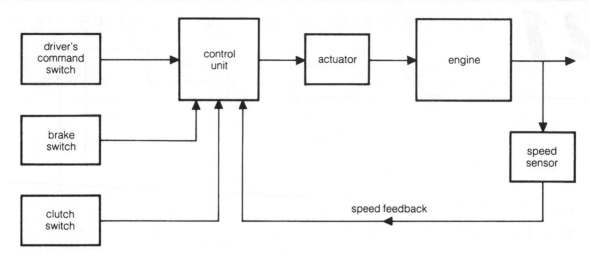

Fig. 21.2 Main components of cruise control system

response of the cruise control system during the time that a gear change is taking place.

The main parts of a basic system are shown in Figure 21.2.

Driver's command switch Normally the command switch is a stalk-type switch mounted on the steering column and positioned so that it is in easy reach of the driver's hand. Most switches have three positions such as: 'activate/set', 'off' and 'reactivate'.

In the first position the vehicle can be accelerated as long as the button is depressed. When the desired speed is reached, the button is released; this 'sets' the cruise control unit so that it holds the vehicle to the speed that existed at the time the button was released.

The 'reactivate' or 'resume' position is used to reset the system after it has been switched off by brake or clutch pedal operation.

Actuator Movement of the throttle valve is obtained by means of an electric or pneumatic servo motor. This unit is capable of moving the throttle smoothly and gradually in both directions.

The electric-type actuator is often a d.c. permanent-magnet motor so in this case the return motion is obtained by reversing the direction of current. This current is supplied in the form of pulses of short duration of the order of a few tenths of a second so this enables the throttle to be moved through small angles in a smooth precise manner.

Pneumatic actuators are similar in construction to the vacuum unit used in a distributor to control ignition timing. 'Vacuum' for the operation of the actuator

can be provided by the engine-induction manifold but great precision is obtained when the 'vacuum' is developed by an electrically-driven pump; this ensures that the pressure is constant. Return motion of the servo diaphragm is given by a spring.

Brake and clutch switches In addition to the electrical cut-out switches, the pneumatic system also incorporates brake and clutch vent valves. These valves allow the 'vacuum' in the servo actuator to be dumped to make the system inoperative when either the brake or clutch pedal is moved.

Electrical servomotor systems often have a disconnect-relay to perform a duty similar to the pneumatic dump valves. This relay switches off the complete system and cuts off the fuel pump to overcome the problem that would arise if the servo motor failed to return the throttle due to seizure of the motor. In the event of this type of malfunction, the accelerator pedal is fitted with an extra switch, called a *drag switch*; this switch reactivates the pump when the driver depresses the throttle.

Speed sensor The speed sensor is normally connected to the speedometer drive. In cases where the speedometer is electronic, the signal from the speedometer transducer is also used to provide the feedback signal to the ECU.

An alternative type of sensor uses permanent magnets glued to the drive shaft to generate an a.c. pulse in a pick-up coil situated adjacent to the drive shaft.

Whereas some speed transducers generate an analogue signal voltage which rises proportional to speed,

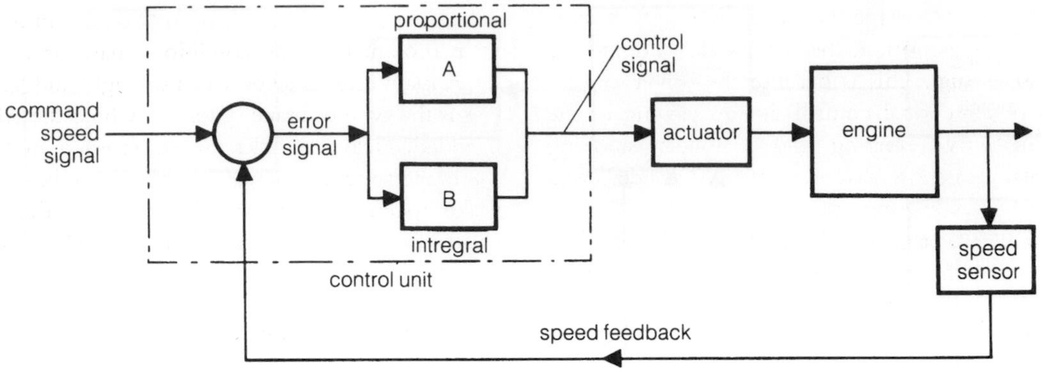

Fig. 21.3 Proportional-integral cruise control system

other systems use a digital signal. In the latter case an increase in speed produces logic level pulses the number of which is in proportion to the speed.

Control unit This unit is the brain of the system; it provides an output signal to the actuator to adjust the throttle whenever it detects the actual speed of the vehicle is above or below that set by the driver.

The closed-loop controller fitted in the control unit compares the system's output measured by the sensor to that indicated as an input command. Difference between the two signals, obtained by simple subtraction, is called an error signal; this is used to adjust the control signal so that it is proportional to the error signal.

A *proportional control system* by itself lacks sensitivity since a comparatively large error signal is required to make final adjustments to the speed. To overcome this problem, vehicle speed controllers generally use a *proportional-integral system* as shown in Figure 21.3. In this diagram it will be seen that the command signal is the sum of the outputs from the two blocks A and B. The circuit of the proportional block A gives an output that is in proportion to the error signal, whereas the integral block B produces a variable-rate output designed to reduce the error to zero in a short time without oscillation.

The cruise-control system can be designed for analogue or digital operation. The analogue system uses a capacitor charge set by the driver by the switch operation to represent vehicle speed. Detection of the charge on the capacitor is achieved by a very high input impedance amplifier; this outputs a voltage to an error amplifier to represent the command speed.

A digital circuit stores the input speed command and the vehicle speed as numbers. Feedback pulses from the sensor are counted against a clock signal and these are subtracted from the command speed pulse to obtain the error number. This is then passed through the two paths previously outlined. Alternatively, the error signal can be fed to a microcomputer for processing, so with this method of control a more sophisticated programme can be used.

Data in a digital system is stored in the form of digital codes; compared with an analogue controller, the digital system is less affected by changes in temperature and humidity.

Fault diagnosis

Electronic operation of this system is similar to many other sensor–ECU–actuator systems, so fault diagnosis is carried out in a similar manner.

Many systems have a cruise indicator lamp on the instrument panel that illuminates when the system is in operation. If the self-diagnosis facility detects a malfunction, the lamp blinks to alert the driver; at the same time the fault is memorized by the cruise control ECU.

'Trouble codes' can be retrieved either by connecting a code reader to the diagnostic plug, or by reading the indicator lamp blink pattern; the latter is activated by bridging certain terminals in the diagnostic plug. In addition to the fault-code lamp-blink pattern, the lamp can also be used to check that the system is serviceable. By following a given test sequence the technician is able to see from the lamp signal pattern if each part is functioning correctly.

21.2 Anti-lock braking system (ABS)

The majority of drivers cannot judge the point at which a wheel starts to skid because far too many factors are involved. This problem, combined with the driver's over-reaction to an emergency, normally results in skidding of the vehicle. When the wheels are skidding the accident risk is high; this is because the driver experiences loss of directional control due to yawing of the vehicle, ineffective steering and a longer stopping distance. Statistics show that over 10% of accidents are due to the brakes locking-up.

An anti-lock or anti-skid braking system overcomes these problems; this makes the vehicle much safer to drive especially when tyre-to-road adhesion is poor. The system is called ABS; an abbreviation for the German term *'Anti-Blockier System'*.

Basic principles

Anti-skid systems are used on cars and heavy vehicles. Articulated-type heavy vehicles benefit considerably from ABS because these vehicles are prone to *jack-knifing* (rear wheels of tractor locking) and trailer swing (trailer wheels locking). Cars that tow caravans are also subject to jack-knifing.

Both the car and heavy vehicle require a similar electronic control layout (Figure 21.4). This has a sensing system to measure the wheel speed so that a control unit can determine when the wheel is at the point of skidding. When this critical point is reached, the control unit operates a valve in the brake system to release the pressure on the brakes. Having averted the initial skid, the ECU then opens a brake valve to increase the pressure until the skidding point is reached once again. This cycle, involving a pressure release–apply–release–apply, recurs at all times that the brakes are fully applied. By repeating the cycle between 4 and

10 times per second, maximum braking can be achieved even though the road conditions may vary.

A main difference between the light and heavy vehicles is the type of brake system to which the ABS layout is added. Heavy vehicles use compressed air to operate the brake system, whereas a light vehicle has a hydraulic brake system. This means that although the electronic control system is similar, the method of control of the actual brake system is different.

Hydraulic brake ABS components

The layout of a typical ABS unit for a rear-wheel-drive car is shown in Figure 2.15.

Wheel-speed sensors Normally three wheel sensors are fitted: one to each non-driving wheel and one to the propeller shaft flange on the axle. An inductive-type sensor is used which gives a voltage impulse-type signal as the tooth on the rotating reluctor ring passes the sensing head.

Electronic controller This ECU evaluates the signals transmitted from the sensor. After processing, it determines whether the brake pressure needs to be decreased, maintained constant or increased. The computer in this module is programmed to recognize the rate of change of wheel speed which immediately precedes the lock-up point. At this instant, it gives an output signal to lower the brake pressure slightly.

Hydraulic modulator This unit is the actuator part of the control circuit and its duty is to vary the pressure

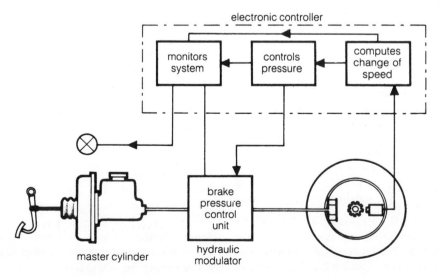

Fig. 21.4 ABS control system (closed loop)

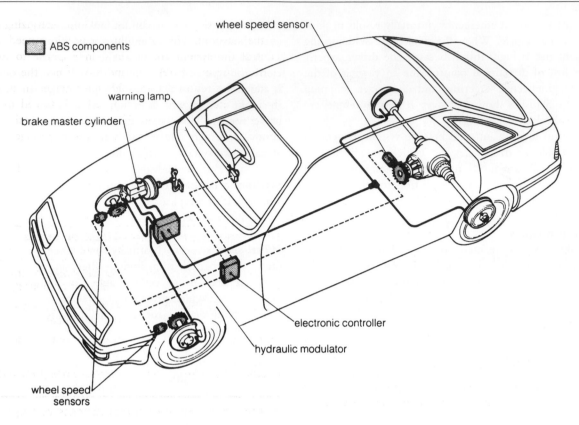

ABS components

wheel speed sensor

warning lamp

brake master cylinder

electronic controller

hydraulic modulator

wheel speed
sensors

Fig. 21.5 Layout of a typical ABS system

in the fluid lines in accordance with the electrical signals it receives from the ECU.

Fluid passage to, or from, the brake lines is controlled by solenoid-operated valves; one valve is needed for each brake circuit. Fluid released from an individual line flows to an accumulator. This is a chamber fitted with a spring-loaded piston which temporarily stores hydraulic pressure so that it can be re-supplied to the brake line if the ECU signals that extra fluid pressure to needed. Return of fluid to the lines via the accumulator is achieved by a pump.

The solenoid valves have three working positions:

(1) Open to the reservoir to release pressure.
(2) Open to the pump to increase pressure.
(3) Closed to allow either pressure to be maintained during one phase of the anti-lock cycle or normal operation of the brakes by the master cylinder.

(For further information about the mechanical details of an ABS system see *Fundamentals of Motor Vehicle Technology*.)

4-channel system The single sensor fitted at the rear of the vehicle as shown in Figure 21.5 can detect when one rear wheel skids but it cannot signal which wheel it is. In this event the system reduces the fluid pressure in the common rear brake line with the result that the total braking torque of the rear wheels is diminished.

Most modern vehicles overcome this problem by using a *4-channel system*; this provides each wheel with its own sensor and independent fluid line.

A further improvement is the total enclosure of each wheel sensor; this reduces the risk of damage due to dirt or impact.

ECU operation
The digital controller consists of an input amplifier, computing unit, power stage and monitoring unit.

Input amplifier This unit filters and reshapes the a.c. waves from the sensors into rectangular pulses suitable for operating the computer.

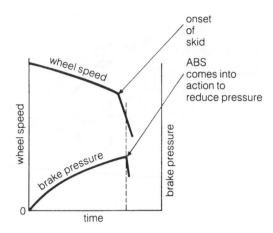

Fig. 21.6 Wheel speed change at onset of skid

Computing unit A computer with its microprocessor and memory circuit reads the signals sent by the sensors. After comparing the signal with a reference signal obtained from the wheel diagonally opposite the sensor, it is able to detect the approach of a skid by computing the rate of change in the wheel speed (Figure 21.6).

Power stage This provides an output signal to operate the solenoid valves. Digital pulses from the computer allow the power stage to deliver a regulated current to the appropriate solenoid; this moves the valve in the desired direction.

Monitoring unit Every time the vehicle is started or stopped the circuit is monitored. If a fault is present, a warning lamp on the instrument panel is illuminated. A defect discovered by the monitoring circuit when the vehicle is in use causes the unit to activate the warning lamp; for safety reasons it also switches off the ABS system. In this state, the vehicle can still be driven but the driver loses the anti-lock feature.

Control system

Many ABS systems use a similar principle to the solenoid arrangement shown in Figure 21.7. In this diagram only one of the four valves is shown.

Fluid flow through the valve is determined by the solenoid plunger, the position of which is controlled by the current supplied by the ECU to the energizing coil of the solenoid. The three plunger positions needed to control the system are obtained in response to ECU current outputs of 0 A, 2 A and 5 A. When the output is zero, the return spring holds the plunger in its rest position and when 5 A is supplied it is forced to the upper end of its travel. The weaker magnetic flux produced by a 2 A current only moves the plunger part-way up its stroke.

Table 21.1 shows how solenoid position and pump action provides brake control.

Solenoid plunger position	Pump	Effect on brake
bottom of stroke (at rest)	off	normal brake operation (ABS not activated)
top of stroke (5 A)	on	ABS activated – pressure being reduced
mid-stroke (2 A)	on	pressure being held steady
bottom of stroke	on	pressure being increased by pump

Table 21.1 Brake control process examples

The ABS does not come into operation until one of the roadwheels starts to skid. At this time the ECU activates the pump and supplies the appropriate solenoid with a 5 A current; this reduces the fluid pressure in the brake line (Figure 2.17b).

When the wheel sensor signals that brake pressure has been reduced sufficient to overcome the skid, the ECU reduces the solenoid current to 2 A. This allows the hydraulic units to hold the pressure steady.

Any change in road conditions may allow more braking than that given by the *holding pressure*, so this is tested by de-energizing the solenoid and allowing the pump to build up pressure until the sensor once again detects the start of a skid (Figure 21.7c).

Repeating this cycle of events many times per second allows maximum braking to be obtained from all wheels.

Fail-safe If the self-diagnosing facility senses any malfunction, current from the ECU to the actuators is cut off; this isolates the ABS system and allows normal braking.

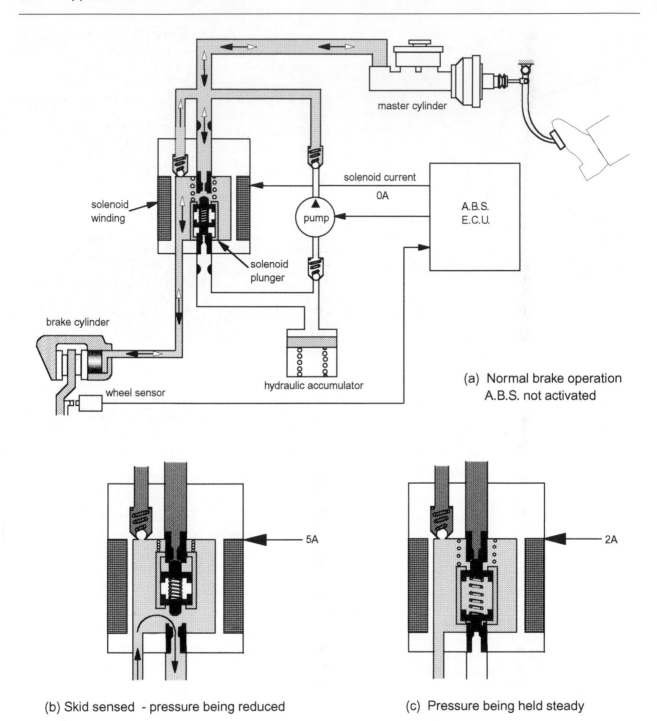

master cylinder

solenoid winding

solenoid plunger

brake cylinder

wheel sensor

solenoid current

0A

pump

A.B.S. E.C.U.

hydraulic accumulator

(a) Normal brake operation
A.B.S. not activated

5A

2A

(b) Skid sensed - pressure being reduced

(c) Pressure being held steady

Fig. 21.7 Solenoid valve operation

Fault diagnosis

When the anti-lock function is in use, the brake petal may pulsate and the vehicle body and steering wheel may vibrate. This effect is due to the rapid on–off action of the ABS system.

An ABS warning lamp on the instrument panel shows when the ABS system is in use. Each time the engine is started, and again when the vehicle speed has reached 6 km/h (4 mph) the lamp illuminates for a few seconds to show that the system is in order.

Any ABS fault detected by the self-diagnosing facility is stored as a code in the memory unit and signalled to the driver by the warning light. Technicians can identify any stored faults in the normal way, for example by using either a code reader or by observing the warning lamp to establish the blinking code.

21.3 Automatic transmission control

Most automatic transmission systems use hydraulic controls to activate the clutches and brake bands to obtain the various gears. In the past, these operating units relied on a collection of mechanical cables, rods and levers to sense the operating conditions of the engine and vehicle. Modern electronics have made these clumsy sensing and control systems obsolete, but hydraulic actuation of the planetary gear-set, clutches and brakes is still retained.

Much of the information required to manage a gearbox is already available when electronics are used to manage an engine. This data includes information on engine speed and load as well as vehicle speed.

Basic system

The layout shown in Figure 21.8 is an early design in which an electronic system is substituted for the normal mechanical control arrangement.

In this system the ECU is programmed to control the gear changes in response to data received from various input sensors, especially those giving a feedback of load and speed. Since this feedback is readily available, the system can easily be converted to achieve closed-loop control.

On many systems that use this layout, the actuator is a solenoid-controlled ball valve fitted in the hydraulic circuit to control gear changes. Two or three of these valves are used to provide the various gears.

Modern systems

Today, an *electronically controlled transmission* (ECT) incorporating an intelligent management system takes into account engine and vehicle conditions to control:

- vehicle speeds at which gear shifts occur
- lock-up clutch timing
- hydraulic pressures over operating range
- reduction of engine torque during gear shafts

In addition to gearbox control, the ECU can be programmed to provide the driver with two or more gear patterns to suit the driver's 'mood'; two typical modes are *sport* (power) and *economy* (normal). These patterns are selected by an ECT switch situated next to the gear selector; the position of the switch indicated on the instrument panel by a signal lamp.

Electronic control unit   Since data from some sensors is needed both by the engine and transmission unit, the advent of new powerful processors has allowed designers to use a single ECU to manage both units.

The electronic control features of a typical transmission system are shown in Figure 21.9. Driver instructions, together with the comparison between the various inputs and ECU-mapped values, dictates which actuators must be energized.

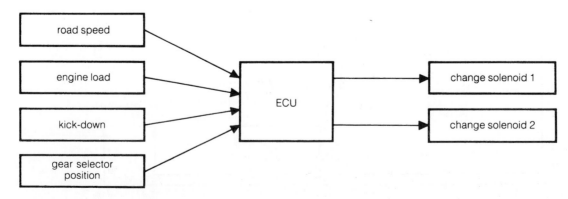

Fig. 21.8 Transmission control system

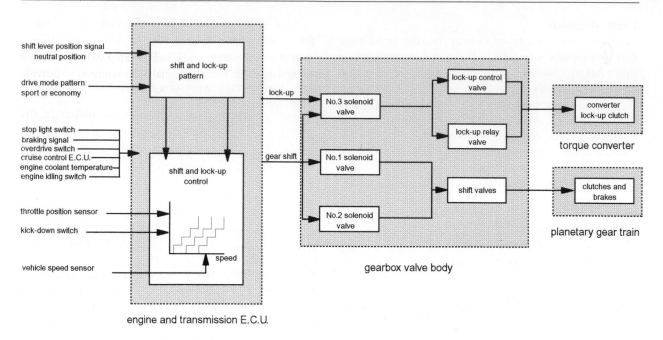

Fig. 21.9 ECT control system

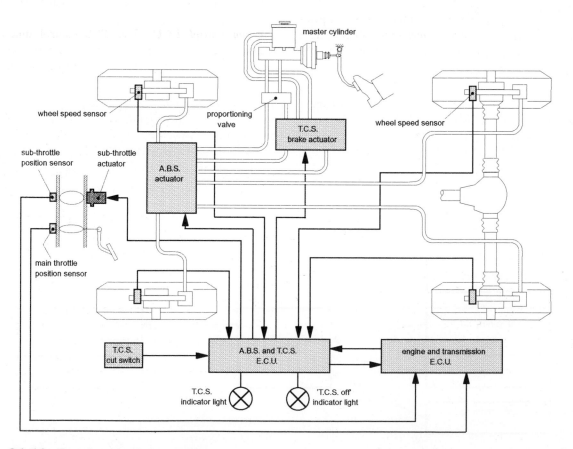

Fig. 21.10 Tractive control system

Fault diagnosis

The system is monitored by the on-board diagnosis facility and this indicates any malfunction, especially any fault that affects engine emissions, by a panel warning lamp. Some faults are identified by a blink code; other fault codes stored in the memory need to be down-loaded to an off-board code reader for interpretation.

21.4 Traction control

It has long been known that safety and vehicle performance is improved if spinning of the roadwheels could be prevented under driving conditions. When a wheel spins, traction is lost and vehicle control is jeopardized. This control problem arises because spinning of a rear wheel causes the back of the vehicle to move sideways and loss of adhesion at the front results in a loss of steering control.

Since many vehicles are now fitted with ABS, the speed sensors on each wheel can also be used to signal when a wheel starts to spin. The existence on the vehicle of this sensing equipment means that it is a comparatively small step to a *tractive control system* (TCS). This fact suggests that new luxury vehicles are likely to incorporate a traction control system.

TCS system layout

The similarity between the construction of a tractive control system and an anti-lock braking system is shown in Figure 21.10. The additional units required to provide an integrated TCS/ABS package are:

- *throttle controller* – varies the torque output of the engine;
- *electronic control unit* (ECU) – detects spin at any wheel and overcomes it by applying the brake on that wheel and simultaneously reduces engine power.

Throttle controller   Engine torque is controlled either by fitting an additional throttle (electronically controlled) or using an actuator on the main throttle similar to that employed for cruise control.

When an electronic actuator controls the position of the throttle, the traditional mechanical linkage becomes redundant, so a *drive-by-wire* control system is a natural development. Vehicles fitted with this *electronic throttle control* system have the accelerator pedal connected to a potentiometer; this sends to the ECU an analogue voltage signal which increases as the pedal is depressed.

Traction control ECU   The TCS control unit constantly receives signals from the four speed sensors; this data allows it to calculate the speed of each wheel. Also

---

REMEMBER

Cruise control:
- is a closed-loop system
- uses feedback from a speed sensor to allow the ECU to control engine throttle
- is deactivated if the brake or clutch pedal is touched

Anti-lock braking:
- uses speed sensors to detect the onset of a skid
- has four sensors for a 4-channel system
- uses a hydraulic modulator to vary fluid pressure in each brake line
- ECU detects the onset of a skid by comparing input signals with a reference signal
- ECU controls brake pressure by pump activation and solenoid current
- ECU energizes solenoid with current of 2 A or 5 A
- operation is felt by a driver by pedal pulsation
- operation is signalled by a panel lamp

Automatic transmission control:
- uses solenoid actuators to operate hydraulic valves
- has an ECU programmed to give various gear-change patterns
- ECU is often integral with the engine ECU
- provides smooth gear changes by varying the operating pressure and throttle setting

Tractive control system:
- works in conjunction with an ABS system
- sometimes uses a second engine throttle
- uses a wheel sensor to detect spin
- ECU compares the speed of each driving wheel with a target speed
- limits engine torque to avoid excessive spin
- applies brake on driving wheel when adhesion is broken
- has a self-diagnosing facility similar to other wheel control systems

it estimates the vehicle speed (the target speed) by using the signals from the non-driving wheels.

When the accelerator pedal is depressed sufficient to cause wheel spin at any wheel, the ECU senses that the wheel is turning faster than the target speed. This causes it to partly close the throttle and, using the ABS control, slightly applies the brake on the spinning wheel until its speed is reduced to the target speed.

TCS switch and indicator lamp A TCS switch is provided to allow the driver to cut out the system; when the switch is operated a *TCS OFF panel lamp* illuminates. Normally the TCS system is programmed to be operational when the engine is started.

When the TCS system is selected, the lamp blinks to inform the driver when the system is in action, but if there is a malfunction the light remains on.

Four-wheel drive

FWD vehicles fitted with TCS have additional control units to vary the proportion of driving torque between front and rear wheels. This ensures that each wheel exerts its maximum tractive effort.

Fault diagnosis

The ECU has a self-diagnosing and code storage facility. These codes are accessed by a reader or by using the blink signals displayed by the TCS lamp after two terminals in the diagnostic plug have been bridged.

PROGRESS CHECK 21

Questions 1–5 relate to a cruise control system

1. State the purpose of the system.

2. Why are microswitches fitted on the clutch and brake pedals?

3. What feedback signal is required to operate the system?

4. Which vehicle component is used to drive the speed sensor?

5. What method is used to signal a malfunction?

Questions 6–10 relate to an ABS system

6. State the method used to measure wheel speed.

7. State the method used to detect the onset of a skid.

8. What action is taken by the ECU when a skid is detected?

9. State how the ECU controls the solenoid valves.

10. What method is used to signal a malfunction?

Questions 11–15 relate to automatic transmission control

11. State the purpose of the system

12. Why is the transmission ECU usually integral with the engine ECU?

13. How does the driver alter the gearchange pattern from sport to economy?

14. What type of actuator is used to control hydraulic pressure?

15. What method is used to signal a malfunction?

Questions 16–20 relate to a traction control system

16. State the purpose of the system.

17. Why is the TCS electronic control unit usually integral with the engine ECU?

18. State the method used to detect the onset of a spin.

19. What action is taken by the ECU when wheel spin is detected?

20. What method is used to signal a malfunction?

22 *Supplemental restraint systems*

What is covered in this chapter

⟹ air bags
⟹ seat-belt tighteners

By law, all new vehicles manufactured in the UK must be fitted with 3-point seat belts. These belts must be worn by the driver and all passengers unless a special exemption is granted.

In addition to this legal requirement, many manufacturers now offer a *supplemental restraint system* (SRS) to give added protection to the vehicle occupants. This system embraces two main arrangements:

- airbag
- seat belt tighteners.

22.1   Air bags

An SRS airbag installed in the steering wheel centre lessens the shock to the driver's upper body in the event of a front-impact collision (Figure 22.1).

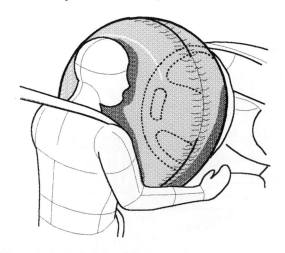

Fig. 22.1   Driver's airbag

When the impact is severe, sensor switches signal a control unit in the steering centre to inflate the airbag. The near-instantaneous inflation takes place in about 30 ms after triggering, but the bag only remains inflated for a short time (about 100 ms); this allows the driver freedom of movement after the initial impact.

On many cars an airbag is provided for the front-seat passenger. Also some cars fit extra airbags to protect the occupants against side impact.

There are two types of airbag, *electronic* and *all-mechanical*; only the former is considered here.

Electronic airbag system

Figure 22.2 shows the layout of a typical airbag system for the protection of the driver. The main components are:

- inflator and airbag – mounted in the centre of the steering wheel;
- front sensors – two sensors placed at the front of the car;
- airbag control unit – centrally mounted: it incorporates additional sensors, battery back-up and self-diagnosing facilities;
- SRS warning lamp on the instrument panel.

Inflator and airbag   This self-contained module houses the nylon fabric bag, the gas generant capsules (nitrocellulose and nitroglycerine) and igniter squib.

When a very small electrical current is applied to the squib, the igniter charge is fired and heat is

---

SAFE PRACTICE

Only a very small current is need to ignite the squib and inflate the airbag, so squib resistance must NOT be measured with an ohmmeter

---

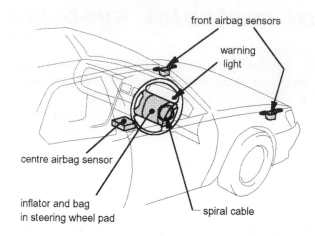

Fig. 22.2 Airbag system layout

produced. This causes the gas capsules to generate nitrogen (or carbon dioxide) gas to inflate the airbag.

The volume of airbags used on European vehicles is approx 30 litres (driver) and 60 litres (passenger). These sizes are smaller than airbags used in the USA, because they are intended to be used in conjunction with a 3-point seat belt.

Figure 22.3 shows the construction of a typical inflator system. The connection between the squib and the steering column is normally by a flattened cable wound in a spiral shape similar to a clock spring. This maintains a sound connection in all steering wheel positions.

Front sensors

A front sensor is a mechanical switch that is closed when it detects a forward deceleraton at a rate sustained by a vehicle that is involved in a serious front-end collision (many front sensors activate when the deceleration is greater than 4 g).

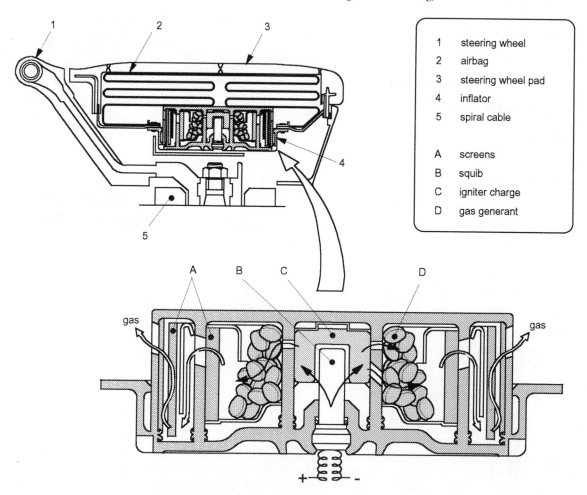

1	steering wheel
2	airbag
3	steering wheel pad
4	inflator
5	spiral cable
A	screens
B	squib
C	igniter charge
D	gas generant

Fig. 22.3 Section through inflator and airbag

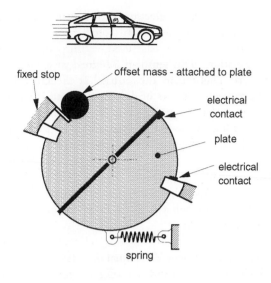

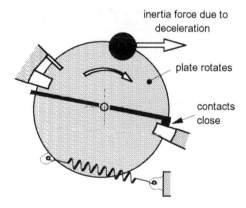

Fig. 22.4 Principle of deceleration sensor

The principle of a decelerometer is based on the inertia force produced on a mass when the velocity of the mass is changed. In simple terms this means that when the forward speed of a body is suddenly reduced, the body will be thrust forward; this force increases with the deceleration.

The type of sensor shown in Figure 22.4 has a spring-retained circular plate onto which a mass ('weight') is mounted; the mass is positioned so that it is offset to the plate spindle.

Sudden deceleration will force the mass forward, the amount of movement governed by the strength of the

spring that opposes plate rotation. When the force is sufficient to allow full travel of the mass, a switch is closed.

By altering the strength of the spring, the decelerometer can be made to signal when the force of impact is large enough to need airbag inflation.

Some manufacturers do not use front sensors; in these cases the sensors are built into the central control unit.

Airbag control unit

Mounted inside the vehicle for protection, this ECU consists of:

- centre sensor
- safety sensor
- back-up power supply
- air ignition and drive module
- diagnosis and memory module.

Centre sensor   Usually this is a solid-state sensor that maintains its characteristics for a long period of time. The type shown in Figure 22.5 is a cantilever onto which is attached a pair of strain gauges; these are connected to a Wheatstone bridge circuit (see page 34).

Impact due to a collision causes the cantilever to bend and alter the resistance of the strain gauges. When

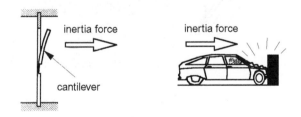

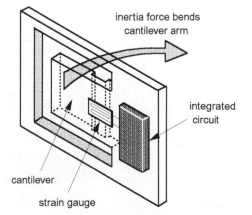

Fig. 22.5 Airbag control unit centre sensor

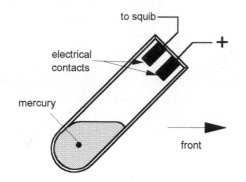

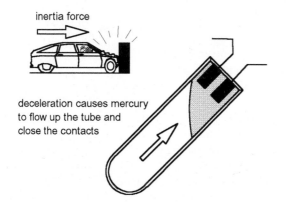

Fig. 22.6 Mercury-type safety sensor

the extent of the deflection shows that the impact is severe, the sensor 'switch' is closed.

Safety sensor This sensor is designed to prevent unintentional ignition of the airbag. It is activated at a comparitively low rate of deceleration and is connected in series with the power supply; the airbag will only inflate when the safety sensor switch is closed. Figure 22.6 shows a mercury-type safety sensor.

Back-up power supply A capacitor, charged by the battery, provides the system with electrical energy for about 150 ms when a collision causes an interruption in the battery supply.

Airbag ignition and drive module The brain of this module is a microprocessor (Figure 22.7). Since front and centre sensors are all connected in parallel, any impact detected by any one of these sensors is signalled to the processor. The processor will ignite the squib when the safety switch is closed and the input data compares with the programmed crash data stored in its ROM memory.

Diagnosis and memory module This works in conjunction with the SRS indicator lamp. When the ignition is switched on, the SRS lamp is illuminated for about 5 s to show that the system is serviceable. If no malfunction is detected, the safety circuit is deactivated and the squib is made ready for ignition.

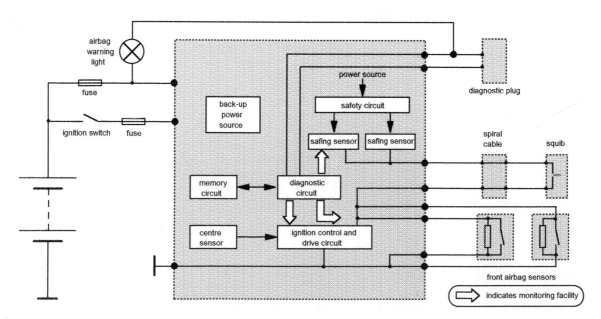

Fig. 22.7 Simplified airbag circuit

When the vehicle is in use, the system is being continuously monitored. If a malfunction is detected, the SRS lamp will illuminate and the fault will be stored as a code in the memory.

Fault diagnosis

The ECU has a self-diagnosing and code storage facility. These codes are accessed by a reader or by using the blink signals displayed by the SRS lamp after two terminals in the diagnostic plug have been bridged.

In view of the dangers associated with tests and repairs of a SRS system, it is essential that the manufacturer's instructions are read and understood. For identification purposes the main cable harness is normally coloured yellow. After an airbag has been inflated as the result of a collision, it is recommended that the airbag assembly and various other named components are renewed; this is to limit product liability.

22.2 Seat-belt tighteners

In the event of a front-end impact, vehicle occupants are subjected to a very large inertia force that can exceed forty times the weight of their bodies. To improve the chance of surviving a collision of this order, the occupants must be securely restrained to a strong structure; the vehicle body.

Wearing a conventional seat belt improves safety considerably, but the need to allow the occupants freedom of movement generally means that the belt tension does not prevent a person being thrown through the windscreen.

Vehicle designers now realize that, in the interest of safety, seat belts must be tightened during the time that the large inertia force is acting.

Electronic seat-belt tensioner

These systems use a similar principle to that used to inflate an airbag; normally the crash sensing system is common to both units.

REMEMBER

SRS airbag systems:

- inflate bag in about 30 ms and keep it inflated for about 100 ms
- are either *all-mechanical* or *electronic*
- use crash sensors that trigger when the deceleration is greater than 4 g
- have a 'safing' provision to avoid unintended operation
- use a capacitor to provide *back-up power*
- must be handled and tested with extreme care
- used on European vehicles have smaller airbags than those used on vehicles made in the USA
- have front sensors that work on the *inertia principle*
- have the front and centre sensors connected in *parallel* and the safing sensor in *series*
- use a *squib* to ignite the inflator
- have an SRS warning lamp
- **should not** be serviced without reading and understanding the manufacturer's instructions

Seatbelt tighteners:

- reduce the risk of occupants being thrown through the windscreen
- work on a similar principle to the airbag
- use the same sensors as the airbag
- use the gas generated to act on a mechanical tensioning system

Each belt is fitted with a gas generator and squib; this is ignited in the normal way by current from a SRS control unit. Various methods are used to link the sudden release of gas with the belt-tightening mechanism. This is achieved either by discharging the gas into a cylinder to drive a piston, or by directing the gas onto a turbine wheel.

PROGRESS CHECK 22

1. What is meant by the abbreviation *SRS*?

2. State the purpose of an airbag.

3. Why does the airbag deflate after about 100 ms?

4. State the method used to generate the gas.

5. State why an ohmmeter **should not** be used to test the ignition system of an airbag.

6. State the purpose of the sensors that are connected in parallel with each other.

7. State the purpose of the sensor that is connected in series with the battery and control unit.

8. State the method used to operate the system in the event of battery supply failure.

9. Why are European airbags smaller than those made in the USA?

10. State the principle of:
(a) a front crash sensor;
(b) centre sensor;
(c) safety sensor.

11. What method is used on SRS systems to indicate a malfunction?

12. State TWO methods used to identify the cause of a malfunction.

13. State the purpose of a seatbelt tensioner.

14. What method is used on a seat belt tensioner system to sense an impact?

23

In-car entertainment and communication equipment

What is covered in this chapter

→ radios
→ tape cassette players
→ compact disc players
→ in-car telephones
→ navigation systems

Not many years ago a radio in a popular car was only available as an optional extra; often this was fitted by the dealer when the car was sold. Today the majority of cars and commercial vehicles are supplied with a wide range of *in-car entertainment* (ICE) systems. These range from a comparatively basic radio/speaker arrangement at the cheaper end of the market to a sophisticated radio/cassette deck/CD player and high grade multiple speakers at the expensive end.

In addition to entertainment systems, many vehicles are used by their owners as a portable office; this means that communication equipment such as a telephone (and in some cases a fax machine) becomes an essential part of the vehicle.

Present day road congestion, especially motorway delays, has brought about the development of special communication equipment that informs the driver of road conditions. The availability of this navigation equipment is intended to reduce the stress that arises when a driver is held up in a traffic jam for a considerable time.

The intention of this chapter is to provide an overview of the systems and highlight the main terms used in this specialized field. Detailed descriptions of the installation of these systems is not covered. When fitting or fault rectification has to be undertaken, either the services of an audio specialist should be sought, or the manufacturer's instructions should be carefully followed.

23.1 Radios

Besides giving advice, the after-market is often required to upgrade the standard audio system.

Radio waves

Electromagnetic radio waves travel through the air at 300 000 000 m/s. The strength of the a.c. wave cycle is called the *amplitude* and the number of full cycles that occur in one second is the *frequency*; this is expressed in hertz (Hz). Broadcast frequencies are given in kHz or

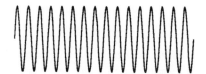

carrier wave - constant amplitude and frequency

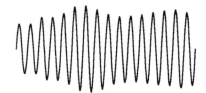

A.M. AMPLITUDE MODULATION
amplitude varies, frequency constant

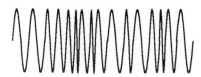

F.M. FREQUENCY MODULATION
frequency varies, amplitude constant

Fig. 23.1 Radio waves

387

MHz. As the term suggests *wavelength* is the length of one complete wave; this is expressed in metres.

Radio signals are transmitted by using a *carrier wave*. The frequency of this wave is controlled by the transmitter station, e.g. Radio 5 uses a wavelength of 433 m and frequency of 693 kHz. In the past the tuning scale of a radio was calibrated in metres, but today frequency scaling is preferred. Nevertheless, the terms *long, medium* and *short wave* are still in common use.

Transmitting sound signals via the carrier wave causes changes in the wave amplification pattern; this is called *amplitude modulation* (AM). Tuning the radio to select this particular frequency allows the signal to be received and amplified to drive a speaker (Figure 23.1).

An alternative method of modulating the carrier wave is to vary its frequency; this is called *frequency modulation* (FM). Transmission of an FM signal at a *very high frequency* (VHF) gives excellent reception and is the preferred method if high quality sound, such as stereo broadcasts, is to be transmitted over short distances (normally about 100 km max.).

One disadvantage of FM is that the VHF waves travel in straight lines, i.e. in the line of sight from the transmitter. This means that the signal is easily interrupted by any hard obstacle in the line between the transmitter and receiver.

Receiver sensitivity   Sensitivity is the minimum voltage measured at the antenna that the receiver requires to provide a noise-free sound signal. For an average-priced radio tuner, values of 5 μV and 50 μV are typical for FM and MW respectively.

Tuner functions   Driving a vehicle safely whilst tuning a radio to obtain and hold the transmission from a given radio station is very difficult. Various improvements have been made during recent years to simplify this task; some of these are included here.

Phase-locked-loop (PLL). An electronic tuning feature which locks the radio onto a station. The drift-free reception cuts out most interference.

Station presets. Allows the station to be selected at the touch of a numbered button. The feature minimizes distraction at a time when a driver retunes the radio.

Auto memory. Allows the radio to locate and store the strongest stations (normally six) in the selected MW or FM band. Afterwards any station can be selected by pressing the appropriate pre-set button. Using this facility is the easiest way to allocate stations and preset buttons on a new radio. Various names are used to describe this feature, e.g. autostore, best station memory.

Scan tuning. Selecting this feature causes the tuner to cycle through the wave band until it finds a station. Once a station is found, the scanner holds it for a few seconds before it continues with its search. When the driver wishes to retain a station, the auto-scan button is pressed.

Seek. Similar in action to the auto-scan, but in this case the facility selects and holds the station until the seek button is pushed again.

Pulse noise suppressor (PNS). Reduces ignition and static noise on FM.

Radio data signalling (RDS). This tuner receives data broadcast from the BBC and IBA on the FM radio waveband to instruct the radio to interrupt its programme in order to receive road and traffic condition reports. Since the system is localized it provides the driver with up-to-date traffic information.

Radio code. An anti-theft feature that makes the radio inoperative unless a secret code, applicable to that particular radio, is keyed-in. If the battery supply is disconnected for any reason, the code has to be re-entered.

Amplifier functions

To amplify means to enlarge, so in the case of audio systems, an amplifier strengthens and enlarges the signal sufficient to drive a speaker.

These are two types of amplifier; a *pre-amplifier* and a *power amplifier*. The former intensifies and modifies the input signal and the latter is an extra amplifier to boost the output signal from the basic system to power a sophisticated speaker array.

A number of terms are associated with amplifiers; some of these are considered at this stage.

Tone control   Varies the frequency response of an amplifier to alter the treble and bass sound quality. On low-cost sets one controller is used; turning it one way boosts the bass and cuts the treble and visa versa. Today mid-range units have either separate bass and treble controls or a *graphic equaliser*. This sophisticated tone control unit divides the output into separate frequency bands to allow individual balancing.

Loudness   The limitation of a human ear prevents low frequencies being picked up when the volume is low, so this feature restores the natural sound balance by boosting the low frequencies.

Power output Net useful power delivered by an amplifier. It is measure in watts and relates to either the maximum or continuous (r.m.s.) power output. The former is a measure of the power supplied for a very short period and the latter a more realistic guide because it relates to its power over a much longer period of time. The amplifier output governs the speakers that are used in the system, e.g. a power amplifier having a max/r.m.s. rating of 100 W/80 W would not be effective if the speakers were incapable of taking this power.

Speakers

A speaker consists of a coil winding, connected to a paper cone, that is placed in the centre of a circular shaped permanent magnet (Figure 23.2).

When an amplifier passes a variable a.c. current through the coil winding, the electromagnetic reaction causes the speaker cone to move in and out. This vibrates the air in the cone and produces a sound; the lower the vibration, the lower the frequency of the sound wave.

The diameter of the cone governs the frequency range that the speaker can handle. Large cone speakers, (*woofers* and *sub-woofers*) handle very low bass notes, whereas small cone speakers (*tweeters*) produce high frequency sound waves.

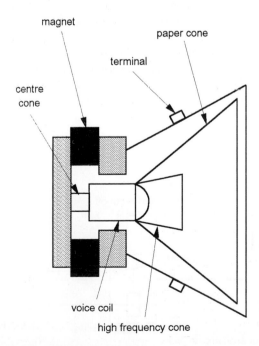

Fig. 23.2 Construction of a twin-cone speaker

Phasing of speakers When two or more speakers are fitted, all the speakers must be connected in the same polarity to ensure that all cones move in the same direction at the same time.

A strange sound effect is produced when the speakers are incorrectly connected. To prevent this out-of-phase problem, the speaker terminals are marked '+' and '–' and one of the two cables has a coloured stripe along its length.

Power rating A speaker is rated in watts in a similar way to an amplifier, namely maximum/continuous (max./r.m.s.) power rating. The closer the two power ratings are together, the better, and more expensive, is the speaker.

Normally the power rating of the speakers should exceed the amplifier rating by about 50%. For example, if an amplifier delivers 20 W (max) per channel (per speaker), the power rating of each speaker should be 30 W (max).

Impedance When upgrading audio equipment, attention must be given to the speaker impedance (see page 24). Normally speakers have an impedance of 4 Ω or 8 Ω, so it is necessary for the speaker array to match the set. Sound quality will suffer if speaker impedance is higher than the set and damage to the set might occur if it is too low.

Speaker set-up

Figure 23.3 shows a 4-speaker system that is now fitted as original equipment (OE) to many cars. In some cases

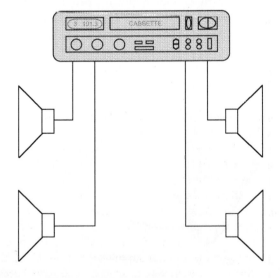

Fig. 23.3 4-speaker system

component speakers (mid-range and tweeter) are used at the front.

Radio installation

The majority of cars now have a radio fitted as OE, so ICE specialist activities have changed from installations of basic units to work associated with personalization of existing systems.

In view of this change, the following topics have been included to cover replacement of defective items and work that is needed when audio equipment has been disturbed during mechanical repair of the vehicle.

Aerial position   The aerial (antenna) converts electro-magnetic radio waves into a signal which the radio can process and amplify. Ideally an aerial should be one quarter the length of the radio wave, but since this length is impractical, modern electronics allow the length to be reduced to about 100 cm and made telescopic for stowage.

To minimize radio interference due to ignition pulses, the aerial should be situated at the back of the car. When this is not convenient, it is mounted at the front of the car and made so that it can retract into the roof of a pillar. The angle of an aerial mounted in a pillar is a compromise between the vertical and horizontal positions ideally required for AM and FM respectively. An alternative type of aerial uses a grid in the window glass such as a heated rear window; this works in conjunction with a signal amplifier.

Electric aerial   Extension or retraction of an aerial can be achieved with a remotely situated permanent-magnet rotary motor. Often this reversible motor acts through a reduction gear to drive a cable by means of two crimped plates (Figure 23.4). The cable, often made of a plastic material to avoid radio interference, is joined to the top rod of the aerial. When the aerial is retracted, provision is made to enable the spare cable to be wound in a coil adjacent to the driving plates.

A two-way switch reverses the motor polarity to give the up and down motion. Often the aerial switch is incorporated in the radio to operate the aerial when the radio is switched on and off.

Aerial installation   A good earth between the aerial body and vehicle body is needed to obtain good interference-free reception. In addition the metal screen of the coaxial lead must make a good connection with both the aerial body and radio.

The aerial lead must not be cut; instead the lead should be 'snaked' (not coiled) in a body recess.

Fitting the radio   Provision is normally made in the fascia panel to accommodate a radio. Since the aperture size is made to conform to a ISO or DIN standard, a normal type of radio can be slid into the recess in the panel.

The radio supply should be taken from the recommended feed point (normally ignition-key controlled) and the unit protected by an in-line fuse. In this feed it is often necessary to fit a suitable *in-line choke* (as close as possible to the radio) to minimize line-borne interference.

After ensuring that the radio is connected to a good earth and the aerial plug is securely fitted, the unit is slid into the panel and fastened. Prior to this operation, anti-theft measures should be considered. Some people

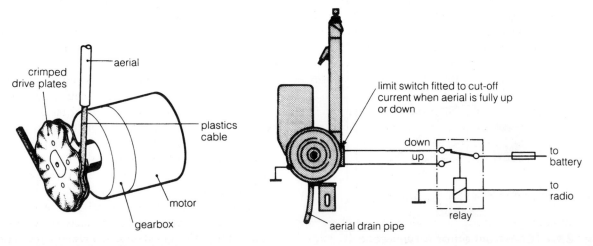

Fig. 23.4 Electric radio aerial

fit a coded radio, others find it safer to use a QRB (quick release bracket); this allows the owner to easily remove the radio.

Trimming After a new aerial has been fitted, it is necessary to trim the aerial to match the radio. This achieved by tuning-in to a strong station midway along the MW band and then adjusting the trimmer on the radio until the strongest clearest signal is obtained.

Radio interference

Radio interference is either *line-borne* and/or *aerial borne*. The radio can be operated with the aerial disconnected to establish which one of these is the source.

A line-borne voltage surge is caused by the electro-magnetic effect that follows a change or rapid interruption in either the supply current or consumer load. The interference is minimized by smoothing-out the supply current by fitting a choke, in series with the feed, or a capacitor, in parallel with the radio.

Air-borne interference is caused by components that are subjected to sudden voltage changes, especially when arcing is present. One of the following is used to minimize air-borne radiation:

- supply to the component is smoothed with a capacitor;
- radio wave is suppressed at its source;
- cable is screened to resist radio wave penetration.

The source of the interference is found by using a process of elimination together with clues gained from factors such as frequency and operating conditions.

Circuits of electronic management systems are designed to minimize interference, so external capacitors and chokes should not be fitted to these systems.

Crackles and clicks on a radio can also be caused by *static electricity*; this is generated by friction between two running surfaces, e.g. brakes, clutches and body components. To avoid this interference, the two rubbing surfaces should, where possible, be connected together with a conductive bonding strip and securely earthed.

Glass-reinforced plastic (GRP) bodies require special attention because they have no metal screen around the engine. The problem is solved by lining the engine compartment with special metal foil.

23.2 Tape cassette players

Miniaturization has made it possible to combine a cassette deck with a radio and accommodate the integrated unit in the normal DIN aperture in the fascia panel. Sound reproduction obtained from a player depends on both the tape quality and the special features incorporated in the unit.

Cassette tapes

Many manufacturers make the three main types of tape; these are classified as types I, II and III according to the material used to magnetically record the sounds. Material used for each type is:

Type 1 – a normal bias tape that contains gamma haematite, a ferric oxide material. Can be used with all cassette equipment

Type II – high bias chrome dioxide (CrO_2) tape that produces a much better sound from a wider frequency response. A good all-purpose tape.

Type III – high bias metal tape having a high reluctance that relies on the need for a stronger recording signal to cut out residual noise and avoid distortion. This expensive type of tape needs a high-grade metal-compatible cassette deck

Tapes are made in all lengths; the most common are C60 (30 minutes each side), C90 and C120. As the tape length is increased, the thickness is decreased. In view of this, the very thin C120 is not recommended for ICE because it slips on the rollers or jams.

Cassette deck features

The number of special features included in a cassette player is governed by the initial cost and, as with other audio equipment, 'the sky's the limit'. Some of the main tape and deck features are:

Auto-stop. At the end of the tape the player is automatically switched-off.

Auto-reverse/auto-play. At the end of the tape, the deck drive rollers reverse and play the other side of the tape; this gives continuous play.

Auto-metal selector. Automatically switches the play head to suit the type of tape in the machine, i.e. switches between normal, chrome and metal tapes.

Dolby system. Designed by Ray Dolby for reducing tape hiss on playback. There are two systems in use at present, Dolby B and Dolby C. The latter gives better results but it is necessary to record and play on equipment that is compatible.

Balance control. This control is fitted to a pre-amplifier to adjust the output of the speakers in relation to each other. When used on stereo systems, the control balances the left and right speakers. Systems having

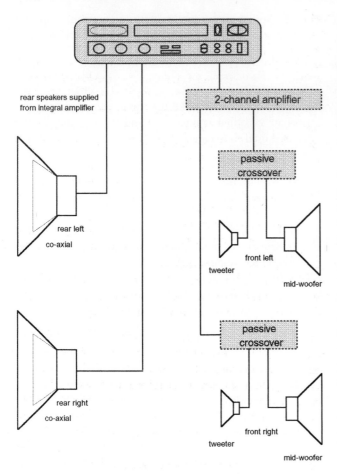

Fig. 23.5 Speaker system with power amplifier and crossovers

four speakers sometimes have a joy-stick to balance left/right and front/rear speakers.

Fader. A control fitted to either the pre-amplifier or power amplifier to balance front/rear speakers.

Speaker upgrade

To obtain the full effects of a good cassette deck, it is sometimes necessary to consider upgrading the speaker system.

Figure 23.5 shows the layout of a system that uses a 2-channel *power amplifier* and *crossovers* to drive the front speakers.

Crossovers These are needed to separate and distribute the appropriate frequencies to the speakers e.g. treble to a tweeter, bass to a woofer. There are two types of crossover, *active* and *passive*: the former divides the sounds before amplification and the latter after amplification.

23.3 Compact disc players

Introduced by Philips, the *compact disc (CD)* has many advantages over a tape; these include superb sound quality, long life, and high storage capacity. Since the digital signals are read from the billions of microscopic pits in the disc by a laser-light beam, there is no physical contact. This means that the disc does not deteriorate with use provided it is handled and stored carefully.

As with other audio equipment, sound reproduction depends on the quality of the CD player/speaker system. If the system cannot handle the very wide frequency response obtained from a compact disc, then the overall effect will be little better than that obtained from a tape.

CD player

Various options are available when deciding on a layout. These are dictated by the space available to accommodate the CD player. If the unit is to be fitted in the standard DIN aperture in the panel then the tuner/cassette player must be replaced by a tuner/CD player; the alternative is to mount the CD unit separately.

Many CD players (or CD/tuners) have a 50 W integral amplifier, so in these cases a 4-speaker system of about 100 W is necessary if the full benefit of a CD is to be gained.

Changing a disc while driving can be hazardous, especially as a disc should only be handled at the edge. This problem is overcome by fitting a *multidisc autochanger*. This is a magazine that holds a number of discs; these can be selected and changed at the touch of a button.

In addition to the function controls used on a cassette player, the CD player has other features such as:

- *Repeat* – allows one track or the whole disc to be repeated
- *Display* – shows either the time left on the disc or the elapsed time of a particular track
- *Mix (random play)* – shuffles the tracks, or discs, to play in a random order
- *Oversampling* – expressed as ×2, ×4, ×8 and ×16, this indicates the way in which the digital sound is produced; the higher the number the better the sound quality.

Speaker upgrade

Figure 23.6 shows a sophisticated speaker system that allows a very wide frequency range to be obtained from a combined tuner/cassette/CD system.

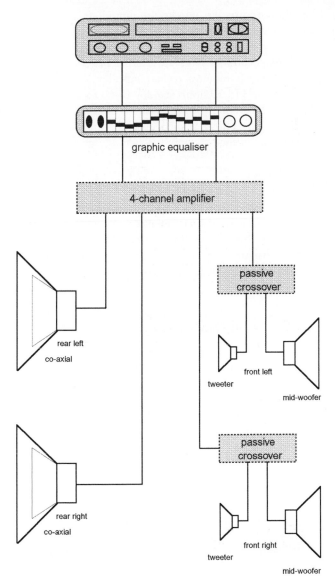

Fig. 23.6 Audio system with graphic equaliser and 4-channel amplifier

Equipment selection and use

When it is necessary to recommend audio equipment, the following items should be taken into account:

- Equipment requirements of the owner in respect to sound quality, ease and type of use, system preference and preferred refinements
- Purchase price
- Difficulty/cost of installation
- Reliability
- Robustness

- After-sales service/repair
- Guarantees and warranties

Owners of vehicles fitted with powerful ICE systems must be aware that the playing of equipment at high volume can involve the driver being charged with causing a public nuisance.

23.4 In-car telephones

It's not many years since the initial purchase price and operating cost of an in-car telephone was prohibitive; this restricted their use to the emergency services and rich businessmen. The advent of cheap, hand-held mobile phones, together with intense competition, has made the portable telephone very popular.

Cellular network

Short-range transceiver The mobile phone is a transceiver that works as a radio transmitter and receiver. To send a message over a long distance, the transmitter has to send out strong microwaves. These are dangerous to humans so to overcome this problem the power of the phone is restricted to a safe level.

The method used by an air-time supplier is to divide the country into a number of cells so that the receiver and transmitter in each cell is within the range of the mobile phone. Blanketing the country with this cellular structure allows the mobile phone to automatically select and communicate with the nearest cell. Travelling from one cell to another presents no problem, because when the phone detects that it is out-of-range, it switches to another cell that is nearer.

Operating system Mobile phones are either *analogue* or *digital*. Since the latter type offers the caller greater privacy and gives a clearer speech quality, it is gradually taking over from the older analogue type. The GMS system (global system for mobile communications) uses digital technology to enable the caller to use the phone in many overseas countries.

Mobile telephone equipment ranges from base station systems (car phones) permanently installed in a vehicle to mobile handsets that can be carried around. The personal telephone offers many advantages over the car phone, but if a large transmitting range is needed then the powerful Class II car phone, with its 2.8 W RF power output, is more suitable.

Car phones

A basic system consists of a handset, transceiver unit and a short aerial. Powered by the vehicle battery the transceiver is positioned in a protected area such as in the car boot or under one of the seats. The permanently fixed or magnetically mounted aerial should be placed as high as possible. It is earthed and connected in a similar way to a normal radio.

Handsets are normally retained in a cradle positioned for easy use without causing severe distraction for the driver. A safer alternative is to fit a voice operated telephone. This arrangement uses a built-in microphone and speaker to give *hands-free operation*.

SAFE PRACTICE

The Highway Code states that:
a hand-held telephone should not be used, except in an emergency, while the vehicle is in motion or when parked on the hard shoulder of a motorway

---

Telphone features

The handsets of modern telephones, car and mobile, incorporate a number of features; these include:

- *service indicator* – shows when the phone is inside the network area covered by the service provider
- *battery alarm* – illuminates when the internal battery requires charging
- *memory* – stores a given number of names and telephone numbers
- *notebook* – allows numbers to be noted and stored while the phone is in operation
- *auto-redial* – if a number is engaged the phone will automatically redial a set number of times
- *last number recall* – pressing the recall button redials the last number called
- *call waiting* – allows a second call to be answered while keeping the first call on hold
- *call divert* – redirects incoming calls to another phone
- *call timer* – monitors and displays the elapsed call time
- *silent ringing* – allows incoming calls to be displayed without ringing
- *password* – prevents unauthorised use.

Portable mobile phones

The reception obtained from handheld portable phones having a class IV RF power rating is sometimes poor when used in poor reception areas from within the vehicle. This problem can be minimized by using a car-

kit; this consists of a window-mounted aerial, hang-up cradle, speaker and microphone that can be conveniently placed for hands-free calling.

Portable phones have an internal battery (normally Ni-Cd) which requires recharging after a period; this ranges from 8 to 30 hours standby or 60 to 140 minutes talktime depending on the make of phone.

When the phone is used in a car, the cigar lighter socket can be used to supply a portable charger.

Interference

Sometimes electromagnetic waves radiated from powerful car phones can interfere with vehicle electronics, especially ABS and engine management systems. In view of this, it is essential that installation and operating instructions given by phone and vehicle manufacturers are followed.

23.5 Navigation systems

Throughout the world various systems are available to guide the motorist from one point to another. These range from expensive satellite navigation and position locators to portable receivers that provide information about local road conditions. As electronic communication systems develop, the range of in-car traffic information systems is expected to increase considerably. The systems mentioned in this chapter are available at this time.

Fig. 23.7 Trafficmate™ navigation system

REMEMBER

Radio:

- signals are transmitted by a *carrier wave*
- signals are transmitted by *amplitude modulation (AM)* or *frequency modulation (FM)*
- signals transmitted at VHF give excellent reception, travel in straight lines and have a limited range
- *data signalling* (RDS) is a method used to transmit road and traffic conditions
- amplifiers are classified by their *max/continuous* power output
- speaker power rating should exceed amplifier rating by about 50%
- speaker *impedance* should not be lower than the tuner if damage to the set is to be avoided
- aerials should ideally be positioned remote from the engine ignition system
- aerial coaxial cable should not be cut or coiled
- interference is either line-borne or aerial-borne

Tape cassette player:

- tapes are classified as normal, CrO_2, or metal
- must have a special head if metal tape is used
- Dolby system reduces tape *hiss*
- balance control adjusts the output of the speakers
- having *tweeter* and *woofer* speakers incorporates *crossovers* to distribute the treble and bass frequencies

Compact disc player:

- uses digital signals read from microscopic pits in a disc by a laser-light beam
- requires a good speaker system to obtain best sound reproduction
- having a multi-disc autochanger improves safety by reducing driver distraction

In-car telephones:

- use a *cellular* network to compensate for their short range
- are either *analogue* or *digital*
- are classified by their RF power output
- fitted in the vehicle are more powerful than hand-held mobiles
- should not be used by a driver when a vehicle is in motion
- having a *service indicator* show the user when the phone is inside the network area
- may interfere with the vehicle's electronic systems

Navigation systems:

- use a cellular network to broadcast traffic information
- use sensors on motorways to detect traffic movement
- transmit a signal of low power to the vehicle from a transmitter in the vicinity

Trafficmate™

The technology used in Trafficmate is more sophisticated than that used for traffic bulletins selected by RDS radio (see page 388). Information transmitted to the receiver (Figure 23.7) from a cellular network of infrared sensors situated on the main motorways give information of traffic conditions in the area in which the vehicle is operating.

Low power digital signals (433 MHz) from the transmitter nearest to the vehicle are picked up by the onboard receiver and relayed by a speech synthesizer to the driver. Since the information is sensed and transmitted twice per second, drivers are able to plan their route accordingly.

Access to the service is controlled by a key that is purchased at 12-month intervals from the service provider.

Trafficmaster™

Trafficmaster YQ is a screen-based portable unit that fits on the dashboard of the vehicle to give drivers an up-to-the-minute bird's eye view of the traffic situation. At the touch of a button, the information displayed on the map of the national motorway network allows the driver to choose the least congested route before travelling or whilst en-route. By moving a cursor to the area of interest, the driver can zoom-in on specific section of the motorway.

Using an infrastructure of trunk road sensors and transmitters, the unit shown in Figure 23.8 provides details of delays including traffic speed, location and length of tailback. Also the YQ unit has a text facility to access news, weather information, news about the cause of any congestion and provision for a personal messaging service.

A battery duration of 8 hours standby and 3 hours airtime is common; the unit can either be recharged by the cigar lighter socket or permanently connected to the vehicle battery.

Access to the service is controlled by the purchase of an information key from the service provider.

Fig. 23.8 Trafficmaster™ YQ

PROGRESS CHECK 23

Questions 1–10 relate to car radios

1. State how a change in amplitude and frequency alters the shape of a radio wave.

2. What is the difference in wave pattern between AM and FM?

3. Compared to AM transmission, state TWO disadvantages and ONE advantage of a VHF FM broadcast.

4. What is a *RDS* broadcast?

5. State the purpose of a radio code.

6. An amplifier is rated as 100 W/80 W. State the significance of the two values.

7. Two speakers are connected in a way that makes the polarity of one opposite to the other. State the effect of this.

8. How should the power of the speakers compare to the power of the amplifier?

9. A new aerial has been fitted. State the method used to trim the aerial to the radio.

10. Radio reception is poor due to severe interference. Describe the method that should be used to locate the origin of the interference.

Questions 11–15 relate to cassette and CD players

11. State TWO types of tape. Indicate which one will give the best performance.

12. Name the tape system that is designed to minimize tape hiss.

13. State the purpose of a balance control.

14. State ONE reason why the life of a CD disc is longer than a tape.

15. State why high quality speakers are normally used with a CD system.

Questions 16–20 relate to communication equipment

16. State why a *cellular network* is used for mobile telephones.

17. Why are car phones more powerful than portable mobile phones?

18. Name TWO vehicle electronic systems that can be affected when a powerful car phone is used.

19. Name TWO items of information conveyed to the driver by a *Trafficmate*™ unit.

20. How is traffic data presented by a *Trafficmaster*™ system?

24 *Other electronic applications*

What is covered in this chapter

➡ auxiliary systems
➡ multiplexing
➡ electronic developments

Many electronic systems and features that were regarded as innovations a few years ago are now commonly used on popular range vehicles. These new ideas were first introduced on luxury cars and as the costs come down, their use spread through the vehicle range.

In this chapter the systems have been divided into two sections; auxiliary systems in common use and systems in development. In a short time many of the features in the latter section will be regarded by the general public as essential systems.

24.1 Auxiliary systems

Electric seat adjustment

A number of vehicles in the mid- to upper-price range are fitted with an electrical motorized system that adjusts the front seats to suit the occupants. Initially these systems only gave fore-and-aft movement, but today provision is made to control all the seat adjustments; in some luxury cars ten seat adjustments can be made.

Soon after the actuator system has been introduced, an electronic controller was added. The memory function in this unit stores information previously keyed-in to set the position of:

● each front seat
● door and interior mirrors

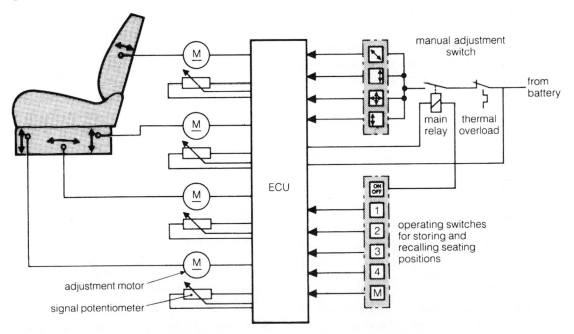

Fig. 24.1 Electrical seat adjustment

- steering wheel position
- seat belt.

Figure 24.1 shows the layout of a typical system. This uses four electric motors to adjust the settings of the seat and a separate memory unit to store four seating positions.

Rotary motion given by the motor is transmitted by shafts, flexible and rigid, to gearboxes sited in suitable positions to give the required seat movements. These gearboxes often have a worm and wheel drive, which acts directly on to the seat frame to control front and rear height adjustment, or uses the worm wheel to drive a rack and pinion gear to provide the longitudinal adjustment.

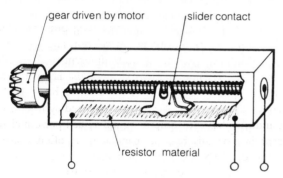

Fig. 24.2 Potentiometer for sensing seat position

The memory feature uses four potentiometers to sense the seat position; these signal the settings of the four adjusters. Figure 24.2 shows one of these potentiometers. It consists of a threaded spindle that drives a slider along a resistive surface; its operation is similar to a conventional potentiometer (see page 35). The voltage signal transmitted to the ECU depends on the position of the slider, so when the seat position is set, the driver operates the memory button; this commands the ECU to store the voltage signal for future reference when it has to reset the seat position.

Electric seat heaters
Introduced by Saab, the seat heater provides comfort in cold weather conditions and is intended to relieve the occupants of backache troubles associated with long distance driving.

A series of heater elements are positioned under and behind the front seat occupants. The temperature of each seat is regulated independently.

Electronically controlled steering

Power assistance Ideally a power-assisted steering system should give the driver considerable help for low-speed manoeuvring, but the assistance should be minimal once the vehicle has reached a reasonable speed. Normally pure mechanical systems cannot meet this requirement; as a result the vehicle is either hard to steer at low speed or very sloppy when it is moving fast. Once again electronic systems provide the answer.

Since existing sensors already input speed data to engine and transmission electronic control systems, it is possible to communicate this information to separate steering control ECU. By using mapped values, the ECU signals the actuators fitted on the mechanical steering box to either vary the hydraulic ram pressure or change the characteristics of the steering torque sensing mechanism.

Arrangements that use an electronic system to control a mechanical power-assisted steering unit are given names such as *variable steering system* and *progressive power system*.

Steering wheel position The position of the steering wheel makes it difficult for a driver to enter and leave the car. This problem can be minimized by fitting an electronically controlled *tilt and telescopic unit* to move the steering wheel away from the driver when the ignition key is removed. The memory of the ECU that controls the system sets the wheel in the position previously programmed by the driver.

Steering wheel adjustment can be integrated with the system used for automatic seat and mirror positioning.

Suspension systems
Various systems are used to control the ride of a vehicle. These systems range from sophisticated *active suspension systems* to arrangements for controlling either the damping or ride height (or both).

Adaptive damping system (ADS) It is claimed that this system, offered as an optional extra on some models by the Ford Motor Co., improves driving comfort and vehicle handling.

The microprocessor-controlled ADS system selects either a *firm* or *soft* setting of the dampers to suit driver actions, vehicle speed and road conditions. The main components of the system are:

- *steering position sensor* – infra-red optical sensor (working with a multi-holed disc attached to the steering mast) detects steering angle, direction and speed of movement of the steering wheel.

- *ADS control module* – contains a microprocessor and a sensor to detect vertical acceleration of the vehicle body.
- *vehicle speed and accelerator sensor* – shared data with the engine management system.
- *driver's selector switch* – allows the driver to select either *'automatic'* or *'sport'*. The latter position sets the dampers to the firm position; this is indicated by a panel light.
- *damper actuators* – a solenoid valve fitted to each telescopic damper opens or closes a fluid by-pass passage to give soft and firm settings respectively.

Continuous monitoring of the system is performed by the ECU. If it detects a fault the ECU selects the firm setting, stores the fault as a code and illuminates the panel light. A diagnostic plus is provided to enable the fault code to be read.

24.2 Multiplexing

The increase in the size of this new edition shows that the electrical content of the average motor vehicle has increased considerably over the last few years. In the past features such as electric windows, central locking, electric mirrors, anti-theft systems, etc. were restricted to luxury models; today they are standard equipment found on comparatively basic models. This trend is likely to continue.

In order to control the various systems, a labyrinth of cables is needed; these cables occupy valuable space as well as being heavy and costly. Multiplexing is one technique that has been developed to overcome these problems. At this time it is only being used on top end-of-the-range models, but history of auto-electronics shows that 'highline today leads to lowline tomorrow'.

Principle of multiplexing

The principle behind multiplexing, which was introduced earlier in this book (see pages 142 and 329), is to replace several current-carrying conventional cables with a databus. This bus has only one or two wires to transmit digital signal information around the vehicle. Some additional electronic circuitry is then required to code or decode the signals at each end of the bus.

Many occasions arise where data, such as vehicle speed, that is supplied by a sensor to one ECU is also required by another ECU. Using a multiplex network to connect these control units together provides an

effective solution. In the automotive world this interface arrangement is called a *controller area network* (CAN). Intercommunication between the units is possible provided that all ECUs in the network 'speak the same language', i.e. in this case they are all equipped with a *serial CAN interface*. This type of *interface* (circuitry for connecting two devices together) is used when each character or piece of data is transmitted in order, one after the other.

The CAN system has been recognized by the International Standards Organisation (ISO) as the standard for automotive applications, such as engine management systems, that require data streams of over 125 kbit/s (called the *baud rate*). Other standards are used for body systems that do not have to respond so fast; these only need a baud rate of about 10 kbits/s.

Use of CAN   Apart from the operating principle, the techniques associated with the installation and servicing of a multiplexed system, are quite different to the well-tried conventional system. In view of the large step to the new technology, many manufacturers have wisely delayed the adoption of a full multiplexed system until the industry has the equipment and skilled personnel to accept it. For this reason, manufacturers often restrict the use of CAN to non-critical body systems such as the electrical units contained in the doors.

Protocol   Although all units in a network may use the same serial transmission, the order in which the data is sent will vary unless manufacturers agree to adopt a common form; the recommended pattern is given in the *protocol standard* (J1850) as published by the Society of Automotive Engineers (SAE) in the USA. This standard also includes recommendations to cover items such as system layout, diagnostic facilities, etc.

The system considered in this chapter relates to a CAN system similar to that being used on prototype test vehicles by Lucas Rists.

Lucas Multimaster System

This system consists of eight *active junction boxes* (AJB) and one *passive junction box* (PJB); these boxes are interlinked by a databus and common feed cable (Figure 24.3). A conventional cable harness from each AJB supplies the electrical body components in the region adjacent to the AJB.

Junction boxes   The single PJB, mounted behind the dash panel, acts as the 'star point' for the databus. The box sends a digital signal along the databus at a time

database harnesses
local harnesses
passive junction box
active junction box

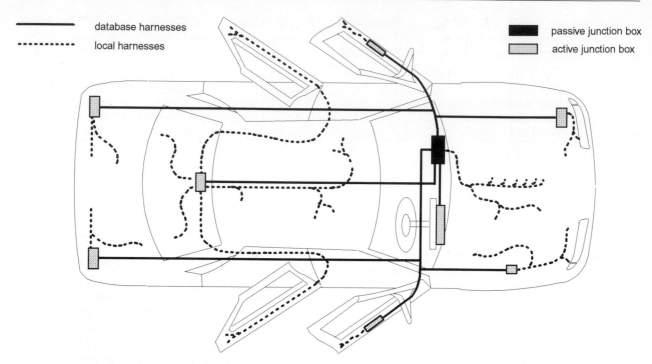

Fig. 24.3 Layout of multiplex system

when one or more of the AJBs is required to initiate a switching action to control a component in the local region.

Besides receiving and acting on broadcast messages, the AJB also has to monitor the local components and report any malfunctions to the PJB.

Since the system operates on an event-driven basis, the databus is idle unless some switching or monitoring action is taking place. When some action is required, the relative data is broadcast. If an AJB recognizes that the information is addressed to it, the full message is explored and action taken.

Databus The databus is the communication link between the boxes and its purpose is to broadcast extremely low voltage digital signals in the form of a message. This means that only a very small bus cable is needed; also the connectors fitted in the circuit must be effective.

Message structure The databus uses *Standard Corporate Protocol* (SCP); this is Ford's implementation of the SAE J1850 standard for Class B (low baud rate) data communication. The message format used for SCP consists of a number of bytes, each made up of a series of binary digits (bits), and arranged in the sequence shown.

(1) *Priority/type.* Used to determine priority when two modules are attempting simultaneous message transmission.

(2) *Generic function code (GFC).* Describes the function to which the message pertains, e.g. lighting, windows, locking, etc.

(3) *Source address.* Message destination. Ensures that only one module has control of the databus.

(4) *Data.* Defines action to be taken; e.g. 1 = brake light on; 0=brake light off.

(5) *Cyclic redundancy check (CRC).* Checks for corruption of the message. The code is sent back to the PJB and if the two codes do not agree, the message is distroyed and a new message is sent.

(6) *End of data.* End of message.

(7) *Acknowledgement.* AJB sends its source address back to the PJB to confirm that the message has been received.

The generic function code is a loose description of the function to which a message applies. The *functional message look-up table* stored in the memory of each AJB microprocessor contains a list of relevant GFCs. Only when a module recognizes a code that is identical to one in its store, is the message data investigated. The data that follows the GFC indicates the action to be

GFC code (1st byte)	Meaning	Data (2nd byte)	Meaning
0000 0001	lighting	XXXX XXX1	brake light on
0000 0001	lighting	XXXX XXX0	brake light off
1000 0000	windows	1XXX XXXX	start window up
1000 0000	windows	0XXX XXXX	stop window up
0000 1111	locking	XXXX 1111	lock all doors
0000 1111	locking	XXXX 0000	unlock all doors

Table 24.1 Message data examples

taken; this is done by assigning bit positions within the data bytes to represent specific functions. For example, the information contained in an 8-bit lighting message is given by the code:

bit 0	brake light	1 on, 0 off
bit 1	dip beam	1 on, 0 off
bit 2	main beam	1 on, 0 off
bit 3	left indicator	1 on, 0 off
bit 4	right indicator	1 on, 0 off
bit 5	front fog lamp	1 on, 0 off
bit 6	rear fog lamp	1 on, 0 off
bit 7	sidelight	1 on, 0 off

If the data byte in an 8-bit message is 0000 1000, the action required (reading from right to left) is to switch on the left indicator.

Table 24.1 shows examples of 2-byte messages that use this code pattern. The X means 'don't care'.

Diagnostic capability Each AJB processor has built-in 'intelligence' to monitor signal voltages and sense the power consumed by the components. Feedback information about the consumer load is achieved by using *field effect transistors* (see page 66). When used as an 'intelligent' device to perform this duty, the FET is often called a *smartfet*.

In addition to its role as a diagnostic tool to inform the driver of a fault, the microprocessor also has the ability to minimize the effect of a failure; e.g. if it detects that a bulb has failed, it can switch the power to another bulb.

Diagnosis of faults is carried out by using either the blink code facility or by connecting a code reader to the J1962 diagnostic plug. This feature is useful to carry out a self-check at the end of the assembly line and essential when the technician needs to find the cause of a fault, especially one that is intermittent.

24.3 Electronic developments

Developments are continually taking place to find better ways of controlling the various automotive systems. These improvements are often dictated by national legislation or international recommendations. Anti-pollution and safety measures have brought about the biggest changes, but the improved availability and reduced cost of electronic chips has encouraged designers to spread the use of electronics to other automotive fields. Whether it is wise or not to saturate a vehicle with electronic gadgets is open to debate, but their existence makes an attractive selling feature and this, no doubt, creates customer appeal.

Many interesting developments are currently taking place in the automotive electronics domain. Every year sees the introduction of some new feature; the following list shows some of the newcomer items that are offered or being developed by one or more manufacturers.

- *Headlamp directional control.* Moves the headlamps with the steering.
- *Automatic headlamp dipping.* Overcomes the need for the driver to dip the lamps when approaching oncoming traffic.
- *Automatic light switching.* Switches on the sidelamps at dusk.
- *Intelligent front lighting.* Headlights are automatically adapted to suit direction of vehicle movement, condition of road surface and light conditions. Additional sidelamps are switched on around sharp bends.
- *Automatic wiper control.* Wipers are automatically switched on and speed-controlled to suit the conditions.
- *Engine valve timing control.* Sets the opening and closing positions of the valve to suit the engine speed; called variable valve timing.

- *Engine air intake ram.* Varies the length of the air intake to improve cylinder filling by utilizing 'ram effect'.
- *Front screen heater.* Controls a heating element in the windscreen for defrost purposes.
- *Tyre pressure sensing.* Monitors and adjusts the pressure in all tyres to suit the driving conditions.
- *Automatic door locking.* Locks all doors when the vehicle is moving.
- *Mirror dipping.* Automatically dips the mirror when it is exposed to a high light level.
- *Radar headway control.* Detects obstacles in front of the vehicle at times when visibility is poor.

REMEMBER

Multiplexed systems use:

- a single databus to control the switching of several components
- digital signals to control the switching action
- a databus to provide an effective communication link between several ECUs
- a *serial CAN interface* to connect ECUs
- a standard CAN system to transmit data when the *baud rate* is greater than 125 kbit/s
- THE *J1850* standard as a basis for the self-diagnosing facility
- a standard message format
- a *binary code* for databus communications
- *smartfets* as an intelligent device to monitor consumer load

PROGRESS CHECK 24

The following questions relate to multiplexing

1. State THREE advantages of this system compared with conventional wiring.

2. Name the part that carries the broadcast message.

3. Write in full the abbreviation *CAN*.

4. What is meant by baud rate?

5. State a typical baud rate for an engine management system.

6. State the protocol standard that is normally used for automotive applications.

7. A system uses a PJB and a number of AJBs. Why does the system only have one PJB?

8. What action is taken by an AJB when it recognizes its 'call sign'?

9. Show, by examples, how an 8-bit binary message can be constructed to switch on and switch off a particular lamp.

10. Write in full the name of the electrical component that is used to sense the consumer load.